The Backstage Clan

CHEN YAN

Translated by
Hu Zongfeng and Robin Gilbank

SINOIST

ACA Publishing Ltd
University House
11-13 Lower Grosvenor Place,
London SW1W 0EX, UK
Tel: +44 20 3289 3885
E-mail: info@alaincharlesasia.com
www.alaincharlesasia.com
www.sinoistbooks.com

Beijing Office
Tel: +86(0)10 8472 1250

Author: Chen Yan
Translator: Hu Zongfeng and Robin Gilbank

Published by ACA Publishing Ltd in association with the China Translation & Publishing House

Original Chinese Text © 装台 (Zhuang Tai) 2015, The Writers Publishing House Co., Ltd, Beijing, China

English Translation text © 2023 ACA Publishing Ltd, London, UK

ALL RIGHTS RESERVED. NO PART OF THIS PUBLICATION MAY BE REPRODUCED IN MATERIAL FORM, BY ANY MEANS, WHETHER GRAPHIC, ELECTRONIC, MECHANICAL OR OTHER, INCLUDING PHOTOCOPYING OR INFORMATION STORAGE, IN WHOLE OR IN PART, AND MAY NOT BE USED TO PREPARE OTHER PUBLICATIONS WITHOUT WRITTEN PERMISSION FROM THE PUBLISHER.

This novel is entirely a work of fiction. The names, characters and incidents portrayed in it are the work of the author's imagination. Any resemblance to actual persons, living or dead, events or localities is entirely coincidental.

Hardback ISBN: 978-1-83890-537-8
Paperback ISBN: 978-1-83890-536-1
eBook ISBN: 978-1-83890-564-4

A catalogue record for *The Backstage Clan* is available from the National Bibliographic Service of the British Library.

THE BACKSTAGE CLAN

CHEN YAN

Translated by
HU ZONGFENG AND ROBIN GILBANK

SINOIST BOOKS

1

Smooth Diao had been so busy lately assembling the stage for the modern drama troupe that he didn't catch the sunlight at either end of the day. Still, he did manage to squeeze in enough time to see that his new wife – the third – was fetched home.

It was not as though he particularly wanted to marry her. The ghosts seemed to be piloting his course, and so he consulted the feng shui almanac to divine an auspicious date, before hiring a taxi to shuttle her over.

His eldest daughter Daisy was cursing upstairs by scolding the locust while pointing at the mulberry. She kicked deliberately at a yellow, autumn-flowering potted chrysanthemum by the doorway that somersaulted base over rim and shattered into pieces on the patio below. The lame dog was startled awake and belted into the room, yelping for Smooth, her one and only guardian.

At that moment, his third wife, Cai Sufen, was emptying her bladder in the privy in the corner of the courtyard. A potsherd bounced in through the half-length curtain covering the doorway. Her shank was left grazed and her noo-noo narrowly escaped impact. She was so stricken with terror that, tugging up her knickers, she crept swiftly along the foot of the wall back into the house.

Shuddering, the lame dog bunched her buttocks under Smooth's leg. She could only tiptoe warily and fearfully as she stuck her head out to woof. The anxious Cai Sufen stared at her husband, anticipating that he would take matters in hand. To her surprise, his mouth merely mumbled, "Spoilt rotten. No manners. Shitty dog." He then fell silent.

Daisy had been cursing for half that day. Cai Sufen hoped that Smooth would do something about it. But he only vented his anger in private, muttering nothing stronger than "wretched bugger". He didn't even risk going outside, let alone climb the stairs. Since it was Sufen who had proposed marriage to him, she could not afford to argue with her new stepdaughter. Hesitant as he had been about making up his mind, Smooth felt a twinge of embarrassment about bringing her home. Daisy's termagant turn was quite unexpected. That very first day, she spelled out to her stepmother how impossible cohabitation would be.

Cai Sufen buried her head under the quilt and wept. Smooth leaned on the bed and attempted to coax her out. He peeled a banana and tried to slip it into her mouth. Sufen raised her hand and broke it in half. He retrieved the piece deftly from the pillow and crammed it between his own lips.

Smooth was inarticulate and prone to seesawing the same phrases back and forth. "Daughters are bound to get married sooner or later... It's me you live with, not her, so why be afraid? Every family has its own cryptic crossword to tackle... Weather it through, and things will get better."

His words sank in, and Cai Sufen gradually stopped sobbing. She covered her bloodshot eyes and half of her face with the pillow case, leaving her mouth and nose exposed in order to breathe. Smooth peeled another banana and rubbed it around her lips. She opened up abruptly and gave a forceful bite, catching his thumb together with the fruit. Smooth let out an "Ai yah" and Sufen seized the opportunity to pull him onto the bed.

It was only slightly after 9 pm, and Smooth turned off the light.

The dog became agitated over this premature blackout, but was able to make out her master and that woman cavorting on the bed. She barked endlessly in their direction. "You bitch with no conscience," Smooth cursed. "You can't bear to see someone else's wok with something good in it. You hate me for having something oily in mine?" His jibes made Sufen chuckle. With several gasps of hilarity, she became soft and weak as if her breath was spent.

As they were enjoying these blissfully affirming throes, Daisy scuttled around downstairs. She approached the lavatory and then went to the tap, opening it fully so that a torrent of water crackled against the ceramic. The din echoed like the skies were being torn up by a storm. Smooth and Sufen were so frightened that they dared not breathe aloud. Frozen *in flagrante*, they waited in silence. As soon as Daisy reached upstairs, she spat out one more cruel barb that pierced the window and struck their hearts in the manner of a poisoned arrow. "You'll lead anything to your bed. Just so long as you find it's female when you lift its tail. Humph, you bitch, slut."

Smooth's tolerance was exhausted. He rolled over and sat bolt upright, ready to let rip.

Sufen gripped his waist and pressed her face to his back. "Let it lie, let it lie," she pleaded. "Everything will settle down soon."

His paternal dignity was deeply hurt. How he'd exerted himself to raise her and now she was scorning her own dad without scruples. Today, he must give her a stern reprimand.

Sufen wouldn't let him leave the bed. She clutched his waist firmly and tightly until he sighed in resignation and shrank slowly back.

That night afforded Smooth no opportunity to display any power or prestige as a man.

When the dog detected no more sound or movement on the bed, she licked her broken leg and dropped off early.

In the middle of the night, Sufen moaned that her body was itching all over. "What is this? An outbreak of lice?"

"Nonsense," Smooth mumbled in a daze. "There were some here before, but I haven't seen any in ages."

"Ah, they're all over me. How can you say they've gone?"

Smooth switched on the light and found that there were ants – and not just one or two of them. The longer they stared, the more abundant they appeared. Uniform black specks the size of bristles, when walking individually they were difficult to notice. But trooping en masse, they morphed into a relentless battalion.

Smooth noted the direction in which the insects were advancing. "Those ants are heading home," he said. "It's not a rare thing. This village has plenty of them. When I was a lad, I'd often see them doing this."

He realised that the ants were crawling beneath the door, so he opened it to take a look. As he had thought, a grand black army in a five-inch-thick phalanx was surging across the eastern wall of his

3

house in the moonlight. After seven turns and eight bends, they finally disappeared into a narrow hole in the corner at the foot of the western wall. Those tiny critters. Most of them were carrying loads heavier than their own frames, with their forelegs bowing under the weight. The ones that strayed into the bedroom had perhaps come scavenging or else had sneaked off.

"What should we do?" Sufen asked.

"Let them carry on what they're doing, and we'll carry on sleeping. I guess they'll be done before dawn." With those words, Smooth hauled up the quilt from the bed and shook it.

Sufen stamped on the pests that pattered down onto the floor. Her husband stopped her, crying, "Don't squash them." He swished a broom and gathered them into the cinder basket, then tipped them back to join the troop.

Sufen smiled. "Are you a Buddhist who's sworn off meat?" she mused.

"Poor blighters. Running for their lives all over the world, just for the sake of a bite to eat."

When they rose in the morning, the grand battalion had left as predicted. Only on the route where they had travelled, there was a trail of rice grains, insect eggs and the corpses of sundry other creatures. Odd stragglers and deserters wended hither and thither. They could not assemble into a battle array, and a number of them were trodden inadvertently underfoot. Smooth even splattered a few himself.

"You're squishing them now," Sufen crowed from behind him.

"Oh, that's their fate. Nothing personal."

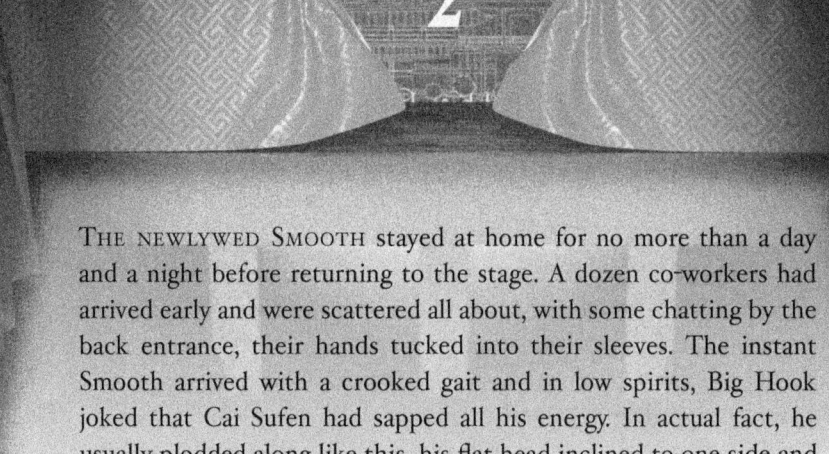

2

The newlywed Smooth stayed at home for no more than a day and a night before returning to the stage. A dozen co-workers had arrived early and were scattered all about, with some chatting by the back entrance, their hands tucked into their sleeves. The instant Smooth arrived with a crooked gait and in low spirits, Big Hook joked that Cai Sufen had sapped all his energy. In actual fact, he usually plodded along like this, his flat head inclined to one side and his legs like two inner tubes from an old banger. Today those inner tubes were wobbling along especially slackly, so everyone burst into laughter.

"Over, it is all over," Monkey said with a jeer. "She's squeezed the 'man eggs' in Smooth's crotch until they've cracked."

Even Mound, the youngest among them, crinkled his eyes and commented, "Brother Smooth is over fifty and married for the third time. He really has got a death wish."

"You know shit all. In the past, well-heeled men would take loads of women as their wives. Being old didn't matter. They just wanted to keep their peckers up. That's exactly what Smooth's great grandpa did, and the apple hasn't fallen far from the tree." Before Big Hook could finish, Smooth had drawn close to him.

"You dirty dog, how are you bad-mouthing me now?"

"I said your diamond drill bit is hard. You can bore through the toughest porcelain."

All of them erupted into guffaws again.

Monkey, who had scrambled onto the dragon throne – just a

stage prop – added, "They say you have healthy kidneys, which make you capable of doing all sorts of things. You've had three wives, but your legs are as floppy as worn-out cotton wadding."

Smooth kicked Monkey's backside. "Ivory tusks never sprout from a filthy dog's mouth. You never noticed what time it was until I came along. Early this morning, Chief Qu phoned me and said we must be set up by tonight. There'll be an important performance tomorrow."

"My dick, always so many urgent things. We've worked non-stop the past two days and nights to put up the stage for the modern drama. Tonight, we'll have to build one for the opera troupe. I haven't had a decent sleep in days. This'll be the death of us."

"Monkey, don't be a killjoy. We live by building stages. If you don't want to stay up late, you should go eat the wind and fart it out the other end. Get a move on and no more of this kak." Having said his piece, Smooth headed backstage.

"You could throw in a chicken drumstick for everyone's lunch," Monkey nagged from behind.

"I'll toss in a cock, if you prefer?" He then issued orders. "Mound, you guys deal with the hard scenery and backcloths. Big Hook, you four erect the lights. Chief Qu said we must arrange it as if they were performing in Beijing – sixty-four computerised lights and a hundred and twenty strobe lights. Not one less."

"We can't do all this at short notice," replied Big Hook, kicking the light box hard.

Smooth turned around and barked, "Even if it's impossible, we must pull it off. There'll be a bonus. Monkey, go and lay down the boom." He took the lead and shouldered a light box, and walked towards the side light slot. The box weighed at least a hundred pounds, and his legs trembled visibly as he tottered forward. Prattling and sputtering, all the others followed his example and busied themselves.

Smooth was the boss of the dozen-strong gang, though no one addressed him as such. He had a pet phrase: "We live by hard work. If you can keep pace, carry on. If you can't, then bugger off." As a new and developing profession, stage building was not counted as one of the Seventy-Two Walks of Life in Chinese tradition. If it could be included as Number Seventy-Three, then Smooth and his colleagues were insistent that it should be regarded as the toughest. They worked routinely day and night without interruption and led the lives of ghosts. All the various troupes typically held rehearsals during the daytime, so the stage had to be constructed at night. However, the builders were not free to idle away the hours of sunlight, as they were required to wait on the sidelines.

The directors of the troupes all had dirty mouths and would abuse people as readily as savouring a homely meal. Even female directors shared the same trait. "Fuck" regularly tripped off their tongues, accompanied by a flash of the middle finger. But one thing was for sure, they all spoke clipped Standard Mandarin. Many of those who signed up for the job could not bear the insults, let alone the gruelling toil. They stuck it out for a while and then found another means of making ends meet. Only Smooth held fast and earned a reputation in the field.

At present, whenever someone in the Western Capital needed a stage erecting or dismantling, or some arts and literature organisation had a haulage job, they would invariably seek out Smooth. Others could not break into this business even if they wanted to. As time went by, a gang of hands flocked around him, eager to scrape a living together. Some of them suggested that he should set up his own enterprise, a kind of cultural company. He duly visited the Bureau of Industry and Commerce and filed for a business licence. Despite his certification, he never allowed himself to be addressed as "manager" or "boss". When people spoke to him in that way, he would say they were ribbing him and pulling his leg. He maintained that he got by through sheer graft alone.

There were no middlemen under Smooth's leadership, only a few steady retainers charged with recruiting personnel. They were divided into loose teams, tasked with dealing with the lights and the scenery and backcloths. Most of the time, they attacked the project like they were fending off a rabid dog. Without fail, Smooth would set the ball rolling and allocate their funds in the open air. Precisely how much the troupe had paid him was as clear as a mirror in the hearts of everyone present. The business was earned in his name, so it was logical that he took a larger cut. And yet Smooth was never greedy. He always told others that the money was garnered by collective endeavour. Hence, those in his retinue were all old hands who had been with him for seven, eight or even ten years. They had honed their specialist skills so that the mere wink of an eye was sufficient for them to know whether a hammer or a pincer was needed, or if a boom should be lifted or lowered.

"Every last guy around Smooth is qualified to be a senior stage technician," Chief Qu often opined. "Better them than the idlers who plant themselves on the bench and stare vacantly at their bowls of cold bean jelly."

Smooth was quick to downplay the compliment in case it gave rise to envy and discord in the troupe. "We live by our labour," he replied. "What skills we have were picked up on the job from the best in the business. We grind away at what we do with a good heart. None of us wants to rob anyone's limelight."

Qu beamed. "Don't belittle Smooth," he warned. "He's the most cunning bloke under the sun."

Smooth answered with a smile, saying, "Hard work. I'm nothing more than a hard worker."

They had just hung up several backcloths, and the lights had yet to be moved into position when Chief Qu arrived. A popular expression stated, "Become an opera chief if you want to lead a life of grief." Many of those in this profession looked well and truly downtrodden, having the air of a doormat made flesh. Qu was the exception. Nobody dared blunder in his presence, and Smooth knew he was seldom the target of backbiting. The local epithet "tender ears" could have been coined for him, since he showed forbearance to demanding divas, respecting them as "grandpas" and "grandmas" or "aunties". That is not to say there was any fault on his part. These players, some of whom were headliners, would try the patience of any impresario.

Chief Qu was by training a composer, and he turned out music for his own company's productions. As a freelancer, he might have raked in 200,000 or 300,000 yuan per score. The fact he sought no remuneration from the troupe counted in his favour.

Opera company hands were in the habit of addressing the leaders without using their full title as a prefix. For example, they called Section Chief Liu "Sect' Liu", Captain Nan "Cap'n Ah" and Team Head Zhao "'Ed Zhao". Accordingly, Chief Director Qu was known as "Chief Qu". As it came across almost as a term of endearment, Smooth followed their example.

Chief Qu upheld very precise aesthetic criteria. Even though he wore a pair of spectacles and had a gentle and learned countenance, when rankled, he too would spew out expletives. Smooth had witnessed first-hand how he could hurl away the microphone during a public address. However, most of the time his mood was mild and collected. Smooth had been collaborating with him for years.

Smooth remembered that the first time he met Chief Qu was when he had just become the head of the company. Back then, the troupe was about to go to southern China to perform two dramas: *A Journey to West Lake* and *Zhou Ren Returns Home*. These were standard repertoire and had been staged countless times. Maybe because of this, the performance was "old wine in old bottles". The staging and light effects lacked a fastidious touch. When the performance company in southern China sent inspectors to monitor the progress of the production, these experts made exacting demands about how the stage effects should be organised. They feared that the drama would be derailed by slipshod technicals. The freshly minted Chief Qu did not have the measure of the troupe. He found it hard to push for changes, and in fact there were those among their number who were setting him up for a fall.

One day, when Smooth found nobody around, he approached Qu and said candidly, "Chief, this time you might need me to go."

"You, what for?" the chief asked in confusion and bewilderment.

Owing to the reach of his renown, Smooth thought that Chief Qu ought to know who he was. During those days of rehearsals, he had been on-site constantly and made a point of milling around Qu time and again. Contrary to his expectations, and much to his disappointment, the chief didn't recognise him let alone acknowledge his importance.

Smooth introduced himself briefly and then said, "You're a new hand at laying on important performances of this kind. Did you notice the state of the troupe? They're practically blowing around about like loose sand. This happens when a horse tries to lead a pack of bulls and gets no co-operation. There could easily be trouble in the evening. If I don't go, who is going to keep an eye on things on- and offstage for you? I'm afraid you can't even put up the stage properly."

Chief Qu shot him a scornful glance. "There are more than thirty stagehands just on the artistic side," he retorted. "Does it need you to come and spectate? Go off and do your own thing."

When the stagehands resumed work, Qu soon came to appreciate the complexity and magnitude of affairs. He endured agony and many headaches in constructing and taking apart the stage, with hiccups in the lighting and scenery eliciting sardonic applause from the audience. The chief was forced to realise the complicated clashes that commonly arose between the various stage designers. This time, Smooth had left a deep and enduring impression on him. Through their constant comings and goings, a firm friendship was cemented. The members of the troupe poked fun at him, saying, "Smooth is Chief Qu's golden boy." He would always answer with the same parry: "Sure, quite the golden boy – I'm just a hardworking fella."

The moment Chief Qu entered the arena today, he started shouting for Smooth. "Hey, Smooth, get a move on. The lighting engineer will drop by tonight to adjust the focus. The actors and orchestra will come in at eight in the morning for the combined rehearsal. If things are not ready on cue, it'll be on your head."

Smooth slid down from the lighting balcony, his whole body and even his hair covered with dust and cobwebs. He clapped his grainy hands together and swept the powder from his face. "Chief Qu," he said. "You see, we brothers are so busy we don't even have time to fart."

"Brag as much as you like. Does farting have anything to do with this job?"

"Ha ha, just a turn of phrase. But Chief Qu, today's a tough set. You see, usually we only install just over twenty computerised lights, and about forty strobes. Some of them are ready made. This time, all the rig has to be carried in from outside. We can't even let a single screw go astray. All my brothers are cursing me. They complain how this job is like the emperor's mother combing the field for bits of grain after harvest."

"Come again?" Chief Qu seemed not to understand.

Smooth smiled. "Ha, they are not in it for the money. They just want to imagine what it's like having to rough it like the poor."

"Don't give me this, Smooth." Chief Qu's tone seemed quite earnest.

Smooth then changed tack, noting, "I wouldn't dare. We just live by our labour. Chief Qu, my pussy mouth just likes to flap."

Chief Qu then grinned and admitted, "I was told by the office that they can throw in a bonus for building this stage."

"Yeah, they'll give a bonus. Only a thousand yuan. They're all cursing me."

"Who is cursing you, Boss Smooth?" the chief asked.

Monkey hastily raised his hand and said, "I'm cursing him."

Mound did likewise, chiming in, "Me too."

Everybody laughed.

"You see, it is difficult to deal with them," Smooth explained. "They only have the glint of cash in their eyes. Do you want them to learn from the model soldier, Lei Feng, and do things for free?"

"I tell you, Smooth, tomorrow night's performance is a benefit do. We won't make a cent out of it. I'm not even sure where we'll find the subsidies for the players. The office is doing an extraordinary favour by giving you that grand. Be content and get a move on." After saying this, Chief Qu was about to leave.

Smooth resorted to his tried-and-tested method of bartering, saying, "Chief Qu, you see, they all know that you never abuse honest workers. We don't demand extra pay, but can you throw in a chicken leg for each of us for lunch? You've come down here in person. You should reward the fighting army."

"You really are a cunning gaffer. Button it now and there'll be an extra chicken leg, two wings and a carton of milk all round. But if you cut corners, Smooth, I'll tell the office to dock the money from your fee."

"Don't worry, Chief Qu. We don't want to lose face."

The chief left.

Mound took the lead and clapped his hands. "Brother, Brother," he exclaimed. "You can needle him the same way tonight. Cadge us all a pork bap and a bottle of beer too."

"Go ram a carrot up your arsehole."

While they were chuckling and chatting away, Smooth's mobile rang. It was Cai Sufen. She did not speak, just wailed loudly. Whatever he said, there was no answer from the other end, and her wail became more pained. Smooth feared she might have got into an altercation with his daughter Daisy. Anyway, he must go back to check. He left Big Hook with some pointers and then sped out through the backstage.

3

THE WORK SITE was not far from Smooth's home – ten minutes or so by tricycle cart. A whole host of literary and fine arts bodies serving both the province and the municipality crammed into this one thoroughfare named Shangyi Road. Having these places on his doorstep was Smooth's sole reason and consolation for shifting stages for a living.

His family had something of a history hereabouts. It was said that in the 1950s this was an execution ground and that unmarked burials lay wherever one trod. As literary and fine arts units peeled away from their military affiliation at the Communist base in Yan'an, they began to cover the land with row after row of buildings so that gradually a whole street took shape. Smooth's forebears were affluent and able to reside within the city walls. However, following the Communist liberation of the Western Capital, his great grandpa was caught harbouring a senior member of the defeated Nationalist Party and summarily shot. Rumour had it that he met his doom on this very patch, and nobody dared lift a finger to move or bury the corpse. The family property was also confiscated, and they left the downtown area to become market gardeners here. Later on, Smooth's grandpa, being a shrewd businessman, restored the family's wealth by becoming a fruit and veg magnate. His fortune, which ran to tens of thousands of yuan, went undiscovered upon his death for instead of depositing it in the bank, he wrapped his hoard in an oilskin and secreted it in a false bottom added to the household piss bucket. Meanwhile, he maintained the pretence of eking out a miserable and shabby life, like a hungry ghost pining for what he seemed to lack.

Following the start of the reform and opening-up policy in 1978, Smooth's father was the first in the neighbourhood to construct a modest multi-storey abode. Of his three sons, Smooth was the youngest and the other two only succeeded in frittering away the property before the old man was even in his grave. The firstborn turned out to be a compulsive gambler and the second an opium fiend. Once the building was gone, the addicted son vanished as rapidly as the narcotic plumes. The elder sibling took up gaming as a vocation and, in the course of three decades, became a seasoned hand at its every form. Canny though he tried to be, the odds at last tipped against Big Army Diao. His wife bolted too. This period he referred to as the "low tide of revolution", and he roughed it out in a ramshackle, rented, one-room, oddly tubular apartment, with not even the amenity of a street lamp. Once every fortnight or so he might bed down there, but most of his time was spent in the thick of combat at some gambling den or another across the Western Capital.

A piece of hearsay once placed him in Chang'an County, where it was rumoured that a debt collector had been buried alive. Nevertheless, ten years ago the "high tide of revolution" came coruscating down on him. Nobody knows what happened exactly. For a time, Big Army's fortunes were mesmerising, and he appeared able to triumph at mahjong with his eyelids clamped closed. That winning streak continued virtually unbroken, and no one had the courage to sink their stake into a match with him. The last that was heard of Big Army, he was exiled to Macau as a so-called "career gambler".

Smooth's current bijou home was acquired by mortgage about a dozen years back. Rising at 3 am each day, he would speed out of the city on his trike. The field-fresh produce he bought on a shoestring would be hawked for a hefty mark-up on Shangyi Road. As he was reduced to being a spectator while his older brothers squandered the family home, Smooth developed gumption. He knew he had to salt something away for a rainy day. His vegetables furnished him with a house of his own, the small dwelling proving modestly affordable. The only drawback was that the home was encircled completely by other properties, with no aspect facing out onto the street. He might have piled on an additional storey or two, but the neighbours around him beat Smooth to it. Were he to follow suit, he would be depriving them of sunlight or robbing them of the privacy they savoured on their balconies. All those householders were testy, and he found it impossible to parley with them on affable terms. Having neither the time nor the money to negotiate further, any renovation plans of his own were abandoned.

Smooth's two daughters currently occupied the upper floor. The elder, Daisy, was the offspring of his first marriage, and the younger, Plum Han, a stepchild brought over by his second wife. The year before last, Plum sat the entrance exam and entered Shangluo Higher Education College, returning home infrequently save for during the summer and winter holidays. This left Daisy as the lone full-time occupant. Nearing thirty, she craved a proposal of marriage, though her looks were decidedly plain. She sought to plump out the flat physiognomy she inherited from her father with several rounds of cosmetic tweaking. Her budget could not extend beyond minor repairs, and nothing could be done to remedy her narrow forehead or elongate her stubby chin. The more one studied her face, the clearer the folly of those investments became.

By the opposite score, her temperament was erratic and utterly inscrutable to everyone who came into her orbit. For the past few years, she struggled to rub along pleasantly with others. More recently, even her own father found himself on her wrong side. She was apt to hurl projectiles and curse people in an offhand manner, needing neither occasion nor obvious provocation. Now that Smooth was belittled to a nobody, if he were unable to remonstrate with her in a calm voice, then who else could?

Smooth took the pre-emptive step of informing Daisy about his forthcoming marriage to Cai Sufen. That very day, his daughter asked him for the money to buy a new mobile. Initially, he was reluctant since the one she currently owned was still perfectly functional. Daisy protested that Apple phones were now *de rigeur*, and she suffered great embarrassment at having to slip out her mediocre brand in public. Rather than scolding her, as had been his first instinct, Smooth gritted his teeth since he knew that he needed to show a little lenience in return. On handing her several thousand yuan in cash, he began to talk about his intended.

The young woman's stare grew fierce and upbraiding. "What?" she exclaimed. "Are you sick in the head or something?"

Any response Smooth might have made was stuck firmly in his throat. His silence lasted for what seemed an age.

Much to his relief, Daisy spoke first, reflecting, "Well, as long as you go on making a living, what's it to me if you have a harem of ten?"

From then on, not a single word on the subject left her lips. Sufen had been pushing him to bring her to his home, so he did so without further thought of taking precautions. Neither was ready for the trouble that was to come. It was midnight before the first bout of commotion ended. On the second day, who could know what fresh turmoil would strike? As Smooth parked the tricycle at home, his legs barely had the energy to dismount.

He pushed the front gate open gently. The yard was strewn with shattered pots, bowls, plates, bottles and jars. Even Daisy's favourite statuette – a replica of the bare-buttocked *David* – had been fractured into eight small shards, with the naked lower portions tossed into a cracked pot containing a cactus.

As Smooth crossed the threshold, he heard Cai Sufen wailing. The very first thing to catch his eyes on the ground was a broken porcelain bowl. Its fragments, together with the two poached eggs and fried dough sticks it must have been holding, lay all about like shrapnel.

To begin with, he peered upstairs and heard not a peep, for Daisy's door was firmly closed. To be blunt, she was the creature he feared more than any other in this world. He could not even recall when exactly this terror began, but it was certainly deepening as time wore on. There were occasions when he heard her lobbing objects about on the first floor and his hair would literally prickle on end. Fortunately, he rarely found himself at home, since matters relating to the stage kept him busy all the year round. His residence had assumed the air of a guest house, with Daisy taking on the role of live-in landlady.

Gingerly, he applied pressure to the bedroom door and found Cai Sufen curled on the bed, weeping. As he approached, he noticed how half of the pillow was sodden. Goody the dog was cowering at the base of the wall, licking her injured leg. On seeing her master, she began to stumble over excitedly and follow his every move.

"What's the matter?" Smooth asked.

She did not answer, only wept more.

He sat down and reached out to embrace his bride. Her tears became morose.

"What's up?"

"You go ask your daughter 'what's up'."

Not knowing what atrocity Daisy had committed, Smooth found it awkward to continue this line of questioning. He could only deduce that it was somehow connected with the bowl of poached eggs. Sufen must have really been intimidated to have broken down like this. Before bringing her here, he had made a point of describing his daughter's vexation at being trapped at home, not having found a decent family in which to marry. He advised her not to let this vexation rub off on her, and without much deliberation, she agreed to try to make a go of the situation. Sufen also mentioned her own difficulties in keeping peace with her ex-mother-in-law and former sisters-in-law when all of them had to live together under the same roof. She coped, though. In under forty-eight hours here, matters had deteriorated so terribly. Smooth experienced a pang of uncertainty about what the future would bring.

"What on earth's up?" he asked, drying his wife's cheeks with a small towel.

Sufen's tears rained down heavier. Through the sobs she rasped, "Your daughter's... so wicked... this morning I... was being kind, and cooked two eggs especially... bought two dough sticks. I... I... kindly... carried them upstairs. She ... she ... told me to my face to eff... eff off, and cursed me... said I was a mental nympho..." Sufen was choking with livid tears and had to stop.

In a flash, Smooth's hand started to stroke her spine with affection. "Don't let her get to you," he comforted her. "Disgusting. Shameful. Don't let her get to you... so disgusting." Several times with vehemence, he repeated, "Wretched bugger."

Sufen's indictment continued. "I didn't... make a nuisance, just laid the poached eggs... on her table. As soon as I got down... from upstairs she... threw the bowl. The bowl only missed... my head by a foot. I... I was nearly... killed."

"Wretch!" Smooth's words were still terse, although his pitch was higher than before. "Wretch!"

"All this... I was able to tolerate. I didn't say a word... but she... still cursed... cursed me as no better than a pig or a dog... and... eff off again..."

"Wretch." This time, as he repeated his assessment, he stood up in fury as if ready to brain somebody.

On seeing her husband's clear and resolute attitude, not to mention his upright posture, Sufen's anger dissipated. "I'm to blame for being a penny-pincher and being set on living here," she said coquettishly. "You see, if we can't live together, I... would rather leave." With this vow, she blew her runny nose fervently and was about to get to her feet.

Smooth's blood was as hot as lava. Gripping Sufen's hand, he reassured her, "Now, try to pull yourself together and wait for her. I am her father. Wretched bugger, but it's not as though she can turn the heavens upside down." He turned to ascend the stairs.

"She went out ages ago," Sufen informed him in a tone that was neither frosty nor warm.

"Wretched bugger! I'll deal with her when she's back. Wretched bugger!" Those last two words were spoken with such volume that, had Daisy been upstairs, she would have heard them clearly.

"I can see you're capable of snarling like a wild hound when nobody's around to listen," Sufen grumbled beneath her breath.

Smooth had been bracing himself to summon up a more powerful air with which to impress Sufen. Unexpectedly, his mobile rang. It was Big Hook, urging him to come back without delay. He described a host of problems awaiting his attention at the stage and complained that Monkey was being workshy again, for the most part dangling in the air reeling off witticisms. This didn't sit well with Smooth, who growled back, "Imagine if I were dead. You'd be incapable of making money and feeding yourselves." Sufen couldn't hear what Big Hook then said at the other end, but it made her husband even angrier. "I go away for one moment," he shouted. "Does that mean the sky has to fall down? Dumb dicks. I'll be over there soon." He closed the mobile and told Sufen, "Must dash. Too many things nipping at my heels."

"If you go now, what am I meant to do?" She seized hold of his body and placed her face close to his while shaking his thin shoulders. For a second, Smooth smelt a softly fragrant, feminine sweetness. It dawned on him that among his three wives, she was the most captivating. Despite not being far off forty, her face and neck remained taut with barely a discernible line. No wonder Big Hook quipped about him taking a dainty young bride. Sufen was indeed a decade or so his junior. As he inspected her eyes – worn peach red from crying – he held her in his arms with tender affection.

"You can stay at home and do whatever you must. She isn't going to swallow you whole."

"I can't. I'm scared." Sufen purposefully wriggled deeper into his embrace. "I can always offer you a hand at the stage."

"What help can you offer? It's a skilled business. What use are you where stages have to be built?"

"Oh, it's hardly assembling aircraft or making cannons – stuff I can't dabble in. Let me tag along with you."

Smooth considered her proposition before capitulating. Today, he was so busy that if he left her at home and then she tussled with Daisy again, there would be no chance of handling the problems on both fronts.

Having no alternative, Smooth allowed Sufen to be his shadow. The lame mutt was restless as well, so she too was lifted onto the cart behind the tricycle. "Who'll take care of her?" Sufen asked. "She might run away."

"Hmm, maybe so. So much the better if she did."

4

ALL OF SMOOTH'S "BROTHERS" were elated when he brought Cai Sufen over to the stage. Monkey, who was dangling mid-air lashing a boom, whooped out a long and hearty wolf whistle, crying, "Brother Smooth is so stuck on her. You'd better stay home and wait on our sister-in-law. If you have a sudden burst of passion, there's no bed handy here!"

Even the usually earnest Third Skin cajoled, "Hey, Brother. You know there's a 'dragon bed' in the corner of the stage – the type the emperor used to service his concubines on. If you want to give it a go, I could put up a screen for privacy!"

Mound, who was tying into place a backcloth depicting "the sun rising beyond the sea", let it sink to the floor with a laugh.

"Go on. Mind your own business. See what a pig's ear you've made of it. None of the gauze is hung yet, none of the backcloths are up, and only seven or eight lights are ready. But your pussy mouths are busy enough. You bleated for me to come over, so what's the matter?"

Big Hook wanted to say something, but glancing at Monkey, he chose to remain silent. "All of us are working hard," Monkey protested. "Don't listen to all their crap."

Instead of badmouthing Monkey, Big Hook switched to venting another irritation. "Hey," he said. "You see, we brothers are not happy. The head of supplies didn't follow through with the promise you and Chief Qu made us. There's been no chicken wings let alone legs for lunch. Not a drop of milk, either. All we had was cabbage and tofu simmered in plain water with a couple of meatballs. And those so-called 'meatballs' were kneaded out of flour without even a hint of meat in them. You should tell Chief Qu and make sure his underlings don't always trick us."

"You nagged for so long on the phone just because of that? I got to thinking that the sky must have come tumbling down. Do you ever think about work, or are your minds always in your bellies?"

"Heavy work of this kind warrants a good feed," Big Hook maintained. "Since Chief Qu made that promise, how can he take it back?"

Smooth had thought that the chief was not like other foremen and would keep his word. What precisely had gone wrong here was still not apparent. Much as he wanted to call him, it felt somehow improper. Everybody said he kept on good terms with him, but wasn't he the only one intimately familiar with Chief Qu's character and the sensitivities of his position? The mainstay of stage shifters' income in the Western Capital had to be the Shaanxi Opera Troupe. Whereas other groups might perform sporadically, they trod the boards nearly every day and multiple branches were out on the circuit. This one troupe really was the "parent" that fed and clothed them. Come what may, they couldn't afford to spoil this bond. Sometimes, maintaining amicable relations with junior post-holders made more sense than courting their senior colleagues. A missing chicken leg or carton of milk was no big deal, after all. If one of the links in the chain broke down and they couldn't shift stages, then there would be no income for anyone. "Don't get riled up over trivial stuff," Smooth declared. "If others heard about it, we'd be a laughing stock. Can't I treat you to hotpot instead?"

"You already owe us," Big Hook moaned. "When you brought your bride home, you didn't treat us to any 'nuptial liquor' then, and we missed out on teasing the happy couple on their marriage bed."

Smooth grinned. "No need for nuptial liquor," he said. "When the bedroom suite's worn and second-hand, is there any smutty joke it hasn't heard?"

"This can't go on forever," howled Monkey from up above. "You must treat us sooner or later."

"Since none of you gave us nuptial money, why should I treat you? Had you given me that, I'd have splurged the lot on treating you."

"What a stingy sod!" Third Skin grouched from behind the curtain. "Some bosses treat their employees many times a year. Smooth, though, is a real miser. If he had a louse for lunch, he wouldn't even pick off a leg for us."

Originally, Third Skin had been named Hu Bo. Whenever he signed for his pay packet, the strokes of the character "Bo" (波) would be written in too open a manner, so it resembled two separate words, "Three" (三) and "Skin" (皮); hence his nickname. Third Skin was a diligent worker who took charge of minor matters, which nonetheless required care and consideration. His natural disposition was far from garrulous, so his colleagues often forgot that he still existed. Consequently, these comments he spat out from behind the curtain had great impact.

"Third Skin, if you really must fart, come to the front to blast it out," Smooth charged. "Am I really so stingy? On red-letter days when members of staff are meant to treat their bosses, do you ever shout me a single cent? No, you sons of bitches even nab my fags. Should I treat you? Treat your arses to a good kicking, more like!"

"It's such a relief that Smooth never became an official," Monkey concluded. "If he had, he'd be greedier than Prime Minister He Kun back in the days of Qing."

"Mither less with your mouths and speed up your work." Smooth hauled a computerised light onto his shoulder and went to the optical slot.

Sufen had been standing to one side all along, not daring to walk centre stage. Smooth asked her to linger in the wings as an onlooker to begin with. Stage work was a case of each radish having its own hole. No matter how tired a person became, they never forgot that their post had a designated salary. None of them was prepared to lend anyone else a hand lest it "peel a layer from their flatbread". Sufen sat there for a while before announcing that she couldn't bear being a spare part. She started to assist the overstretched Third Skin in binding the curtain, but was met with a disapproving glare. "Sister-in-Law," he said. "Take a rest. I can cope by myself."

Sufen understood his drift and quickly reassured him. "I'm not after a cut of your pay. Just can't stand watching others busy and doing nothing myself."

Her words caused him a twinge of embarrassment. "I didn't mean that. You're our guest. You can size up the place. No need for you to muck in."

"I only wanted to try it for a bit of fun."

Everything here was novel and fresh in Sufen's eyes. In the past, she had watched operas in the countryside. Those productions had minimal sets and the simplest of props. This was totally different. Each item was an exact replica of some real-life counterpart, and only on very close inspection could the difference be discerned. Smooth must have done an outstanding job, since on realising the deception, his wife found the fakes rather funny. To be able to hobnob with actors and actresses every day and be sheltered indoors from the rain and the searing sun, he must be positively surrounded with happiness.

"Smooth, Chief Qu is coming," blurted Third Skin in the direction of the stage. "Chief Qu is here."

The chief nodded at Third Skin and entered the stage from the wings.

"He's the boss in this place," Third Skin whispered to Sufen. "And he and Smooth get on pretty well."

She heard another shout from up above. "Smooth, Chief Qu is here."

"I'll be down soon."

"Chief Qu, we never had those chicken legs and wings you promised us," the swinging Monkey observed. "We don't know who got hold of our milk."

"What's up?"

The crew all took turns to rant about their meagre lunch. By the time Smooth joined them from the lighting slot, they had exhausted their grumbling. He heard nothing of what was said and reported hastily, "Believe me, Chief Qu, we'll be ready to hand over to the lighting division at eleven tonight."

"Can't you bring it forward?"

"Really, we're doing our best."

The chief left without responding.

Quite unexpectedly, ten minutes or so later the head of supplies swept in, towering with fury and gall. Even before drawing to their front, he flung out curses. "Smooth, I'll fuck your mother, you son of a bitch," he began. "You have the nerve to bite me in the dark! Do you all have such hungry pussies for mouths? When did I refuse to give you what you wanted? When did the chief give his word in the morning? Was I given time to prepare? All those lunches had to be ordered to a fixed menu in advance. Still, having hungry pussies for mouths, you wanted chicken wings. What about abalone wings, too? What kind of people are you to go biting me in the dark? If you don't want the job, call it a day. There are plenty more queueing to take your place. You sons of bitches, just remember my surname is Kou. I'll change it by deed poll if the company hires you mob again." Iron was a very apt given name for Iron Kou, for his speech and actions had a metallic ring. By the time Smooth had innocently clambered down from the lighting slot for a second time, he had missed this visitor too.

He asked what had happened. Big Hook recounted how Monkey and the others had whinged in front of Chief Qu. "Hungry pussies for mouths sounds about right," Smooth yelled ferociously. "So petty. If there's no stage to shift, there'll be nothing to pad our pockets with. Must you always aim for the yuan and miss the cent just because your greedy mouths tell you to?"

Smooth bore another computerised light in a hod-like fashion. He left no empty hand for climbing, instead clutching a spool of leather-clad wires. Sufen noticed how his body swayed as he reached halfway up the ladder. Restoring his balance in an instant, he continued to ascend. Stage shifting was gruelling as well as hazardous. When Smooth reached the summit, Sufen realised that her own tensed palms were perspiring with anxiety.

All of a sudden, her thoughts turned to the lame dog. When they arrived, they left her on the back of the trike. "No dogs are allowed in the stage area," Smooth had said. "Goody knows that for herself, so there's no chance of her wandering in. She's done that a few times before and was taught a lesson."

Sufen was curious about how a pet could be so obedient as to willingly stay put for so long. On going outside to check, sure enough she discovered the creature sprawled out on the cart at the rear of the vehicle. Smooth had even parked it in a sunny position to prevent her from feeling cold. When the dog saw her mistress approaching, she stood up and wagged her tail. Imitating her husband, she called out "Goody", to which her tail wagged more joyfully. Sufen stroked her out of love and pity, and fed her some of the dog food Smooth left on the trike. It was at this moment she heard another bout of cursing and hurried back to the stage.

5

IT FELL TO IRON KOU to arrange for a street pedlar to deliver chicken thighs, wings and milk in two cardboard boxes. The containers were deposited in the centre of the stage. "Smooth," he called out, kicking them. "Come over and eat. Gorge yourself to death. Things are chaotic already, but at least you won't be moaning on top of this. I've never seen a shabby stage shifter who was able to kick up such an almighty fuss."

Smooth, whose face was peppered with specks of dust from the lighting rig, wiped his sweat away with the towel tucked into his waist. "Director Kou," he insisted, "I absolutely did not say a thing to Chief Qu. My brothers didn't mean to slander you. We're all workhorses, and wouldn't be able to do our business if you didn't tend to us. How could we be ungrateful? How could we lower ourselves to bite you in the dark? Just now, some of them pestered Chief Qu about giving them food and drink. I've already criticised them. I'll come to your home later and apologise to you on behalf of the team. Director Kou, I hope that like any great man you'll have the grace to overlook the faults of those humbler than yourself. Don't look so meanly on us."

"Get lost. Don't give me that. You're herding me into a corner and then trying to flatter me. I'm in charge here, and this is the last gig you'll get. Eat up, quick. Finish this stage and then get away from here – the farther the better." He swanked off pugnaciously.

On hearing his footsteps peter away, Monkey resumed his nagging from up the ladder. "Fierce – my dick! A skivvy to a drama troupe, but so much bluster. Maybe he thinks he's the grandpa we must obey, some top-of-the-bill actor or even the company head?"

"Monkey, keep that second arsehole in your face shut. As long as nothing comes out of it, nobody will take you as a cretin. Does money really scorch a hole in your hands? Every time you spout more shit, there's always trouble and I'm the one left to wipe it away. Just keep your hands busy. This isn't some radio or TV station. Chatter is as helpful here as a limp dick." The moment Smooth lifted another computerised light onto his shoulder, he could hear Big Hook and Monkey quarrelling behind him.

"Big Hook, you like to act the boss. So what if I chatter?" Monkey shouted down from the ladder.

Big Hook, who was installing the ground lamp in the rear lighting rig, bellowed back, "So skilful. Keep up your crowing. When you've pissed off everyone else here, you're bound to still have stages left to build and tons of cash."

"A pittance – but I still go after it. I've wanted to give up this lark for so long. Your shitty mouth has no good reason to curse me." While swearing away, Monkey raised and lowered the ladder with great commotion, pivoting from left to right on its rungs like an acrobat in full flight. Where these manoeuvres were concerned, Monkey had no equal among the team, and his midair agility meant he earned only a little less than Big Hook. Still, this discrepancy stung him like a searing brand, and he wondered how Big Hook could install himself as second-in-command when he only had eighteen months' experience on the job. Whenever Smooth was absent, Big Hook would deputise. The problem was that he was the type to wield his cock's feather as though it were an arrow. On such occasions, Monkey would become lackadaisical and act the comedian until all the green hands were reeling about the floor with laughter. Monkey only wanted to undermine Big Hook's pretensions to power. The joker showed loyalty to Smooth and Smooth alone, with nobody else being bold enough to wag their finger at him. Just now when Smooth had criticised him, Big Hook murmured sarcastically how "Monkey has the verbal squits". He thought his jibe too quiet to be heard, but Monkey caught it and hurled a furious blizzard of slurs from on high, in effect gagging Big Hook.

Smooth was well aware of what lay behind their constant bickering. He didn't want to intervene and was content to let them squabble away as long as the stages were built and the wages covered. His years of experience could be summarised in two words: "sheer graft". Whatever task was allocated them, he had to lead by his own labour. Once motivated, his team could tackle any assignment. Moving the lights up to the suspended rigs was invariably the heaviest task, and Smooth chose to be the first to volunteer. Even now in his early fifties, he could still lug more than fifty kilos of iron on his shoulder. His worst fear was that the day would come when he lost the brawn to pull off this task. Smooth's command would be compromised if he was no longer the standard bearer in his own battalion. While his muscles were still in form, he would continue unabated, the weightiest instrument on his scapula being the mace that allowed him to holler and micro-manage as he pleased.

Imperfectly executed as other tasks might prove, he stood assured that by 11 pm the lighting would be perfect. Every lamp would shine brilliantly when the lighting division took over. Smooth knew the capricious nature of the head of the lighting division; if the rig was less than pristine in any way, he would flounce out of the exit with not even Chief Qu being able to bring him back. Mr Ding was an auteur in the field. Each time, he set his fee for one lighting design at 150,000 yuan after tax. Concessions were not considered. He would stay precisely three days and two nights, parting at the earliest juncture as soon as his wallet was replenished.

Sometimes, when a number of national tours were running simultaneously, Ding would deal with multiple productions. Tonight, he might be on Hainan Island and tomorrow in Xinjiang. By his own admission, he pocketed a steady 5,000 yuan per hour. Money gushed his way effortlessly, with his fixed price of 150,000 yuan being as much as Smooth's gross annual income. That Mr Ding could often make this sum several times over in a single fortnight made Smooth and his comrades smack their tongues in admiration.

Well-acquainted as they were, Ding did not know Smooth any more intimately than the other members of the troupe since he eschewed spending very long in their company. He would always be launching off somewhere in the world or else be mid-flight, only materialising when his presence was crucial to a production. Smooth formed the impression that Ding never shot him an earnest glance.

The initiative always fell to him to flatter him with honeyed phrases. Words of praise from the lighting division were in truth more potent than anything else heard on or about the stage.

Smooth's mind was dexterous and clever. He would only approach Ding and flatter away when he was sure he was in a buoyant mood and content with the job as it had been done. Should the maestro appear sullen, despite Chief Qu being around, Smooth refrained from seeking his attention. At prickly moments such as this, Monkey was the only hand who knew how to inject levity. He had cleaved his own haven of favour in Ding's critical eyes.

Tonight, Maestro Ding did happen to be satisfied with the lighting arrangements. Clad in a jumpsuit, he claimed to be fresh from the fitness suite. The back of his head was home to only a compact island of hair, arranged into a comb-over so that he bore a resemblance to Beethoven. This clump was growing sparser and he attributed his somewhat vulture-like mien to too many late nights. A small strap now lashed the remaining hair together, so it bobbed about as a ratty tuft.

Ding's assistant tailed him with a buff-coloured leather holdall in one hand and a cup of tea in the other. The cup looked like a cannon shell and had the capacity of a thermos. Director Kou also offered up a bag of fried soya beans, for Smooth knew that the master had his own inviolate working routine. While adjusting the lights, he would claw unconsciously for some beans, which he chewed meticulously one by one. Some said this was a habit he acquired from Marshal Lin Biao. The origins of this quirk are of no real consequence. One thing did matter, though. If in the depths of the night the maestro dug into the bag and found it empty, he would immediately declare himself exhausted regardless of how urgent the project was. Ding would head off for his constitutional sleep, immune to others' pleas. Not surprisingly, the caterers made sure there were beans aplenty, and it was not uncommon for the bag to be still half full at the end of the night shift.

As soon as Master Ding took his seat, the assistant unfolded the script and the lighting blueprint before him. Chief Qu could be seen mouthing something to Kou, who then relayed the order, "Stop all action onstage. Start to adjust the lights. Who's meant to be moving the scenery? Put that down first, put it down. Start adjusting the lights."

Finding Ding to be in a rather agreeable mood, Smooth slowly approached him and reported, "Teacher Ding, we've installed all the lights according to the plan you gave us. If you find anything out of place, we're on standby, waiting for your orders."

Ignoring him, Ding instead focused on the script. Smooth stood by his side, perfectly upright. After a long silence, the maestro asked, "What's that fellow's name, the lanky one…"

"Monkey. He's waiting there onstage for your orders. Monkey! Monkey! Master Ding is calling you!" Owing to the intensity of the light, Monkey could not perceive clearly what was going on downstage and had to shield his eyes with his fingers.

"Come quickly," Smooth shouted. "Master Ding is calling you."

Just as Monkey was about to leap down from the stage, Ding yelled, "Stay there! Let's start to reposition the lights. First, lower the fifteen lamps in the first row by fifteen centimetres, then adjust the second and third rows. Move the eight lights pointing in reverse from suspension forty-three to forty-five. Add six reflecting lights on the side of the second curtain in the entrance and two soft lights. Oh, scrap that, four on the third curtain at the exit." After issuing his edicts, the maestro opened his cannon-shell tea cup and poured some tea. He took a sip and then chewed slowly and patiently at his beans.

Smooth was too angry for words. All the lights had been arranged according to Ding's own exacting design, and now he wanted them altering with all the disregard floodwaters have for riverbanks. That evening spelled further grind for them. Whatever Smooth truly had on his mind, he answered obediently, "It'll be redone right away, Master Ding. We'll redo it at once."

He then walked over to Chief Qu and showed his determination. "Rest assured, boss, we'll do whatever Master Ding requires." However, he pointed out, "It was already done as he demanded, but we'll change it as he's demanding now. It only needs a bit of extra energy. Our power never runs out. Just rest assured. We're doing it for your sake. I'd never put conditions on you. As long as you remember we're here to work, that's reward enough."

"Get going. Quickly," instructed the chief.

Smooth did not forget to sidle over to Kou and share some words of loyalty. "Director Kou, you've witnessed everything. We followed Master Ding's outline, but then he had a burst of inspiration, so we're not to blame—"

"Get a move on, beat it. Get on with your work." Kou didn't even make eye contact as he swatted Smooth away with his hand.

"Director Kou," Smooth continued unfazed, "you're still angry with me. Great minds never keep record of the slip-ups of small fry. Later, I'll visit you at home and apologise properly in person."

Kou turned his face away disdainfully.

When Smooth climbed onto the side stage, he could hear Big Hook swearing under his breath. "Lighting division, my dick! Does he have a mouth or an extra bumhole? He's not kept his mouth under control, and now we'll be busy half the night."

"Shut it," Smooth interjected. "We're labourers. A spot of hard work isn't going to kill you. Go and move those lights." With these words, he seized two reflecting lights and heaved them up to the gantry.

Big Hook dealt the lighting box a kick and it slid some distance, colliding with a mobile lamp and bracket, which tumbled to the ground. One bulb flopped down and shattered. "What's going on?" Kou's voice boomed at once. "What's happening backstage?"

"Nothing," yelped Big Hook.

He knew he had landed himself in bother, since that bulb was imported and cost about 320 yuan. That was enough to erase his whole salary, and when he saw no one else around, Big Hook kicked an imported speaker even harder. The front of his sole was almost bent double, and he leaned forward in agony.

Sufen, who had been helping Third Skin in the wings, had only exchanged looks with Smooth a handful of times during that half night. Mostly, she caught sight of him clambering about, and it seemed that his feet never made contact with the floor. When somebody shouted downstage that a light needed adjusting, vibrant beams would flash onto the performing space, giving Sufen an almost mystical frisson. She continued to survey the scene from afar, and Third Skin told her to take this opportunity to drink in the mystery. Slipping down into the auditorium, Sufen chanced upon a corner where she could crouch until her form was practically invisible. Quietly, she watched on as the various "magic spectacles" unfolded on the stage. Later, she dozed off, and sometime later had the sensation of bodily contact. Waking, she discovered that Smooth was stretching a coat over her. The spectacles had still not come to an end, though the stage shifters too had made a beeline for the theatre floor seeking out a place to catnap. Sufen asked what time it was and her husband said 5 am already – daybreak was imminent.

"All done?"

"The lights are in place, the adjustments nearly finished. I need a brief kip. Expect more bother when the production director comes at eight."

"You keep the coat, then. I'm not cold."

"No, they might call me at any time. Covering and uncovering myself is just asking to catch a chill." As he was speaking, Smooth sought out a vacant patch near the lighting director and prostrated himself there.

In Sufen's eyes, Ding with that tiny pigtail was the spitting image of some village hoodlum. Still, his character was tenacious, and he thrust his crop around unchallenged in this place. When it was almost 6 am, he decreed, "Raise those first lamps in the front row another fifteen centimetres, and put the eight lines on suspension forty-five back to suspension forty-three. Be quick about it, don't drag your heels. Time is pressing."

Sufen saw a still-dozing Smooth rise to his feet and stagger with a rocking motion over to the stage, which he ascended.

6

DAISY STAYED OUT THE ENTIRE NIGHT, not returning home until almost dawn. She was accustomed to her father being absent throughout the daytime. Whatever season of the year, he would sling a careworn army overcoat over his trike to serve as bedding should he need to nap on the floor. There was no regular domestic routine as Smooth remained outside until close to daybreak, leaving Daisy on her own in the house.

His elder daughter now preferred not to wait around for him. Rather, she would play mahjong or sing songs at the karaoke. Nothing had prepared her for the fact that having passed the age of fifty, he should take a third wife. At first, she thought he was jesting and there was no substance behind his talk of an engagement. What she found most intolerable was that he should choose a bride only eight or nine years older than herself. Worse still, her appearance was not just modestly pretty, but positively alluring. Sufen was decidedly younger, more charming and more entrancing than her immediate predecessor. Those breasts of hers were ostentatious and shuddered beneath her jacket at the least disturbance. They heaved too much to the point of caricature and came across as confrontational and an assault on the eyes. "Surely, Smooth has married Daisy's sister?" was one of the comments she overheard from the neighbours. The minute this sex-soaked cow crossed the threshold, she knew there was no prospect of compromise or yielding ground.

In the space of little more than ten hours, Daisy had discarded whatever belongings she could lift and smashed every immoveable article. Even so, this female interloper was thick-skinned and had gone so far as to make her breakfast and carry it upstairs as a gesture of flattery. Since her faithful retainer had gone out to shift stages, Daisy took this as her opportunity to discharge a round of pernicious verbal arrows. The poison was concentrated, and the arrows struck their intended target. When she finally heard an anguished wail, she went out humming a ditty. Daisy joined a few fellow singletons in watching a movie double-feature and went on to sing and drink at the karaoke. They kept company until nearly sunrise.

When she came home, the door was locked. She asked herself: have my poisoned arrows shooed that slut away?

The bowl of poached eggs with fried dough sticks that she threw down from upstairs were still strewn about the yard. She flashed a glare at Smooth's room. The window curtain was wide open and there was nobody on the bed. Had the slut been driven away? She dealt the door a series of deliberate kicks and found that not even the lame mutt was inside. Perhaps both the dog and the slut had been taken to work by their keeper.

The belligerent passion Daisy had been harbouring in her chest suddenly dissipated, and on starting up the stairs, her legs became like jelly. Climbing was something of an ordeal and barely had she entered her own room when she lolled down limp on the rush floor mat. Brandishing a mirror, Daisy inspected yesterday's make-up job and, feeling it unsightly, smashed the glass and began to whimper. She didn't know why she had become so teary. Suffice to say, at that moment her lot struck her as a pitiful mess, more pitiful in fact than every last one of those left-on-the-shelf spinsters with whom she had been socialising.

As far back as she could recall, her pa had been transporting and assembling sets for opera troupes. In the early days, this duty fell to the members of the company themselves. If stage shifting were an art in its own right, how could the practice be taken up by jobbing hands off the street? Apart from working for the troupe, her pa used to help transport produce for stallholders, provide household removal services and deliver gas cylinders for people. She had been so excited when he would let her sit at the front of the trike and then pedal so fast they'd even overtake cars. How fond she had been of the times he moved and put together scenery and props for the troupes. The whole range of curios would be left on full view and she could study, touch and fiddle about with them until she was tired. Sometimes, she had to mind this trove while the adults went for their meal. Left alone, she could pose in a succession of multifarious hats and manipulate props of her choosing to emulate how she had seen them employed on the stage.

She also remembered how her mother would linger out late every day and then compensate her with a hot dog or a lolly. After lying in until noon, she would head out again in the most garish make-up, her lips vampiric red. Quite without warning, at the age of six, she arrived home from school one day only to be seized by her father's arms. "Your ma has run off with someone," he spluttered. "Why would she do that?" asked Daisy. "'Cause your pa is hard-up. He's a good-for-nothing. Only a measly coolie on a trike." Torrential as the girl's tears were, her mother never came back. Later, as time went by, she became habituated to her absence.

Daisy and her pa weathered the situation in tandem. While attending school in term time, during the holidays she was able to tag along with the troupe for fun. As the players and company relinquished the handling of the stage, her father increasingly had to work in the evening. She still followed him, but out of fear of being left marooned in the house.

As Daisy made a habit of slumbering on the edge of the stage, troupe members and their children came to know her as "Smooth's spawn". A few years later, it dawned on her that "Smooth's spawn" carried a derogatory undertone. Thereafter, she stopped coming out to play like this and ceased fraternising with the theatrical types.

Her stepmother appeared on the scene when she had reached junior high school, and Smooth was careful to give Daisy advance notice of her arrival. "What I need is a stepmother to cook and wash for you," he told her. "My hands are full right now making us money." Not long afterwards, the woman arrived together with a younger daughter by the name of Plum Han. The two girls grew acquainted quickly and initially rubbed along without friction. Matters soured when Daisy failed her senior high school entrance exam, whereas Plum not only passed, but gained a place at university. A silent frost set in between the two and yet, when the stepmother succumbed to uterine cancer five years ago, Daisy was still prepared to attend the funeral decked out in the mourning attire of a full-blood offspring.

Now this new woman, Cai Sufen, was insufferable. Come what may, she must not be allowed to establish roots in their home, and Daisy must engineer her exit by whatever device came to hand. The injury that this might cause her pa did not deter her. Daisy had simmered with unseen resentment towards him ever since her stepsister had enrolled at high school. How her beloved pa had been enchanted by the adopted creature and held her dearer than his own flesh and blood. Hmm, after her mother's passing, Smooth even supported Plum's tuition at Shangluo Higher Education College and would brag in public about how adept she was at study. Puh, how could somewhere hidden among the remotest hills and gulleys call itself a "college"? Plum had been brought originally into the household like a precious carafe of oil, so how could she now be counted as one of his own?

Once, when Smooth had been boasting yet again before others, Daisy was so affronted as to nearly spit on him. At other times, she reviled her father's willingness to lower his head and crick his back before all-comers. He exuded the air of a skivvy. She entertained the suspicion that this very visible servility was hampering her prospects of finding an intended at thirty. When he brought this slut home, his daughter was more obdurate than ever of the need to sever relations with him. Whether Sufen brought him contentment or not, and whether he agreed or disagreed, she had resolved to eject the slut from their home.

Daisy sobbed a little as she pondered in this way. She then fell asleep. In her dream, the accursed Cai Sufen was perched in a sedan car like a diva. Meanwhile, her father wore a sleeveless jacket and brandished a whip as he escorted his mistress home. Ever since her pa brought that slut back, it was as though he had swallowed some elixir of ecstasy and needed to be fused to her all the day long, relegating Daisy to being the rogue member who ought to be evicted. When she was leaving home in her dream, that woman pelted piping-hot poached eggs and fried dough sticks at her back. She sat up straight and gazed dumbstruck at the bedroom wall.

A knot of plans as to how to rid herself of the slut was now taking shape in her mind.

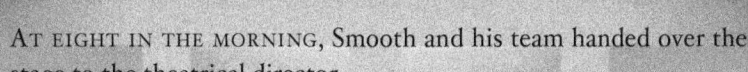

At eight in the morning, Smooth and his team handed over the stage to the theatrical director.

The director was in her fifties and weighed more than fourteen stone, so the chair she occupied at work had to be custom-made to support her bulk. She was not one to assume airs, and the play script and a tankard-like tea mug were the sole items she carried in with her. The ceramic sides of the mug bore a slogan painted in red. Heavily chafed, the characters were just about legible: "It is good for young intellectuals to go down to the countryside."

Once on the stage, she scanned around in several directions before calling for Smooth, who scurried over.

Her surname was Jin, and although Smooth followed the others in calling her "Director Jin", he prefixed that with "Teacher" to burnish further respect.

"Smooth, move the third plum blossom net behind the fourth dangling curtain. Make it snappy," Director Jin ordered. "It's too near the front and looks out of place."

"Director Jin, Teacher Jin, please don't fret. We'll do it right away and the schedule won't be disrupted." As he spoke, Smooth led colleagues across the gantry.

Cai Sufen was half awake and half asleep in the auditorium. Eight o'clock came around and she didn't straighten her spine until the directors and then the actors filed in. Before long, more than a hundred people were scattered about the floor. Someone shouted repeatedly that they should gather together and a few moved tardily towards the centre. It was as though a tattered net had been cast over too broad an area and no amount of shouting and bawling was capable of gathering them as a shoal.

Chief Qu was the first to speak up. Some of his jargon was incomprehensible to Cai Sufen. The bare bones were that tonight's performance was of great importance and several foreign nationals would be among the audience. If the proceedings were deemed satisfactory, an international tour might follow. Other provinces had been competing for the same opportunity. This time, going abroad would not be an ordeal. Rather, they could showcase their art in its authentic form in major opera houses across a number of European countries. Cai Sufen overheard two men alongside her carping, "They seem to enjoy being tricked by foreigners. These past few years, we've invited plenty of them over to poke around and inspect what we do. Fussing like a gynaecologist about every corner and cleft. But was any kid pulled out in the end to be sent abroad?"

After Chief Qu had finished his address, the substantial Director Jin took up the lead. Even though Cai Sufen was unaware of the exact remit of her job, she could see that the matron plied the whip on the stage. "In recent years," she began, "these foreign agents have screwed us royally." Sufen thought her ears were playing tricks on her. Laughter erupted, and she resumed, "Now they're back here again. Chief Qu tells me that they're still those same horny guys with their fancy beards. This time they claim they're here to choose shows to transfer to royal opera houses. I hope they're not going to try to bust my muff again!" Every sentence she spoke stirred up laughter, applause and even whistles. Cai Sufen caught the wit and pith of her words, being drawn in by the grand dame's charisma. Once she had said her piece, the crew began to prepare for the rehearsal.

Smooth was the first onstage, shielding his eyes from the lights with his hand and dashing over to ask volubly, "Director Jin, Teacher Jin, can you take a second look? Is the plum net OK like this?"

"OK," she replied.

"Well, in this position no light is cast on the net," Smooth further explained. "Last night, the light was coming from the first column. It can't reach it now from that source, so we'll have to resort to using the second column."

Somebody downstage chuckled.

"This is Maestro Ding's – Teacher Ding's – responsibility," Smooth noted. "Whatever advice I give is amateurish."

"Point noted," the director called out. "Chief Qu, couldn't we promote Smooth and give him a position in the lighting division? Ding Bai, please reposition the light onto the plum net."

Master Ding, who was by now too exhausted to lift a single pea, drowsily ordered, "Switch to using the second column of lights."

Someone clapped their hands and squawked, "Smooth has come out on top. Master Ding just asked us to use the second column."

Smooth scratched the back of his hand rather awkwardly and retreated hurriedly backstage.

The rehearsal officially began. Smooth and his team had a brief window in which to relax. He bowled down the stage from the side and presented his wife with steamed dumplings. Not wanting to eat in an ungainly fashion before others, she professed she had no appetite. Smooth wolfed down a few, being too shy to sit close to Sufen lest his colleagues rib him. He happened upon a space in the front row, but the moment he crouched down, he nodded off. No matter how raucous the band and actors were, his ears were insensible.

Had she not observed Smooth at work for a whole day and night, Sufen would not have appreciated the strenuous nature of shifting stages. To be honest, she could not endure such an existence. Last night, she had managed a stretch of shuteye, though those hours slumped over in the theatre did not constitute sound, refreshing sleep. Somehow, Smooth had the ability to segue one shift into another almost seamlessly. Now she wanted to cover him with the greatcoat he had given her as a blanket. To do this in front of his men would invite taunting. These chaps had sharp eyes and keen tongues, and would jump at every opportunity to tease their team leader. She didn't want to court ridicule by being so visibly attentive. While she was mulling this over, the portly director started to growl, "Hold on, hold on, hold on. Smooth, Smooth." He could not be wakened. Cai Sufen was tempted to shout, but froze once she saw that constellation of eyes fixed on her. She lowered her head at once.

"Hey, why's Smooth dead to the world? He's dreaming of an angel? Someone give him a shove!"

Before Director Jin had finished speaking, Monkey quipped from the wings, "Marriage seems to have wrung him dry."

"Who's got married? Did Smooth tie the knot again?"

"This is his Number Three, didn't you know?"

"Ha ha, I never took him as being so ambitious! Stage shifting has given him new wealth."

"Who is this Number Three?"

Monkey jabbed a finger in Cai Sufen's direction, his pupils stealthy.

"What an eye he has," said one. "Young enough to be his kid."

Laughter broke out spontaneously.

Cai Sufen wished that a chasm could open in the ground into which she could crawl.

Smooth was oblivious to these exchanges until one of the crew roused him. His dozing brain responded immediately to her order. "Director Jin, just tell me plain. I wasn't asleep, just waiting for your cue."

Further laughter ensued.

"Smooth, you're quite a guy," she complimented him. "You look gutless on first sight, but you've taken a third bride. Why didn't you even give us some sweeties to mark the occasion? Watch your health."

"It's not an issue, not a big deal." He surreptitiously stared at Sufen as his lips moved. She was already too ashamed and fled outside.

Everybody laughed again.

"I know you work so hard, but there's no time to rest," said Director Jin. "Adjust the plum net back to its original position. The scenery was placed too far back and it would be getting in the way of the performance. It's me that's to blame. Sorry for putting you out once more."

Inside, Smooth was one thousand per cent unwilling to comply. Still, his face and mouth affected an attitude of obedience. "No need to talk that way," he told Director Jin. "We're all grafters. Things need to be moved and we've boundless strength. This is for the sake of art, Director Jin. How can we not cooperate with you, Director Jin, Teacher Jin? We'll do it straight away." He clambered back onto the stage.

Once she had left the scene, Cai Sufen didn't know where to head. She went to the trike to check on the dog. It was already the depths of autumn and the morning felt very crisp. The hound was cowering beneath the moth-eaten quilt Smooth had prepared, sleeping effortlessly. When she saw her mistress approach, she slunk out from under the cotton, shook her body and wagged her tail. Sufen realised that the dog was very fond of her, and she took pity on her gammy leg. She held her in her arms and stroked away.

A short time later, Smooth appeared.

"Why is everyone here so weird?" Cai Sufen asked with chagrin.

"Theatre types are all jokers. You just have to accept how they are," her husband answered. "You'd best get inside and see how the play pans out. It's parky out here, watch you don't catch a cold."

"How can I go back in there? They all look at me in such an odd way."

"Take no notice. Just enjoy the play. Once the rehearsal's over, there's not much left to do. Right now, I can't tear myself away."

"You keep busy with your own stuff. I'll stroll about awhile, then come indoors."

Smooth had never before taken the time to observe Cai Sufen on such a clear and well-lit morning. Despite a whole night's exertion, her face still appeared creamy and smooth. Aside from the lightest of crow's feet at the corners of her eyes, she had barely a discernible wrinkle. Big Hook and Monkey, those sons of bitches, had cooed about her vast cleavage. As she now stood at an angle to him, Smooth held that they might in fact be able to smother somebody to death. They were what nature had blessed her with, and now she was his woman. Nonetheless, a kind a vacant, un-moored sensation still dogged Smooth. What with Daisy trying to whip up a tsunami in a teaspoon, his marriage felt far from settled, as if he were a camel rider trying to lasso his mount with a frayed cord.

The outdoor labour exchange was located close to his home. That had been where Smooth first caught sight of Cai Sufen. Every day, he would cycle past without noticing what was in the offing among those surging throngs. Big Hook, Monkey, Mound and Third Skin had each been signed up from here, and so by then he wasn't short of hands. That was the type of place where the most innocent of glances could entice a person over and stir trouble – rather like how a bee becomes infatuated with a flower. Sufen was ensnared in precisely this way.

That morning was cloudless and sunny. Following a whole night at the stage, Smooth tried to cycle home in spite of his woozy head. A flash of absent-mindedness caused him to collide with Cai Sufen. That second, their faces were brought within a hair's breadth of direct impact.

It was a relief that the brakes were so sensitive and the woman didn't take a tumble. In these situations, the victim might look to create a brouhaha. The slightest unintentional contact with a stranger could be twisted into something catastrophic. Had his front wheel bashed her shin, she could have keeled to the ground and feigned injury, raising the prospect of an unofficial lawsuit – blackmail, in other words. To his relief, Cai Sufen did not end up on the floor and did not even lose her temper, instead smiling coyly for the trike had only brushed against her inside leg. She dusted herself down. "No harm done," she said gently. Smooth was immediately touched and dismounted, repeating how he was sorry. Each apology was met with a gracious demur, and Smooth couldn't help looking at this lady. Perhaps these avid eyes of his would prove the catalyst for trouble. Every time he passed by this area, he would scan the scene and should he fail to see the young woman, his mood would sour. He would then double back and comb the whole market once again, ruing his misfortune if he failed to pinpoint her.

The majority of the time her piquant, spicy eyes were easily found. Marriage had not really crossed his mind, for he only perceived her as pleasant and her countenance comforting. That was as far as his thoughts led him. He never anticipated the consequences of his eagerness to glimpse her so often.

One rainy day when he was pedalling home after work, all the jobbing hands pressed together, seeking shelter under the eaves. Much as he wanted to see the woman, the downpour restricted visibility to a few short metres. He cycled more emphatically towards the little lane leading to his residence. Quite without warning as he was turning into the alley, a figure crossed the road. The pedestrian pitched over on being struck and Smooth, leaping from his vehicle, tried to prop him up. What he had taken as a man was actually the very same woman he had been seeking. He still did not know her name, and the whole of her body had blanched through immersion in the muddy drain water. Her legs were unsteady too and his offer to ferry her to the hospital was refused. The woman's flesh was shivering, so Smooth lifted her onto the cart at the back of the trike and took her the short distance to his home.

It just so happened that Daisy had gone on a tour around Lake Qinghai with a group of friends. Her absence emboldened her father to bring this strange woman back to their house. The darker side of Smooth's conscience suggested that he had an ulterior motive. Had she been checked into the hospital, the welter of tests and checks might very easily swallow up thousands of yuan. Several days as an inpatient would sear a hole in the bottom of his money pouch. Fetching her home and dishing up some pleasantries and a square meal may well have been sufficient to assuage the distress. Later, when wrestling over this episode again, he wondered: did this woman actually set this trap? Considering and reconsidering what had just transpired, he discounted the notion. The rain was shuttering down and nobody could see further than two or three metres ahead. How could she have predicted his arrival and staged such a stunt? No, it must have been a heaven-sent encounter.

The day after the accident, he rummaged around upstairs and retrieved some of Daisy's cast-offs. He also boiled some water so she could bathe. The bath did nothing to stop her from shivering, so he again raised the issue of going to hospital and once more she denied it was anything serious. She would soon get better of her own accord, so any expenditure was senseless. Smooth felt encouraged by her reasonable and rational words. He tried to fix a hasty meal for her, including vacuum-wrapped sausages and luncheon meat. Both had been bonuses from the opera troupe. Fond as he was of these treats himself, he had wanted originally to take them home to share with Daisy. His daughter was emphatic, though, that she wanted none of his junk food. It was laden with preservatives and probably carcinogenic. He kept the processed meat, allowing himself a nibble now and again when she wasn't around. Today, he could utilise the whole package.

It was almost nightfall by the time their hearty meal was over. The rain seemed heavier than ever before. Casting his mind back over a number of years, Smooth struggled to recall a wet spell quite like this one. In the meantime, he had learned that the woman's name was Cai Sufen, that her husband had passed away and that she had come to the Western Capital in search of work. Later, she grumbled that her legs hurt, so Smooth boiled some alcohol and applied it to the skin as an analgesic. While his hands were rubbing, his mind began to wander. Her eyes were captivating and her body so soft that anything he caressed was at risk of melting. His coarse hands lost their restraint and the territory they were prepared to treat enlarged. Angst began to set in as he knew that once his fingers ventured further, it would be hard to remove them. His force of will was weak and he made an ethical blunder. In hindsight, he accepted that he had acted the hooligan and done nothing to rein himself in. More than once, Cai Sufen had grasped his cunning hands and pushed them back, only to have them rear up again and surge like untameable serpents. Finally, once he had unbuttoned her dress, the whole frame was exposed. "Oh heavens," he sighed, dumbstruck. "How can there be such bounty in this world!"

The rain continued unabated for seventy-two hours. Many quarters of the city experienced flooding. Smooth, being at a loss, sprawled out on his bed for the duration. On the fourth day, Cai Sufen raised the issue of marriage. She was not placing him under any duress, yet he found himself powerless to refuse. In fact, he willingly accepted. As soon as matters had run their course, he brought her home a month later as his bride.

Everything was satisfactory. The only niggling hurdle was his daughter. Some resistance was only natural, but her objection turned out to be resolute.

Working on the stage for a whole day and night, Smooth's hands and feet had been in constant motion. Behind this outward show of industry, his brain was preoccupied with how to settle future domestic discord.

The rehearsal went on glitch-free. His crew could now unwind. Smooth tried to usher Cai Sufen back into the auditorium and the pair sat far apart, watching the performance in silence. The plot of the opera related how an emperor had become bored of life at the palace and so he absconded secretly and fell in love with a country maiden. After various twists and upheavals, he successfully insinuated his beloved into the imperial court, but the young woman could not adapt to the rules and etiquette, and was exasperated by the cruelty of the empress and princesses. She left the palace in the guise of a eunuch. In this way, the opera that had been simplistic in plot and rambunctious in execution, drew towards its sad denouement. When the performance ended, Smooth found his other half damp-cheeked. It was not until the theatre lights had been switched on that she could shrug off the sorcery of the drama.

A colleague poked fun at Smooth, to which a jovial Director Jin replied, "Smooth, you shouldn't let these people in the palace bully your country wife."

There were chuckles on every side.

Director Jin stood up and said, "OK." Smooth took this to mean that he had done his work well.

All of a sudden, as she was mincing forward, Director Jin spoke up again, "Sorry Smooth, but that plum net has to be moved to the fourth curtain where it belongs. Please sort it out."

Servile as Smooth was, he choked back any curses that might be brewing inside and did as he was instructed, without a word.

"Not happy?" the director continued. "Chief Qu, I don't care how it's dealt with. Just see that it's removed."

Smooth was before the chief in a flash, saying, "Move it, remove it, who's saying 'no'? Director Jin, well Teacher Jin, gave the orders. Since art is at stake, who are we to refuse? It's our job to move and remove."

The whole crew seethed with malcontent as they were making the modifications. Mound accidentally tore the corner of the stage cloth depicting plum blossoms and a foot-long gash was rent in the fabric. They all knew that removing items from the stage was not factored into their pay packet. As they were so disgruntled, Smooth sent them on their way. Only he, a new hand and Sufen stayed behind to reposition the plum net properly.

It was already approaching 3 pm when they left the stage. Tiredness was causing Smooth's head to tingle, yet he ordered Sufen to crouch on the rear of the tricycle. The lame dog jumped up so she could cradle her in her arms. The present task had been dispatched. Smooth knew only too well that what was awaiting them at home was no less ominous. As he pedalled, his foot kept on cranking up into the air and he nearly tumbled off the seat. "Too much load,"

Sufen called out, clutching him from behind. "I should get down and walk."

"No problem. You just try to sit steady." Smooth attempted his damnedest to maintain his rhythm before a brainwave struck him. Why had he been so timid and weak before his daughter? How could he be a slave to fear? When all was said and done, he was her father. His energy now rallied, and his feet moved with confidence.

8

DAISY DID FINALLY PERCEIVE A NOISE FROM DOWNSTAIRS. In spite of how gently the couple shuffled about on tiptoe, nothing could mask the familiar sound of her father's trike. She was spoiling to launch an assault, but then reasoned that it was better to wait for the opportunity to arise and then unleash her tirade. She could hear them cooking downstairs, followed about twenty minutes later with a call from her father, "Daisy, come down and eat." She was unresponsive. "Come down and eat. Your auntie has made egg noodles. If you don't have them now, they'll get all claggy." How revolting. What could possibly have happened to elevate that slut to the status of an "auntie"? Whose auntie was she now supposed to be? Humph, her mind was overwhelmed with anger once again. Still, she would not answer.

"Daisy, did you hear me?" Her father's shouting became more emphatic. "I asked you to come down and eat. Do you want someone to come up and feed it to you?"

She was still silent, biding her time for a riper opportunity.

At last, her father downstairs lost his temper. "Eating or not eating? Give us the word."

In the past, she would have been unnerved by his temper. But now, she pretended not to notice. She realised that this spectacle was a show put on for the benefit of the slut. Today, she also would do something for the slut and then she would see whose word was law around here.

Daisy remained unmoved, sitting on the margins and waiting for the optimum time to swoop. The voice of the slut could now be heard too, suggesting, "Let me carry hers up there."

"Don't do that. Leave well alone." These were unusually decisive words from her father. The slut still pursued her instinct and climbed upstairs. In Daisy's mind, this was a low tactic on her part, and since she was stooping so low, the slut courted whatever bile might be flung her way. The daughter's resentment extended to Smooth himself for being so gutless here.

"Come on Daisy. Eat up." Before Cai Sufen could hand the bowl over, her arm had swung with a malevolent swipe, splashing scalding soup over the stepmother who cried in agony. Daisy's roiled face struck her as formidable and she dashed away. As she was retreating downstairs, the younger woman raised her foot and propelled the bowl so it hit Sufen on the shin. "Get away, you lowdown slut! Bugger off, slut!" She reached for a Tibetan dagger that was lying on the bedside cabinet. That weapon, bought at Lake Qinghai, was utilised as a deterrent to ward off her terrified adversary. Sufen missed a step and completed the rest of the descent, skidding down on her back. This mortal dread only stoked in Daisy a sense of the utmost hilarity, and she cackled, "Ha ha, look how far the lowdown slut has fallen. Ha ha." Once she was done gloating, she stabbed the blade into Plum Han's bedroom door with a thud. As her stepsister had been away for months studying at Shangluo Higher Education College, the door was garlanded with cobwebs.

Smooth had an inkling that matters upstairs were less than congenial, so he planted his bowl on the table before he'd finished gulping down the last of the noodles. He saw Cai Sufen reaching the bottom of the stairs as if she were a piece of discarded door panelling. Grabbing a stick he cried out, "What a wretched bugger!" As he bounded onto the stairwell, his wife clawed feebly at the hem of his trousers. Cursing "What a wretched bugger!" once more, he rushed to the upper floor in desperation. He had never before laid a finger on his daughter, so this fracas was unprecedented. Daisy was pouting at her door with an expression of disdain.

"Hit me," she yelled. "Go ahead and beat me to death. You wouldn't be fit to call yourself Smooth Diao if you didn't clobber me to death." It had slipped even his mind that his surname was Diao, and to hear his name called out tauntingly in public like this was an unmistakable act of provocation on her part. Raising the stick in outrage, he suddenly felt his wife trying to restrain him from behind. The power of her grip astonished Smooth. She clasped him there until his lungs almost collapsed.

"Get away! Fuck off!" Daisy was still in a frenzy. Smooth's own face became crumpled with wrath. Cai Sufen wouldn't loosen her hold.

Without warning, Daisy screamed out the word "Mum!" and dived onto her bed with a wail. She twitched convulsively so that the rush mat beneath her rustled with her every twitch. All at once, the atmosphere in the room froze.

Smooth had never expected Daisy to play the abandoned daughter card, and this tactic brought a welcome calm to the household. The club in his hand was removed in timely fashion by Cai Sufen.

For so many years, the one thing he could not tolerate was the sound of Daisy crying in this way. However tough and unyielding his disposition might seem, her moans and tears still had a dissolving effect. Daisy's mother bolted when she was only six years old, and it was all down to his ineptitude that he allowed her to be charmed away by a rival.

Tian Miao had been her name, and it was fair to say that she was the great beauty of the neighbourhood. On account of her fine looks, droves of men harassed her. As this intensified, her character morphed into being somewhat open and loose. There were rumours that she began bed-hopping at around fifteen or sixteen. To begin with, Smooth never contemplated taking a girl like this as his wife. For her part, Tian Miao didn't look on him as being anything more that an errand boy, useful for sorting out menial tasks for her. He would love to watch over her shoulder as she played mahjong. She might say, "Smooth, go and buy a hot dog for your big sister." Actually, she was his junior, though this didn't prevent him from purchasing the snack in a mood of contentment and flattery. He would also fetch her an ice lolly as a bonus.

As Tian Miao became entangled with further suitors, Smooth was increasingly averse to doing these little favours. She found work as a door woman in a hotel foyer, and it was there that she took on a lover who was black. She even gave birth to a lovechild, the paternity of which was plain to see. It passed away in infancy, though the notoriety this earned her made her family fearful that no man would consider her for wedlock. At this juncture, some around her recalled how Smooth had apparently shown affection for her. He rejected matrimony at first because he thought it was an invitation to be a full-time cuckold. He wouldn't be made to sport a single pair of horns then, but a whole herd's worth of antlers was awaiting him. Someone tried to enumerate her conquests and reckoned that the tally must run into three digits, including the black lover. Smooth swore that he would rather stay a lifelong bachelor than be spliced to such a vixen. The tide of events is unpredictable, though. Smooth may not have been in Tian Miao's sights, but when she heard that he tried to berate her, she decided to set a small trap that would capture him with ease.

After their nuptials, the new husband took life rather lightly. In response to comments such as "Nice horns, Smooth", he would reply, "They are just so-so right now," while all the while knowing that his scalp was flat. Former lovers of Tian Miao who lived in the vicinity were apt to make coarse remarks such as, "Her pliers are awfully tough. Watch she doesn't snap your dick off." Smooth would reply, "Best mind that your own dick is safe." Rankled as he was deep down, he never let this discontent bubble up at home, and he never lost composure around his wife. He knew all there was to know well in advance, and their marriage was an instance of one party being willing to wave the truncheon and the other being willing to be beaten. There was nothing rational or constructive about disinterring whatever escapades took place in the past. Besides, he was too busy and too tired to care. After the day's work was over, he would slump on the bed like a dead sow. Tian Miao acted with consideration, bringing in a tray laden with tea, water and food. He could accommodate himself to this situation.

Ever since Tian Miao's liaison with the black lover, her father and elder brother had been exasperated. In fact, they tied her up and flogged her until she was half dead. In the years that followed, her demeanour became calm, and marrying Smooth brought out her domesticated side. Then, when Daisy was five or six, she began a fresh liaison with a TV dealer from Guangdong. Her old weakness had reared its head again, and she mercilessly abandoned her daughter to elope with him.

The affair continued for months, unnoticed by Smooth. Back then, he was not only assisting opera troupes in transporting equipment, but had a sideline running odd jobs for stallholders. When he found nothing to keep him occupied, he would rise at 3 or 4 am and cycle out to purchase fresh produce, which once sold on could guarantee the household a buffer of at least a hundred yuan. Tian Miao dared not show her face in public, so she devoted herself to domestic management. Eventually, when she did start to frequent the mahjong tables again, she could be absorbed in the game until dawn. Neglectful as she was as a parent, Smooth was reliable enough to stay home in the evening and see that the kid was put to bed at the right time. And then a rumour reached his ears that Tian Miao was involved with a TV salesman from Guangdong. Allegedly, they had met over mahjong and she would always accompany him back to the hotel where he stayed. A certain choosiness became evident in what she ate and wore. Smooth shadowed her more than once, but even if he caught them entangled in an assignation, his position would still be futile. Curse her as he might for her brazen promiscuity, she would challenge him with rebuttals such as, "Guilty as charged. So what? If we can't handle this arrangement, let's get divorced." His anger was apoplectic, yet his primary concern was for the pitiful lot of little Daisy. At her tender age, she couldn't fail to be scarred by the dissolution of her parents' marriage.

Ultimately, Tian Miao did leave him for the Cantonese guy, whose face was creviced with a multitude of scars. No news was heard of her from then onwards. There was a rumour that the elopement was short-lived and that she had succumbed to an Aids-related illness. Smooth doubted the veracity of this yarn and held on to the hope that they could have some kind of reunion in the future. After all, she was Daisy's mother.

His daughter had thus been his charge since the age of six. A motherless child has an endless appetite for concern and comforting. Smooth felt he had such arrears in this regard that he owed the child a colossal debt. Her disposition was growing trickier and more contrary, especially since the arrival of Sufen. She never showed him face and was prone to rowing with him when others were watching.

A period of quiet reflection drew him to thinking that she deserved mercy. The altered circumstances were hard for her to accept. Given that Sufen was of a rational and reasonable disposition, he saw the potential benefits of sharing a candid talk with Daisy.

And yet, as he sat down opposite his daughter, her posture changed. She reared herself up in a way that suggested the seeds of further mania. "Smooth Diao, get out of here! This is my room! Get out!"

Her father was too agitated to put any of his thoughts into words. He tried to exercise self-control and not initiate any confrontation that would leave too much debris. His day job entailed bowing and submitting to all-comers, so wasn't it only natural for him to appear cowed before his own daughter? He swallowed the words in his throat and sat there without uttering a thing.

Daisy was unwilling to let up. "You get out," she screeched. "This is the last time I want to see you!"

"I'm your dad. Why should I leave? Wretched bugger!"

"Are you really my dad? Do you think you have the face to claim that title? Do you behave as a father should? You scurry after one woman, then another. Has our home become a knocking shop?"

Smooth could bare it no longer and bounded forward, slapping Daisy with force.

Daisy was affronted and retaliated like a lioness, pinning him into the corner of the room. Sufen, who was waiting outside, rushed in and wrenched them apart, installing herself as a human shield. Daisy delivered her stepmother a series of brisk slaps, though Sufen simply stood there erect and didn't repay the blows. Smooth's patience was exhausted, so he straightened himself and shoved Daisy with a single hand down onto the rush mat. His hand was firm. As she tried to gather herself together, shamefaced and galled, any counter-attack Daisy might have been hatching was curbed by Sufen's grip. "Daisy, he's your dad. He's your dad. Don't act up like this. I'll leave, then. I'll leave. Fair enough!"

"Fuck off," snarled Daisy. "Get out." She kept on trying to break free, swatting with her hands, kicking and biting like an animal at Sufen. The older woman winced from the pain, though she didn't loosen one bit. At last, Smooth's patience was spent. "What are you, a maniac?" he bellowed.

"You're the maniac – a sex maniac. And you're in your element."

"Wretched bugger!" Smooth was desperate to lash out at Daisy again, though Sufen blocked his access from both the left and right sides.

Daisy suddenly took on a haughty air. "Go ahead, go ahead. Strike me, strike me. You two can team up and do me in together. Then you'll have the home all to yourselves. Go ahead, hit me. Outside, you're as obedient as a turtle. Now you have found the balls to be a brute at home. Go ahead and hit me. Show the world your bravery, Smooth Diao. Punch your own daughter to death. Hit me, you just hit me..."

Daisy once more wailed, making Smooth come over impotent.

He glanced at her dressing table, which was chockful of various bottles and canisters of peculiar shapes and design. He realised that each one was far from cheap. Daisy would spend more than a thousand yuan of her monthly salary on cosmetics, while Smooth had to make do with a cheap tube of lanolin to salve his chapped hands in winter. He wasn't reluctant to spend money on her, but the results were underwhelming. He would respond by saying, "Carry on. Do whatever you must. If I can't keep you, find somebody who can."

"You're driving me away. When you brought that slut home, wasn't it your intention to drive me away?"

"Wretched bugger! How can you call your auntie a slut?"

"Auntie? Oh, humph, the slut!"

"Daisy Diao, you've no right to sit in judgment about who I choose to marry and bring home. All I possess has been earned by these two hands of mine. I've brought you up, supplying everything you eat, wear and use in everyday life. That's all come from me sticking my arse up and my head down. How much must you waste on face paint each month alone? I know you look down on me and think I've lost face for you. I can do no better. Just pedal my trike about and shift stages for others. I only scrape a pittance. If you think the food is not up to scratch, you don't have enough to spend and your life's not cosy, then you can leave. I'll come to believe I never had a daughter. You just leave. Wretched bugger!" Smooth at last spat out the bitterest words.

"I'll leave," Daisy lashed back. "All the more room for you couple of bitches. I'll leave this minute. I'll not spend one more cent of your rotten money. Humph!" With those words, she gathered up the pillows and whacked them down on the dressing table. The bottles and canisters pitched up into the air and fell down, sploshing all over the floor and filling with room with a pungent, floral smell.

"Daisy, Daisy. Your dad is swearing because he's annoyed," said Cai Sufen, trying to mollify matters. "Don't take what he says so literally."

"Humph. It's you, you slut, who brought it all out."

"Let her go. Wretched bugger!" Smooth's voice took on a kind of ferocity.

Cai Sufen had no choice but to release the reeling captive Daisy. She was still bouncing and jumping, kicking and cursing. She picked up her mobile and Louis Vuitton purse and thundered out in a frenzy. They could hear her kicking the lame dog out of spite and slamming the iron gate shut with the boom of an exploding incendiary. The sound nearly cracked Smooth's heart into shards.

"Hurry, and bring her back," Sufen advised.

"Let her go. Wretched bugger!" Smooth was now the one left bleary-eyed.

9

DAISY WAS UNSURE WHERE TO GO after stepping out of the front door. Staging a disappearance of sorts formed part of her ongoing master plan. She believed firmly that her father's affection for her still trumped whatever he felt for that slut. In addition, he was kind-hearted and made himself as pliable as mud to those he dealt with outside. Why should his daughter be any different? Should he want to actively drive her away, he would need to become sterner and more cunning.

Her plan had been to lie low at her maternal uncle's home for a few days. This would not be ideal, for she wanted to maximise her father's torment rather than reassure him that all was well. Better if she were to check into the express hotel opposite home. She was quite familiar with the boss, and they regularly shared a round of mahjong. When she told him her father would pick up the tab, he let her check in with no questions asked.

Once installed at the inn, Daisy flounced in and out, making herself as conspicuous as possible. Anybody prepared to listen would hear tell of how she had been ejected callously from home. Both within and outside the lane, the word was that Smooth had wed a scheming harpy who had bewitched him into wanting rid of his own girl. This was exactly the sort of furore Daisy desired.

The day Daisy left, Sufen had been convinced that her departure was also for the best. When Smooth examined her following the tumble down the stairs, he discovered a bruised area on her back measuring almost a foot in length, as well as numerous bite marks, welts and scratches across her arms and torso. A chill disturbed his heart. He could not deny that Sufen had acted sensibly throughout and had done nothing to incite things. That she had shown consummate patience in the face of ignominy meant there was no reason why she should be the one to leave. Sufen had a special flavour and quality of her own, and he could not allow himself to be parted from her until he had explored it fully. "Why should you have to go?" he asked. "Don't go. Spend the rest of your life with me. Wait and see what she dares do next. Wretched bugger! To think I raised her!" He wiped her injuries gently with some gentian violet and staunched the trickling blood with gauze and sticking plasters. Such repairs were common in his line of work, so his dressings looked quite professional and deft.

Sufen relished Smooth's care and attentiveness. The physical pain might well have been his to bear. In truth, she had no wish to leave. She just exuded the impression of being content to remain neutral amid this civil war. When her husband made his position clear, she saw no need to dwell on the subject.

Daisy had deluded herself into believing she was a lamp that could burn inexhaustibly on her own oil. The tale of how her father's hussy had made her homeless was trotted out implacably, so that when Cai Sufen went outside she was greeted with wagging fingers.

Smooth always reassured her in the same way, saying, "Never mind, you're under my roof now. You don't need to look elsewhere for food and drink. If anyone has farts stored up, they can let rip as they please."

This outward confidence concealed a mesh of anxieties. Of all the people in the world, his daughter ought to be the one he cherished, yet she had been the one to decamp. How could he sit by as she chose to live in a hotel instead of at home? What's more, the bill would be running to a hundred or two hundred yuan per day. He might be able to tug a bit of surplus wool from his own coat, but would Daisy be willing to part with a coin or two of her own?

Predictably, on the second day of her stay, when Smooth was passing through the lane, he happened to catch the eye of the hotel manager. "Hey Smooth," he yelled. "Your lass is living here on credit. That's not how we do things here. If this was anybody but you, we'd never allow it."

Smooth's head was throbbing as he had seen all of this coming. "Boss," he answered. "This is nothing to do with me. If you want to give girls freebies, that's up to you. I'm a manual labourer without a coin to spare. How could I think about living in a plush hotel? You'd best not reason in this way."

Actually, those words were spoken in the hope that Daisy might be listening.

The manager smiled. "I don't care one bit who actually pays," he went on. "When the room's in service, the water and electricity costs have to be covered. We've got our taxes to deal with, staff wages to pay, and on top of it all there's a franchise fee."

"Well, who you're paying a cut to is certainly none of my business. I'm too busy to jabber like this with you."

Smooth rode away, his legs now a little limber. He wasn't inclined to enumerate every fine detail. All he knew was that if he had to subsidise Daisy's banishment there any longer, that would leech away all his earnings from shifting stages.

At present, there was no prospect of him giving way to his daughter, since that would entail asking Sufen to depart. How could he do such a thing! They had a marriage licence and she wasn't some overcoat he could slip on or toss aside at will. He still needed a pretence for saying something robust to Daisy. Silence was more potent right now than small talk. She had started to address him provocatively as "Smooth Diao" rather than as "Dad". What mighty rhetoric could he, a trike-riding stage shifter, intone to overawe such a girl? It was like trying to crack a nut forged from steel.

Another, not dissimilar nut was waiting for him at work. A few days previously they had antagonised Director Kou, and Smooth had not found the time to visit him in person and apologise. Chief Qu held no fear for him, but he was concerned about the possibility of riling those petty ghosts who sneaked about below him. Once that type was so incited, they might find ways of ensuring his crew was denied work. Then everything would run awry.

He had been trying to contact Director Kou, but either his calls were cut short on the flimsy pretence of him being busy or else were simply left unanswered. Messages were sent ad nauseum. When at last Kou did agree to receive him, Smooth was unsure about what conciliatory gift to buy and how much to spend. He called over Big

Hook to seek a second opinion about what was proper. "Two hundred and fifty tops," was his benchmark. "But what are we hoping to earn back from this?" Their discussion led to the purchase of a case of milk, a box of apples, a bunch of bananas and a basket of oranges, for a total sum of about three hundred yuan. Acting like a troop of Japanese trying to capture a mine in an old movie, Smooth stealthily approached Director Kou's home. He didn't even offer his visitor a seat and talked with him while standing. Of course, Smooth punctuated the conversation with bows and kowtows, requesting assurances of help and support in the future.

Kou's wife was an actress, always cast as a young female opera lead. As the two were talking, she lay on the sofa with a damp white sheet of tissue applied to her face so that only the lips and eyes were exposed. This was her beautification routine. Before Kou could open his mouth, she chipped in first, "Oh, Smooth, you're so strong. Already onto your third wife. It's like they say, a carrot sprinkled with pepper will surprise those who taste it. Over fifty and you're a better man about the house than Kou. If you've got a secret recipe, please do share it with him."

These sentiments made Smooth blush. "Ai, I'm just a hard-working fella. I get home and find no hot meal or tea on the table. So I need to find someone to boil the water, cook dinner and keep my feet warm."

Kou was discomfited by his wife's interjections, and took this as the sign to engineer Smooth's departure. Saying "I know", he showed his guest to the door. Once outside, the voice of the diva indoors struck up the aria "Missing Mortal Being" with her voice in its natural tone, free of falsetto.

Visiting Director Kou turned out to be most efficacious. Early the next morning, he sent Smooth a memo: "Come this pm to take down stage once show over."

During the day, he twice cycled to the northern suburb to courier materials for decoration. He earned 160 yuan. By 10 pm, he had summoned his team and they were loitering about the corridor backstage. Cai Sufen accompanied them since there was nothing to occupy her at home. Smooth knew that her real motive was fear of being in the house alone. Big Hook and Monkey spouted some innuendo about the situation, and she tried to be neither calm nor flustered. It was Third Skin who spoke up in her defence. Then Monkey made a crass comment about how Third Skin wanted to nibble their sister-in-law's "warm tofu". Eating "warm tofu" was a metaphor for groping a clothed body. Stallholders wrapped their warm tofu in a cheesecloth, but it still wobbled suggestively.

After the curtain call, the actors withdrew backstage one-by-one to be replaced by the stage-shifting crew. Chief Qu was still onstage talking with Director Jin. Smooth purposefully approached them, his hands crossed in front of him. "Congratulations, Chief Qu. Congratulations, Director Jin," he gushed. "Such a success."

"How d'you know it went so well?" asked Director Jin, who was partial to this tenor of praise.

"I overheard the audience – all kinds of stuff like 'Director Jin's – Teacher Jin's – surpassed herself', and 'Chief Qu's steered the team towards a triumph'." This was pure blather because Smooth was in no position to hear a thing. He knew that only honeyed words were welcome among their kind, and contrary comments were unpalatable. Who wanted to listen to a squawking raven?

The director did not forget to reciprocate Smooth's appreciation. "This time you boys pulled off a great feat," she declared. "There's every chance the agents have chosen our drama. Several days straight they've been around here and never missed an evening performance. They even suggested a few improvements. This hasn't happened before."

"Congratulations, congratulations," Smooth complimented them in turn. Then he set about dismantling the stage.

Dismantling the set was less of a hardship than assembling it. The heaviest task was transporting the props to the warehouse. This was a four-storey structure located behind the stage, and this particular troupe owned storage space on the top floor. A total of about two hundred iron cases with handles needed to be put away. The building was of some age and its stairways narrow and low. Each case had to be carried individually on one's back, a chore that lasted until 3 am. Smooth always put himself at the head of the pack with the larger items. Sufen came afterwards with her hands full of prop bags and backcloths. After moving the last case, her husband was felled with fatigue, slumping down on the stairs, and only being able to rise again with her encouragement. "Don't put yourself out with those bigger cases," she said with compassion. "There are younger guys who can cope better."

"If I don't force myself to tackle the big ones, I won't have the strength to manage small ones. It's not in folks' nature to tax themselves. People who lie on the ground don't want to stand up. People who stand up don't want to walk. People who walk don't want to run. In other words, use it or lose it!"

On the way back, Sufen refused to be a passenger on the tricycle. Worried that Smooth was too tired, she followed on foot. Her husband moaned that keeping a pedestrian's pace was slowing them down. Sufen reluctantly agreed to sit on the back and enquired, "How much do you take home each time after it is all divvied up?"

"Varies. Depends on the type of job and whether the boss is a tightwad or not."

"What about tonight?"

"At most, about a hundred and fifty yuan apiece. As the head, I get double." He told her that after discussing it with Big Hook and Monkey, they had agreed to give Sufen half of the standard wage – about seventy or eighty yuan. She was invigorated by the news.

On passing the express hotel, Smooth's mood sank again. No matter how hard he worked, he could not fund Daisy's defiant extravagance. Though he couldn't bring himself to share what he was feeling, his heart was in tatters, as if someone had hacked away at it with a dagger.

10

It was Goody the dog who woke Smooth the next morning. Smooth peeked at his watch and realised he'd slept only four hours. The day had by now fully broken, and the tricycle was stacked with goods, scheduled to arrive in Chang'an County by 11 am.

Sleep had made Sufen muddleheaded. She lifted her leg and hooked it over Smooth's body, murmuring beguilingly, "Oh, rest a bit longer. I'm still so drowsy."

"You go on sleeping. I've a delivery to make." Smooth crawled from the bed, still dreadfully fatigued.

Her hands intercepted his waist. "Rest a bit longer, just a little bit longer."

She really was a charming specimen of womanhood. They had not arrived home until nearly 4 am, but now she was enticing him into some sunup servicing. Goody barked throughout their tryst, not being quite sure of what it meant. After he was finished, Smooth came over slightly queasy. He had almost tumbled down the stairs last night and then they writhed beneath the sheets with the minimum of noise. "This takes more stamina than lugging cases up to the fourth floor." Sufen pinched him in a way that made his skin itch. He then thought: for better or worse, this is what a man's life is about.

Smooth slid back onto the mattress and reclined a while. His wife deliberately tweaked his flesh all over in a manner that made him reluctant to get up. He then suddenly recalled a verse from the opera *Concubine Yang*:

> *The hairpin, the flowery face and golden feet all sway,*
> *Tented by lotuses the spring night is restfully gay.*
> *Short lasts the darkness, the sun rises with bright beams,*
> *The emperor never visits court early, or so it seems.*

As he trolled away, he placed himself in the position of the greedy Tang Dynasty emperor who was willing to throw over his courtly duties. He asked if "carrying the prop box to the fourth floor" once more was a possibility? "Nobody said 'no'," Sufen replied. "As long as you have it in you, you can try as many times as you like." And so he did.

Goody again barked at the bed, pawing the ground until the motions had ended.

"You're a charming fox fairy," reflected Smooth.

"So what if I want to be your personal fox fairy?"

Now joyful, Smooth thought he could be a permanent fixture on this bed, or lie there until he took his terminal breath. This was not to last, though, for his mind soon switched to how Daisy was holed up in the express hotel. The entire flesh of his body ached and drooped at that prospect.

Smooth was able to resist Sufen's enveloping thigh and stood up. She bolted up too and went down to poach four eggs for him. Those first three days she had stayed at his home, he outlined the extent of his demands in life, deducing that as long as he had four eggs and a fried dough stick before going out to heave sets, that would be sufficient for him. Hence, that was the first meal she prepared for him and Daisy upon arriving.

Smooth ate with relish, tears beading his eyes. This was an unprecedented shaft of delight. Finding himself temporarily rid of his obstreperous daughter cast a fresh complexion on his mundane life.

Once he had cleared his bowl, he readied himself to leave. Sufen's request to tag along was rebutted on the grounds that it was blustery outside and the journey would take more than an hour. Besides, there was no room in the cart since the load consisted of glassware that couldn't be squatted on. Sufen no longer pestered him.

The second he crossed the threshold, the tribulations of Daisy once more invaded his thoughts. No matter what transpired, the present situation could not be allowed to continue. If this was the template for things to come, he would be the one to shoulder all the adversity in the world. How could he refuse to cover the hotel bill, though? What kind of a reprobate did his reluctance make him! Submitting to Daisy's precondition was utterly unthinkable, though. He could not drive Sufen away. On top of that, she had done nothing to warrant this rejection. The fuss she had stoked up on Sufen's first day made him regret his failure to take Daisy in hand a long time ago. Today, he felt not one shred of regret. He had yet to reach his seventies or eighties, so life was not a strain on him. Even in his early fifties, he could keep pace with his younger colleagues. Now was the time to look to the future with a broader perspective. It was far from easy to cross paths with a woman of whom one was fond. As the saying goes, you might well pass a village without noticing the inn. As for Daisy, she would get hitched sooner or later. Once she was a wife herself, how could she endure seeing her father without a companion? The more he mentally revisited this ground, the more logical his actions appeared. She was his daughter and his alone, so there was no outsider who could mend matters for him. The best tactic would be to persuade her to return home.

A go-between was what he now needed, since none of these issues could be broached face-to-face with Daisy. Among his relations and extended family, there was no one who could perform the role of intermediary. Those closest to him disparaged Smooth for having taken a new wife before his grown-up daughter was safely married off. This was a source of consternation for Daisy herself, and to recruit a relative to be the peacemaker would be to stoke the pyre higher. Having taxed his brain cells, Chief Qu came to mind.

From Smooth's point of view, Chief Qu was a man of uncommon quality. His hair had turned snowy, it was said, as a consequence of the incessant troubles wrought by the troupe members. He maintained his keenness and composure, weathering the most irksome of challenges. As a local saying puts it: "Better to lead a legion of troops and steeds than an opera troupe of motley talents and leads." Chief Qu had served in this capacity for dozens of years and could dispatch the thorniest of problems. How, Smooth thought, could Daisy be smarter than his colleagues? She had tagged along with them since early childhood, and Chief Qu would tantalise her with treats and drinks. Once, when New Year's Eve came around, Smooth had been too entrenched in shifting a stage to be able to go out and purchase a new outfit for his daughter. The chief gave him a dress he had bought for his own girl, maintaining that it was a touch small for her figure. This favour was still lodged in the memories of both Smooth and Daisy. He knew that the chief was the most suitable candidate for the present task, but fretted that there would be no opportune time to enlist his help. Their customary banter made others assume they were close. Some even insinuated that Smooth was precious to him. The very act of asking such a favour brought with it the risk of a repudiation. Smooth ruminated over this dilemma before deciding that once the glassware had reached its destination, he must be the one to call on Qu.

The chief dwelt in the oldest block in the possession of the troupe, his apartment being on the top storey out of five. Last year, a new building had been completed to accommodate younger staff. Chief Qu decided to set an example by not adding his own name to the waiting list for rooms, lest the veteran staff scramble with each other after the better flats. This earned him the gratitude of the junior personnel.

Smooth had never once been inside Qu's home, though he knew precisely where it was. That year when he passed on the dress for Daisy, he cycled to the suburb very early on the sixth day of the Lunar New Year. The consignment of fresh produce he bought out of gratitude was left silently and strategically on the doorstep. The chief later criticised him for this, observing, "It's not easy for you to scrape by. Anything you spend on me will make me feel guilty. Never do this again." From then on, Smooth gave Qu's residence a wide berth. Should he ask him for a favour now, it would be incongruous to drop by with nothing by way of a sweetener. In due course, he settled for four types of gift: a case of milk, a box of apples, a bunch of bananas and a basket of oranges. In short, the same perishables he had offered to Director Kou. Smooth was self-conscious that others might take note of his actions. For him it was inconsequential; the chief's name could end up sullied, though. The two colleagues ran into each other unexpectedly at the foot of the stairs and Qu was insistent that the goods shouldn't leave the trike.

The interior of his home seemed extraordinarily plain to Smooth. He had seen deluxe apartments on his delivery rounds, and a few of them were so disconcertingly sumptuous that he dared not contaminate them with the soles of his shoes. The chief's unadorned surroundings filled him with disbelief, too. The outer door opened directly into the reception room, which was in fact spacious enough only to house a dining table and an upright refrigerator. Guests were entertained in a somewhat larger room containing an ancient piano, a five-drawer desk and an outmoded three-piece suite. Chief Qu unfastened the balcony doors leading off the sitting room. A barricade had been created here in the form of a series of bookshelves. Although a window was left at the centre of the room to let in light, every cranny and crevice around it was stuffed with books and musical scores.

Smooth stood there, not bold enough to take a seat. Whenever he entered a customer's home, the householders would be so unconcerned that it wouldn't occur to them to encourage the deliveryman to have a rest. Chief Qu's invitation to sit down felt odd, and so he only planted half of his buttocks cautiously on the edge of the sofa, until his host repeated the invitation. The chief was keen to know why he had visited, and Smooth could only murmur slightly incoherently, being too abashed to spell out his true purpose. He then began to digress to other topics, saying, for instance, "Chief Qu, you've contributed so much to the troupe. How can you still live in such a shoebox?"

"It's not that small," he answered. "Three rooms and about seventy or eighty square metres. Besides, my daughter's married now, so it's ample for the two of us."

His wife entered with a cup of tea for Smooth, who was now so uneasy that he was unsure whether to rise or sit. He knew this lady had been a teacher in a primary school and was said to be kind-hearted, though every time he caught sight of her there was no opportunity to engage in conversation. Smooth proceeded to reflect on the chief's good name and how the troupe all stood united behind him. What he took as fact was intoned more loudly, and other embellishments were sprinkled in as well. Anyhow, he had nothing but effervescent compliments for Chief Qu. That was until his host cut him short and again asked the reason for his visit. Smooth laid out the truth very simply, and a lengthy silence ensued. "Perhaps I've overstretched myself?" Smooth said. "Me a hired hand, and I've come to the boss for his assistance. Call it conceited. I'm a hardworking guy who happens to be in a hole. Chief Qu, you've got broad shoulders, so ignore me if I'm behaving like a petty fellow. Pretend I said nothing to you."

Smooth rose to leave, a gesture of retreat a little like hiding one's needle in a bundle of cotton wadding. He made one final gambit to apply pressure to the chief. "You know they all spin stories about me, calling me your 'can-do-no-wrong wing man' and 'honoured member of staff'. Some even jeer at me as 'the backbone among your middle-level comrades'. I tell them I'm only a hired hand. How could I be your backbone? Only Director Kou should be counted as that. How can I compare to him? It's only because Chief Qu takes me as a somebody that I can take pride in my name and my position. Chief Qu, please get back to your business and I'll not detain you any longer."

As Smooth was on his way out, the chief said, "Let me have a stab at it. It's not that I'm reluctant to help. My concern is that you two can't be easily reconciled. Your daughter is grown up now, so likely she has her own sense of face to think about. There may be too many things lurking beneath the surface. If we go into it half-cocked, our opening words might only serve to repel her forever."

"Chief Qu, if you can't sort this out, nobody else in this city has a prayer."

"Don't think too highly of me. I'm not at all confident right now."

"I was told that there's been more than one couple in the troupe who talked about divorce. You were the one who persuaded them to go on living together. Quite a few families have had long-standing feuds, but you calmed those rifts. As long as you are determined, I am certain you can succeed."

"Never expect too much from me. I am prepared to have a try, mind. I'm just worried that she could really have taken umbrage this time. Living in the hotel is a strategy for bleeding away your earnings. You sweat enough as it is, and can't afford this much more."

Smooth's eyes almost melted at the chief's words.

There was nothing further he could share out loud. He cupped Chief Qu's hands in his own and shook them repeatedly. That was the signal for his tears to trickle. Bowing his head, Smooth withdrew from the room.

11

BEFORE LONG, Daisy had reached the eighth day of her sojourn at the hotel. Her room overlooked the street, so she could monitor her father as he rode past every day. That slut always followed on behind or else sat proudly on the tricycle with him as if she were royalty. Daisy used to do the same as a girl, and would pester him to build up speed. Sometimes he cycled at such a lick that he could overtake motorists. Now, a queer cuckoo had usurped her perch. One evening, she duly noted how the slut sat so louchely on the trike and knitted her fingers around her father's waist. The woman's own midrib seemed to flex so very kittenishly. Daisy grew bilious inside.

She had never been entirely unsatisfied with her present condition. When she gazed at herself in the mirror on the dressing table, she could neither bring herself to sob nor cackle. Eventually she found an outlet for both, and the laughter carried a greater note of tragedy than the tears. Maybe there was something wrong with the mirror? When denuded of cosmetics and gaudy clothes, her reflection appeared unbearably commonplace. She had grown up in this city, as had her father. One time in her teens, she eavesdropped on a few of the ingenues in the troupe who were nattering. "She's a city girl, isn't she?" the conversation went. "How could she turn out like that? Goes to prove that townies have problems just like the rest of us!" Later on, the gist became clear to Daisy when she learned that most of the staff were originally from the countryside. The performers were at least either a little handsome or fetching, yet city locals would taunt them as bumpkins. Naturally, they accrued a seam of hostility to native folk, which in this case meant Daisy became their target.

Daisy remembered her mother as a woman of not inconsiderable beauty. As she neared adulthood, she heard tell of her exploits, the riper morsels being truly nauseating. She was routinely branded a "loose bitch", and even her own brother seldom mentioned her out of shame. They also viewed the trike-riding, stage-shifting Smooth with an air of condescension. For this reason, she was became partly estranged from that maternal uncle.

Daisy did sometimes wonder if her mother's life would be the prototype for her own. Any partiality her mother experienced for a man would soon mushroom into fondness, and in the grip of heartfelt affection she eloped so readily. As for the reality, Daisy had passed thirty with only one dalliance of her own. That transpired the previous summer. Her father happened to be out all day shifting stages. At around 9 pm, he sent over a young assistant to fetch his toolbox. Smooth had been on a delivery job in the afternoon and then had gone directly to the stage, so there was no chance to drop in himself. When Daisy beheld the errand boy, she had no clue that anyone so head-turning worked under her father. Nothing about him betrayed the fact he was a migrant labourer from the countryside, for he wore crisp shorts and his vest was peeled upwards so that his honed midriff was exposed. At the sight of Daisy, he covered himself up. She felt a deluge of hormonal energy and her words came out as an incoherent babble.

Daisy knew where the toolbox was kept, though feigned ignorance and pretended to scour the house for it. The young man stood poker-straight in the centre of the room. That night was sweltering, and she wore only a night robe with nothing underneath. She had originally expected that the countryman who came on this errand would be grubby all over and that his body odour would be detectable from afar like her father's. He did perspire, but the sheer force of his virility proved intoxicating and could not be constrained by his modest shorts and vest. Her heart was at once stirred and aflutter. She beckoned for him to sit down and handed him a flannel with which to dab off his sweat. It was her own personal towel used for drying her face, neck and even her breasts. Usually, her father was forbidden from touching it. In that fraction of a second, she yearned to be the one to wipe the visitor's angular face. He just took the towel, remained motionless and could not bring himself to be seated. The young man stood there, his head drenched in sweat.

The light in the yard was dim and far from enlightening. One solitary beam reflected over from the neighbourhood. When that young man entered, a strong residual glow illuminated his face as if he were a statue on the stage. From being a child, she knew about optics and could draw him into a prime position where his contours would be shown off to the fullest. She was not about to switch on any other lamps, for she hoped that he would not see her features in their entirety. This obscure sensation emboldened her, so she had no hesitation in asking him his full name. Smooth may have had to pedal his own trike, but he was the head of the stage-shifting team and de facto boss, even though he shrugged off that title. For an instant, Daisy realised the stature that came with being the boss's daughter. At last, she persuaded him to sit down.

As she searched for that toolbox, the object of her quest was forgotten. The young man was quick-witted, and he detected how she appeared vacant all of a sudden. Not wanting to trample over the etiquette of the situation, he sat there in silence during her fruitless rummaging. Actually, he had already spotted the toolbox and was similarly keen that she keep up her charade. He drank with a gurgle that encoded anxiety mingled with a thirst that must be quenched. That was his implicit signal.

"Is it upstairs?" She asked this both opportunistically and with more than a hint of the seductress. In hindsight, she knew the man was not to be blamed for leaving without uttering a single word. When she revisited the minutiae of the episode, she knew that he too was not a lamp that could burn inexhaustibly on his own oil. "Might it be upstairs?" she asked, with a palpable tremble to her voice. He offered up nothing in response, but followed her upstairs. Everything proceeded according to a pattern of tacit understanding. She entered her bedroom, only to turn around and, in a state where her soul and mind seemed rent asunder, spoke out what she was thinking at random.

"Coming in... after the toolbox?"

"Yes." His voice sounded thinner than hers since he had downed copious quantities of water. Still there persisted the thirst and anxiety, now almost fusing his jaw so that words had trouble escaping.

Presently, she discerned how this man, who stood a head taller than her, was edging behind her and his breath felt so hot and potent that it might be flammable. She was, at base, a girl and this was the first time she had known such intimacy with the opposite sex. It would be improper for her to assume the initiative. Instead, she should wait and be receptive. At an opportune moment, he touched her waist with one hand while pretending that the contact was accidental. She shyly blocked that advance and he seemed prepared to withdraw his caress. Daisy now indicated that she was not objecting. He stretched out both hands, so that what had started as a loose grip around the middle intensified into a possessive clench. Throughout the entire process, she knew he was making a move on her. She once again put up flimsy resistance and was convinced he may be about to withdraw his hands. Daisy pivoted backwards, ostensibly in retreat, but in reality she was trying to locate the edge of the bed. She tumbled down where she was, just missing the mattress, and her body landed heavily on the reed mat. Her suitor took advantage and pitched to the floor like a mighty trunk that had been felled. Even if she wanted him to call it off, he had no desire to withdraw.

The visitor's name was Shusheng. The next day, as she and her father ate lunch together, she probed him incessantly about this man. Smooth, who was unaware of the nocturnal goings on, was asked if it was possible for Shusheng to return and assist in smartening up the home. It never once occurred to him that Daisy would have fallen for a migrant hand from the sticks. What never occurred to either of them was that Shusheng would dematerialise without a trace. Daisy's father was perplexed as to why a hired hand would vanish without even collecting his pay packet. Only she knew what had spurred his departure: he had observed her true countenance in the merciless light of the sun. That very day she had done herself up in what she regarded as her foxiest outfit. Shusheng was caught unawares the second she came into view. His expression of astonishment became welded into her mind. Quite beyond her expectations, he was more handsome and cool that he had been after dark. Before her was a virtual replica in flesh and blood of the statuette of David she venerated. Little wonder then that on the night in question he had finally been straight with her and related how he wished to become a performer, belting out the folk songs of his native northern Shaanxi in the city. This was a career that legions of people wanted to follow, so the strenuous work of shifting stages provided him with a temporary toehold.

Daisy dropped countless romantic hints, both subtle and more brazen. That afternoon her father was out on deliveries, leaving them with a few hours in which to become more acquainted. They vowed to discuss outstanding matters, but the conversation only slid into banter. After repositioning just a few plant pots, she feared that he might become fatigued. As darkness fell, she tried more than once to coax him upstairs on the pretext that the reed mat needed to be spread out in a better spot. Shusheng's only response was to murmur that he had to slip outside and purchase some things. He would be back shortly. Daisy waited and waited, with not even the hint of his shadow to be glimpsed by the time her father came home after 10 pm. The angry young woman complained to Smooth, being adamant that he should recall his lackey. She told him that there were still many chores left unfinished, though when Smooth tried to reach him on his mobile, the power was off. He then phoned Big Hook, who shared digs with him, only to learn that Shusheng had rushed home, packing all of his belongings hastily together before leaving. His explanation was that some emergency had arisen back in his hometown. And so it was that Shusheng had disappeared for good. Daisy did make enquiries at a number of restaurants specialising in northern Shaanxi food, but none of his compatriots even knew anyone by the name of Shusheng.

Daisy slid into a prolonged depression. With the passing days, she ceased to devote quite so much emotional energy to this affair. Her disappointment was supplanted by a feeling of urgency about being wed. She knew that in the past she had not considered finding a boyfriend too herculean a task despite being a perpetual singleton. Now she had been thrown over by a measly migrant farm hand angling for piece work in the city. Her heart had been gored.

Daisy's marriage was indeed on her father's mind too, and he would consult almost anybody in the hope of them introducing a potential match. No shortage of willing helpers stepped forward, but the courtship always sketched the same trajectory: men were happy to be involved in chapter one of the story, but made an exit before taking it any further. Daisy's shrewish instincts broiled away inside, further fuelling her outlandish thoughts. Intermittently, she could entertain the idea of having a suitor in his forties or fifties so long as his character was proper. The best outcome would be if she could be spirited away from this place like her mother – the more distant the destination, the better. She was tired of living in such a state.

Her father bringing that slut home had soured this environment – extra tedious, extra boring, extra shameless and extra futile. There were periods when she had the urge to torch this godforsaken dive to the ground. As angry schemes festered within her, she snatched the cup from the hotel table and pelted it at the distorting mirror. Who cared? Smooth Diao would cover every breakage.

Beforehand, she had been planning to head to the karaoke that evening. Her mood was even harder to mend than broken shards of mirrored glass. She sent out the message that she would not be joining the assembled group. Instead, she would sleep, and sleep alone. That way, the commotion and stimulation from outside would be held to a minimum.

The doorbell chimed and she asked who was there. The hotel porter told her that some fellow from the opera troupe had called by. He said that he went by the name of "Uncle Qu" and he was waiting for Daisy downstairs in the foyer.

What could Chief Qu have come to meet her here for? Then the thought struck her that he had been recruited as her father's go-between. She thought this a little peculiar, for what had Smooth done to be so honoured? He was a simple coolie on a trike, so how could he enlist Chief Qu? How was that possible? "Just tell him I'm not in," Daisy replied.

Minutes later, the bell rang again. "Daisy, this is your Uncle Qu. Please open up. It really is your Uncle Qu."

Since it really was him outside, she was obliged to open the door.

12

Daisy spent her formative years in the midst of the theatrical company. The children of the troupe were her playmates. Nobody deterred her from romping and larking around with them. However, their homes were strictly off limits. On occasion, she would scamper to a front door, only to have it slammed in her face. It was not only the adults who shunned her, but the kids too reinforced this domestic embargo. Once she inserted a tiny foot into a doorway, only for her friend to ram it closed. Her ankle was swollen and bruised, and she could not put pressure on it for days. Another time, when flush with fun and looking for fresh amusement, she followed a crocodile of youngsters into the decorated wedding chamber of a famous actor who was about to marry. All at once, she felt her ear being yanked as she was led outside. She could do nothing more than press her throbbing lobe against the door and listen as that ragbag of kids battled over wedding sweets and red envelopes of loose change. She had to wait until they too left the room before being able to enter herself.

Subsequently, she gained a whiff of what was happening at these social gatherings. Each time the young folk congregated, items would go astray, and there were those who secretly accused Daisy. She had never been a magpie. Her father pounded it into her that to pinch even a single needle was a crime, and that no perpetrator had the right to hold forth or raise their head in company. She was apt to pick up scraps of cardboard, empty bottles and plastic bags, but these were items of refuse rather than contraband. Should anybody let a re-useable article drop to the ground, she would naturally retrieve it and pass it on. The thought that she was a thief was ludicrous. Daisy had no clue as to why people nursed groundless suspicions of her. Only Chief Qu – Uncle Qu – was kind enough to invite her to eat at his apartment and be his daughter's homework buddy. Staying there that one night was no imposition either.

Daisy would never forget the events of her twelfth birthday. Her father had been stage shifting unremittingly for three days and nights. The troupe was to participate in a national tour and each fine detail had to be sorted out. Her mother had been gone for a few years, and during summer and winter holidays she would be her father's shadow, scuttling to and from the stage. On the night in question, she did try to rest in their home. A member of a neighbouring family had passed away and the creak of the bugle and rattle of the drum combined eerily with the piteous weeping. Daisy became so unnerved that she tried to bed down on a square of cardboard at the corner of the stage.

As midnight neared, Smooth saw Chief Qu approaching. "Ah, Chief Qu," he said. "Three days and nights straight. Not a wink of sleep. You're in charge here and the honour will be yours. A national performance. As a troupe, we have to take care of our corner, but the province is in the spotlight too. We can't bluff our way through it. I'm not putting on airs. Today's my Daisy's birthday – her twelfth, so the year of her birth animal. I'm too busy to spare her any attention, though. Poor lass. The old chap next door's croaked it. She daren't sleep in her own bed, so she's curled up here like a dog. I feel really bad about all this, Chief Qu. She's no mother any more, and so I owe her so much. Don't worry, Chief Qu. We're hardworking fellas, and we'll do a decent job for you. Have I ever lost face for you or sold you short? The stage is bound to be perfect when the director takes over. Just be at ease and don't fret."

Chief Qu strolled a circuit of the stage and was about to assume temporary custody of Daisy. "Smooth, don't fuss. I'll take the kid home and she can share my daughter's bed. You should take it easy, too."

Daisy could see how dumbstruck her father was. He rubbed his hands endlessly. "She's filthy all over," observed Smooth. "How can you let her into one of your beds!"

Chief Qu made no reply and led the girl away. She turned around and could see how tears glistered in Smooth's eyes. From that day forwards, everyone believed he must be the darling of the chief.

When Daisy arrived at the apartment, Qu's wife and daughter had already turned in. She didn't know what the chief had said to them, but the pair rose to help. The wife drew water for Daisy to take a bath, and his daughter fished out some garments for her to change into. They presented her with an array of tasty fare before tucking her in. The daughter, named Susu, handed Daisy an outsized doll, even taller than her, which she could hug and have double up as a pillow. Her sleep was deep, and in her dream she imagined what it would be like to be Chief Qu's daughter. The two sisters were clad in identical white one-piece dresses and were playing away on swings beneath the azure skies and cotton clouds. From then on, she tried to visit his home, but her father warned her not to make this a part of her routine and to ration their time together. He was convinced that people should be conscious of boundaries in their social lives. If someone gave you a wheat stalk, it shouldn't become your walking stick.

Daisy found that Susu was fond of study and was constantly practising English vocabulary or attending to her homework. She had been learning the violin since she was barely one year old and had won first prize in a national competition. Their pastimes and interests did not overlap. Eventually, Daisy visited less and less and Susu went to study in Vienna.

The whole Qu family displayed the greatest solicitude to her, and this generosity left an indelible memory. Thus, when the chief banged on her door, she was duty-bound to open up.

Uncle Qu did not enter. He merely asked her to come to his place and take a look at some photos of Susu. She complied.

It was her first time in that apartment for a number of years, and her shadow hadn't even darkened the courtyard of the troupe. She couldn't bear how the residents stared at her, for one glance chilled her backbone to ice.

Uncle Qu's wife was also at home, and it seemed that the two of them had prearranged what was to ensue. The second Daisy appeared, a mug of coffee was awaiting her. She invited her to sit down before withdrawing to tutor some violin students. This was her job on the side, and purportedly every pupil paid more than 120 yuan per hour. How the young Daisy had wished she could be one of these students. As her father clawed in less than a hundred yuan a day, wouldn't it be shameful to labour this matter with him? She recalled how Susu once showed her how to handle the bow, and even praised her tunefulness. Susu also told her that musical talent should be nurtured early on. Older kids could not acquire the skill. Back then, when Daisy was twelve, Susu had already passed the Grade Ten violin examination.

As promised, Uncle Qu laid out swathes of photos that Susu had snapped during her overseas doctoral studies in music. The young woman's grace, romantic air and poise roused in Daisy's mind just four words: "Don't you feel ashamed?" She did not actually envy Susu and was glad that her friend should be basking in such praise and fulfilment. The nub of Daisy's regret was how she lacked parents like the Qus and how the environment in her own home was not conducive to education.

After studying the photos for a while, Uncle Qu at last broached the topic, asking, "Have things not been so good between you and Dad lately?"

Daisy did not answer. She crooked her head and continued to look through the photos.

"This is your father's fault."

Daisy was stunned and gaped at Uncle Qu.

"When it comes to an important matter like marriage, yes, he should have discussed things with you first. How could he leap into it? I've criticised him about this and made him admit that it wasn't handled sensitively."

Daisy further lowered her head.

"If you can't accept what's going on, I'll have more words with him. I can help you persuade him to make her leave."

Daisy was still unresponsive.

"Do you lend a hand with cooking and the laundry these days?"

Daisy lowered her head even further. In the first few years, she had prepared their meals. As her father's workload snowballed, home-cooking was one activity that was allowed to slide. She ate at irregular times and now and then subsisted on snacks. As for noodles, she preferred to buy in ready-pulled ones of the rice or wheat flour kind. Gone was her inclination to cook, and she even became downright lazy, gagging at the odour of oil and smoke. The young folk in her community were mostly of the same bent, and found nothing stimulating in their surroundings. Surfing online had been a fad a while back, though even this had come to be deemed dull. Whiling the time away was daunting for them. Whereas formerly Daisy had taken care of her father's washing, there was little now to launder for his work attire consisted of a simple four-seasons blue coat that needed a rinse about once a month. Given the erratic schedule of stage shifters, they might only meet every two or three days. Mostly, his return was marked by the sight of her father's jacket freshly washed and flapping on the line. Daisy was not at all curious about this relic, for whether laundered or soiled, it sported a perpetually crumpled appearance. And so life puttered on without grief or vitality.

Daisy wanted to answer, but did not.

Uncle Qu allowed himself a sip of tea and said in a measured tone, "My child, in the future you'll have a life of your own. Your dad is not easy to get along with. Perhaps you could offer him more space. We all understand it must be hard for you as a daughter to stomach. From your father's perspective, his actions are not unreasonable. You can't spend all your time under the same roof. He's in his fifties, so will need a carer someday. It's too much of an imposition to expect a daughter to do that. You'll be much less put out if there is another person to look after everything. For once, you should forgive your dad. His life is far from easy."

Daisy had never expected that Uncle Qu would share such an exchange with her. Blunt as those words were, she did not grab the bait and simply listened without saying anything.

She had envisaged that Uncle Qu would reproach her father and chitchat relentlessly about him. Without warning, he moved the topic onto her unmarried status. This was the subject she hated being broached most of all, and Qu happened to be rubbing a tender sore. "I heard from your dad that it's been a bit of a palaver trying to find a man of your own."

Daisy was about to let her disdain flare into the open, but she exercised self-control. There was no malice behind his intrigue, but she was simply loath to being drawn on the subject.

"My Susu's just the same," Uncle Qu continued, beginning his subterfuge. "Past thirty already, and still no other half. It causes us no end of stress, but she never seems concerned. You kids all behave the same."

In an instant, her fondness for the avuncular Qu had returned. By juxtaposing Daisy's experience with that of his daughter, he succeeded in placating her. Apparently, he did not attribute Daisy's spinsterhood to the conditions in her family or her own physical appearance. Rather, this was a social epidemic that affected nearly all young folk. Excellent as she was, Susu herself was not immune.

All of a sudden, Daisy discovered some dignity in this debate and could open her mouth in response. "So Susu hasn't found a boyfriend either?"

"No. We've been urging her, but she's adamant there is no hurry. Now she tells us that she believes there's no shame in celibacy."

At last, Daisy laughed heartily and admitted, "I'm on her side. No need to look for Mr Right. You can find contentment alone. Times have changed. Talking about marriage is a bit vulgar." In that one second, she seemed to have discovered her sturdiest spiritual crutch, and straightened her spine on the sofa.

Chief Qu sat back slowly and with a slight sigh, and reflected, "There's nothing vulgar about you. It's just we worry as parents. If a decent match comes along, then getting married is the best option. Of course, if you don't find a decent match, you can't just surrender yourself to marriage. Marriage shouldn't be about surrender."

Daisy had never conceived that Uncle Qu could speak in such a tenor. Their small talk meandered between miscellaneous topics before reaching her father's marriage. She was nonplussed.

"My child, what on earth is bothering you about your father's wife? Can't you tell your Uncle Qu?"

His words rendered her mute. This was not the place to call her a cheap bitch. What other reasons did she have to be disgruntled? She couldn't hone in on a single one. Frankly, and by rights, the woman had tried every means to flatter her from the second she entered their home. Even her own father took pains to calm Daisy. Beyond saying that she was dissatisfied with having a new stepmother, she couldn't pinpoint a tangible reason.

Her head sank again as she fumbled through the leaves of the album. She could not answer Uncle Qu's question.

"Your Uncle Qu has a bit of advice. Could you suck it and see? Try to tolerate your father's choice for a time. If that's impossible, call on me and we'll talk it through with him. OK?"

Daisy still did not speak. She listened placidly to the notes from the violin in the next room. These were the efforts of a novice – say twelve or thirteen years old – the same age she was when she wanted to learn.

"I think it's better you don't live in that hotel," he resumed. "It's not the place for a single woman to be for long. If staying in your own home proves inconvenient, you can bunk down at mine. Your auntie is retired now and has nothing else to do apart from tutoring a few kids."

"No, no. How could I do that!"

"My child, each day in that place must swallow up a couple of hundred yuan. It's like driving a blade into your dad's heart." Uncle Qu's voice modulated to a serious tone.

"Your dad is a prickly customer," continued the chief. "I'll tell you one incident, then you decide whether being angry with him is warranted or not. Do you remember last summer when he caught his foot on a nail?"

She did not. Cuts and bruises came with the territory of stage shifting. He never told her about his latest injuries, nor did she hear him groan in agony or discomfort.

"I was there when he had that accident. A few of them were carrying pieces of set, and he stood on a rusty nail. It was a pretty long bugger and went right up through his sole and out. His face turned blue with pain and drops of sweat as big as beans ran from his cheeks. Some of the boys hauled him pronto to the hospital. I thought he might be laid up for days. After the wound was dressed, he limped straight back. In the evening performance, he was scheduled to push the iron frame. They use that rig in *Journey to West Lake* to make it look like the ghosts are floating. It might take four beefy men to shove it forward or pull it back. When actors are hovering mid-air, pushing and pulling that thing is tough. His foot was wounded terribly, but he refused to let another chap stand in for him. Guess why? Those dozen minutes earned him about forty yuan. By the time he was done, his foot was soaked red and so was his mouth from all that chomping of his lip... my child, can you bear to live in that hotel and bleed two hundred yuan from him each day?"

After that, she failed to catch the essence of what her uncle said. Sadness and shame engulfed her, and her brain throbbed. Daisy barely had the prepossession to walk out of the flat. Her cheeks were pulsing crimson and even her neck seared. She told Uncle Qu of her resolution to check out the very next morning.

However, it was to the home of her maternal uncle, and not Smooth's, that she relocated.

13

AT FIRST, Smooth was emphatic that he would not foot the hotel bill. Each time their paths crossed, the manager would press the issue. With Sufen's urging, he mustered the courage to clean the slate. Daisy had spent eight nights there at a daily cost of 240 yuan. Smooth winkled a thirty-five per cent discount, and throughout his bargaining the staff exhibited nothing but the most respectful of expressions. About 800 yuan-worth of food had been bought on credit, as she had hankered after snacks, beer, mineral water and chocolates. The disposable towels had been soiled and a mirror broken, those damages running to nearly 400 yuan. All told, he was liable for in excess of 2,000 yuan even after the most generous discount. When he drew the notes from his pocket, his face convulsed with fury. Still, she had checked out and a bung had been fixed in that bottomless crater. Smooth was extremely grateful to Chief Qu and went to his home to underline this sentiment. The chief said that the young lady was blinkered and stubborn. She had to be handled carefully, and he asked her father not to do anything on impulse. Things should be left to unfold by themselves.

At this juncture, Smooth landed a bankable task. One of the real estate moguls had secured a large plot of land in the east of the city, and wanted to organise a thank-you soiree on a massive scale. The roster of acts was said to include first-class vocalists from Hong Kong, Taiwan, Macau and mainland China, in addition to an American rock and roll legend. Nothing short of a superlative stage arena would do. Smooth had no involvement between the initial plan and the implementation of the festivities. Instead, his portion of cake was desirable and flavoursome in a fashion he had never known before. His team was tasked with building the shell of the platform within a two-week period. Smooth was summoned by the executive director to join a gathering at the most lavish five-star hotel in the city. It wasn't the first time he had been to such an establishment. Usually he delivered goods via the service doors, so didn't know the charm of entering a social event through the main entrance. A sort of unspoken excitement washed through him, and his morale was rejuvenated. His reputation might be about to reach the heights, much as this evening party would. In the future, any mention of this event would be incomplete without referring to the stage builder by name. It was the handiwork of Smooth and his team. Recognition was the key to maintaining a monopoly in this field.

Smooth shivered with anticipation as he heard the executive director's description of the party. Apparently, he was a big fish from Beijing and spoke with the brogue of the capital. He was known to have contacts at the seat of national government in Zhongnanhai. When the general stage manager introduced him, he reeled off a dozen of the more fabled evening parties he had overseen without catching his breath. In spite of not having heard of a single one of these events, the atmosphere and air of grandeur made Smooth listen attentively, almost kowtowing on the floor out of reverence.

The executive director sported exuberant facial hair not unlike Osama Bin Laden, who had by then been captured by the American military. His pate was smooth, lending the impression that his follicles had decided to invert convention. While the racing torrent of his speech outlined the lofty vision of the soiree that was to be entitled *Ode to Golden Autumn Fields*, he incessantly ran a delicate comb across his bare scalp. This gesture was hilarious to behold, but the earnest solemnity of the occasion ensured the audience didn't break with decorum. The executive director claimed that the time had come to launch an authentic work of art. He was certain that the Western Capital, the nation and the world would remember forever this evening spectacular. His slogan went, "Shock the nation, stun the world." He asked that every section involved should not fight for glory or personal advancement but dedicate themselves to art night and day until final victory was secured. Elated at hearing these words, Smooth still couldn't shed his old habit of calculating every figure he might net in the process. His mind wandered from the task at hand to working out what his fortnightly haul might amount to this time.

It had been Iron Kou who introduced him to this job. Iron Kou only took responsibility for the building of the stage, and the general stage manager had a distinctive Beijing accent too. Iron Kou was under the charge of a separate stage manager with Smooth as Kou's subordinate. When Kou came to fetch him, he revealed that the total budget for the stage came to three million yuan, but two million of that went on the rental of stage equipment and was beyond his remit. The remaining million was earmarked for erecting the stage and the al fresco seating, as well as prettifying the outdoor environment. One hundred thousand yuan was all Smooth could expect for hiring thirty personnel to be responsible for the three aforesaid components. After Smooth protested, Iron Kou agreed to add a further 5,000, bringing his share to 105,000 yuan. This was on the proviso that Smooth signed a contract which stated that the total budget amounted to 300,000 yuan. Kou maintained that this deception had been the stage manager's idea and they had to oil the hands of every senior official involved.

At first Smooth was unwilling to sign the contract, being under the apprehension that the men he mentioned were hawks, and requested that he be given 200,000 yuan for putting his name to the document. Iron Kou upped his offer to 110,000 yuan, saying that this was the absolute limit. It occurred to Smooth that every person has their own approach to doing calculations and this was the largest contract he had ever received for building a stage. His crude arithmetic told him that, barring catastrophe, one fortnight might yield him a personal net income of more than 10,000 yuan after wages and deductions. If he factored in Sufen's salary, then that would be 15,000 yuan. Looked at from every angle, this was a worthwhile proposition. That was not even considering how such a prestigious project would boost his own profile and lead to mastery in the field. His only worry was not being able to pull it off to perfection.

After the executive director wrapped up his speech, Smooth, as was his wont, stalked up to the man, seeking a brief exchange. As the headman of a pack of dozens, he was obligated to make himself known. Once he had struck up a little bonhomie with the boss, future discussions could be initiated more freely. His years of stage shifting, moreover, had taught him that this was a tactic to circumvent potential losses.

The air and demeanour of the executive director did indeed overawe those in his presence. Smooth was a little tense as he approached, saying, "Ex... Executive Director, that speech was astounding. No wonder you got to where you are today – a great and golden director who made it in the capital. Really great. Rest assured, sir, I shall do a phenomenal job of your stage. It'll be turned over to you on time for rehearsals. We won't stand in the way of art."

The executive director was puzzled and asked, "You? Who are you?"

The stage manager alongside Iron Kou moved hastily forward and said, "This is the fella in charge of shifting the stage."

Iron Kou was afraid that the introduction was too fuzzy, so stepped over and clarified, "He represents the premier stage-shifting company in the Western Capital. He is the head and known as Smooth Diao or Manager Diao."

"Is that Diao as in Diao Deyi – the sly Nationalist officer in the Peking model opera?" The executive director's interest was whetted.

"Yah, that Diao – Diao Deyi," Smooth answered, nodding.

"You seem better suited to playing Diao the Bum." The executive director's quip made all the onlookers chortle.

"I am a hardworking fella. How could I play a famous role like Diao the Bum?"

"Ha ha, sounds quite professional. You must excel this time. Everybody there will be a big shot in their own way. They're super picky about stages, so any cock-up will be noticed. If someone injures themselves, that'll be more shit than you can bear." He went towards his room along with several assistants, not even aiming a glance in Smooth's direction.

The stage for *Ode to Golden Autumn Fields* was to be constructed in the middle of a colossal wheat field. Adjacent to this farmland stood a plant for manufacturing steel pipes, once operated by the village. It had fallen into disuse ages ago and the row of empty, ramshackle workshops that had not been demolished were available to serve the on-site needs of the crew. Smooth led his troops over and commandeered the largest workshop since this had its own cookhouse. He persuaded Sufen and Third Skin to assume the catering duties. And so it was that the spectacular and raucous feat of moving the outdoor stage began.

The first task for Smooth and his team was to surface a road. The highway lay several metres from the boundary of the field, and a route of conveyance would enable them to move goods to where they were required. The terrain stretched out flat and almost level. Nonetheless, in order to create a link, Smooth's team of thirty had to dig and spread aggregate, toiling away for fully three days until the trucks had a pinched path of access for carrying their steel cargoes.

Not even Smooth, the former market gardener who had been digging food from the earth since he was small, had undertaken such a backbreaking job before. After three days, he could not even straighten his waist. Those who had thought the work would be easy now started to rebel. Monkey was extremely cunning, and he knew that for such a grand stage the pickings ought to be far healthier than for run-of-the-mill jobs. He tried to discover the total amount invested in the performance. When he heard that it was thirty million yuan, he told Big Hook that there must be shenanigans with the books. Under pressure, Smooth had to disclose all. The contract had stated 300,000 yuan, but they were only actually entitled to claim 110,000 yuan. It was a little like a mute person eating boiled dumplings. They know in their heart exactly how many they have consumed, but cannot share the truth. Smooth comforted them by saying, "We're just hands who labour hard. As long as we have a bone to gnaw on, we mustn't care how much meat others have. If no meat ends up in our bowls, it's pointless making a fuss about it. Sure, this time there's a bit more flesh on the bone than usual." They clumped together and calculated the budget back and forth. The 10,000 yuan in their hands was little more than a down payment, earmarked for covering meals. Smooth collared Iron Kou plenty of times to remind him how the crew depended on that money for their livelihoods. But whenever Kou approached the stage manager, it proved a fruitless task. Kou related how he had been told that there were no such rules under heaven. The money would be transferred after the stage had been installed. Kou explained repeatedly to others how there should be no anxieties about the pay. The real estate boss had so much money he could fuel a bonfire with his spare banknotes.

Although it was mid-autumn, the noonday sun on the uplands was still excoriating and the workers could find no sanctuary from it. Ten days and more here turned the warriors in Smooth's army into dark ghosts who appeared to have emerged from a charcoal kiln. Faces and hands peeled in the overpowering solar glare. At long, long last the stage was completed, and all the lights had been hoisted onto the iron frames. Once the power source was connected, the lighting division descended. The general manager of that division also spoke like a Beijinger. He turned up shortly before sundown in a green army overcoat, followed by a small retinue. Throughout the procedure, Smooth never caught a clear view of his face, though intriguingly Master Ding from the provincial opera troupe had come along as his overseer. It was only then that Smooth twigged the true rank of this newcomer. He had been Ding's mentor years before, so it was little wonder that the maestro deferred to him as a subordinate. With the full set-up being switched into life, Smooth caught the grandeur of the epic composition. Fully 1,200 bulbs were used in configurations not seen in standard stages. As the director made several rounds of adjustments, the plateau was turned into a chromatic arcadia.

Sufen, having no yen to rinse the vegetables or smash the garlic for the evening meal, dashed outside to imbibe the "exotic scenery". Third Skin, being by his own admission more of a man of the world, had the decency to let her stay out and watch while he went ahead and mixed the dough. The lame hound had been tailing her mistress all the time. As a crowd clustered together, Sufen grasped Goody in her arms, fearful that she could be trodden on, and squeezed into the throng beneath the stage.

Smooth continued to pace about the platform. Ten or more days of this had made him so fatigued that his haemorrhoids flared up. Only Sufen was privy to his bitter suffering. When he walked it was with his legs splayed apart, prompting Monkey to jibe that maybe his third wife had caused his bollocks to swell and his legs could no longer carry them.

Smooth did not forget to put on a show before the "Lighting

General". He had heard others address him as General Pi. In truth, he looked rather affable and benevolent. Judging by his appearance alone, had he been seen walking casually on the plateau without so many people around him, one would likely take him as a vegetable seller. Smooth crept in his direction with great respect. He had been on the verge of striking up a conversation with Pi more than once, though he was always wrapped up with someone else. Smooth had noticed that a large bowl of fried beans was standing on the temporary lighting platform. From time to time, General Pi would forage for one, cracking it open with a succession of bites and then swallow it down. He ate bean after bean without pausing.

Master Ding's partiality to legumes had been inherited from his teacher as a result of countless evenings spent adjusting lights together. The process of digesting beans invariably produces a surfeit of gas, and General Pi was a prime offender in this regard. While simultaneously gnawing and chuntering away, these fumes would leak loudly from down below. Everyone was apparently accustomed to this brazen habit, and for Smooth it removed something of the general's lustre. Eventually, as he was sipping water, Smooth decided the time was right to accost him.

"General Pi, if you find fault in how any of the lights are installed, please don't hesitate to inform us."

Pi did not seem to catch his meaning and stared at those around him. Smooth then repeated himself in Standard Mandarin.

The stage manager had no patience for these kinds of exchanges. "Go, go away," he shrieked. "Just go and take care of your own business. How does anyone have the nerve to report matters directly to General Pi? A splendid performance of this kind needs hierarchy. If people don't stick to their own stations, the whole thing will be anarchy. Don't approach this platform unless there is something crucial we should be notified about."

Smooth left red-faced. Even that dog-fucked Monkey who was swinging from a lighting boom had taken this as a kind of comedy sketch.

They treated Smooth as a nobody. Oddly, this brought him great relief. While the big potatoes were in the middle of their discussion, Smooth took his leave. He patted Sufen on the shoulder and told her he wanted to run some water to soak his piles. She followed him to the workshop.

Sufen carried water to the ridges behind the building. Every night, the crew would take a shower here. Smooth's haemorrhoids had been bleeding and his underwear was glued to his buttocks. Sufen helped to douse the region with warm water and gently peel the fabric away. The pain was excruciating, though attenuated somewhat as he regarded Sufen's kindness towards him. She wanted to take care of the whole cleansing procedure, though he refused. A topical analgesic cream as the last stage made him feel comfortable.

A chilly breeze pierced the mid-autumn evening on the plateau, leaving Goody pawing to get into Smooth's arms and Sufen slumping her head against his shoulder.

"Look!" she suddenly screamed.

"What's up?" Smooth asked.

"What's that dark thing on the ground, all wide like a belt? It's moving."

They drew cautiously near to discover that it was ants swarming home. Oh, heavens! The dark belt emerged from an indeterminate spot and then twisted and zigzagged before becoming invisible.

Smooth clicked on his flashlight and was able to make out how these insects were heftier and more unruly than those in the city. They were trying to lift bulkier loads with their forelegs and ended up staggering clumsily. The more ambitious among them could raise a bean several times their own body weight. Others were capable of kidnapping ladybirds, swinging their captives aloft and scuttling away. Still more tackled unwieldy targets, heaving up out-sized objects before collapsing, then repeating the act in desperation, not wishing to concede defeat. "Why bother when you know you don't have the brawn?" Sufen sighed.

"How can you say that?" her husband asked. "There might be a load of mouths waiting at home. What other choice do they have?"

They watched the insect flurry for a while before walking to a mound of earth, which gave them a fine vantage point to survey the Western Capital. The nocturnal cityscape had a glamour quite beyond their imagining. For those dozen nights, that same vista must have been available to these two citizens. Only now did they have the opportunity to look on from afar and dissect the view. The couple searched for that modest courtyard where they made their home.

"It's yours, not mine," pointed out Sufen.

"It's ours," Smooth corrected her. "Doesn't belong to me alone."

Daisy flashed into his mind, but he tried to exorcise her at once. She made his head ache. As he was thinking, an announcement on the microphone blasted through the night sky, penetrating every inch of the plain. "Smooth, Smooth, Smooth Diao. I'll fuck your mum. Where are you hiding? The lights need adjusting. Where are you, where are you?"

Smooth recognised this as the voice of Iron Kou. He answered without hesitation, though his words were drowned out by the sheer volume of the mike. Smooth howled his reply from the wilderness and was dealt an earful of ever fiercer curses. In spite of Sufen urging him to steady his pace and be careful, he sprinted to the stage. He couldn't afford to be remiss where that stage was at issue, so hastened over a series of ridges as if they were hurdles. When it came to the last one, Sufen saw his legs falter. He paused ever so briefly, then limped onto the stage in a hurry.

14

THE PERFORMANCE WENT ON AS SCHEDULED, with Smooth and his team on the job for almost an entire forty-eight-hour stint. The first night, as they repositioned the lighting rig, General Pi was afflicted by chronic flatulence. His farts were cacophonous and battered away one round after another for the whole night. No one could ignore this and it roused much hilarity. Big Hook whispered, "Pi, pi, pi, pi – the General's arse is spelling out his name!" At the brink of dawn, the lighting section were ready to down tools, and a group of them accompanied General Pi back to the hotel to rest. Smooth removed his team from the stage and they set about fixing the audience seating. Early on, the wind-breaking had injected a kind of comic energy to proceedings. But by now, they were too exhausted to open their mouths. Monkey, inured to contrary voices, decided to slumber in the workshop. A clearly disgruntled Big Hook accused Smooth of spoiling him, to which he replied, "Look, he's been dangling in the air all night. He's entitled to a bit of rest." This left Big Hook dispirited. Mound suggested that everyone should be allowed to doze awhile, but Smooth knew that once they lay down, their legs would want to remain horizontal. He advised that they should first install the larger banks of seats. If the inspectors happened to swoop down, there ought at least to be the barest outline of an audience arena.

It was a matter of no small consolation that the roller had packed the ground flat and solid. They initially arranged 3,000 chairs, of which 2,500 were of a plain polyurethane form and five hundred were upholstered for VIPs. When they were arranged accordingly, a battery-operated plastic clapper in the shape of a hand was laid on each seat. The intention was that every audience member could wave this novelty to the rhythm of the music as the star singers did their turn. Once all of this was settled, they began to install iron frames and pillars along the four sides of the square. Massive curtain-like banners, similar to those used to advertise new-build show homes, were hung from the pillars, so the square was surrounded on all four sides. Viewed from afar, it seemed that a miniature simulacrum of a modern city had sprouted unannounced in the middle of a wild and barren plain.

For another eight or nine hours, they persisted in girding their already numb bodies. They would not lie down until everything was fixed and sure to prove visually satisfying to the inspectors. The rehearsal was scheduled for the evening, yet there was still an interminable to-do list. None of them had the vitality to stumble very far, so returned to the workshop and took the floor as their mattress in expectation of the director coming to start the rehearsal.

Smooth had the sensation that his rectum was now prolapsed, so hid behind a stage curtain and tried to poke it back into place. As he touched his trousers, he realised that a quantity of sticky blood had seeped out. He wanted to sneak back to the workshop and ask Sufen to warm some water to tidy him up. But his body simply would not comply and he could only sprawl out motionless. In no time at all, somebody's foot dug into his side and he heard the vague signal that the director was here. He opened his eyes to see that it was Iron Kou. Smooth crawled up at once and winced out loud as though his back passage had been lanced open. Kou asked what the problem was, to which he replied, "Nothing at all." He then scrambled up the side ladder to reach the stage.

The evening rehearsal was meant to involve the whole contingent of stars, though apart from the two singers native to this province, only the trio from the US appeared. Smooth learned that they were not in fact the authentic group, but three black stand-ins intended to mime their role. In order to save money, the organiser had planned for them to arrive the following day and then leave the day after that. Unexpectedly, the group came two days early and claimed that, since it was their first time in China, they wanted to go on a short tour first. In addition, a troupe of acrobatic performers came from Guangzhou, with fifty or sixty backing dancers from a performing arts college in Shanxi Province. They boasted that they had formed part of the chorus line in the Spring Festival Gala on CCTV. The executive director was not present, only a few deputies who scrutinised their own area of responsibility.

Smooth was hailed by the deputy director in charge of backstage affairs. He too spoke in a Beijing dialect, which sounded as though his tongue was stubby and the words kept on getting trapped in his mouth as grunts. Smooth struggled to catch what he was saying. He was fond of using the verb "do" in sentences. At last, Iron Kou managed to interpret his instructions for the benefit of Smooth. The crux was that he was to "do" again the passage used by the actors backstage. The surface was uneven and the floor panels were not properly joined. As so many performers opted to wear high heels, a mishap was more than likely. "If they do that to themselves," he warned, "will you take the blame?" Those stern words were immediately clear to Smooth. He bowed his head and then, in a nodding gesture, promised, "Your Honour, Director, Teacher. Rest assured, we'll redo it at once. We are sure you'll be pleased with the result, our honoured elder." After saying those last three words, it dawned on Smooth that the person before him was a corpulent gentleman in his twenties or thirties. Smooth's attempts at praise in clipped Mandarin had been lost on him.

The official rehearsal commenced on the front stage. The names of the leading figures were announced, but only their deputies and assistants were to be seen on the performance platform. The run-through mainly sought to fix locations on the stage and ensure synchrony between the lighting and dancers. The director general of the lighting division was not present either. Master Ding filled in for him with a few of his assistants. Smooth and his gang began to "do" the passage again in accordance with the instructions. No sooner had they prised away several of the tiles did the bark of the corpulent gentleman call out above them, "Oh, ah, ah. What are you doing here? Who asked you to do it now? Don't you know they are trying to do the rehearsal out front? Don't you know we are trying to do something artistic here? If you want to do this tunnel warfare here, how are we meant to do our art on the stage? Stop, stop at once. Do it after the rehearsal is over. Why must you do it now?"

Smooth and his companions stopped. He invited them all to take a breather in the wings as he himself sat there awaiting the next order. The rehearsal was brisk and arrears piled upon arrears. Not only did they have to redo the backstage, but the lights in many areas also required readjustment. The whole night was an unremitting ordeal and closure only came at the break of day.

Ultimately, rest was what all the company needed. This time, two migrant workers had joined the team as a one-off and were now nagging to receive their wages from the previous day. Otherwise, they would not lift another hand. This was no work for a proper man, so they claimed, and one of them had a dodgy kidney so couldn't stay up late. The other felt nauseous from high blood pressure. Smooth paid them out of his own pocket, reasoning that since he knew nothing about their personal details, it would cause a great rigmarole if either collapsed on the stage. He could rest certain in the knowledge that fellows including Big Hook, who had been in his team for a dozen years, were sturdy enough and had stamina. Wither as they might like a frost-bitten cucumber, they wouldn't shirk their duty and would toil on until the job was done, however protracted it turned out to be.

Stage shifting was a profession where there was no day or night. A run of sleepless nights was nothing exceptional. What made the difference here was being forced to labour in the wilderness, feeling half scorched to death during daylight and half frozen to death after nightfall. The way it sapped their time and energy caused resentment among the crew. Big Hook said he'd rather "rent out his arsehole as a male whore" than sign up to anything of this kind again. Monkey teased him by saying that playing this role would be a waste of his finest asset. "Big Hook" was actually a nickname bestowed on him by Monkey as a tribute to his awesome manhood. He once spied that part of his anatomy in the washroom and was stunned at how it seemed to touch both the heavens and the Earth. At its root was a kind of "grass-thatched roof", while the shaft extended plumb straight in the direction of the crap hole. From then on, the moniker became popular. Smooth took the name to mean that he was robust like a towering crane and willing to exert himself to the full, not carping about petty oversights. Mound grabbed the baton from Monkey, saying, "Here's a proverb for us – 'if Big Hook turned tricks as a rent boy, he could make a fortune from his special toy'." Big Hook was tired by then, but not too tired to kick Mound's posterior. He growled, "To make a killing from sexy stunts, why not ply your mothers' cunts?"

Smooth's own rear end knew no relief, and during the day he found no corner in which to tend to it. Sufen, similarly, was too busy to care. Smooth gritted his teeth and reclined. No matter how sore the prolapse became, they only had forty-eight hours left on-site. In his dream, he imagined that the performance was a rapturous success and that all the bigwigs, including the singing stars he had only so far seen on the TV, headed to a palatial hotel for a celebration. The executive director invited him over by name and declared that the success of the event would have been impossible without the fine execution of the stage building. He raised his cup to the responsible parties. Iron Kou pushed Smooth, Big Hook, Monkey and Mound so that they were amid the press of celebrities. Almost to a person, each of those great names wanted to clink glasses with them. The goblets were filled with some kind of foreign, scarlet wine and after a number of refills he became dizzy and sensed his face was now bigger than his body. "Little Diao," the bold executive director then remarked, "you've excelled this time, and the performance was a triumph the like of which we've never seen. This cuts new ground even as far as the whole nation is concerned. I've decided to up your wages." Gladness enveloped his entire being, and he woke from the dream to find himself still clapping. He shuddered with chilly apprehension, realising that whatever we dream about, the reverse might transpire in reality. He started to wonder if there may be some glitch with how they were to be paid.

Everyone else was still slumbering, but Smooth's rest was over. He picked up his mobile and thought about calling Iron Kou. Today, he would try to secure an advance. He searched among his contacts, though held back from ringing Kou himself, afraid that he might scold him and ask what were a few mislaid coins here and there when you get to participate in such a magnificent event? His sense of upset remained, and his eyes began to twitch as he had the intuition that those bosses were not to be trusted. He slid down from his bedding. Just before dropping off, he'd taken a dose of ephedrine and the pain had lifted. His suffering arsehole appeared improved.

Marching onto the stage alone, he diligently stamped down the tiles one-by-one both on the front platform and in the actors' passage backstage. Afterwards, he gave them another once-over to check they were holding steady and sound. To his mind, they should leave no room whatsoever to be criticised.

Iron Kou appeared close to midday to inform him that the florists had delivered, and many bouquets and displays were ready to be laid out on the stage. Smooth thought this would not require a lot of personnel, so was taken aback to discover that truckloads of red begonias were parked by the stage and the idea was to have the whole route from the entrance to the main road carpeted with them. This meant everyone had to chip in.

The labour fee bothered Smooth again. He was compelled to remind Iron Kou once more and did not care whether he appreciated it or not. Kou berated him for behaving like a small-town blacksmith who would never make a big fortune. To be honest, what might have been regarded as a diatribe put Smooth rather at his ease. Since the job had been arranged by Kou, he couldn't duck away now. There was no need for him to worry about whether the organisers were trustworthy or not.

At 5 pm, the military band and the group of waist drum dancers arrived. Gone was the silent tableland of the past, and the whole earth was reverberating. They could now appreciate why such a spacious parking lot had been designated. Oh heaven! In barely an hour, more than a thousand vehicles had streamed into the temporary car park, and an interminable queue of honking cars was still left to be accommodated.

VIP tickets were priced at 2,800 yuan, and regular ones were 1,600 yuan. The word was that every last one was a complimentary gift, and no money changed hands through the box office. Smooth and his team retreated before the business of ticket collecting and driving away non-ticketholders began. He consulted Iron Kou on whether there was any hope that he and his brothers could take in the show and savour the festivities. Kou's requests for a viewing area for the lads were refused, and the front and rear of the stage were patrolled by helmeted police officers and security guards. Much as Iron Kou tried to flatter the manager, he was ignored and became the last straggler to be shooed out of the auditorium.

Having spent a dozen days constructing the stage, the men were considerably frustrated at not being able to even glimpse the faces of any of the big names. They crushed towards the passage leading to the stage, hoping to have their inquisitiveness sated. Three layers of bystanders flanked both the interior and exterior of the corridor, so their line of vision was eclipsed. Now and then a star might be seen beyond the ranks of the curious, but their faces would be half covered with sunglasses and monstrous upturned collars. Smooth was experiencing a relapse of the intolerable burning pain down below. He opted for sleep, since an entire night of dismantling the stage lay ahead.

As he began to doze, the dream he had in the morning was picked up once more. This time the action had relocated from the hotel to the stage venue. Post-performance applause cascaded in waves, bearing all the entertainers to the front of the stage. Praise came from all corners and the executive director again drew a connection between the success of the production and the judicious assembly of the stage. Thus, the stage shifters were invited up front to take a curtain call with the stars. Smooth, Big Hook, Monkey et al were shoved into position. The executive director repeated his earlier sentiments before the entire audience. He announced that the stage shifters were the genuine heroes behind the curtain and would be festooned with awards and bonuses. Theirs was the success of the production too. The applause and clapping of the plastic hands could, without risk of exaggeration, be described as "thundering" and a "tumult". The corpulent deputy director swung by with a large red envelope that the bearded director presented personally to Smooth, who duly counted it. The figures spiralled on and on, surpassing 200,000 yuan, then... he awoke. He always thought that dreams ran in contrary cycles, but now he had dreamed the same thing twice. This was certainly not a good omen.

Sure enough, the next morning the ill fortune of the dream would come to fruition.

15

Smooth was none the wiser about how the main performance had gone off. He wasn't on site for the duration. Judging from all the echoes and vibrations, it was an unqualified hit. The 3,000 replica hands clacked in one almighty din. He later slipped over to the plateau in an attempt to peek inside. The hands were shaking frenetically and without end, their rhythm regular as if machine-operated. A whole psychedelic spectrum of colours was on display.

That night, the wind on the plateau whipped up more intently than before. A succession of gusts rent the brightly printed banners around the square into strips. These pretty textiles would have ended up shredded were it not for the ranks of security guards being deployed there to rescue them. Smooth, being too sore to sit down, crawled onto an earthen hillock and tried to focus on the scene below. That 3,000 people should be willing to swarm into the wasteland in the dark was a truly surreal phenomenon to behold. They were dauntless in the face of the sandy gusts and flapped those plastic trinkets as they whooped and hurrahed. Such a mysterious facet of humankind!

The performance drew to a close amid the most vehement of loess squalls. Smooth could observe the wind swirling over from the west and had a portend of trouble. For starters, or so he later heard, the banners were reduced to ribbons. Then, after a tumult of whoops and clacks, a power line was fractured. This coincided with the final number, and while the stage boomed to the strains of *An Unforgettable Night*, within moments the voices had been stilled, leaving only the instrumental backing track. The audience dispersed in a fraction of a second. Led by instinct, Smooth charged towards the stage as if it were his own property he was defending. Saving the stage was akin to dousing a raging fire, and he knew he must lead from the front in this crisis.

The spectators dispersed in no time. It was of some solace that this was an exposed environment and escape made possible in every direction. Chaos and stampedes were thus averted.

Once all the assembled had retreated, Sufen was able to gather a basketful of discarded stilettos from the ground. The real havoc came with the 1,000 vehicles. Smooth watched the "terrestrial dragon" of traffic weave for more than an hour, horns ablaze. As no party volunteered to give way, nobody was able to depart in a hurry.

The director general, general manager, head of the lighting division and their associates accompanied the stars to their hotels following this unforeseen denouement. As soon as he saw the director general withdraw, Smooth ventured to step forward and offer him flattery. This was his personal habit as well as being a piece of etiquette he felt appropriate for the stage shifter to extend to the stage user. Smooth flicked up his thumbs and cried, "What a success! Great! Such a great day for you, Director General!" The director general appeared to have forgotten who "Little Diao" the stage shifter was, and his eyes didn't even hover in Smooth's direction. He muttered something inaudible in a low voice to the general manager and swept out to the blast of a fart. Smooth could gauge that this must have emanated from General Pi for it burst out as unscrupulous as a trombone.

Save for the stage managers responsible for specific duties, just Smooth and his team were left behind. An affair of this scale would take the whole night to dismantle, yet once the wind quietened down, the project could advance unhindered. As they got stuck in, Smooth heard the lowdown on the performance from Mound. He and some young local guys had gatecrashed the arena once the first banner had been split. The security personnel didn't challenge them. In his words, the party was a con. None of the heralded high-flyers were there, and only two or three of the headline acts appeared. Their voices were so strained, they couldn't hold the notes, and so resorted to lip-synching to recordings. The big-name performers, including the comic Zhao Benshan and the compere Liu Huan, were impersonators. That was the deception. They did resemble the acts they were imitating, yet were certainly not the real thing. Mound alleged that if the tickets had not all been complimentary gifts, a riot would have broken out and laid waste to the site. The real estate boss was said to have been fuming and in the middle of the performance asked how this had come to pass. At the end, he thundered off, cursing savagely, "Cheats, what a bunch of dog-fucked cheats!"

Smooth's nerves tensed as this story was relayed in his presence. He dropped in on Iron Kou to try to establish the fact of the matter. Kou was unsure too, and he remained sullen-faced.

"Director Kou," said Smooth, "perhaps you should go back and check on them PDQ? Watch out, that bunch might try doing a runner."

"How could they? Our folks would tail them."

"Why not?" asked an agonised Smooth. "Even the real estate boss felt swindled. How can we expect anything good to come of this?"

"I rented out those dozens of trucks full of iron frames myself. If any of them were stolen in the confusion, I couldn't cover their loss."

"Better get onto it. My group's more than thirty-strong. They are up to protecting your frames. The most pressing thing is to get our money."

Iron Kou left. The knot in Smooth's heart was swelling more and more. In the middle of the night, he phoned Kou countless times and was always told that his mobile was not in service. They worked until dawn, and Smooth had still not connected with him despite everything now being packed away. He instructed Big Hook to take charge of the loading, and then pedalled to the five-star hotel. When his rectum became too painful, he removed his blue coat, and wrapped it around the saddle a number of times. He reached the hotel with his bottom half on the seat and half crooked into the air.

It was past 9 am when he got to his destination. Iron Kou's mobile was still not in service. As he remembered he had a room in that establishment, he made enquiries at the front desk. The receptionist told Smooth that eighty rooms had been block booked. About thirty guests had checked out the previous night and the remainder this morning. On asking when the latter group left, the answer was 5 am and that all of that cohort had been taxied to the airport. He stood forlornly in the lobby for a while, then left when it became unbearable. He couldn't hitch himself onto the saddle of the trike, and thought about depositing it in a shed nearby while taking a bus to seek out Iron Kou. The storage fee was quoted as twenty yuan per day, a sum he was less than eager to subtract from his hard-earned wage. And then there would be the hassle of returning to retrieve it. He could only wheel the tricycle to the gutter and use the height of the kerb to help lever himself into place. As he rode away, his eyes were ready to dissolve. But who was there to see his tears? He bit his lip and continued to pound. How could those organisers have so little conscience that they'd be willing to rob small fry like him? This thought besieged him as he cycled on his way.

Smooth again dialled Iron Kou's number, this time from the opera troupe compound. The call was answered, though the voice at the other end sounded fragile and short of breath. He held back from moaning about the lack of communication and learned that Iron Kou was at home. His request to drop in on him was sanctioned, and upon dismounting Smooth saw that the overcoat that had been swaddling the saddle had become bloody. He inched towards Iron Kou's front door, steadying himself by running his hand along the wall. Now Smooth could hear cursing. It was the familiar voice of Iron Kou's wife.

"Ah, look at them. They fathered kids without holes in their arses. What a thing! They cheated you. Sue them, those sons of bitches!"

"Calm down, calm down," an impatient Iron Kou counselled.

Smooth knocked gently on the door and the actress opened up. Her assault resumed. "Hey Smooth, surely you can tell us. Are those bastards human? They even fleeced your Teacher Kou. What kind of person does that make your Teacher Kou to be cheated by such bastards?"

"Calm down, calm down!" said Iron Kou, waving his arms.

He was slouched on the sofa with a warm compress on his forehead and beckoned for Smooth to take a seat. Wary of his physical malaise, Smooth didn't move. He knew that as soon as he eventually stood up, his ailment would be betrayed. Iron Kou intermittently let out a sigh, making it hard for the reticent Smooth to ask what he needed to know. He had an icebreaker of sorts: Director Kou had given them this job, so it was urgent that he check the books on behalf of his team.

The actress was still tearing up the sitting room. Even when she paused to brush her teeth, she was able to squeeze in some profanities. "Those sons of bitches, let their planes fall out of the sky. And if not today, that's what they deserve at some point. That bunch of bastards."

Iron Kou's patience was at last exhausted. "Can't you put a sock in it? Aren't you afraid the neighbours will get wind of this? Keep it shut."

The actress was now apoplectic and hurled down the cup she used for rinsing her mouth. Gritty shards of porcelain ricocheted across the apartment. Smooth's face now looked as if it had been hammered by a rainstorm.

"You, Iron Kou, can only play the hero behind closed doors. Those guys from away robbed you and now you come and try to twist faces at me. Twist your ma's pussy! Hundreds of thousands you've lost. Eight generations of your ancestors feel your shame!" Gobbets of foam from her toothpaste-filled mouth sprayed out onto Smooth's neck. There was a "bang" as the door slammed closed and her obscenities were muffled.

Smooth's body was constricted into an S-shape and his legs trembled, though he tried to brace himself.

After an age, Iron Kou opened his mouth. "Fuck, those guys cheated us!"

Smooth said nothing.

"Sorry, I put this work your way out of kindness. It turned out such a hash."

Smooth didn't allow himself to contemplate the full extent of the mess and kept silent. Iron Kou had been the middleman and as long as he was around, Smooth still had someone to lean on. If the organisers had cheated him, that was between Kou and them. Smooth had thirty steadfast brothers waiting for what they were due. As he was pedalling along the roadside, Big Hook phoned to say the trucks were loaded and they expected their fees. He could only reply that that money was not about to sprout legs and run away, so they should rest in the meantime. He hadn't envisioned an outcome like this.

Smooth did now cogitate for a time, before saying, "Director Kou, you've been a good promoter and helped me loads. I'm only a hired hand. To be frank – and I don't worry that you'll laugh at me for this – I've worked so hard that my colon started to squirm its way out. Half of the thirty chaps under me are temps and they don't care about anything but the wage. These days, they've been demanding cash-in-hand for everything. Understandable, since they sweat and bleed for what they earn. Nobody's life is easy." Smooth avoided mentioning the outsiders involved in this fiasco. He couldn't lump them together with Iron Kou since he was the only one with whom he had a relationship. By the same score, he couldn't drive Kou too hard into a corner because in normal times he was their lifeline.

Iron Kou was speechless for an eternity. As Smooth stood there, he assumed more of a hangdog expression.

"You can go back over there first," suggested Kou. "I need to think if there is a road out of this. Come what may, I don't want you to have been put out for nothing."

This came as a crumb of reassurance. Knowing Iron Kou had nowhere else to flee, Smooth left his home.

He fumbled his way downstairs, and Sufen rang to find out his whereabouts. He answered that he was at the opera troupe compound, and she asked him if he'd had the lock on their front gate changed. Smooth reminded her that neither of them had been back for the last fortnight, to which she complained that her key didn't work and she couldn't enter.

He contorted himself back onto the tricycle and rode home. It was true. The lock had been replaced, and he immediately thought Daisy must be the culprit. His indignation surged as he reached for a hammer from the cart to smash it open. Before Smooth could raise the tool, he slumped down by the side of the trike, his body as limp as clay. He could faintly hear Sufen calling, "Eeeek, you're shitting blood." He would later have no recollection of how she took him to the hospital.

16

Daisy stayed in her maternal uncle's home for just a few days. To begin with, there was an air of freshness and her aunt treated her as a guest. As the end of the first week came around, the hospitable ambience was gone. She had difficulty dropping off and often stayed awake until 4 or 5 am, not rising until the early afternoon. Her aunt ran a small store specialising in crickets and grasshoppers, so customers would call early in the day, and the proprietor chose to turn in by early evening. The uncle had no steady business of his own, yet would keep himself occupied all the year round. Whatever small investment might yield fast dividends, his hook was baited. For instance, a few years back philately was a fad. He would visit the post office and ask his pal who worked there to reserve newly issued sets of stamps. Those that became rare and valuable he would sell on for profits of 8,000 or 10,000 yuan. Another example was ticket scalping. His friends in the management sector were entitled to free seats at superstar concerts. Sold on at a generous discount on face value outside the venue, these might haul in 7,000 or 8,000 yuan for him once he had replenished and exhausted his supply. One time when the Taiwanese crooner Qi Qin was here on tour, the uncle made in excess of 20,000 yuan from his customary ruse. He advised that such enterprises were predicated on by judgment, and the grooves in one's brain played a part too.

Daisy's uncle was not an inveterate bragger. He was simply so adroit that his schemes never floundered in practice. The hair on his scalp had grown sparse, and in recent times he opted to shave it so his ears appeared bigger as though someone strong had tugged his lugs. Viewed from afar, he might have been a clan godfather in an American sci-fi epic. He spent none of the proceeds from his wife's business and occasionally hived a little to her. Daisy's aunt had learned neither to depend on him nor poke about in his capers. In other words, they tolerated each others' avocation. What they did share in common was a sense of condescension to her trike-pedalling coolie father Smooth, which intensified after he took to shifting stages.

Before Daisy's mother eloped, she would follow her to this house from time to time. After she disappeared, her relatives were compassionate and full of pity. Once she visited alone, there was always someone around to clasp her in their arms and sob and sigh about her lamentable state. As time wore on, their concern dwindled. On occasions, she would be met with a kind of deliberate coldness, and so her visits tapered off. As an older girl, she comprehended what was happening. Her uncle and aunt spoke of her parents with a blanket disdain. More times than she could remember, she had tried to persuade her dad to change his profession and make money by other means. Whenever she attempted this, he would reply that pedalling the trike and shifting stages was all he was fit for. Were he try something else, the two of them might as well live by drinking the northwest wind. This explanation left her impotent with rage.

Within their neighbourhood, the Diao family to which Smooth belonged was a venerable clan and a long-established household. Stranded as he was in the old neighbourhood of the Western Capital, he made ends meet by running his tricycle and doing errands for opera singers. That his livelihood seemed no better than country labourers who had recently migrated here was a source of scorn for fellow residents. Most locals could simply live off the plot they inhabited. Either they could rent out rooms or gain a share of the compensation when the community sold off land for redevelopment. Not so long ago, the neighbourhood covered an area of approximately forty hectares, but at least half of that had been disposed of in parcels. Each household reaped a portion of the revenue, the peak period being in the early 1990s. Back then, one family could anticipate a cut of 200,000 or 300,000 yuan. This set up the kids so they didn't need to study hard at school, and virtually every family ran mahjong tables for an income. Daisy grew up in this environment. Her dad never learned this game and took riding the tricycle as his sole talent. Once he was in the saddle, not even a cyclist on two wheels could outpace him.

Among the Diao clan, Daisy reserved her admiration for her eldest uncle, Big Army. His path in life was what could be termed "overwhelming". Years ago, he started smoking cigars, a Cuban cheroot hanging perpetually from his lips. Each of his fingers boasted a chunky gold ring, and a gold chain as thick as his little finger was draped around his neck. Later on, when the trend moved towards diamond clusters and jade ornaments, he made sure not to be left behind. During those years, whenever she met him and addressed him as "Uncle", he would blithely pull out two or three hundred yuan in cash, their serial numbers running consecutively. She still recalled that one year when he returned from Macau in a Bentley worth more than six million yuan. The neighbours' eyes all smarted with admiration. The young men in the community took brother Big Army as the model of what a genuine male should be – chic and elegant. He hadn't returned at all in the past few years, and rumour had it that he was now a shareholder in a casino in Macau.

Daisy always wondered how it was possible for two blood brothers from the same womb to walk such different courses. Her dad, at the very least, should strive to gain his income in a dignified way like her maternal uncle. However, he opted for the life of a wretched hound. Smooth related how, as a teenager, he started out hauling night soil to fertilise the fields. Once the vegetable plots were sold off, he acquired the trike and began to shift stages. This meant she could not raise her head in the community. To make matters worse, he replaced his first wife in an underhand manner. To make matters worse still, he replaced that one through a still more wretched manoeuvre. Whenever Daisy brought this history to mind, acrimony bubbled in her heart with ever greater toxicity. She grouched to her maternal uncle and aunt about this. "Doesn't this show your dad's sick?" the auntie opined. "Him in that poor condition, always thinking of women." Although she resented her father, these words of contempt made her stomach queasy.

During that period in the aunt's home, Daisy grew to understand that there was always a subtext to her comments. As their daily routines were so out of kilter, her aunt's sense of irritation grew so that one day she flew into a tantrum in front of her husband. She complained of insomnia and felt that she was about to die from chronic mental fatigue. Another time, a dozen pairs of giant golden crickets all died mysteriously on the same day, incurring a loss of several thousand yuan. Her aunt wailed and growled that this was down to her home being plagued by ghosts and evil entities. She demanded that her husband spray powdered disinfectant and burn touch paper to ward off the malevolence. Daisy interpreted this as a slight and left their place for good.

She concluded that wandering outside like this was no sensible solution. At home, she could luxuriate and relax. She could sleep for as long as she desired, smash whatever she pleased and curse whomever she wanted. As right was on her side, why should she be the one to erupt before others did? Leaving home posed no distress to Smooth, and that slut could not be expelled remotely. She resolved to return to their residence and initiate a war of attrition until Sufen was ultimately broken.

Unexpectedly, on her return there was not the least sign of Smooth or the slut for days.

Then, one day as she was brooding over that woman yet again, she appeared. Before Daisy had the chance to toss her banana peel at her feet, the slut called out, "Your dad is in the hospital." She did hear this, though pretended she hadn't. There was no chance of her engaging in conversation with the slut.

It was not until the evening that Daisy determined which hospital he was checked into. The doctor in charge described his diagnosis of a prolapsed rectum in conjunction with haemorrhoids. Daisy reasoned that this couldn't prove fatal. Also, since the slut was keeping him company, her continued attention was not required. In the hospital corridor, she even caught sight of that woman supporting her dad with her arms wrapped around him. He said something to her and the slut responded by flexing her slender, soft waist and rubbing her hip against his. How vile! An untold emotion was churning in her heart. She swore secretly that only one of them could be mistress of the house: her or me.

17

Smooth's prolapse was protruding as much as five or six centimetres by the time Sufen had him examined in hospital. The doctor was indignant, asking, "How can anyone be this careless as to delay treatment?" Sufen could say nothing smart in defence. She actually didn't know his condition was so serious, and Smooth himself cracked jokes to downplay the drama. After the surgery, he gradually came to. Sufen's eyes were swollen red and peach-like from crying, while Smooth affected his characteristically silly yet honest grin. "All for a bit of a pain in the arse. You get teary-eyed like this, but other people might laugh at you for making such a fuss. Nothing serious." For the next few days, Sufen had to pick each nodule of fresh faeces from his rectum piece by piece. He was reluctant to let her do this at first, though soon had to rely on her in his incapacity.

As he recovered, Smooth's mind turned to the labour fees for that concert soiree. Big Hook rang him repeatedly to relay how those dozen temps were being extremely demanding. Smooth didn't mention that he was an inpatient at the hospital. He was reluctant to have others squander money on visiting him here. Life was not easy for anybody. He preferred instead to state that there was a pressing situation keeping him at home. The wages were being processed, he maintained, so everyone should remain tolerant. In truth, flames seemed to be licking at his heart and the redness downstairs still throbbed. By now, sores had appeared on his lips. He tried to connect with Iron Kou, but this was futile as his mobile was out of service. Text messages might not go ignored as Kou would see them as soon as he turned the device on. Still receiving no reply, he was desperate to thrash matters out face-to-face. Sufen was having none of this and forced him to stay seated. His next text message had a decidedly robust tone.

> Honoured Director Kou, how are you keeping? This is Smooth. I called you a lot but your mobile was turned off. I sent texts and there was no answer. As a leading director, your workload must be huge. I still want to discuss the business of our shifting stages with you. The thirty guys under me have left me feeling skinned. I have no way out of this. We're all hardworking fellas and I daren't cheat my people. Recently I've been struck by a rectal prolapse and the area around it is blistered. It might be retribution for past crimes. Director Kou, you're a high-flyer and we're dwarfs. I do hope you can give us what little money our labour has earned. I kowtow before you.

The message was left unanswered all day, and Smooth found himself unable to continue lying in bed. In the evening, when Sufen was laundering his clothes, he sneaked out of the ward and hired a tricycle bound for Iron Kou's place.

He was not at home, his wife being the one to open the door. She was still badmouthing her husband as a gullible cretin. He'd lost more than half a million yuan without recouping a single cent. Her demeanour made Smooth feel like he was the guilty party. He opted to try to dig in his heels, refusing to leave the house until he was paid. She drove him out before he was able to say his piece. Indoors, the actress persisted in cursing those cheats as "sore arses". Smooth's own rectum now itched as if cauterised.

Faced with no alternative, he returned to the hospital and lay back down on the mattress. Blood was weeping visibly from his backside and the sister upbraided him in the severest of terms. While changing the dressing, the young nurse tugged too hard at the gauze and he could sense that tissue had been flayed away with the fabric. His incarceration there lasted another two days, for that was as much as he could tolerate. The cost tore into him as well – more than 4,000 yuan for five days. Were he able to recover the lost labour fee, almost half had been gobbled up already. The entire affair was still wrapped in a pall.

Smooth knew that Daisy was back, since Sufen kept him updated. He also knew that she was aware of his hospitalisation. He had thought a visit from her was not beyond the bounds of reason. He waited and waited, but still no daughter. At night, when Sufen was dead asleep, heartbroken tears moistened his cheeks. He couldn't hold back. She was his daughter, and for thirty years he had raised her, acting as both father and mother for most of that time. His reward was to be maligned as her enemy. Sufen was the catalyst and this he knew. Just one month into the marriage and she had shown herself to be a worthy wife. Especially since he was admitted to this place, he quaked to think what an ordeal he may have faced without her. A daughter waiting on her father was a far from congenial situation, but spousal care was something different. Much more than this, Sufen was compassionate to him. From the day she entered his home, she had to contend with relentless bullying. This meant that she never replied to curses with bile and never retaliated when struck at. In particular, during the first few nights of his hospital stay, she barely blinked at anything. She served him food and refreshment, gave him a bed-bath and rubbed his back, legs and feet. Neither of his previous wives had demonstrated such attentiveness. He was already in his fifties, so how many more years could he graft like this? Some day in the future, he would be too decrepit to continue. What a boon it was to have a woman of her stripe, tending to him and vouchsafing his comfort. He was more than pleased with her. If anybody schemed to force her away, he would rally in her support.

Smooth was at last discharged. When Sufen assisted him back into the courtyard, Daisy was listening to music upstairs. The nature of the track could not be readily discerned, though the sheer racket emanating from the speaker caused the ceiling to shudder. Smooth prostrated himself. In his annoyance, he wanted to go up there and sort it out. Sufen stood in his way. She poached him an egg and prepared a second for Daisy. The bowl was carried upstairs to be met with a firmly closed door. Sufen balanced the bowl on the windowsill adjacent to the architrave. Smooth could make out her every move and was unburdened. However, he blurted out "So humble" under his breath, as if to scold her.

Smooth seldom spent any time on his mattress save for when

sleeping. Thus it was a princely, yet incongruous, turn of events to be able lie down wide awake. In spite of his unease, Sufen insisted on a further day of respite. He listened to Daisy's tunes all day and night. In the early hours, his daughter cranked the volume louder so it sounded like the God of Thunder was rearranging the tables and stools in heaven. She tapped the floor rhythmically as well with some mystery object. Smooth's heart seemed ready to burst out of his chest cavity. Sufen once more restrained him from going upstairs. "I don't know what sins I committed in my past life," he said loudly. "Such a noise at an ungodly hour. Our neighbours must be cursing our ancestors for lumbering them with the Diao clan." Sufen was silent. She rolled a pair of cotton balls and slid one into each of his ears. She then massaged his lobes and temples to soothe him to sleep. When he awoke the next morning, the din was still blasting out on the upper floor. He no longer had the time to let it irritate him, though. His mind was honed on the labour fees, which amounted to a hefty sum. His comrades cajoled him with text messages many times a day. There was no means of contacting Iron Kou. In his despair, he thought of Chief Qu. Yes, Chief Qu was the only one who could wrap this up in a rational way.

18

SMOOTH FOUND CHIEF QU in his office and related everything to him, including how Iron Kou wasn't answering his calls. The chief had not seen him in days either, so rang his landline. The diva at the other end caterwauled like a banshee, cursing that she hadn't a clue if he was living or dead. Her voice was head-splitting, and Smooth caught every consonant. Qu then texted Iron Kou on the pretence that there was a pressing matter in the troupe and he should reply at the earliest opportunity. He told Smooth to return home and he would contact him as soon as there was word. Smooth left and then turned back to plead, "Chief Qu, please don't mention that I came to complain. I'm cornered myself in all this." His boss was understanding and did not ask him over until noon the next day.

On his return to the office, Smooth was filled in on every point.

The day before, just after Smooth left, Qu fired off another message to Kou, insinuating that it was urgent – perhaps along the lines of a colleague being indicted for fraud. In the evening, Iron Kou did pick up and Qu probed about his whereabouts. He was lying low at the home of a friend. The chief reiterated that an important circumstance had arisen that required his presence at work. Sensing his reluctance, Qu dangled the option of meeting outside and duly the pair rendezvoused at a tea house.

The chief couldn't fail to see how Iron Kou's face had grown long and drawn and unkempt with stubble. His appearance was oddly wilted, as though the sinews had been extracted from his body. He drove right to the point and asked what had happened. His reply was in-depth, the long and tall of which was that he couldn't bear his wife's days-long onslaught of cursing and had no choice but to flee.

Sure enough, Iron Kou had been cheated. According to his version of events, a friend introduced him to the stage-assembling project at issue. Aside from being employed at the stage, he kept up various second jobs, including serving as an independent performance broker. In recent years, hordes of work units were keen on staging evening parties. These enterprises might not be yet one year old, but they were as enthusiastic about entertainment as companies founded twenty or a hundred years ago. An endless carousel of after-hours events evolved into being. Culture-oriented firms actually branched out into planning and preparing parties or forums like this. Iron Kou joined in too. He had two or three casual staff who congregated when there was a job on and went their own ways once the task was accomplished. In other words, nobody was left sitting about idle in the office. The dividends were carved up and each was a free agent.

As for *Ode to Golden Autumn Fields*, another friend formed this connection for him. Iron Kou was a little hesitant at first to know that a capital cushion of tens of thousands of yuan was required to win the stage-shifting job. His doubts were assuaged once he saw the full potential. He felt that they had the strength to fight lions and tigers into submission. He studied the apparent influence of the organisers, and then went home and persuaded his wife to stump up 200,000-plus yuan. Two of his associates footed a further few dozen grand apiece. The initial stages of the project unfolded without hindrance. Nevertheless, the shady side of the operation didn't remain hidden for long. The whole business of securing "big names" was hogwash, for most were not the authentic article. The disparity in value between the real and the fake was as glaring as the distance of the heavens from Earth. As might have been predicted, once the performance was over, the organisers withheld the last fifteen per cent of the proceeds. They absolved themselves of financial responsibility, for the contract itself was a labyrinth of verbal riddles and fuzzily phrased conditions. The proposal for the programme listed a line-up of fifty major acts, with the guarantee that at least half of them would perform in person. The fifty per cent that did appear were has-beens, whose star had waned long ago. Some of them sang a medley of four or five numbers for a 30,000-yuan fee and then were unwilling to depart the stage. As far as the entertainers "Zhao Benshan" and "Liu Huan" were concerned, the word "tribute" prefixed their names in the contract, and the fogginess of the surrounding passage made the deception hard to notice immediately.

When the head of the organising side travelled to Beijing to talk business, the agents invited along a clutch of stellar female entertainers, the ilk of which he had never encountered before. They accompanied him to play mahjong and drink alcohol. Before the dinner was over, he waved his pen and signed the contract flamboyantly to the admiring applause of the starlets. The agents had earmarked eighty-five per cent of the total budget for themselves in two instalments and the remaining fifteen per cent was assigned for local logistics – ground rent, labour costs and the like. Following curtain-down, they pursued an elaborate escape strategy. Knowing in advance that there would be peril, they checked out of the hotel surreptitiously in the afternoon. By the time the performance ended, they fled to their own cars and sped several erratic circuits around the streets nearby to throw off the pair Iron Kou had sent to tail them. So desperate were they to recover what they were owed, they staked out the hotel the entire night, not realising that their quarry had left the scene earlier.

Iron Kou and a few of the local stage assistants had spent these days searching for the real estate boss in the hope of recovering the lost fifteen per cent that rightfully belonged to them. The boss's subordinate alleged that the matter would have to go to litigation, and so an impasse was reached. They also tried phoning the director general and the general stage manager, but they had used locally bought mobiles for the project's duration and discarded the sim cards afterwards. They consulted friends in the legal profession, who told them that the contract was cunningly worded and it was impossible to detect flaws they could exploit. Even if they did locate the miscreants, there was no redress available. All of the fraudsters were accomplished in their chosen fields, otherwise they wouldn't have had the front to act so brazenly in public.

When Iron Kou and his friends realised their strategy was futile, they decided to temper their steel in the direction of the local boss. They had heard that the twenty million yuan was not all from his own wallet, and business friends of his were prepared to offer two or three million each towards the evening ceremony. His own outlay was only a few million, so Kou and his men thought it just and reasonable to demand their pay. Feeling harassed and anxious about his safety, the boss agreed they could have their ten per cent now and the outstanding five after he had recovered the money out of which he had been tricked. Sympathy was surely due to a man of his calibre who had fallen prey to the same scam. They chose to accept the ten per cent for starters. This meant that Iron Kou was reunited with his "capital cushion", though that fortnight of round-the-clock toil as yet had no recompense.

Chief Qu's first priority was finding justice for Smooth.

Iron Kou freely admitted that Smooth and his team earned every cent with their sweat. But he was simply unable to fulfil his earlier promise and could, at most, hand them an additional 60,000 yuan. This time, the loss had to be shared across the board. He was certainly not holding back the cash because he himself had been welshed. Before anything else, he had to mend the hole in the family finances lest he be devoured alive by his harridan of a wife.

Once the chief's narrative had ended, Smooth was left speechless. He knew only too well that Iron Kou was a fellow victim, but 60,000 yuan was too grievous a blow. If he didn't dig into his own pockets, he had nowhere else to look for a solution. His headhanging silence continued, and he knew he had to face his hardlabouring brothers.

Chief Qu offered him a cigarette and lit one for himself. After a deep drag, he said, "Smooth, I know what a fiasco you've been sucked into. But here we are. We must each give at least an inch. I know Iron Kou. He would never stoop to begging if he could help it. Since he's asked me to beg you on his behalf, you should take on a little of his burden. He promised to put work your way in the future. At the last moment, I pushed him to add another ten thousand for you. His life, after all, is a touch more comfortable than yours. Let's do it like this. I've done all I can."

Since Chief Qu had been the one to approach him, he couldn't mouth a contrary word. The outcome was less baleful than he had imagined. His debt to the chief was massive, as without his intervention, that 60,000 yuan would have evaporated like water.

To Qu's embarrassment, Smooth bowed three times in respect before leaving. He wanted him to desist, but he wouldn't.

Smooth returned to find Sufen locked out of their home. Daisy again.

19

Sufen was settled on the stone step beside the entrance. Smooth asked what had happened. She had merely gone to throw out the rubbish and returned to find the gate locked. Perhaps Daisy had left in the meantime. Not uttering a word, he borrowed a hammer from a neighbour, and despite his wife's opposition, smashed the lock with a succession of blows.

Sufen had tried to give Daisy a wide berth, mindful that there could be a fresh round of mischief. "She has no right to act this way," Smooth swore. "After all, it was me, not you, who wronged her. How could we tumble into this storm?" Back indoors, he related what the chief had told him. Smooth was disconsolate about the magnitude of the loss, though his wife reasoned "falling in the pit strengthens your wit". He shouldn't let it weigh too heavily on his mind. There are times when losing a fortune may actually stave off disaster, so maybe a greater misfortune had been averted through this. Sufen was trying to offer up a salve and, in fact, Smooth was left with a warm-hearted feeling.

The mid-autumn wind assailed the room from every quadrant, and it made Smooth's lips tremble. His wife told him that if he lay on the bed, she would find a way of making sure he stayed snug. He crouched down there as she set about scrubbing a basinful of clothes in the middle of the room, chatting while she did so. With her body squatting in this position, he had a commanding view of her plump breasts. His heart flickered with excitement, which soon turned to ardour.

He invited her to lie alongside him on the mattress, to which she coyly replied, "In broad daylight? Why?"

"We almost never have free time. Mostly, we're like a couple of dead sows once we get home."

Sufen didn't shift from the floor, still fumbling with the garments, her head bowed. He restated his invitation and she wouldn't budge. Her fingers kneaded one piece of clothing after another.

Unable to control himself, Smooth leaped up and kicked the basin so it flipped over behind the door. With a spurt of energy that came from nowhere, he pinned his wife to the bed.

"Fully recovered, I see. And with the strength of an ogre? How can you still have the urge?"

"Right now, my arse is the least of my problems."

Smooth slipped off his watch and flung it onto the rickety sofa. Goody, who was sprawled on the upholstery, yelped at her master's manic behaviour.

As the couple were in a post-coital doze, they heard the rattle of the front gate being opened from outside. Instinctively, Sufen gripped Smooth's waist and he pinched her arm in return to assure her not to be afraid. He knew it was his daughter. After breaking the lock in the afternoon, he had left the door on the latch. Right now, he was reluctant to let her in. Even so, the banging was becoming as fierce as marauding bandits intent on looting the place. A petrified Sufen hastened to throw on some clothes. Smooth did not want her to be the one to open up, so he dressed too, being fully prepared for another onslaught from Daisy and ready to challenge her flagrant disregard.

The moment he withdrew the iron latch with a creak, Daisy kicked from the other side, propelling him to the ground. "Are you crazy?" he cried.

On witnessing her husband being reduced to anger and shame, Sufen came forward at once to mediate. In the process, Daisy was at last able to capture her in one lingering stare. Sufen crooked her neck to discover her buttons were all fastened unaligned. What was more, her hair was as messy as a chicken's nest, and so she set about neatening it with a sweep of her hands.

"Utterly shameless," Daisy could be heard to sneer.

"Who's the shameless one?" her father shouted. "Who are you cursing?"

"The middle of the day, and the old hen is perched on the bed! Bah!" Daisy reared up on her stilettos, the heels of which were chopstick thin, and went into her room.

Smooth had thought that today he could exercise a measure of authority, but he ended up being steered back to the bedroom by Sufen. He thought that this behaviour should not be tolerated, either as a father or as a man. Not a semblance of domestic discipline. But no matter how his flames of ire sizzled, Sufen doused them with cold water. Having reprised this routine a number of times, Sufen proved his conqueror.

Upstairs, Daisy turned up the stereo, which ought to have brought on a cardiac implosion in Smooth. She simultaneously stamped on the floor to the beat of the music. "How could this be my fate?" he began to wail. "What evil thing did I do in a past life?"

Sufen rubbed his back. "If I've brought no luck with me, then it's better I leave," she said.

Smooth took hold of her. "If someone has to leave, we two will leave together. I'd like to say I've never encountered such a wicked child as this."

They massaged each others' backs, and then Iron Kou rang to ask them to come over and collect the money. Smooth led Sufen out of the house.

As Chief Qu had demanded, Kou handed more than 70,000 yuan to Smooth. The gloomy look on the director's face gave the appearance of neither man nor ghost. For his part, Smooth had few words of comfort for Kou. Once the money was in his hands, Smooth went after Big Hook and Monkey to determine how to split it. Those two had followed him for years and, while cursing the fraudsters, they also helped him to find breathing space with those whom he owed cash. Smooth announced that he would forgo his cut, and apologised profusely to all involved. Big Hook and Monkey held back 2,000 yuan for Smooth and 1,200 yuan for Sufen, who had been their cook. This magnanimity convinced Smooth that it was worth retaining such a band of people around him.

Stage shifting was the kind of trade where once one door shut, another would open.

For starters, they had to oversee a performance of *Swan Lake* given by a Russian company. The theatre manager in charge called Smooth and hired his men to load the truck and attend to everything else involved in shifting his stage. A fee of 6,000 yuan was mooted, though Smooth's persistence saw this upped by 500 yuan. As this was a foreign production, the stage shifting was less elaborate, for there were few sets and props and the principal tasks involved adjusting the lights and hanging soft scenery fabric. That was the easiest operation of all, so much so that the lads tugged off Mound's trousers and forced him to dance a routine from *Swan Lake* in the nude.

It was rumoured that this too was a tribute show, for the original company was massive and renowned.

On the heels of the *Swan Lake* job came stage shifting for a Henan Opera troupe. The Western Capital had many residents of Henan descent and people of native stock such as Smooth knew that essentially everybody who dwelt on the northern side of the railway track was Henanese. Locals nicknamed them "north-of-the-liners". During famines in the early twentieth century, wave after wave of refugees migrated from the neighbouring province. At first, they erected lean-tos, which sprawled into endless shanty towns. It was here where the Henan Opera diva Chang Xiangyu was purportedly raised and began her ascent to stardom. Back when Smooth was young, city-dwellers would switch freely between the local dialect and that of Henan in conversation. This was one characteristic that marked out authentic locals. Those who didn't have this ability were impostors.

In recent years, Henanese had been the object of inexplicable animus and censure, so much so that they dared not use their mother dialect openly. This did not prevent others from enjoying Henan Opera. Smooth, for one, loved its emphatic rhythm, overwhelming passion and graceful gestures. He always carried a transistor radio with him so as to listen to the news and opera in his free moments. He tuned into the news programmes to keep abreast of developments in the city and possibly to hear where new projects might become available. Tuning into the opera was a pastime. Maybe because he had been in the stage-shifting line for so long, he could appreciate Shaanxi Opera and Henan Opera and was partial to Peking and Huangmei Operas too. He had such a sense of intimacy and kinship with those who sang and spoke on the stage. Of course, this fondness also served him well in terms of securing work. He was a stage shifter. People must love what they love, be fond of what they are fond, and like what they like.

When the head of the Henan Opera troupe came over, Smooth raised his thumbs and raved, "Great! Fantastic performance. Before you got here, news of your reputation spread like wildfire. My phone almost blew up with so many folks wanting tickets for your wonderful company." The head asked discreetly who this fellow was and the theatre manager told him it was Smooth Diao, the prime mover and main operator in stage shifting hereabouts. "We just labour hard. Just hardworking fellas," Smooth added out of modesty.

The troupe were to stage five performances. Smooth's team toiled away for seven days and nights. The first two days were occupied with installing the lights and frames on the stage. The scenery for the opening night turned out to be most tricky. Opera troupes invariably paid much attention to the premiere, especially when the venue was in the Western Capital. They were acutely aware of how this was an ancient centre of culture, and many seasoned opera fans expected to be wowed by new productions. What is more, locals were as familiar with Henan Opera as the homegrown variety. Consequently, exacting standards were imposed on the stage-shifting group. The suspended "sea of clouds" had to be rehung numerous times, causing Big Hook to curse, "Just a scrap of pissing cloud. Whether it slants to the left or right, hangs high or low, it's still cloud – it's not going to turn into a gold plate!" Smooth begged that everyone be patient and warned them of the high bar set for opening night. Once the premiere had kindled the flame, the rest would be largely hassle-free. Nonetheless, every evening the stage had to be re-installed and the next day the lights readjusted. Then there were rehearsals and last-minute alterations. Days and nights of this routine left their eyeballs almost fused still in their sockets.

This time, Sufen accompanied Smooth on the job and Goody kept her company on the tricycle. The relentless regime left them no time to go home for a rest. Once exhausted, Sufen would snuggle into a padded seat in the auditorium, and Smooth could catch a dozen minutes shuteye wherever there was room to spread a sheet of paper as his nest. This particular night, at the stroke of 4 am, Smooth happened to be climbing the lighting tower with a computerised lamp on his back, when a text message reached him. It came from Daisy and consisted of nine curt words: "Send three grand to bank account, make it snappy." Smooth was reluctant to answer straight away and eventually sent back the question: "What's the money for?" Her reply: "To survive."

Smooth was left in quiet consternation for some time. Daisy was certainly high maintenance. Each year, the neighbourhood gave every household a dividend of 15,000 yuan and from the previous year onwards he instructed the administrative office to transfer it directly into Daisy's account. He didn't even touch that sum. Beyond this, he gave her a monthly allowance of 1,500 yuan, and this was topped up with pocket money whenever she asked. That made a total of between 20,000 and 30,000 yuan a year. Based on her form of late, she likely just wanted to punish him by squandering his wages. This was disconcerting enough, for he couldn't cope with her shrewish behaviour. Whenever she opened her mouth to demand something, he felt powerless to decline. He then asked, "Whatever you truly need, your dad will provide, but you should at least tell me what it's for." Shortly afterwards, Daisy fired off a further message, "So if the slut is free to spend your dough, why aren't I?"

Irritated, Smooth replied, "What kind of a creature are you?"

"So what? I am the creature I am."

Someone was now calling out for Smooth, requesting that he carry the lamp to the second gantry. He suspended his text duel with Daisy for he didn't want to battle her any more, being destined to lose. As he was her father, what was the use of berating each other? Life had to go on and there was no alternative. Sometimes he came over ever so guilty. For all four seasons of the year, he was wrapped up in work and seldom had the chance to show Daisy his concern for her. Since she was asking and he could afford it, he should cough up the full amount.

Early the next morning, Smooth went to the bank next door to the theatre and transferred the 3,000 yuan. After it was done, his disquiet didn't abate.

20

Daisy had no clear purpose in asking for the money. She acted out of greed and the desire to not let her father's heart be without burden. If he could keep a woman like that, he should spend more on his own daughter. That was all fair and just. What money she received was hers; the money she did not receive was the property of others. That slut had gone out stage shifting with him and didn't return home. Her plan was in theory similar to placing a frog in tepid water and slowly increasing the heat to boiling point. This temporarily had to be put on hold.

Daisy found her life tedious in the extreme. Lately, she was so idle that she didn't even turn on the stereo. Who was there to irritate if she did? She had no wish to listen for her own sake. Those songs she had relished in the past all of a sudden seemed insipid. She could only stare blankly at the ceiling, with no motivation to do anything for herself.

Years ago, she had run a small cosmetics shop. This had been her favourite job so far. Every day, she found enough time to daub her own flesh with an array of beauty products. Five months down the line and she had lost more than 20,000 yuan. Her pals all told her to shut up shop, for this was a profession that favoured pretty faces. Cosmetics were best sold by assistants who were born beautiful and could entice customers into believing they could achieve similar results. Even her closest chum "Princess" Wu said, "Oh, my Daisy, give it up right now. Our looks are more suited to being a female general or a chief prison warden. We're fit for weightlifting or throwing the discus, not for peddling blossom extracts, grasses, bottles and jars of stuff. Let's grow in the way nature intended, not keep on ramming our heads in the door jamb in an effort to flatten our features." Daisy did as she was advised and wound up the business, reverting to her habitual routine of being a night owl with the Princess. They played mahjong as if night were day.

In fact, all the children in the community frittered their time away in this manner. They had no pressures about clothing or food. Upon graduating from junior high school, their parents were unable to drive them about any more. They couldn't find employment and were averse to either being met with the long expressions of neighbours or having to admit that they themselves had lost face. Naturally, they were condescending towards grafters of Smooth's sort.

Still, the menfolk of the community might have broader experiences to quest after. For instance, there was Daisy's Uncle Big Army, the scourge of the casinos in Macau. Most women in the neighbourhood remained phlegmatic, harbouring no illusions about matrimony. Simply because the land beneath their feet was more valuable than gold, it didn't matter whether you were mute, deaf or mentally backward, providing you were a member of this community you could chip away at 10,000 yuan without moving a millimetre. More land was there for the selling, and those unexploited hectares would bring a cascade of compensation.

As a result, this was a colony for ever-increasing numbers of "female bachelors" and "tough girls". Daisy didn't want to be a kind of "tough bachelor" hybrid, and craved the opportunity to marry as far away from here as possible. Alas, she remained all alone, for no one was willing to accept her hand. This left her irritable and always on the lookout for some doormat to oppress. She was even apt to attack the litter bin on the roadside.

One day, bored as usual, her beloved Princess Wu called and invited her to the spa. She maintained that she was not in the mood. Wu's reply was ardent, "No, you must come at once. We're going to meet somebody."

"Meet who?"

"It's a male somebody. What else could it be?"

Daisy smiled and agreed.

They bathed themselves for a while and Daisy quizzed her about the identity of the impending arrival. Wu was typically enigmatic, saying it was a male for sure and they had only been acquaintances for less than a week. The gentleman was a sales rep for a famous liquor firm, and they were introduced by a third party. He had claimed to be in his forties, but appeared older, perhaps even going on sixty. Wu giggled and twirled in the water.

Daisy's grin belied a tang of jealousy. Wu was thirty years old too. It was said that her grandpa was of pure Mongolian stock and had taken a Han Chinese wife. The young woman still bore the strong imprint of her cosmopolitan genes. To Daisy's mild relief, her friend, who was three months her junior, had no boyfriend either. Princess Wu, with her high-bridged nose and defined facial features, was clearly far prettier than her. Daisy had acquired some make-up techniques and had a little fashion sense, so could suffuse her appearance with a kind of animated charm. The Princess, meanwhile, had no time for cosmetics, and would just dab on Vaseline as protection against the winter cold.

Wu had grown up kicking a football about with the boys from the neighbourhood. They played in streets and lanes, with no hope of sporting fame. Her kicking technique was accomplished and she could topple an adversary in seconds. More than one potential suitor found himself floored as she rebuffed his advances. In due course, she earned the reputation as a "tough girl". Frankly speaking, men pursued her in their herds, though her character was carefree and Princess Wu even let the prospect of being loved pass her by.

After Daisy and Wu had finished their soak and had put on Japanese kimonos to rest in the tepidarium, the liquor salesman was already waiting for them in a pre-booked side room. Daisy chuckled on seeing him. How could he be in his forties? The top of his head was barren and he had tried to concoct a thin, grassy comb-over. Unfortunately, when he moved his head on seeing them, the grass slid to one side in a foot-long strand. He fumbled hastily with it a couple of times trying to resurrect the comb-over effect. Daisy laughed and quickly put her hand over her outsized mouth.

The agent's name was Tan Daogui and he spoke in Sichuan dialect. He wore a kimono as well, but the jacket was insufficiently generous to cover his belly which hung in folds. His face was so round that it might have been drawn with a pair of compasses, and his eyes resembled glaring bulbs beaming away above floppy bags of skin. Daisy's first impression was that Princess Wu was in jeopardy. She had discarded her own standards by allowing such a man into the scope of her consideration.

Tan flattered Wu at first by thanking her for bringing over another beauty. Daisy was well aware that this was the sort of claptrap men spouted to flatter women. She then noticed how Tan's stealthy eyes were scanning Princess Wu's half-exposed cleavage. Daisy deliberately looked the other way.

"Fatty Tan, can't you shave that long strand off?" Princess Wu asked with absolutely no decorum. "Grow old with a little dignity. Don't coax the straggly rice noodle like that. It makes me uneasy." Daisy felt she had gone too far and so pinched her friend on the thigh.

Tan, who had a sense of humour, said, "Aren't you partial to a straggly rice noodle? It's there fresh for you every day. A good deal, don't you think?"

"Don't you know, the more you try to cover up, the more you end up exposing." Wu's mockery continued in this vein.

"There's no way it can cover it adequately, but better than having no cover at all. It's just like how they are currently 'greening' the city. Do you really want to see bare concrete slabs everywhere?"

Tan's wise technique for neutralising embarrassment made Daisy realise there was something different about him. He didn't come across as trustworthy and she was even disinclined to want to have tea with him. Worst of all was how his stealthy eyes studied her thighs. It was like being pestered by a greenfly, and she felt uncomfortable and nauseous. Even though Tan did punctuate his praise of Wu with some flattering phrases for Daisy, she could not bear to continue sitting with him. Wu sensed her displeasure and followed her out, thereby leaving to waste a tableful of fine dishes ordered by Tan.

On coming out of the spa, Wu asked Daisy how she was.

"Want to know the truth?"

Certainly Wu did.

"Is there something wrong with you? Even if you end up as an old maid, there's no need to subject yourself to this kind of misery." In actual fact, Daisy had been pondering this matter herself. If things really did worsen, she could contemplate marrying a man of fifty or sixty. Still, the prospect of having a Mr Noodle Head was too wretched to consider. Wu's natural endowments were not so poor. And yet how could she lower herself into this wretched situation?

Princess Wu explained that this fellow was quite fond of her. They had only played mahjong and shared a meal a few times. What she did know was that he was male and loaded. Her interest in him was practically zero. She only wanted Daisy to give him the once over and she had no further aspirations.

"Well, it's OK to play mahjong and have dinner with Mr Noodle Head," Daisy conceded. "As for marriage – absolutely no way."

"Who's thinking about marrying him?" With that question, Princess Wu raised her heel and lunged her foot at a wrought iron litter bin on the roadside. It flew a few metres.

As soon as Daisy parted from Wu, she received a call from a stranger. She ignored it at first, but answered when the caller persisted. It turned out to be Mr Noodle Head himself, who proceeded to praise her, then begged Daisy to put in a good word for him with Wu. He also promised her a gift and hoped she would accept it. She refused. In the evening, he rang again, once more extolling her fine qualities and then insisting they meet so he could hand over the present. Daisy declined.

The next morning, as she was still sleeping, there was a pounding at the door, and there he stood, an elegant and decorative gift box in his hand. She had no choice but to open up because he had spied her through the crack in the door. Daisy accepted the present, though didn't invite him in for a seat as it was obvious that he would install himself there and never move. Again and again, he flattered her appearance and reflected on how the Western Capital was a den of beauties. She was not in the least bit moved by his words and felt them hypocritical. She stood at the gate as she saw him off.

Once Mr Noodle Head had gone, she opened the box to reveal what must have been in excess of 10,000 yuan-worth of imported cosmetics. No wonder Princess Wu had testified to his wealth and generosity. Daisy ruminated over whether to relate the incident to

Wu or not. Rice Noodles had told her that it was between the two of them. He only asked her to put in a good word with her mate. After much thought, she decided that secrecy was the wisest policy for there was no need to generate unwanted friction. Indeed, she had no intention of saying nice things about him. In her mind's eye, he was not a viable option.

21

THE FINAL PRODUCTION of the Henan Opera cycle was one of Smooth's favourites, *Fresh Wind Pavilion*. A tale of karmic justice, it was also performed under the alternative titles of *Zhang Jibao is Struck by Thunder* and *Revenge by Thunder*. The scenario was straightforward. On visiting a country fair, an elderly man named Zhang Yuanxiu chanced upon a foundling left in the Fresh Breeze Pavilion. After bringing the baby home, Zhang and his wife decided to raise him as their own. Later, following an extensive search, the child's biological mother discovered where her son was living, and the old couple relinquished their custody of little Zhang Jibao. From then on, the pair waited by the door, hoping that their ward would visit them again. The years of expectation inflicted a grievous toll on the health of both. Zhang Jibao had in fact gained first place in the imperial examinations and was elevated to a high post in officialdom. On passing by the Fresh Breeze Pavilion, he was greeted by an ecstatic Old Zhang and his wife. However distinguished he was in worldly terms, they found him a flinty and aloof officer, who refused to embrace anyone wearing what appeared to be a beggarly garb. So great was his adopted mother's distress that she pounded her head against a wall until she died. Old Zhang himself sought to remonstrate with Jibao, but was kicked by the young upstart and died of his injuries. The heavens were outraged at this spectacle, and as the final breath left the elderly man's body, thunder and lightning battered the skies. The ungrateful and merciless Zhang Jibao was slain on the spot at the Fresh Breeze Pavilion, sliced clean in two by a cleaver-like bolt of lightning.

Having watched scores of productions of this opera, Smooth had memorised many of the lyrics in their Shaanxi dialect form. Whether the drama was performed in its Henan, Peking, Shaanxi or Shanxi variants, the core plot remained unaltered. Never could he behold the scene of the elderly couple waiting for their ward's return without his face becoming awash with tears. These past two days he had been humming their duet:

Old Ma: Your ma isn't maligning her wayward son.
Old Pa: But why did you run away like water, never to return?
Old Ma: I cannot hear the calling of my dear son.
Old Pa: Why don't I see you beg me for food and clothes in turn?
Old Ma: I cannot see you helping Ma turn the grindstone.
Old Pa: I cannot see you helping Pa in the mountains to mow.
Old Ma: The kids all return home when lessons are done.
Old Pa: I cannot see my son's shadow and smile mellow.
Old Ma: Zhang Jibao.
Old Pa: Dearest son.
Old Ma: Your ma calls out for you repeatedly. (She faints.)
Old Pa: She is old and pitiful, collapsed by the roadside.

It had been a masterstroke to choose this drama as the finale to the trilogy. "*Revenge by Thunder* is the perfect climax, truly fantastic," Smooth had told the head of the troupe a few days earlier.

He hailed the head with his thumb and started to extemporise about theatre like a connoisseur. "The best drama in the world has a bitter kick. You can do no better than *Revenge by Thunder*. Let's wait and see. The venue is bound to be packed this evening."

"If it's not a sell-out, you should buy up all the leftover tickets," Big Hook interjected.

"I shall," replied Smooth.

The turnout was as Smooth predicted. Every last seat was taken, and there were even people crouching in the aisles.

Feeling in the mood to brag, Smooth accosted the head backstage. "Wasn't I right, sir? A full house! A great performance built on great leadership. A great troupe, a great drama, a great leader." He once more made a gesture by waving his thumb.

"Thanks," replied the head. "If we come here again, we'll definitely have you take care of our stage."

Smooth seized the chance to hand him his business card.

He would go to any lengths to be able to watch *Revenge by Thunder*. As long as the drama was a classic, he could see it a hundred times without ever tiring. As the stage for that evening's performance was already fully installed, he was able to search for a place to nap backstage until it was time to dismantle the set. Today, however, he knew he must imbibe the drama. Since there was no room in or around the seating area, he dragged Sufen to the lighting slot beneath the stage. They sat there on the floor, and from time to time he would offer a commentary to her on the plot. Perhaps because she was tired and the lamps exuded considerable warmth, Sufen nodded off on his shoulder after only taking in a little of the show. When she awoke, she found her husband tearful. He had soaked all of his tissues and used hers up as well. There was no end to his trails of weeping.

"It's all make believe," Sufen said. "How can you act like it's for real?"

"I know it's a drama," he responded. "But it does show real human emotions. Look at how Zhang Jibao's pig-headedness breaks that old couple's hearts."

"And you think that a disloyal child can really get whacked by lightning?"

"That's the dramatic touch. The parents might be heartbroken, but still nobody wants to see their child cut in two and burnt to a crisp like that."

After the curtain came down, Smooth and Sufen were about to join the others in taking apart the set. They heard Mound cry out that a fight was in the offing backstage. Smooth rushed over to investigate. It turned out that during the performance when the character Zhang Jibao was meant to kick his ancient guardian to the ground, the actor had laid into his co-star for real. The man playing Old Zhang peeled back his costume and bent over so the head could inspect. Sure enough, a blackish-purple bruise had appeared on his haunches, with the clear impression of a thick-heeled boot. Again and again, the head promised to mollify the situation as soon as they returned home. The veteran actor was having none of this and became quarrelsome. Those employed in the dramatic field had a special hierarchy of relationships. Either they were master and disciple, or pupils of the same master, or else shared an equal footing as kinsmen. In daily life, these colleagues maintained the pretence of warmth and congeniality, but as soon as something adverse arose, these dividing lines suddenly became stark.

There were those among the troupe who sided with the veteran, while others sympathised with his junior colleague. As they began to thump and kick each other, matters ceased to be civil. Smooth tried to plant himself between the main antagonists and pacify the situation. Several stinging kicks forced him to withdraw, but the head assumed his place as the human shield and managed not to be deterred by the pain. Calm was restored.

While dismantling the stage afterwards, Smooth learned of the root cause of the hostility. It long predated the violence seen this evening. Apparently, the younger actor had aspirations to be a leading thespian and his colleague was a member of the selection committee at his state-level audition. A few acerbic words from him had been enough to skew the voting and ensure the candidate's rejection. The discord had its genesis there, and the two men disseminated vinegary slights against each other through the network of theatre players. Before long, many became embroiled in the feud. They held their tongues during this provincial run because far too much importance rested on it being an unqualified success. Now that the last performance had come around, all the pent-up hatred was unleashed. One blow from a fist left the head's eye blue, and he was still hovering around backstage trying to seek a resolution when the last of the actors departed for home.

Smooth approached him, hoping to offer up comforting sentiments. "I know that opera troupes are tricky to deal with," he said, "but you coped very well. You're an able man and when you were willing to put yourself in the middle, the trouble really did die down. I've seen so many things of that kind. Some of them, when they really got out of control, needed the police to come and break up the brawl. The performance was sensational. Didn't you hear all of that applause? Folks in the Western Capital are hard to win over. Such a stir."

To avoid the embarrassment of revealing his black eye, the head remained ducked down. He had been counting cables and lights in this position. He didn't leave until they started to load the truck. It was already 4 am by the time Smooth and his team had filled the backs of three vehicles with lights, costumes, props and settings.

The checking of the books was completed without incident. In the course of seven days and seven nights, they had erected and pulled down stages for five separate dramas. Including the task of loading and offloading the trucks twice, they earned in excess of 20,000 yuan. The director wrote out his signature before he went, but the manager refused to pay them until the loading had been finished. Fifteen hands were on the payroll at the outset, though this temporarily shrank to eight. Their number then needed to swell by another five on account of the physical arduousness of removing the stage. Once the truck had departed, everyone followed Smooth out of the building and beneath the dim illumination of the street light, he divided the wages according to their pre-established rules. Big Hook and Monkey were entitled to 2,500 yuan, and Mound, Third Skin and the loyal old crew of the second tier each received 2,000 yuan. A few were limited to 1,500 yuan, and Sufen a mere 1,200 yuan. Still, the yawning team went away with a semblance of satisfaction, for seldom was the pay presented to them in such an easy and timely fashion. Smooth found that even the powerfully built Big Hook could barely raise his leg over the tricycle. Their exhaustion was acute. "Don't sleep so heavily tonight," Smooth advised. "Maybe there'll be work to be done tomorrow. I'll call you when it's fixed."

A dozen tricycles disappeared into the dark night like a fleet of galleons.

Once everyone had departed, Smooth asked Sufen to try to mount the tricycle. She asserted that he should take to the saddle instead.

"You don't know how to ride it?" he asked curiously. She smiled. "Have a try."

As Sufen slung her leg over the frame, the dog was still curled in her own little corner. On seeing her master, she shook her bedraggled pelt and snuggled into his arms. Sufen climbed into place in no particular hurry. After gripping the handlebars rather gingerly, her control steadied. Pedalling hard, the trike surged forward at a confident pace.

"You do know how to ride," Smooth cried in disbelief.

Sufen didn't answer. She simply cycled on.

"When did you learn?"

"Just picked it up these last few days."

"How could you learn so quickly?"

"Not possible?"

"Well, for sure, it mustn't be impossible."

As Sufen realised how exhausted the stage shifting left her husband, she set about teaching herself how to ride. She wanted to relieve him of the duty of being her midnight chauffeur.

To the west of this particular theatre was a large square, which became her practice site when nobody else was around. Since she had already mastered the two-wheeled bicycle, little special adaptation was required, and, with a number of test runs she could complete a circuit of the courtyard. Her only intention in acquiring this skill was to be in a position to transport Smooth home in the depths of the night. He had been labouring hard, but tonight his energy was not fully spent. Her husband, being rather merry, assumed a sharp falsetto voice and sang an aria from the young female lead in the Shaanxi Opera *Fifteen Pounds*:

> *My dad sold me because he was greedy for money.*
> *Unwilling to be a slave I duly fled.*
> *I went to Tall Bridge to visit my auntie,*
> *For her help I anxiously pleaded.*
> *I ran into a stranger after straying afar,*
> *And then heard how villagers were on my tail.*
> *They accused us of adultery and of killing my pa,*
> *Then fleeing with the spoils along this trail.*
> *This was a catastrophe rained down from the sky.*
> *One person's misfortunes surely cannot run so deep,*
> *I beg you, your honour, to investigate why,*
> *Root out the truth, let not justice sleep...*

His voice resembled the whining of a goat. The effect was so comical that Sufen couldn't pedal for laughing. He asked her what she thought of his vocal talents and she replied that it was "like the howl of a pained billy whose head's been trapped in the gate of its pen". Smooth claimed to have learned the tune from listening to a master by the name of Mr Ma as he fumbled away in the light slot. He was convinced that his intonation was identifiable as being of the school of Ma.

"Don't go around saying that," Sufen warned. "Master Ma might slap you in the mouth if he heard you."

Smooth was undeterred and simply wanted to sing as an outlet for his joy. In spite of a week of around-the-clock grafting, he kept only 3,200 yuan for himself. Once that 3,000 yuan given to Daisy was factored in, he was left with a piffling 200 yuan. This was not such a deathly blow to him, for he now had somebody to make him the object of their love and concern. As a trike-pedalling stage shifter, to be the recipient of love and solicitude was as much as he could hanker after in this life. And so it was fitting that he should sing. When he resumed, he warbled a few strains of the Henan Opera *Hua Mulan*:

> *Brother Liu spoke in a manner unfair,*
> *How could a woman savour idleness rare?*
> *She might sow seeds in the field all day,*
> *And in the evening weave cotton away...*

His tone was a little unearthly and the stray dogs hungry for a feed or a screw fled into the remotest alleys upon hearing him. Sufen laughed so much that she nearly choked, and yet Smooth sang on all the more energetically. Those shouts that resounded about the hollow, desolate streets were unmistakably from Henan Opera.

As they neared the home gate with Smooth as the passenger and Sufen as the rider, the silence was all-pervasive. Smooth pushed at the gate to find that it had been latched from the inside. He thought to call for Daisy to come down, though refrained on second thoughts. He asked for Sufen's assistance and, shattered as he was with no residual energy, tried to scramble over the wall. Now inured to pain and numb throughout his frame, he dropped down the other side like a piece of discarded wood. Hauling himself to his feet, he let Sufen in and then carried her in his arms. Gently fumbling their way into the bedroom, she suggested boiling water to clean his feet. As he couldn't even open his eyes, he dismissed this notion. Once on the mattress, his body was too weak to turn around. No sooner did he close his eyes than the music began to roar out upstairs together with the clack of stilettos above him. Much as he wanted to retaliate, there was nothing left to fuel him into action. He waved a hand and groaned, "Wretched bugger..." Sufen scrambled to locate the two cotton balls and plugged his ears. Scarcely had she done this, when his snores began to growl out.

22

Smooth's second daughter came home at the beginning of winter. As she would graduate at the end of the academic year, there were no lessons to occupy her on campus.

Daisy was at home when Plum Han returned and even opened the door for her. Years ago, she had actually been quite cordial and kind to this adopted girl, who had no blood ties to the Diao family. Daisy was indeed relieved when her father married Plum's mother and brought her home. She was contented to gain a baby sibling and a playmate. They shared the same bedroom for a number of years without any conflicts flaring up. It was only upon growing a little more mature that she became uncomfortable whenever others praised Plum for being pretty. This worsened as she entered high school and Smooth supported Plum as she covertly studied hard to enter college. Her attitude began to alter towards that ambitiously minded younger stepsister.

After Plum began her higher education, the two barely ever communicated and they in fact avoided meeting whenever she was home during summer and winter breaks. To onlookers, the sisters did not appear at odds. This time, however, Daisy's pent-up fury erupted, for Plum brought back a male classmate with her. Standing more than five feet eleven inches tall, he bore something of a resemblance to the Japanese Golden Age legend, Takakura Ken. Daisy opened the door to them and had retreated upstairs, "humphing" before their introduction was even complete. She slammed her bedroom door with a thump and turned up the track *Inconsolable* by Gong Linna to full volume, making even the window panes shudder.

137

Plum shrank into her own room with the young man. Since she had not forewarned her stepfather, cobwebs were strung everywhere inside. Normally, Smooth would make a habit of dusting and cleaning her room in advance of her arrival, even drying out the quilt and bed mat in the sun.

Her stepfather had been tremendously generous to her. She was nervous about telling others about this tricycle man, but deep in her heart she felt nothing but gratitude towards him. This classmate was in fact her boyfriend and the two were already a year into their courtship. As his family were common farmers from Cai Family Ridge in Zhen'an County, she didn't have so much hesitancy about sharing the truth of Smooth's profession with them.

The boyfriend's name was Zhu Mancang, and he was a foolishly kind-hearted lad who treated her with candour and compassion. She had visited his parents at home and even sought permission to become his bride the following year. Actually, she was very fond of him too. The only factor holding them back was her fear that they would have to live together forever as husband and wife in the countryside. Should Zhu be unable to claim residency in the Western Capital, she would have to surrender the city life she knew and reconcile herself to moving to the sticks. As these uncertainties swung back and forth, she believed it was the opportune time for him to meet her stepfather. Hence her decision to take him home now.

Through her college years, Plum became attuned to Daisy's creeping hostility, though she tried to accommodate her. Today, her brusque welcome for Zhu left her feeling rankled. Never could she cast aside her true position in the household. From her mother's death onwards, she could read in Daisy's eyes how she repudiated Smooth's claim to take her as his full blood daughter.

Her stepfather came back in the afternoon with his new wife. Plum Han had not expected her to be so young. Prior to signing the marriage certificate, he had called her and discussed the matter. Plum's own status in the family meant she was in no position to object, but she offered them her blessing as long as the lady brought him happiness. Moved by her sincerity, Smooth's voice over the phone became choked and he sobbed.

Both her stepfather and his new wife were hospitable to her and

Zhu, Smooth even requesting that she address Sufen as "auntie". The young couple both obeyed. Industrious Auntie Sufen prepared seven or eight dishes, and then her stepfather asked her to call Daisy down for the reunion feast. She was unsuccessful and so Smooth went up in person. They could hear his gentle "hello", but this appeared to stir a still greater maelstrom within the bedroom. There was a noise like the wailing of a ghost or the howling of a wolf. A disgruntled, but still composed Smooth at last came and sat with them at the table. "Your sister says she's had her meal," he informed them. "Don't let's be distracted by her. Tuck in." The boyfriend and girlfriend shared the spread with her stepfather and Sufen.

Plum Han's stepfather had been busy in recent days, having been contracted to do another stage-shifting job. The auntie was his constant companion as he went about his work. Similarly, Goody, the broken-legged dog, crouched on the trike in an attitude of obedience. Exhibiting genuine concern towards the situation with Zhu, Smooth once asked his stepdaughter if they were going steady. "It's no big deal," she replied. "I brought this classmate to the city for a little fun." Smooth enquired as to where Zhu would be put up at night. "He can find a small hotel nearby," she answered with feigned anger. "There's certainly no space at home."

Her stepfather went to a private hotel in the neighbourhood and placed a 500-yuan deposit for a 100-yuan per night room.

"He has money of his own," declared Plum.

"He came to our home as a guest. How can we let a guest pay for a hotel!"

Plum was touched by this sentiment, and when her stepfather left home without his gloves, she chased after him with a pair. He claimed that it really was not so cold outdoors, but nevertheless slipped them on gratefully.

The younger daughter could detect that the atmosphere at home was far less congenial than before. Daisy had neither been exactly glacial or warm to her previously, but had never before refused to engage her in conversation. Talk was now invariably truncated.

The two young women's doors stood adjacent to each other. Daisy inhabited the larger corner room and would have to pass by

Plum's door on her way in or out. She no longer exchanged greetings, nor stepped over Plum's threshold for a quick word. These days, Daisy's door was flung wide open, yet she would flounce along the passageway without casting so much as a glance in Plum's direction and would increase the volume on her stereo until everyone else was agitated and uncomfortable. They had once shared a meal from the same wok, but this time Daisy avoided the dining table, preferring either to order food in or go outside and dine alone. It was clear that her dagger was sharpened especially for Auntie Sufen, and she was uncommunicative with her father as well. Even Zhu happened to comment that "Your elder sister is weird". Plum Han was cagey about revealing too much about her family, so merely replied, "Everyone has a bad mood now and then."

Zhu Mancang had been to the Western Capital only once before. Everything was novel and fresh to him. As Plum accompanied him in some sightseeing and took him back to his hotel in the evening, she was seldom around the family home. During this sojourn, she discovered how Zhu was becoming more and more attached to her, so much so that she had some difficulty in constraining her own passion.

It was almost 11 pm the previous night when they returned from the Big Wild Goose Pagoda. Zhu invited her to come and sit in his hotel room for a while. Unable to bear being parted from him, she followed her lover. The usually clumsy fellow kissed her and then proceeded to try to plant her body beneath his on the bed. Her first reaction was to resist, though she knew deep down how she yearned for him to see his plan through. Plum's resistance was obviously flimsy, and on sensing the hints she was unconsciously generating, he became emboldened like a bull and wanted to pin her down. What surprised her even more was how this normally doltish sloth found himself able to prise open the first button of her coat with some dexterity. Next, the second button came loose. She was still resisting to a degree, though seemed more prone. By the time the third button was undone, she fended off the bull with an abrupt swipe of her hand.

Plum knew that there had to be a bottom line, and that once this had been transgressed, she would assuredly be spliced to this bumpkin from the deep mountains. This was the main point of contention, which was constraining her from confirming out loud whether he was her classmate or boyfriend. Shy as she was, she pretended to mask these feelings with a show of anger. Plum watched as Zhu consigned himself to a corner of the room like a cowed schoolchild, waiting for the teacher to scold him. He dared not even raise his head. This was why she loved Zhu. He once told her he could rotate a 100-kilo grindstone and was capable of devouring a kilo of meat-stuffed dumplings in a single sitting. This grandsire of a bullock could easily conquer his forty-kilo "feather" if he so chose. What was more, she knew that she herself was half eager and half reluctant. It was a relief that he had not tried to assert himself with force. He reciprocated her ardour, and this was why he was prepared to follow her back to the Western Capital.

Leaving the hotel, Plum Han decided that it was best for Zhu to return home the next day. If they stayed together for a few more days, the carnal conundrum would surely swing beyond their control. She sent him a message suggesting that he travel back to Zhen'an. When he replied that he wanted a little longer in town, she advised that he make his own amusement and not ask her to escort him. Being an obedient fellow, he agreed to go home the next day.

Early the following morning, on accompanying him to the bus station, he tried to persuade her to come along to Zhen'an as well. She dismissed the idea as there was already enough to deal with at home.

The moment the couple parted, Plum was desperate to be hugged. The marvel of being embraced by such a strapping young man in a crowded public place would earn her unprecedented kudos. Some lovers were kissing ardently as though nobody else could see. Zhu now clambered onto the coach with his two canvas bags like an uncultured oaf. The vehicle got into gear and they waved to each other. As she flapped her hand, she knew her heart was entrapped by this uncouth country bumpkin.

Back at the house, Plum Han discovered that everything around her was icy to the touch. Her stepfather and auntie had not returned for two days and two nights, nor had Daisy come home after leaving the night before. In the kitchen, she found nothing but mice scurrying about. On catching sight of her, they plunged into a newly dug hole behind the stove. Not wishing to cook for herself, she bought a roasted sweet potato and an omelette on the street. These she ate crouching on the bed together with some swigs of plain boiled water.

Early winter in the Western Capital was quite chilly and the house lacked central heating. While she was revising for her college entrance exam, her stepfather bought her a freestanding electric heater, which kept part of her room warm, while the walls remained like a freezer. The bed proved to be the snuggest place. During the years of preparation for the test, she spent the majority of her time in winter snuggled down here. This fourteen-square-metre enclave was her only foothold as a citizen of this metropolis. She knew that since losing her mother, there was no one in all the vast city with whom she could claim a close blood tie. Kind as her stepfather was to her, he already had a biological daughter of his own. In her mind, though, a barrier persisted. She ought never to relinquish this small territory, for that would spell the end of her fastness in the city.

The moment Zhu Mancang left the city, she had thought of following him to the countryside of Zhen'an for an excursion. There she could sit by a charcoal brazier and be warmed as a precious pearl and as one worthy of being loved for a lifetime. As their courtship grew more formal in character, it made sense to keep her distance from that country family. Once she found herself too close to them, there would be no reversing out of the situation. When she was not even one year old, her father and mother had brought her to the Western Capital, sacrificing their very lives in the pursuit of a dream. Were she to head back to the countryside, it would be tantamount to bringing sorrow on her deceased parents.

She must keep hold of this small room of hers in the Western Capital. Here, there was optimism and the prospect of leading a life of a different order. Sometimes she felt that this was like defending a bunker. Frigid as it was inside and tricky to protect, she must not surrender.

This time, when she came back, she needed the courage of a rifle-wielding sentry on duty.

23

SMOOTH'S LATEST JOB was to assemble the stage for a Buddhist evening party to bestow blessings on New Year's Day. The project was taxing since it had to be built on the flat ground of a temple courtyard.

The ancient temple complex was situated dozens of miles from the downtown area. It was torched during the Cultural Revolution, and the current halls and rooms were freshly reconstructed. Keen to extend the influence of the foundation and attract disciples on pilgrimage, the forthcoming evening party was planned on a fabulous scale.

The abbot of the temple was the maternal uncle of Iron Kou, and the contract came via him. The investment was alleged to run into millions, having been subsidised by the directors of a number of local enterprises. Kou was charged with coordinating the programme and organising the lighting and stage designs.

When he called Smooth to introduce the operation, Iron Kou emphasised explicitly, "Smooth, this time I'm letting you earn some readies. That'll make up for the fiasco of the last evening party." He said that he had been tricked out of tens of thousands of yuan the previous time and he was still cursing those silver-tongued cheats who were responsible. He wished that cancer would rot their mouths away until they died. Smooth had expected that he would be antagonised by the way he had enlisted Chief Qu to recoup his losses. Far from it. Kou had taken the initiative to soothe matters over. "My great and honourable Director Iron Kou," his staccato answer began. "Smooth would be a moron to fail to tell what is good from what is bad. Today, we can scoop up some cash from hard labour, and it's all down to your consideration. For what it's worth, we'll toil hard and won't demand any conditions from you. Really, how could a great director like yourself be indebted to a poor trike pedaller like me? Just give us the nod and we'll be on site in a blink."

Smooth led his team of around a dozen to the temple early in the morning. All were pedalling tricycles, save for Sufen who was balancing on the back of Smooth's trike.

The air in the suburb was rather bracing. The sun had just risen and its golden beams enhanced the complexion of all the group. Even their grey hairs took on a soft and sheeny bounce as if nourished by medicinal shampoo. These stage shifters, who seldom saw the day at its fullest, had to steel themselves not to break into song and catcall at this uplifting weather. Big Hook began to croon *My Younger Sister Sits on the Prow of the Boat,* to much hilarity from Sufen, who pummelled Smooth's back with her fist. As the highway was so broad and devoid of traffic, the tricycles swarmed into a configuration with Smooth at their centre. Actually, it was Sufen who was the draw. Beneath the sunlight, these unoccupied grafters began to see how jovial and becoming she truly was. Their work with the drama troupes had allowed them to encounter many starlets, but at this moment Sufen with her wavy tresses was not a jot their inferior. "My sister-in-law turns heads like nobody else in this city," Mound extolled. The crew then started to compete at singing all the love melodies they knew, cheering their spirits and Sufen's too.

Beating her husband's back from time to time was in fact a method for registering ebullience. Of course, Smooth knew how fortunate he was and was intimately familiar with his wife's endowments. How could his enthusiasm to pedal possibly wane?

"Big Brother, you're the head," yelled Monkey. "Eat more and own more. You've got a babe on your trike so can make it a real knee-trembler. You've plenty to keep you fuelled as you pedal. What about your brothers?"

Sufen was concerned at how much Smooth was perspiring, so to lessen his burden leaped onto Monkey's trike. "Now this babe belongs to you," she exclaimed. "Do as you like, but don't lose your pace. Happy now?"

Everyone took this as a ribald stunt.

Their arrival at the temple coincided with the morning session of sutra study. The abbot, several monks and dozens of layman were applying themselves earnestly to the Zen scriptures. Smooth and his team stood agape at this by the front gate until a small monk led them away and enjoined them not to encroach upon the courtyard and spoil the ambience of their recitals. Smooth's attention was captured by a smoking censer in the Buddha Hall. He felt the compulsion to light three incense sticks of his own before kowtowing three times and offering them up with the greatest reverence. He was seen to murmur prayerful words as his eyes looked towards the Guanyin Hall.

"Asking for his fourth wife, I'll bet," remarked Monkey, causing Sufen to flush.

"Monkey, you son of a bitch," scolded Smooth. "Can't your pussy mouth even produce civilised words in a holy temple! I was praying for more jobs. For us all to be touched by fortune. Praying for a fourth wife for your grandpa?"

"If you could pray for a fourth wife for Monkey's grandpa, he'd burn incense to thank you in the underworld," jested Big Hook.

"Fellas, this is a temple," Smooth reminded them. "Keep your filth to yourselves."

No sooner had he upbraided them in this way, did Mound produce another tactless comment. "Hey, that statue of Guanyin's the spitting image of your little Plum Han."

"Enough of this guff. Bad luck will come back to bite you if you don't give it a rest right now."

To be candid, in his first glance at the statue, Smooth did see the likeness of his second wife, Orchid Zhao. Facially, there was little to distinguish her from her daughter, and Plum stood just a little taller. Before she went away to college, Mound had told Smooth of his desire to marry the girl. Plum naturally refused him, and Smooth himself did not want to see her with his underling. Mound had long been simmering with resentment towards him on account of this slight.

Once the chanting of the sutras had ceased, Smooth led them on a promenade about the courtyard. When the abbot came out, he was keen to approach him, though did not know the appropriate form of address. "Director", "manager" or "leader" all sounded similarly unsuitable. Suddenly, it occurred to him. "Great master," he declared, "I am Smooth and these are my men. We've come to take care of the stage. Director Iron Kou introduced us to this job and said that the party is designed to try to bestow blessings. I am sorry for whatever trouble we may be putting you through." As he spoke, Smooth bowed with his hands folded formally in front of him.

The abbot nodded his head without replying. He whispered briefly to a junior monk and then proceeded to the Grand Hall in the company of monks and laypeople.

The young brother told them of how the stage designer had examined a set of iron frames in a nearby village. Since these were satisfactory, they were to fetch them over. On their return, Iron Kou, the stage designer, the director, and the heads responsible for lighting and music had already arrived. The abbot was discussing some matter with them, underlining his words by recourse to physical gestures. The core personnel were drawn from the Shaanxi Opera Troupe and the Song and Dance Troupe, so they were all on very familiar terms.

Smooth saw his opportunity to step forward. This time, he was answerable solely to Iron Kou. After his venerable uncle had given him an overview of the party, the tasks on site were divided up. Apart from a few on the creative side who convened an extra meeting in a wing room, the stage shifters were given the liberty to begin their operation. For the first time, Smooth heard the proper parlance. The older monk was to be referred to as "abbot" and the monastery was, in fact, a "temple".

"Abbot, rest assured," said Smooth when he sensed his moment. "The stage will be completed without any hiccups. Your honour, you govern this temple so dutifully that even the city folk want to come here and burn incense. The party is sure to swell your influence. Word will get around as quick as a stinky fart." He regretted immediately the use of that vulgar term. Much to his relief, the abbot went about attending to other business without sparing him so much as a glance.

The most challenging undertaking was to assemble a freestanding stage of irregular design. One option would be to obtain a ready-built rustic stage and add an armature of iron frames, fastening the wooden boards into place with rivets and introducing a suspended curtain. That could look attractive for the setting. Nonetheless, the director stipulated that the grand hall must constitute the backdrop for the performing space and the dozens of steps leading up to the building should be utilised. He asserted that a panoply of different performances needed to be presented on it, so the stage-shifting task could not be simplified too much. Indeed, the key problem was the irregular shape. Only a few of the iron frames they brought over were amenable, with the majority needing to be fused in some way. Most of the first two days had been spent sourcing materials. Smooth and Big Hook shuttled between the city and the temple, hiring out iron frames from a number of troupes. They also laid their hands on acetylene welding torches and cutting machines. If the iron skeleton did not fit into place, they would have to crop and splice on site. Eventually, by the fourth day, the stage was finding its embryonic shape, though Smooth was troubled by having to bend his waist constantly.

The monastery served meals every day, and yet enforced strict rules of vegetarianism. However much they ate, hunger would set in soon afterwards. If Mound and the others wanted a taste of something meaty, they had to head to a nearby town. One day, absent-mindedly, Mound brought back a half-eaten portion of pig's trotters. His infraction was duly reported by a junior monk to the abbot, who then reprimanded Iron Kou in the sternest of terms. He in turn passed on this reproof to Smooth, seasoning it with a hefty dose of profanity. Whoever wanted to jeopardise their income was told they could fuck off this minute. Kou asked him if he was unaware that it was a sodding act of blasphemy to consume pig's feet in the Buddha's holy house. Smooth assembled his crew and relayed the prohibition on eating meat, reinforcing the point again and again. To his relief, nobody had noticed him and his wife earlier as they munched on those two chicken wings Sufen requested he bring in from outside.

They made their lodgings in the Bodhisattva Hall after Iron Kou lobbied the abbot repeatedly for accommodation. This entailed waiving the embargo on outsiders being allowed to stay, though made practical sense since it was too time consuming to travel home each day. The abbot supplied them with several quilts to keep them snug on the floor of the Grand Hall. As a female, the same hospitality could not be extended to Sufen, who lived temporarily with a laywoman who cooked for the brethren.

The appearance of the statue of the Bodhisattva did arouse a twinge of excitement in Smooth. Much as he told himself not to dwell on this, he became increasingly convinced that Orchid Zhao must have been the sculptor's model. As they stayed here overnight, a thin beam of moonlight tilted gently and obliquely in through the window. In his drowsiness, he formed the impression that Orchid herself was alive and walking into the room.

The couple had first encountered each other when Smooth rode his trike to the wholesale clothing market on Shangyi Road. Since stage shifting was not yet a regular gig, this was a prime spot to loiter, waiting for casual business. Nothing special was happening on that particular day. As they chatted away, he and his fellow pedallers heard a cry of "Oi, trikes!" They all sprang into motion at the same moment, questing after this female caller. They struck their target simultaneously but the woman singled out Smooth as "My one".

The other couriers did not immediately take this as a signal to back off, and so the woman firmly lodged the bolt of cloth she was holding onto Smooth's cart. Now, the stragglers recoiled. Later, when Smooth asked why she had showed him this favour, she only answered, "No particular reason. You had the look of a trike rider and I felt safe letting you help me." Smooth was left puzzled as to what feature of his person made him come across as a trike rider?

The first thing he noticed about Orchid was her diminutive stature. After loading the products, it took her a number of jumps before she could land on his cart with the cargo. He eventually realised that she stood no taller than five feet two inches. Despite this, she had the countenance of a holy Bodhisattva.

Orchid Zhao inventoried a delivery that would fill the whole cart. There was curtain fabric, nylon hooks, buttons and miscellaneous cloth. The composition of this haul branded itself on Smooth's mind as in the coming days he was to order and deliver everything in person.

She was a seamstress by trade, renting out a compact booth in one of the narrow alleys outside the South Gate of the City Wall. Space was pinched, though business prospered. All types of goods were on sale in the area, making it a convenient location. People tended to rent out apartments here as its proximity to the city centre inflated prices. Most residents commuted about the local area.

Zhao had begun her working days as a stitching apprentice in one of the towns around Hanzhong in rural southern Shaanxi. Upon marrying, she followed her husband to the county town. He himself was a skilled mason under a contract foreman. Once the foreman gained a project in the Western Capital, the couple relocated again, taking with them their daughter Plum, who was still less than one year old.

At the outset, life traced an easy pattern. Whatever they coveted never seemed unreachable. Her husband thanked Orchid, praising her as his star of good omen. In response, she claimed that never since they first met had she sewn on buttons askew. Formerly, it was not uncommon for her to stitch on sleeves the wrong way around or scorch garments with the iron. Each year, she would be penalised and have to cover those ruined clothes with her salary. Now, being on a far steadier keel, it appeared the right time to contemplate buying a place of their own in the city.

Then, a thunderbolt struck without warning. Droplets of blood had begun falling regularly from her husband's nose. They treated it as a minor ailment, only to be informed when this persisted that he had leukaemia. The medical bills gobbled up all their savings, and at last she was left a widow with a young daughter. She had that nauseating sensation of dangling without an anchor between the heavens and the Earth.

Orchid Zhao's initial instinct was to retreat to her native Hanzhong. On reasoned reflection, however, she calculated that the little booth could furnish Plum and her with more than enough to get by. She would stay put. After two years of widowhood, she met Smooth, who had not been anticipating a new relationship. Zhao had not been overly regardful towards him, for on delivering and offloading the first order, she squared the bill with him and didn't even suggest taking a seat for a while. Too shy as Smooth was to have name cards printed, he would pull out a notepad and scrawl down his contact number for potential customers. He noticed how Zhao tossed the paper beneath her trestle table without bothering to look at it. But then, about a month later when he was waiting in the same place, he once more heard the call of "My one". Another job was agreed, only this time when she struggled to jump onto the cart, Smooth lent her a hand. Afterwards, his fellow pedallers started gossiping. They asked if, when the task was over, he bundled up the little woman in his arms and set her back down on the ground?

Once again, she failed to invite him to rest his weary feet. However, she did request his phone number on the pretext of needing a regular courier. About a month later, he lifted his receiver to hear the voice of Zhao on the line. She informed him that she was in the process of ordering goods and required his assistance. He had already agreed to undertake a different job that day, though passed it on to somebody else as he was keen to cultivate this client. He even turned up in person to "ferry cargo and passenger" back to her place.

Now, noticing how his hair was slick with perspiration, Zhao bought him an iced soft drink from a neighbouring shop. He downed it in a single gulp like parched land receiving rainwater. He advised Zhao that since he was now familiar with her requirements, he could carry all the goods to her door without her needing to be personally present. If she didn't trust him, she could defer payment until receipt of materials. Zhao looked at him for some time and then said that this was worth discussing in the future. She still accompanied him on two more occasions before trusting him to deal with it alone.

Almost every month without fail, Zhao drew on Smooth's services. Sometimes when he arrived, she would be busy and he would leave, telling her they could settle up next time. No matter how trivial the affairs seemed, Smooth would obey in a flattering manner. As their contact became more frequent, he feared that he would start to feel bereft if they went more than a few days without meeting in person. Orchid Zhao also showed more latitude towards him. One time, he interrupted her afternoon meal. Without hesitation, she presented him with a bowl of braised pork over rice. He showed a polite face and was told, "If you don't want to eat, make the most of your hunger. Carry on." Her demeanour and expression were those one would display towards a family member. He ate with great zest, conscientiously communicating to her his sense of approval.

What sealed their decision to tread the same track was the intervention of Zhao's daughter, Plum Han. She was barely four years old at the point of their first acquaintance. Each time he couriered goods for her mother, she would want Smooth to carry her on his cart and play around. As matters developed, Orchid entrusted him to fetch her from the kindergarten when she couldn't break away from the booth. He alternated between pursuing business and entertaining Plum. Soon, entertaining Plum did become his business, and a family one at that. She adored being allowed to perch on the trike and even appeared disappointed when her mother rather than Smooth turned up to collect her. In this way, his involvement in the lives of both mother and daughter intensified.

Since Daisy was by then in junior high school, he could make a routine of carrying Plum home, before returning to his apartment and firing up the wok for his elder daughter. As Daisy ate, he would peel away and either make more deliveries or shift stages. Often being gone overnight, he did worry about her safety and study regime. Thus, he bought her a mobile for use in the advent of an emergency. Not infrequently, she experienced nightmares and cried for him to come and comfort her. It was then that he understood his household needed a woman, and Orchid Zhao was the natural candidate.

He never actually thought that the pair would be a suitable match. Despite living in the city, he was a lowly tricycle pedaller, clad from morning to night in a grubby blue overcoat. As a seamstress, Zhao had an affinity for immaculate, tailored clothes. Should her blouse have a white collar, it had to be pure as ivory without a single blemish. Her milky skin was complimented with made-to-measure, crisply ironed trousers. As for her white measuring tape with red printed numerals, she took pains to drape it around her neck so the two ends hung at equal length.

On their first meeting, he perceived that she was something of an imp, since the top of her head drew up level with the base of his neck. She needed a hand up onto the trike. He subsequently found that her nature was elevated, so high that initially she was beyond his reach. As Zhao's kindness flourished and Plum became dependent upon them, the chasm between them attenuated, with him climbing in her direction.

When Spring Festival came around, Smooth purchased for himself a suit costing more than a hundred yuan following a not insignificant discount. A customer let him have it at the wholesale price, so the retail price tag may have exceeded 300 yuan. He already owned a tie, brought back from Macau by Big Army. Despite having tried it on at home, he had not yet ventured to wear it in public. A new white shirt set him back a further few dozen yuan, but on the first day of the Lunar New Year he found himself able to deck himself out in full formal wear. Before visiting Orchid Zhao's home, he bought two pounds of De Mao Gong crystal cake and two pounds of Old Iron Family marinated beef from the Muslim Quarter. In addition, he stuffed a hundred yuan note into a red envelope as a gift for Plum.

He had not expected to receive such warm hospitality from his hostess. "What's this in aid of?" were Zhao's first words to him. "You're dressed up like a bridegroom. Do you have a date or something?"

Smooth felt he had the chance to be brazen. "Yeah, I do have a date."

"With whom?"

"That's the luck of New Year. Whoever I might happen to bump into."

For a while, the two of them exchanged phrases that seemed to conceal covert meanings. As he sweated with nerves, he unfolded the secret note and divulged its contents, so to speak.

Orchid Zhao clearly did not have so high an estimation of herself. She declared that her husband had died and asked if he was afraid of the widow's hex or not. She then said that she had a "burdensome flask of oil" in reference to her little Plum. As a migrant to the city, moreover, her habitation was as modest as a needle hole. She was worried that he would become tired of them both before long and drive the pair away. Smooth was not so reticent in announcing how his feelings were steadfast and she mustn't fear instability.

Then aged only twelve or thirteen, Daisy saw no reason not to accede to her father's wishes for the household. Orchid Zhao's kindliness and benevolent nature were not in any doubt, for even before moving in she produced a custom-made wardrobe for Daisy so the girl now looked presentable. The first time the couple came back together, it had been she who served Zhao the maiden cup of tea, addressing her without hesitation as "mother". Plum was to share a bedroom with her stepsister, and Daisy even hauled a quilt upstairs for that purpose, making the bed so it was crisply neat and inviting. In retrospect, how carefree and merry Smooth had been in those years! Nobody could have foreseen the benighted fate of Ms Zhao. She contracted a rare illness, which ravaged her body without mercy. That rarest jar of honey and sugar Smooth cradled tumbled from his palms and crashed into smithereens.

Tonight he had been enchanted by this statue of the Bodhisattva and dozed off as his thoughts wandered back and forth. He dreamed that Orchid Zhao stepped out of that marble likeness. Her appearance was unaltered in its generosity and sincerity, though she was wearing the garb of the Bodhisattva and held some kind of bottle in her hand. As she drew nearer, he recognised it as the IV drip on which she had been reliant in the final year of her life. With that pristine measuring tape still adorning her shoulders, she stepped towards him. "I placed Plum in your hands," mouthed the spectre. "She was pitiable, an orphan. I beg you to show her more tolerance. Help her acquire a home. As long as she has a bowl of her own to eat from, all will be well." She vanished after expressing these words. Smooth reached out his hand to grasp at the wide sleeve of her habit, though failed and awoke there and then.

His mobile was vibrating. He opened it and saw a text message from Plum. "Dad, when will you come back?" it began. "Am I right in thinking I'm not welcome here any more?" He checked the time and realised it was 1 am. He messaged her back to ask, "Daughter, what's up?" Minutes later came the answer. "Nothing. You please rest. It's too late now, Dad. Goodnight."

Smooth found sleep impossible.

24

AFTER GRAPPLING WITH AN INTRACTABLE INNER CONFLICT, Plum Han sent the text message to her stepfather. Her patience was spent, for this time the atmosphere in the household seemed irrevocably peculiar. She had perceived her elder sister Daisy's unease around the newcomer, but she too had been in receipt of her viciousness.

Another victim was the lame dog, originally owned by her mother. The day she received her diagnosis of uterine cancer, that stray came nosing around their front gate. More than once Smooth had driven it out of the alley, though it kept on limping back. Later on, when he had a delivery job in the eastern suburb, he plopped it on the back of the tricycle and dumped the dog outside the Eastern Gate. Two days later, it reappeared at their home. The whole family could not fathom what was going on, so the mother adopted Goody. She thought the animal worthy of pity and had a hunch that its presence was somehow predestined. They should let it into their home and see that it didn't want for food. Her stepfather even pinned his hopes on this being a gift from the immortals sent to save the life of Orchid Zhao.

At that time, Daisy appeared not to object to their new canine companion, yet made no effort to be kind to it either. Plum once heard her curse, "Showing pity to dogs!" Then continuing with, "How so? What qualifies it to be doted on like that?"

The dog was not the harbinger of good fortune. Her mother passed away in the second year following the diagnosis. They all said that the tumour was in remission and that ninety per cent of patients in her position would go onto make a full and lasting recovery. Orchid Zhao happened to find herself among the unfortunate ten per cent, and the cancer metastasised and caused necrosis of her bodily tissues. She expired with a look of regret on her face. As she was nearing the very end, the dog became frenzied and yelped wildly day in day out, tugging at the hem of her stepfather's trousers to indicate she wanted to go out. Smooth was sure Goody wanted to be reunited with her mistress, and Plum Han told her mother all about it. "Such a pitiable creature," her mother gasped. "Whatever happens, don't shoo it away. It's a living thing, after all." She was never to be discharged from the hospital, and at the very time she died, the dog was banging her head against the kitchen floor until her scalp was broken and bloody.

The newly orphaned Plum took to nursing the dog in her arms. She sensed that she had some esoteric connection with the soul of her mother. The two saw each other less often after she pursued her further studies in the mountains of Shangluo. And yet, every time her return was imminent, the dog would become hyperactive, pulling at her stepfather's trousers and scratching at the door. It was a sure prophecy.

When she brought back Zhu Mancang, the dog was not at home. Smooth related how it had barked frenetically on the back of the tricycle, and when pondering over the matter Plum could pinpoint this to the very moment she was crossing the threshold. Her pity towards the dog intensified, as did her compulsion to show her kindness. The pet did not fare so well with Daisy, who had no scruples about kicking her whenever the creature got under her feet. Goody knew to be subdued and lie back in silence when Daisy was in the house. In fact, today the dog proved to be the catalyst for the fracas between the two sisters.

When Plum arrived home with Zhu, Daisy maintained a stony silence. This was a first, and she didn't know why her sister was incapable of mouthing a simple "hello". It was her custom to return from Shangluo with specimens of local produce as gifts. Typically, she might present fresh fruit, Shangluo walnuts, Zhen'an chestnuts, sweet potato brittle or persimmon cakes. Never once did she fail to offer something. This time, the couple opted for market-fresh produce and dried fruit. The day after giving these to Daisy, she discovered them consigned to the bin. Fearing that they were out of date or had gone mouldy in the box, she sifted through the contents of each and turned the packages over, finding nothing awry. Plum didn't raise this issue before Daisy, though was sure that there was a problem on some level. Daisy continued to act as if she were invisible, and after Zhu's departure Plum herded Goody into her own small bedroom, read books, went online and prepared materials for her dissertation.

Daisy listened to her music as though oblivious to the presence of anyone else around. She danced and pleased herself, much of the time generating unnerving and inexplicable noises. Plum took this behaviour as a kind of assault aimed at her, but tried to tolerate it. She knew her position in the home. Daisy was the legitimate daughter and heir, whereas she was the burdensome flask of oil. Now, the thread that bound her to this household had been severed, and it was merely charity that prevented this flask from being tossed out of the door. She tried her utmost to be resilient until the tension between them reached its flashpoint.

Plum took the initiative to try to flatter Daisy. The chill had to be lifted, otherwise continued cohabitation would be impossible. That day, she visited the Muslim Quarter and bought items for her elder sister. She knew she was fond of desserts such as rock-hard sugar, southern fried sugar, sticky milk sugar and peanut brittle. She also thought of purchasing head meat from a sheep and boiled lamb pluck. In the past, when her stepfather took this route, he would pick such fare up for them as a treat. She remembered that the meatier morsels were savoured by Daisy and so decided to take a selection over as an unprecedented peace offering.

Daisy was in the middle of performing her beauty ritual. Only the tip of her nose and her eyes were exposed through the holes in the facial mask. Her mouth was completely covered over, but she could still emit short syllables that sounded like beans frying in a cast iron wok. "Quick, quick, quick. Out, out, out. Stinks, stinks, stinks. Humph, humph, humph." Plum obliged in taking the treats out, though couldn't find anywhere to hide her face after this encounter. As the younger sister, she just tried to lay her sense of shame to one side.

The following lunchtime when she was cooking downstairs, she asked Daisy what she would like. Her sister snubbed her, so Plum boiled a few more balls of sweet glutinous rice flour and poached an extra egg. This was how her late mother would tantalise Smooth and herself. Plum took the bowl upstairs, only to be met with further chants of "Quick, quick, quick. Out, out, out." The door swung behind her as she began her retreat, and half of the wall appeared to shudder precariously. This again she tolerated. After all, she was a student at university and thus she and Daisy must have formed contrasting impressions of the world. Much more than that, her tuition rested on the blood and sweat of Daisy's biological father.

Plum was able to bring to mind how her mother would handle bickering between the two girls. "No matter whether it's something big or small, yield to Daisy," Orchid Zhao whispered. "Your presence here makes her own portion of cake a little smaller." These words scored themselves in her memory. Once orphaned, she took them as a sobering touchstone and resolved that she must receive a higher education.

Her tolerance was finally exhausted when Daisy kicked the poor dog and made her nose bleed.

Plum did not know precisely when Goody had slipped into Daisy's room. She seemed to have been crouching on one side of her bed all along. She disliked how muggy and stuffy her bedroom had become, so when the mesmerising noonday sun was aloft in the sky she opened the door ajar, perhaps giving Goody the opportunity to sneak out. All at once, she heard the agonised, unnatural yelp of the hound, who had clearly been struck by a heavy object. Next, she heard Daisy's salty cursing. "You tiny slut. How dare you come in here again!" she roared. "I'll kick you till none of your four legs works. Slut, get as far away from here as you can!" Goody squeezed out through the door with her nose dripping red. Now not one, but two of her legs were injured. As she entered the room, she couldn't support her own body and so slumped onto the floor, then rolled over, licking at her freshly disabled limb. Her belly wheezed as if assaulted by cramps, tears trickled from those tiny eyes. As Plum stared at her puny, trembling form, she could not help feeling moved and was so incensed that a confrontation was inevitable.

When Plum stormed into Daisy's room, she was polishing her

black boots as if about to go out somewhere. Plum noticed that the tapered toe of the boot still bore traces of blood and canine hair.

"Sister, what is the matter with you?" Plum demanded to know. "How could you assault Goody like that?"

"What did you say?" replied Daisy with feigned disbelief.

"I said how could you kick Goody like that?" she asked in a firmer tone.

"Ah, you mean that tiny slut? It was crawling along the ground and happened to collide with my toe." She did not pause for a second, still polishing her footwear.

"If there's something you want to say to me, be direct, Sister. There's no need to bully a dog who's already disabled."

"Smooth Diao is clueless about how to raise a family. He even clings to a broken-legged little slut of a she-dog. Even the name's odd – Goody. Get lost, get away. Don't stand there swaying. I'm getting bored." Daisy swished one of her hands dismissively as she spoke.

Having reached the nub of the matter, Plum Han didn't want to back down now. "Don't point at the mulberry and scorn the locust," she snarled. "Sister, I don't know what I've done wrong this time I came back. You've been awfully mean to me. Spell out the reason, please, so I can correct any mistake I've made." Plum was trying her best to be politic.

"You've done nothing wrong. You've got everything. Smooth Diao let you enrol at college and you've found a man. He's even come back here to sleep. What else could you possibly want?"

"Don't spew nonsense. Who's been sleeping in this house?" Plum's face was by now tinged blue with anger.

"Humph, humph, humph. I feel sick just mentioning it."

"Don't be silly. We're only classmates."

"Honestly, who cares about your shitty business? Ah, this household has been looted by outsiders. Since you've got yourself a man, go to him. Can't you bear to leave? Are you waiting to share these broken windows and doors in the future?" Daisy's final words carried the headiest venom.

Plum was too furious to answer coherently. "You... you, how can you say this?" she just about gasped. "I always call you my elder sister, so how can you come out with things like that?" She genuinely could not find the right words.

"You have a nerve to keep up this 'elder sister' charade. I'm the only child my mother gave birth to, so I don't have any brothers or sisters. Shift, don't get in my way." Having uttered these words, Daisy bowled out of the room like a blast of wind, with the door slamming shut without any assistance.

Plum stood there, truly aghast. She did not recover her composure until Daisy had clicked the iron latch of the front gate behind her. This was unbearable. She spreadeagled on her own bed and broke into a protracted wail.

After weeping for a while, she packed her belongings with the thought of leaving this home that didn't belong to her any more. The young woman wanted to go to Zhen'an to be with Zhu Mancang. On more sober reflection, if she did travel down there it would be troublesome to disentangle herself from the village. Her only sanctuary must be the campus. Once everything was packed, it dawned on her that should she leave, it would be permanent. After all, her stepfather was good to her and the fourteen square metre room was under his protection. She then slowly unpacked her bags. Plum also knew that her stepfather was busy and chronically fatigued. She wanted to call him, though didn't have a comfortable feeling about doing so. In the silence of the night, she realised her limits had been reached and so tapped out a text message. To her astonishment, he came back seated on his trike the next morning.

On being probed, Plum recounted tearfully the mishaps of the previous day. Goody's mouth was still swollen and her leg lame. Smooth lifted the dog with care and tenderness. It was a relief that Daisy had not yet returned. He was still engaged with matters outside, so he suggested taking her to the temple in the suburbs so she could unwind. As this home was no longer hers, she bundled the dog up in her arms and went away with her stepfather.

25

THE DAY AFTER HER FINAL ESTRANGEMENT FROM PLUM, Daisy accompanied Princess Wu to the ski slope at Yuhua Palace in Tongchuan. Mr Noodle Head was their chauffeur. From the fondness that was evident between them, much progress had been made in their relationship, and the very fact that Wu could allow a man of his type into her affections caused Daisy to now regard her friend as being totally ruined.

Mr Noodle Head was sporting a watermelon-red beanie hat that gripped his cranium tightly. Wu tried to whip it off, insisting that "truth is beauty". His strands of hair slid down again, and the Princess wove them into a pigtail, clasping the end in place with a faux sapphire butterfly clip. When the plait fell to one side of his head, the other side appeared stark, and Daisy nearly choked with laughter at the grotesque sight. Tan Daogui caught a glimpse of himself in the rear-view mirror and, instead of being annoyed, merely simpered. His swollen and squinting eyes appeared like two consecutive ruts. "Split those two lines wider," exclaimed Princess Wu. "This is an expressway." Tan sat up straighter, tried to open his eyes wider and slammed his foot on the accelerator of his Land Rover.

Daisy was pondering over what had induced her friend to be lured into this trap. She even derived a shred of relief from the knowledge that although her life was miserable, she had still not sunk to this level. Tan really did make her stomach turn. She suddenly thought of the Takakura Ken-lookalike Plum had brought back. Had he been born in the Western Capital, girls would stick to him like flypaper. From her point of view, Plum had no distinct advantages. True enough, she had been a mite bonnier in the past, but Daisy looked on her as a nobody and just a flask of burdensome oil dragged into her home. Having grown into womanhood and being on the cusp of graduation, she was in a position to ensnare at least one male, and that in itself stoked Daisy's ire. This time that Plum came back, her unhappiness was absolute and she couldn't identify the reason. The worst part of it was her bringing that five foot eleven inch tall "wild bull" with her and parading him about the house. Daisy's contempt for him was equal to the contempt she felt for Cai Sufen. Well, Smooth Diao had brought home a slut while Plum had a breeding stallion. As the only one who had a true right to reside there, how could her life be worse and less cosy than those of the slut or a wild animal? How could she tolerate such a topsy-turvy situation? Actually, she had no illusions about Smooth's fleapit with its dilapidated decor. What she was enraged and perplexed by was how blatantly he maintained and nurtured two female interlopers. She had not minded the crippled dog in the past. She would even stroke and bathe her, and trim her nails. But now this slut seemed to have thoroughly ingratiated herself with the two women from outside. The home was now infested, and all these creatures of the soil had united to marginalise her and were gnawing away at her share of the cake like gluttonous silkworms. Daisy had to safeguard her legitimate rights in the most robust and resilient fashion.

To be truthful, the lame dog hadn't sneaked into her room. Leaving the door ajar would never have been construed as an invitation from her. When she was preparing to leave, the little slut was sunbathing by the rail in front of her door. Since their home was encircled by neighbouring properties, sunlight could only penetrate the building through a tiny gap, leaving a bright patch no larger than a handbasin. The canny hound positioned herself right at the snug centre of this patch. She opened one eye as Daisy was crossing the threshold, though closed it again, displaying neither the coquettish eagerness she doled out on Plum, nor the ardour she reserved for that slut Sufen. Daisy unleashed her anger in an instant, digging her toes into the animal's body and then repeating the action. Both blows were sharp. Knowing that the dog owed her home to Plum's mother's intervention, Daisy allowed her to become a proxy for all the sluts who were wronging her. She intended to kick her and then send her flying down the stairs. However, the moment she was struck on the posterior and tummy and bumped her head against the wall, the dog managed somehow to limp on two injured legs and squeeze into Plum's room, thereby escaping the mortal strike.

She did regret her subsequent quarrel with her sister. Her expressions had been far too mild and vapid to have a deep effect. When Plum's words of reproof drifted back through her memory, how she wished she could revisit the scene and fend them off more acerbically. She was soon brought back to the present, for Princess Wu and Tan had already parked the car by the entrance to the alley. Daisy had to climb on board.

Daisy had not conceived of the liquor salesman as being an entertainer, but he made the journey lively and light-hearted through his constant banter. Far better than watching a comedy film. When they arrived at Yuhua Palace, the Princess forbade him from unpicking his pigtail and this caused many to look on in disbelief as they traipsed through the ski resort. As a southerner, he didn't know how to ski, and Wu was content to let him make an exhibition of himself. This appeared to delight him as he was naturally so outgoing. His attempts at skiing were risible, yet he keenly climbed the slopes both low and high, and took what was presumably an accidental tumble. No limbs were injured or broken, though on account of his bulk the seat of his trousers tore wide open at the seam. Rolls of fat filled the red underwear beneath, so that it bore the shape of a huge inverted wok. Worried that he might be badly hurt, his two companions skied hastily to his side. "Nothing's damaged," Tan joked. "Just my bum's got a big crack in it! Still usable."

Après-ski, they decided to check into a nearby hotel at the resort. This being the weekend, countless visitors had come over from the Western Capital and there were no standard rooms available. Tan gladly paid for the emperor suite. Daisy didn't want to be a spare part, so volunteered to lodge at a homestay farmstead. Wu was firmly opposed to this idea and suggested that they could sleep in the room while Tan remained outside on sentry duty. He at once agreed, repeating "OK" several times.

After checking in, they sought out a barbecue. Since it was so cold, Fatty Tan ordered kebabs to takeaway and collected wine, spirits and imported beer from the boot of his car, so they could drink inside the suite. To his credit, Fatty was patient and considerate where women were concerned. When he noticed that his friends appeared to be sitting awkwardly, he gathered together every cushion in the room and saw that Daisy and the Princess were propped up comfortably before he even dared take his seat and drink. He started to knock back the booze and from time to time cajoled the ladies to have a try. He said that wine was fine stuff, but one had to be sure that it was the genuine article. Tan could guarantee the authenticity of every last bottle he placed on the table.

"Don't you just sell fakes for a living?" the Princess interposed.

Fatty Tan smiled enigmatically. "Nonsense," he said. "Completely real. Come on, let's drink."

Their host became gradually intoxicated and loose. He extended his hands with the intention of planting one on Wu's thigh and the other on Daisy's. Wu simply smirked and showed no sign of disgust. Daisy had an uneasy, defiled feeling inside and tried to shake her leg free.

Now rowdier than ever, he turned to his forte of cracking jokes. Vulgar as his comedy was, the women nevertheless were tickled. When telling a joke, Fatty would self-consciously evoke the situation using his body language. For example, when describing how a monk got caught up in a tryst, he tried to imitate the holy brother by bumping his bald head against Wu's commodious breast. As for the one about the "improper fling" between an old grandpa and his daughter-in-law, he mimicked how a woman would groan in the throes of passion. In the joke, the foolish son and his mother mistook the noises for a cat's satisfied purrs as it lapped up millet porridge.

By now, the guests in the next room had become irritated. They banged against the party wall and asked them to keep the noise down and have a thought for others at this time of night. Princess Wu rolled around on the sofa, laughing. So as to poke fun at Fatty, she removed Daisy's gigantic hooped earrings and pinned them onto his lobes. Daisy was displeased, but didn't show it as it was actually rather rare for them to share in such hearty fun. When Fatty was completely intoxicated, words gushed endlessly from his mouth.

What stood out for her was how he said that ten years ago he too had been a tricycle pedaller. Despite being flushed in the face to begin with, she was eager to hear about how he bettered himself.

Fatty Tan recounted how he had been a teenager when he first started to ride the trike. He initially earned ten yuan a load, rising soon to fifty. Later, he heard about how one of his colleagues had given up this work to sell liquor instead. Fatty trained his sights on this guy, noting his every manoeuvre, and then tried to copy him. He made 15,000 yuan effortlessly. Good gracious! From fifty yuan serving other people, he was now making 15,000 yuan as a freelancer. Only a buffoon would turn down such an opportunity. He continued to operate independently until he accrued his first million, then transferred to working for a genuine brand. This was far less risky than trading in counterfeits. To date, whether he had sold real liquor or fakes, he never failed to succeed in what he did...

Fatty Tan droned on about his achievements, still being awake when dawn came. His trousers were by now visibly damp at the crotch and while the Princess chuckled at the sight, Daisy thought her friend set the bar very low for what she considered humorous. In her eyes, Fatty Tan epitomised one thing: vulgarity. One might even call it cheapness. His jokes raised a titter at first, though wore very thin on retelling. The anecdote about his former life as a trike rider caused her to disdain him all the more. But for the gaudiness of his Italian fur attire, he was every bit the image of a filthy old goat. Daisy could not hear the words "tricycle" and "pedaller" without feeling that they were an assault upon her ears, eyes and heart. She came over uneasy, became warm in the face, and had a stinging sensation in her ears that meant she couldn't raise her head from its drooping position. From believing that Fatty lacked grace, the knowledge of his past line of work made her want to see this obese heap of flesh banished to some dank corner.

Fatty gritted his teeth, snored and farted as he lay comatose on the carpet. Daisy lifted his head using her foot and removed her earrings. She went into the bathroom and rinsed them before snapping them inside her clutch bag. If they hadn't been forged from pure silver, she would have tossed them straight in the bin. Nonetheless, Princess Wu still chuckled when he either broke wind, ground his teeth or snored. She even mimicked these noises.

"Do you really love this tub of lard?" Daisy asked.

"So funny."

"There's really fun to be had here?"

"Isn't being funny enough?"

Midday had already come around by the time Princess Wu kicked Fatty Tan awake. He was embarrassed at having wet himself and asked if he had talked gibberish when drunk.

"Just acting the rogue all night," Wu replied.

Tan claimed that this was his habit and he was only trying to make his two beauties happy and was at base a decent sort.

"Previously, you told us that you used to be a sommelier," Wu observed. "But last night you said you rode a trike."

"A load of crap. That's just crap," retorted Fatty without hesitation. "Just drunken babble. I am a trained sommelier, a professional taster."

The Princess then startled him by adding, "And you also claimed to know how to make fake wine. You implied that even now you mix black market stuff with honest trading. Take care or you'll end up in jail, you damn pile of fat."

By now, his face had distorted into a bluish hue. "Don't talk drivel," he said. "I, Tan Daogui, am a law-abiding businessman through and through. You've seen those medals in my office. My hometown named me as one of its Top Ten Entrepreneurs of Integrity. How could I dare deal in counterfeit goods? You must have been sozzled and misheard me. Isn't that right, Sister Daisy?"

"I heard nothing of this sort." Daisy did not want to be a participant in this cross-examination.

"You see, you see. Absolute drivel, isn't it." As he spoke, Tan gurned at Wu in such a way that tickled her funny bone.

In ancient times, the site of Yuhua Palace had served as a military camp before the emperors commandeered it as a leisure resort. It is fabled that the monk Xuanzang, who features as a hero in the novel *Journey to the West*, used it as a base for translating the Buddhist sutras he brought back from India. Consequently, the place was reconsecrated and to this day is a foundation accommodating numerous monks.

Following lunch, Fatty proposed that they visit the monastery and burn incense. He declared that it was his habit to kowtow and show reverence to the Buddha. Whenever and wherever he passed by any kind of temple, he had to fulfil this ritual. Wu and Daisy accompanied him, bearing witness to how, at the sight of the statue of Buddha, he sank to the floor in a kowtow, murmuring various incantations in a loyal and devout manner. Princess Wu chuckled again as his gross buttocks elevated in their direction. Afterwards, she asked what he had been saying.

"Praying for fortune, for peace and for you," was his reply.
"Why me?"
"Praying that you would be my better half."
"Your better half or your mum?" She laughed again.
"Well, I could call you 'Mummy'. Little Yummy Mummy."

Princess Wu was paralysed from laughing so much. Meanwhile, goosebumps crept over every millimetre of Daisy's body.

26

Smooth promised to take Plum to the suburbs for a spot of recreation, and she obliged. Regardless of any pain the now severely injured dog felt, Goody jumped from Plum's arms onto the back of Smooth's tricycle.

To be seated once more on her stepfather's trike gave Plum no particularly special sensation, only one of familiarity. She was so familiar with the vehicle that she knew exactly how to jump onto the saddle without requiring a hand to steady her. As they drove on further, she felt rather ungainly. From whatever angle she looked at her surroundings, her depth perception seemed awry and despite the weather being cold, her back began to sweat. At the age of four or five, she adored perching on this tricycle. Before her mother and stepfather had started to go steady, he would take her around for rides on the back of his cart. After the couple married, this became both her main source of amusement and the family's sole mode of transportation. She could even remember her reaction when her mother shared the news that she and Uncle Smooth were to be wed. "Oh, oh," cried Plum. "From now on, I can sit on the trike every day!"

In spite of her stepfather changing the tricycle more than once, she was acquainted with the anatomy of each one. She knew every dint where paint had been flaked away as if it were the contours of her own palm. Plum remembered how, when she started school, he would come to drop her off and collect her. He would even give lifts to classmates who lived in the same community, referring to them as the "partners" he carried for his girl. It was rumoured that other trike riders followed suit and that whereas Smooth pedalled his passengers for free, they would try to load a group on each time and charge seventy or eighty yuan per child per month. Only her stepfather regarded it as a favour for her little pals. As the tricycle belonged to her family and it was Smooth who pedalled it personally, for a time Plum relished a certain pride and superiority. Still, with his burgeoning workload, she found it necessary to learn to ride a regular bicycle, relying on him less and less. He made an exception when there was a downpour or snow. In such circumstances, he would fashion a canopy from oiled cloth and pedal jerkily through the treacherous streets.

On one occasion she could recall, it was snowing and the ground was frozen. He made too swift a turn at the crossroads and the tricycle tipped over, spilling out Plum and her classmates. Her stepfather's mouth was bloody, but having cleaned it with his sleeve, he limped over to massage or knead the arms and legs of each child. It was of great relief that everyone escaped injury and was only stunned for a brief time. Smooth turned the tricycle the right way up and loaded each child onto the cart one by one. After transporting his charges, he went to the hospital to be examined and was informed that he had sustained a cracked rib.

Plum still remembered how his taxi duties continued into Year Twelve. She went down with a severe cold and was too weak to ride her own bike in time for class. He escorted her for several days when she was sitting the college entrance exam. Of course, he dropped her off some distance from the school to spare her the indignity of being seen shinnying down off a trike when plenty of parents were driving their kids in cars. Plum did not think in this way, and felt only indebtedness that her stepfather should support her high school and then college studies with the money he earned with his own sweat and blood. It never escaped her that she was not his biological daughter, and he even ferried her to the station when she was departing for university. As long as she notified him in advance, he would postpone any task in hand and come and collect her when she later returned for the holidays.

Nonetheless, as she now sat on the tricycle and passed by Chang'an Avenue, which she knew only too well, there was a stinging at the back of her eyes as if burrs had become stuck there.

Her first response was to shield her head and try to avoid making eye contact with passersby. As the journey progressed, she could not sit still any more for her posterior was aching from the bumpy terrain. She asked her stepfather to pull over.

"Dad, you've carried me so far, you must be exhausted," remarked Plum. "You tell me where this place is, and I'll get there by bus instead."

"You weigh less than fifty kilos. I can carry loads four or five times that. You hardly use up any of my energy. Quite light, really. I'm not tired at all. Just sit still and I'll begin again when I'm ready." He then prepared to flex his feet once more.

Plum jumped down from the trike. "Dad, I can't force you to do this," she said. "I'll catch the bus."

Sensing that something was out of kilter and being mindful of the inquisitive eyes all around them, Smooth told her the destination and which bus to catch, together with the stops where it was necessary to change. He would not leave until everything had been fully elucidated.

It took two changes of bus for Plum to reach the allotted place, and her stepfather and Auntie Sufen were already waiting for her at the stop when she arrived. Goody beamed at her tenderly from the cart. Smooth pointed out that there was still another mile to go before reaching the monastery and that it was best if she got on the back once more. This being the suburbs with fewer prying bystanders, she complied. Goody bounded promptly into her arms, while Sufen maintained that as there was an uphill gradient ahead, she would be of greater assistance tailing them on foot and giving the trike an extra shove when needed. Plum wanted to do the same, but her auntie would have none of it. As Smooth arched his back and pedalled at full pelt, Sufen had to trot to keep up. The number of pedestrians increased the closer they drew to the monastery, and so Plum dismounted. Auntie Sufen had already prepared everything in the home of the Buddhist laywoman.

Her hostess was a laywoman whose husband had travelled to Guangdong as a migrant farmhand. Once he made a tidy sum down there, he fathered a baby with a local. By the time his legal wife learned the truth, a second lovechild had come along and was already a month old. Owing to the temple's proximity to her home, the lady volunteered to cook there when it held a fair or a lecture on the sutras. Duly, she was admitted as a lay sister with Serenity as her Zen name. She was a capable woman of forty or so, and her home was orderly and clean. Female lay Buddhists who visited there from afar to worship and burn incense would frequently lodge with her for a day or two. Having several spare beds about her rooms, it was perfectly convenient for Sufen and Plum to sleep there. At the outset, Plum was concerned that their disabled dog would not be welcomed. On realising the severity of Goody's injuries, Serenity clasped her to her chest and whispered some words of sutra as a prayer. Plum was able to relax.

Since there were so many to cater for, Serenity was kept just as occupied as her stepfather and Auntie Sufen. Plum amused herself randomly. She discovered for the first time how Smooth was prepared to humble and abase himself. He bent his waist and bowed to all-comers, repeating phrases like "I'm just a labourer who works hard" in a poor and pitiful tone, as if his objective was to win over the sympathy of every last soul in the world. Plum had no inkling of this when she was small. She only thought him to be kind, affectionate and witty by character. Other tricycle pedallers bordered on sycophancy when dealing with adults, though exhibited a fierce attitude towards children, demanding that they did not touch their vehicles, let along romp and frolic on them. Uncle Smooth was the exception. Kids would pile onto his cart like a pack of monkeys. He didn't mind if it capsized and would make light of the matter by shouting, "What naughty tykes you are!" Sometimes, he would cycle a broad circuit of the alley at speed before allowing them to climb off. She could never recall a time when his back was plumb straight, but then again it was never as crooked as it was now. It seemed to have become kinked into the shape of a bow, and the curvature was accentuated by perpetual bending before others. His dirty blue overcoat now appeared much longer at the front than it did at the rear.

Plum never thought that such a relaxing tour would compel her to confront the sorry spectacle that was to follow. Her stepfather was slapped twice by another person and he got down on his knees in public. By noontime on the second day, the stage in front of the grand hall was already exhibiting its completed shape. She sat on a stone pier and surveyed a pile of fragmentary statues as she soaked in the rays. Every carving dated back to Tang Dynasty, and she could tell from the inscriptions on the steles inside the temple that it was constructed during the Kaiyuan Period. In the course of its history, there were several rounds of desecration and the buildings were almost razed during the Cultural Revolution. The broken stone carvings had survived because they had been hidden by locals and then donated back in recent years. None of the present buildings was more than twenty years old and since she had no interest in these replicas, she snapped photos of the ruined stones and bricks, and shared them with Zhu Mancang who was messaging her on WeChat. He professed to her that he was no longer a wild bull, but had grown into a fat table pig. The previous day, when he went to the mountains to chop wood, he had caught a palm civet in a hole. He described the entire process of capturing the animal, and though he infused the story with his own sense of fun, Plum knew deep inside that this was not the type of life she wanted for herself. Her decision to send the images of historical ruins took on the air of reminding him how different they were. She was, ultimately, a citizen of the civilised ancient capital.

As she was snapping away with her mobile, she witnessed a tall man on the stage delivering two firm slaps to her stepfather. Smooth stumbled forward, stunned, cricking his waist and nodding his head to the point where he could barely stand steady. She got up and was about to dash over, though paused for some reason. She then saw the livid face of the abbot. Her stepfather knelt down before him, kowtowing so that his face struck the ground as if he might be trying to crush a bulb of garlic with his forehead. Auntie Sufen attempted to mediate and was kicked in the crossfire. More monks surged over, as did men from Smooth's crew. There was deadlock. Her stepfather kowtowed yet again in an effort both to apologise and to keep his colleagues at bay. The abbot and then the monks filed away, so that Sufen could at last aid her husband. Plum was desperate to rush down and intervene, but she couldn't muster the courage and so waited until she saw that the couple had found refuge by a grapevine.

Unlike in former days, Plum maintained a distance from the stage. She had once treated such places as a playground and amused herself on the platforms. Tagging along with her stepfather had given her great joy. From her college days onwards, this fell into abeyance. Only once, when she was eleven or twelve years old, had she seen Smooth on the receiving end of violence at work. He had been hauling a piece of artificial rock down from a mountain set piece and had the misfortune to collide into the waist of the hero. The actor retaliated by kicking Smooth's belly. The stage shifter had been apologetic, though his brow was damp as he reeled from the pain and retreated backstage with the prop. Plum had seen everything from the auditorium and sped to the rear of the theatre to mop his sweating brow and cried as she asked if he was hurting. He said that it was nothing. But from then on, she could not forget the sadism of that so-called "hero". She made a point of puncturing one of the tyres on that guy's motorbike. Then subsequently, when her father was busy, she sneaked down to watch the performance again. When the hero forgot his lines, she took the lead to boo and jeer at him.

Today, though, she was reticent and did not want to publicise the fact that she was Smooth's daughter. However, a lot of the team did know her identity and there was even talk that Mound wanted to marry her. What a joke! This time, she steered clear of the stage and never made herself conspicuous.

Once the situation had calmed down, Plum slid secretly out of the monastery. She boarded the bus alone, pretending to have witnessed none of the drama.

She left a message for her stepfather, stating that something urgent had arisen and she was needed back at the college.

27

Smooth could never have conceived that such a calamity would strike him. Elsewhere it might have been a small trifle, but within these surroundings the magnitude of the incident swelled incalculably.

It turned out that the junior monk had reported a misdemeanour on Mound's part. In the middle of the night, he had been masturbating behind a statue of the Bodhisattva and sprayed semen all over it. A group of monks investigated the scene of the alleged offence and found that there was ejaculate on the marble surface, and a startling quantity of it. At first, they tried to conceal what had happened, since the abbot was not on site. All suspicions pointed to Mound as the perpetrator of this desecration.

Mound was a shrewd customer. When he realised that fingers were wagging in his direction and brethren were stalking to and fro to the rear of the statue, looking as though the heavens had collapsed before their very eyes, he surmised what was going on. The previous night, he actually had the vague sense of being fixed by the beady stare of the little monk who supposedly slept before the Ksitigarbha Bodhisattva. He thought nothing of it, however. As far as wanking was concerned, Big Hook, Monkey and Third Skin all did it too, only he, like them, pretended not to notice. No ordinary guy would take such a thing seriously.

Yesterday with the appearance of Plum, her allure awoke in Mound some dormant delinquency that he was powerless to control. In the past, he had shared with Smooth his feelings for the girl, but was told to go away and not broadcast the daydream. He had to revisit this fantasy time and again in private. But that night, he couldn't bridle himself and was attacked by lust in the holy cloister of that religious house. From the stern expressions on the monks' faces, he could tell that this was an act of gross violation. He even noted how those brothers, with their gaping eyes and upraised brows, had gone about informing the thin monk of what they had witnessed. Alert to the impending peril, Mound scampered out as if heading to the privy, though instead tried to escape over the courtyard wall. This structure being rather high, one of his arms fractured with a discernible crack. Some attributed the injury to divine retribution since it had been the same limb that offered him nocturnal relief.

It was heard said that Mound's accuser had appeared here as a beggar in an earlier life. Since the holy brothers had food and drink in abundance, in all conscience they could not drive him away. The abbot attested later on that it was the boy's destiny to be among their community, and his head was shaved as a mark of acceptance. One duty no brother had claimed as his own was refilling the lamps in the Grand Hall with oil. So he lay down there before the Ksitigarbha Bodhisattva with a quilt – half of it folded underneath him as a ground sheet, and the other half draped over him as a cover. In this way he came to serve as nightwatchman.

Having to slumber in the darkness sharpened his already perceptive vision. It was rumoured that the brother's eyesight was so acute that he could see the twitching whiskers of a dormouse in the depths of the night. When others had to fumble even to find the doorway in darkness, he could throw a shoe as a projectile, and then go and fetch back a squashed rodent from where it landed.

The inhabitants of the monastery nicknamed him "night owl". To be frank, from the first day Mound had lodged there, the brother found this chubby guy rather peculiar. Everyone else slept in front of the holy statue, since this was supposed to bestow good fortune. They could literally bask in a pool of blessings, with a prayer upon their lips as they dropped off. Mound, meanwhile, bedded down behind the statue, and as the others snored away, his body switched from side to side. Later, in the middle of his quilt, a bulge appeared that seemed to swell and take on a kind of fuselage shape. In the darkness, the monk could perceive how Mound's jowls were flinching and he was groaning, even sucking at his teeth. It then dawned on the brother what was going on.

When the junior monk had been a street beggar, other homeless men also observed how he groaned and sucked in this way at night. They told him that this was the most comfortable pastime in the world. From the first time he tried it, he became addicted. On entering the monastery, the abbot informed him that their number one edict was a strict prohibition on self-abuse. If he were to carry on with this vice, it would ruin all his merits and virtues, and the benefits of reading the sutras and practising benevolence would moulder into self-deception. Following several months of lashing his wrists together with a leather thong at night, the young monk was able to suppress this desire.

Now, to his consternation, the fat fellow from the stage-shifting crew was committing this very same lewd act, and behind the niche housing the Bodhisattva statue no less. As the responsibility for guarding that effigy fell on him, his "magical eyes" opened miraculously wider. The first night he saw that fuselage thing bobbing about rhythmically, another sleeper rose to empty his bladder and on walking close by him the tumescence fell flat. Perhaps he had worn it out and didn't have the energy to wake it up again? Mound began to snore once more.

During the second night, the fat one slumbered like a dead pig. As soon as he reached the Grand Hall he fell to the floor, not even bothering to undress from his work clothes, and pulled the quilt over himself before dozing off. It would be the third night before the young brother would have evidence to implicate this bad egg. The very worst part of the crime was how the obese chap was keen at the last moment not to contaminate his bedding, so brushed it aside. His ugly member was now exposed and a geyser firing several feet into the air was unleashed, splattering the two-metre-tall holy relic from its knee right down to the lotus pedestal on which it stood. The little monk was so incensed that, had he a blade to hand, he would have emasculated that sinful bit of flesh. He succeeding in controlling himself, though. As there were a dozen or so guests in the Grand Hall, if he aired his accusations right now, he couldn't be guaranteed a conviction. After daybreak, he enlisted the monastery supervisor to conduct an inspection. The abbot had gone out to issue invitation cards and would return in the evening, so the supervisor sought the opinions of fellow monks. None of them had encountered such an event before and shared the feeling that this was a grievous matter and should await the attention of the abbot himself.

The trouble had been fermenting the whole morning without Smooth or his co-workers having any intimation. He was busy beneath the stage, adding struts to bear the load and prevent possible collapse. Abruptly, Big Hook called out from above that Director Iron Kou was seeking out Smooth urgently. He came from under the stage, his face as blanched as a spectre, and saw how Kou's eyes were gleaming emerald. Without enunciating one word clearly, he screamed for Smooth to accompany him to the Grand Hall.

The area around the Bodhisattva was gloomy at this time of day, so a flashlight was required to expose the evidence. There was some kind of deposit that had made an impact high up and then trickled down, leaving only a moist arc across the grey surface of the statue. Iron Kou related to him what they thought had happened and insisted that he track down Mound. To the best knowledge of the workers backstage, he had gone to the washroom two hours earlier and never returned. Next, the abbot appeared and Iron Kou slapped Smooth twice hard on the face. In his pain, he toppled to the ground and kowtowed and bowed to the leading monk. No matter what excuse he might produce, the abbot said he would withhold forgiveness. He demanded that the sinner responsible be located and be made to confess his offence while burning heaped incense on top of his head. A Buddhist cleansing rite must then be enacted, in which the filth was removed and the niche rendered sacrosanct again.

Mound had turned off his mobile in the process of making his escape. Smooth dared not try to call him back, lest the monks degenerate into a mob and slaughter him. He was adamant that he would find him, but secretly sent a text pleading with him to go and hide in his hometown, and not to show his face in the city for the time being. "You son of a bitch," he typed. "This time you've thrown us in it good and proper!" Needless to say, Mound disappeared, leaving Smooth to be scapegoated in his stead. In the evening, when the cleansing rite was underway, Smooth was the first to be called upon. Four monks, all of them sturdily built, came from the temple to collect him. One of them, who had a mole on his face, was not even fazed by giving the stage shifter a hard shove.

As a teenager, Smooth had witnessed a Buddhist rite in his home community. Three members of the same family had perished in close succession. The first was a man of seventy who had succumbed to an illness, then his wife died a fortnight later and a grandson was maimed in a car crash. The household invited a party of monks over to perform the rite. Smooth helped the relatives to make touch paper. This was created by rubbing miniature fake ingots against sheets of rice paper, in effect to transfer the wealth to the underworld when burnt. Through this process, he saw the monks recite sutras and shoo away the evil spirits and ghosts. The scale of the ceremony was impressive, and as the drums and gongs began to be beaten, they summoned over half of the street to share in the clamour. It was indeed clamorous, but lacked the grandeur and solemnity of the ritual being held today. To prevent the truth being known by more people, the abbot asked for the doors of the Grand Hall to be closed firmly. They did so with a pronounced creak. Smooth's heart sank as he wondered what kind of Buddhist trial awaited him.

Big Hook, Monkey and the others were terrified that the monks would beat Smooth. So they ordered that two of them should go in together and both kneel and burn incense. The abbot declined. Sufen was so anxious that she paced back and forth outside the Grand Hall. As a woman, it was nigh on impossible for her to enter. She even got down on her knees before Iron Kou and pleaded with him to protect her husband. "It might not be so serious," he responded. "After all, who would dare beat someone to death inside a temple?" His facial expression conceded that he too was unsure what would happen. Sufen, Big Hook, Monkey, Third Skin and their comrades tried to peep through the crack in the door of the Grand Hall. Iron Kou also strained his ear to try to tell what was unfolding within.

Smooth was hauled in front of the Bodhisattva and someone kicked his shin to make him bend to the floor. A monk balanced a censer on his scalp, which must have been about two kilos in weight. His head was very sensitive to the weight of objects, since for so many years he had been in the business of carrying loads. Not only his hands, but his feet, back and diamond-shaped head could accurately estimate mass to within a margin of error of about half an ounce. Once, when a troupe came over from Shanghai to perform, during the process of assembling the stage, they heard it rumoured that one of the team had hands, feet and a back as proficient as weighing scales. They all took a wager on his skill. When he held a light box in his left hand and a costume box in the right, his estimate was dead on. He then lifted a coil of cables with his left foot and a coil of iron wire with the right. His estimate for the former was only half an ounce out. Next came a box containing gongs, cymbals and wooden clappers. Again, only half an ounce shy. Finally, he weighed a carpet bag of caps and hats and was again spot on. Stingy as the Shanghai punter was, he still bought a bottle of beer, a pig's trotter and a baked flatbread for each of the stage shifters.

Although the incense burner was not heavy, it might still cause fatal fatigue if worn for a long time. As expected, a monk brought over a long and thick coil of incense. Smooth had seen this kind of holy object before. It was made especially for being burnt on the top of the head. Upright sticks were unsuitable, since they would collapse while burning. And so, the "head top coil", which consisted of a great quantity of material but maintained its centre of gravity thanks to its shape, was invented. It did not appear large, though could burn for an extended period. Smooth estimated that it might last the whole night.

The abbot knocked at the chime of summons three times and was the first to kneel in front of the Bodhisattva and confess. "Oh most merciful and kind Ksitigarbha Bodhisattva," he began. "Forgive thy disciple's shallow karma and poor virtues. We have not waited on thy honourable person with the greatest diligence, but have let a wild layman from the countryside pollute thy holy and immaculate body, thy honourable and perfect fame..." He started to weep silently. "With all the sand particles from the Ganges, we could not grind away the filth with which this dirty world has besmirched thee. With all the waters from the river, we could not rinse and cleanse away the heinous sin brought upon thy body. The rest of our mortal lives may prove insufficient to atone for how we have ruined our virtue with transgressions. We could not achieve this even if we were to suffer nine deaths... Now we have brought this miscreant, who is baser than swine and hounds, to grasp and clean the hand of the Buddha, light incense and beg for thee to mercifully forgive us." Smooth could not understand the abbot's words precisely, though he did catch their gist. It was a diatribe against him, insinuating before the Bodhisattva that he was worthy only to be reincarnated as an animal.

Why had his subordinate desecrated the Bodhisattva? In Smooth's heart, the Bodhisattva was holy as well. Mound, that son of a bitch, was the culprit in this evil business. It would serve him right if in the next life he was reborn as a man, only gelded like a donkey with his cock being dished up as a delicacy for the table. Smooth was rightfully judged guilty by association.

As he reflected on each facet of the abbot's incantation, tears of contrition flowed. The crying degenerated into sobbing, with his eyes and nose becoming sodden and his cries obscuring the sound of the sutras being chanted. Smooth confessed to the Buddha repeatedly. "I, Smooth Diao, am a sinner," he admitted. "Oh, most honourable Bodhisattva, I did not take strict enough charge of my men. That one ran amok like an animal. If he doesn't mend his ways and stop those evil habits, sooner or later his fleshy thing will become rotten like a strand of... He deserves to be slain with thousands of cuts. How can he harbour such wicked desires behind the Bodhisattva? Somebody of his kind will remain lonely and single all this life. In the next life, his children will be born without arseholes, his head should be cut off and his piece of meat stolen by a dog. Those who upset the immortals invite a painful death..." His confession was enough to make one of the monks nearby almost titter. But the expression on his face remained sincere and honest, so the abbot's rage dissipated.

The abbot recited sutras again, and the supervisor joined him. He let Smooth carry the "head top coil" and proceeded slowly to the back of the Bodhisattva, whereupon he set about removing the residue. A monk had already prepared a copper basin of water, a red cloth for rubbing and a ladder. The supervisor instructed Smooth to wash it thoroughly. He wanted to take off the censer in case it fell, but the supervisor shouted, "Wash with it on your head!" Then, like an acrobat, Smooth ascended the ladder and started the tricky and involved act of cleaning. Mound, that son of a bitch, was a youngster and had somehow coated such a big area. As he set about this task, Smooth cursed Mound in his heart, thinking, what a damned piece of work! You could've pulled it off anywhere, but you chose here! May your doggy eyes go blind from it!

As he was cleaning the statue, all the monks recited the Buddhist sutras with such gusto that the entire Grand Hall shook. Smooth did not understand a single word of their incantations. The supervisor and the junior brother monitored his work, with the brother being able to detect remote and isolated stipples of semen. Smooth continued for more than half an hour until the supervisor brought the abbot over to inspect. He did not move from the top of the ladder until the abbot gave a nod of approval.

"Go back over there and kneel down," the supervisor commanded.

Smooth retreated slowly back to his original position and bent down as instructed. The abbot led the brethren in the recital of what sounded like just a single paragraph of sutra before leaving. The other monks filed out one at a time until only the junior brother was left. Smooth had overheard the supervisor tell him to keep vigil, in case he became lazy. He also gave the order for the chime to be beaten three times every hour, and when the incense had been expended, the next morning there should be nine valedictory strikes to end the ceremony.

The junior brother closed the door of the Grand Hall once the other people had left. He had been polite to the stage shifters upon their arrival, though his attitude soured after Mound's misdemeanour and he was now less hospitable than his fellow brethren. He levelled at Smooth with vulpine eyes. After securing the door, he blew out the candles, half filled the copper basin opposite the Bodhisattva with oil and then sat down on a mat to meditate. When Smooth saw the junior brother close his eyes, he tried to extend his legs to work the cramp out of them. Without even opening his beady eyes, the monk yelled, "Don't move." Smooth was inanimate from then on.

Mulling this predicament over, he knew that without Iron Kou, there would have been no amenable solution. Even though Kou had slapped him twice and then kicked him, he did so knowing that this display would likely serve to mitigate the punishment. The abbot appeared not to want to downplay the significance of this heinous act. Kou reminded him again and again that the invitations had been issued, and the stage shifting could not be completed without his team. Moreover, there was no group more capable of doing this assignment. The abbot had to yield and ceased mentioning the idea of tracking down Mound, agreeing that Smooth could be his substitute.

Plum's text reached Smooth, but he was embroiled in too many matters to respond to it. He set the problem to one side, being unsure if Plum had witnessed him being slapped. Had she seen that spectacle, doubtless the young woman would have suffered a loss of face. Smooth regretted bringing her over here in the first place. The issue of whether the two were linked by blood or not was immaterial, for she was his greatest source of pride. Ever since she had enrolled at college, he had been itching to show her off in public as his "second daughter". Plum, however, kept a low profile in this instance, for never once did she approach the stage area. She merely wandered around the temple grounds, taking photos and shunning all the crowds. Her frame of mind made sense to him. As long as she was happy, she didn't need to be paraded for other's attention. Still, he felt gloomy in his heart over her disappearing like that.

"Don't move."

Smooth flinched. Not only were his legs numb, but his neck was too sore to support his head. As he thought the junior brother had fallen asleep, he let his body sway, then steadied himself for he appeared to be following everything with his eyes closed.

He could now hear the voices of Sufen, Big Hook and the team conversing outside the Grand Hall.

"Kneeling like that for so long is enough to kill him," said a sobbing Sufen.

"There's no other way," said Big Hook. "Just now I pleaded with Iron Kou. He told me not to poke around in what we don't understand. This is the lightest punishment available, after all."

"No problem, sister-in-law," explained Monkey. "In the countryside, when an old relative dies, all the family must kneel in vigil night after night."

"But he's been made to wear a bronze incense burner like a hat."

"That's no different from what the sons of dead country folk do. To show they're filial, they must put a basin of ashes on their head."

"Let's try to cut a secret bargain with the little monk," suggested Third Skin. "Maybe one of us could take his place for a while?"

Without warning, the junior brother swept over towards the doorway, tugging at the handles. "What are you doing?" he demanded to know with a decidedly adult timbre. "What are you wanting to do? Don't you know this is a Buddhist rite? If you disturb the Bodhisattva, some retribution may follow."

"Little Master," said Big Hook, "you see, we only meant–".

"Go, go away," the monk said. "You're daydreaming. If you're feeling so relaxed out here, how can the Bodhisattva channel her powers?" He started to close the door but was blocked by someone's leg. "If you don't move," the brother warned, "hands will come and deal with you."

With his back to the door, Smooth shouted hastily, "You all take a rest. I'm fine. It's quite warm in here. I'm saddled with this burner for the duration. Go back now. Tomorrow, there's some heavy stuff to tackle."

"Retract that leg," sneered the monk. "You too. Pull it back, right now. Pull." Soon, the great chamber was sealed again.

Sufen still grizzled outside. Smooth could hear Big Hook coax the team away. Following Mound's desecration, the stage shifters had been barred access to any of the halls. A makeshift dormitory had been made by suspending a curtain cloth so they could shelter on the ground beneath the stage. Smooth could hear how blustery it was outside. On a winter night like this, hunkering down under the stage was truly a feat of endurance.

Smooth had been unprepared for the sober conduct of the junior brother. As his eyes were flickering drowsily, still with the censer as his crown, a rustling sound reached him. He spied the monk removing one of his shoes without opening his eyes. There was momentary calm and then an almighty thwack as the slipper pelted into a corner of the Grand Hall. A rodent shrieked in agony. The brother crossed his arms and pressed his palms against his chest. "Amitabha is most excellent indeed," came the chant. He then scuttled into that dingy corner and retrieved the corpse of a mouse.

In recent days, Smooth had become familiar with the miracle stories about the monk, yet treated them with scepticism. Since he had just slain a tiny vermin like this, there was no reason to doubt that his "magical eyes" had indeed caught Mound fiddling with his caterpillar under nightfall. He was convinced of the veracity of his power and wanted to brown nose a little.

"What a miracle worker you are, Little Master!"

"Button it!"

After a pause, Smooth tried once more. "Little Master, you are bound to achieve fame in the future."

"Didn't you hear me? Keep quiet."

He was relegated to silence for the last time. The junior brother's regimen of closing his eyes and drawing in refreshment to his spirit was remarkable. He exuded a kind of ethereal maturity that placed him ahead of even the abbot.

Sleep was so inviting to Smooth. He fought back his tiredness for he knew that if he did nod off, the burner would likely smash to the floor. Instead, he raised his eyes in the direction of the Bodhisattva. On their arrival, Mound had noted its resemblance to Plum, whereas for him the statue's look of mercy was deeply reminiscent of her mother Orchid Zhao. She had transformed his "messy pigsty" from the first day they cohabited, tidying up and cleaning everything and culling the dated and misshapen wardrobe to which he and Daisy still clung. The grey denim overcoat he wore like all the other trike riders was replaced with one tailored from blue cloth. She stitched three identical garments and requested that he rotate them as soon as the present one became infused with grime and perspiration. In the past, he had been timid about standing in company, for he knew his body could be ripe with sweat. As he neared others, polite folk would inch themselves away as subtly as possible, whereas blunter people would tell him to give them a wide berth.

Orchid's arrival signalled the end of unseemly odour and sweat-soaked clothing. The first New Year they spent together, she sewed him a beige windcheater. He told her that it was a little swish for someone in his line of work and onlookers might laugh their teeth loose at the sight of him wearing it. Nevertheless, on the first day of the New Year, she forced him to give it a try as he strolled out arm in arm with Daisy and Plum. This was ever so snug.

Her kindness extended to her stepdaughter, who she attempted to make more feminine. Despite Daisy being a plain girl, Orchid knew that fine feathers furnish a fine bird. Once attired in the clothing of the stepmother's choosing, Daisy's looks were enhanced significantly. Orchid Zhao had an instinct for which fabrics were becoming to the wearer and knew how to sew modish and attractive dresses for her. Smooth noticed that after Orchid passed away, Daisy's appearance suffered. She now cocooned herself in make-up and invariably exposed more flesh, sensing that this was the fashion. Smooth couldn't look at his daughter with a straight face any more. It was as though her whole body was bedecked with pieces or patches or dangling trinkets, which gave inadequate coverage to her breasts or left her back totally exposed. Sometimes, the waist of her trousers would be pitched so low that her navel was on full view. Despite having passed thirty, she aped the trends of teenagers. Much more than that, she applied strokes of wisteria or mauve make-up to her cheeks. That made Smooth seethe with anger.

In bygone years, Orchid had given them a home that was so regimented and spotless. Smooth found it painful to put on those best clothes that she had crafted for him with her own hands. The harmony of the household was almost perfect. Daisy and Plum bonded as though blood was no barrier. Then, the tragedy of the cancer turned it into a living chaos, like trying to stir-fry porridge in a wok.

Orchid first entered the Diao home in a rose-coloured trouser suit. It was neither quite red nor purple in hue, just as it wasn't blue or black. She had ironed the collar and hem of the skirt so they were flat, yet flexible. She held the hand of the six-year-old Plum who was dressed as elegantly as a blossom. Smooth wore the dark blue suit she had tailored for him, and a scarlet tie. Daisy and their neighbours welcomed the new family at the gate, with some of them passing asides to the effect that Smooth was so lucky to have snagged such a neat and able woman. How could he hope to keep her safe and sound?

Orchid pinned a rose corsage stitched from leftover material onto her jacket. She had fashioned this little adornment before Smooth's very eyes... Somehow, Orchid appeared to be levitating in midair. After she made her landing, her pace was very nimble and spry. She handed Plum to him and then took hold of Daisy's hand. "Smooth, since I am here," she promised, "I shall try to make our lives better and better." She made this pledge with the benevolent and merciful expression of the Buddha. "From now on, Daisy is my real daughter, just as Plum is yours. As long as we have these hands of ours, we won't fall behind any other family in the Western Capital."

Smooth was roused awake by a crash. The censer had slid onto the floor. The little monk hastened to him with a broom and kicked him repeatedly without a word before slapping his back with the makeshift weapon. These brutal acts did not deter him from his incessant chant of "Amitabha, Amitabha". Smooth picked up the burner and was ready to wear it again. However, the half-burned coil of incense fell into a number of fragments, which extinguished themselves among the spent ash. He apologised again and again to the monk, who replied, "This business hasn't a fart to do with me. It's all about worshipping the Buddha. You don't show enough respect to the Buddha, so what should you expect? You're risking some kind of retribution."

Perhaps the Grand Hall had no replacement "head top coils", for the monk only presented three sticks of the thickest vanilla incense borrowed from the niche. These he planted on Smooth's head. "Watch yourself," he warned. "Doze off once more, and you'll have to do it all again tomorrow night."

Smooth was too anxious to let his eyes fall closed again.

After midnight, the Great Hall began to feel rather draughty. The monk struck the chime diligently every few hours. He would then kneel and kowtow deeply three times before the Bodhisattva. Smooth was struck by the piety and rigour of the monk. He himself took pleasure in bowing and burning incense whenever the chance arose. In fact, the kind and merciful face of the Buddha heartened him. In his mind, the Buddha enjoined people to strive to do good deeds and not bad, so warranted his holy name.

The junior brother had been a Tartar when it came to his captive's kneeling position. As midnight came around, Smooth knew he could not persist and life in this state appeared little better than death. "If you don't do it, well, sooner or later, there'll be retribution," his instructor hissed. "The Bodhisattva is most astute. I've found that you are a man of good character, so want to see you receive a blessing. If some reprobate comes along to burn incense, then I don't care how he kneels. No matter how long that sort kneels, he kneels in vain."

Smooth found a kind of spiritual fortification in these words, and his knees felt less leaden. As the pain cranked up beyond endurance, and the aching, the numbness, the stiffness and the swelling became insufferable, he tried his best to retain a positive focus. This kneeling in the utmost obeisance may restore harmony to the household and cause Sufen to stay. This kneeling in the utmost obeisance could bless Daisy so that she would find a family willing to accept her as their daughter-in-law. This kneeling in the utmost obeisance might bless Plum so she would find a decent job after graduation. He even thought it could bring blessings and healing to his lame dog. It was so pitiable to have to watch her totter along, her mobility compromised... Then, at last, his body was unable to move. He had become a rotten wooden stake, bored into that spot. The lightest touch of a finger may cause him to collapse. He braced himself one last time in agony, and held on, not daring to appear absent-minded before the Buddha.

Daybreak did come after an interminable wait. The sunlight outside penetrated the large windows positioned high up in the walls of the Grand Hall. It shone stronger and stronger, giving Smooth the illusion that halos were leaping about the top of his head. He once more trained his eyes on the awesome statue of the Bodhisattva. Apparently, she was gazing at him too, her eyes half opened and half closed. Here was at last a countenance engraved with tolerance, forgiveness and the rejection of all that was trivial. Her mouth broadened and unfurled into a smile that concealed no harshness, no conspiracy, no misfortune and no venomous secrets.

"Oh, Bodhisattva," he meditated in his heart, "please bestow your blessings. Mound did not behave through malice. He lacks heart and lungs, and has not the guts to challenge a deity. He is twenty-six or twenty-seven and still cannot find a wife. That son of a bitch really cannot restrain himself. His water pistol exploded into fire. Oh, great and honourable Bodhisattva, please forgive the error of this measly guy..."

At once, the Bodhisattva's head seemed to motion infinitesimally into a nod. Now bathed in sunlight, the figure smiled more incandescently than she had done on the first day they met. Her likeness to Orchid Zhao became more preternatural too. He dared not fasten onto that thought or speak it out loud. Wouldn't doing so be to incur further iniquities?

"Well, the incense is burnt away. You can get up now."

At these words from the small monk, Smooth keeled over sideways onto the ground.

28

Cai Sufen endured a night without sleep, for her thoughts kept turning to how Smooth had been forced to kneel down before being slapped, kicked and beaten. She did not understand the reason for his punishment. Meek as he was, Smooth had prostrated himself before the assault and was already kowtowing as if he intended to smash garlic on the ground with his brow when the admonishment began. All night, he had been so intimidated by the requirement to kneel before the Bodhisattva with a burner on his head. He was as impotent as a turtle. How she pitied him and even wanted to take his place on the floor for a while. The temple vetoed the idea, and she could only keep him company by sitting outside the Grand Hall until others persuaded her to leave.

When she reached her lodgings, Serenity was in the lotus position on her bed, muttering incantations. Not wishing to disturb her, Sufen went to the room opposite and lay down. Moments later, she heard the voice of her host at the foot of her bed. "Don't worry yourself," reassured Serenity. "To kneel before the Buddha is a beneficial thing. It can prevent disasters and scotch misfortune. It's rare for anyone to be permitted to kneel in the Grand Hall."

As soon as she had been made aware of the incident, Sufen approached Serenity in the hope that she could mitigate matters for Smooth by speaking with the abbot. At that time, however, Serenity seemed even more outraged than anyone. She said that the guy who blasphemed before the Buddha ought to be sentenced to death and boiled in a wok of oil. She even cursed that his impure member should have been lopped off at birth and fed to a dog. That would avert so much trouble across the planet. So acute was Serenity's anger that Sufen never again mentioned the subject in her presence. Now, though, it was her host who was raising Mound's sin.

Serenity was indignant towards the pervert who sprayed his seed on the statue. She also had a quiver of questions of her own. How old was he? Was he married? Did he habitually misbehave? "I mean," elaborated Serenity, "does he like to use filthy words or fondle women's bodies?"

Sufen found herself unable to answer.

"Well, as long as that strap of flesh at his waist is still working, you can't expect a man to behave himself outside." Serenity moved the topic back to her own husband. He had a penchant for coarse expressions and his legs would freeze at the sight of a female. He was free with his hands, and would find ways of making contact with women's breasts, or pinch their thighs and buttocks. As one might expect, a single year of working outside was enough for him to father a lovechild. It was said that he had now begun an affair with a third lady. Whatever could a woman do if she found herself lumbered with such a creature? Serenity believed that men were no better than beasts, and to prove her point, she cited other affronts to public decency committed by men in her village. Finally, she concluded that women could only shed their sense of gloominess and stay away from trouble if they took on a religious habit and set a distance between themselves and vile men.

Once her host left her alone, Sufen wriggled restlessly on the bed. She had no fears about Smooth philandering, only that he might continue to be pitiful and put upon in life. Her own story was interred deep within the recesses of her heart. Much as Smooth might try to dig it up, she remained uncooperative. She had to keep it private and chew over its aftertaste alone.

Sufen was a native of Gansu Province and grew up far from any sizeable city. Her beauty was evident from birth and the renown of this fine blossom spread far and near. Decent men competed over her affections, and after completing high school, she was assigned to work as a substitute teacher in her home village. She was never sure of the exact circumstances, but one of her fellow teachers lost half his ear in some kind of brawl over her. Soon afterwards, she didn't know how, the stubbornest braggart in the community managed to entice her. He would pester Sufen relentlessly from dawn until nightfall, and his attention was unremitting. She ended up being cajoled to the city by this man, whose name was Sun Wuyuan, and the two spent eight years together there.

Cai Sufen found herself unable to conceive, let alone give birth. Tests revealed she was infertile. No medicine could remedy the problem, and the Sun family complained about her being a wicked moth, and divorce must follow. Sun Wuyuan was having none of it, especially while she was receiving treatment. As an unyielding man of peerless resolve, he could not tolerate having even a grain of sand fall in his eye. He fell out with a succession of bosses, though harnessed his stamina and skill to stay up late and perfect the craft of masonry. Sun was dauntless, and should one workplace not be to his satisfaction, he would turn around and choose another. His earnings never fell short of what the family required, nor did he experience stretches of unemployment. Sufen was forbidden from having a job, for he fretted about her once she left the home. His main preoccupation was the thought that no man under the heavens must be able to resist his wife. While this nurtured in her a sense of grievance, she also knew her married life was contented, steady and sure. She would spend her time reading a book, watching TV or going to the market to buy vegetables. This was surely the kind of envied lifestyle enjoyed by only a few women married to city professionals. Unfortunately, it was not to last, and she would run into a despicable lout who would claim the life of her husband.

The man in question, who had the surname Jiang, hailed from a neighbouring village. He earned a packet hawking medicinal herbs and had been one of her old pursuers. Jiang's wandering hands had even squeezed a purple bruise on her chest, causing Sufen to curse him a number of times. His business having branched out into the city, he could boast of extensive trade with pharmaceutical factories and hospitals. Many of the key players in these institutions, he claimed, were his "good brothers".

Sun and Cai encountered him one day at a small snack bar run by someone from their hometown. It took only the exchange of a few words before Jiang was telling Sun that he should quit chiselling stone. The toil was heavy and poorly remunerated, not least because as he was straining himself, he was having to pitch high his posterior and have torrents of sweat run back down his body. Following him in selling medicine and medical equipment could furnish him with 10,000 or 20,000 yuan a month. On top of that, there was the chance to enjoy fine food and drink. If he was adept at transacting deals, his earnings could rise to 30,000 or even 50,000 yuan. In the course of his boasting, Jiang's eyes started to take in Sufen's features.

Coincidentally, at that point, Sun Wuyuan was on unenviable terms with his then employer and was looking for a reason to leave his job. He promised to hand in his notice there and then. Sufen could gauge from Jiang's eyes that there was some form of ulterior motive, but not being able to bring this to Sun's attention, she could only stamp on his foot underneath the table. However, as the proverb goes, those seated at the gaming table are insensible to the future. He failed to pick up on his wife's prompt and agreed to drop in at the company the next day.

Catastrophe was not far away.

Sufen was convinced that this was all her responsibility. If she had been more determined, she could have put up a better resistance and seen that things wouldn't pass beyond her control. She had no doubts that Jiang was scheming, but still let Sun do as he pleased. Jiang sent her husband to broker contracts in or transport pharmaceuticals to a number of distant places, meaning that he was away for many weeks at a stretch. Jiang went about pestering Sufen daily like a rabid, horny mantis. She slapped him several times and kneed him in the groin. When he realised that his actions were destined to fail, he began to grind away softly at her resolve. He declared that she was the last and only object in life that he was yet to savour, and that not being with her etched a hole in his heart. Moreover, if he could not have her in his arms, he would die discontented and aggrieved. Sufen was powerless to put up a concerted resistance. After all, her husband was his employee and the present salary was much greater than that received by a mason. She did not want to wither Sun's prospects, and felt that as long as she could prevent anything untoward from happening, the situation would right itself.

Her attempts at restraint were a shower. Jiang invited her to sing KTV at a bar and also promised to put her in touch with a specialist who could restore her fertility. She did accept this counsel and consumed huge quantities of imported medicines, but to no discernible effect. Subconsciously, she knew she owed far too much, and one night while intoxicated shared his bed.

The indiscretion soon came to the attention of the ever-suspicious Sun Wuyuan. In a red mist, he murdered Jiang in his office. The court stated in its ruling that "Criminal Sun was inhuman, sadistic and a barbarian". He had used an eighteen-inch-long pig slaughterer's knife to wound Jiang fatally. He stabbed him twenty-four times, severing his head and genitals, before hanging them on the door frame of his office. He then strode away with his head raised high...

Sufen spent days in criminal detention before being released without charge. She preferred to wait and see if the sentence of execution was implemented by the court. She lay low, concealing her identity and after having cremated and interred Sun's remains, went to the Western Capital in search of work. Sufen hung about the labour exchange on Shangyi Road for about six months, taking on minor tasks each day in order to get by.

As a newly single woman, she refrained from dressing smartly, and her appearance may have come across as dowdy or even slovenly. Even so, there were men who looked on her with aspirations. Finding a new husband might better her lot, providing he was not another example of the strong-willed, unbending type. Her priority was to shun the kind of relationship that might lead her into trouble once more.

It was at this very point that she noticed Smooth pedalling his tricycle. She had been observing him for a few months and even tailed him to see where he went. After she had learned circumstantial information about his home and family, Sufen began to stand in the road, so she could glance at him in an enticing manner as he rode past. Since the execution of her first husband, she dressed demurely out of fear of courting trouble. But once Smooth was in her sights, she set about engineering a collision between the trike and herself. That rainy day, he carried her home and the raw rice was now cooked, so to speak.

Her initial experience of life with Smooth was satisfactory. She could withstand Daisy's insults and bullying because their relationship was firm and dependable. But with the passage of time, would doubts set in? From being in the arms of a man who was confident and determined to one who was puny and downtrodden, that contrast would assail her thoughts and wake her in the middle of the night. She questioned whether she was truly the old Cai Sufen of the past? Was she really in the world of the living? Since she felt pain when pinching her own flesh, it was obvious that she was alive and inhabiting this reality.

It was not that Smooth failed to adore her, he was just a little tousled and careless about his person, with a build that was not well defined. Even when he clasped her in his arms, he had the look of a fatigued elastic belt. Of course, that tiredness was not an act. But Sun Wuyuan would never let his exhaustion show. Whatever the circumstances, he could clamp her like a steel hoop, causing her to gasp for her very life.

The day before, when Iron Kou hit Smooth, the image of her former husband slid into view. Were it Sun Wuyuan on that stage, his blood would already be boiling and he would have punched the guy back so his teeth scattered across the ground. As it was, Smooth rolled and crawled wretchedly, knelt down on the floor and kowtowed, in readiness to be kicked like a ball of mud. Since Mound had fled the scene, there was no need for him to volunteer as the scapegoat. Her husband gave off the impression that being abused and maltreated was somehow his forte. He offered to go to the Grand Hall and have incense burned on his head. Faced with this situation, Sun Wuyuan would rather surrender the chance to make money than submit himself to insult and shame. The dissimilarity between the two men hovered back and forward before her. The placid, balanced feeling in her heart was gone, and it was now restive.

There could be no reconciliation between herself and Daisy. Try as she might, none of her efforts produced any effect and even served to aggravate the breach. She was now consciously striving to ignore her. Plum was far more personable, though their bonhomie was mostly superficial. A bulkhead appeared to separate the two of them. Intimate words had yet to find occasion to flow between the two. Owing to Plum falling out with Daisy, Smooth had brought her over here to share Serenity's guestrooms. The stepdaughter was now more garrulous, though what she said were words of resentment, which could not sit comfortably in the ears of her seniors. Sufen was clear about one crucial detail. That was that, although both women acknowledged her as Smooth's wife, neither afforded her with the esteem due to an elder family member. Indeed, had she said anything improper at this point, it might very well be recycled into ammunition for future gossip.

Cai Sufen had witnessed too much familial discord when she was the two daughters' age. Today, they could squabble and become sworn enemies, then tomorrow there would be a reversal and one girl might be willing to lose her head for the other. Such things were plodding melodramas according to Sufen's way of thinking. She dared not take any of these posturings for solid fact. As if to confirm this reasoning, the pair had regarded each other as full blood siblings for years.

From Plum's words, she could infer the desire to forge a united front together with her new stepmother. She had herself been hankering after such an opportunity, but was in no place to request or initiate it. Had she accommodated herself to Plum's strategy and it became known to the others, the contradictions in the household would multiply and grow fiercer. She was loath now to court calamity. No matter what the young woman said, she only offered crumbs of advice and mild encouragement. When Plum realised her stepmother could not provide any substantive help or support, she became less communicative. If consulted, she would mouth a word or two without laying down the book she was reading.

Sufen could make out the figure of Plum in the distance as Smooth was being attacked that day. In a split second, the girl had disappeared out of the gate. Only after a lengthy interval did she receive a text explaining, "Auntie, something urgent has come up. I am needed back at college."

The message pinged on her mobile just as the abbot had finished scolding Smooth, who promised to support the burner overnight in Mound's place. Sufen waited by the door of the side hall, tense about the prospect that the monks might attack her husband. Smooth was compelled to retreat backwards from the Grand Hall and while doing so crossed his hands before his chest, murmuring, "Thank you, your honour, for your gratitude. Thank you, father abbot, for your gratitude." His posterior landed awkwardly on the cement floor by the side hall, and he was unable to rise to his feet for some time.

"Are you badly hurt?" she asked.

"No, not too bad. Just had to wear that burner thing all night."

Smooth reached for the mobile in his pocket and flipped it open. "So Plum has gone back to college?" he asked.

"I got that message too. Something she must do there right away."

Smooth thought over his situation for a few minutes before remarking, "It's better if she doesn't know about all this to-do we had here, don't you think?"

"I don't know if she's aware of it or not," replied Sufen, peering at a snowy cumulus in the distance. "Maybe she's no idea."

"Agh, Mound. That son of a bitch." Whenever Smooth thought of him, it would be with a shake of the head.

The stage was at last complete and the evening party was on schedule.

For such a remote religious house, the temple was inundated with concertgoers. The abbot wore a brand new kasaya surplice and greeted a succession of guests. The first group of attendees were senior abbots from various mountains, and then came local officials and their spouses. In Sufen's eyes, the abbot was a straight-faced and earnest man, yet when confronted with such fame and prestige, his neck and waist were every bit as flexible as Smooth's.

The junior brother was appointed to oversee the car-parking arrangements. A Mercedes Benz of exactly the same model as the one owned by the murdered Jiang purred over, though the monk blocked it at the gate. They were at an impasse for some time as the brother was adamant that this was sacred ground and no one should be entitled to enter without explicit permission. The manager at the wheel was outraged and about to slap the monk. He had two young female passengers, and one of them came out and flicked the brother on the head, then puckered up and left a red memento on his cheek, saying, "What a lovely lad. Let your big sister in, eh?"

The brother wiped his face in fury and declared stonily that rules had to be followed. Next, the abbot appeared, and the junior brother pointed at the trio, blaming them for intruding in a rational and calm tone. Instead of being praised for his diligence, as he fully expected, the monk received a whack from the abbot, who said, "Be off with you, you blind dog." The young man staggered and capitulated.

"That's a colliery boss," someone nearby whispered. "On good terms with the abbot. This time he stumped up two million yuan." Sufen, who was close enough to witness every sordid detail, then became less than enamoured with the religious life. Business here seemed to operate much like it did in the world beyond the cloister.

The evening event began with remarks from the abbot and associated entrepreneurs, as well as congratulatory comments by the senior brethren from mountain monasteries. This was followed by monks reciting the sutras on a magnificent scale. Sufen had eavesdropped on the director backstage and so knew that these were actors who had shaved off all their hair under duress in order to look the part. Each of them demanded a bonus of 500 yuan, for why else, they reasoned, would anybody be willing to go about in winter with a head as bald as a gourd? Iron Kou totted up his sums. For a line-up of 120 men, that would cost an exorbitant amount. Even halving the number of chanters would add 30,000 yuan to the budget. The cost was punitive, but the director was clear that to limit the personnel would be to diminish the grandeur of the spectacle and rob the sutra segment of its arresting impact. After discussing the dilemma back and forth, they resolved that each player should slide a nylon stocking onto his head, or two if one was insufficient. One pair of tights would set them back just one yuan. Still with a mind to expense, they decided that further savings could be made if the actresses from the chorus doubled up as some of the 120 monks. To hide the anachronism of a mixed-gender community, the director instructed that the lights be dimmed low to create a mysterious and vague ambience. As predicted, once the monks were illuminated in full, applause cascaded down from the audience.

No one could have anticipated that, for all the innovations and overwhelming charisma of the performance, a cracking sound would then be heard. Barely had the performance begun, when the centre of the stage began to buckle from the sheer weight. "Damn it," cursed Smooth from the side. "The whole rig is shot to buggery!"

Smooth and Big Hook craned down to inspect underneath. A number of the triangular struts had been knocked down by the children who milled back and forth. Two of them were nowhere to be seen. Smooth and Big Hook tried to make the repairs in situ, crouching like crabs, so their legs were tensed and splayed while their backs brushed against the shaking and swaying stage. The sound of sutras being recited and feet pattering around above them were ringing in their ears. Sufen came to their aid by attempting to locate the two missing struts. With Third Skin's help she found one, which was restored to its correct position. Still, the whole structure was unsteady, and Smooth and Big Hook had to remain below, primed for any emergency.

Cai Sufen hung around backstage for some time, though for her such entertainments were unfathomable. She could watch as the actors and actresses sped to play one scene and then changed costume for another. First, they were being monks, then ancient musicians and then background dancers in one-piece dresses. Only the opening and closing scenes were of any discernible relevance to Buddhism. The rest of the programme featured numbers like *Let Me Have My Fill of Love* and *Ten Thousand Years are Not Enough*. These were belted out by teen idols and thickets of high school children from the Western Capital crammed into the arena. They either squeezed through the crowd to take photos or bumped towards the stage in the hope of a kiss or a hug, many of them damp-faced with ecstasy. This too was lost on Sufen as she was not even familiar with the names of the headline artists.

Backstage was a tumult of players and spectators. Out front, a mass of faces filled one's line of vision. A few brought stools on which to stand.

Sufen discovered nothing appealing or original in what was yet another boisterous event. The air in the courtyard was decidedly muggy, so she set out through the gate alone in the direction of the wheat fields. All of a sudden, she became conscious of somebody tailing her at close quarters. It was Third Skin.

Third Skin was pushing thirty and as his wife stayed behind in their home village, he only had the chance to see her once a year. His careful and attentive manner earned him the responsibility of taking care of fiddly odd-jobs about the company. When Smooth first took Sufen to work, he had let her give Third Skin a hand collecting props for this was light and elementary stuff. In the run-up to the previous evening party, *Ode to Golden Autumn Fields*, her husband had arranged for them to operate the cookhouse for the team. Smooth recognised that he lacked brawn, but such a careful, assiduous and meticulous colleague had his use in minding seemingly trivial matters. Besides, he called Cai Sufen "sister-in-law" and had been polite and considerate to her on the job.

Third Skin seldom looked at her straight in the face. This he blamed on his astigmatism that called for the wearing of spectacles. She suspected, though, that his eyes were actually rather agile.

During their time cooking for that production, there was no toilet designated for women anywhere near the kitchen. Sufen had to amble down into a gulley to empty her bladder. Once, she had just finished and stood up to realise that Third Skin was gazing at her like a hook hungry for bait. Bashfully, she tugged up her knickers, and he claimed to have seen nothing. He said that the coal heap was exhausted, so he needed to gather firewood to cook over. Sufen thought it diplomatic not to mention the incident to Smooth. She could handle it herself. Life had taught her that there are certain things that a man is happier for not knowing. Third Skin behaved with the utmost honesty after that, so she could reconcile herself to the likelihood that he had indeed seen nothing. He still showed great concern about her, and Sufen thought that she had no reason to be on her guard against this weak-eyed mole of a man. That vulnerability, however, was a cover for his degenerate side.

It dawned on her that Third Skin was following her. "How are you able to see anything?" she asked. "It's so dark. Why come out?"

"You're out too."

"Well, I have good eyesight."

"If my sister-in-law is able to lend me a hand, I can find my way too."

"Don't talk nonsense. Get back while you still can."

"It's so stuffy back there. Let me follow you out here for a bit."

Sufen could detect the sincerity in his words, and how considerate his manner was, so took his hand.

Holding hands felt like the natural thing to do, since they were familiar and he needed a guide. Before long, he switched the subject to Mound. "Sister-in-law," he said, "are you aware of what Mound did? He was playing with his todger backstage... That's not the first time I've seen that kind of thing."

"Please change the topic," Sufen blurted out in an attempt to nip this in the bud. "It sickens me."

"Actually, Mound is not the only one. Big Hook and Monkey do it, and me too. If we don't play with ourselves, then what other option do we have—"

"No more of this. If you don't shut up, I'll shove you into that ditch!" With these words, Sufen let go of his hand.

Third Skin was trembling all over and became direct. "I love you," he declared. He then grasped her hands again as tight as pliers so Sufen could not escape.

She was so furious and screeched, "Let me go or I'll scream."

"No use. There's no one else out here."

Inside the temple precinct, the audience was caterwauling and shrieking along to the song, which went "little sister must cross the river, who is willing to have me on their back..." As Sufen and Third Skin were right behind the courtyard wall, the huge speakers made even the wheat stalks underfoot quiver. No matter how hard she shouted, her cries would go unheard.

Third Skin took this as his opportunity to go further. He held Sufen in his pincers like a voracious wolf and proceeded to pounce. He was not his usual passive self. She had never guessed that the mildest man could be so carnal. Sufen may have had the strength to free herself from him, though decided to wriggle rather than struggle. At last her hands were freed through calm manoeuvring. She lay flat under his body. "Who am I, Third Skin?" she cried.

"You are... Sister-in-Law."

"Whose sister-in-law?"

"Everyone calls... you Sister-in-Law."

"Why do they do that?"

"Smooth is... our senior."

"Anything else?"

"Smooth... is... Mr Big."

"How do you usually address him?"

"Call... call him Big Brother."

"Is Big Brother Smooth good to you?"

"Different thing... not the same."

"Just answer me. Is your big brother Smooth good to you?"

"Yes... but... different things run in different ways."

"No, this is the same thing. I'm your sister-in-law, the wife of your big brother Smooth. Your elder brother is your boss. He is very good to you. He knows your eyes are not so sharp and always shows you understanding. If you go ahead with this, it's unfair on him. Don't you know? Get off me, get off, off."

Third Skin's body became limp, and he rolled off from on top of Sufen.

29

SMOOTH SLEPT SOUNDLY FOR THE ENTIRE DAY after returning from the temple. Two truckloads of cargo had to be loaded and dispatched, but Sufen figured that he was too exhausted. Besides which, his haemorrhoids were stinging again, so she switched off his mobile and made him stay at home. While he was resting, she bundled together all the dirty clothes they had changed out of and cleaned them.

Plum knew her stepfather would be back that morning, so planned to arrive home at noon. Rather than going to the campus, she had in fact slept over at her middle school classmate's apartment for two nights. This girl knew her family well and advised that now was not the time to yield. In the Western Capital, even the tiniest hovel of a few square metres could be handsomely compensated in the event of buildings being demolished and residents relocated. It might warrant a full-sized apartment as part of the settlement, but once she yielded, that would earn her nothing. What was enduring a few petty annoyances compared with having an apartment of one's own? The latter was far more appealing and valuable. Plum had not been thinking the predicament through in such a business-like manner, for she was more fixated on the loss of her roots and a place to stay.

Her classmate's comments introduced a sense of perspective to the affair. Once back home, she knew her confidence and courage to defend her corner would grow. Hitherto, she had opened and closed the front gate with the hesitancy of a guest. She had not wanted to disturb and enrage Daisy. Today, she found her stomach and even turned the key in the lock with a loud clank. Auntie Sufen greeted her on entering and she responded in a shrill voice. When Goody limped forward, she greeted her by shouting, "Ah ha, ah ha, see how nice!" She entered her own small room and kicked the door behind her. The clear, crisp sound of the lock catching sounded like the opening shot in a contest.

Sufen could immediately understand Plum's intention from her mien downstairs. She hoped above all for concord among all family members. Meanwhile, she took up Smooth's blue jacket, which had been heavily soiled. Its condition should have required the enlistment of a laundry paddle to finish the task. As she didn't want to cause a commotion with all that thwacking, she would have to scrub hard with her bare hands.

Daisy heard Smooth and the slut return in the early hours, trying to be as quiet as possible. She had been out until almost daybreak playing mahjong with Princess Wu and Tan, and was too tired to pay them any attention. Then, Slut Number Two arrived, teasing the dog noisily and clattering the gate hard so that Daisy couldn't drop off. Much as she wanted to open her eyes, they drooped closed again with exhaustion. That little bitch had been making mischief ever since day one.

Now it was deepest winter. Plum flung open her window wide and turned up her African American rock and roll tracks to maximum volume. In spite of the absence of loudspeakers, the sound was loud and particularly tinny and hissing in texture. Perhaps her computer was old, for sometimes the music sounded like a strangled man trying to catch his final breath. Otherwise, it had all the finesse of effluent gushing down a freshly dredged sewer pipe. Daisy was unable to rest.

What made the racket particularly unbearable was how the little bitch then tried to show off her English proficiency by joining in with the songs. The sound fell somewhat short of an electric saw chewing through wood, but was at least as sickening as a cat on heat. Daisy scrabbled for a stiletto, which she then pounded against the wall. When there was no reaction, she threw on her pyjamas and stalked over to the bitch's door, which she kicked.

"Hey, hey, can't you throw me a lifeline?" growled Daisy.

"Who's trying to kill you?" asked Plum.

"How are people meant to live through this braying of donkeys and howling of cats?"

"What donkeys and what cats?"

"Isn't it you making that din? How can the human body produce such a noise?"

"You... went too far bullying others. I ... I did at least call you Big Sister for years."

"Hold it, hold it right there. Don't call me that. I told you I've never had a sister. You calling me that made me feel sick."

"You..." Plum was spoiling for a set-to with Daisy, though knew that once a verbal duel flared up, she could never resort to using vicious words. Only Goody could spring to her aid by barking.

Daisy kicked the door, but Plum refused to open up. Instead, she went to stand by the window. "Throw that slut dog out right now," Daisy hissed. "Or I promise I'll do it in today."

Goody continued to yelp at her.

Daisy readied herself to break the window covering.

Plum held on to Goody protectively. "Why lose your temper on a dog?" she asked. "If you stop shouting, she'll stop barking."

"Go ahead. Let it bark. Let it bark at me. You can watch how I kill it. I'll rid myself of these sluts one by one." With that, Daisy ripped off the window screen in a single tug, leapt onto the windowsill and then landed on Plum's floor. The two began to skirmish over the dog.

Plum screamed in desperation.

Sufen, who was washing clothes, dashed into the main bedroom and woke her snoring husband, telling him there was another battle upstairs.

Smooth could hear how Plum was screaming in a devastated and heartbroken drone, and that the dog was wailing in fear too. He pulled on his long johns and raced out. As soon as he reached the courtyard, he could sense the pet's cry of distress was coming from midair. He raised his head and saw Goody plummeting towards the ground. Somehow, despite slipping onto his back on the damp concrete, he managed to catch the dog. Goody burrowed into his arms and rested motionless against his chest. When Smooth tried to lift her away, the animal began to twitch in shock. The next thing he heard was scratching and pawing between Plum and Daisy.

Smooth wanted to stand up, but his back felt creaky. Sufen came to his aid and helped him upright, while still nursing a stunned Goody. She recovered the dog from his hands and Smooth attempted to crawl up the stairs. Realising the unprecedented virulence of their altercation, he strove to gather speed. His waist seemed fragile and the slightest movement of his leg set off torturous backache. Regardless of the pain, he persisted in the ascent.

Daisy's lunge for the dog with the intention of hurling her downstairs had incited Plum to become a little lioness. While they were sparring over Goody, Daisy, whether intentionally or unintentionally, had dealt Plum body blows. The final capture and expulsion of the dog had fanned the flame of rage in Plum's heart, so she caught hold of the collar of Daisy's dress. Her rage now equalled that of her sister. Plum's eyes smouldered with fury. "Why break in here?" she demanded to know. "Why jump in through my window? Why? Why?"

"As you so correctly surmised earlier, this is the house of the Diao family. That's Diao, not Han. It already stood here before you were brought over as a flask of oil. Does it have a single fart to do with you?" At this, Daisy raised her arm and rammed her elbow hard at Plum's hand. She didn't budge.

"Even if it's under the name Diao, I live here too. You have no business breaking into my bedroom like that."

"Because it's under the name Diao, I can roam wherever I see fit. I can jump in through windows. I can even bore a hole through the ceiling and skydive in here. This is the business of me, Daisy Diao. Nothing to do with Little Plum." By now she had become highly aggressive, and she placed special emphasis upon enunciating their two names.

Plum was at first too angry to speak, then shrieked, "Even if this property belongs to you, you've no right to invade my private space while I'm still living here."

"Well, since it is my property, please vacate it at once. Look smart, get away, go." As she spoke, she again elbowed Plum, but Plum would not release her hand.

On fixing the furious little lioness before her, the irrational anger within Daisy swelled to a noxious level. It had been a while since she had looked at her from such close quarters. The bridge of this little slut's nose was exceptionally high and straight, and her oval face was slightly reminiscent of Audrey Hepburn. Damn odd. Plum's skin was so tender and delicately milky, that nearly every pore radiated the unmasked charm of youth. Daisy had picked up some of the rudiments of female beauty care. She knew that this type of face required no special modifications and without even the lightest layer of powder could draw attention to itself like flowers entice butterflies and bees in March. How could the daughter of a seamstress, a crummy flask of oil, have become so alluring that Daisy felt ashamed to show her own face? When the right moment came around, she would pilfer a brick from the Ming Dynasty city wall and pound this angular, flawless visage until it was as flat as a washboard.

Daisy finally struck Plum's face with her fist so her nose bled like a pig's when slaughtered. Sparks ricocheted about her eyes, so she could not see a thing. And yet her hands still gripped Daisy's collar tightly. In the process of breaking free, she kneed Plum in the abdomen. Plum wanted to return blow for blow, but being shorter than her assailant, her legs could not lift that high. Instead, she transferred her fingers from the collar to Daisy's hair, eventually clasping onto the cape at her rear. Now it was she who imitated a swine being butchered, for she let out an agonising howl. Daisy then reached for Plum's hair too, only to be interrupted by the appearance of her father. "What are you doing? What are you trying to do? Take your hands off her. Hands off."

Neither of them were deterred by his call of intervention, so he had to place himself in between them and loosen their claws. The more he tried to prise them apart, the faster those fingers clamped closed. Whichever side he sought to aid, it would only magnify the pain meted out on the other. Utterly helpless, he knelt before them. "Both of you now, let go," he begged. "My children, two strangers couldn't hurt each other like this. You've been sisters for a dozen or more years. Your dad is pleading with you now. Please give in. Your dad is pleading, I am pleading." He went so far as to bang his forehead against the ground in a kowtow.

None of this was to any avail as they still grappled away. Smooth turned to Plum first, since she was usually the obedient one. "Plum," he said, "you're the younger. You take your hands off first. Your dad has never begged you to do anything in the past, but now he is. Let go first. OK, let go, let go." Plum released her grip, then Daisy yanked her sister's mane in one last show of spite, and left.

Cai Sufen now entered, giving Daisy the chance to fire off a last shot. "All those sluts must be banished from the Diao house," she vowed. "Once and for all."

Smooth's sufferance had worn out. "Your mother's fart!" he cursed as he got to his feet.

Daisy stood erect and countered the attack. "I am a fart straight from my mother. So what?" she asked. "All these sluts can beat it."

"Who is a slut?" Smooth lashed back. "Who are you calling a slut? Who are you commanding to leave?" He was raring up to tackle her out on the balcony, though Sufen blocked his path.

"Even the dog's a slut," she cursed from outside the door. "Who's the slut, indeed? Humph." She slammed her own door shut.

Sufen hurried to mop the blood from Plum's nostrils with a tissue.

The floor was strewn with tufts of hair, most of them formerly belonging to Plum.

Plum wailed volubly.

"It's too cruel and merciless," Smooth tried to console Plum. "Take no notice of her. This home is yours too. Your dad is here and you're welcome to live here." Smooth was fully aware that Daisy's words were aimed at Sufen too, so he added, "As long as I'm here, even Goody is one of us. Nobody can drive her out. If they tried, I'd bring her back. Humph, aren't there still laws under the heavens!" He intentionally raised his voice.

"Don't grope about blindly when you haven't a club to kill the tiger," Sufen reflected. "Once you flush a tiger, you can't hope to defeat it."

"Humph, you think she's able to turn the sky upside down?" shouted Smooth from behind the door.

Music blasted out once more. It was the song *Inconsolable* sung by Gong Linna. The piercing vocals at once eclipsed Smooth's barks.

That evening, the family discovered that the ants were abandoning their nest.

From a narrow hole in the west, they were migrating eastwards. Who knows why, but they chose to make a detour via the upper floor of the Diao residence. They marched out through a narrow crevice and across the wall. It was quite feasible that some should have wandered into Daisy's room. So riled up was she that she boiled a kettleful of water and poured it along the route, scalding the thousands-strong battalion to death. The next morning Smooth's heart shuddered with a chill as he surveyed the genocide. "This kid really is too cruel, too cruel," he sighed as he swept up the carnage.

30

That Plum should put her life in order was an issue of urgency. She had no idea what type of terrain she was treading on and could not foresee which direction to pursue. Her first thought had been to seek out a lawyer and determine the legal basis of her predicament. Until now, this never required any thought. She had entered this household with her mother at the age of five or six, and in spite of some initial problems, had become acclimatised to the environment. Her own past had been forgotten, and this had become her one and only home. After fifteen or sixteen years had passed, suddenly her claim on the place was bluntly repudiated, the seamstress's booth being identified as her rightful home. She was now branded a flask of burdensome oil and, like the lame dog, labelled a "slut" and given an ultimatum to leave.

Plum knew that her stepfather loved her in his own rough, unvarnished way, and would never tolerate her being ejected. His fatherly love showed no discrimination between herself and Daisy, and on occasions the balance even tilted in Plum's favour. This much was transparent to her. Even so, within the home he was browbeaten by Daisy, and especially after marrying Sufen, did not know where to position himself for the best. Plum believed that had it not been for her stepmother, she and Daisy might have kept on convivial terms. Sufen had supplanted Daisy, wedging herself into the centre of the household, and cultivating an affinity with Smooth that held them together like resin, whether the environment was blissful or baleful. They ate and drank together during the day and shared a bed at night. Plum had been relegated to the status of a gallbladder, a tumour or fingernail. Once judged superfluous, she could be cut away or vanish with no fatal detriment to her family.

She left after her fight with Daisy. Her nosebleed had not been entirely staunched, and her nostrils were swollen visibly. Sufen was keen to take her to the X-ray department in case the nasal bridge had been broken. She insisted on going there alone, and her stepfather stuffed a thousand yuan in notes into her pocket.

The physician examined her and diagnosed damage to the connective tissue. He washed inside the cavity and prescribed a course of antibiotics before Plum departed.

All at once, she was struck by how much she missed Zhu Mancang in the countryside. Lately, he had been calling and sending messages, though she never answered him properly out of fear she would become drawn in too deep. In her heart she missed him a great deal, especially at this moment.

She reminisced about the day when they visited the Double Dragon Mountain Reservoir with classmates. Since neither of them could swim, the two stayed on the bank and guarded the clothes of the others who scrambled down to bathe. She noticed someone chewing on a golden apricot and told Zhu that her mouth was salivating over the thought of eating one herself. Without uttering a word, he ran to a stand two miles away and bought a bag of them for Plum. In the meantime, she was being pestered on the shore by three hooligans. Each one wore hipster jeans and struck a tough, macho stance. They chuckled as they hit on her and, in turn, demanded a hug and a squeeze. She was a beauty of the kind they had never seen before, and they begged for just a single embrace. They said that whoever pressed her for more would be a jerk. That type of behaviour, they reasoned, would not go unpunished in the next life. The jerk might be reborn as a pig or a eunuch. The shorter of the trio spoke glibly, saying that as a true man he couldn't bring himself to brush past an authentic beauty.

Plum was by now petrified and screamed desperately as she tried to recoil from them. Their cheeky grins seemed to be pressing ever closer in her direction. Zhu happened to return at this point. He gathered speed as he saw she was in peril and shot them a gallant and undaunted expression that engraved itself on Plum's memory. They no longer acted loutishly, and the taller one who had dragon's talons tattooed all over his body patted Zhu on the shoulder. "You look like a fool, but how lucky you are in romance," he said. All three left laughing, as Plum was engulfed by a single thought. Zhu was her guardian. Today, when Daisy climbed in through her window, he and not her stepfather was the first man she thought could protect her. Only when he was present could she repose in safety.

Plum made a phone call to Zhu, who was delighted to hear her voice. She even sensed that he might be about to weep. He said he was mucking out the cattle pen. He shovelled up the dung and then spread it on the fields where they would sow corn next spring. When he asked her what she was doing, her answer turned into "Missing you".

She had never spoken such tender words to him before, and he sobbed as they conversed. "You could come here," he suggested. "There's so much fun to be had. It snowed yesterday and all the mountains and fields are silvery white. Extremely beautiful." He was prepared to collect her, though she didn't clarify whether she was willing to come or not. The signal at his end was weak. Zhu described how he had scaled the walnut tree in front of his home. The reception flickered on and then off, so she eventually hung up.

Plum located a law firm, and the middle-aged partner received her warmly. She outlined the details of her domestic situation. His response was concise. "According to the letter of the law, you and your sister share the same right to inherit the property," he said. "Family law stipulates that no discrimination can be made between biological offspring and those who are adopted or wards." The lawyer then stressed, "You entered the family at the age of five or six. Your stepfather raised you, so your relationship is classed as the adoption of a minor. Had you come into the household when you were eighteen and had already reached legal adulthood, that would not have been the case." He then asked if she was considering pursuing a lawsuit. "I can take you on as my client. Providing the facts are exactly as you just described them, we are bound to succeed."

Plum said she needed time to think about things and would perhaps consult him later.

On stepping out of the office of the law firm, Plum received another call from Zhu. He said he had found her mood out of sorts, so was thinking about visiting her overnight in the city. She replied that this was quite unnecessary and she felt fine. Zhu had already changed his clothes and was about to head for the station.

"Don't," Plum snapped resolutely. She explained that many matters required her time and attention, so she couldn't offer hospitality to an old classmate right now. Plum then closed the mobile.

Striding with consummate confidence, she approached the house. Yes, it was Daisy's home, but it was hers as well. The law told her so.

31

SMOOTH WAS INCREASINGLY OF THE OPINION that he lacked the authority to keep order at home. Daisy was, of course, the hardest to appease, and he was certain that as long as nothing served to provoke her, Sufen and Plum would also be at peace. However, his elder daughter was the main antagonist and as the situation degenerated, the other two were encouraged to emulate her. To begin with, Plum adopted an aura of stubborn anger, whereas in the past she had been yielding by nature. Now, when confronted with the prick of a needle, she would jab back with her own awn of wheat. On observing the deadlock between the two sisters, Sufen blamed Smooth for being too preoccupied with securing work outside. Whenever they clashed, his patriarchal pronouncements were no more potent than the paff of a fart. If matters were to drag on like this, she feared some cataclysmic denouement.

Smooth was a man without alternatives. In a packed household like this, everybody needed sustenance and refreshment when the sun came out. He would claw at his scalp, asking pensively how they could cope if the daily quota of income was not met. He had no idea how others in his community survived, and how he himself could scratch by in such a bitter and meagre estate. The leaner matters became, the deeper grew the contempt of his daughters and their stepmother. Sometimes he worked like his own life was at stake, but still made no progress and never experienced the feeling of being at leisure. What a fucking dick of an existence this was!

He did have the consolation of knowing foolproof ways of raking in the pennies. As long as one was unafraid of physical toil, there were always cargoes that needed ferrying by trike. That was even the case at midnight.

As his reputation spread, Smooth could be confident of more stage shifting in the Western Capital. The very day the temple job was wrapped up, the father of the head of a village committee just outside the northern gate passed away. They were set on having an opera stage erected and that the structure be assembled well. The performances were overseen by a promoter named Geng Shen, who discreetly assembled players and approached Smooth to undertake the manual work. He, along with Monkey and Big Hook, conducted a site survey and concluded that the area was too cramped to fit in a stage. All the buildings were arranged in a terraced fashion flush to the road. It took some time before they could locate a street with sufficient room. This happened to be the main thoroughfare in the neighbourhood, and they believed instinctively that no such erection would be allowed. The headman received word of this request and said that any place meeting their specifications was within consideration. The street was duly cordoned off.

The stage shifting advanced with ease. Seemingly, miracles could be realised. Bridleways were cleaved when hills were encountered and pontoons flung out when faced with water. The erection of several pillars entailed the removal of the cement surfacing of the street. This was sanctioned. Similarly, the units on either side of the street agreed to have basin-sized holes drilled into their outer walls in order to accommodate a pair of horizontal beams. Finally, when they found the voltage was insufficient, one phone call from the head conjured up a truck with a transformer.

When the stage was close to completion, that son of a bitch Mound returned.

One of his arms was wrapped in a dirty gauze of indeterminate colour, apparently an attempt to plaster a fracture. Big Hook asked what had happened. Too ashamed to admit it had been broken falling from the high wall of the temple, he claimed to have stumbled carelessly on the road and let the impact be absorbed by that single limb. Monkey asked if that was the hand he'd used to tickle his todger that night. Mound laughed in response and cursed, "Fuck your mum!" On catching sight of Mound, Smooth just wanted to boot him out. He had been the reason for his torture, and why his bruised knees had not yet fully healed. Were he to bend down, the pain was enough to make him grimace.

To date, Iron Kou had not handed over the money for that job, and since he had incurred tremendous trouble at the monastery, Smooth felt ashamed about asking for it. Leaving that place had come as no small relief, yet here now was this fellow grinning knavishly as if in a state of triumph. When he smiled, his eyes were reduced to tiny creases in the flesh, barely the width of a cotton thread.

Smooth cursed Mound to his face, using the most abusive idioms and channelling the most incendiary anger. "You mangle-dicked bastard, how come you're still alive? What gives you the fucking face to swagger around here? You son of a bitch, don't you know you nearly bloody killed me? Just looking to shoot your own bastard juice. Don't you see how you've made me fucking suffer?" Smooth tugged up the legs of his trousers to reveal two unhealed lesions on his knees, which were still scarlet. Mound stopped laughing and offered to help roll the trousers back into place. Smooth kicked him. "Get the fuck away from me," he yelled. Mound laughed again, looking around the assembled group, though still not opening his smiling eyes.

No one believed that Smooth would take Mound on. Contrary to their expectations, Mound became clingy and obliging, being more than willing to do odd-jobs such as feeding wires through holes and binding curtains. At first, Smooth was inclined to pretend he wasn't there. When Big Hook made enquiries around the group, he was told, "What else could we do? This fuck-up has a crippled mother at home waiting for him to send a little back every month."

Smooth, meanwhile, told Big Hook to try to ensure Mound remained on edge, in case he caused others to stumble in the future. Big Hook naturally obliged, adding some seasoning of his own. "Hey Mound," he would cry out purposefully. "Your elder brother Smooth wants to know if you really want to stay or go?"

"Me? Of course, I really want to stay."

"If you are serious, he has something big to ask of you."

"Just spit it out, brother."

"He demands that you slice off your cock and let his lame dog take care of it. Once you've mended your ways, you can have it back."

"Fuck your ma, Brother Big Hook!"

Mound duly rejoined the team.

Since he tried to make a pass at Sufen, Third Skin had always been embarrassed to catch sight of her. He dared not look Smooth directly in the face either. He was panic-stricken that Sufen would tell her husband. As it was, a number of days had passed without any change in Smooth's treatment of him. One day, the gaffer did pace in his direction with an ugly expression on his face and Third Skin winced and began to hotfoot it away. In reality, Smooth was still agitated by the situation at home. He announced that Daisy had asked him for money again. So acute was his rage that he shared the news with everyone, claiming he'd been reduced to being her bank runner. This nagging persisted until Sufen reminded him how foolish it was to share trivial domestic matters with all comers.

She had been lending a hand as Third Skin's assistant, so the incident in question made her uncomfortable. Sufen would rather work with somebody else in case this wasn't the end of the matter. The problem was that in the world of stage shifting, every team member had his area of specialisation and once they were slotted into a particular place, they couldn't easily second themselves elsewhere. For this project, Smooth had assigned them to take care of the catering, negotiations and odd jobs. What went by the name of "negotiations" in fact entailed wheedling as much as they could out of their host, the headman. The odd jobs came in blizzards. The pair of them had to read others' minds, beetling intuitively to where an extra hand or two might be required.

For such a grand ceremony of mourning, the protocol demanded that tables of food were served and replenished like a never-ending stream. As the host was a gentleman of repute and position, the number of guests was stupefying. To lay on two benches of food for the labouring hands should have not put a dent in their economy. However, unbeknownst to them, Geng Shen had arranged with the host that no spread be laid on for staff. When Smooth heard of this, he spoke to the general manager and was told that the budget didn't cover their food. Thus, Sufen and Third Skin were tasked with preparing meals. In the evening, Big Hook and the others said they wanted something hot, meaning their caterers had to trail to another street for red bean porridge and steamed dumplings. Finding no one in sight, Third Skin tried to confide in Sufen. "That thing," he began. "You shouldn't have blabbed to Brother Smooth about it."

"What thing?" Sufen asked with an air of deliberateness.

"That... that thing."

"Your sister-in-law has forgotten all about it," she claimed, laying especial stress on the "sister-in-law" component.

After a while, Third Skin sighed bitterly. "My sister-in-law," he remarked, "have you ever heard the saying, 'My big bro's bride's tooty is more than half my booty'?"

"Stop this rubbish. Are you such an animal that you have to fling yourself blindly at me?"

Third Skin wanted to continue. When they carried the porridge and steamed dumplings back in the iron bento box, his steps were intentionally slow. "Get a move on," Sufen urged him. "It's getting chilly. They're expecting all this piping hot." The pair then broke into a trot.

The stage shifting lasted another whole day and night. The promoter Geng Shen arrived with the actors and band the following day at noon, there being more than thirty of them in total. They had been engaged to perform selected opera highlights in the afternoon, including a cappella solos by big-name actors. Smooth was quite familiar with every member and greeted them before leading Geng on an inspection tour of the stage. His plaudits were effusive, not least when he described how this degree of perfection screamed that only Smooth could have been the overseer. So magnificent!

Mr Geng invited all of them over to partake in a meal and explained how the host had set aside several benches for them already.

"I doubt they're keen on letting the labourers graze like this," Smooth reminded him.

"Keep your beak out of this," came the response. "For a grand do like this, there's no carping about having a few extra mourning hats like yours. Just eat your fill."

Smooth called on all his brothers to take their seats. As soon as their chopsticks began to flex into motion, somebody flew out and started to curse. "Who let you eat?" he shrieked. "Who brought you to this table? Guests only. Who said you could touch it?"

Geng, who had just taken a bite from a marinated trotter, was so rattled by the man's scream that the meat nearly fell from his mouth.

Smooth, having sharper eyes, calmly gulped down the piece of shank that balanced on his palate. As Smooth ate, he repeated how he was sure that they were not welcome at the feast.

Geng chewed the trotter steadily. "And who are you?" he asked.

"Lay down that pig's foot," the fellow snarled. "Who said you could eat? Is there any mention of catering in your contract?"

"Damn it!" said Geng. "What day and age are we living in? Do we still need to spar tongues over a mere meal? Call your manager over."

"I am the manager."

Geng, who had seen the ways of the world, now patted the table. "Manager," he scoffed, "go manage your ma's cunt. Eat, yes, I'm the poor sod who told them they could eat."

At this very second, the general manager swooped in. His voice may have lacked volume, but it was full of self-assurance. "You can't eat," he pronounced. "All of you please lay down your chopsticks because the guests are coming. If you want a bite of something, just slip down the corridor over there. The mourning band have some pork noodles they can share with you. This is a set table and rules are rules."

"What farting rules?" replied an irritated Geng. "People aren't even allowed to eat?"

"It's clearly stated in the contract that food is not included," stressed the general manager. "If you want to eat, that can be done, but it'll cost you two thousand yuan per table. However many tables you require can be totted up and then deducted from your fee."

Everyone remained silent, waiting to see how Geng would respond. He knew that the locals hereabouts were obstinate and that all these dirty dishes were not worth sacrificing their fee over. He rapped his chopsticks on the table and led them off with a parting parry. "You guys only know how to pick at sparrow's cunts."

Multi-talented as they were, the actors among them cared about losing face. They claimed they would all leave at once, being unwilling to perform for such despicable charlatans. Geng then recalled how they had been happy to sign the contract and so should not dare incur a lawsuit. After all, the fees for the performers were not miserly. A renowned player was assured of anywhere between 3,000 and 10,000 yuan for their services. Dirge singers were guaranteed at least 2,000 yuan, and those in supporting roles with the band would perhaps pocket 800 or 1,000 yuan. They might bluster about their sense of upset, but no one could bear to throw back a pile of crisp red notes. Smooth too was anxious that these performers could flounce out, leaving their construction of the stage to have been in vain. He helped Geng to persuade the others by sticking to the same strategy. Folks who lived barely ten feet outside the city walls were all bumpkins, he said. Their outlook could never be reconciled with that of citizens of the Western Capital like themselves. This technique proved persuasive.

Following this episode, there was a curious twist to the business. One of the leading actors, who was driving himself to work, turned up late. "Where's our spread?" he asked out of force of habit. Smooth knew that this was the self-same phrase used in countless dramas. A prankster nearby gave a teasing answer. "The master has ordered that upon arrival your honour should head directly to the guest table in the main chamber and receive his meal there. The wine and dishes are prepared and the serving girls have been waiting in the courtyard for some time."

With a measured gait, the veteran actor strode towards the main chamber, grasping a large tea bowl. He sought to loosen his vocal cords by intoning, "Yi, ya, yi, ya."

Two of the provocateurs followed on behind, keen to witness the clash. As soon as he entered the room, the actor sat down on the couch and twice pointed gently at a bystander using two fingers, indicating that he should tilt his ear towards his mouth. The man didn't heed these instructions precisely, instead querying out loud what it was that the visitor wanted. "Go and tell the manager that Teacher Chen of the troupe has come." He began to outline his requirements by stating, "Tell him not to go to too much trouble. Just lay on two taels of beef, pig's ears seasoned with raw garlic, a smashed cucumber and a toasted flatbread. The flatbread should be crisp and golden. No need to serve liquor. I'm about to sing *Dragon and Tiger*, so can leave that until afterwards. Beer would be fine for now. Room temperature is OK."

To his consternation, the server launched into a blunt rebuttal. "There'll be no meal for the actors. That's our manager's policy. If you want something to eat, you can grab some pork noodles in the corridor down there."

The two mischief-makers couldn't suppress a giggle at this scene and the actor, who realised he had fallen into a trap, stood up and demanded to know what was going on here. The pair recounted what had just happened to them, upon which the gentleman climbed into his car and sped off without a single word. No matter how Geng pleaded with him on the phone, the actor reiterated that he had no interest in their money. Geng promised to pay him more, but the actor retorted that even if they paid him a gold mountain, he wouldn't sing for those tight-fisted bastards. The promoter responded that although it was a privately organised affair, it was in fact a form of serving the people. The actor likened them to turtle's eggs, buried in the beach and left to hatch without parental supervision. How could such bastards be considered "people"? He added that he would rather make his own grandson his master than pander to them. Without any more excuses and knowing that continuing in this manner was futile, Geng had to draft in another vocalist as a stand in.

There was no paucity of spectators, and the audience packed into the cordoned-off street. After Smooth and the team completed the stage, the host asked them to drape some bolts of black funerary cloth, so they pinned them up like curtains. Mourning wreathes lined both sides of the thoroughfare. Glancing casually at the inscriptions on the wreathes, Smooth could pick out condolences offered by officials from provincial, ministerial and departmental divisions, with some including the names of work units with the prefix "China XXXX". Foreign envoys were among this number too. He heard onlookers discuss how this small community head had a welter of connections and even knew folks in Beijing. Every inch of land here was worth an inch of gold, and too many people were trying to ingratiate themselves with him.

The same gossip continued in cryptic fashion. "Didn't you notice how, in recent days, the headman only received cadres from the provincial ministries and their wives? As for heads of departments, whether he meets them or not depends on their position. When it comes to department heads with no real power, the general manager receives them after their gift money has been handed in."

On hearing this, Smooth clicked his tongue. Not only had he spent his life dwelling in an urban community in this city, but his family belonged to the old citizenry of the Western Capital too. A suburban headman putting on such airs left him mystified. Usually, Smooth found some opportunity to come into contact with a top manager or senior official, and express his resolve to fulfil his word. He accepted this as the duty of a boss, and also as a means to grease the wheels. In this particular locality, it was as though from the outset he was barred from having access to the village head. As folks pressed in around him, Smooth realised how uncertain he was in fact about this job.

Prior to the opening number, the village head stepped up onto the stage and offered thanks on behalf of his kinsmen. One of the elders of the community, who was said to be his maternal uncle, was assisted onto the platform too. He wore a pair of antiquated copper-rimmed spectacles, the frames of which had been resoldered using an alloy of copper and red bronze. This looked like a striking anachronism, though the man held himself with all the grace of history and age. He was wearing a purplish-red coat tailored in the style of the Tang Dynasty and was invited to declaim an elegy. He burnished his address with phrases such as "Alas, so mournful" and "Please savour the donated delicacies". In the middle portion, he even broke into grandiose expressions, such as "The heavenly pillars have slumped earthward in the south", "The riverbeds are desiccated in the north", "The sun and moon mourn so melancholy" and "The wind wails in grief". He extolled the merits of the late father of the village head with epithets that made him sound as consequential as Chairman Mao. Next, he switched topic from describing the father's paternal diligence to saluting the illustrious achievements of the headman. His vocabulary modulated again, embracing terms like "bringing far-reaching changes to this world", "adding glamour to the moon itself", "endowing all living creatures with benefits" and "stellar virtues recognised far and near". The village head took the lead in the applause, so that as far as he could make out, he was whipping up blasts of thunder.

When the headman left the stage, the general manager talked at length, noting how benevolent and lofty the host was, and how he felt unworthy of being tasked to handle such a grand ceremony. He then thanked the mourners as the host's proxy, reeling off a list of names that ran to dozens of pages until his mouth was dry and his tongue chafed. Still facing the microphone, he attacked the compiler of the list. "What a motherfucking bollocks-up you've made of this," he cursed. He mentioned how such-and-such VIPs had been omitted. After a further apology, he announced the opening of the show.

First in the opera highlights came the customary *Dirge at the Bier*. Were the deceased a man, *Dirge for Liu Bei* from the drama *Great Revenge* would be the selected. For a woman, *Dirge for a Lady* from *Washing Clothes at the River Bend* was considered most appropriate, especially in the mourning customs of the Guanzhong Plain around the Western Capital. Smooth had known these numbers as a small child, so when the accompanists got to the end of the "bitter and slow" rhythm that formed the prelude, he squatted by the stage, closed his eyes and started to hum to himself.

> *All three armies in the camps mourning attire do wear,*
> *Banners and flags unfurl as snowflakes float mid-air.*
> *White people, white steeds and white banners,*
> *Silver bows, jade arrows and pale feathers.*
> *Officers wear mourning caps with trains of three feet,*
> *Generals don war robes the colour of sleet...*

The host had scheduled three days of opera singing, with the addition of dancing and modern songs to engage the younger audience members. Geng Shen was the organiser of these elements as well, and it was bizarre how he was able to recruit so many dozens of nubile and brightly attired youths. Most of them showed as much flesh as dignity allowed, with backs denuded of fabric, breasts only half concealed and navels exposed brazenly. A flash of pink hot pants assaulted onlookers' eyes, though nobody could avert their attention from this parade. Once it was over, several elderly residents criticised these "dramas". To their mind, every kind of performance was to be classed as "drama". They complained that there was nothing funereal about them and that they might obstruct the peaceful passage of the soul to the Western Paradise. "Mind your own business," an old man cut in. "The village head's dad always loved a touch of this. The year before last, some young folk slipped him into a strip club. That last show was him to a tee. I'm sure his honour travelled west with a grin on his face." This made Smooth laugh.

Although the others left once the stage was assembled, Third Skin, Mound and Smooth remained behind to monitor the set up. Smooth soon obtained another job, though was made to realise how in this world events unfold as chains of coincidences. It was claimed that the band who chanted sutras were drawn from four different temples from four different directions. One of these so happened to be the monastery where they had just built their last stage. Even the senior abbot who had punished Smooth in person had come along to lead the expedition. That was a clear indication of the importance of the ceremony. Also among their number were monks who had been baying for revenge. On spying them, Mound wet his pants and thought instinctively about running away without any word to Smooth. To his relief, the monks who recited the sutras and petitioned for the soul of the dead to be released from torment did so while encircling the bier. The dramatic performance was held roughly two or three hundred metres from the mourning hall, so the two groups went about their own business without ever converging, somewhat like the waters of the well and the waters of a river. Smooth and his team shied away from the hall, thus avoiding encountering those holy brothers.

The five days and nights drew to an end, so Smooth and his crew set about taking apart the stage. The promoter Geng Shen pointed out how the host had deducted 10,000 yuan from what they were owed in order to cover the substitute who had sung *Dragon and Tiger*. This had not been stipulated in the contract. Geng jousted with the general manager in a protracted manner, before even consulting the headman. As a filial son in mourning, he maintained that he was divested of all such worldly responsibilities and had entrusted their discharge to the manager. It was his orders that commanded respect. Geng Shen could infer an aura of might from the person of the community head. In his experience, there were even some senior cadres who were incapable of mustering quite this much clout. He saw no benefit in arguing with them any more.

As the saying goes, "When the city gate catches alight, it's bound to unnerve the fish in the neighbouring pond". Geng Shen could not deduct this sum from other participants' fees, and so, discussing it with Smooth, he admitted this as a loss and asked him to bear a share of it as well. He took 5,000 yuan from Smooth's fee on the understanding that he would find a way of making up for it later on. Smooth knew these pleasantries were crap. He could not remember how many years he had been shifting stages and how many promises of that kind had been made to him only to be broken. His response was neither overly irritated nor impatient. For more than an hour, a succession of gripes issued from his mouth, about how "we all just labour by our hands" and "it's hard to let down any of my team".

Eventually, Geng Shen patted his thigh. "Button it and I'll sub you two thousand," he said. "I'll take this as letting the emperor's mother comb the field for bits of grain after harvest – it's a foray for fun and relaxation." Once the loss of 3,000 yuan had been factored in, Smooth distributed the cash with curses flying from every corner. Before the task was done, he received a phone call. His brother Big Army had returned from Macau.

32

BIG ARMY DIAO'S RETURN to the neighbourhood was a noteworthy event about which almost every household was speculating.

They all remembered how, on his last visit a few years back, he breezed in at the wheel of a Bentley worth six million yuan in the company of a new wife. Their admiration for him soared, and the young in particular regarded this uncle as the very model of a modern, upwardly mobile gent.

This time he flew rather than drove, but the new wife was considerably newer than the previous one. She was certainly in her twenties, whereas he must have reached fifty-seven or fifty-eight by now. He didn't call Smooth until the plane began its descent on its approach to the local Xianyang Airport. The message was simply that, after a long absence, he would spend New Year in the Western Capital. When Smooth asked whether he expected to stay in the family home or not, his brother answered that it was of no consequence and hung up. Of course, there was no question of Big Army lodging with Smooth. He ordered the presidential suite at the same hotel where Bill Clinton stayed on his trip to the Western Capital. After checking in and arranging every pressing affair, he sashayed into the old community with his young bride on his left arm and Daisy on his right.

His niece had no idea that his return was imminent until her dad called and told her. This made her tingle with anticipation, for in her view the uncle was an object of pride. She could not account for the gulf between these two brothers. While one spent money like it might soon become extinct, the other zipped around on a scruffy tricycle. How bloody peculiar!

On reaching her uncle's hotel, he told her to wait in the lobby for a short time and that they would be down presently. Daisy immediately thought that the "they" referred to the significant other he showed off last time. But when "they" appeared together, the couple was not the same as before. It had been her intention to bound over and wrap her arms effusively around her uncle, though she felt inhibited about doing so as soon as she saw that the female he was holding was even younger than her. Her uncle, being still carefree and unrestrained, introduced the lady directly with the local twang of the Western Capital. "This is your new auntie, ha ha," he announced. "What do you think? A pretty creature?" Both she and the girl stood still in amazement.

Big Army grinned hastily. "There's no need to call her 'auntie'," he explained. "Her name is Marti, and that is enough. You know 'ma' means the horse you choose to ride, and 'ti' tells us how all Americans are imperialists. It's not the local slang for 'damn it', even though they sound similar. Ha ha. This is our niece, Daisy, the one I mentioned."

Marti seemed a touch disappointed by this new relative and tilted herself further into her husband's arms without showing a shred of emotion. She did not even nod her head in recognition, as if to say Big Army was sufficient for her and his kindred were excess to requirements. Daisy escorted them from the hotel.

They took a taxi back to the old community. As they readied themselves to enter, Daisy grappled hold of Big Army's spare arm that Marti could not contort herself to grasp.

He had brought with him some souvenirs, which he asked Daisy to hand out. Now the whole neighbourhood was astir, he could not cross his brother's threshold until the news of his return was upon every pair of lips. Big Army Diao was back from Macau.

On going through the gate, he started to yell out loud. "You see what kind of life your dad leads? The iron gate is all rusted up and hasn't been replaced."

"Hum, but he changes his women quite regularly," Daisy responded in anger.

After that jibe, she looked at Marti and realised she had spoken somewhat out of turn.

"What?" her uncle asked. "Did he find someone new?"

"Didn't he share the glad tidings with you, Uncle?"

"No."

"Well, he probably didn't have the face to tell you." Daisy released a nasal hum.

"Hey, Niece. Your father needs a woman at his side. How can you talk like this? Is she a looker?"

"You can see for yourself soon." Daisy was nonplussed.

Right at this moment, Smooth swept in on the tricycle, with Sufen as passenger.

Despite it being winter, Smooth was covered in sweat. Dust from the stage he had been taking apart was mingled with perspiration, so his skin was blotchy like a tabby cat.

"Brother!" he called out warmly upon seeing Big Army.

"Is this your daughter-in-law?" he said upon spotting the abashed and timid Sufen. "Great. It's only right you should find yourself another half. How else would you cope with life? Very good choice. Such a fine and pretty lady." He then threw in the local expression, "Quite a bonny piece."

Naturally, Smooth was glad to hear these words. "Greet our elder brother," he urged Sufen.

"Elder Brother," she addressed him. Her first impression of him was on the whole positive. He was not only tall and had etiquette, but his tone and body language were appealing.

"This is your new sister-in-law," Big Army went on. "Her name is Marti."

Smooth and Sufen were taken aback to find themselves staring at such a green and delicate young acquisition.

"Just call her Marti," Big Army insisted. "'Sister-in-law' sounds cumbersome. 'Ma' means like the horses of the Terracotta Army, and the 'ti' is about royal imperialism. It's not the local slang for 'damn it', even though they sound similar." His words made everybody chuckle.

"Now, you had another daughter, didn't you? What was her name?"

"Plum, Plum Han."

"Where is she?"

"She should be home. Plum! Plum! Plum Han!" Smooth hollered.

A short while later, Plum's door opened and she walked out.

"Your big uncle is back," Smooth informed her. "Come down, quick."

"Uncle!" Plum called from up above and made a neither slow nor speedy descent.

Much to Daisy's jealously, Big Army embraced Plum on first sight even though neither experienced any especial sense of intimacy or estrangement. Her uncle's attitude towards women unsettled her. When she saw him heading to her father's room, she slipped upstairs alone.

As they sat in Smooth's bedroom, Big Army groused about his failure to notify him about his remarriage. "We're an old couple, just got hitched together," Smooth explained. "We wanted to get ahead and make a go of life, so didn't tell anyone."

They chatted for a while before Smooth changed tack. "Big Brother, it can't have been easy for you to come back here. If it's no bother to you, let's make some dishes together and have a family reunion feast."

"Today, I feel the need to taste mutton with flatbread. I'm salivating at the thought of it. We can go to Tong Shengxiang. My treat."

Smooth told him that he had grafted five days and nights, so was not presentable enough to be seen in public.

Big Army said his brother could have an hour to take a shower while he would spend that time trailing around Shangyi Road. In the five years that had passed since he left, many of the stores were no longer in business.

Smooth shouted for Daisy to serve as an escort.

Daisy was only too delighted to accept this task, and she and Marti both hooked one of Big Army's elbows as they left through the gate.

While the couple were alone downstairs and Smooth showered, Sufen was adamant that she would not partake in the meal. Her husband riposted that this was merely showing the most basic respect to his elder brother. He also elaborated on how Big Army had been a careless and lackadaisical man. His intentions were never malign, but he had a propensity for loafing and playing. After learning mahjong at the age of eleven or twelve, he became the one to beat in the village. When fortune came his way, he might own a mountain of gold and silver. When it failed him, he might be left sitting bare-arsed in the gutter. On balance, fate appeared to favour him and he was able to gamble his whole life long without the need to sweat and toil. Such was his luck that latterly he expanded his success to Macau. In this world, Smooth could only claim one true blood brother, and this happened to be one who never looked upon him condescendingly for pedalling his trike around. By all means, Smooth and Sufen should display their heartfelt respect to their kin.

Sufen agreed, but Plum stood firm, leaving her stepfather to have to cajole her. To his relief, Plum's hesitancy around Big Army was not rooted in aversion. She simply could not recognise or cultivate a deep relationship with him, and was reluctant to fuel Daisy's envy by giving the slightest hint of wanting to compete with her for the old man. In the end, she followed Smooth out, almost with the demeanour of submitting to a command.

Smooth was elated to have the entire family seated around a huge circular table. He had no prior intimation that the reappearance of Big Army would be sufficient to twist back together their fractured unit. He secretly prayed that his elder brother could stay long enough to ensure that this awful mess was righted.

33

Spring Festival was drawing around in less than a month and the Shaanxi Opera Troupe had been busy rehearsing a fresh New Year's show with extra shifts and overtime. Smooth assumed responsibility for creating the set, and he promised to meet Iron Kou's every requirement. Once started, the job revealed itself to be as difficult as cracking a steel-like nut. It was necessary to have an articulated platform capable of accommodating forty players. Added to that, they had eighteen days to paint six curtain backdrops, running to a completion rate of one every three days. Even so, the director dictated that the stage assembly should begin on the twentieth day of the final month of the lunar calendar. In effect, they had to be done in fifteen days. That was not including the need to create five backdrops of gauze and the pair of peach trees that had to have canopies stretching one and a half metres across. Visually, the upper branches of each should intertwine with its counterpart, framing the stage in the fashion of an arbour. Also, the trees had to reflect the passage of the seasons, from the falling of the foliage to the formation of buds in spring, and finally full blossoming. According to the director, only if the audience applauded rapturously when the lights came on could the floral spectacular be judged a triumph. "Don't let this get to you, brother," Mound murmured to Smooth. "When the time comes around, I'll sit among the audience and start the clapping. Those dimwits are bound to follow whatever I do." Smooth stamped surreptitiously on Mound's toes out of fear that others in the troupe might overhear.

He distributed the jobs in fine detail among the dozens under his command. Big Hook and Monkey oversaw the platform itself. Big Hook had carpenters and welders on hand, while Monkey was proficient at installing the kind of motor needed to automate the stage. Third Skin and Sufen were put in charge of the gauze backdrops, and Smooth and Mound took on the painted curtains.

Producing these six pieces of textile was the most exacting of tasks. Smooth laid his hands on three sewing machines that were on the go nonstop for three days and nights. Nobody liked to be delegated this job. Sewing bundles of white cloth into a curtain with a width of sixteen metres and a drop of nine appeared fairly elementary. The challenge came in turning the corners while stitching, and being sure that the cotton remained sheer. When used as scenery, flatness was essential, for any flaw or crease would be magnified under the powerful beam. And so it was common for curtains to have to be painstakingly adjusted. Those who had tried this before were apt to want to shun the task again. Owing to his experience with his second wife, Smooth had become familiar with various seamstresses and knew some strategies to recruit them. It was his lot to suffer their long faces. With Spring Festival approaching, nobody went short of stitching work and to their minds, sewing such curtains proved thankless. Smooth's ears were soon cauterised with all their cursing. He dared not blink as he filed around the three sewing machines, inspecting the finished articles repeatedly to make sure no error went unnoticed. No amount of flattery could remedy a substandard curtain.

Mound had to run after food supplies, bellyaching as he bought every indispensable item. In theory, he should have been supervising in the evening with Smooth, but nodded off on a heap of surplus stage cloths in the corner of the workshop. Not even Smooth's kicking could rouse him. The three seamstresses, who were all in their forties or fifties, gabbled away more pungently and lustily one after another. The previous night, they all complained that it was impossible for them to carry on and they wanted to go home for a rest. If they couldn't head home, could they at least take this curtain as their blanket? The trouble was that the workshop needed to be cleared for the painting work to commence. Hiring somewhere else to allow them to kip was too much. His best recourse was to try to lighten their moods by reeling off as many blue tales as he could remember the troupe members telling him. Eventually, they grew so agitated that they pounced on Smooth and tugged off his trousers, tossing them out of the window. Covering his modesty with a scrap of cloth, he raced out into the courtyard to find them hanging from the bough of an osmanthus tree. That son of a bitch Mound just chortled away to his side. A bare-buttocked Smooth proceeded to climb the trunk and rescue his clothing, but then when he was sliding them on again, it occurred to him that his piles had begun to flare up once more. As the job was already at peak flow, he must try not to aggravate his condition. By daybreak, he sent the women away even before the master painter had arrived. Taking his cue from Mound, he slumped down on a pile of rags.

It was Iron Kou's merciless toes that jabbed Smooth awake, who by now had been dozing for close to two hours. He sneaked out from his nest of waste cloth to find himself the object of hilarity among several of the painters. Smooth could not tell what was so funny until one of them told him to take a look in a mirror. His reflection betrayed how the textiles had secreted their dye onto his skin. Where he had salivated at the corner of his mouth there was a purple scar, and his face was now the countenance of a jagged-toothed phantom. Even he himself couldn't help but be amused.

"Take your time," reassured Iron Kou. "There's no room for error. A fault in any link will spoil the whole ensemble. It's one thing being cursed by Chief Qu for not having the Spring Festival show ready on time, but you might miss out on a tidy wad as well."

"How can you put it like that?" asked Smooth. "We were already assured of a tidy wad at the outset. We daren't run through every fine detail, otherwise we could find ourselves out of pocket."

Before he had finished, Iron Kou launched a counterattack. "Well, well, Smooth," he observed. "Each time you complain about diminishing returns. Why stick at this game then? It's allowed you to marry a bevy of women, you crafty dog. Here's me stuck with the same old fishwife." These words came across as comical.

"Director Kou is sending me up," said Smooth, also smirking. "I'm just a labourer who grafts. I can't get a woman to stick by me. If I could, why would I have to keep on starting again from scratch? I'd be happy to keep the same one, but that doesn't seem to be my lot. How can I savour the rich fate of the honourable Director Kou!"

"Well, well. Less of this glib talk. Get back to it. Get a move on with the platform and the gauze backdrops. The director is coming to check up on the platform design in the afternoon." Iron Kou readied himself to leave.

"Don't worry, Director Kou," was Smooth's brisk rejoinder. "Doing things wholeheartedly and with every muscle is just my style. My heart goes into it. Even if we only have shit and piss as rations, we'll still do it, but... but..."

"But what? You want to bring up the money for the temple job again? You really need to be taught a lesson. Look at the grubby shits who work under you. You kicked off a giant furore and still want rewarding for it. A flash of my prick is all you deserve."

"Ah, ah, Director Kou, I am well aware that there are some shits among us, but what happened, happened. There are dozens in the team and we don't all deserve to be blamed. Most ordinary folk are decent sorts."

"Louse. Be quiet. I'm intending, for Smooth's sake, to go over there and ask. That's on the understanding that you'll do a proper job for me this time."

"Rest assured, your honour. I never take a promise lightly. If I make a cock-up, you can spit straight in my face."

"Your pussy mouth really loves to chatter. Do your stuff well."

Iron Kou left. Smooth felt a touch of discomfort within his buttocks. When no one else was around, he hid himself in a corner and parted the cheeks gently with his hand. He then went to the workshop to unfold the curtains for the painters.

These painters were drafted in, since those members of the troupe who originally performed that work had quit long ago. Among them, a few had gained a measure of fame producing original pieces of art, this being more remunerative. If they encountered an enthusiastic patron, that would keep them in clover. Others, whose talents were less conspicuous, turned to related lines of design work, such as making backdrops for films or TV dramas. What they abhorred most of all was to be referred to as a "curtain painter in a drama troupe". To them it smacked of being a commis chef, left to smash garlic, peel spring onions or trim vegetables, while the stage art designer was the chef de cuisine.

Those who persisted in this field were by now old. Nobody saw their creations as being of professional standard. None of them had either the vision to move into graphic design or the stamina to keep pace with a movie or TV crew, so they were left to create stage backdrops. Drawing sets was still no minor skill, since it entailed being able to enlarge sketches a foot in length so that they could fill a vast curtain. It took confidence to be able to twirl one's brush onto a white cloth, for strokes of different colours could not just be applied randomly or casually. The key was to have a practice run, mocking up the image to scale. Once this had been done, it was relatively straightforward to complete the final article.

Smooth had lost count of how many cloths he had helped to decorate, so there was no misplaced confidence in Iron Kou assigning these six to him. He was the supreme head, and even the painters were there at his invitation. One curtain alone, with the addition of the materials and working fee, cost 7,000 yuan. The white cloth, the iron rings, the binding laces and processing fee added up to 1,000 yuan. On top of that, the painter charged 3,500 yuan for completing the "bare outline" and the final "fleshing out". Smooth and his comrade would fill in the colours during the middle stage of the process. The painter would then move to another shed to begin the next in line, returning to his previous effort if he noticed anything that needed rectifying.

Light and straightforward as this operation appeared, the fatigue could be dangerous. After several days of toil, it was difficult for workers to straighten their spine. Fortunately, Smooth and his team had learned a secret technique. By tying the brush to the end of a long stick, colours could be applied from a stationary, standing position. Should their necks become stiff or start to ache, a tilt of the head could relieve that. Still, being upright in this posture caused Smooth's haemorrhoids to nag. He could only focus his thoughts on how much money he would rake in this time. The cumulative effort was enough for him and his brothers to be in profit. Typically, 150 or 160 yuan per day would suffice for each. As Spring Festival was coming and the job urgent, greater demands were exerted upon them. This upped their per capita income to 250 or 260 yuan for a stint of about twenty days. Everyone was content to seal their lips and knuckle down.

Smooth, by his own calculations, estimated that a flawless run would give him net earnings of 12,000 or 13,000 yuan. With Sufen's salary on top, they would have 17,000 or 18,000 yuan – enough to furnish them with a bumper New Year. His guarantor in all of this was that Chief Qu was in charge, and he lodged enormous trust in these labouring hands. As gleeful as his calculations made him, Smooth could not ignore the hindrance down below. His solution was to purchase a pack of sanitary pads and go to the toilets to make a change once the present one had become bloody. As soon as Mound discovered the pads, he blurted out, "How can Smooth be having his time of the month?" Smooth lashed back with, "Your father is having his period!"

That night when he had finished painting the curtains, he crouched on a ramshackle chair with one eye closed, appreciating the artful morass of rocks and grass. Painting filled him with a sense of achievement. Just then, his mobile rang. Big Army was calling him. He said not a word at first, merely opening his mouth and yawning like a distressed toad. "Smooth, please find a few dozen grand and send it over," he ordered. "I'm playing cards at Uncle Scar's place. I can't get back to the hotel right now, so please be quick. They're all playing for small stakes, so thirty to fifty grand will do. Yes, not another word. Fetch me fifty grand." Following this request, Smooth turned off his mobile and was so perturbed he almost slid off his chair.

Oh heavens! He could speak so casually about 30,000 or 50,000 as being small stakes. Big Army surely didn't know how his little shit of a younger brother subsisted by counting every new coin, and made a living by picking around inside the cunts of sparrows? He may have formed the impression that his younger brother, the stage shifter, had become his bank runner too.

Fifty thousand yuan! Even if he were able to steal such an amount, he'd first have to know where so much money was being stored. He was furious and wanted to call him back and tell him frankly that he didn't have access to so much cash. Thinking again, his elder brother had not shown his face around the community in years and if he was playing in Uncle Scar's home, the eyes of every neighbour would be trained upon him. Were he to refuse to give his brother any kind of face, rumours of estrangement would circulate. By chance, he did have more than 10,000 yuan about his person. He had borrowed that sum from the finance office with a promissory note in order to purchase necessities, in tomorrow's case, pigments and odds and sods. Come what may, he must answer his brother's call. How much should he fetch over, though? He squatted in the toilet, contemplating for twenty minutes and more.

The money had been bundled into his waistband. He took the notes out and counted them over and over again. In total there was 13,240 yuan. A one-yuan coin had rolled out and plopped down into the gutter, whereupon he picked up a couple of thin sticks and tried to employ them as pincers to recover it. Oh, mother fucker! The pincers nudged the coin into oblivion. He wanted to bring 5,000 yuan, but thought that rather too mean. He couldn't bring 10,000 yuan since it might go unreturned. Six or eight thousand – even that seemed improper. More than once, his brother had mouthed off about 30,000 or 50,000. Should a smaller amount be presented, explanations would be necessary. As his brother sported the deportment of a magnate, 10,000 should not be a hindrance to repay. For his part, a pack of loose change would be difficult to raise. Thinking back and forth, he convinced himself that 10,000 was the optimum amount. He replaced the sanitary pad on his posterior and cycled over to the family home.

34

Uncle Scar's gambling parlour had been in operation for more than three decades. He was fond of recounting how his career in gaming had unfolded alongside the reform and opening-up policy.

Smooth was greeted by a foul and rank-smelling pandemonium. People couldn't even keep their eyes open on account of the smoke. He knocked on the door to enter and, once accustomed to the pall, could pick out the faces of a few gamblers. The first to come into view was Uncle Scar himself, who sat facing the door with a cigar as thick as a thumb waggling between his lips. Smooth called the cigar Uncle Scar's "black stick", and some special dexterity was required to balance it on the edge of his mouth so that no matter whether it moved up or down in that position, it appeared moored there. Smooth could conceive that this self-same black stick had been a constant feature for in excess of thirty years and that it had all but merged into the lineaments of Uncle Scar's face.

Uncle gained his nickname during his teenage years when he got into a brawl with the accountant in the production brigade. This man was in charge of the steelyard and presented his family with one pound of sweet potatoes less than the quota they were owed. He had two incisors punched out, and in return, Uncle Scar was struck multiple times in the face with the bar of the scales. This not only caused the copper finial at the end of the scale to break, but it also ripped into his face, even revealing the white bone below. A gash that never fully healed was left behind. This ran all the way from his supraorbital ridge down to his lip.

The year when that accountant died, Uncle Scar went to the mourning hall. "Dead at last, you old dog," he cursed. "Our karmic debt hasn't been settled. When I reach the netherworld myself, I'll pulverise you back with a metal rod. Then, you son of a bitch, you'll have no face to meet anyone in hell."

It was commonly known that Uncle Scar seldom left the community. At most, he would pop out to a stall in the evening and turn back as soon as he reached the memorial archway at the village entrance. For sure, he had been inside the police station on numerous occasions, though would usually return in the dead of night. He might be hauled off in a police vehicle, though would come back in a car belonging to one of his gambling chums. Even if he were released in the morning, he would sit firm and wait until dusk before heading home, since he did not want to be noticed outside in the community during the daytime.

Smooth could remember when Uncle Scar first set up a gambling den in his home. Back in those days, the stakes were genuinely small. Once he lost sixty yuan in a single night, which was hard won by sweat and blood, being the equivalent of pedalling the tricycle for three days solid. He experienced such heartache and pounded his head with a hammer once he got home, vowing that this was one mistake he would never repeat. As the saying goes, "Nine out of ten gamblers are losers, and the tenth is on the run from debt." Uncle Scar set up his fiefdom in that self-made dive, never finding himself challenged. To begin with, locals dubbed him "Damned Scar", "Rotten Scar", "Festering Scar" and "Son of a Bitch Scar", only to be succeeded by "Uncle Scar" and "Grandpa Scar". This was because, apart from the fact he was advancing in years, he took an ethical approach to gambling and was highly skilled in every game. His leanness and demeanour lent him the appearance of a transcendent being. He wore black silk attire all day, which in his words was rather comfy. In the eyes of others, this encapsulated Uncle Scar. He himself never claimed to be some kingpin, though he did seem to embody that mantle.

Smooth was aware that Uncle Scar too looked down upon him. He derided Smooth's dismal existence. "Man comes into this world to enjoy a fleeting journey," he repeated several times to his face.

"You pedal a broken trike, work yourself into the ground like a dog and shift stages without seeing the sun. Don't you cower from light like the dick in your crotch?" A dick was a dick, anyway. Since it was not his destiny to be victorious as a gambler, he had to pedal the trike and shift stages to cover his next meal. Besides, Uncle Scar was the one who shied purposefully away from being seen in daylight and had made himself the dick cowering in his crotch. Who was he to laugh at Smooth? Of course, this thought remained confined to his heart, and he knew that as far as the fame and honour of Uncle Scar were concerned, he was not qualified to either cast aspersions or form judgments.

Smooth could see his elder brother sitting with his back to him and that girl Marti was letting her hands crawl along his spine until they settled on his neck. Besides them, there were a few acquaintances from the community and strangers from outside. The eyes of every last spectator were absorbed with the succession of miracles that were materialising on the table. Smooth stood there for a time without anybody noticing his presence.

It had been years since he had hung around a pit like this. The last time he was here, mahjong was still the gamblers' game of choice, but later it was agreed that "kneading the tiles" was tiring and took too long to reach a conclusion. Hence, they switched to playing cards. Smooth was surprised to see that each hand was reeled off with the same velocity that a gale might whisk away the bitumen roof of a shed. In his teens, he had stood guard over the vegetable patch and observed just such a hut at the centre of the field. Many had been the time when a gust had divested the shed of its roof, never to be spotted again. In one round, his brother surrendered his hand after fanning the cards so slightly that only a glimmer of the number and suit were visible to him. He pushed the pile of chips towards his opponents with a rattling sound.

"Big Army," said Uncle Scar. "Smooth has come over to bring you some readies. He's been here a while." This startled Smooth, for seemingly Scar had noticed his presence all along without actually turning around and looking in his direction.

Big Army gave a leisurely and simple glance at his brother, just as though he had prepared him a mug of cold tea. "Put it here," he instructed and nodded with his chin before continuing to rub his cards. The cards could be plied apart with just two fingers, though each of them appeared to be anchored by an iron gate weighing a thousand pounds. They could only be cinched one hair's width apart at a time. The iron gate would then be closed firmly, and the hand revealed with a frenzy or else tossed away gloomily. Those chips were pushed back and forth in vastly different quantities. One moment they might be stacked like a hillock and the next not a single one was left behind. Smooth knew that at the very end, these plastic counters would be metamorphosised into bales of banknotes.

Smooth had already dug his hand into his pocket for the money. He was loath, though, to withdraw the contents. That 10,000 yuan could fund a round or two at the table, but for him it represented a month or two of blood and perspiration. From now on, once he unleashed it, the booty belonged neither to him nor his elder brother. And yet the two of them had been apart for years, with him returning this Spring Festival for the sake of his kinsman. He had not forgotten their fraternal bond. As he had opened his mouth, it would be very embarrassing for the stash to remain lodged in his work clothes. What was more, the fellow gamblers could look on it as small beer. His brother suggested 30,000 or 50,000 on the phone before finally plumping for the larger figure. Fifty thousand was quite beyond his means and even if it were not, he couldn't just expel such an amount all at once like a mammoth fart. He really could not bear to go through with this, even though folks mocked him for making a living from "picking at the cunts of sparrows". He also admitted to himself that this 10,000 had virtually left him penniless. In the end, he forced himself with trembling hands to pick the notes from the belt inside the blue overcoat. He even flattened out those that had become rolled up in there and placed the lot where his brother had indicated with his chin. This series of complicated gestures did not arouse the attention of all present, yet when the 10,000 had been deposited on the table, every pair of eyes directed itself at Big Army, keen to gauge his reaction.

Big Army was the first to turn around and fix Smooth. "Mid... midnight," Smooth's throat choked as he stammered. "I couldn't find more... even this... this is public money."

"You're quite a somebody," sniped a fat fellow who was trying to gain the upper hand over Big Army. "Now even Smooth is starting to dabble around in the public purse. Since it's public money, why such a measly amount?" The chips in front of him were already piled like a knoll.

"I'm just a hired hand who labours hard, shifting stages for people," Smooth answered. "This time, they offered me an advance to run errands and take care of minor matters."

"You're a boss," said another player as he shuffled the deck, "but you're still at the beck and call of others? They say you hire dozens of men, so you must be a boss. How can someone in your position not have a hundred thousand yuan readily to hand? Your brother called, and you only brought ten grand! Do you mean to insult him? Is that a significant amount for a man like your brother? He didn't ask you for more, and I don't believe you couldn't get fifty grand," nagged the other gambler while rearranging the cards. "You want to pull the plug on your brother's fun?"

"I just pedal a tricycle, so how can I count myself as a boss!" Smooth explained hastily. "My gang gets together when there is a job to be done. We make only a little, which is usually shared fairly. Our palms would be sweating if we were asked to handle eight or ten thousand yuan, let alone eighty thousand or a hundred thousand. We couldn't make that much even if we were to stick our heads down and our arses up for a whole year. You're just taking the piss."

"You can't criticise Smooth," Big Army interjected. "It's midnight, so it's hard for him to find any stake. I thought we'd just be playing for small sums, so I only brought a hundred grand with me when I came out this evening. I didn't expect to be such a dud. Marti, you go back to the hotel and fetch a top-up."

The young lady who had been draped on Big Army's back appeared too tired to even acknowledge Smooth. "I can't be bothered," she cooed. "If you want it, go yourself." She didn't detach herself from his body.

Big Army raised his hand and patted Marti's face tenderly, as though coaxing a child. "The more spoiled you get, the worse you behave," he said. "OK, let me throw in this ten grand. If I lose the lot, I'll go to the hotel and collect more." He then lifted his left buttock and emitted a series of noisy farts. Marti tugged his ears as Big Army lifted his right buttock and followed it up with another three.

Uncle Scar was tickled. "Smooth, you must follow your brother's example," he said. "See how he lives, enjoys a carefree and graceful life, feasts, drinks and has fun. Even his farts caress the sky like spring thunder. You arrived here like a dick on a broken trike. You've lost face for the whole community. Your roots run deep in the Western Capital. Damn it, how can a citizen do something so despicable? Building stages for actors brings shame on all the ancestors of the Diao clan."

Smooth was incensed. He was all but ready to blurt out how ironic it was that a paltry gambler should want to look down on him. His approach was more circumspect, though. "So in your mind, Uncle Scar, making a living from gambling is more honourable and fashionable than pedalling a tricycle and managing stages?"

"For a city-dweller, certainly," he answered without a moment's rumination. "If you want to do something original, you should try trafficking aircraft, cannons and munitions. At least then you could experience both ecstasy and ice. When you were at a loose end, you could drink tea, cut cards, take your caged bird for a walk and chat. Why be the one to wait on others? First of all, take a rest. Then resolve to follow your brother Big Army's lead. Let your farts ring out loud and be heard."

"Well, you must surely have things to be getting on with," Big Army pressed Smooth. He felt Uncle Scar's words had strayed too far and wanted his brother to leave while nobody's eyes were trained on him. Smooth wished to grumble further, though on surveying Uncle Scar's blanched, bloodless face, and his paws with no muscles, only protruding bones and corpuscles, he suddenly lost the impulse. He sensed that this old man was a worthless shit and nobody would spare the time to bury him. Arguing any longer would be futile.

The minute Smooth departed, he heard a loud onslaught of flatulence behind him. After a brief silence, there was a roar of laughter like vegetables being stirfried in a wok. The heat of Smooth's embarrassed face soon subsided, for he had become accustomed to others treating him with condescension. Today was worse, though, for it had occurred in front of his elder brother. Not only had he lost face on behalf of the returning Big Army, but that slip of a young sister-in-law as well. He had the sudden urge to break wind, but however much he tried, he could not channel his rectal gas into something audible and tangible. This failure was in fact a relief, for it would have knotted his haemorrhoids until his waist gave way in pain.

Winter nights in the Western Capital are characterised by their propensity for strong, dry winds. Tonight, those squalls were especially sharp and dislodged hoardings and billboards, so they rolled randomly across the ground. When Smooth left the stage, it was windy but dry. On his way back, the sky was filled with snowflakes. They pirouetted higher and higher, borne aloft by the breath of the night. Not a single one was consigned to the ground.

Smooth's posterior was too sore to make pedalling possible, so he dismounted and wheeled the trike along the roadside. His legs felt doughy and tired. It was not far from home, though he was desperate to sit down by his own doorway and never rise again.

Smooth had actually known how to enjoy fun in former days. Years ago, he raised birds and chirping insects like other families. As he grew so busy that even preparing a hot meal could be considered a luxury, his life tumbled into a disarray where even forging a clarion fart proved a labour. He had never been so alert to the chill of such a winter's night in the Western Capital. The wind tickled his collar, running up through his sleeves and trouser legs until it stung his body. Owing to the nature of his work, he didn't find it practical to wear a cotton-padded jacket at this time of the year. He only put on long johns beneath the jeans he left unwashed for the entire season. His top half was clad in a sweater knitted by Orchid Zhao, and then darned and mended by Sufen. As his entire form was enveloped by that blue greatcoat, he was nigh on oblivious as to what should be worn underneath.

Tonight, even with a panoply of layers, he was frozen and his teeth clattered together, almost severing his tongue. He did not want to take another step forward, being desperate only to find himself back at home this instant with a quilt covering him so he could sleep unburdened. He would take care of the infernal curtains in the morning.

Hardly had his front wheel reached the entrance to his home

when he heard the two girls playing music in their own rooms at full blast with complete disregard for those living next door. He peered at his watch and saw it was past 2 am. He was fully aware how much the neighbours despised his family. For one thing, its head was a good-for-nothing stage shifter who wore rags and pedalled a tricycle all day long. To make matters worse, there was the obnoxious Daisy with her music at antisocial hours mimicking the sounds of noisy phantoms and lone, mournful wolves. It was not unknown to find a brick flung into their courtyard or shit slathered across their gate. Daisy would pay not the least heed to Smooth, and he was belittled and helpless. Sometimes, he did try to circumvent the hostility. In the face of the neighbours' profanities, he would bow incessantly with his hands crossed before his chest.

Since he was a teenager, Smooth recognised that hard graft dogged him. He would always be crouched somewhere, his buttocks tilted in the air, trying vainly to catch up with the lives of others. He not only worked the hardest out of all the residents of the neighbourhood, but knew the severest adversity too. Each family raised their kids believing they might turn out promising, fetching, obedient and filial to their parents. He hadn't been able to spend much money or thought on that daughter of his, but it still mystified him as to how she could turn out like this. How could she shun her own father? He didn't know where to locate the precise fault or how to steer her back to something like normalcy. As long as she could at least bring herself to smile kindly at her old man, he would exert himself until he dropped dead.

None of this had any effect. It seemed that even the money he brought home was somehow intrinsically different from the pay packets of other parents. Daisy could not spend his earnings with a sense of ease, for she felt that money earned in this manner was somehow shameful. In her eyes, demeaning himself into the role of a fool and doing menial chores divested any salary of his of the glamour it may have otherwise possessed. Even so, he knew no other means of work and dared not contemplate a change.

Of course, he did not stew about this issue. Even were he to do so, it wouldn't change anything. Perhaps he was destined to ride his fate in this bitter way?

The snow fell heavier. Leaning by the gate for a few minutes, he reasoned it would be better to stay in the troupe's workshop tonight. The wind had pressed scores of snowflakes into his nape and he shuddered with cold. The wheels rotated, precariously slippery. All along the length of Shangyi Road, he must have been the only trembling pedestrian.

35

Daisy shadowed Uncle Big Army for days until it became clear that Marti resented her presence. Laziness had dulled her enthusiasm. To aggravate the situation, she found that somehow she was always the one to settle their bills with her own money. The returned Big Army split his time between gambling at the card table, snoozing or being Marti's chaperone as she savoured the local specialities of the Western Capital. At first, Daisy was only too keen to cover everything and she would duly comply whenever she heard "Ah, Daisy, your uncle left his wallet at the hotel. Please can you pay?" She would not be overstretched in buying the marinated pork cakes at the Fan Family restaurant, soup dumplings from the Jia Family restaurant, or steamed beef mixed with flour or lamb chitterlings and head meat prepared by Hui Muslim chefs. The same was not true of mutton broth with bread cubes at the Tong Shengxiang restaurant run by the Old Song Family. Their menus covered a la carte dishes such as the fried tail, tongue and stomach of a bull, and venison, with several bottles of Phoenix brand liquor to cleanse the palate. Throw in the company of those gambling pals he hadn't seen for an age and the bills mounted exponentially.

Every mealtime, Big Army would drink until almost bursting point, with his friends having to restrain him. Marti would sit there, not mindful at all about the expenditure, leaving Daisy to take care of their victuals. One day, her uncle fancied mutton cooked in a massive iron wok, and decided to treat a dozen primary school classmates to table talk over this repast. Once he got to the restaurant, he spotted the renowned Hengshan County Mutton at eighty yuan a pound, so ordered a fifteen-pound heap for starters. His classmates gave flavoursome accounts of their past jaunts as the hefty portions of meat caused their cheeks to puff out. When one of the chaps spoke in admiration of Big Army's wristwatch, he unfastened it and offered to swap. The disparity in value of the two timepieces must have amounted to tens of thousands of yuan.

All the men around the table praised Big Army for being so "upper crust, generous and sumptuous" in his demeanour and hospitality. The thirteen of them dispatched sixteen bottles of Phoenix liquor, a score of beers and an additional five pounds of mutton. In the end, only a dribble of broth was left at the bottom of the wok. Beyond that, they requested that the male and female house vocalists give renditions of dozens of traditional folk songs from northern Shaanxi. Each number cost about ten yuan.

Daisy took the situation as a total washout and made an excuse to sneak away early. Before she reached the apartment, her phone rang to tell her that her uncle was beset with sorrow. Sure enough when she returned, Big Army was still at the table, weeping with trails of tears mingled with snot. He bemoaned how his little brother led such an impoverished life. For dozens of years he had ridden that trike, carrying materials for actors and setting up their stages. Not even migrant workers from the countryside would stoop to doing such a thing. He did not enjoy the lifestyle of a true citizen. A few years from now, when his legs grew too old to pedal, Big Army vowed to bring him to Macau to live out his days in indulgence.

Daisy found herself habitually uneasy in these situations where others might glean information about her father's state. In this instance, she was touched to realise that her uncle was so magnanimous. He was by now dead drunk and needed the assistance of his comrades to reach his hotel suite. Daisy footed the bill, which exceeded 5,000 yuan. She was truly rabid at this and called Smooth for aid, claiming that escorting his elder brother had set her back over 10,000 yuan. Her father's response caught her unawares. "You love to pay for him really," he observed slowly and calmly. "He lives in the lap of heaven, but does that mean he needs you to buy his meals? He won't starve to death if you say no."

These words provoked her. "Hai, Hai, Smooth Diao, don't you think you've got it wrong?" she began to curse her father. "He's your elder brother and has no farting business to do with me. Let him die. If I have to go out with him again, I'll end up in the nuthouse." She promptly cut the call and resolved not to be so solicitous to her uncle in the future.

The next morning, Big Army once more called on Daisy. He told her he wanted her to guide him to Zhen'an County to eat soya bean butter sliced pork in the southern foothills of the Qinling Mountains. More than twenty years ago, he recounted, he had tried that dish and the flavour still seemed to linger on his palate even now. His niece wanted no part in what would be another costly escapade. Quite unexpectedly, Big Army drew out two bundles of banknotes from a holster in his waist. "Your uncle is really fond of a glass or two. The trouble is that when he's potted, he always forgets to pay. You can take charge of what we eat. Try to find all the best restaurants and watering holes. We'll do a trawl of them one by one. I'm back here for long enough this time, and your Auntie Marti is something of a gourmet herself. You can arrange it so we eat a new treat each day." Daisy found it was a fresh batch of 20,000 yuan in banknotes with the serial numbers in running order. Her uncle's "upper crust, generous and sumptuous" manner was indeed no myth. Daisy's mood was restored and she grabbed her purse, ready for their jaunt to Zhen'an.

As Plum's door was ajar, he suggested to Daisy that she should join them. "No, she's a wretched bugger and don't I know it?" she asserted firmly.

On leaving the house, Big Army started to scold her. "Don't behave like this. Since we've walked through the same home gate, this must be our fate. Don't be pigheaded for the sake of it. Being estranged benefits nobody." No matter how her uncle tried to persuade her, Daisy was unyielding.

Whatever activity Big Army engaged in, he always revelled in having the company of others. And indeed, there was no shortage of hangers-on wanting to share the Macau tycoon's boisterous sightseeing with all its free food and drink. Daisy even thought to invite Princess Wu and Mr Noodle Head. Eight or nine people travelled to Zhen'an, with Noodle Head driving one car and a gambling buddy from the neighbourhood the other.

Big Army had not anticipated that Zhen'an would be so accessible from Xi'an. Soon after they passed through the Qinling Expressway Tunnel, somebody shouted, "We're here." That was barely one hour after departing.

The seasoned gambler admitted that he had once been to Zhen'an in his twenties. Staring at his gaming partner, he asked enigmatically, "And can you guess what for?" He then shot a glance at Marti.

"Some lurid business, no doubt," replied the fellow who must have been almost the same age as him. "Eating or boozing, or betting. A bit of the other?" He clicked his tongue. "What else?"

"Bang on," said Big Army, not being in the least evasive. "I chased a girl right into the depths of the mountains. There wasn't even a train in those days, let alone an expressway cutting through the rock face. I had to take the bus across two huge ridges, the Qinling Range and the Yellow Blossom. I set off from the Western Capital at first light and it was dusk by the time I reached the county town. My body nearly fell apart."

"No shit," exclaimed his buddy. "Did you manage to get your leg over, then?" His voice sounded urgent.

Big Army smiled again enigmatically. "You've got a one-track mind. So dirty. Let me tell you, I ate and drank my fill and was given some marinated pig's arse as a souvenir."

"Brother, what kind of a delicacy is that?"

"Well, you must remember. Back in the eighties, a ten-pound pig's bum was no tiny treat."

"Never mind the marinated arse. Did you get it on?"

Big Army sighed. "To be honest, no," he answered. "But I can still recall the pork in Zhen'an. It was delicious and so full of flavour. Unforgettable."

Even Princess Wu was eager to know the outcome of the tale. "So you brought us here to relive the taste," she remarked. "What about the girl? Did you ever meet her later on?"

"No. Much as I've thought about it, there's always been so much else to keep me occupied. Her appearance, though. So striking, so flawless."

"How did you come to notice her, Uncle Big Army?" Now the Princess was his chief interrogator.

"She caught my eye at a barbecue stall in the Hui Muslim Quarter. The owner was an old-timer from the West End here in Zhen'an County. They hired a few girls from back home as dishwashers. She was one of them. As I hung about there, knocking back beer and eating kebabs, I became familiar with her. Later on she disappeared, but I did have her home address and so was able to track her down without saying a word. At that time, she had a boyfriend in her village. He always wore a machete on his waist for chopping wood. The blade must have been a foot long and four or five inches wide. Whenever I approached her house, he would be there grinding his machete at the door. The girl's mother pleaded that I keep my distance in case something kicked off. A little later on, the lad's father got a machete of his own and he would grind it next to the door as well. I was told that this pair had gone with their weapons to the city and menaced her until she fled back home. Then it dawned on me that this was all too risky and withdrawal was the only option. Her mother gave me the pig's arse as a parting gift."

A sentimental air seemed to descend on Big Army. "Uncle," chuckled Princess Wu, "this is maybe what we call touching a chilly butt against a warm cheek."

Everyone saw the humour in this. Daisy was convinced that Marti would feel jealous at hearing of such exploits. But quite the opposite. She listened with interest and relish. When Big Army finished his tale, she asked, "Why didn't you go looking for her again?"

"I simply didn't."

"Since you're such an upstanding gent, how could she not want to go with you?"

"How would she possibly escape from all that? If she was free to go, how could she resist coming with me?" said Big Army proudly. He scratched the high bridge of Marti's nose and she squirmed into his arms, gasping, "You're disgusting."

When they arrived in the county town, the whole group was thirsting to have Big Army introduce them to the fair maid he had known twenty-odd years earlier. He observed that she had lived far away in a place called Cloud-Covered Temple, so the cars sped off, their passengers ravenous for home-cooked pork. The vehicles carried them to the temple, where Big Army announced that they must cross about twenty miles of mountains and valleys before reaching Black Kiln Ditch.

"Uncle," Princess Wu called out heartlessly, "you must have been so crazy to want to run after that blossom all those years ago. This area is undeveloped virgin land."

"Ha ha, at that time I was crazy. I'd never seen such a bonny and unspoiled girl, so innocent, so beautiful. She was what they'd now call 'clean, organic food'."

Marti's envy was roused. "Be quick and find her," she snapped. "If you can, it's not too late to take her back for a bite."

Big Army beamed and hugged his wife closer to his chest, whereupon her attitude became more submissive.

Daisy saw in her uncle a man of six foot two, whose body was in outstanding shape. In particular, the bridge of his nose stood out as full, erect, bright and healthy. His slicked-back hair was always combed tidily in a manner that might even be perceived as prim. He had an affinity for white suits, and a belt and leather shoes of the same colour. Added to that, his sunglasses had to have white frames. Since he was young, his facility with the ladies had been masterful. It was said that in his youth he never had to purchase tickets for football matches or headline concerts, for there would always be several brothers ahead of him, beating a path through the crowds. The security officers elbowed bystanders aside with calls of "Give way, give way, yeah, it's you, give way". Big Army would then stride into the alleyway with a broad smile and feeling self-possessed. He would go so far as to shake the hands and pat the shoulders of the ticket collectors and security guards before swinging into the venue. People could never quite deduce who exactly this VIP was. His outward appearance was consummately assured, leading no one to doubt that he must possess status. This despite the fact that he seemed to travel with a pack of idlers in tow. Rumour had it that at a concert given by Qi Qin, he brought in twenty-one handpicked guests of his own. One of them wanted to turn back at the gate in case the ruse fell flat. "Follow me," Big Army declared. "Just don't look shifty-eyed or crane your neck to peep in all directions." At last, the whole cohort was granted admittance.

Someone once surmised that Big Army had the mindset to haul himself to any summit. Daisy was always perplexed, however, that there was such a canyon between him and his brother when both shared the same parents. Apparently, genes were not the ultimate determinant of how someone turned out.

Big Army tracked down the right household and discovered that the sometime belle from the 1980s was tending to the pigsty. He could not reconcile himself to this being the "clean, organic food" who lingered in his heart even after infinite conquests. Now appearing all of her fifty-plus years, the woman's head was swaddled in a black towel, and her body covered in a padded cotton jacket and trousers. Her footwear consisted of shabby hiking shoes, which had been mended so many times it was hard to say if they were originally black or white. Blue and purple blotches caused by the cold gave her a mottled complexion. Still, judging merely on the bone structure, that face in her youth must not have been so ungainly when it was plumped out with a little more fat. As of today, there were so many fissures running up and down and intertwining on her face that it was as if someone had begun to whittle her flesh. All that when Big Army's description evoked the fresh contours of apples and oranges.

The woman was carrying a slop pail, and she was hollering for the swine to come get their feed. A white sow planted its trotters straight into the trough, trying to install its body as a barricade to prevent the others from eating. The woman whacked it on the head three times with her wooden ladle. "You'll be dead from fever. Grab, grab. You just like to grab it away from others. Go on and stuff yourself alone and not let the others get any, then you'll burst and die of fever." The white pig couldn't bear her violence and straightened its frame and withdrew its two trotters. Big Army and his companions grouped around the sty.

The middle-aged woman looked on at all the visitors timidly.

"Hey, great siren," Princess Wu burst out. "Can you still recognise him?"

She pointed at Big Army.

The woman peered at him, apparently without comprehension.

"Peach Blossom, Peach Blossom Yang, don't you remember?" he asked.

Responding to her name, she raised her head and gasped at him in surprise. "Ah, you…"

All the onlookers applauded.

It was obvious that Big Army had left his mark on her too, for girlish shyness and coyness flooded back into her face.

"A true reunion between old flames," the gambling buddy pronounced.

Tan Daogui, keen to see how the eyes of the former sweethearts appeared, half craned his body into the sky. Just then, he lost his footing on the icy ground and nearly pitched headlong into the feeding trough.

Raucous laughter followed.

"Still feeding the pigs?" probed Big Army. "I recall back then you had two, but now there are so many."

"Not that many. Just seven or eight at any one time. The whole family depends on them. Such a lot of rare guests. Come and rest in the parlour."

"I still remember your mother's smoked bacon and the soya bean butter sliced pork she steamed for me. They've all come to try the pork."

Yang's face creased into a light smile. "Sure," she replied. "If you're partial to it. My mother's gone, though."

"What happened to her?"

"Passed over last spring. Come indoors and take a seat, all of you."

Big Army led the way.

Inside, it was pitch dark everywhere. From what Big Army could remember, nothing had been altered. The house and its decor were quite unchanged. With familiarity, he showed them around the courtyard, before at last directing them via the wooden stairs to the upper floor where the bacon was smoked. As might be expected, flitches hung above the kitchen, occupying half the building space. Grease oozed down in globules. There was a batch of pork from last year and the year before, but the older vintages went back eight years or a decade and were rumoured to become richer with age. The very oldest required no cooking, and the lean parts could be torn off and eaten directly.

Smoking bacon was the skill for which the people of Zhen'an were rightly renowned. Cypress leaves were used in the curing process, and whenever the aroma of meat being boiled in a wok wafted around, neighbours as far as eight miles away could tell which household was enjoying this delicacy. Princess Wu and Daisy tilted their necks, surveyed the ceiling and counted joints. More than two hundred of them lined the rafters, and dozens of freshly prepared cuts were strewn about the kitchen downstairs. Perhaps one sow had been slaughtered in the last months and its remains were still being smoked above the fire. What drew everybody's curiosity were the marinated rear ends of ten pigs. At first, they appeared so dark against the wall that they could have been mistaken for cave paintings. Big Army referred to them as the acme of smoked pork, which no one could refrain from eating. That one he had been given by Yang's mother all those years ago was much rangier than those currently before them.

While they were touring the upstairs and downstairs, along with the front and rear courtyard, Yang had been rinsing a pig's posterior and was boiling it in a hanging crock. The cooking vessel was thrown from clay and stood suspended in the main chamber all the year round. Big Army outlined how the local custom in the depths of these mountains was to start to burn wood for warmth in late autumn. The heat could also be utilised for boiling water, and families who could afford it would stew their pork in this way, removing a chunk to eat as they so pleased. Meat that was torn by hand was known as "straight from the pot" and the rest which was sliced on a board called "platter". Soya bean butter sliced pork was prepared by cutting the boiled marinated pork to particular dimensions. The lardons should be the thickness of a chopstick and roughly the same length as the diameter of the mouth of a bowl. According to the texture, they would then be assembled on a bed of fried bean paste and steamed for an hour or two. It was ready when the residual fat had sunk into the paste, while the pork should be so tender that it would fall apart before it could be chewed. Hence the name "melt in the mouth meat".

"I didn't expect that Uncle Big Army's sweet memories of life here could have stayed so lively and fresh," said Princess Wu.

"I spent a few days and nights in this village and it just stuck with me."

"I've always doubted that you got it on," the gambling pal leered.

"No, and that's the truth. The girl was too naive by far and I didn't dare try anything. Honestly, I didn't even hold her hand. One day when her parents were out and we were warming ourselves in the main room, I tried to take her hand. I ended up being shoved against the stove and almost barbecued."

There was hilarity all round.

Peach Blossom Yang, who was hidden away in the kitchen, felt puzzled by the laughter but was in no special hurry to join their company.

They ate the straight from the pot, the platter and the melt in the mouth meat. The man who once ground his machete by the door returned at noon when lunch was nearly ready. He had been chopping wood to the rear of the mountains, and was puzzled as to why there were so many guests. His wife beckoned him into the kitchen and they spoke at length. On coming into the room, the man offered tea and cigarettes to all present. The gambling chum joked that Big Army was the "hooligan" who had come from away to duel over his wife. He asked if he still had his machete so the two could settle the matter today.

The husband smirked foolishly, exposing the absence of his two front teeth. In spite of not yet being fifty, he appeared to be in his sixties and nothing about him was identifiable as that machete-grinding young man who had once terrified Big Army away.

After his father had lost his life in a mineshaft collapse in Shanxi Province, the man had come to this residence as the live-in son-in-law. Consequently, Yang's own son had gone to Shanxi last year to excavate coal. An accident had broken his backbone and that lad of twenty-one or twenty-two now slept in the side room, being unable to get to his feet. As the woman of the house had already related, they raised seven or eight swine each year, but even that wasn't enough to pay for the medical treatment of a quadriplegic. He said that he wanted to seek work outside, but nobody would hire him because of his age. The son's infirmity had dragged down the whole household.

When they were about to leave following the meal, Big Army cast down 20,000 yuan in banknotes on the table in the main hall. Everyone thought that this was his inimitable style. "Upper crust, generous and sumptuous" as he was, this was no mere bravado. He was the sort who could let out a ripe fart whenever he had the yen.

Daisy noticed that the two bundles of banknotes were a fresh run with the serial numbers in sequence. How could she not respect an elder uncle of this redoubt? Whenever he made this kind of gesture, the world-weary image of Smooth would flash in her mind. She could only conclude that she had been reincarnated in the wrong home.

That night, they lodged at the Mountain of Flowers and Fruit Inn in the county town. Each had a single room to themselves. At around 1 am, Mr Noodle Head knocked at Daisy's door. She didn't want to open up, though his banter was relentless, and he eventually said that something urgent was bothering him. She could hear that he was almost weeping. Daisy let him in and he crumpled to his knees spontaneously. "Sister Daisy," he wailed. "I beg you. I know I shouldn't have tried to use force. Just now after Princess Wu went to bed, I used my ID card to puh... pry the door of her room. Damn it. I have no shame..." He slapped his cheeks in the process of making this confession, the coil of hair sliding clear off his pate. Daisy was sickened and didn't want to look him in the face.

"What have you done to her?"

"Nothing terrible, just... mounted her, and... she pushed me down onto the floor. Damn it, I'm possessed by demons. Damn me!" Tan pounded away at his face, which was the size of a basin.

"Yes, you deserve to be damned if she wasn't willing. How can you act like this?"

"Possessed by demons... really possessed. My room is next to your uncle Big Army's, and I could hear them getting it on. The first time I could control myself, but the second time... that Marti... she screamed ecstatically... and I... I couldn't stop myself... damn me, damn... Wu... she dialled one-one-zero... called the police..."

"Serves you right. Get lost. Fuck off. Get out of here, quick. How do you have the nerve to tell me this? You'll get what you deserve. Smelly rascal. Fuck off!"

Daisy elbowed him from her room with a pushing and shoving motion. She then called Princess Wu to ask for her version of events. Wu could be heard laughing in her room until she nearly hyperventilated. She outlined in detail how Tan had sneaked in. Daisy asked her how come kicking him a few times wasn't enough, and why she felt the need to call the cops. Wouldn't that cause repercussions? Wu giggled. "I just wanted to knock the wind out of him. Stinky shit. He actually believed me."

The next thing Daisy knew, there was the sound of an ignition in the courtyard. She lifted the curtain to one side and spied Mr Noodle Head beginning his fugitive flight.

36

The sheer rigour of the present job surpassed anything that Smooth could have envisioned. As it ground on, the behaviour of the painter alongside him worsened. He knew that nobody else was his equal to this task and that as Spring Festival was drawing near, no one would be willing to take over this post. He grouched unceasingly about being underpaid, and his brushwork became slapdash. When the stage designer examined the first curtain, he scolded Smooth for being a potboiler, not an artist. Smooth then tried to explicate his bind. "If you have the balls, go take it up with Director Jin," the designer answered plainly. "If she agrees with you, I'll voice no objection." Smooth was all too familiar with the tricksy Madame Jin. She had no qualms about pelting a musty shoe at a star who underwhelmed in rehearsal, so a manky stage shifter could expect little leverage with her. He grovelled once more and coaxed the painter to modify his work by promising to sub an extra 200 yuan per curtain.

The problems with the stage platform itself, under Big Hook and Monkey's supervision, also exceeded what Smooth could imagine. Big Hook was so wrung out he was ready to quit there and then. He'd had enough of those "grandpas" – senior personnel who wanted others to wait on them with the servitude of far younger relatives. The team was forced to alter the designs time and again. No sooner had they finished welding the base of the platform into a twelve metre by four metre oblong, did Iron Kou pass on the director's injunction that it should be expanded to thirteen by five-and-a-half metres. All the materials had been ordered, so to change course now would be a waste. Furthermore, Kou himself stipulated that the budget was capped and that there was no surplus to accommodate a bigger stage. The director backtracked to the original design, saying she was merely toying with the idea of having more space and that in practice the extra size might affect the performance. Hardly had the crew finished their modifications when they were told by Iron Kou to undo them.

The director then took issue with the incline of the platform, suggesting the gradient be adjusted from 35 to 45 degrees and be capable of moving as a whole, as well as splitting into independently moving sections. Extra money would only be added for the purchase of the motors, with no further allowance made for labour. Big Hook and Monkey were incensed, and they called Smooth over to say that their brothers had laid down their tools and were wanting to head home for Spring Festival. On leaving the curtain-painting workshop and joining them in the shed where the platform was being crafted, he found all his men disconsolate. The place was in a corner of the courtyard, and as it only had an old scenery curtain as a roof canopy, snowflakes drifted in through every opening. In the early days they had kindled a fire in the middle of the shed, using offcuts, wood shavings and refuse as fuel. Once the flames were homely, they found themselves lambasted to their faces by the deputy health and safety officer. He accused them of being lunatics and felons in the making. If they were so keen to end up on a penitentiary farm, he said, they should volunteer directly and not cause trouble for him by risking arson in this courtyard.

The faces and mouths of the team members turned to a kind of cobalt colour. Some jigged around as they worked to assuage the chill. Big Hook caught a cold, which was advancing towards fever. Smooth told him they could swap places, so he would be left indoors painting curtains. Now installed in the other workshop, the leader asked them why they were on strike. He explained how they relied on this troupe for their livelihood and how sabotaging a New Year's performance at this crucial point would seem an act of hostility. It would likely limit their chances of finding work in the future. Just think, whereas top-rank acting talent was hard to come by, stage shifters were not at such a premium. Each day on Shangyi Road alone, thousands were waiting for this kind of work. Having your bowl filled daily was a blessing, for once broken it was not easy to repair. Smooth took up a hammer and started to drive nails into the platform, encouraging the others to roll up their sleeves and join in.

In truth, Smooth was once more in the grip of haemorrhoidal pain. On a secret visit to the hospital, the doctor had advised him that medicine could do little to help, and that lying down and resting was the best therapy. Failing that, an operation would have to be scheduled. But how could he take it easy in the face of the huge workload? He purchased a roll of gauze and stretched a length of it from the front of his crotch to the back, in case the piles started to protrude. That son of a bitch Mound joked that it seemed as though the boss was smuggling a football down there. Smooth was unprepared to disclose the nature of his ailment, since he was aware that everyone in his team had pains of their own. Monkey suffered from a stomach disease, which when it seized him aggressively would cause him to expel sour water through his mouth. His face remained bitterly pale, as if the final drop of blood had been exsanguinated from his body. On occasions, when the pain started to sting, he would bump his stomach against a solid surface, pressing and rubbing it in an effort to alleviate the internal cramps.

Big Hook had a slipped disc, which sometimes left him bedridden. He was still willing to come to the stage even when immobile, arguing that in order to survive, a man must endure hardships. Smooth was conscious that these migrant workers from the countryside were hardy. To lie down and eat and sleep without doing anything in return was anathema to them. A day without work cost dozens of yuan, meaning that a staple daily two bowls of noodles was eating into their savings. How shabby. Factoring in the cost of rent and medicines, they might as well chance it by turning up to work and trying to suppress the agony. It came as some relief that the team had their own tacit agreement whereby if one of them was temporarily unable to graft, they pooled together to see that he did not suffer. For instance, when Big Hook could not bend his waist, they refused to look on as bystanders, and tackled his bulky boxes for him.

In stage shifting, everybody had a clear sense of what and how much they should do. A glimpse could tell how many crates required loading and unloading, how many people were to share in that fee and how much they could make. This was rather like a mute person eating boiled dumplings. In their heart, they knew how many they had consumed, but just couldn't spell it out loud. Mutual assistance was encouraged, though the crew were also attuned to who were malingerers. They would become pariahs, because in the long-term nobody was willing to overexert themselves for the sake of those not up to the slog. For this very reason, Smooth found it necessary to weed a few hands from his team.

If the gaffer himself paused for a rest, no one would begrudge him or argue over it. He was the one who sourced all the jobs, took care of expenditure and wages, and tackled every matter of basic courtesy. Were he to adopt the mantle of a boss, dictating orders without mucking in by carrying boxes and lights, painting curtains and nailing boards, he would still have had the same share of the spoils and not one penny less. Usually, he had no appetite for personal gain. If the host short-changed them, he would only claim the stipend of an average labourer. Should there be a bonus, it would be distributed on the basis of everyone sharing the extra. All was so transparent that those who had followed him for a dozen or more years couldn't bear to leave his employ.

Smooth pondered how, if he had chosen to be a skinflint like Iron Kou, he and his crew would have parted company long ago. Scratching bloody furrows into others' backs to extort more money was not his style. None of them, not even Big Hook or Monkey, were less shrewd than him. As Big Hook had formerly served as a village cadre, it would not be a massive challenge for him to establish his own small crew – perhaps ten strong – to do business. However, would they be willing to work for him and, if so, for what motive? Once he overheard Monkey telling a new recruit that Smooth was deserving of their loyalty for he was altruistic and never did anything contrary to his conscience. Another time later on, a university student joined the team during his summer vacation. On his departure, he informed the others that Smooth's plain exterior belied a tremendous sense of responsibility. When Chief Qu voiced similar sentiments, Smooth could not at first understand what was meant. As time went on, the hint sank in. It was their way of saying that he took the job in hand seriously and strove to treat others fairly. On second thoughts, Smooth believed that this was nothing remarkable. If it could be regarded as something remarkable, then all the capable people in the world would already have poked a huge hole in the sky.

In the process of nailing the boards, Smooth's mind turned back to his teenage years when he stood guard at the vegetable plots. Summertime was not a period of taxing labour. Apart from an overabundance of mosquitoes, being outdoors felt more comfortable than staying at home. In the cool breeze, he could catch crickets and fireflies. When the greenhouses needed security in winter, that was more arduous by far. The chill wind on the hinterland of the Western Capital sharpened itself against people like knives. Each night he went out on patrol with a stick in his hands, protected by cotton clothes and long johns, and a quilt wrapped about his person. Back from his patrol, he thought he was about to turn into a gigantic ice lolly. However much he might massage his limbs, they didn't seem to thaw.

The fields were supposed to be guarded in shifts, with each security guard earning 1.5 yuan per night to cover their meal. At that time, although just a single yuan was sufficient to buy two chicken legs, he was left as the lone watchman. Everyone who started the job complained about its hardships, especially in winter. Some even paid others more than the going rate to avoid their duty on such a night. In his own mind, Smooth was contented and even entertained the worry that this 1.5 yuan could be snatched away from him. Presumably, it was during these years that he cultivated his calm, resilient nature. If others complained that it was too cold to bear, he would reply, "Don't always dwell on the cold. Think of how this is tolerable. Not so very cold, perhaps a little on the warm side. Unless a man feels cold in his heart, his body won't be chilly."

"You think you've won a spiritual victory, like Ah Q in Lu Xun's story," jeered Monkey.

"Never mind what method I used, it got me through those winter nights on the allotments."

"But what era was that when you were working there? Everywhere must have been cold. You wouldn't have had central heating at home. Nowadays, we are used to being able to stay warm, so we feel frozen even when it's a touch cold like this."

"Monkey, your mouth's good at chattering. I'm no match for you. If you do keep on thinking about being cold, you can expect to freeze to death, you son of a bitch..."

One advantage of this workplace was the presence of a heating pipe not far from the side of the outdoor workshop. The outlet was covered with a small, round cast iron lid, and when snowflakes landed on it they melted straight away with a hiss. The snow adjacent to it had banked up to a height of around one inch, so the lid appeared to be wearing an ivory collar. Hot steam gushed from the seam, intermittently drawing the attention of those who worked in close proximity. After midnight, they took turns to warm themselves by the lid. In these half-hour-long breaks, a few would slumber with their head resting on the hot spot, and could not be woken until their bodies were dragged through the snow.

When Smooth's shift came around, he curled himself up like a silkworm, with the lid serving as a kind of platter for his whole body. The curling steam around him created the illusion that he was taking a hot spa.

"You see," shouted Monkey, "isn't that Concubine Yang taking a dip? Oh, sorry, it's Brother Smooth with his bare arse."

"Is Brother Smooth's arse worth a peek?" joked Mound. "If the Emperor Xuanzong was offered that instead, he'd be inclined to hang himself."

All the company thought this was a hoot.

Someone living in the nearby high-rise flung down a stinky shoe. "Laugh, your mother's cunt," their voice cursed. "It's midnight, don't you want others to sleep? Pack of swine."

Monkey picked up the shoe, scanned the tall building, and was ready to hurl it back. Smooth awoke at once and wrested it from him, trying to prevent a flare up.

"The swine fucked your mother!" Monkey fired back. Any further curses were gagged by Smooth's hand, which clamped across his mouth. He could feel that Monkey's lips were like two shards of ice.

"Keep your pussy mouth closed," he ordered, repeating his pet phrase. "Don't stir up more bother." He then went back to the lid to refresh himself.

Not long after Smooth had laid down, in his imagination Iron

Kou came over. Never before in real life had he worn such a sunny smile, and his manner towards Smooth was positively fawning. "Manager Diao, Director Diao," he began. "How can you take a pleasure bath here when dozens of theatres are demanding your skills? Which will you choose first?" Behind him pressed a sizeable crowd, with every individual claiming that their performance was of peerless significance and imploring Smooth to assemble their stages.

"We can do any of them," said Smooth, assuming a semblance of self-importance. "But we must have heating. Otherwise, it's out of the question. Beyond that, we can work overtime until midnight, though never after the stroke of twelve. A deposit of thirty per cent must be paid. That's a precondition. After the stage is installed and has been checked over by the director and drama manager, the remainder of the fee must be provided. That's a further precondition. And one more thing, for lunch and dinner there must be two chicken legs and a bowl of egg soup for each of us. No egg soup, no deal."

To his surprise, all those assembled argued over his preconditions. Iron Kou even spoke up. "General Manager Diao," he said, "I'm afraid the time has come where you will have to expand the scope of your business. Shangyi Road is on course to become the Broadway of the Western Capital, and you'll have to adapt to meet the demands of the market. If you are willing to be the boss, I can be your lackey."

In no time at all the "Smooth Stage Shifting Company" received its business licence and the number of employees mushroomed. Big Hook and Monkey were appointed general managers, with Cai Sufen as director of the office, and Mound and Third Skin the managers of market development and the scenes and props research department. Several times, Iron Kou visited, bearing gifts and pleading to be offered a position. Smooth forgave the events of their chequered history, and willingly assigned him to be Sufen's subordinate.

And so, the headquarters of the Smooth Stage Shifting Company stood proud on the most prosperous stretch of Shangyi Road. The building looked a little like the "Giant Underpants" skyscraper housing the offices of China Central Television. In spite of its comical appearance, it became a landmark in the Western

Capital, with Daisy, Plum and Plum's boyfriend all occupying managerial posts. Oh heavens! Now the Western Capital was the centre of theatreland, with venues filling the big streets and small lanes alike. Subsidiaries of Smooth's corporation became as ubiquitous as express inns, vibrating rhythmically with energy like hornets. Some foreign troupes even approached him through the back door, eager for him to arrange their stages. The business of whether a stage was to be built or not required numerous steps of ratification. It must pass through the subsidiary, Daisy and then Smooth himself. The crucial part was that every component that went into a show in the Western Capital, including those luminaries who trod the boards, must seek approval here. Show business and stage shifting were now the most honourable and modish professions in the city...

Smooth sensed several stiff blows to his posterior and awoke to find they were coming from Iron Kou's outsized leather shoes. "Hey, it seems you've found a pleasant place to sleep," he noted. "That lid's your comfy mattress. Don't you know what time it is? The director's here to inspect the stage." Smooth looked at his watch to see that it was already 7.30 am. He asked Monkey and the others why they didn't wake him. No one answered. He realised that he had got more rest than anybody else. At least two hours on that warm lid. They must have been showing their consideration for the boss by not disturbing him. A warm stream seemed to percolate outwards from his head and toes.

It was comforting to know that Director Jin was satisfied with the platform. She even raised her thumb to indicate that Monkey had been clever in his execution. Only after her departure did Smooth begin to air some grievances before Chief Qu. He alone could risk venturing this face to face. Were Iron Kou in the room, he might be stonewalled with a response like, "If you're finding it too tough, plenty of others are queueing to take your place." So Smooth sought no such confidence with him. Tender-hearted as Qu was, he still cut Smooth short. "Today, we must see that the outdoor workshop is surrounded by a windbreak. A bit of scenery curtain should stop gusts and snow from interfering." He also demanded that Kou procure additional electric heaters so that every worker should have a place to toast their hands. Iron Kou's promise was observed only partly. Two heaters appeared that evening, though the periscope-like outlet of one did not rotate as it should and the other had only a single functional bar. Fortunately, the curtains provided respite from the full-on assault of the elements.

    That evening, Smooth was trying to apply some topical ointment to his anus and secure the area with gauze when his brother phoned. Marti had gone off with his wallet, leaving him at the Arc de Triomphe Sauna, unable to settle his account. Smooth was so affronted that he pelted his phone against the floor with a thud.

37

ONCE HIS REAR END WAS TIDIED UP, Smooth reached for his mobile. Its back cover had been bashed against the iron pipe of the urinal and one component was missing. The battery had landed in the trough, so he rinsed every bit of the device in water and rubbed it against his blue overcoat before holding the lot under the hand drier. The display screen was already pitted with scratches and cracks, to which more were now added.

"Why not get rid of it?" Monkey suggested. "Two or three hundred will buy you a much better one on the black market."

"My dick. What are you chuntering on about? It can still be used, so why shell out two or three hundred on another?"

Smooth had been using this phone for eleven, perhaps a dozen years. Daisy had originally spent more than 1,000 yuan on it, a sum he would never even contemplate parting with if it were up to him. In those days, Daisy had been considerate and, saving up all her loose change, purchased the model as a New Year's gift. He asked her to return it to the shop, though she refused and it became his possession. He didn't mind showing it off, but even a year or two after he was given the mobile, he still emphasised how it was a present from his daughter. Much as he wanted to curse her for splurging recklessly, Daisy's generosity made him glad. As the battery had dried out, he reconnected it to find that it was still functional. The screen flickered on and off, and not all the horizontal and vertical strokes lit up on the digital display. Still, it was not yet dead. He slid it into his pocket and returned to work. He knew it was improper to try to sort out his brother's affairs while on shift. It just so happened, though, that he was short of nails and brackets and he would have to get on his trike to obtain some more.

The Arc de Triomphe Sauna was not far away. Turning into the next street, Smooth found himself before the building. All the vehicles in the front parking lot were luxury brands like Benz, BMW, Land Rover and Cadillac, and the staff would not allow a tricycle to join them, so Smooth rode to the entrance of a narrow lane nearby. The bathhouse was close to his home, though he had never been inside this establishment. At the doorway, he encountered seven or eight female security guards all kitted out in the same aquamarine uniform, with high boots and wide belts. They put him in mind of the SS officers one would see in war movies, minus the holstered pistols. Their bearing and manner were formidable, and these tall females formed a phalanx, standing to attention and saluting visitors. Even from afar, Smooth felt self-conscious about whether to attempt to put his left foot forward or his right. He knew they were not standing to attention and saluting for him, but rather for the male visitors ahead of him. Wanting to sneak in behind them, Smooth's sluggish legs would not stretch out to their full length and slumped instead like a couple of chitterlings that couldn't be made to progress straight or gracefully. He had been raised at the foot of the city wall and believed that he had seen something of the world. For more than fifty years he had been a pedestrian on Shangyi Road, but how come he now suddenly lost the ability to walk? His left leg reeled against the right, causing him to stagger. Those stately female guards could not help giggling. One of them blocked him with her hand and asked him what business he had in being here. He answered in a rather manly tone that he had come to settle the accounts for another customer. The troops looked at each other. These days, even the most improbable things were conceivable. Then they let him in reluctantly and with perplexity.

Once inside, Smooth could perceive what a rampant enterprise bathing had become. Decades ago, a handful of bathhouses had opened for business on Shangyi Road and he had visited all of them. People came to have a bath, a body rub and a shower. In the winter months especially, those leisurely, balmy baths could remove the grease from one's body. When your frame assumed a rich brown hue, you might dive into the water and come out shuddering from refreshment. Sheer paradise.

In his teens and early twenties, he had shared this ecstasy many times with Big Army. In the meantime, admission to the public baths in the community had risen from five cents to fifty, and then to five yuan. He envisaged this as having something to do with the gap between the old city areas and the urbanising villages, and also the disparity between the lifestyles of civilised city-dwellers and those fresh from the country. Those bathhouses on Shangyi Road closed their doors one by one, and in the summer Smooth had to make do with tipping a pail of water over his head. In winter, this was replaced with a heated basin, and he would massage his own body with a towel.

For ages, Smooth had not kept abreast of the times and so missed out on what was considered the fashionable way to bathe. Right now, it was so chilly that he craved the chance to immerse and resuscitate his ice-cold bum, legs, wrought iron back, chilblained feet, hands and ears. It wouldn't matter if the fee was five cents, fifty cents or five yuan. But all those deals were consigned to the past. He had heard that the Arc de Triomphe charged as much as 100 yuan for a basic dip. Further personal services were like the arsehole of a snake. You couldn't guess how far it would stretch into the distance, and the costs might wrack up inexorably. Not surprisingly, he had never frequented this establishment, for his body was not a rarefied artefact put on this Earth to require 100 yuan's-worth of ablutions.

The sight of the private parlour where Big Army was relaxing came as a shock. His elder brother was sprawled out on a massage bed with his limbs splayed in every quadrant and his body occupying the entire surface area of the couch. A foreign girl was kneeling on his back, gibbering away. He later learned that she was Russian.

Smooth could not tell whether he was stark naked or not, for his back and thighs were fully exposed, with a bath towel draped over his buttocks. Since childhood, Big Army had always been a man of great physical stature, yet for a time he lost weight and became as thin as a stalk of hemp, so that it appeared he could be toppled by a stray gust of wind. In middle age he filled out, and on account of his height he never appeared corpulent, only majestically masculine. Today, he was bare and Smooth was reluctant to look in his direction. That back of his had the appearance of a door panel upholstered in leather, landscaped with thick, fleshy and greasy bumps, now collapsed onto the massage bed.

As the masseuse moved her hands, Big Army's flab glistened and swirled before settling back into position. Those naked thighs were almost as thick as an elephant's, the girth neither widening nor receding between his knees and ankles. Smooth doubted that this was a symptom of dropsy. The bath towel gave partial coverage to his bulky backside, and the foreign girl knelt down and then sat square upon it. Her dainty posterior was barely the size of one of his buttocks, so it took a great effort for her to thud, sway, rub and knead away as she tried to steady herself by clutching at the other cheek. "Paff, paff, paff." Suddenly, three cannon blasts came from his crack. The girl pinched her nostrils and turned away, though could not help smirking as she slipped down off her perch.

On seeing Smooth enter, Big Army filled him in on how Marti and Daisy had gone to the beauty parlour next door. He had decided to bathe here, but when it came to needing cash for tips, he realised that his wallet was in Marti's pocket. Given his character, this was not the kind of mishap that required indepth analysis. Smooth asked him how much was needed, to which he replied that 3,000 or 5,000 was sufficient. The flesh on Smooth's body began to quake. His big brother always gabbled away in such a carefree manner. To him, 3,000 or 5,000 yuan might as well have been three or five cents. The sound of those figures made Smooth feel his muscles had been diced and his blood siphoned away.

"So much for a bit of a wash?"

Big Army looked at him and then at the Russian girl, who apparently could not catch their conversation. "You put it down there," said the big brother rather unhappily. "I know money does not come your way easily. I promise to repay you later. You know, it's not convenient for me to ask Marti to fetch some change over."

"Even if you do have money, there's no need to burn it away in places like this," Smooth nagged. In half a century, these were the most pointed words he had ever dared to direct at his brother. As boys, even when Big Army kicked, beat and cursed him, he respected his seniority in age and never once fought back. Later on, his brother lived far more comfortably, while Smooth lost face for him by pedalling a tricycle and building stages. Here today, he sensed there was nothing more he could say in his presence. In the past, he knew that Big Army was fond of such pastimes and turned this into the stuff of jokes. Querying or interfering were not Smooth's style, but spending this amount of money on a mere bath session was not something he could let pass without criticism.

"Go and get on with your own stuff. If you don't have the money on you, it's no problem. I can call Burger and Banger over to sort it out." Burger and Banger were two of his gambling mates.

His brother's response caused him a twinge of embarrassment. Even the way Big Army was mildly annoyed one minute, then seemed able to be understanding the next, made Smooth somewhat ashamed. He was being irrational. Big Army had come back from Macau to spend the Spring Festival in the Western Capital with his useless brother. Were it not for him, this tycoon would be free to bathe, gamble and celebrate the New Year anywhere he liked. There was no need for him to suffer the elements in this northern city for a month. As Marti had put it, people's ears could drop off with cold as soon as they stepped outdoors here. And yet Smooth did not have 5,000 yuan about his person. The contents of his pockets added up to 2,500 yuan, and besides which, he had various materials to purchase for the stage. "I didn't bring much with me," was all he could say. "I didn't think taking a bath could be so pricey."

"How much did you bring?"

"A little over two thousand."

"Then put it all down there for me."

Smooth laid out 2,200 yuan, while secretly retaining three banknotes in his pocket.

"If it's really not enough, I... should I go and get more?"

"Well, well, if you've your own things to be busy with, I'll try not to be so adventurous."

As Smooth was about to leave, he turned around. "Sorry, Brother," he apologised. "I'm painting scenery curtains and building a stage. It's so pressing that I don't have more time to stay with you. When this log jam is over, I'll–"

"Well, well, I see. Just get on with what you need to do. I can extend my stay and make sure we have time. Get along if you must."

Smooth proceeded to leave.

Before crossing the threshold, he heard the massage bed behind him creak as if it were about to collapse. He turned his head around inquisitively and saw how the girl had now flown back up and was nestling on his elder brother's yet-to-be-massaged buttock.

On leaving that place, something lay heavily on Smooth's mind and he could not quite put his finger on what it was. Mounting the trike was an effort again. The snow persisted, making the road surface slippery. He pedalled at a measured speed, tacking purposefully along Shangyi Road to maintain traction. Without warning, a car screamed to a halt. A woman craned her neck out. "Are you looking to end up in a coffin?" she yelled.

The hour was late and the street lamps subdued. He could not make out the motorist's face clearly. Smooth thought she must be cursing somebody else and so scanned his surroundings.

"You, you measly trike pedaller. I'm cursing you and how you ride."

It occurred to him that he might have scratched her expensive car, and so, scared into action, turned into a narrow lane. He could still hear her swearing behind his back. Part of the knack of the seasoned tricycle rider was that, whenever trouble reared its head, one must hit the pedals and duck into some narrow passage inaccessible to wider vehicles. The farther one could retreat, the safer. Otherwise, those in the profession could face twin penalties: loss of time when facing up to accusers and loss of precious income.

Three or four turns about these alleys took him to where Sufen and Third Skin were gluing the fabric backdrops. After a few days apart from his wife, he was ready for a visit, so parked the trike.

38

THE NEW PRODUCTION by the Shaanxi Opera Troupe was designed on a stupendous scale. The fabric backdrops were being pasted together in one of the larger classrooms in a vocational tech school. A classmate of Iron Kou's was the principal of that institution, so had allowed them to use the space during the winter holiday.

Sufen followed Third Skin's supervision as he had extensive experience of this kind of task. At the outset, she was apprehensive and feared botching the scenery. As soon as the designer had demonstrated exactly how the peach blossoms needed to be gummed into place, the simplicity of the operation became evident to her. First of all, rolls of red gauze were snipped into the shape of peach blossoms, then manipulated so they took on three dimensions. Once these had been glued securely, they were affixed to the nylon net, completing the arrangement. The workload, however, was intimidating. The nets were the size of scene curtains, measuring nineteen metres by nine metres, and able to hold between a thousand and two thousand blossoms per curtain. The flowers should be arranged in a naturalistic fashion, bearing the correct botanical density and distribution. The areas of thickest bloom required layer upon layer of flowers. Third Skin, who was tasked with creating the effect of blossoms, branches and leaves on the nets, knew how to evoke profusion. He bought and dyed cotton wadding, which he spread out in large fillets, then poked holes into it. Blossoms inserted into this backing would stand out with a realistic sense of perspective.

When the first curtain was completed, the stage supervisor

praised him for his meticulous workmanship. However, he added that this ought to be positioned to the rear, since the front two curtains were in close enough proximity to the audience for them to notice how he had cut corners. The illusion would be marred if viewers could pick out where the rig was joined together at the seams. And so, the later nets should be characterised by their sheer delicacy and refined execution.

To cut and craft blossoms was a novel task, in particular for the newly hired women. They would whoop and laugh with joy now and again. One of them was mocked for cutting what appeared to be a pumpkin blossom, or a knotweed. Overall, this was light-hearted work, boosted by the addition of a free meal on top of the 100 yuan or so daily fee. Projects like this only came by rarely.

As time went on, their buoyant spirits were deflated. Hands soon broke out into blisters, and the job required them to bend their heads for more than ten hours at a time. This being the winter holiday, the heating in the classrooms had been turned off, and their bodies as well as their hands became stiff with cold. The cutting stage provided an opportunity to sit, but applying the decoration required squatting down. It took a further twelve hours in that position for the gum to dry. The women felt dizzy and came close to passing out on rising to their feet. Worse still, the gum smelt awful and made them almost black out. A woozy Sufen herself went out to retch several times.

Third Skin tried to show special concern towards her, handing her a tissue whenever she appeared ready to gag. He also came to her aid when she did in fact have to go out and throw up. In response, Sufen was anxious about the strange looks people gave them. She reminded him of this when nobody else was around. He continued regardless, even tipping his own portion of fried eggs and tomatoes into her bowl since he heard this was her favourite. This made her so discomfited she was keen to leave. When she called Smooth and asked to switch posts to somewhere else, he reminded her that this was lighter work than most. As there was no means of elucidating her predicament, she was compelled to stay put.

Smooth arrived to find his wife lancing the blisters on her palms with a red-hot needle. Once the pus had been released, they cured rather quickly. Third Skin offered to assist, by which he meant affixing his mouth to her hands and trying to suck away the fluid. Before she had chance to recoil, one of her fingers had been caught between his lips. "It's not a nipple," someone joked. "Don't be so coy." Smooth entered and Sufen wanted Third Skin to stop. As his two hands clasped hold of hers, her husband looked on in bewilderment. "Blisters," Sufen yelped. "Poking them with a needle..." Third Skin raised his head with an expression of humiliation on his face, but her hand remained in his.

"Just carry on," Smooth said. "Give your sister-in-law a good suck and she'll soon get clean."

There was laughter all around, though Smooth couldn't figure out why. Third Skin released Sufen's hand.

Smooth wanted to be brought up to date on the progress of their work. The answers came in a disorderly and random fashion, though he seemed to understand. He unfolded the finished net to study their handiwork. "Rather delicate," he noted. "Good. This time, the troupe is doing a creative drama, a highlights show. After the New Year's performance, they'll take part in a national competition and so we must be thorough now."

"Thorough work calls for thorough pay," someone cawed. "New Year's a-coming. We all have urgent things to do at home."

Following this interjection, everyone felt compelled to chip in. One complained that she had to arrange for her child's engagement, another woman said that she couldn't even find the time to launder the bedclothes for her whole family. They all buzzed like a box of bees, their drone being the same: not enough money!

Smooth's reaction was that it was uncouth to act like a greedy snake, desperate to swallow an elephant. In no respect was the troupe paying them below the going rate and there were no grounds for whinnying for extra fees in the festive season. They should train their minds to where their next meal would come from when this assignment was finished.

He was certain that they would all break out in blisters from the blossom cutting, so had prepared two bottles of iodine and made sure everyone applied a dab to avoid infection. While talking to his wife, he cracked open one bottle and wanted to treat her calluses. The moment he made contact with her hands, he recalled how supple and soft they had been the first time he held them. They were every bit as milky and refined as those of city women who had never done manual work. In those six months she had been at his side, they had roughened to the texture of glass paper. It was not that he was unable to provide for a spouse by pedalling the trike and building stages. The stark reality at home had coerced her into his world of masculine toil. Not only did she bear blisters, but chilblains too.

He was stung with pity as her eyes became bloodshot at the application of iodine. She studied his busy hands in silence. Those fingers were stubby and encrusted with both calluses and chilblains. The moment they were scratched, white flaky residue became visible. Layer upon layer of this coating mimicked the symptoms of psoriasis. For as much as Smooth was an authentic city dweller, one would be hard pressed to find a compatriot who exerted themselves as he did.

"Why don't you wear gloves?" she asked.

"I can't when the task calls for such a fine touch. This is no great catastrophe. Come spring, my hands will recover. This has been my cycle, year in, year out."

As he spoke, Smooth asked her to slip over to one side. He inserted a dozen chocolates into her trouser pocket as he knew she was so fond of them. This was also a usefully calorific snack. She was adamant he should keep a little for himself, though he told her he was not partial to them. Smooth could recall how, as a lad, he and several local boys had been clouted by a storekeeper for pinching chocolates. Now that he could eat them as often as he desired, they no longer held any appeal to him. What he had purchased for Sufen cost forty-five yuan, and he had deliberately left the packet outside, having emptied it of the contents. Since this was a luxury, he couldn't flaunt it in the face of others and risk having to share them.

As he prepared to depart, he stared in Third Skin's direction. "Take good care of your sister-in-law," he called out. The crew guffawed more loudly and wildly, there obviously being an element of unspoken mystery behind their response. Sufen's face reddened all the way down to her neck, and even Third Skin hung his head sheepishly. To Smooth, though, nothing was amiss and he beamed on his way out.

Sufen was well aware that Smooth was a man whose heart was

not clouded by suspicion. For more than six months, she had been engaged in the tasks he earmarked for her. Had he been at all mistrustful, he would have separated Third Skin from her immediately. Finding that the boss was not suspicious of him and the wife, Third Skin became ever bolder. In the middle of the night, when they had been taking it in turns to nap in a storage area outside the classroom, he decided to embrace her and try to kiss her, as nobody was around. She slapped his face, leaving him stunned, and hoped that this might prove a deterrent.

Third Skin's reaction could not have been predicted. Sinking into melancholy, he took her rejection of this kiss as an invitation to go on hunger strike. How would she react if he went two days without touching a morsel? Fearful that their colleagues might infer the cause of the problem, and that this would snowball beyond control, she decided to carry his meals to him in person. She did not even resist when he tried to slip her his fried eggs and tomatoes. When it came to the emotional setbacks between men and women, Sufen could certainly not claim to be any kind of novice. Still, it occurred to her that this little headache had the potential to evolve into something pernicious.

39

DURING THIS PERIOD, Daisy became rather fatigued from chaperoning her uncle. He was indeed "upper crust, generous and sumptuous", yet at the same time random-headed. In the vernacular of the Western Capital, "random-headed" referred to a person who was impulsive and never thought about the consequences of their words or actions. Someone of this disposition would make ostentatious arrangements with scant concern as to what the ultimate result would be. The day after Uncle Big Army had given her a crisp, neat run of 20,000 yuan in banknotes, Daisy became the cash dispenser, covering all of their expenditures wherever they went. That money was soon gone, and she expected a top up. However, Big Army was either at the gambling table or drinking, or else asked her to take Marti to a salon while he did something unspeakably shady. She was afraid that her uncle might splurge every last yuan he brought with him, leaving her in arrears. And so, whenever her uncle asked her out these days, Daisy would always concoct some excuse. She switched off her mobile when mealtimes were approaching, and only kept company with Big Army when he came around in person and escape was impossible.

Another source of irritation was how Princess Wu tried to pester Daisy to persuade Big Army to take her to Macau as a way of furthering her career. This is what Daisy had long coveted for herself. In the past, her uncle had mentioned such a possibility. Smooth stood in her way as he knew he lived off the proceeds of gambling and in his mind that was not a decent profession. What would she do if she found herself with nowhere stable to settle down? She realised that her uncle was full of hot air and that he wouldn't have taken any steps towards enacting a plan for her. Things just ran on without incident.

Prior to this visit, her uncle's contact with home was at best sporadic, and though he might get in touch with Smooth, his younger brother had no way of returning calls. Either his phone was turned off or the number he supplied was indecipherable. Daisy had thought of travelling to Macau and seeking out her uncle following Smooth's remarriage. She gave up for want of any line of communication. This time, when Big Army was reunited with her, she was eager to bring up the topic of her father, though there never seemed to be an opportune time. When Marti was present, in particular, there was no way she could steer the conversation. Then, one day, a chance arose when they visited the Old Airfield for a barbecue.

Big Army regaled them with tales of how he had grown up eating Old Airfield kebabs. That sounded rather incredible since he was in his late fifties, and the establishment appeared to go back barely three decades. Great as the changes to the city had been, Big Army's recollections were vivid to the ear. The cabby who drove them was new on the job, so was uncertain about which route to take. Big Army could reel off place names on the way, so their destination was soon reached.

By now, the Old Airfield barbecue was a renowned local delicacy in the Western Capital, and its name had been appropriated by a slew of stalls in the city. Daisy was an avid fan of grilled meat, though rarely ate such choice and dainty cuts. "Who would haul themselves all this distance for a handful of skewers?" she remarked. Big Army related how once, after a game of mahjong, they would nibble the kebabs at the Old Airfield until the break of day. If anything, this place deserved to own the name of barbecue, for its meat was tender and fresh with no off cuts. It was grilled to distinction with a dash of invigorating cumin, sesame oil, hot paprika and a single clove of garlic.

As Marti headed off to powder her nose, Daisy began to share her idea about going to Macau with her uncle. But to her dismay, he pretended not to hear a word. The venue may have been boisterous, but not sufficient to smother out all she said. Daisy's confidence was dented and yet she repeated herself verbatim, knowing that he could not recycle the same excuse. Now he nodded without expressing anything negative or affirmative out loud. His head movements were perhaps directed towards the grill master for he never relinquished the premise of being upper crust, generous and sumptuous.

Marti rejoined them. While munching on barbecued meat and swilling beer, Big Army shared with the grill masters his deep memories of this place. "Has the 733 Military Unit been wound up? What about the factory, Yan Guang? That was such a famous military unit. If you didn't know somebody on the inside there, you had no chance of getting past the gates. It manufactured aircraft engines initially, though branched out into washing machines and electric fans..." As he spoke, he sounded increasingly intoxicated. Daisy and Marti had no way to transport him home, and all the cabs declined to pick up a pisshead. Daisy had no option but to call Tan Daogui, otherwise known as Mr Noodle Head. He was the only one willing to undertake the mission.

The spectacle of the night before went unmentioned. Daisy was perturbed. She intentionally avoided Big Army when he called and invited her out.

Princess Wu had fended off Mr Noodle Head's nocturnal advances, which infuriated her friend. Still, after returning from Zhen'an, Wu didn't manifest any great aversion towards him. Whenever he phoned, she would go out and play and eat with him with Daisy in tow. It felt as though not one guilty thing had transpired and she couldn't understand her old soulmate Wu. She was perplexed by her attitude towards him.

If Wu were eventually to marry someone like him, it would be truly astounding. Daisy's motives for dwelling on this issue were far from chaste. Her own life was a twisted farce and so it would be consoling to see Wu ruin herself with Fatty Tan. Such a fall and with somebody so irredeemably unprepossessing would relieve her misery over having no fiance of her own. Daisy wanted to withdraw from being either Big Army's chaperone or their third wheel. Letting them have more time in each others' company should serve to better cement that ghastly bond.

Instead, Daisy redoubled her spirits and energy into the dilemma of Plum.

Recently, Plum had tucked herself away at home reading books. Now and then she left the house to find some materials relevant to her studies. Daisy could overhear the calls she made to classmates on this subject, and as her neighbour came and went, she pricked her ears to try to discern what was going on next door. Plum set the audio volume on her computer to low. Save for a rare bark from the lame dog, barely a single decibel could be detected from the calm and peaceful haven Plum had made for herself. In Daisy's eyes, this was a provocative counter manoeuvre, for there was that saying about how still waters run deep. The elder sister was uneasy. When her uncle failed to answer the question about taking her to Macau, that needled her into a more combative mode, and home was the arena where this would be unleashed.

Now stirred, Daisy knew that change was inevitable. To her, having somebody slumbering in tranquillity so close by was enraging. Early one morning she came across the dog sunbathing and took it on herself to boot her down the stairs until the poor creature was seized with cramp. Goody had heard the creak of her door and was already reeling, though could not gather enough speed to dodge her onslaught. In her defence, Daisy claimed the dog had defecated in front of her door at either Smooth's or Plum's command. As Smooth was not at home that day, who else must have ordered this vile prank? Wasn't it as obvious as spotting a louse on a bald man's head?

Hostilities were resumed.

Daisy had prepared herself mentally for the latest bouts of attrition. She even unfurled her arms in the knowledge that she was older than Plum and physically stronger. That kid had frittered away too much energy on trying to maintain a waiflike and delicate body. To Daisy, she was some kind of malevolent imp who could be floored by a stray breeze. Having tested her mettle in the last conflict, she was confident that as long as she primed herself, victory was assured. What was more, hers was a just war, for she was the true blood heir, albeit of a down-at-heel family. How could she suffer to see other women divvy out, scratch away and plunder the meagre savings of her father? In their community, brothers had battled bitterly over a stake in inherited property. There were matters in this world where merely talking and being fixated on losing face could not facilitate a settlement. Ultimately, those who channelled their strength would overpower the puny, and simply sidestepping any potential altercations would serve no advantage. The latter was bluster to her. As Uncle Scar would say, "A man ought to be high-handed. When one is high-handed, even the American imperialists can be driven into retreat." Daisy had primed herself, though Plum was decidedly uninterested.

Plum rushed down and took hold of Goody, staring daggers at Daisy above them. Then, with her shoes half hanging off, she charged out of the gate, howling, "How evil!"

Daisy had learned all the machinations of Big Army. She heard those words and yet feigned partial deafness. "What are you nagging about?" she scolded. Plum was apparently far away. She was furious and descended the steps, locking the iron gate with a loud clank. Flakes of rust fell from the distressed metalwork.

Once back on the upper floor, Daisy had intended to return to her own room. Curiosity drove her to snoop around Plum's little haven in the hope of finding any evidence that could serve as a pretence for attack. Surveying the place, there was nothing of interest, save for the computer, a few old books, a quilt and a portable heater still emitting warmth. She kicked the switch and the two bars in the element died. Her envy was roused by a row of photos. Shot in a studio, that pipsqueak bitch did have the look of Audrey Hepburn. Although the prints were recent, the use of sepia emphasised the resemblance, as did her hairstyle and the charming and winsome positioning of the eyes. The nasal bridge was so high that it radiated brightness.

Daisy was on the verge of seizing the scissors from the table so as to gouge out those seductive eyes and disfigure the sculpted nose. She stopped. That bitch had shown no will to retaliate, so this was the wrong time. She spat at the faux Hepburn and kicked the heater back on. Skulking back to her own room, she thudded down heavily and impotently on her mattress, then kicked her stilettos so they whacked against the ceiling. She did not know what she wanted to do and had no plan formulated. A half-bottle of wine sat on the table, so she picked up a goblet with the intention of sipping it with all the finesse and class of a movie actress. But instead, she took up the bottle and swigged down half the contents with aplomb. She then slumped back comatose, alcohol now being her preferred sleeping draught.

The iron gate banged and clattered, Daisy wasn't sure quite when. On waking, she thought instinctively that the pipsqueak bitch had returned. However, the sound was not hers, and she soon sensed it was her uncle. Looking down from the balcony, she could make out that Big Army was among company. He had led workmen over to replace the aged gate.

"Hey, Uncle. What are you doing?" she shouted.

"Must be some heavy sleep. You barely noticed strangers making off with your own front entrance! What am I doing? You see how manky and broken this gate is? It couldn't keep sheep out, let alone burglars. I'm giving you the finest gate in the Western Capital."

"But the entire home is manky. There's nothing worth protecting against burglars. Why choose the best?"

"Hey, how can you talk like this? Your grandfather always said this broken-down house was worth tens of thousands of taels." Had these words been spoken by anyone else, they might have carried a touch of solemnity. Coming from Big Army's tongue, Daisy found them downright comical.

"What are you laughing at?" her uncle continued. "In your pa's eyes, this is the Kremlin, Buckingham Palace, the Belém Palace and the White House. Didn't you know that? Had he the money himself, he'd install barbed wire mesh, buy a strapping hound and hire bodyguards." To begin with, these words were meant in jest. The workmen installing the burglar-proof entrance were tickled. Daisy withdrew, unwilling to carry on talking at the mention of her father's name.

The existing gate, rotten as it was, fell to the ground with a shove from the workmen. As Big Army had told them the dimensions accurately, installing its replacement was no great feat. He tried to chat with his niece as the operation was progressing. Daisy's lofty impression of him had taken a nosedive, though. Upper crust, generous and sumptuous he may be, but that had nothing to do with her. She didn't even brew him a cup of tea. Big Army fished out a 100 yuan note from his pocket and asked one of the workers to buy a box of mineral water. As it was the dead of winter, the bottles were left untouched. Big Army uncapped a few for himself before suddenly bringing up Daisy's request to go to Macau. "Hey, you said you wanted to accompany me there, didn't you?" he asked. "How about after Spring Festival?"

"Ah really?" Daisy thought her ears must be deceiving her.

"How could I be lying?"

Twenty years seemed to peel away from his niece's age, and she jumped over to him and clasped his hands. "What can I do there?" she asked.

"Do whatever you like," he stated simply. "If you don't want to do anything, just sponge off your uncle."

"Really? I can help to manage your finances as your agent. I can cook as well."

"Do whatever you like."

Elation took grip of Daisy so that she felt on the cusp of soaring away on invisible wings. Her age and appearance vanished as hurdles, as she pirouetted about like those "tiny cygnets" in a kindergarten dance class, her body half squatted to the ground. Her hands arranged themselves into the graceful "orchid fingers" pose she had learned in the opera troupe as a girl. She clapped, too, in the manner of a highborn lady, her palms never making direct contact. Even the workers were aghast at her junior showtime antics and cast their eyes towards the floor.

At this point, Plum strode into view with the dog in her arms, face still mortified. The two women would likely have torn into each other were it not for the presence of Big Army and the workmen. Daisy was tenderer than earlier, her uncle's invitation having initiated the first stage of defrosting her heart. Finally, she had the intimation that she might be able to cast aside these unseemly surroundings, that is to say the lair of a tricycle pedaller. Only a few minutes earlier, she had been pensive, wondering where she could reside if she left this shithole. Now she could recline on her uncle's broad back, and so this place and its contents held no value to her. The other two poor cows could compete for all that, if they so wished.

As she was thinking along these lines, Plum and Goody reappeared. For Plum, everything had altered incomprehensibly. Daisy strutted forward and fondled the dog's scalp. "Little thing, how could you do that outside my door?" she mouthed with apparent sincerity. "How could your bowels flap open like that? I just moved ever so gently, and you got so scared, so scared, ever so scared, didn't you?" As she repeated the phrase "so scared" with increased volume, she pretended to scratch the pet's nose, pat its head and stroke its mouth. Goody became so vexed that without warning, she reared her head and bit at Daisy. Had Daisy's reflexes not been so sharp, her fingers would have ended up clamped in the canine's jaw. But she refused to show anger. Rather, she prolonged this show of kindness, teasing Goody some more. "You're so fierce," she cooed. "You carry on, carry on." Her performance left Plum genuinely flummoxed. Perhaps it was a charade put on for the benefit of the assembled guests. This behaviour was most unlike Daisy. Unwilling to stay any longer, she just exchanged greetings with Big Army and climbed the stairs.

"Your sister doesn't seem so happy today?" Big Army asked after she was gone.

"She's a tiny thing, but with a towering temper."

By this time, the gate was already finished and the workers had left. Daisy wanted to treat her uncle, and Big Army suggested that Plum should join them. Daisy picked up a copy of the new key and went upstairs.

Since Plum was accustomed to her elder sister trying to evict her in her tirades, she had not anticipated being able to gain admittance with Goody. Daisy appeared to have been changed along with the gate. Further surprise came when she brought her the key in person. That really was akin to the sun rising in the west. Plum declined to go out with them, for as a family member by adoption she felt incongruous. Even when Big Army came up to try to cajole her, she maintained she felt uncomfortable just at the moment.

Daisy was reinstalled as her uncle's enthusiastic companion. She gripped his arms even tighter than she had on his first return. His grace and gravitas were tangible to her, and strolling along the pavement like this was bound to win second glances from passers-by. She leaned her head against her uncle's shoulder and held his arm more firmly than Marti. "Be gentle, be gentle," he said. "Your uncle's arm is starting to feel cramp." At this, he withdrew her grip, and his arm twitched like a chicken's foot.

40

WHILE ON THE JOB, Smooth browbeat Iron Kou about the fee for building the temple stage. His tone and words were carefully weighed, for he could not afford to be either too tough or too timid. Spring Festival was only ten days away, so kids had started to let off firecrackers as a lark. Smooth's heart was discomfited as though it were being jabbed with a stick.

As Chief Qu was on the scene, there was no need to vex himself about receiving the forthcoming money from the troupe. The temple project stuck out like a swollen pustule. Big Hook and Monkey had been pressuring Smooth to receive their wages. The pair asked him to leave aside his painting and wheedle Kou to see what further lies he might spin. They maintained that the money was necessary to pay their fares to return home for New Year. Smooth jiggled along as he walked, for his anus was in agony. Chasing after Iron Kou wherever he went, he was fended off with accusations of being greedy and brazen, together with the threat that he would offer no fresh work to him. Perhaps it was that Kou hadn't been paid by the temple? He made Smooth fidgety by adding, "The monks still have a warrant out for Mound. How can I press them for it? If you think so highly of yourself, why not send Mound over with the invoice?" Smooth was so infuriated that he kicked Mound's behind, making him yelp.

The set-making had nearly drawn to its conclusion. Smooth had already spent the allowance of 12,200 yuan given to him by the finance section. Big Army promised to repay it in full, but he hadn't yet found the time to meet his elder brother and arrange the reimbursement. Given who it was that was concerned this time, Smooth was steeling himself to call this another loss. On reconsideration, his brother had never taken money seriously in his life and it was far wiser for him to keep hold of what he won by blood and sweat rather than let Big Army fritter it away at Uncle Scar's place or the spa. This was no small sum, and it was hard-earned indeed when one had to work with a prolapse.

Smooth felt it improper to ask for money directly, so he phoned his brother to verify his whereabouts. Big Army answered that he was having a lie in at his hotel. Smooth insisted on visiting him, since the pair had spent such a paltry amount of time together since his return. Big Army being willing, the younger brother made a point of first dropping by at home and changing into a fresh outfit. Plum opened the new gate to him and told him it was a gift from Big Army. A warm current ran through his heart at the realisation that his brother could pay such attention to fixing the family home. He pedalled his trike to the vicinity of the E'pang Palace Hotel and parked it in a bicycle shelter. Smooth spent over 200 yuan on fruit as a present. These were varieties that normally he wouldn't eat. It was his custom to swing by the stalls shortly before the shutters came down and purchase whatever bruised, broken and withered specimens were about to be discarded. How could he now be choosing such eye-catching produce? Still, it was his brother who was visiting all the way from Macau. As he was accustomed to living so lavishly, how could Smooth begrudge him a smidgen of hospitality?

He entered the hotel trembling and approached the door to his brother's suite. Big Army opened up after a protracted bout of knocking. He was clad in pyjamas, though his thick, pale legs were on show and he was yet to give his face a rinse. This was a spacious suite, replete with a sitting room and bedroom, the door of which was still sealed. Likely Marti was in there, resting. Smooth arranged a selection of the fruits on the table, expecting them to be received with words of politeness. "You can take them all with you when you leave," Big Army suggested. "Marti won't touch these. She only eats imported fruit. Leave them here and they'll be a perk for the domestic staff." Smooth was deflated.

The room was roasting. Within the space of a few minutes, the visitor was perspiring heavily, and his brother invited him to remove his coat. This jacket formed the upper half of the suit Plum's mother had tailored for him, and which he reserved for these few days at Spring Festival. His sweat did not abate, however, since the room was far too sultry. Glancing at the thermometer, it registered 26 degrees, compared with minus 7 outside.

Smooth couldn't bring to mind anything to share with his brother. It was much the same when they were boys. His brother was a kind of hedonist, always questing after fun. Smooth didn't have this inclination, and when the other kids went to fish with iron wires in the River Ba, he would stand further up the bank, guarding their clothes and shoes. Other times, when they configured a human pyramid in order to pilfer apples, pears or apricots, he would be left at the bottom of the heap, and be rewarded with fruit that had already been discarded by the rest. Then, when others hid among the vegetable patch to kiss or play "one stack upon another", they would ask him to stand guard and whistle should anyone pass by. He had joined their playtime without ever actually playing. Later, he refused to participate at all, in spite of Big Army's coaxing. As they grew towards adulthood, there was no overlap between what each brother took pleasure in. Often, Smooth just fell back into the role of listener.

Today, he happened to initiate the conversation. "How come you fitted me a new gate?"

"The old one was on its last legs. The iron had festered so badly you could knock it down with a single kick." Big Army put the kettle on for Smooth.

"There's nothing valuable in there. If anybody did kick it, they wouldn't find enough change inside to pay the cobbler to fix their shoe."

"When did you learn to be so mealy-mouthed? You weren't like this when you were pedalling a trike all day, but have grown this way now you're a boss."

"A boss? Just a hardworking fella. Even those actors wouldn't see me as fit to pick up their shoelaces."

Big Army knew what was meant by picking up somebody's shoelaces. It referred to chores done by a young errand boy or girl for their master. What his brother was implying was that stage shifters occupied a far more menial position in the opera field than even those humble assistants. He poured out half a bottle of mineral water into his cup and topped it with several ice cubes from the freezer. "You see, you're so hot," he observed. "Fancy some iced water?"

"No, it's the middle of winter. That'll do my tummy no good."

Big Army smiled. "Has your life become so precious?" he asked. "When we were small, we never had a taste of hot water. We'd just stick our mouths straight against the tap and twist the handle." He took a sip of iced water and sat down opposite Smooth.

"That was cold water, not freezing cold." In fact, when they were parched, Smooth and his colleagues did still sometimes treat a tap like a teat.

The room was silent again. That was until a delicate, charming voice chimed in. "Mister," it crooned, "I want some water."

Smooth had learned a few words of English in primary school and still remembered that term of address, "mister".

His brother got to his feet and carried a cup of water into the bedroom.

Smooth noticed how Big Army had really filled out. It took two goes for him to raise his body from the couch.

"It's too hot," wailed Marti. "Turn the heating down a notch."

"OK." He could hear his brother tapping at the LCD screen. "Isn't it time you got up?"

"Sleep, just a little more."

Smooth looked at his watch and saw it was almost noon.

His brother returned to the lounge, closing the door and lowering himself back into his former position, but not without difficulty.

"Brother," said Smooth, "you ought to slim down. What's your weight now?"

"Two hundred and thirty pounds. Not so easy to shed the flab. I am always sitting down or staying up late."

"You must try dieting. Excess fat is not good."

"Sure, when I get back. How's your health?"

"Fine, oh, fine. Always the same." He fidgeted while offering this response, for he was sweating and feeling a stabbing pain in his rear end.

"Aren't you a bit on the lean side? Do you eat enough meat?"

"I eat whatever's going, and it doesn't affect me one bit."

"Your brother wishes he could be trimmer, but it's a struggle. Marrying that wife of yours must have been a good thing. Remind me of her name."

"Cai Sufen. Yes, she's pleasant and not afraid of a bit of hard work."

"You have an eye for pleasant and pretty women. Prettiness goes a long way."

"Well, no matter how pretty they are, once they're hitched to me, they'll never be without a dusty head and cheeks."

"Is Daisy not on good terms with what's-her-name?"

"Cai Sufen. Well, we just carry on. What's done is done. Since she arrived in my home, she's been very busy."

"I'll find time to talk with Daisy. This can't be allowed to go on. She can't keep on resenting her pa's choice. You just carry on with what you're doing as long as you're content." Big Army stressed these sentiments rather earnestly.

"Oh, it's not a case of contentedness or otherwise. I ran into her. Will she stick by my side in the future? Who can tell?"

"What's that girl's name? Your second wife's daughter."

"Plum."

"She's personable, and a looker with it."

"Personable, yes, and college educated."

"The key thing is to find a suitable husband. Nature's blessed her. Try to offer her more chances, let her travel and see more classy places."

"In my position, how can she get to visit classy places?"

"Take it easy. Kids these days know how to get around. Let them have a few trysts and they'll gather so much about life and society." Smooth could not reconcile himself to these comments. How could he let his own child weather affairs and repeated heartache? He had known the tribulations of marriage, so how could he not wish to spare his daughter blind suffering? His brother always behaved like a chicken that had no idea what it was like to be a duck. He thought he should reply, though demurred.

"Let's do it this way," his brother went on. "After she graduates, she can come to Macau and I'll set her up on a new track."

Inside, Smooth fumed at the thought of an innocent being finagled into the company of an inveterate gambler. Try as his brother might to cultivate a plush life, he could not look upon him with admiration. Better that Plum follow a trike pedaller like him than be dragged into idle dissipation in Macau. Still, he kept silent.

His silence did not go unnoticed by Big Army, who took two gulps of the iced water. "Daisy was a little..." He tried to broach a new topic. "Hasn't she found a fiance yet?"

"No."

"When she was a girl, she was less plain than she is now. What's gone wrong? Growing old seems to have been unkind on her looks."

"Brother, please don't go there. Daisy complains enough as it is about being my daughter. She tells me stories about the daughters of such-and-such boss or high official. They were plain like she was before, yet matured into beauties. She blames her appearance on me being a trike pedaller. How can you say these things?"

"I'm just telling you straight. How can I call her plain to her face? You must give her more attention and not always set your mind on just shifting stages. It's urgent that you find her a good family to marry into. Otherwise, staying at home all day might send her crackers."

"I've asked plenty of people. It's far from easy."

After a pause, Big Army resumed. "Daisy is keen to go to Macau. She asked me about it a while back, but I didn't give her an answer. When I saw how unhappy she was, I made her a promise. On second thoughts, there's no guarantee that if she went down there, she could live as cosily or as idly as she does now."

"Brother," Smooth interrupted, "there's no need to concern yourself with such things. Don't take her with you. I'll tackle this myself. Once the cart reaches the hill, it will find its own passage. Maybe the frozen river will melt by itself in the future." Inwardly, Smooth was certain he could not let her go off with him. His older brother had spent his whole life in disreputable pursuits.

"Well, you're already in your fifties, mind. How much longer do you count on pedalling that tricycle? You might be able to flex your legs a few more years, then follow me over and live out your days in peace and calm. We two brothers can share our old age together."

These words at last gave Smooth a sensation of gratitude. It was not the first time he had made promises. Prior to leaving for Macau, he once vowed that when he made his fortune, he would construct a big mansion in the foothills of Mount Zhongnan. Each brother would occupy half and share a swimming pool. The garage would accommodate four cars. Smooth had forgotten the rest and never really gave it any further thought. What heartened him was that his elder brother always kept him in mind.

Big Army suddenly grasped Smooth's hands and stroked the layers of chilblains, crisscrossing cracks and calluses. "How can you work with hands like this?" he asked. This was not a pair of hands that most people cared to look at, let alone inspect and caress. Try as he might to straighten them, his fingers remained bowed, and when they were extended fully, they shook as if they were bearing some heavy, invisible weight. Big Army stroked and rubbed them. To Smooth, his brother's hands had the texture of cotton and instead of bones, there was more silky soft, enveloping flesh. Smooth wanted to withdraw his hands, but Big Army would not release them until his massage was complete.

The elder brother was ready to rise, which once more took two attempts. He ambled to a safe and typed in the pass code before opening it. Inside was sheaf after sheaf of banknotes. Smooth's heart thumped. He had come in pursuit of 12,200 yuan, but their time together made this request seem mean and imprudent. It was far from simple for his brother to come back, so how could he have the face to demand his outlay be returned? He wanted to let go of the topic and leave, but then his brother revealed that bounty.

Big Army removed five stacks of notes. Bending down to gather them, he let rip three times. His flatulence had a clear, crisp, unabashed ring to it.

"Take it. I didn't buy you anything when I returned here. Fifty grand – that should be enough to give your daily life a shot in the arm. It can serve as a congratulatory gift to my young sister-in-law too." Big Army did not mention the 12,200 yuan specifically, but what he was offering far exceeded that sum. Smooth now thought himself stingy for having dropped by in person like this. He dared not look his brother in the eye lest he see how flushed with embarrassment he now felt.

For whatever reason, he was reticent to accept the gift. Smooth tried to push it away and make for the door, but he forgot to pick up his suit jacket. Big Army's dragging and pulling were difficult to resist.

"Do you take your brother as a stranger?" he asked, becoming rather indignant. "This money's nothing. Just the kind of loose change I lose in one night. See how hard it is for you to accept a few pennies? Take it, or I'll fling it out of the door after you."

Smooth knew he was hard pressed and tried to agree on just 10,000 yuan. Big Army was in no mood for debating and crammed the five stacks of bills into his hands, pushed him outside and closed the door with a slam.

Smooth heard further blasts from his brother's rear.

He stood by the door for a while before gathering the money together dexterously and setting off back in earnest.

Outside the hotel building, a man with no legs stretched out his bowl, pleading for alms. Smooth dropped in a one yuan note. On turning around, it dawned on him how pitiful the man looked. He slipped him another five yuan. A few steps further and he turned to see the beggar was kowtowing to the sight of his back. Returning and bending down, another ten yuan was pressed into that dirty bowl. Normally, thirty or fifty cents felt a reasonable amount. Today he was flush and hadn't been forced to toil hard. It was only right that others should share his windfall.

41

THE DRAMA FOR WHICH SMOOTH AND HIS TEAM WERE PREPARING was entitled *Peach Blossom Cheeks*. The rights to the libretto were bought from a third party and it was said that the troupe parted with half a million yuan for them. Since they were perpetually involved with the theatre, the stage shifters knew that the "script was the core, that great drama would ensure". Chief Qu maintained that finding a good text was the toughest part of theatrical life. One might scour the nation and be surprised what scant pickings were to be had. Through the help of his chain of friends, the troupe had secured the present script, which was the work of a southern playwright. It was about a romance in the ancient Western Capital.

In spite of leaving school after Year 10, Smooth did know of the Tang Dynasty poet Cui Hu and as a teenager had watched the opera *The Gold Hairpin*, adapted from his verse of the same name. In recent years, a local form of opera called Old Qiang had grown in popularity and taken this story into its repertoire. Veteran actors found great merriment in being able to thump bricks and pound wooden benches as they sang its rambunctious numbers. Rumour had it that the players had been invited to tour abroad, and Director Jin mentioned in her speech how films and TV serials had borrowed from Cui Hu's work. The poem in question was only four lines long, so dramatists could imbue it with their own sense of fancy. Playwrights occupied an elevated place in Smooth's imagination, with his own preference being for "bitter tragedies". He never tired of watching *The Story of Chen Shimei*, *Snow in Summer*, *The Orphan of the Zhao Family* or *Zhang Jibao is Struck by Thunder*, each of them prickling his tear ducts. Monkey would jape that "the prostates in his eyes are playing up". *Peach Blossom Cheek*s was purported to belong to this genre too, and in rehearsal the actors became overly emotional, struggling to shrug off the sentiment of the plot. Smooth was itching to see it being performed.

Only one painted curtain, depicting the "Snowy Peach Tree Slope", was left to be finished while a single fabric backdrop, "The Weathered Branch in Deepest Winter", required embellishment. The sections of the platform had been assembled somewhat skew-whiff, though appeared to meet Director Jin's technical demands. They could not be opened or closed very swiftly, and did not coordinate well with the fast or the slow stage directions. Time was at a premium and no rejigging was possible. Iron Kou cursed and snarled that everyone should put the stage into position.

The crew had endured successive late nights and Smooth's swollen and aching arse resisted all his old wives' remedies. He went to the hospital repeatedly to have it cleansed, and the doctor warned that without rest, it would become infected and weep pus. This advice had to be ignored, since the stage work was now like a runaway stone roller on a downward slope. He couldn't bring it under control even if he wanted to. He was so busy that the heel of one of his battered leather shoes was torn away by the platform, and, having no time to mend it, he had to limp around. Iron Kou berated him for being slow and slipshod, asking if his swaying body and flighty mood were down to him, having swallowed an ecstasy tab. Smooth knew that the time had come for the "troika" of the production team to convene. The stage designer, actors and orchestra must all assemble. The tempers of those who had responsibilities, whether significant or trifling, would be on a hair trigger. Smooth had warned the team to be resilient if they found themselves being hectored or abused. Even if the emperor's mother died, they had affairs before their faces that needing managing. As long as nobody was flayed with a dagger, they should serve patiently, submitting to their lot as stage shifters.

The project continued for a further three days and nights, with those who flaked out lying down on the rows of seats at the back of the stage, taking a curtain cloth as their duvet. The stage manager, designers and supervisors alternated in shifts to allow each other several hours of rest. Only Smooth and his colleagues worked around the clock, with even Big Hook, the brawniest among them, becoming bandy-legged and mute out of fatigue. Smooth could see Sufen's eye sockets becoming recessed and her hair messy. He suggested that she go home for the night, but she would only allow herself the same amount of nap as the men. Smooth spread a piece of curtain fabric over his wife and humped a lighting box backstage. As he was turning around, he glimpsed Third Skin laying his greasy army coat on her as a coverlet. To his mind, that young chap was really attentive to his "sister-in-law".

Chief Qu stayed up late with everyone on the final night. As the New Year was so near at hand, there was much bitching among the troupe. Iron Kou could not browbeat them into action, so it was left to the chief to stay there for the duration with a mug of tea in his hand. Qu was accustomed to late night vigils at critical moments, but this overnighter was unprecedented. Usually, he could be persuaded to head home at 3 am at the latest. Tonight, he heeded nobody and stayed put until daybreak.

Smooth exchanged many rounds of words with the chief. Mainly, he stressed the taxing nature of the present job. His principal gripe was that as Spring Festival was approaching, should there be any dispute about securing the full fee, he would have no way of placating his co-workers. Lately, Smooth had heard talk of a shortfall. The troupe had spent lavishly on the drama, with the funds from on high being far from adequate. Some staff had begun to fret about their end-of-year bonus, and once the ripple effect took hold, others became furious and resentful about being involved in this production. One guy from the props team, who was in charge of shoes and hats, kicked the bole of the peach tree on the backdrop. "My dick, how did we get dragged into this shitty new drama?" he raged. Those in Smooth's crew were unsettled by the mood among the staff in the troupe. They were afraid that any financial constraints could put their service fee in jeopardy, and not for the first time. They urged Smooth to speak out, to confide in his retainer Chief Qu.

On listening to these concerns, the chief was rather irritated. The section head had just reported a brouhaha among the troupe. The male lead from Group B was complaining that only Group A had been given the chance to rehearse, and took exception to being asked to perform a walk-on part for them. He asked for leave. The diva cast as Peach Blossom resented having to step in as a supporting maid, for she said that it caused her to lose face. The ladies-in-waiting found their number cut from four to three, as did the extra quartet of walk-ons.

"You want me to wear a frock?" Chief Qu thundered. "In future, we should refuse to give leading roles to those who won't lower themselves to doing walk-ons too. You tell them that word-for-word. It simply isn't on."

At this very moment, Smooth tried to cut in with his problem.

"Who told you that you wouldn't get your service fee?" the chief answered bluntly.

Smooth wiped away the ice-cold drop of saliva that had flown from the chief's mouth onto his own lips. "No... nobody said it," he tried to explain. "I was just... raising this casually."

Temperamental as Chief Qu was this evening, Smooth could feel in the clear about the service fee. He turned around to Big Hook, Monkey and the others. "Close your pussy mouths tight shut and get on with the job," he shouted. Everyone realised that detente had been reached between him and the chief.

The "troika" now came into play.

Smooth and his team had learned so many lessons. As the festive season was close, preparing a grand spectacle was bound to unpick a mass of contradictions. For starters, Director Jin clashed with the lighting division. As the lamps were being adjusted the night before, she felt underwhelmed. There weren't enough ceiling lights, and the blossoms didn't glisten in effulgence. Master Ding ignored these criticisms and merely added two tracking lights at the ends. Actually, everyone knew that he was dissatisfied with his share of the troupe's budget. The 150,000 yuan he would garner for outsourcing his services dwarfed the pittance to which he was now entitled. This production swallowed up months of his time and enthusiasm. Rumour had it that in taking on *Peach Blossom Cheeks*, he was forced to turn down a far more lucrative deal. That would have seen him organise a huge New Year's evening party for a renowned enterprise, netting something in the region of 200,000 to 300,000 yuan. Maybe he had tried and failed to negotiate a way out with Chief Qu, leaving him disconsolate and working as though his head and face were somehow dislocated. Smooth was so on edge around him that he instructed all his men to seal their pussy mouths. Iron Kou and the catering division prepared fried beans, according to Ding's wishes, and even bought in beer. This did nothing to alleviate the core problem. Chief Qu was incensed and his face flickered periodically from ashen to dun and back. Director Jin, meanwhile, was restrained, though she suspended the rehearsal until the proper adjustments were made.

Chief Qu had to flatter and sugar Ding with his words. Smooth overheard him promise that if a few personnel were shortlisted for the title of Expert with Outstanding Contributions, he would guarantee that Ding was the victor. After that, the Maestro wore a face as long as an ass and called upon Monkey and his assistants to readjust the ceiling and bar lights until Jin was heard to exclaim, "Well done!" Unexpectedly, just as the lamps had been fixed at the right angles and in the correct positions, and the orchestral conductor had mounted the rostrum for tuning up, a shout came from the backstage. "Oh, my dick," it yelled. "The leading man isn't here."

The chief, who was sitting to the side of Director Jin, asked how could this be. All the company dancers, who had been wriggling about the stage in the posture of peach blossoms about to bud, sat up and gazed around to see what the head would do. The team leader moved to the fore. "Cui Hu caught a cold," he said. "He's on an IV drip in the clinic outside the gate."

"Why an IV drip so early in the morning?" asked Jin.

"He was dead set on it, so how could I stop him?"

"Didn't he know it's the 'troika' this morning? The stage designer, actors and orchestra are all here and waiting."

"How could he not know? He wouldn't have been put on a drip if he didn't know."

Everyone chuckled. All eyes were on Chief Qu to see how he would respond. His look became serious. "Make him come over at once," he ordered.

"How can he come here with an IV bottle?" the team leader asked.

"Bring that thing with him," the chief said flatly.

That instant, all who were present were feeling nervous, but sensed that the outcome was bound to be interesting one way or the other. Those who had been scattered around and were chatting at the corners of the stage and in the orchestra pit grew flustered. Quietly, they fumbled about beneath the stage in twos and threes, trying to find out how the show might proceed.

Smooth, too, was stirred by this turnaround. For so long they had been nauseated by the showy air and manner of the leading players. He himself knew every secret from the years of being in the company of those in artistic and literary circles. Should the head of a troupe abdicate responsibility, there was no means of remedying the situation. In many ways, it was like screwing with one eye open and one eye closed. The big names owed their stature to the perception that they were irreplaceable. In the old days, there was a saying that "a troupe with one prima donna will make its head a goner". Wily heads recognised that the success of a production rested on having a pair of leading men or women on hand for each opera. Otherwise, the situation would be unmanageable. One of the pair being absent meant the performance could still go ahead, whereas relying on a single protagonist put the manager in a bind.

Nowadays, the fashion was to divide the troupe into a Team A and a Team B. Sometimes, a C would be added as well. The leading player in Team A was regarded as the most bankable performer, since if the troupe was keen to gain renown and notices, they put the most talented actor out first. As soon as he had garnered fame, he became like the meat inside a dumpling. Nobody dared try to make this dish without him as the essential filling, and it was only natural for him to assume airs thereafter. In turn, others stewed with envy, simultaneously admiring and despising those big shots who accrued elevated professional titles, a big apartment, public fame, heftier bonuses and the most outsized red envelope to glint under the moonlight. What was more, few of these individuals had much schooling and so were not tutored in the etiquette of restraint. When they were tired and sensed they were not being pampered enough, they would turn on others as though they were minions, firing off questions like, "Who is it you think keeps you fed and watered?" This attitude was inflammatory, and so when they made a fuss in the troupe over something large or small, it inevitably swelled into a crisis. Everyone was on tenterhooks, wondering if the head would dismiss their protestations by saying "tough shit" or something similar. Smooth routinely allied himself with Chief Qu, so couldn't take such challenges lightly.

All the assembled were waiting without noise for the appearance of the protagonist. In situations like this, the director would use the time to explain the roles of the other actors. Today, Director Jin sat firm, as if she were carefully creating a mood of suspense for the appearance of the leading man. Almost everyone glanced surreptitiously at Chief Qu's face. A few of those alongside Smooth were less than restrained with their tongues. "Let's see how Old Qu deals with his 'grandpa'," said one. "Well how?" asked his companion. "Massage? Massage the guy's balls and make him cosy. Or else he'd only flash his dick." Finally, somebody rushed in and made eye contact with everyone, pouting his lips as a sign. The "grandpa" was on his way.

Even the orchestra pit became silent.

The leading man swept in, a drip line attached to his left hand and his right arm inside the sleeve of a beige overcoat. The rest of the coat was draped over his body, and a scarf was wrapped around his head. His clothing couldn't help but put Smooth in mind of a pregnant woman. Flanked by two apprentices, one steadied his arm as the other carried the drip bottle and steered its frame. This big shot did not make eye contact with anybody, simply taking a chair by the door. He coughed heavily several times, causing the one clutching his arm to pound therapeutically against his back. Next, someone quickly closed the door that had been left open.

Once more, all eyes focused on Chief Qu, and Smooth's heart beat with a thump. Were he the head, he would have found a nook in the earth in which to hide. Chief Qu was in no hurry and walked in the direction of the primo uomo. "You see, Old Qu is going to massage his grandpa's balls," a bystander next to Smooth quipped. He, in turn, wished that he could press forward and hear how Qu would deal with this gang of ghosts. Smooth could only look on anxiously, for rising and drawing any nearer would seem inappropriate.

Chief Qu felt the star's forehead with the back of his hand and then pinched his temples and crown.

"Is this what we think it is?" the voice next to Smooth piped up again. "Is he about to massage his balls?" One of the mockers slid off his chair with laughter.

The chief bowed his head very low and continued to knead the actor as he talked with him. Smooth thought this somewhat lamentable, for whereas Qu was not far from retirement, the other fellow must have been in his early thirties. His manner of pleading came across as both cringeworthy and mean. More than a hundred people were waiting for the chief to display his "cutting power". From time to time there was a bum note from one of the instruments, which elicited peculiar laughter.

Smooth came across Iron Kou fiddling with his mobile in a corner. He stood up and poured out two cups of water, pretending that one was for himself. The other he carried over to Kou, who humphed in acknowledgement. Smooth then positioned himself in a flattering way alongside him. The topic of his chatter soon advanced towards the fee for the temple party.

Kou glanced sideways at Smooth. "If you press me any more," he threatened, "I'll stop trying altogether. You see, I've gone there begging for money rather than offering donations. Is that so easy? Besides, you haven't exactly flexed your own dick to help matters, have you?"

Smooth slapped his own face quietly and apologised again and again.

"Well, don't try pulling your tricks on me," Iron Kou warned impatiently.

Smooth could not find anything else to say. Maybe the heating in the pit had come on unannounced, for he became conscious of some kind of stench emanating from his own body. Kou turned his head away, which Smooth took as a signal to get up and leave.

Smooth surveyed the auditorium and could see his wife sitting in the back row, looking perplexed about the situation. He walked in her direction. On catching sight of him, Sufen asked quietly, "Is the big shot not even afraid of the chief?"

"Now you see, the big shot in the group can play the grandpa. He's even more superior than the chief."

"Your piles are better?"

"Much improved." In fact, there had been no improvement whatsoever. Smooth knew his condition was deteriorating, though wanted to spare her the worry. At the present time, he was too preoccupied to be concerned with the pain.

"The drama will still go ahead?" Sufen was rather upset as she looked on at the gaggle of people in the pit.

"Take it easy. As long as Chief Qu is here, everything can be ironed out." Smooth used these words as a cover to conceal the turmoil in his own heart. The crux of the matter was that time was tight. If the dress rehearsals could not be completed before New Year, the troupe would naturally withhold their service fee because the task was left unfinished. As he had dealt with the troupe on countless occasions, he knew to trust Chief Qu to spread lineament on the gaping wounds.

"Ready to begin!" shouted the chief on cue to Director Jin.

The next thing Smooth saw was the apprentice detaching the drip line from the leading man's hand.

Warm applause eddied through the pit.

Smooth was mildly elated and thought to flash his thumb in Chief Qu's direction. Before he could, there was a call from Daisy. Sobbing, she related how her uncle had gone without telling anybody. To aggravate the situation, he had left massive gambling debts. Right now, Big Army's mobile was not in service.

42

DAISY WOULD NEVER HAVE EXPECTED that the "upper crust, generous and sumptuous" Big Army Diao could leave without saying a word to anybody. He had given her 20,000 yuan for sundry expenses, but her whole outlay amounted to nearly 30,000 yuan, leaving her with a deficit of about 10,000 yuan. As she would be heading for Macau after New Year, there was no cause to worry about money. She parted willingly with her savings, not anticipating that her uncle would abscond. The 10,000 yuan was just for starters, since he also owed gambling debts to Uncle Scar, who presently would send hands to search for him. She could only call her father because, as Big Army's brother, he was next in line.

Smooth raced back home after receiving her call, and, upon interrogating her about what had happened, Daisy wept and scolded her uncle. The allegations could very well be true, but since Big Army was Smooth's brother, those curses and criticisms made him feel his own skin was being pared away. He had to cut short her nagging, for a stabbing pain was coursing all around his body. Daisy found the whole business insufferable. She segued from admiring Big Army for being "upper crust, generous and sumptuous" to lambasting him as a "swine, shiftless and a parasite of a liar". Without pausing for breath, she re-branded the "timeless hero" as the "timeless clown". Her cursing went on to the effect that he was "a bullshitter, a swindler and the biggest arsehole in the Western Capital". Given her ferocity, Smooth might very well have been forgiven for believing that he was the one who had wronged her. A bloody, angry fire flickered in her eyes as if she had become a flamethrower in an old movie, which was now directed at his face.

He tried to concoct words of mediation, even suggesting that perhaps his brother might still be in the city, having just switched hotels. Daisy then asked why it was necessary for him to turn his mobile off and for Marti to do the same. She had been to the hotel and discovered that the couple had ordered a car to the airport. Smooth tried to get through to him as soon as Daisy rang. No reply. Funny, since this was not his brother's style. Daisy then reported how she had heard from Uncle Scar and his gambling clique that Big Army had lost more than a million yuan, all of it taken on hock at exorbitant interest. Smooth was forced to believe that all of this could be true. He intended to stay at home to comfort his elder daughter, yet Big Hook called to say that Iron Kou was fuming backstage over his absence. He fled in a panic. On his way out, Daisy was still screeching. "This is your business," she pronounced. "You must square up with me for your brother. What a piece of shit!" This was followed by the sound of a flowerpot toppling down from upstairs. A dull thud was audible from the ground level. Smooth had heard this kind of noise before, only this time it was very loud. He surmised that she had dislodged his pomegranate plant, which he had been tending for more than a decade.

A fog of uncertainty now cloaked Smooth's mind. Owing to his brother's departure, New Year would be rendered less meaningful. In these preceding days, no matter how taxed he had been, the thought of his brother waiting for him at home provided a stimulus. There would be a rare reunion to look forward to, not only in the form of a fraternal meeting, but he also knew that Daisy was habitually obedient to her uncle. The thought of this made him unreasonably excited.

The current turn in events soured his mood. He had visited Big Army at his hotel in the hope of recouping that 12,000 yuan of public money and without any anticipation of a 50,000-yuan windfall. In his deepest guts he had been a reluctant recipient, but then again his brother, in all his generosity, ejected him from the suite and refused to accept the cash back. Since then, Smooth had been pondering over what New Year's gifts to purchase for his elder brother and his young bride. He even discussed the matter with

Sufen, who figured that since they were loaded anyway, no present they could choose would have much of an impact on them. It was during these deliberations that Big Army sprang his surprise.

Upon leaving the house, Smooth tried his mobile again, only to find that his brother's number was switched off. Next, he answered a call from Uncle Scar. "Smooth, what kind of a dick is your brother?" he rasped. "Gives the appearance of being 'upper crust, generous and sumptuous' but far too tight. Doesn't he know it's taboo to borrow cash at the gaming table? They lent him some readies for the sake of your Uncle Scar's face, but then he blew the lot and crawled away with his arse in his hands. Such a fucking shit, no? You grew up right here in front of me and he moved away for a while. How could he turn into such fucking crap? If he can't afford to cut his losses, he should have a word with me. All he can do is fart uncontrollably as if he thinks he's the president of the World Bank. In the end, he farted dumbly and sneaked off. What a fucking loser! Let me tell you, he might have fled, but his little brother is still here. New Year is around the corner and everyone wants what they're owed. Find your brother or find a means of dealing with this yourself. If not, don't blame your Uncle Scar for being unfair. I've lived in this community for nigh on seventy years and never smashed anybody's wok and stove. Today's the Festival of the Kitchen God, and your wok and stove may not be safe!"

Smooth quickly promised to try to track him down, but couldn't be made to take on the responsibility for his brother's debts. As far as he knew, there was no law that made a younger brother liable for what an elder sibling owed. While saying this, he knew that whoever crossed Uncle Scar in this life would never again be able to reside in peace and safety. He now felt positively cursed, as though he himself was spread so thinly that he couldn't even be made to form a layer of distemper on his own household walls. Now, Big Army's return had brought more shit his way. He lost the energy to pedal on.

The weather turned, and it started to snow. These were not actual flakes, but had the texture of grains of rice, which stung pedestrians' faces with a smarting sensation.

No sooner had Smooth arrived backstage than Iron Kou's curses begin to fly. "You son of a bitch. Think you're a big shot now, putting on airs? How dare you skulk away when we're doing the troika today? You think you're a somebody? Director Jin just criticised the petals on the first and second peach blossom curtains. They're too dense and need to be thinned out right away. Where did you up sticks so we couldn't find you?"

Smooth swiftly replied that he had some business to attend to.

"This troika is the day of judgment," he continued. "How dare you let your own business interfere? Scrabbling about for your mother's pussy or whatever. Director Jin just cursed me."

Smooth bowed and apologised to him. Big Hook related how Director Jin had indeed unleashed her towering temper. She observed how the backdrops were not glued properly and the scenery curtains were so roughly finished that they might have been the handiwork of a county town troupe. Everybody knew that her hackles had been raised by the leading man who protested that he was out of sorts during the rehearsal. When she asked him to repeat his lines, he was reluctant and projectiles ended up being hurled. Director Jin was again resorting to veiled abuse. In fact, Smooth could recall how, when they were adjusting the lights last night, she had praised the scenery. This was some reversal.

"She's just throttling a chicken to warn the monkey," Big Hook said.

They all knew that at this tense juncture, nobody could afford to offend the leading man. He alone was off limits, so the rest of them were fair game. Once he felt incensed, the trouble would only spiral inexorably. Awesome as Jin's directorial abilities were, she still needed to vent her anger by victimising either the understudies or the stage shifters.

Smooth's solution was to address himself to Director Jin directly. He might be able to reassure her that he had not ventured far and was actually awaiting her next injunctions. She should not be allowed to form the impression that he was lax or hapless, or willing to forsake his post at such a critical point. At the same time, he ought to permit her the chance to express her fury. He knew that she was a great cannon of a woman and that once the ball of iron had been well and truly expelled, she would revert to her more pleasant disposition. Diligent as she was, she could be relied upon to offer hints on the work in progress and lobby the troupe for a little extra for the stage shifters. In fact, the troupe didn't observe her advice on the last point, but Smooth was still touched by her effort.

He admitted upfront that he had been in error, though lied by saying he was in the toilet. He had been forced to squat there for an eternity because his stomach was uncomfortable. As he had missed her volley of criticism, he was here now to receive his due portion. She screamed at him to begin with, though he sensed that this was actually for the benefit of those up on the stage. Otherwise, such volume was uncalled for. "So you're really somebody now, Smooth? You even dare to shirk away from the troika. Don't you know this is art? Don't you know it's an artistic creation? This isn't going to end up as a jumble sale, don't you know?"

"I see, I know. Director Jin, it's all my fault. I'm to blame. You'd have every right to spit in my face. I'm to blame because I clung on to a shred of pride. Last night you praised our painted curtain, so I became a touch complacent. I admit I'm to blame and am willing to criticise myself." Of course, Smooth had an ulterior motive in pivoting to mention the praise she had doled out last night. He was afraid that if Jin stressed the flaws, Iron Kou might take it out of their labour fees.

Today, however, Director Jin's attitude was rather curt and unkind. "Those painted curtains are poorly made," she said. "Last night, I wasn't seeing them in conjunction with the face paint and costumes. This morning, I could take in the full effect and realised how dull those curtains are. They clash with the scenery front stage. Old Qu, do you hear me? What Smooth's men have done is not up to scratch. You can't pay them in full for that scenery as it stands. Perhaps you can reconsider if they are repainted properly."

Smooth was ready to collapse to the ground in anger.

Director Jin clapped her hands and the next run-through began. Smooth stood by her for some time. Once she was swept up in a stage spectacle, she became insensible to anything else. Perhaps craving tobacco, she slipped a felt pen into her mouth.

Unconsciously, she tried to light it with a Zippo several times. Smooth offered her a real cigarette, which she accepted as if it were a pen and attempted to scrawl on the script. He then scurried away, afraid that he might somehow trigger a further outburst.

Smooth saw that Chief Qu was sitting behind her, so he

approached him and explained that the director had in fact praised him last night. The chief was not in a good mood either, so advised him to button it. Smooth retreated to a corner, cursing himself and his own pussy mouth, acknowledging that he shouldn't have pestered Jin just now.

The rehearsal continued apace, as other issues flickered through Smooth's mind. Every last one of them was serious. If there really was to be a penalty for the painted curtains, he couldn't give his brothers their entire salary for the New Year. He had entertained the thought of using the money from Big Army to sub them all. Then, there was the matter of covering the debts demanded by Uncle Scar. And there was still no news about the payment from the temple. Within three days, everyone was expecting to leave with cash in their hands, and he was clueless how to cover each expenditure.

Smooth was struck by the intense heat of the pit. He was sweating all over. Normally, he would have watched the performance in silence. Today, he had no such inclination. He just wanted to sneak out of the emergency exit and stand in the snow for a while. No sooner had he crossed the threshold when there was a cry, "The motor's lopped off Monkey's hand!"

43

IN ADDITION TO HIS WORK WITH THE LIGHTING TEAM, Monkey was also in charge of the articulated part of the stage platform. The director had insisted that both separate portions of the stage and the whole entity were able to move freely. The electric motor malfunctioned constantly, so Iron Kou thought to draw Monkey away from the lights to oversee the platform.

In the third act of the play, Cui Hu and Peach Blossom were supposed to chase each other and cavort. All of a sudden, the moving platform shuddered to a standstill and the leading lady was nearly flung from the stage. In order to salvage the situation, Monkey sped over and wrenched the leather belt from the motor. Equally abruptly, the platform jerked back into motion and one of Monkey's hands was dragged into the gear. With a sharp howl, he lost consciousness beneath the stage.

Big Hook and others carried their gore-soaked friend to hospital on the back of a trike. The examination in Casualty revealed that four fingers had been fractured, the middle one most grievously so. As it was impossible to reset, the consultant recommended amputation. When Monkey was asked for his consent, he agreed, figuring that it was something of a relief that it was not the most used of his appendages.

Chief Qu followed the party to the hospital and encouraged the financial officer to do likewise. With sweat falling from his head in torrents, Monkey managed not to release a single yelp of pain, instead beaming with a smile more tragic than any frown. Smooth's heart felt like it had been pierced with an awl. As the nurse carried away the amputated limb on a tray, one glimpse of it was enough for Smooth to lose his composure and slump to the foot of the wall against which he was leaning.

As he squatted outside the operating theatre, he cupped his head in his hands. Chief Qu patted him on the shoulder. "I'm so very sorry," he said in consolation. "How could this possibly have happened?"

Smooth grasped hold of Qu's hand. "My brothers are so pitiful," he lamented. "They put their safety on the line for a pittance. You just think about it. Grafters must rely on their hands. Losing a finger to us is like an actor having his vocal cords ripped out. Monkey has both young kids and old parents to support. Where does that leave him in the future?"

Smooth realised that he was exaggerating to be emotive. Among his team, there were those who had lost a thumb or an index finger, but they could still pedal a trike and shift stages. These labourers lived under the threat of being felled by accident or injury. So far, Monkey had been a lucky one among the unfortunates. All the same, Chief Qu held Smooth's hand firmly and apologised again and again, reassuring him that they would provide the maximum compensation as permitted by the policy.

Monkey pleaded that Smooth must not phone home on his behalf. He feared that such a call would cause distress and amplify the severity of the incident. Smooth then offered to let his wife take care of him on the ward, but Third Skin said this was no task for a woman. The business of his bodily functions would be too undignified. How could she carry his drip bottle and look on as he peed or emptied his bowels? Was it proper to help him pull up his pants? Smooth agreed with Third Skin's rationale and suggested he could stay as well. When Sufen got wind of the arrangement, she told Smooth her presence wasn't needed and she would be of more use on the stage.

Her husband stood firm. With New Year around the corner, the injured Monkey would feel better for Sufen's care. She could attend to him and prepare three nourishing meals a day. If the hospital facilities were inadequate, she could cook dishes at home. Monkey should in no way be allowed to sense that his boss put profits ahead of welfare. Sufen smiled and said that at last he was referring to himself as the man in charge. "Ah," sighed Smooth. "I recruited him. Now he's lost his finger, how can I act like a turtle and pull my head back into my shell?"

Before Smooth had left the hospital, he received a ferocious call from Iron Kou. He pointed out that there was no need to have so many people over there. The troika was hard to run with so few personnel. They must remember that a number of orchestral players were drafted in especially from outside at a rate of 200 yuan per day. Hiring twenty musicians pushed the costs of the accompaniment into thousands. If one considered the stage shifters, the outsourced designers, the cost of the dry ice and the snow machine, the troika required tens of thousands out of the budget every day. The director endlessly changing the settings and the actors' stage calls meant that the positions and the sizes of the sets had to be altered ad nauseum.

"You can all die in that damned hospital since you don't give a fuck about the stage," Kou seethed. "Leave me over here to act the doormat. Still pressing for what you're owed, Smooth? Dream on, fucking dream on. If you don't come back right now, you son of a bitch, you'll not get a single coin from me. Just you wait and see."

Smooth replied that he was coming, and Kou hung up. Monkey's hand was horrifically injured, and apparently Iron Kou thought it had nothing to do with him. As he cycled back, Smooth dwelt on just how cruel and loathsome he was.

The streets were already teeming with festivities for New Year. Pedestrians were undeterred by the shimmering flakes. Parcels of every size could be seen as people lifted merchandise onto their shoulders and weaved in among the spacious streets and confined alleys. Certain places Smooth found impassable by tricycle. He drew his thumb to sound the rusted bell on his handlebars, producing nothing but a series of numb clicks. Bystanders gawked in irritation rather than giving way. A few kids thought to affix a kind of Catherine wheel known as a "country mouse" to his empty cart. The whizzing firework startled and repelled those in his tracks. They dodged away and broke the encirclement.

Back on the stage, a hush fell. Smooth could only hear the voice of Director Jin growling through the microphone. He was reluctant to approach Iron Kou and relate how Monkey had undergone an amputation. Not that Kou was in any mood to listen. "The director is giving us a fine tongue-lashing," he said under his breath. "Listen up with your dead sow's ears." Smooth took up his position at the corner of the side stage.

"...Barely a single one of the sections understood what was going on between the lines of the script. I'm not just blaming the stage management division. They were too sloppy, too careless. If they'd thought ahead and taken it seriously, couldn't this bloody mess have been averted? I've stressed again and again that painting scenery and creating sets should be done with feeling. Don't just waggle your toe in the water. Look at those 'finished' sets. Some of them aren't even in proportion. What was going on with the supervision? Did you just have your minds on the money? You can't expect to earn a thing by churning out this crap. Thinking artistically and thinking materialistically are two different things. An artist is not a businessman, nor can a businessman become an artist. Is Smooth here?"

On hearing his name mentioned, Smooth was so frightened that he nearly sank to his knees as his legs started to give way. In a fraction of a second, all eyes were on him.

"Get up there to the front of the stage!" Iron Kou commanded.

Smooth dragged himself in that direction. As soon as he reached the entrance to the stage, someone shone the spotlight on him. This was a special piece of equipment imported from Germany and intended to draw attention to the hero and heroine. Smooth had carried that very lamp with great caution into the lighting slot as they assembled the stage.

Some of those in the orchestra pit tried to add levity to this dressing down. Copying the signature tune of a TV talk show, they played *The Japs are Entering the Village*. Laughter sprung up from both on and below the stage. From within that spotlight, Smooth could see nothing clearly and struggled to shield his eyes. "Director Jin, I am here," he tried to report in an official-sounding tone. Before the last syllable came out, the amplifier in the pit had emitted a loud creaking sound that made him shudder. More laughter followed.

"Smooth, it isn't that I want to single you out for criticism.

You've been in this field for ten or twenty years. You may not claim to know much about art, but you do know a thing or two, at least compared with the rest of us. You often give me suggestions about when something isn't quite pretty enough or if a beat has been skipped. If I do acknowledge you know a little about art, you turn vacant and just think about the pennies. Whenever you deal with anybody, you start to worry that your labour won't be paid for in full or on time. How can you apply yourself to stage art with that mindset?"

Smooth nodded. "Yes, yes, that is fair criticism," he agreed. "My weakness is that I am prone to talk about money. I should correct this in the future."

His words were received with more giggles. Smooth could not bear to be singled out and made to look so awkward. As he was retreating, the spotlight followed him to the wings and impromptu music once again provided an accompaniment. The new tune was *I Really Want to Live Another Five Hundred Years*.

The chill atmosphere, which felt like a bomb was about to detonate, was gone. Aided by Smooth's outlandish style of entrance and exit, the director had stirred the theatre into a glade of dancing bees and wheeling butterflies. However, he himself remained doleful, as though his heart had been somehow deflated with a jab. The balance of blame was apportioned to the set makers. Through all their hardships and protracted ordeals, they might have succumbed to insanity or illness without the prospect of financial reward at the end of it. Fair enough, if people wanted to pursue art they could become an artist, accruing apartments and titles, and serving as representatives and committee members. What were Smooth and his kind after? Were it not for the scale of the duress, they might have been able to breathe more freely and discharge their duty with greater diligence. As it was, they were driven so hard that they didn't have the room to fart. Twenty days-plus without sound sleep rewarded with the severest cursing and scolding. Smooth's heart had become a tangle of icy knots. Why should they be willing to expire on this lonely road of shifting stages? If their superiors begrudged them making money, then why persevere at all?

"I stressed to you again and again," continued the reproving voice of Director Jin down the mike. "Read books about the Tang

Dynasty. Learn something about the material and spiritual lives of the people of the Western Capital in those days. Did any of you do that? This drama tells the love story of the famous Tang poet, Cui Hu. Our goal should be to let the audience experience life back then in its every dimension. But nothing in what you've come up with sets this apart from the romances of princes and princesses in the Song, Ming or Qing dynasties. I told you that you can think of the Tang Western Capital as being like New York today. People came from more than three hundred states and countries to make their home here. Fifteen per cent of the whole population were foreigners. They didn't come along for the sights. No, they found wives or husbands, started families, traded in properties, and set up singing and dancing troupes, acrobatic companies and orchestras. Some even sat the imperial examinations and became government officials here. What an open-minded, cosmopolitan place! Just think how free, romantic and unrestrained society must have been, and what imagination and creativity people surely had! Such a pity! You went into this like a turtle pulling back its head. There's only two words for this: pitifully sad. It's really pitiful and sad..."

When Madame Jin reached this point, the actor playing Cui Hu stood up and left in anger. The head of the team could not stop him. His parting words were, "Whoever else can play the role, let them try. I'm not willing to wait about here!"

With the male protagonist gone, the stage became chaotic. Director Jin was perhaps unaware of his departure and did not let up with her verbal cavalcade about all things Tang.

Smooth was too antagonised to linger about the theatre. This time, his hurt was genuine. No sooner had he left through the eastern exit of the building than he heard snatches of a conversation between Iron Kou and Chief Qu. "You shouldn't take it on yourself to be so kind," Kou was saying. "Chief Qu, a contract has been signed, and if an accident should happen, it's their responsibility. At most we can cover the medical costs. Anything beyond that means we can't operate in the future."

When the chief witnessed Smooth passing by, he made no answer.

Smooth did not speak either and continued straight ahead.

"Watch where you're scurrying to," Iron Kou shouted. "Director Jin might start fuming and cursing again."

"Fuck this rehearsal," Smooth said. "The leading man has quit." With that, he tramped across the snow-covered ground without turning back.

Chief Qu and Iron Kou both froze with shock.

44

EVER SINCE BIG ARMY DECAMPED WITHOUT WARNING, Daisy's spirits slumped. She had pinned so many of her aspirations on him. A few years back, when news of his ascendancy in Macau reached the community, neighbours urged her to follow him. Try as she might to phone her uncle, no connection could be made. Rumours spread, some to the effect that he was in police custody and others related how he was an all-conquering magnate. Anecdotes placed him at the wheel of a Maserati down there, with a foreign girl in his arms and servants aplenty to open and close doors. In short, nobody from that neighbourhood had surpassed Big Army in the outside world.

After his recent return, Daisy could drink in the glamour and swagger of his lifestyle, but was also privy to his wanton spending. He wouldn't nod his head in agreement to begin with, though her dream of going to Macau won emphatic support in the end. This had been her towrope out of an abyss, not least because she could now shake off the stigma of that trike-pedalling father of hers. But now, not only had her travel plans been thwarted, but a good deal of her savings were gone, too. All this bile she directed towards Smooth. Her contempt for Sufen and Plum diminished somewhat since the trip to Macau was all about self-betterment, and to shrug off thoughts of these two local turtles was surely good for her health. With the fading of her dream, this conflict once again drew more sharply into focus.

Cai Sufen was clever and followed Smooth day and night like a Pekinese, wagging her eager tail behind him. Daisy found no chance to interpose. Meanwhile, Plum remained at home around the clock, feigning an air of entitlement that implied she had the same rights and position in the household as Daisy. She would read English vocabulary aloud, listen to music, and watch films or TV shows. Sometimes she smiled to herself in her room, laughing with the crispness of a pealing silver bell. Humph. How could this be known as a "silver bell"? All of her music tracks were so tender that it made her want to recline in somebody's arms. What was more, the crackling of her decrepit computer provoked Daisy and made her want to dash over and snap the neck of this nuisance neighbour. The older sister pondered every means to drive this pair of sluts away. This was not done on behalf of the family property, since that was really not worth the mental exertion.

Having those two grains of sand ground into her eyes was irritating enough. The sight of them gambolling away plunged her into despair. Her life now being a study in monochrome, she could not stand the vibrancy apparent in others. She remembered how a philosopher once said that "hell is other people". She was not sure of the full connotation of this sentence, yet its object was striking. Her "others" consisted of those two women. Although she was a natural misanthrope, this pair had an egregious influence and spurred her to moan. Were she not to pour out her rage, boredom would set back in and she would yearn for all the cheerful people in the world to live as piteously as she did. How Daisy hankered for that psychological redress.

She suddenly felt it was time to show her hand to Plum. That dwarf couldn't be banished from the family unless the conflict was driven to an extreme. She must deploy barbarian strength to make the unyielding bow flex into action. Thus, she devised a plan and then invited over one of her former classmates who worked in interior design.

Daisy rapped at Plum's bedroom door with a confidence and purpose that evoked a landlady seeking long-overdue rent.

As her elder sister had been rather friendly of late, Plum opened the door with a smile and asked, "Sister, what's up?"

Daisy's demeanour implied that her mission was non-negotiable. She led her classmate inside and began to make gestures with her hands and feet. "Put a door here," Daisy indicated. "My room can remain as the bedroom, and this will become the sitting room. Install a flat-screen TV here with a drop box. A closet can be made here and a shoe cabinet there. I think rounding off the ceiling is far better on the eye than leaving it square. The door can be widened as well, with the lintel forming a semicircle..."

Goody, who had been behind her mistress's ankles, realised that their visitor had malevolent intent. She tucked her rear under the bed and craned her neck out to scan the room with vigilance.

Plum understood this to be a direct invasion, and could see that her room was being trampled over. Her eyes grew bloodshot. Daisy, by contrast, appeared to be flouncing around her own territory. On leaving, she casually turned off the ceiling light.

"What are you doing?" cried out Plum.

Daisy cast her a disdainful glance. "I'm getting married," she said. "And sorting out the house. You can stay here until the fifteenth of January, and then you are evicted."

"What do you mean?"

"What do I mean? I am getting married, so need the space. You're not required here any more. Don't you get it?"

Plum's face became blue with anger. "What do you mean?" she kept on repeating.

"Don't pretend you don't understand. That's twenty days' notice. Enough for you to find someplace else." She slammed the door.

After Daisy saw her classmate off, Plum came out from her room. This time she was the first to speak, having obviously braced herself for this exchange. Still she repeated the same question, "What do you mean?"

"How you love to waste your breath. You might as well ask that same question a thousand times. What do I mean? You've lived in this room rent-free for years. It's high time you moved your nest. Clear enough now?" Daisy's tone was firm and blunt.

"On what grounds?" asked Plum, contorting her face.

"On what grounds? On the grounds that you have nothing to do with this family. I'm protecting my rights."

"Don't you know the letter of the law? I've been living here legally and reasonably. How can you hope to do this?"

"That's actually easier said than done – 'legally and reasonably'. At the beginning, Smooth Diao showed you pity as a flask of burdensome oil. Your mum died long ago and any relationship you have with us went with her. You ask for a reason? The Diao family has shown you charity, raising you until the age of eighteen. The truth is that from the ages of six to twenty-one or twenty-two, you sucked and squeezed the last drop of milk from this family. It's high time you packed up and left. Have some sense of shame."

Plum perhaps had not been expecting Daisy to be so brusque. The courage she had been mustering collapsed. "You... how can you curse me... you...," she stuttered. "On what grounds can you make me pack up and go—"

"I've made it perfectly clear. There's no need to repeat it. I've given you a deadline. You can stay until the fifteenth of January, but the next day, you must fuck off!" Daisy had thrown away her every inhibition, so would say whatever sounded most provocative and callous.

Plum seethed with outrage. Finally, she coughed out the most vicious words that had ever crossed her mind. "You're... you're plain abnormal."

"I'm abnormal, so what? This is the house of the Diao family. I can be as abnormal as I like around here. I can paste a moustache on my top lip or fix a fox's tail on my backside. It's none of your business. So what? So what? So what?" Daisy thrust out her legs and hips in the obscene manner of a vixen on heat.

Plum shut the door with a furious clatter. "Off her rocker!" she snarled.

"I'm off my rocker, so what? If I'm totally deranged, what does that matter? If you don't cut the crap, you'll not be spending New Year here. I'll see to it. You don't believe me? I mean what I say. I told you to fuck off, so fuck off is what you must do." She dealt Plum's door a single punch as she enunciated those last three words. The younger sister could be heard sobbing inside beneath her quilt. "Don't try to trick others with your pussy water. I'm not Smooth Diao. I'm not buying it."

The lame dog barked a number of times.

"Got a death wish?" Daisy cursed.

The iron gate creaked and Daisy spied Sufen returning alone. Possibly, she had heard the ruckus from outside as she looked up on entering. "What are you staring at? Thieving now?" Daisy couldn't withhold her contempt.

Sufen hurriedly bowed her head and went into the downstairs quarters.

Daisy believed that she had conquered Plum effectively. She now wanted to capitalise on this achievement and abuse Sufen. The thought of knocking, punching and menacing them thrilled her. When Smooth was not on the scene, she found it particularly simple and pleasurable to teach that duo a lesson. What enervated her even more was the thought that it came as easily to her as chopping vegetables or boiling noodles, and that this mess would soon be concluded. Whenever she recalled Sufen's turtle-like manner, and her refusal to make eye contact, she guffawed so hard that she almost regurgitated her food. Daisy could now hear Sufen entering the kitchen, so she decided to bide her time and listen to what she was up to. There was the sound of a meal being prepared downstairs, so she carried over a stack of unwashed bowls and chopsticks.

Daisy swept in and threw her load into the sink. A few stray chopsticks and a couple of ceramic spoons came flying out, with one of the spoons breaking into pieces. Sufen, who was frying tomatoes with eggs, bent down and picked up the detritus. As she was about to gather the shards of spoon, Daisy ran her foot over the pieces and exclaimed, "So humble!"

Sufen withdrew her hands, those two words making her face and ears hot. She didn't speak a word and continued with her chores.

"So, just slipped back for something to eat? Wherever's Smooth Diao got to?"

Sufen was by now accustomed to her short manner with her father. "He's at the stage," she answered. "Somebody's lost a finger and was put in hospital. Your father asked me to come back and cook a meal for him." Whatever Daisy said or did, Sufen maintained her composure.

The stepdaughter was deliberately trying to provoke Sufen at every turn, but with no success. She would have to stab lower than ever before. "Hah, you surely can't be serious about wanting to settle down here?" she asked.

Cai Sufen remained silent.

"I'm talking to you. Didn't you hear me? You're living in my home, and that's making me unhappy. Don't you realise? I'm miserable. Can't you tell? You're the third one Smooth's got himself hitched to. The first eloped and maybe died someplace. The second one pegged it too. Aren't you afraid he'll bring disaster on you too? When Number Two died from cancer, they all said it was Smooth's matrimonial jinx. You're not scared to die at his hands?"

Regardless of what Daisy said, Sufen was unresponsive and concentrated single-mindedly on the cooking.

At last, Daisy lost her cool. She took hold of the cutting knife and beat it resoundingly against the chopping board. "How can you have such a strong face? I've been talking to you like this and you still refuse to go. Happy enough to be fed and watered. Aren't you worried I'll put rat poison in your food?"

Sufen still didn't flinch. It had been her intention to cook two dishes, but once the first one was ready, she slipped it into the bento box. Daisy was still haranguing her as she was on her way out. "Hai," she cried, "make sure you're on the lookout. Think ahead and be sure you have a place to go for when you're driven out of here!"

45

SMOOTH RECEIVED A PHONE CALL from Plum, though he couldn't leave the theatre at that moment. He told her not to let the "abnormal" one bother her and to just read her books at home in peace. It would be several days before the job was over and he could return to her. "Rest assured, Plum," he stressed. "You are your dad's true daughter, and nobody can change that fact."

The leading man left in a huff, and Smooth too wanted to release his pent-up frustration. He loathed Director Jin for humiliating him in public, and Iron Kou too for stirring the pot in front of Chief Qu and for trying to absolve himself of responsibility for Monkey. Those negative emotions found no outlet as he circled about in the snow and then came back when Qu called for him. The stage scenery required attention. Madame Jin now regarded the whole crew as amateurs with not a whit of artistic sensibility. She branded their output as "fucking nuts", "a stinking louse" and "a heap of bullshit". Even Smooth's newly bought broom failed to escape her bile, for she said that articles from daily life had no place on the stage. He picked it up and took it down to the pit, asking with a hint of satire how it could be rendered "artistic". Jin plucked out a few of the bristles, roughing up the head slightly, then after looking at it left and right, pronounced it a worthy theatrical prop. To Smooth's eyes, a broom was a broom and making it a touch distressed didn't make much difference. He thought of how she had claimed to have perfected it. "Artwork, my arse," he cursed under his breath.

As the lighting, scenery, costumes and settings were being put right, Chief Qu visited the leading man at home to attempt some political chicanery and mild persuasion. Staff members at the troupe blamed outbursts such as his on the actors being spoiled. The more they were indulged, the more irrational and entitled they became. Tougher rules could potentially curb their behaviour. Then again, others observed that there were a shitload of rules already. Were these all bound together in a single volume, it would be thicker than the epic *Romance of the Three Kingdoms*. New rules were thus fucking obsolete. Should his language be too brisk and firm, Qu's intervention might cause him to develop an aching back. Someone else commented that even if the King of Hell were the head of an opera troupe, he would still find himself put upon. Whether willing to cooperate or not, a player could torpedo a production by simply claiming that their throat was a touch sore. The stereotype of pampered lead players was thus uppermost in the minds of troupe members.

Still others reflected that Chief Qu had ensured their troupe was a paradigm of the "broken windows theory". The visible disorder of the theatre set invited further laxity in its occupants' behaviour. They were interrupted by the doorkeeper craning his head into the room. "You've no need to cosset Smooth," he quipped. "He'll come and shift the stage even if he isn't summoned over. Everybody he meets, he flatters like his old grandpa." They all laughed out loud.

Smooth already had a stabbing pain inside and when he heard himself being mocked, he cursed under his breath, "Why rip the piss out of me? Have I dug up your ancestors' graves?"

In the evening, the "big shot" leading man did finally appear after much cajoling. He entered together with Chief Qu. No matter what people had been nattering about or who they had been badmouthing, as soon as the big shot was in the room, all that talk died down.

A number of the hands believed that since Director Jin had been so critical earlier in the day, she would at least display tact in broaching the leading man's shortcomings. Smooth had conditioned himself psychologically. He was ready to be the "mountain" she would hack away at by means of warning the "tiger".

Tonight, Director Jin showed her powers of self-restraint. During the half-hour wait for the leading man, her patience had been trojan. She sat and tapped a table rhythmically, without so much as a peep. At other times, Smooth would have taken the initiative to greet her or have found a pretence for praise that would soften her outlook. Today, he thought her a traitor who had shafted longstanding friends. It was like she had cracked open his egg and was sifting around inside for bones. Her eyes were now honed into finding anything she could brand "improper" or "inartistic", and Smooth was made to feel that his very involvement endangered the production. She had made him lose face in public and turned him into the fall guy. He hid his face before the troupe as though it bore the heavy and ignominious smuts from the bottom of a wok. Smooth thought that if her use of him as a punch bag proved salutary, she could also learn from the leading man's disobedience. He seemed to care about nothing, leave his phone off the hook and bide his time, waiting to see what her next manoeuvre would be.

Anyhow, Smooth was contemplating giving up shifting stages. When there was still money to be made from ferrying cargo, why should he hang himself on this lonesome tree?

While he was deep in thought, a shout came from Director Jin. "Smooth," she called. He rose almost unknowingly with a thud and answered, "Yes." Sounding like he was replying to a drill sergeant, his response was received with giggles. People in this field are amused at the smallest of things and Smooth at once regretted using such a tone. He was still as sycophantic as before. If he had a tail, he would have wagged it until it broke. But even doing that was an act of obligation rather than will.

"Have you seen where the second platform has gone?" Director Jin asked.

Smooth spotted that it was in the right location, but peering at it a second time, he saw that it was out of alignment, having drifted a few centimetres from its correct place.

"Just a little out," he reported.

"How much is a little?" Jin demanded to know.

"About three centimetres."

"Could this 'about' become more precise?"

"Three and a half centimetres."

"There shouldn't be the slightest error." She was emphatic. "This is art, not a kid's Wendy house." Smooth knew all too well her strategy. Throttle the chicken to scare the monkey. He himself was the chicken and could be used and abused to put the rehearsal in the best order with the minimum cost.

The rehearsal finally began. Smooth dragged his weighty frame to the toilet and changed the cotton gauze that had become bloody and putrefied. It was much to his relief when a new dressing was in place, and on returning to the pit he slumped down in a position neither too close to nor too far away from Director Jin. He must be primed for the next order from the Night Ogre.

Despite all the time spent on preparations, Smooth was not entirely familiar with the plot of the drama. He couldn't immerse himself in the opera during the early stages, for his mind was swirling with thoughts of his elder brother Big Army, Daisy, Plum and Sufen. A great uncertainty hung over how they would spend the coming New Year. He was also preoccupied with how to file a claim for Monkey, the arrears from the temple job and the fee for the present project. All these anxieties seemed to constrict his heart like a snare, reducing it to a pulp. How he wished he could pluck out each problem and then rearrange them into neat order.

Despite these preoccupations, Smooth was still able to admire the finished scenery made by his team. Leaving aside Director Jin's carping, he felt a semblance of accomplishment. After all, he had chosen to shift stages because of the escapism he found in opera as a child. Back then, his home had been close to a theatre and he knew which walls and sewer pipes would allow him to gatecrash a play when he had no ticket. He had no intimation in those days that he would end up among the theatre crowd, so in spite of it all, he retained a seam of contentment for having landed such a job. Still, nothing could rid him of the enmity he felt towards divas and poseurs. When these types appeared on stage, it was impossible to resist defying one's conscience and applauding their inborn talent.

The leading man of the current production was about thirty-two, yet he effectively evoked the timeworn grace of a veteran thespian. Were this not a troika rehearsal for staff only, he would have clapped his hands until they chafed. He would also have shouted in congratulation, for as a boy he had once bravoed and whistled endlessly at the performances he watched on the sly. The usher yanking his ear to eject him did nothing to deter him from coming back and yelling until his throat ached.

Watching the Cui Hu before him, that character had both charisma and good looks. From the opening lines of his lyrics, his feet moved and his eyes radiated with delicacy. His gestures were pleasing and totally captivating to the last. Sure enough, he was an arsehole, but some arseholes steal our admiration. When a little tipsy, the "big shot" began to brag to his fans. "Never mind where they... they hide their hands," he slurred. "Once I – your teacher – appears onstage, their hands will rise up and thunder applause. On and on it will go... only Chairman Mao... enjoyed this kind of clapping... when His Honour spoke to the masses." Smooth knew that these ramblings were no exaggeration. That arsehole did indeed bask in the glory of the boards. Among his fans were high officials, tycoons and run-of-the-mill patrons. Whenever he performed, the front and back of the stage were chock-full of fans scrambling after an autograph or a selfie with him. How could his head not expand with the heat and contract with the cold?

The menagerie in Smooth's mind appeared to be forgotten as he surrendered his attention to the plot of the drama and the alchemy of the protagonist.

The scenario was, broadly speaking, as follows: one day Cui Hu went on a spring outing to the suburbs of the ancient Western Capital. As he was taking in the peach blooms, he caught sight of a girl leaning on a door woven from twigs. Her name was Peach Blossom, and upon first glimpse his heart was her captive. On his return from this excursion, he sent intermediaries to offer her his proposal of marriage. She declined as she was already involved with a swain from her village. Later, Cui Hu found a way of moving her heart and married her and brought her to the Western Capital. The girl was from a mountain family and had no schooling, whereas his household was affluent and influential and they dwelt in a sprawling mansion decorated with brick carvings. As the scenery was being created, Director Jin stressed over and over how the gate tower and the screen wall should be painted delicately. Since the images had to be enlarged several times to reach the appropriate scale, Smooth was made to comprehend the grandiosity of that family in Tang times.

Returning to the opera plot, Cui Hu's parents were reluctant to have the girl live with them, and naturally, she ended up being ill-treated. Young and rather wild as she was, Peach Blossom retained the habits of the countryside. She was an inveterate joker and lost face for the Cui family. In the end, she offended her parents-in-law, and Cui Hu was compelled to divorce her. He continued to be besotted with the sixteen-year-old, but was powerless to rebuke family ethics and discipline, so had to let her leave aggrieved and under duress. Peach Blossom was then left with no face to be able to return to her home village. She both adored and abjured her former husband. When she heard that her childhood sweetheart had married, she hanged herself among the peach boughs at the entrance to the village. Cui Hu sped back to that place. The ramshackle door woven out of twigs was still there and the blossoms were brighter and more exuberant than ever. But gone for good was the comely and lively girl. He searched for her all about the forest, first of all singing in the lachrymose and chanting style of Shaanxi Opera. Then, to the tune of *The Old Dragon Weeping at the Sea*, he declaimed a whole lyric running to fifty lines. Smooth was convinced that this would sate every operagoer's thirst for charm. At the end, Cui Hu, with his tear-lined face, reached for his writing brush and set down immortal meters of poetry:

> In this house on this day last year, a pink face vied
> In beauty with the pink peach blossoms side by side.
> I do not know today where the pink face has gone;
> In vernal breeze still smile peach blossoms fully blown.

Smooth was startled to hear the sound of sobs coming from behind him. He turned around and found that it was Sufen whose eyes were crimson and swollen from weeping. As he was about to hand her his tissues, there was a cry from Director Jin. "Smooth, Smooth, the fourth platform is not moving! What's wrong? What's wrong? Stop, stop, stop."

The music came to a halt.

The articulated stage seized up too.

Smooth bounced up with trepidation and mounted the platform.

Once again, the motor on the fourth platform was the problem.

It would revolve once and then seize up. Below the stage, Director Jin's temper was boiling. Smooth and Big Hook climbed down and pushed the platform upwards with their backs. Now bearing less load, the motor started again. They could hear from below how all the people onstage were nearly laughing themselves silly.

"What's the matter?" Director Jin could be heard to bawl. "What's wrong? When we want it to move, it doesn't want to go. When we don't, it does. Stop, stop!"

Smooth and Big Hook crawled out, and it seized up once more.

"What on earth's happened?" the director went on.

"There are too many people on the platform," Smooth replied from down below. "It's too small and doesn't have enough power."

"Originally, we had three dozen flower girls and have stuck to that number," Director Jin observed. "How can the motor not be powerful enough?"

"It's simply not powerful enough," grumbled Smooth.

The people on the stage were giggling again. Someone banged on the boards. "Smooth, try to fart louder," that person said. "Director Jin can't hear what you're saying."

He was then silent.

"Listen up, stage management," Director Jin intoned. "The problem of the motor must be solved tomorrow, otherwise it'll be the thing that ruins the performance."

Later on, they heard that the "big shot" had departed too soon. It was Chief Qu who had personally helped him to slip into his overcoat. Word had it that his cough had worsened, and Smooth had noticed him turn to clear his throat several times in rehearsal.

Although the star performer was gone, Director Jin forced them to rehearse the epilogue twice. As the motor couldn't handle its load, the size of the group of flower girls was cut. Only then did the platform move as it should.

While the director was rounding matters off and had paused to delve into some related issues, Smooth's mobile started to vibrate incessantly. The call was from Uncle Scar, who demanded mercilessly and forcefully that he ought to contact his brother without delay. Should he fail to do so, he must clear his brother's debt. Failure to act would make Spring Festival a very uneasy time for him.

Smooth's incoming calls eventually started to irk Director Jin. "Smooth Diao, did you come here to shift stages or play about with your phone?" she asked. "You're busier than the secretary general of the United Nations, it seems. Switch it off and listen to me!"

He turned the power off.

46

CAI SUFEN HAD NEVER BEEN SO TOUCHED BY EMOTION when watching a drama. She had shed a few tears during *Zhang Jibao is Struck by Thunder*, but did not have the same sentimental and melancholic feeling as she did tonight. Owing to her hospital duties, she only caught the second half of the story from the point when Peach Blossom entered the mansion of the Cui family. On watching how the young bride was brutalised and humiliated, she could not help reflecting upon her own situation. True enough, she was much older than the heroine and far more worldly wise. Yet she could relate to the grievances she endured. Daisy, if anything, had been more vitriolic and extreme than Peach Blossom's mother-in-law. In that mansion, she could at least resist or take her anger out by damaging small items if pressed too hard. At Smooth's home, however, she was so careful as to avoid even treading on an ant. Even then, she could not win recognition from her stepdaughter. Far from it, she was victimised even more. Recalling what had happened earlier when she went back to cook for Monkey, a lingering fear started to brew inside her. Daisy was preparing to eject her publicly, like the mother-in-law who cornered Peach Blossom in the cellar and decreed that she leave the Cui family. Sufen sensed that if she stayed there any longer, she might be done in, for there seemed nothing of which Daisy was now incapable.

But then she reflected on how kind Smooth had been. When she came to the Western Capital as a refugee in a peculiar land at the most wretched point in her life, it was he who accepted her. She understood his dilemma, though there ought to be limits to what she should suffer. In the beginning, she felt she could withstand any pain and embarrassment. As matters persisted like this throughout the year and even degenerated, her resolve weakened and she contemplated bolting. She did not believe there was anything to be gained by telling Smooth what Daisy had done to her at noontime. Besides, he himself was in an unenviable pickle.

Cui Hu, the hero of this drama, was talented, educated and lived a vibrant life, but he remained a loser by nature, much like Smooth. When family members abused Peach Blossom, he could only mope about, not having the courage to defend her overtly. He looked on with his eyes wide open as his sweetheart was driven away to take her own life. Irrespective of how pained his cries were, there was no way to resuscitate his beloved. This made her thoughts turn to her first husband, who had dismembered his rival for the sake of his dignity. What a titan he was! At the time, she had bemoaned his narrow-minded, wild and impetuous nature. Set alongside her present spouse, Smooth was a doormat and a tramp. He had all the backbone of a bucket of pig intestines.

To make the situation more convoluted, there was the issue of Third Skin – somebody she could "never grip, nor give the slip". This guy was too persistent and absolutely obsessed with her. To be frank, she had no time for men who opted to work in shady corners, though he did try to be pleasant towards her. As soon as Smooth stepped into this world of stage shifting, he set himself up single-mindedly as a leader. He cared only about rubbing along with his seniors and those who took charge of practical matters. He was focused squarely on securing the full fees, or whether catering could stretch to an extra egg or chicken leg per person. He often ignored her very existence. Third Skin, meanwhile, concentrated exclusively and implicitly upon her. Were the sky to collapse, he would first of all check to see that she had not been crushed. If she was unscathed, then the sky could do whatever it pleased. Smooth once told her that their colleague was basically decent, only with a streak of selfishness. Should a bottle of oil fall to the floor, he would not offer to help clear the spillage. But Sufen now knew that if she were to fall to the floor instead, Third Skin would crawl on the ground and gather her up. These days, he had been prepared to assist in looking after Monkey, only because Smooth had seconded her to stay too. Otherwise, he would have refused to hang around and wait on others. Formerly, Third Skin would try to make advances on her when there was nobody else around, but would desist if Sufen mentioned the name of her husband, for he knew he had been good to him and shown especial consideration for his poor eyesight. Now his restraint was gone, and there was an endless barrage of touching and fondling. She could neither do anything to deter him, nor could she reveal all to Smooth. His fixation intensified.

A while ago, when they were gluing the peach petals to the fabric, Third Skin had become even bolder since Smooth was nowhere in sight. One day, he tried to kiss her with force, only to receive a slap in return. This was no deterrent, and he pawed her breasts after much pestering and pleading. She felt guilty for having slapped him and perhaps this could prove some recompense, since he had been depressed and refused to work or eat. He caressed them for ages, pinching the nipples and rubbing the sacs of flesh themselves. In his excitement, tears streaked his face.

"I haven't touched a woman in years," confessed Third Skin.

"Don't you have a missus at home?"

"Don't laugh at me, but she ran off with another bloke. I don't want the others to know in case they laugh and tease me."

After all this fondling, Third Skin resisted taking his hands away. He wanted to let his mouth have a go too. She pushed his head from her body as she realised this was not a good precedent. If she were to allow him to get away with everything the first time, there was bound to be a second time. Owing to her emotional fog, she had let her defences slip, and he was free to grope away in spite of her reluctance.

Sufen and Smooth did have a few rather intensely tender periods when they first became an item. Subsequently, the work saw him exerted to distraction and sleep came quickly. Smooth would often not bother to remove his clothes first.

When all was said and done, she was still in her thirties. Besides, her first husband took lovemaking as being more important than eating, and was so voracious that not a day went by without a session. Compared with those times, she was as good as leading the life of a nun right now.

That day, Third Skin tried to seduce her in a dark corner of the tech college. Since it was vacation time, there were many empty spaces around the building and it could be eerie to stroll about the place on one's own. Third Skin caught hold of her breasts and was eager to go further. She refused him in an instant. When he wanted to break the stalemate, she nearly broke his arm in retaliation. "This is the bottom line," she warned him. "Do you hear me?" Third Skin made no response.

While they were taking care of Monkey in the hospital and there was no one else in the lift, Third Skin led his hands down from her collar so that they reached her cleavage before she was conscious of it. She became irritated and kicked him. His groin was the target as she was keen to teach him properly. This did not stop his pestering, though, and it occurred to her that violence was not the right approach. Instead, she tried to loiter about the theatre as a means of evading him. He did try to follow her, only to retreat back to Monkey's ward after she meted out a harsh scolding. Third Skin continued to send messages on his mobile, often resorting to lyrical expressions of love. Where he had learned such things, she was not exactly sure. Sufen was in a quandary about what to do or whether it was now proper to tell Smooth. After thinking it through, the latter was no option. To bring this to her husband's notice would be like presenting him with another hard nut when he already had too many nuts to crack.

After the rehearsal, Director Jin was once again voluble. Most of her monologue concerned Smooth. Several items of scenery would have to be reconfigured overnight, ready for use early the next morning. Sufen saw him stand contritely centre stage. Without a word, he and Big Hook started to disassemble the sets. The birthday party backdrop from the Cui family mansion was hauled down. Director Jin maintained that the chosen shade of red did not seem authentic. She demanded that an extra coat be added before the next day. The set pieces all cascaded down, knocking Smooth to the ground. At first, Sufen noticed how he sat up straight before slumping back into a lying posture.

She raced over to check on him.

"Guess what I want to do now," he whispered to her angrily.

His wife shook her head.

"Slay Director Jin, the Night Ogre."

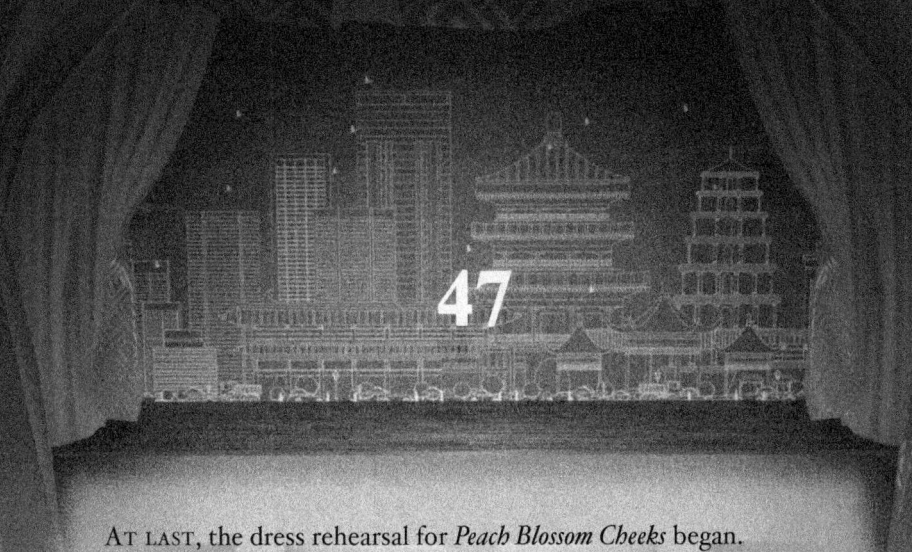

47

AT LAST, the dress rehearsal for *Peach Blossom Cheeks* began.

Smooth and his crew were running around in a frenzy, sorting sets and stage until the very last minute. Director Jin was living up to her title as the Night Ogre. She grumbled about this and that, cawing and lambasting anybody she encountered. Even Chief Qu was careful not to draw too near as he was wary of her scattergun rebukes.

"Old Qu, you see what kind of troupe you're leading?" she would typically begin. "How can they churn out 'artwork' like this? Aren't they competing to be among the top in the nation? They carry on like a bunch of amateurs. From what we've seen with the rehearsals and the sets, it's time they disbanded. I wouldn't put it past those stage shifters to cock up the evening dress rehearsal."

"Rest assured, I'll make it clear to them again later. Nothing will be allowed to fall short. There'll be no delay in the performance."

"Well, well, well, Old Qu. It looks like you've spoiled this lot. High time you laid an egg with a shell."

He still smiled flatteringly in spite of all her vitriol.

Smooth could not bear to look on at this. "Hey, Chief Qu, is this old boiler crazy?" he whispered in a low voice. "She sinks her fangs into everyone she meets."

The chief grinned back. "Director Jin menaces like the barrel of an old cannon. With her, it's all for art or for nothing."

Smooth couldn't say anything more.

In line with the director's requirements, come dress rehearsal "an egg with a shell" did indeed plop onto the stage.

The management division gathered together all the set-moving staff so that Qu could give them a speech of admonition. "It's not that I'm losing my temper," he began. "More's the pity! When the set was being shifted in the afternoon, it would be hard not to get furious. The ox was dragging away, but the horse was not, so to speak. Eh? Tell me in all conscience, how does this troupe usually treat you? Eh? You might not be on the full-time payroll and have a steady salary, though we've never taken roll call or made you keep office hours. You've been free to gather here when work was available and then bugger off when there was none. What else could you want from a troupe, eh? There are twelve months in a year. Just a few more days until this year is over. We've only asked you to move a few bits of set, so how can you behave like this! Put your hands on your hearts and think it over. If there's such a cushy deal to be had on another planet, you can fly over there right now!"

"Who doesn't want to be a full-timer?" somebody mumbled. "You wouldn't allow that. You split us into different grades and ranks, so how can we not feel put out?"

"Hai, Chief Qu, we don't like what we just heard," someone else shouted. "It's not that we don't want to work. It's just you're not the one to assign tasks to us. All of us have the ability to be a leading man if we were ever asked. Only one or two dogs at a time can eat warm shit. The others have to stare on in envy."

Everybody cackled, Smooth included. He loved to listen to how the crew gabbled away in front of the troupe staff. Any words that issued from their mouths were sure to carry a particular pith.

"It's not that anyone of us hasn't had a taste of shit before," another fellow continued. "The dog's old and has fallen from favour. It's fashionable to be nipped at by a little puppy. If you can get rid of us, why punish us by making us haul this lot about?"

Chief Qu now resorted to tough talk. "Let's do it this way. If any of you want to call it a day, tell the business section and we can change staff. But let me make one thing clear. Those who haven't taken on one task all the year round will only get a basic subsistence allowance next year. Tell us now and we'll change staff. If nobody's willing, we can hire different hands." No one responded to these threats. In the past, Smooth couldn't wait for staff in the troupe to refuse stage-shifting work. That meant his position went unchallenged. Recently, however, he simmered with unrest and wanted to find a way out. With New Year approaching, dependable hands were thin on the ground. Hence, after this topic was raised, Smooth became unnerved and retreated from the side of the stage to the lighting slot.

Chief Qu then said something else, and one of the workers called for Smooth to step forward. He was reluctant to become involved, but in the last day or two had gone through the whole gamut of possibilities to try to safeguard their income. He rose from the lighting slot to be told that Chief Qu was waiting for him.

As Smooth neared Qu, he could see that he was conversing with the man in charge of footwear and headgear for the troupe.

"It's not that I'm shirking my duty," the costumier said. "Chief Qu, you surely know how I've applied myself here over the years? Youngsters who entered the troupe after me have been promoted to the second-class level ahead of me. Here's me, still stuck in third class. Tell me, is that fair? This time you assigned me to take care of the shoes and caps for *Peach Blossom Cheeks*. You can ask Director Jin yourself about what I've done. I've resprayed all the boots and dozens of pairs of dancing shoes. I stitched on all of those peach blossom tassels by hand. I've also now published a thesis, you see. It's entitled *On Protecting Prop Boxes with Liquor*. It cost me eight hundred yuan to get it printed in a newspaper. Hah, Chief Qu, are there any conditions I haven't met for promotion? Surely you'll let me be appointed senior associate this year?"

"Do you think it proper to discuss professional titles now? Besides, as this year's round of promotions has been and gone, what's the point?" The chief's patience was by now sorely tested.

"There's no use in me talking about it now. But when else do I have the chance? I'm busy with work, and no one notices me. I'm guessing that next year, when the promotion period comes, you'll have those tender young lads in your sights. What about me, then? Can't you hang a juicy steamed bun around the neck of an old ox like me?"

"I am sure to keep you in mind. I do remember everybody who performs well. You get back to work pronto. The performance is about to start." He then tried to rid himself of the promotion seeker.

"Gather your guys together," Qu told Smooth. "These are the last few hours, and we must cooperate well with Director Jin."

"She's a nut case, no doubt about it," Smooth replied. "But don't worry, Chief. My men will never drop the ball for you. You're a kind sort and we labour hard because it's for you. The only thing is that everyone is worried about their pay. Tomorrow is the last day but two before New Year. They all have to head home for Spring Festival."

"I don't like this habit of yours. It's a character flaw, actually," Chief Qu said suddenly and stiffly. "You always bring up money at a crucial moment." With those words, he turned away and resumed his own responsibilities.

Smooth was also of the opinion that when the rehearsal bell had rung and the conductor had entered the orchestra pit, this was an improper time to mention money. But then again, when was the proper time? Whatever may have been attacking his mind, he warned his men individually according to Chief Qu's commands. He reminded everyone that their eyes should be on their buttocks tonight. However, they all echoed back the same refrain: "But the cash is sorted, ain't it?" This provoked Smooth, and he broke into curses. "Your mother's cunt," he yelled. "Talking about money at this moment! You really do only have the glimmer of coins in your eyes, don't you?" His raised voice was a self-conscious touch, intended to register with them how he too was suffering with repressed anger.

Director Jin lost her composure once again, just before the curtain was to be raised. She was perturbed that there were so many people in the auditorium. It was supposed to be a closed dress rehearsal, so why all this hullabaloo? She grew fixated on the point, demanding that the chief provide an explanation.

"They're the family and kin of all the staff," he answered.

"So that even includes the guy who sells lamb's blood soup with flatbreads at the theatre gate? He's family too? Who's he related to here?"

All directors are dismayed to be faced with too many spectators at their rehearsals, especially if they turn out to be somehow sub-par. Should only a few of those in the stalls decide to invoke unlucky creatures like "ravens", that might scupper what was otherwise destined to be a flawless production. In the world of opera, word of mouth is what counts, especially among stalwart theatregoers. Their comments are weightier than any puffs found in TV reviews or newspaper editorials. "Chattering Charlies", if not brought to heel in the right manner, could easily inflict "venom" on a drama, condemning it to spasms, paralysis and death. It was said that several productions in the past had been literally "euthanised" by a round of "potent pills". The vendor of lamb's blood soup was an aficionado for sure, but also wouldn't spell out his opinions before the troupe. Whatever he blathered the next morning by the theatre gate could signal doom for a debuting opera.

Nonetheless, Smooth was not one to soft soap onlookers. Since boyhood, he had seen almost everything in theatreland. Back then, he was not averse to clearing walls or squeezing through doggy holes to see an opera. He was consummately confident that his eyes were more perceptive than those of "Mr Sheepy Soup". Had he such a gob on him, he too might have won renown as an amateur critic. Based on his storehouse of experience, the present opera was in every sense more than adequate. He didn't deem it wise to pass comment to this effect, since the director had been such a martinet wherever he was brought to her attention.

Whatever Director Jin's foibles and spats may have thrown up next, Chief Qu grinned and reminded her that it was so close to New Year's Eve and those in the stalls had chosen to be there. How could they have the gall to drive them away now? He asked her to allow the dress rehearsal to proceed. She consented, but not until she had lambasted her opposite number as being "as corrupt as the court of Qing, as reptilian as the Empress Dowager Cixi and as wily as her chancellor Li Hongzhang". The list of historical insults wore on and on.

The third bell rang at last, causing the stage to fall quiet.

The dense and concentrated rhythm of the timpani struck up. That rumbling sound from afar shuddered closer and closer.

The dress rehearsal had officially begun.

"Ready to raise the curtain," Director Jin instructed in a low voice into a walkie-talkie. "Raise the curtain on the fourth long note of the pipes. Go ahead. More dry ice. Dim the back lights. Keep the front lights not so bright. Raise the curtain, slowly. Raise the lights, slowly, slowly..."

Finally, with the orchestra reaching a swell, the curtain on the proscenium arch swung wide open.

In fact, once the rehearsal proper had begun, Smooth and his men could begin to relax. Custody of the stage had been surrendered to the troupe, and they simply waited in the wings in case any crack might appear and require a timely fix. Tonight, Smooth really could not unwind. He had to be scrupulously aware of every last stick of setting. Director Jin had bellowed that if, once the curtain was raised for the prelude and the audience did not applaud with gusto at the peach blossom fabric, then the set had been a dud. Nevertheless, Smooth did know that the efficacy of the scenery was allied intimately with the quality of the lighting. His anxiety was such he felt his heart had been pushed beyond his thorax. On the peal of the third bell, it was pounding away in time with the percussion of the kettle drum.

As this was a mere rehearsal, the audience should not be expected to clap like ticketholders. Either those onlookers were there illicitly and stared at the stage with trepidation or thought that the players required no applause at all. Tonight was the exception. Their enthusiasm was palpable and no mistake. The second the curtains opened, applause rattled from every quarter. The protagonist was invisible for a while and the flower girls were lost amid the dry ice. No matter. Wasn't it that they were now applauding to validate the artistry of the stage and Smooth Diao himself? Could there be any doubt? Somebody even leaned over and said directly to Smooth, "Listen, it's you they're clapping for." Smooth's blood was now inflamed and his spirits surging heavenward.

No wonder. Those big-name players were pushing their vocal prowess to the limit. Their numbers, monologues and martial artistry sizzled. No wonder. As they garnered all that applause, they were the only ones who existed. Right now, Smooth felt that just a select few people existed. Iron Kou was rendered invisible, and there was only Chief Qu and Director Jin before him. He thought that this was almost the time to wobble over and make his presence known to them. He must.

With this in mind, Smooth made a beeline from the exit to the entrance. He sidled up to Chief Qu and asked, apparently in a panic, "I heard the acoustics were off. There was a cracking sound that lasted for ages."

"Deaf lugs, if that's what they call you," muttered the curtain operator. "Hear that applause?"

"Applause?" he repeated deliberately while glancing at Chief Qu through the corner of his eye.

Chief Qu winked back, implying that congratulations were due. This one tiny gesture made him feel that the chief was a firm, dependable and reliable champion for his entire group.

They were interrupted by the arrival of the leading man, who was followed by a retinue taking charge of his costume, shoes and hats. The hero was supposed to be sylph-like, elegant and with a graceful bearing. Before coming onto the stage, he wore a down jacket. As he neared the curtain, Chief Qu asked, "Can you hold back?" The star did not answer clearly and just coughed to indicate that he had not fully shaken off his cold. Smooth had the sense that Chief Qu wielded no greater authority over the troupe than he himself did over the team of stage shifters. Although close to sixty, he still had to act lowly and servile before an actor in his early thirties. Everyone in this world appeared to have their own hard nuts to crack.

After that laudatory glint of the eye from the chief, Smooth could only shamble over to gauge Director Jin's reaction and note her attitude and expression in response to those waves of clapping. Once the opening had been completed, she swept through the auditorium and informed Smooth that she was going to stand in the back row. She would settle down in one position until the performance had achieved its customary pace.

Smooth strode around the perimeter of the hall in one vast circle, trying to locate the director. She was in the process of berating the sound engineer through her walkie talkie, moaning that the volume of the bass was too high and it was causing even the floor beneath her feet to vibrate. Smooth pretended to be monitoring some of the key stage effects as he drew closer to her. Once she was done with her cursing, he would try to find an excuse to mention the artistry of the stage design. Before he could do so, there was another sharp creak, which made all the audience cover their ears with their hands. "Are your fingers in spasms?" Jin barked down her walkie talkie. "The sound's high one minute and low the next. Don't jab at the controls randomly. How can you call yourself an acoustics engineer, let alone an artist? You barely have the wherewithal to manage a PA system at a village meeting. What the hell are you doing?"

Following these curses, it was as if Smooth were invisible to her. He turned towards the lighting control panel. Damn crazy woman, he seethed inwardly. You have a backside as big as a basket. Serves you right no one wants to marry you!

Mound sneaked up to him. "Did you hear the applause just now?" he asked in hushed tones.

"Yeah, what of it?"

"It was me who triggered it. Most of them back there are shitty fools. They haven't a clue how to clap, so I hid myself among them and set them off."

Smooth looked down at his damaged hand. "You're a cheating ghost," he surmised. "How can you clap with this thing in plaster?"

"Don't you believe me? I beat the other one against my chest. Just then, the big curtain was being lifted up. The lights were all dimmed and everybody had their eyes on the stage scenery. I unbuttoned my collar. If you don't believe me, you see, there's still a mark here where I hit myself." As he spoke, Mound set about trying to expose his chest. Smooth stopped him, fearing that others might twig what he had done.

After hearing Mound's tale, Smooth lost interest in bragging before Director Jin, and joined the others waiting in the gloom of the stage.

There was only one hiatus in the performance, and to Smooth's relief, it had nothing to do with him. The leading man coughed so hard that it was ten minutes before the action resumed. He would not continue until a doctor had provided him with throat spray. What bothered Smooth the most were the articulated portions of the platform. Three reconfigurations were needed through the course of the opera and, as each one loomed, his heart thumped away within his ribcage. Fortunately, every movement was achieved successfully. Cheers and claps shook the theatre, something that he realised was down to Mound's provocation, since none of the actors elicited such a positive response. Indeed, the audience seemed almost anaesthetised where there should have been applause. Someone joked that tonight was the night when Smooth's work went viral.

In response, he sought out Mound and told him to tone down his drumming. Before long, it might be rumbled as a sham. Still, when the stage moved for the final time and the leading man in all his gallantry became the focal point, the chamber once more reverberated. Now, Smooth could see Mound to his side in the wings, meaning that this response had been merited by the scenery and the platform mechanics.

The curtain fell to prolonged applause and the audience would not budge even when it was lifted again. Smooth watched as the director mounted the stage with a shimmy of her sizeable hips. Next, Chief Qu invited a number of the veteran artists from the troupe up front. They were the "true immortals" who had come to pass keen judgment on the drama. Director Jin then ushered the playwright, the composer and the stage director onstage one by one. They embraced each other and a streak of tears was visible in their eyes. Standing by the main curtain, Smooth experienced surging relief, but this was soon superseded by a sharp sting in his posterior that brought out beads of sweat on his brow. Sufen asked him what was the matter, and he dismissed it as nothing serious, saying he was just waiting to meet Chief Qu for one last time to ask about the labour fee. He thought that the proper moment had come around.

People took to talking on the stage. Smooth was well aware that this was a propitious sign, since if the drama was set to bomb, those "immortals" would only hang around long enough to shake hands and feature in group photos. Tonight, there was no concession to those who wished to leave the theatre early as every orator proved gregarious. Particularly prominent was an octogenarian thespian who lisped and needed the assistance of his daughter. Words trickled forth like a tap that had lost its washer and could not be turned off. He started by discussing the Tang Dynasty, rambled on to the Republic of China era, revolutionary Yan'an, and then the founding of the New China, the Cultural Revolution, and the reform and opening-up. When everyone thought he was done, it was back to the Tang Dynasty. Much as he lauded the leading man, even the big shot found it insufferable and had to go backstage to remove his make-up, coughing all the way. Once more, people thought that the old man would wrap it up. Instead, he moved on to the professional ethics of the minor roles. He again mentioned the troupes in Tang times and noted the striking minor roles in the hard-to-classify dramas of the Yuan Dynasty. He even meandered onto Li Yu, a famous playwright of the Qing Dynasty, and Gai Jiaotian, a renowned actor in modern Peking Opera. The shorthand secretary, who had been scribbling away in his notebook at the corner of the stage, tried to inject some comedy. "This really is stream of consciousness," he remarked. Smooth didn't catch the meaning and wasn't interested if this little river might be home to gliding carp or grass carp. He had been too busy pestering Iron Kou about the money for shifting the stage in the temple. Kou tried to move away, but Smooth clung close like his shadow. No matter how he talked or tried to incite a reaction, the response was always the same. "They didn't give me any money. Can I turn my arse into an ATM?"

The old gentleman's address lasted fully forty minutes, and he started to recount what happened when he created the drama *Li Bai*. Director Jin, who was holding the microphone for him, moved woodenly from foot to foot. At first, her demeanour was rather humble and modest. She promised him repeatedly that she would call on him, especially at home. Nonetheless, "the torrential rain" of this senior citizen was not about to abate. The director could no longer bear to be his stand and so Chief Qu took the mike from her, just as the man had come around to observing that "the key to artistic creation is to be concise".

A few fellow veterans now felt that he was losing face on their behalf. "You chatterbox," one of them called out. "Are you going to talk until New Year's Eve?" Crestfallen, the old man insisted on sharing "just a few last words". Everyone laughed. In the end, even the extras slipped out discreetly to take off their make-up. His daughter too tried to intercede. "Just a few last words," he repeated. This phrase soon became a kind of mantra within the troupe. At last, the engineer switched off all the lamps save for one directly above the stage. It flickered dim and then bright, and by now there were only a few people left. These were the ones who could find no excuse to leave.

The old gentleman then requested that Director Jin and Chief Qu come to visit him at home the next day. He wished to discuss in detail some anachronisms relating to the costumes, shoes, caps and props. Everyone sighed in relief, and Qu and Jin gestured for him to grace the exit.

"You wait and see, Chief, Director," the operational head mused. "The best is yet to come tomorrow. Each of you should take a couple of notebooks."

"Forgive me, Old Qu," Director Jin croaked. "Let me have the day off tomorrow. I'm on the verge of collapsing here."

"Fine, I'll go," he replied. "I'll carry all four notebooks."

Smooth came in their direction, seeking the attention of these senior cadres and ladling on more words of praise when everyone was already afflicted with "aesthetic fatigue".

"It was a hit, Chief Qu. Sure to become popular, don't you think? Four times they clapped just for the scenery. Tickets for New Year must be selling like hotcakes." He stressed the part about the scenery winning applause. This was his opportunity to impress Director Jin before she could go fishing for bones inside the egg.

"Yeah," Director Jin the Night Ogre agreed before the chief could speak. "Old Qu, I tell you, this time Smooth and the others surpassed themselves. They deserve prizes and bonuses."

Smooth was quite astonished at how the Night Ogre, that lioness, that she-tiger, that madwoman, was now speaking so sympathetically and supportively. What he feared was that, after the play took off, she might revert to her pedantic ways. Quite the contrary, her words were daintier than carved ivory and more delectable than a lotus flower at this timely point. He had rediscovered the Director Jin he knew of old, only her frame was more rotund. It was said that she had written off two chairs during rehearsal, though her plumpness could now be regarded as lovely, dear and venerable.

"Director Jin, you are a master artist," said Smooth, scrabbling for some terms of flattery. "Your words are all the credit I need for spending half my life shifting stages. It's not that I want to boast about what we've done. This time, my brothers pushed themselves beyond their normal limits. Since New Year is close at hand, everyone has things to do urgently at home. Still, we exerted ourselves for Director Jin and Chief Qu. There was not one word of complaint and we did everything as instructed. Monkey lost a finger and now has to live with that disability. Even so, he just texted me to ask how the play was going. Truly, my brothers are all decent guys, pretty decent, Mr Chief, Madame Director."

Director Jin turned around abruptly. "Hai," she said, "where is that flower they just gave me? Iron Kou, find it for me. I'm going to visit Monkey."

"It's already midnight," answered Kou. "How will you get there? We can go on your behalf tomorrow."

"No, no, I must go tonight. I must visit in person – me myself. No lackey."

"Go and find the flower," instructed Chief Qu. "I'll accompany you. Smooth, are we allowed into the ward at this hour?"

"We can go in, but it's a big ward with more than ten patients. Director Jin must be exhausted. I can tell Monkey that she expressed concern for him. Once he hears that, his finger might grow back."

Smooth had intended this as a light-hearted quip, but nobody took it that way. As Director Jin was determined to go to the hospital, Smooth and Sufen pedalled there in advance.

The hospital stood a couple of kilometres from the theatre. When Smooth arrived at the gate, the car from the troupe had not yet got there. He told Sufen to slip in and tell Monkey about the impending visit while he waited outside. After all, it was his subordinate who they were coming to see.

Monkey was excited by such an unexpected call. The director held his hand and sobbed without uttering a single word. Had it not been for the other sleeping patients, she might have started wailing. She rummaged around in her pockets and was able to amass more than 2,000 yuan, which she placed beside Monkey's pillow. They all then left the ward.

"That fellow Monkey lost a finger for the sake of this play," she murmured to Chief Qu. "As the director, I must accept a sense of guilt, Old Qu."

"Don't vex yourself. It will be handled properly."

"Thank you, Director Jin. Thank you, Chief Qu," Smooth said, fully intending to switch topic. "All you leaders deserve our gratitude for thinking highly of us labouring hands. Every one of you is a decent and kind person. I'm sure Chief Qu won't treat us unfairly. Since New Year is around the corner, I beg you sincerely to do something for Monkey. Otherwise, he'll have no way to explain to his wife and old parents how he's come home for Spring Festival with a finger missing and no money for it."

"We've thought this through already," answered the chief. "Monkey will receive a cash payment of thirty thousand yuan. The rest can wait until after the holiday."

"The troupe really has no money now," claimed the head of finance. "Chief Qu has borrowed from everywhere, and still we haven't found any way to solve the problem of covering several months of staff bonuses."

"Chief Qu promised us our labour fee as soon as the rehearsal was over," Smooth blurted out. "We're looking forward to that to tide us over during New Year."

The chief looked at the head of finance. "Pay Smooth's fees first thing tomorrow," he instructed.

"But there's barely ten thousand yuan left in the account."

On hearing that admission, Smooth's heart sank cold. He sprang forward, apparently to open the car door for Qu, but in reality barring his way. "Chief, you can't deny us the money," he pleaded. "Otherwise, none of us can go home."

"Old Qu, you must find a way out," Director Jin added. "You can't default on what Smooth is owed."

"Come along tomorrow," Chief Qu said sternly to the head of finance. "Borrow from private individuals if you must, but be certain that Smooth's account is settled."

Smooth wanted to make further sure that the promise would be honoured, but Iron Kou yanked his hand as it hovered by the car door. Kou now worried that there might be other secrets that Smooth would let slip. "No need to worry about a single penny," he snarled. "Let the leaders get inside the car. It's windy out here and not the right place for debate." He stood protecting the door to the vehicle and once the passengers were inside, slammed it shut.

The leaders of the troupe were gone. Iron Kou had come in his own car, and Smooth now clutched the door, asking desperately for the money from the temple job. In fact, this was not his only potential lifeline, as he knew that Sufen had been in touch with the lay sister, Serenity. On making enquiries through her, he learned that the temple had already paid Kou.

"Must I really kneel in front of you, Director?" he pleaded. "My brothers are so pitiful. They need that money to survive, so you can't delay any longer. You must give me a word to pass on to them."

On noticing how irritated Iron Kou's countenance had become, Smooth did actually crouch down on his knees. Sufen, who was watching to one side, was shocked.

It was now 1 am and the shadows of people ghosted by the gate. Iron Kou was wary of creating a spectacle. "Very well," he said helplessly. "Let me borrow some cash for you tomorrow. How would that be, OK?" He drove off in a rush.

The swift movement of the car nearly made Smooth lurch down onto the road.

48

SMOOTH RETURNED HOME and collapsed onto the bed like a pat of sodden mud. Sufen boiled some water and asked him to wash his feet, but he felt unable to sit up. She helped him to undress and dabbed his body with a warm, moist towel. As it approached his posterior, he recoiled stubbornly. Smooth tried to take care of that region himself and a pus-like residue was left on the terry cloth. Sufen wanted to examine it, though he refused, and simply tugged the quilt over his body and started to snore.

He slept until the next morning when he was awoken by the sound of firecrackers being set off by neighbouring children. His eyes could open well enough. Not so his body. Smooth had a numb sensation, as if he had been tied up, and when he flinched his fingers to investigate, the swelling had worsened. He struggled to edge himself off the mattress to allow his wife to lie in.

"Rest a bit longer." She was actually already awake.

"No, I have to chase up the money from the troupe. Everybody is waiting for it." He began to dress.

"Go to the hospital for a check-up afterwards. I suspect it may be another prolapse."

"Nothing serious. Old war wounds."

"Better be careful. From molehills, mountains can grow."

"I know."

Smooth went to a corner of the room and slathered some ointment on his rear end. There was a crinkling sound as he applied the gauze and prepared to go out.

Tomorrow was New Year's Eve, so the morning market would be

packed. He spun the pedals briskly to try to cut a path through all the throngs, watching on as parcels large and small and bags of shopping for Spring Festival were humped and carried all over. His family had not even started any of that. His top priority was to ensure that by whatever means he was able to send his colleagues back to their folks in time. He calculated that the farthest any of them had to travel was four or five hours, so if they had their money at noon, they would easily be home by the evening.

Smooth had spread the word that everyone should assemble in the courtyard of the troupe at 9 am. As he pedalled on, it was as though at least twenty pairs of scorching eyes were trained upon him and him alone.

He headed first of all to the administration building in search of Chief Qu. The chief led him to the office of the deputy director in charge of finance. He in turn took Smooth to the accountant's office where the money was stored. The notes were wrapped in sheets of newspaper, having apparently not been withdrawn from a bank. "You really do have a nerve, Smooth," commented the cashier. "Chief Qu was insistent that the money be gathered from private hands. He said we should cover your labour fees first by any means. Take it, this is the thirty thousand yuan for the chopped off finger. We'll make it legit with the paperwork after the festival. The whole troupe is now on vacation." Smooth thanked him repeatedly.

After obtaining the payment for *Peach Blossom Cheeks*, he once again tried to connect with Iron Kou, whose phone had been turned off. He knew Kou would not take matters for granted.

Smooth distributed the salaries for the present production, all the while praising Chief Qu, Director Jin and their deputies. He told them they should cherish the kindness displayed to them. Next, he asked them to accompany him and wait at the foot of the staff residential building while he went on ahead. More than twenty of them formed a kind of parade, and it was clear from their bearing and manner that they were most anxious. Smooth was left with no alternative. He had knelt down before Iron Kou at the hospital entrance the previous night, so what else could he do? He arranged his crew so that every last one of them should be visible from Iron Kou's window, before climbing the stairs alone.

Smooth knocked on the door and, when there was no response,

tapped again. He had to be bold today, no matter whether Iron Kou was content or incensed, and would continue until the occupants opened up. He had thought that even if Kou was hostile, he would stand his ground and refuse any other jobs from this source. After all, this had become the routine – never to be paid on time or in full for whatever service they rendered to him. Upon the fourth attempt, a woman's voice could at last be heard.

"Knock, knock, knock. Who's there?" It was Iron Kou's wife, the ingenue actress.

"Smooth, it's Smooth, Madame Lu," he replied timidly in a rather low voice. He knew that her surname was Lu and that it was the right decorum to address female performers as "Madame", just as they would say "Chief Qu" out of respect.

"What are you after?" she asked.

"Director Kou instructed me to come."

"He's not at home."

"Director Kou instructed I come," he said once more, this time with sternness. "Director Kou told me to come. I didn't want to, but was given no other choice. There are more than twenty of them down there waiting to be able to go back for New Year. If you don't believe me, take a look out of your window. They're so furious, they've been baying to shove me from the top of a high building."

There was no sound inside at first. Following a short interval, the door creaked open a little. "Smooth, you son of a bitch," hissed a sleepy-looking Iron Kou. "Are you trying to humiliate me? Make your guys fuck off at once, then we can talk about money."

"You tell me what I should say to them, then. Tomorrow is New Year's Eve. They want to go home, but how can they without money? Where should I tell them to fuck off to?"

"I don't care where they fuck off to. You'll not get a penny out of me coming here mob-handed."

The actress now pushed her face to the seam of the door. "Your guys haven't one ounce of shame," she snorted. "Shooting your loads inside a temple. How can you have the face to come and ask my Iron Kou to pay you? You brought shame on us and lost us face, humph."

Iron Kou dragged his wife's head back. "Send that lot away," he ordered. "Then we'll talk money when they're gone."

"I can't drive them away. Honestly, I have no power over them. They've nearly gulped me down whole. Don't you believe me? If I told them I couldn't get what they're owed, they'd be straight up here themselves. These two days they've been sore-eyed and itchy-handed." Smooth thought that even if he couldn't succeed, he should at least fire off some strong words.

"What are you threatening me with? You can't beat me. Come up and hit me, if you've only got the guts."

The actress again put her face to the crack in the door. "Let's see Smooth lay a finger on my Iron Kou," she taunted. "If only he has the guts. A gang of shameless shits."

"Madame Lu, please don't say these disgusting things. How can you call us a gang of shameless shits?"

"You shot your loads in the temple. Isn't that shameless enough–"

Before she could finish her diatribe, Iron Kou had blocked her from continuing. "Just think of it," he now said. "You can't get a penny if your gang doesn't fuck off. Even if I wanted to give you the money, I'd have to take it from the household account. Count yourself lucky the temple didn't fine you."

"You're quite clear in your own heart about whether they paid you or not! Nobody wants to take money dishonestly from a temple."

Iron Kou was shocked by Smooth's sober tone, which hinted that he knew the inside story.

"Never," the harridan shouted from inside. "Let them make money by shooting their loads." With that, the door was slammed shut.

Smooth knocked again. This time it was even louder and with an air of total abandon. He could hear the couple quarrelling inside, seemingly about money too. After several minutes of altercation, the door opened slightly again. Iron Kou tossed out tens of thousands of yuan in cash. Smooth could see that his wife was trying to prevent him from doing so by swiping his arm with a mop.

"Fuck off now, Smooth," cursed Iron Kou. "From now on, you'll never get another thing out of me."

The door slammed shut.

Smooth gathered up the banknotes and found that they totalled

50,000 yuan. This was still more than 20,000 yuan less than the promised sum. Things having come to this stage, he thought it foolhardy to ask again, so took the bundle downstairs. He got his crew to assemble in a quiet place to receive their share. Originally, he was meant to be owed double plus the boss's bonus. The total being well short, he waived these prerogatives and took the same as everyone else. Afterwards, he kicked Mound square and hard on the posterior. "This is all down to you, you son of a bitch," he swore.

He then rode to the hospital to hand Monkey his wage packet. On being promptly discharged, he gave him a lift to the bus station. As they were about to enter the gate, his mobile rang.

"You'd better come back quickly," Sufen said, her voice wavering at the other end. "Daisy's murdered Plum's dog. The two of them are laying into each other as I speak."

Smooth sent Monkey to his seat and then turned around and pedalled home manically.

49

When Smooth reached the house, the bloodied corpse of Goody was already suspended on the railings of the upper floor.

On seeing the carnage, Smooth was aghast with fear and tottered to the ground, being unable to regain his footing.

He had seen various animals slaughtered and even the corpses of humans who had died in rare circumstances. Once, years ago, he had been called upon to help the police haul a body from the city moat. On sweltering summer days, dead bodies can become swollen and fester, with even forensic scientists being reluctant to handle them. Nothing he had seen before was as terrifying and wretched as what he beheld now. How could a poor disabled pet have become the trigger and target for such hatred? Worse still, the perpetrator had been his own daughter. His heart felt icy cold as if his soul had been banished to hell and could not be reunited with his body.

Smooth could hear noises from upstairs, as if his wife were staging some kind of intervention. He tried to get to his feet, but slipped down again since the moment he stuck out his hands, they inadvertently made contact with the hardened icicles of canine blood. "Smooth, come quickly!" he could hear Sufen calling out. He made another attempt to crawl over.

He could quite imagine the bloodbath upstairs, but the truth was far worse than his expectation. In the two bedrooms, there was nothing that hadn't been beaten or torn out of shape. The quilts and sheets had been slashed apart with scissors, and gobbets of long hair and gore soiled the floor both inside and out on the walkway. Daisy and Plum were now grappling with each other on Daisy's floor mat.

Plum wielded a chopping knife, which Sufen had pressed tightly into a quilt to try to sheath it. Meanwhile, her bloodstained face had almost lost any semblance of humanity. Daisy, for her part, took a tubular steel deckchair as her weapon. This was rammed against Sufen's buttocks, as black smoke encircled the filament of the smashed ceiling light. Smooth had witnessed dust-ups like this in movies without ever thinking that it could happen in his own home. He knew the sisters did not see eye to eye, but had never envisioned it degenerating into a mortal struggle. He felt that the family's doom was at hand.

Smooth scrabbled to find anything to salve this hostility, though could find no tool or implement that might pacify them. His recourse in all these years was to face contradictions with the obedient attitude of a grandson. By belittling himself to the point at which he elicited pity, usually even the toughest nut would open.

He held himself unequal to the bullying might of Daisy and was also in no position to cope with Plum's sudden delinquency. He had to fall back on his final option as a means of snatching the situation from peril. He had knelt down for Iron Kou, so reasoned that it was not exactly shameful to repeat this action before his daughters. In well-bred families, one glance from the father was enough to stop anything of which he did not approve. Smooth exerted himself so much that he thought his intestines might be about to squirt out from his arsehole, but he still could not muster any paternal dignity before these two young women. He accepted the reality of holding no dignity, and would do so gladly if it meant that the household enjoyed harmony and safety. Even if their lives were no better than those around them, it didn't mean that they were ready to have corpses dragged out of the door.

Scolding words held not the least potency. In Daisy's eyes, he was not even qualified to count himself as a father in the modern era. Any attempt by him to scold someone else would be met with scorn.

"I am begging you, please don't fight like this," he squeaked, using the very meekest phrase that came to mind. "Isn't there another way of solving this? Whatever the problem is, it can be resolved. Are you starving or dying from thirst? Why the need to fight for life and death? Tomorrow is New Year's Eve. Do you truly hate each other so deeply? Why create this mess? Can't you wait and settle everything after Spring Festival? I am begging you to each give an inch and be tolerant. That I beg." He was already kowtowing on the floor.

Plum shrieked and Sufen scrambled to try to restrain her. The knife dug deep into the quilt.

"Smooth Diao, you're such a loser," taunted Daisy. "A smelly hooligan. There'll be no end to this year if you don't drive these wild bitches out."

Hearing his own daughter denounce him in these terms made Smooth want to lift that tea table and end the life of this miscreant and unfilial creature. He dared not recall the tears of humiliation he had wept and the blood he had lost for his family and for her in particular, only to have these words hurled back at him since he had not furnished her with the life she wanted. Her failure to find a boyfriend brought out a deep sense of guilt in him. Furthermore, he didn't want to antagonise her in this mood, so he shunned the tea table just as he shunned tough words. "I know I am a loser," he admitted. "But is this a reason you can't put up with your sister and aunt?"

"Humph, Sister, humph, Aunt." Daisy's mania made Smooth despise her entire being.

"Well, I'm going. I'm leaving. Enough is enough!" Plum screamed with desperate anger.

50

WHEN IT CAME TO SUFFERING, Plum had gone beyond her point of endurance. Prior to Daisy slaughtering the dog so mercilessly, she retained the will to fight. This bravery, however, had denatured into a kind of swashbuckling panic. She was prepared to take up arms in the form of the chopping knife, though only because she knew that Cai Sufen was alongside them. At that stage, she might still have been resolute, unwilling to withdraw. What made the difference was the ponderous demeanour her stepfather Smooth displayed when faced with major issues of principle. Kneeling down like a rag doll in that way was tantamount to condoning Daisy's act of atrocity. She felt utterly hopeless when she witnessed him bowing and kowtowing. That the head of the family could act in this manner was the final straw for her.

Plum had never thought that Daisy would stoop to murder. Victimising the dog had been one proven way of warning and challenging her. Today, when the younger sister came home from buying breakfast outside, she came across her pet soiled with blood and pinioned against the railings. Her first reaction was that this was not Goody that had been killed, but herself or her deceased mother. She had been a stray adopted by Orchid Zhao and exhibited the character of a supernatural entity. She lay beside her owner in her dying minutes and licked away those tears as her own eyes became damp. On her deathbed at the very last, her mother entrusted two wards to her stepfather: first, her pitiful daughter, and then her broken-legged dog. Smooth grasped her hand possessively. "Rest assured," he whimpered, "I'll take good care of both." But how, when Goody had been slain by his own daughter and he was now kneeling before her, begging for mercy, could Plum depend on such a loser?

As she was packing her belongings in a rage, Cai Sufen entered the room. Sufen tried to pull out the items that Plum had crammed into the bag and Plum in turn attempted to reinsert them. There was no antipathy between the two women. To some degree, Sufen had been generous and quite sympathetic. For a period, she even entertained the idea that they could form a united front against Daisy. Sufen then seemed to skirt away from the notion, preferring instead to avoid her stepdaughter and not be in the house at the same time as her. Duly, no alliance could be born.

On reflection, Plum could pinpoint the time Daisy began to exhibit hostility towards her. It coincided with Cai Sufen entering the home. Maybe without her appearance, Daisy would not have grown so troublesome. From this angle, she did have a streak of aversion to her. Particularly when it came to the abuse meted out on Goody, Sufen was no different from her stepfather in principle or position. Both were anxious to avoid giving offence to her elder sister. Even as she was trying to separate the pair during their brawl, Sufen was largely cowed by the despotic might of Daisy. This deepened her distaste towards the woman.

Now, when Sufen was gripping the handle of the suitcase and appeared reluctant to relinquish it, Plum finally came out with what was the most vicious phrase in her heart. "Don't expect you'll be safe when I am gone," she warned. "If she can murder Goody today and drive me away, she can make you her victim tomorrow. This is my stepfather's evil fruit, but also the consequence of a stepmother who let herself be intimidated and resorted to flattery and evasion. Don't believe that if you stay on here your lot will be any better than Goody's. I'm sure that I'd bear witness to that. Wait and see." With that, she dragged her suitcase and left the room.

"Smooth!" Sufen called out.

He was still in the next room discussing an issue with Daisy, who was unable to hear a syllable of what he was saying for her headphones were blocking out all extraneous sound. When Smooth was about to add something, she kicked over the bedside table for effect. He craned his neck down to where Sufen was shouting for him and saw that Plum was already downstairs with her luggage.

Plum caught a glimpse of the poor hound as she descended the stairs. She burst into a wail of "Mum!"

She had followed Orchid Zhao to this household when she was a small girl, though her mother was dead within a few years. Today, she herself was being evicted helplessly, having no one to depend on, and was bringing almost nothing away with her. She couldn't even protect a poor disabled dog and had allowed it to perish in fear and panic, its miserable death being enough to make an angel weep. Sorrow and dreariness hung coldly from her heart like those icicles of blood had seeped from Goody's nose and limbs. On stepping out of the gate, she might as well have been the lousiest and most pathetic reprobate in the world.

She could hear her stepfather and his wife trying to pursue her from behind. Not even their shrieks prompted a backward glance. It just so happened that a cab was passing by, so she climbed straight in. By the time her stepparents got out on to the street, she was already far into the distance.

The driver asked if she had just been involved in some kind of argument. "It's New Year," he remarked. "It's best to be with family."

"Just drive, please. Don't give me any crap," she retorted.

Plum switched off her mobile.

The taxi drove all the way to the long-distance bus station.

She now had only one place of refuge – Towering Cloud Mountain, the place in Zhen'an County where Zhu Mancang lived. Her choice was settled, for from now on she could not return to the Western Capital. What was that city to her anyhow? Apart from that poky room of fourteen square metres, did she really have any other anchor? Not until this very moment did she fully understand the value and significance of blood ties. No wonder her mother had exhorted her stepfather in that manner before she drew her terminal breath. She had even tried to crawl up from the bed and kowtow three times before him. She was entrusting her daughter and dog to Smooth.

Plum must seek out Zhu Mancang. He was the only man in this

world to fill her with warmth. Even if she was compelled to marry into the deep mountains, she would accept that as her fate.

As the bus was about to set off, she spotted her stepfather Smooth Diao sprinting into the station, perspiring heavily. His mouth was wide open, trying to catch his breath while simultaneously appearing clownish. In the past, Plum did not disdain her stepfather's gawky manner. That feeling only really took hold as she entered senior school at about the age of fifteen or sixteen. One of her classmates had observed how simpletons are in the habit of allowing their jaws to hang wide open. Could it be that her father was one of them? She had tried to correct him and encouraged him to keep his mouth firmly closed when not talking. Even then, he opened it like a fool when his head was turned. Right now, she didn't want her stepfather to intervene. He walked several circuits around the station and she ducked down in her seat, hoping to depart unnoticed.

The bus rumbled into motion. As it passed the gate of the depot yard, the eyes of her foolishly loitering stepfather met with hers. He banged on the door of the bus in desperation, but the vehicle was not permitted to stop in this place. She saw him now staring at her with imploring eyes. As he closed his gaping jaw, he seemed to have remembered something. The wheels of the bus splashed dirty crystals of ice all over him, just as his mouth was opening again.

On the window of the coach hung a sign that read "Western Capital to Zhen'an". She knew that her destination must have registered with him, so there was no need for him to come searching or report her as missing at the police station.

Before long, the bus had left the city limits. She crooked her neck around at the place where she had lived for more than twenty years. Whether her tears were now sentimental or sorrowful, who could rightly say? She realised that her departure marked the severing of her umbilical cord. The Western Capital belonged to others.

51

EVER SINCE BIG ARMY'S VANISHING ACT, Daisy was unsure about whom to claim as her victim. Princess Wu had given her an unforeseen jolt, having just eloped to Australia with an "upper crust, generous and sumptuous" guy of her own. Daisy, despite being her closest friend, had no forewarning of her nuptials. She felt not only deceived but also molten hot with fury. Jealously infused her bones and was even etched into her heart. Try as she might to resist this emotion, she found herself unable to fully open or close her eyes. With her eyes open, it seemed that everyone was looking at her in a strange manner; with her eyes closed, she brought into view Princes Wu and her new husband sprawled out on a Gold Coast beach. Those sands she had only seen on the cinema screen, and they were basking in their timeless love, the flavour of which she had never known. All these churning thoughts just made her want to curse.

In fact, she had met that "upper crust, generous and sumptuous" chap once before. He was an estate agent in his early thirties. His assets were said to exceed 100 million yuan and he had a PhD conferred by a foreign university. He was not tall, at most five feet seven inches. Having an agile body, a sculpted face, a calm temperament and a slightly androgynous manner, he somewhat resembled a South Korean celebrity. Were he taller and stronger, that might have brought him too much unwanted attention. "I love bigger women," Daisy could remember him saying. "They give me such a sense of security." Daisy's response to this was meant in jest. "Princess Wu is tall," she said. "She can double up as your wife and bodyguard." It never occurred to her at the time that he would fall for her friend.

Daisy knew Wu so well, and she lacked the features that men habitually go for. A few years back, it was fashionable for uncouth men to divide the opposite sex into two categories. There were those who were petite and cute, and acted as timid as a bird. They enjoyed great popularity. Then there were the tall, plump and strongly built females. They were derided as tomboys or mocked and dismissed out of hand. Princess Wu happened to conform to all the attributes of the latter group. In the past couple of years, the criteria appeared to have shifted. They should now be "fair skinned, rich and pretty". The Princess was not so blessed, being like an unripe winter melon with its thick, impenetrable rind. What was more, she was giddy, easily amused and a beanpole without many brain cells to call her own. Thinking frankly, Daisy could conceive of someone like Tan Daogui – Mr Noodle Head – pursuing and catching her. She could not stretch her imagination to envisage her going steady with an "upper crust, generous and sumptuous" suitor.

And yet that is what happened. Via WeChat, they sent pictures of themselves cavorting in swimwear on the Gold Coast. Wu's bikini-clad bottom seemed as broad as a country millstone. Her slender companion apparently enjoyed mounting this edifice and gazing out across the distant coast. As if to emphasise the fact that they were actually Down Under, there were photos of penguins, obligatory images of kangaroos bounding about the Bush, and Wu nursing and kissing a cuddly koala. All this technicolour evidence of their Antipodean nuptials left Daisy well and truly deflated.

It had been Tan Daogui who came over to share this mournful news. His eyes were swollen, and his overall appearance resembled a person tasked with delivering an obituary notice. His straggly rice noodle had drooped down and was dangling so it tickled one side of his neck. He tried hard to twirl it up and out of the way before he began to talk. Low spirits appeared to dog his hair too and as the strands fell down, he rearranged them automatically with his fingers. However, they flopped back to their previous position, occupying the thick groves his tears seemed to have worn. These hairs had the pitiful appearance of a stream trickling through a drought-stricken landscape.

"She sure got her honeymoon strip," Tan commented, miss-peaking the word "trip" as if by Freudian slip.

"You knew nothing about this in advance?" asked Daisy.

"No, not at all."

"Weren't you supposed to be an item? You weren't given a look in?"

"I... mentioned the issue. But she... just laughed... never... never answered me seriously."

To Daisy's best recollections, in all the times they socialised, Princess Wu never shared her true impressions of Tan. They just laughed, ate, played and searched for fun when they were outside. Nothing beyond the bounds of propriety had been allowed. Nowadays, there are plenty of girls like this. They help a man to consume whatever is put on offer and lap up both his money and time, but never come close to even mentioning marriage. That night at the inn in Zhen'an County, Tan had sneaked into Princess Wu's room. She was clearly revolted by him and even claimed to have called the police. Daisy knew this was a practical joke, but if her friend did fancy him even slightly, then she would not have caused him to panic and flee like that in the middle of the night. Reviewing the evidence, there were no signs of any love towards him. One could conclude that she was not simply a giddy beanpole or an unripe winter melon, but an old vixen whose heart was as unfathomable as the ocean. She reminded Daisy of the mercenary hero Yu Zecheng in the TV serial *Insidious*.

How could Tan hope to obtain some "balm" from Daisy to help treat his wound? Her innermost heart had now been scalded, so it shrank and twitched convulsively. To Tan, she was repellent.

That night Daisy had barely a moment's sleep. In the small hours she received a text from Princess Wu apologising again and again for having left so hastily and without the opportunity to tell her. She felt a pang of remorse for having sent those cavorting beach photos, though Daisy sensed she was all too ready to exhibit her body. She sent not a single word of reply, being convinced that her friendship with this old vixen had come to an end.

In this ghost town – the Western Capital – why hadn't they banned fireworks and bangers! Her head was fit to explode. Whenever Plum had experienced a pounding at Daisy's hands, she would turn on the track *Lin Daiyu, the Buried Fallen Blossom*. That was a favourite of hers from Shaoxin Opera. She had overheard Plum on the phone telling somebody how Lin Daiyu was the heroine she adored and that this aria would bring her out in tears of catharsis. Daisy found it amusing how the daughter of a seamstress could compare herself to a noble heroine. She wanted to spit in her face and curse her for having muddled along here for years, helping herself to food and drink. She had never displayed any gratitude, but wallowed in bitter disappointment and broken-heartedness like Lin Daiyu. Smooth Diao, however, took this girl as dearer than his very own daughter.

Daisy had a whole arsenal of anger waiting to explode. It happened that on this particular morning, Plum broke into a tone-deaf rendition of *Lin Daiyu, the Buried Fallen Blossom* in her bedroom. Daisy rapped sharply against the window pane with the wonky clothes hanger that Plum had left outside the glass. "Stop that caterwauling," she warned. "There's no tomcat around to give you one!"

Plum took no notice and sang with more bravado. She went downstairs to buy breakfast, consciously leaving the sound at maximum volume. Daisy stormed into Plum's room and intended to toss away that old computer. However, the dog took hold of the hem of her trousers and stopped her. Daisy reached for the fruit knife from Plum's table and plunged it into the animal's back. The dog struggled and bit at her, to which she raised her foot and kicked her away, then stomped on her body several times. Goody the dog was no more. The bones of her fractured leg lay exposed to the naked eye.

As a girl, Daisy had witnessed how the people of the neighbourhood maltreated dogs. Whenever strays began to linger nearby, residents would chase them and beat them to death, so they could skin the bodies and eat the meat. Sometimes this was done for entertainment rather than food. They would brandish rocks, bricks, spade handles, iron wires, crowbars, steel pipes, bicycle chains or anything else that came to hand. No matter how far or how fast the hounds sprinted, they could not escape disablement or death. Especially when two dogs were spotted together, locals would be fired up and want to pursue and attack them. When the pair were in their deathly throes, a morbid curiosity would take over. How the canines would cling to one another fascinated these sadists. Dogs that were beaten as a couple aroused further discussion and would become fodder for anecdotes. Sometimes, long after the event, a guy could be heard recounting how he had dealt the fatal strike with an iron rod. The young Daisy winced at this bloodthirstiness, and would even cry in horror or be left with nightmares. Right now, she had slain this lame dog and was unsure why. The dog had never menaced her and yet her mood was now buoyant and excited, like those idlers who killed for the hell of it.

Daisy had not finished yet. She knew that the slut downstairs was at home too. Another opera came to mind – the Shaanxi play, *Persuading a Wife by Killing a Dog*. She decided to capitalise on her deed by using it to threaten the other slut downstairs.

She had not anticipated that the effect would be so profound. As she was hanging up her victim on display, that bitch slut Cai Sufen looked upstairs. On realising what she had in her hands, she gasped "Oh my God!" and keeled over, unconscious. The basin of water she was carrying flipped upside down onto the ground, spilling out the drenched underwear and cotton shoes.

Next, the pipsqueak slut returned with an omelette in one hand and a cup of hot soya bean milk in the other. She was murmuring the lyrics of *Lin Daiyu, the Buried Fallen Blossom* in soft Suzhou dialect. When she raised her head and caught sight of the body, she spilled the hot drink on to her hand and gasped. The omelette fell to the ground together with the fried dough sticks. Her heart was racing, and she trembled all over. Then, like an enraged lioness, she entered the kitchen, armed herself with a chopping knife and raced upstairs.

Once she regained consciousness, Cai Sufen followed on close behind Plum.

Daisy had no fear of silly rough and tumble games in which the loser was made to beg for mercy. She had played too many of them when she was small. She and Princess Wu could easily make boys beg for mercy if they so wished. A little slut like Plum, by contrast, could be made to spin in circles with the lightest poke of a finger. Today, though, her determination appeared far more concerted. Daisy had to really exert herself to put up a defence and counterattack.

After a while, Smooth came home. To Daisy's disgust, the loser bent his soft legs at the sight of this battle royal. He must have been kneeling for her sake. The big slut and the pipsqueak slut were compliant towards him, so he had no need to abase himself for them. Daisy knew that this was a dramatic trick, employed to try to make her – the bad seed – feel culpable. There had been many addicts in this community and this was a tactic of persuasion their parents slumped to. Few prodigals were saved by it, however.

Studying the crooked and lumpen figure of Smooth on the ground, she remembered that phrase once again, "Hell is other people". Princess Wu's beau, the PhD graduate, had quoted it. His words were vividly apt right now. The more she contemplated the matter, the more she realised how hell had subsumed every facet of her life. In this home, the two women interlopers were hell to deal with, but wasn't Smooth her greatest hell? Thinking carefully, her father's life was the rightful headquarters of Hell plc.

He could continue to kneel if it made him happy on some level. Daisy simply didn't care. Nothing would persuade her to ask him to cease this spectacle and, finally, Smooth stood up reluctantly of his own accord.

The little slut packed her grubby suitcase and parted in melodramatic fashion as if to say "the great river torrent is surging to the east and will never return again". High time she went. Daisy had been dismayed at how Smooth supported Plum's higher education. Now the feral daughter had proved herself more capable and popular than the home-bred one, so that even her father fawned over her as "kind-hearted", "pretty" and "a promising college student". That grain of sand pressed into Daisy's eyes.

Several days earlier, while walking outside, she had been accosted by a fortune teller who couldn't be dissuaded from doing a reading much as Daisy declined. "Lovey, be cautious," he advised. "To start with, your fate will be promising. Then an ill wind with invade your home and usurp your advantages. Deal with it!" The fellow sold her a talisman for 300 yuan and told her to secure it firmly but secretly into the lintel above her doorway. She complied with a note of scepticism. Over the years, she had spent countless amounts seeking divination on finding a boyfriend. Yet she remained single. When the soothsayer predicted an ill wind invading her home, that was something she could easily believe in.

One gust of that ill wind had been tackled today and she credited this to the influence of the talisman.

After the pipsqueak slut's departure, she knew that Smooth had gone searching for her, and failed. In the evening, as he prepared to bury the dog, he stood by her door. "Virtue ruined!" he sighed. "The virtue of the Diao family is all ruined!"

Daisy had expected the slaying of the pet to seriously disorient that big slut Cai Sufen. Instead, the wife laundered the quilt and clothes, even rolling together all the bloody articles from the little slut's room upstairs. These she picked through and cleaned. To all outward appearances, she had such composure that even a hurricane would leave her unruffled.

At night, Daisy suffered from insomnia. On closing her eyes, she recoiled at the image of the dead dog. She thought of Goody, Princess Wu, herself, the atrocious Big Army, the wretched loser Smooth and those two sluts. The longer she stewed over them, the less meaning life held for her. The notion of suicide even crossed her mind. She had heard of a website that was dedicated to introducing the methods of and rationale behind ending one's life. For half the night she surfed online, keen to learn more. She even dabbled in chatrooms, exchanging messages with those teetering on the edge or those who had resolved to bid farewell to this world. In the end, she concluded that life had no meaning, but that actually death was meaningless as well. What had made her so upset and was driving her to distraction was the sound of Sufen doing the laundry downstairs. How could she allow herself to die first while this mule of a woman was still alive?

It was the morning of New Year's Eve. The ripple of firecrackers signified the impending close to her meaningless year. Her discontent was absolute. As she rolled and fidgeted on the bed, highlights of the previous night crackled through her brain. She now struck on a plan. Yes, she ought to die. Die and let Smooth and Sufen watch. Of course, this would not be a genuine suicide. Death was not her aim. Right now, she had no reason to end it all.

When Cai Sufen went to the toilet, Daisy threaded a length of nylon cord through a ring that hung suspended on the upper floor. Normally, an iron pipe was inserted through it and its counterpart to function as a drying rod for clothes. This morning, according to her plan, she slipped into white silk pyjamas, and with the help of a stool, managed to stick her head through the homemade noose. This was in plain view of anybody leaving the toilet. As Daisy anticipated that her stepmother must be about to come out, she kicked away her support.

But Sufen did not appear. She squatted there for longer than was her habit. Daisy immediately regretted having been so keen to kick free. Did Sufen not hear the stool rattle to the ground? Maybe the slut did witness everything and chose not to come to her aid. The game was over. Daisy plashed out her legs a few times without being able to touch anything firm. Her body felt like it had become a cotton strip. Now, this ingenious idea of hers was not so ingenious. Her life could be about to end in such a pathetic and inconsequential way.

52

SMOOTH WENT OUT EARLY TO BUY VEGETABLES. Sufen had spent the previous night cleaning the entire home and, as today was New Year's Eve, they should have some special fare to mark the turning of the year. "Nian", the nickname for this day, where did it come from? There were those who said that in ancient times it referred to a fierce man-eating animal, which every household tried to appease with sacrificial food. They might also let off firecrackers to scare away the marauder. For Smooth, it was as if this were somehow still a threat incarnate. The monster had bypassed him for more than five decades and yet he had never driven it fully away. Indeed, each New Year it seemed to cast a more ominous shadow.

As a boy, he eagerly awaited the festival because he knew to expect decent food and clothes. Later, after his parents passed away, he had to endure the season alone as head of the household. He never worried about what to eat or what to wear. In fact, for him the season had become insipid and uninspiring. In recent times, Daisy would whip up trouble every New Year by crying or making a scene. Last year, she got plastered and smashed the wok into pieces with a brick, leaving Plum and him with nothing in which to boil their homemade dumplings. This year Plum had been ejected, though Sufen was still by his side. From what had transpired of late, it would be impossible for the three to spend this time together in peace and calm. Spring Festival called for celebrations, dumplings, firecrackers and amity. While other families savoured these things, how could they make do with a cold wok and a chilly kitchen? Smooth purchased spring onions and lean meat along with the sort of ingredients that went into cold dish appetisers, such as pig's ears and stomach, lotus root and tomatoes.

His mobile rang and he heard the drone of Uncle Scar at the other end. Since they lived in the same community and he had nowhere else as sanctuary, Smooth couldn't brush him off indefinitely. Scar repeated his request for the money, to which Smooth reiterated that there had been no news of his brother since his departure. As a trike pedaller, how was he able to foot such a colossal bill? Even if Uncle Scar were to take himself as a down payment and swallow him whole, Smooth wouldn't have put a dent in that debt.

"I am due some now, even if it's just a pittance," rasped Scar. "Don't provoke me into being like the brutal landlord Huang Shiren and come knocking at your door on New Year's Eve."

"Uncle, you can come along if you like. I'll make dumplings for you. As for money, there is none to speak of. All I have is the few pennies I've made with my labour."

"Don't give me that. You're a boss with dozens under you. Let's wait and see if you can't cough up some cash. Let's wait and see." Uncle Scar hung up.

Smooth tapped away at his keypad angrily in an effort to connect with Big Army. No luck. "What a scourge!" he cursed.

He had been contemplating cycling over to the Hui Muslim Quarter to buy some marinated beef and crystal cakes from De Mao Gong. That phone call had dampened his mood, and now the anal pain set in again as if someone was trying to sodomise him, only using knitting needles and a knife. He thought that an impromptu visit to the clinic was the best way to assuage any discomfort over the festive season.

Smooth's mobile phone chimed again. This time it was Sufen, in the uttermost distress. "Come back quick! Daisy's... hanged herself..." He started to ask questions, but the line was already dead.

How could Daisy resort to suicide?

He swung his legs into motion. As he was mercifully close to home, the ride took barely seven or eight minutes. On crossing the threshold, he could see the noose still dangling upstairs. Sufen was screeching out Daisy's name, and he ran up to join her, missing his footing at the last moment and hitting the top step with a somersault. He staggered over to her unconscious body, which Sufen was straddling in an effort to administer CPR. The ligature mark on Daisy's neck had by now turned a bluish black colour. On swiftly pinching her philtrum, he shouted out "Daisy, Daisy, my Daisy..." with dripping eyes. Sufen had never experienced a man calling out with such horror.

At last, the corner of Daisy's mouth twitched slightly. Smooth immediately hauled her onto his back. "Going to the hospital," he announced, then staggered downstairs, skidding and almost tumbling.

While Smooth pedalled the tricycle as speedily as he could, Sufen continued to pat Daisy's chest and squeeze her philtrum in further attempts at artificial respiration. Once in the casualty department, the duty nurse gave her a shot in the arm and the young woman was roused slowly to her senses. She refused to receive further care, flinging obscenities at the medical staff. She told Smooth that her time had come.

Despite the good intentions of the doctors and nurses, Daisy knocked away all the equipment, even kicking one of the nurses in the process. Smooth asked the doctor about the wisdom of rejecting extra intervention. He advised that as she had ceased breathing, it was sensible to check for possible complications. With no alternative, they injected her with tranquillisers and she was soon out cold.

Once she was asleep, Sufen told a reluctant Smooth to have a check-up as well. The doctor recommended admission as an inpatient. He wouldn't listen as he had just bought some analgesic to tide him over the New Year. With such a mess at home, how could he afford to lie here on a ward?

As soon as Daisy awoke for the second time, she spied Sufen and created another scene. Her stepmother then fled.

For a while Daisy was silent, and when the IV bag had emptied itself she tried to climb out of bed. Smooth asked what it was she wanted to do. "Die," she hissed back.

Her father asked if it was appropriate for her to be discharged now, to which the physician answered that it was possible, but they preferred to monitor her closely for the time being. Smooth had a hunch that at this time of year the staff would actually be far happier if all the patients could go home, leaving them to return to their families for the celebration. He then pursued the departing Daisy.

The whole of the Western Capital was soaked in the atmosphere of the season, each blast of firecrackers being succeeded by another. Residents scarcely dared put one foot forward in case their mouths and nostrils were assailed with gunpowder. Few pedestrians were outside, and the bulk of the lanterns had been lit in advance. A number of opportunistic trike-riders were offering taxi services, looking in all directions for stragglers who might need taking home.

Smooth shadowed his daughter from afar, not wishing to draw too close lest her temper flare up again. Similarly, he didn't want to fall too far behind in case she disappeared. She first walked along the embankment by the city moat. He was petrified that she might suddenly toss herself into the water. At that time, the contents of the channel had the consistency of slurry. Should a person choose this as their exit strategy, it would be nigh on impossible to foist them out of that quicksand.

He drew closer to Daisy, who quickened her pace and tried to extend the distance between them. The wind now swelled and whirled about all the loose rubbish as if this were its last cleaning sweep of the year. And yet this caused even more disorder. Plastic bags became hooked upon the branches of trees, and one of them wrapped itself around Smooth's face so he had to scrabble to remove it. He eventually tore it away to find that Daisy was nowhere in view. He looked around before heading home despondent, as it occurred to him that he couldn't recover her. The wind was by now impossibly sharp and he had to try to venture forward with his back against it. He bent down to pick up a couple of lanterns that had tumbled on the wayside from who knows where. It proved futile as another gust flung the lanterns out of sight before he could grasp hold of them.

There was total darkness when he reached home. Upon opening the gate, he was aware of a still blacker shadow behind him. He turned to discover it was Uncle Scar. As the old man only ever left home in the evening, Smooth had made light of the invitation to come over. He was now here to settle the debt, so Smooth admitted him to his abode.

Uncle Scar surveyed the room and found no place to sit down.

Wherever one might have sat at normal times was festooned with clothes and bedding, washed and hung out to dry. He gathered together the garments from the sofa, but found the seat underneath was damp. Instead, he stood in the centre of the parlour. "It's not proper for me to discuss this topic on New Year's Eve," he acknowledged. "It's also not proper for me to insist a debt be paid on New Year's Day. Everyone craves status in this life. You yourself are a businessman of sorts. Now your older brother really has gone too far. He owes a packet, but just hauled up his arse and was off in a puff of smoke. That's not how a man of the world conducts himself. You've been resident here for a long, long time. You know about your Uncle Scar's integrity and how he is when it comes to virtue and the honest art of gambling. Whatever a man does, there must be credit. A man without credit has no way to carry on in this world. This time your brother trashed his reputation in the community. You go and ask anyone around here. Your Uncle Scar has lived in this community for dozens of years. He sticks to his guns. Have I ever owed anybody a single penny of gambling debt? With this scarred face, I have a fame of my own here. That's because I stand by my word, and 'sincerity' and 'honesty' are the rules I live by. Whenever I borrow money from someone and promise to repay it by one o'clock, I'll never try to repay it even a minute late. Those who borrow from me should do the same. When the deadline is passed, one's credit takes a nosedive. Your elder brother's conduct is not a question of his credit being no longer good. From now on, I'll just shun him from my circle of associates. It must be a relief to him that he has a brother like you. He also mentioned that he stashed some money in your home. My family needs to celebrate New Year too. Life is hard for everybody. If you can't cough up, then you shouldn't leave that lantern of good fortune lit until morning. How can you raise a lantern this year if you really want to be a deadbeat in the dark?"

Smooth was not about to tell him what had gone on at home, so took out the cash his brother had given him. Twenty thousand yuan had been skimmed off this in advance. Twelve thousand of that was public money, borrowed from the troupe, and the other 8,000 had been presented to Daisy because she made a scene about Big Army owing her that amount from her own purse. He had thought of giving Uncle Scar the full 30,000 yuan. Even if he did so, he would feel uneasy because that wad had not been earned through his own toil.

Still, Uncle Scar was far from satisfied. He nagged about Big Army owing him hundreds of thousands, so how could he send him on his way like a beggar with so little? No matter how Uncle Scar deployed his battery of profanities, insults, mockery and threats, Smooth would not part with one yuan more. The incensed old man struck out at the decrepit tea table with his foot. "Then just you wait," he warned. "Wait until the fifteenth of January when I set fire to the fodder store." Smooth knew that *Set Fire to the Fodder Store* was a one-act play adapted from the ancient novel *Outlaws of the Marsh*. Its villain, named Lu Qian, wanted to burn alive the great hero Lin Chong. Smooth certainly was no gallant like Lin, so how could Uncle Scar cast himself as the conniving Lu? If he wanted to make a fire then go ahead, but could he really bring himself to torch the Diao family home?

As Uncle Scar had been trying to winkle the debt money out of him, Sufen was cooking in the kitchen. After their visitor left, Smooth came in and told her, "I've got to look for Daisy. She ran away from the hospital and I couldn't keep up with her. It's New Year, so if I don't know where she is, I'll be beside myself with worry."

"Eat something before you go out."

"I've no appetite. You help yourself."

"Take care then."

Smooth was already out of the door when Sufen called on him to wait for a moment. He stopped.

She gathered a scarf from the bedroom and wrapped it around his neck, also covering his ears, mouth and nose.

The wind was still fierce and propelled a lantern from nowhere into their courtyard.

Sufen did up one of his buttons he had not fastened. "You can get going now," she said.

At that, he left.

53

SUFEN DIDN'T TAKE A SINGLE BITE OF ANYTHING she had prepared. She covered all the dishes with bowls or plates. Next, she boiled dumplings to fill a bento box and carried the container out with her.

She was not seeking after Daisy, but Third Skin.

Third Skin had not gone back home this Spring Festival and the excuse he gave Sufen was that his wife had eloped with another man, leaving him with no face in his village. He sent some of his pay packet back to his old ma, and as his younger brother was staying there to care for her, it made no practical difference whether he accompanied them or not. In reality, Sufen knew that he stayed behind in the Western Capital simply on account of her.

This chap was as obsessive as her former husband's boss, Jiang, who harassed her unremittingly. Third Skin was a case apart, though, because he was a member of her current husband's crew and loved her with a visceral ardour. If Jiang had been intent only on conquering her for a time to compensate for his regret about not marrying her, Third Skin's admiration was elementally different. He was sincerely concerned for her. During their days of shifting stages together, he was far more attentive to her in this regard than Smooth had ever been. Of course, he had greater time and more opportunities to make his meticulous care and consideration known. Indeed, she had been fearful of what the smouldering remnants of these sentiments would be. After all, she had witnessed first-hand her former husband hacking his rival to death with a knife.

Smooth may not have been at all fierce or tough, and certainly not as powerful as Sun Wuyuan was. And yet he was still a man. A puny ass can kick a man to death as well as any creature. She just could not understand how such an unprepossessing man could display such resilience and endurance. Once he set his mind on a particular track, he would never allow himself to be beaten down or suffer ruin. This previous month especially had seen matters unfold in a way that left Sufen unsure. Her marriage now felt equal parts loathing and loyal compliance – not the healthiest state of relations between spouses. Equal parts loathing and loyal compliance could also describe the assignation she had with the pharmaceuticals tycoon Jiang. She had used her feminine wiles to milk favours from him and then lost the will to be so canny any more. In the end, she became the quarry and submitted to his twisted will.

Comparatively speaking, the situation with Third Skin threw up many emotional complexities and nuances. She felt a little unoccupied when the two were apart for a time. She might as well have been balancing on the brink of a precipice, waiting to tilt forward.

Since Big Hook, Monkey, Mound and the others left the Western Capital the day before, Third Skin had been bombarding her with text messages, imploring her to visit him at his digs. This comprised a basement measuring more than two hundred square metres, and right now he had it all to himself. Sufen replied that visiting was impossible, for she already had a household to call her home and must share the festivities with her husband. She pleaded with him to go back to his village and tend to his parents. "It all depends on you," came his answer. "I'll be in the basement all the time, come what may." After an interval, follow-up messages pinged on her mobile. "Miss U," stated one, then, "Luv U. Waiting 4U." He even typed, "I'm so lonely" and on New Year's Eve, "I cried. Really so sad!" Sufen then prepared to visit him.

Third Skin was in fact weeping when she reached his basement with the dumplings. His wails sounded like an aged ox. The cellar space belonged to a rather old building, and those two hundred square metres he spoke of were pegged into parcels by utilising dozens of concrete piles. Third Skin and his roommates had pilfered discarded scenery cloths and lashed them between the pillars to make various living spaces. There were no "locked doors" here and the flaps to several rooms had been pinned shut with iron wire, while others were left ajar. Packs of rats scurried about the dim space, and Sufen almost planted her foot down on one.

She had heard from Smooth and Third Skin that a few of the men rented out a place like this for a peppercorn rent. It was dingy, humid and devoid of sunshine in every season. People would rather not linger down here for long, since it gave them a suffocating feeling and they feared that a mouldy odour would cling to them even after they left. Sufen was led to Third Skin's quarters by the sound of him weeping. The flap was shut, but she teased it open. He was down there wrapped up in three quilts, moaning like a sorrowful old ox. He may not have been expecting her to come, not least at this time. Presently, thousands upon thousands of families were seated at their reunion dinners. Despite being inside a subterranean chamber, they could still hear the rattle of firecrackers through the open basement door. Were one to close it sealed, the atmosphere would become so stultifying that nobody inside would be able to catch their breath.

"Why do you have so many quilts?"

"Chilly."

"Are all those yours?"

"One is Big Hook's and the other's Mound's."

Sufen could see how the edges of the quilts were all thickly impregnated with grease. She opened the plastic case of dumplings. "Eat these while they're warm," she instructed him.

Third Skin gazed at Sufen foolishly and would not rise.

"So you're wanting me to feed you now?"

He paused for a minute. She noticed how his breath became rushed and he seemed to be about to lift himself from the edge of the bed. Without warning, he cast aside the covers and reached out for her waist, pulling her forward in the direction of the bedspread. He had a hard-on, with nothing to conceal it. Sufen's face changed all of a sudden and she ordered him to dress, otherwise she would leave at once. Averting her eyes, she could hear the rustle of clothes being put on reluctantly, and soon he was holding her and weeping again.

She took out tissues for him to dry his tears. He claimed not to need them and appeared content to have his cheeks trail with brine.

"You'd better go home for New Year. If you don't, it'll only make you sadder."

"No, I'll stay here – closer to you."

"I'm married to Smooth."

"I know you are."

"If you know it, how can you still behave like this?"

"I like you, I love you. I cannot help it."

"This is absolutely out of the question."

"Why?"

"I'm Smooth's wife and he is your gaffer. You shouldn't behave like this."

"What you're saying has nothing to do with me."

"How come?"

"They're two different things."

"So here you go again. Same old, same old."

"No, they are two different things." With these words, Third Skin started to try to loop his hands into Sufen's arms. She blocked him, and so he directed his hands towards her waist and then her chest. As if starving, he took hold of her breasts like they were warm steamed buns. Had she refused him flatly now, he might have yanked the boobs from her body. Seeing that resistance was futile, she shook her head and let him rub them for a while. She stood up resolutely when it appeared that his hands wished to roam around and explore an even more sensitive part of her anatomy. "Absolutely not!" she maintained. "I'm Smooth's wife. He's been so kind to you and you should respect him."

"These are two different things again."

"They are the same damned thing."

No matter how spirited his pestering became, Sufen would not let her morals bend and so she left the basement.

She then went home and collected her possessions before leaving the Western Capital.

In fact, even before she had visited Third Skin, her mind was made up. To be precise, she had been sleeping on this matter for a whole month. The final decision was reached on Plum's departure and galvanised by the business of Daisy's attempted suicide on the last day of the year. This was no simple whim, and Sufen's determination was absolute.

She didn't dare to contemplate once more what had gone on at home in recent days. How Daisy had executed the defenceless dog caused her heart to tremble. It echoed the experience of witnessing Sun Wuyuan slay Boss Jiang. Sun had committed this murder as a culmination of his mania, whereas Daisy's killing merely marked the start of her insanity.

The abuse endured by the dog at Daisy's hands and her coldness and sadism were unfathomable. To make it more disturbing, she could not predict who would be her next target. Plum, or herself? Or even Smooth?

Sufen spent the penultimate night of the outgoing year cleaning. She even tidied the courtyard and kitchen, and took care of the toilet. All the while she conducted these final chores, she had been pondering the question of departure. She dared not turn her back on any corner or cranny as she went about her business, for even solid walls could mask an assassin with a blade to end her life in an abrupt and humiliating way. She was in the grip of a panic she had never known before and realised that the time to leave had come. Should she choose New Year's Eve, some time after New Year's Day or even after Lantern Festival on the 15 January? Come what may, she couldn't remain here any longer. Kind as Smooth was, her continued presence could endanger his person. She tried to wash more and more garments, bedding and household items. Sufen got through all the clothing her husband needed for daily wear, additional warmth and insulating his body in bed. In short, absolutely everything he might require.

The operation spanned a whole night. On the morning of New Year's Eve when the last pair of chopsticks had been rinsed, the sound of firecrackers became denser and denser. She headed for the toilet, her back and waist aching. There she squatted for a while, it being an effort to rise to her feet.

A noise then came from upstairs, and she grappled away to try to stand upright. On identifying the source, she saw Daisy's frame swinging on the upper floor. Feebly, her feet appeared to be kicking and treading water in midair. Sufen screamed upon realising that her priority must be to go up there and tackle the situation.

While climbing the stairs, her knees became so numb that she twice leant forward and bent her legs against the concrete steps.

Finally, she found her goal. Daisy's body at the end of that thick, improvised rope appeared preternaturally elongated. Feeling helpless, she shouted loudly to next door for assistance, but her voice was drowned out by the racket from the fireworks. The explosions continued in courtyard after courtyard and no sensitive ears could hear her hoarse screams.

The chopping knife now glimmered in Sufen's mind. She rolled and tumbled downstairs, removing the blade from the kitchen. Hacking at the rope was eventually enough to make Daisy tumble free, collapsing like a hill. The stepmother now tried to steady Daisy's body with her free hand, but in its unthinking state that bulk pitched forward and smashed into her. In spite of trying to shield Daisy from injury, the mass of flesh and bones proved too heavy and pressed her down. As she lay on the ground, she became Daisy's landing pad.

How the rear of her head, spine and coccyx ached from that collision. Sufen had no time to care about these bumps because someone was about to die in her arms. She had to call as vehemently as she could for help.

As a supply teacher in the countryside, she had been required to teach her students the rudiments of first aid. Step One was to call out the patient's name and try to rouse them. Step Two was to apply pressure to the chest, and Step Three was to administer CPR while pinching several vital acupoints. She followed these procedures painstakingly before phoning Smooth. That Daisy's life had been saved was a matter of great relief. Not that Daisy expressed any gratitude toward Sufen. Rather, her hysteria intensified. The stepmother was confident that she had done all that was within her powers and could now withdraw with a clear conscience.

Had Sufen any residual hesitation about departing after Lantern Festival, the business of saving Daisy's life quashed that. Her plan was settled and she knew there was one person she should call on before leaving. That was her pursuer, Third Skin. This man loved her truly and ardently in spite of everything. A fortnight ago, he had bought her a platinum necklace for about 15,000 yuan, using up all of his savings. He told her that the actress who played Peach Blossom wore a similar one, and it was really striking. She said she couldn't accept it, though he stuffed it in her hands and then ran away. The gift was so precious that she needed to find an opportunity to return it to him. Were her previous admirer, Boss Jiang, to have bought her this kind of jewellery, she would not have regarded it as rare, nor as heartfelt. He could earn thousands upon thousands of yuan in a single day, and on a return trip from Hong Kong might buy dozens of designer handbags or brand-name watches, and dole them out to various people with the power to approve his business ventures. Third Skin was not like that at all. The 15,000 yuan represented his entire life's savings, and he put his heart on the line. How could she be left unmoved? Money was not some kind of barometer to gauge the candour of one man's love, but when he channelled everything into a single romantic gesture, money had been metamorphosed into something unquantifiably priceless. Cai Sufen must find a means of honouring his sentiments.

Before reaching his basement, she had thought out her actions. To begin with, she would hand back Third Skin's gift. Second, she would allow him to have whatever he wanted of her before absconding from the Western Capital. She even took a shower before leaving the apartment. However, when the moment came, she had to turn him down, for to comply now would be to dishonour her vows to Smooth. And yet she knew inside that Smooth could not captivate her heart for the rest of her life.

Sufen had escaped here as a murderer's widow and initially thought that she could settle down with the first man who showed her affection and a degree of stability. The template did not translate to reality. One year with Smooth was enough to confirm in her mind that he was a wretched loser, incapable of maintaining order in his own family. This was not someone who was perpetually dependable. In his own way, though, Smooth exhibited kindness. He was loath to step on a stray ant and deserved credit for having taken on Sufen in the face of Daisy's vicious resistance. His heart was nothing if not sincere, and she couldn't reduce someone of his character to being a cuckold. Moreover, since his underling now stood before her, she should have some regard for his need to keep face. Once she turned down Third Skin's advances, she slipped the necklace into a noodle bowl without him noticing, and left.

When she arrived home, Smooth was not yet back. She boiled dumplings for him, patted them dry and then fried them as potstickers, leaving them in the wok to retain their warmth. Next, she wrote a letter for him, and walked out of the gate with the same suitcase with which she had originally come.

On the evening of New Year's Eve, there was not a single quiet spot in the Western Capital. She zigzagged through narrow alleys, finding a clandestine route of retreat. Her destination was a place where tranquillity genuinely existed.

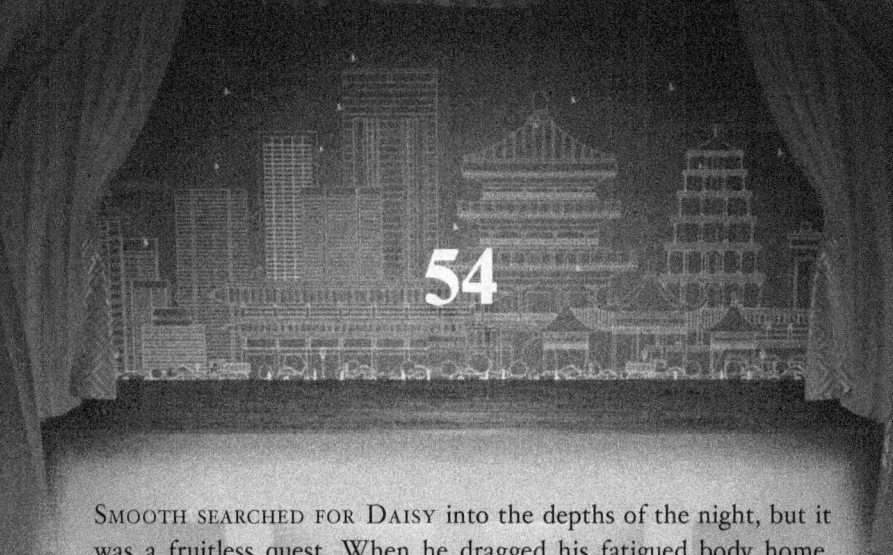

54

SMOOTH SEARCHED FOR DAISY into the depths of the night, but it was a fruitless quest. When he dragged his fatigued body home, there was no Sufen to be seen either. He picked up the letter his wife had left on the bedside table and wailed inconsolably at its contents.

Dear Smooth,
   I am sorry, but I had to leave. I know you have been kind to me, very kind. I shouldn't be doing this, but there is no other way. I can't bear to see you suffer for me. Maybe things will get better after I am gone. Maybe if I hadn't come here in the first place, things wouldn't be in such a mess.
   These last few days, I thought about a memory from when I was a kid. I met a blind fortune teller who told me that I was jinxed. I would cause havoc in any household I joined. My ma even sent me to live in a temple for a while, hoping this might lift the curse. Later, I got married and that first hubby lost his life. You didn't mind about it and accepted me when I was at my lowest. You showed me your heart, and I should be grateful. But I shouldn't have shared my bad fate with you. You are a good man, and the heavens should punish me if I have brought you suffering. After I am gone, you can tell Daisy all of this. Maybe then she will decide to come home. You should comfort her and show her concern. Help her to calm down. After all, she is your own daughter.
   Smooth, I am so sorry. This was the only way out I could

381

think of. I cannot cope with the sight of blood. Lately, I dreamed and dreamed even in the daytime. My dreams were full of blood and dead people. I really cannot live with you because I am afraid of bringing disaster on a good man. Please forgive me for going without warning. I'll always remember you and know you are the best man in the world. You are sure to have good karma, and I'll pray for you however far apart we are.

After you find Daisy, go to the hospital and get yourself treated. Piles is not a serious condition, but you always work so hard. If you don't see a doctor soon, it might get very bad.

One more thing. Stage shifting is too hard. You work day and night. You aren't young any more and shouldn't keep it up for years to come. Better that you get a motorised trike and avoid those long-distance trips. You can make money at your job, but it is costing you your life. That's not worth it. Life is more important than anything else. What's more, getting what you are owed from stage work is so hard on you, so why take on the grief?

Smooth, today is New Year's Eve. I know you'll be sad once I've gone. In the long run, it's better for me to leave than to stay. Please forgive me. Don't go searching for me because you won't succeed. The place I am going is far, far away. Rest assured, I'll still be alive. I don't plan on dying because I know that in this world I still can count on your love and that is enough to keep me warm for years to come.

I've fried some potstickers for you and they are keeping warm in the wok. I've also mixed the vinegar sauce. Steer clear of hot pepper and garlic. Cut back on fermented tofu. None of them are good and will ruin your health. If you have no time for a hot meal, stick to steamed buns with pickle. That's better than the fermented tofu. So sorry to make you eat reunion dumplings alone. Send Daisy a message. Don't go looking for her blindly. Just stay at home and she's sure to come back.

> — CAI SUFEN, WHO WILL ALWAYS REMEMBER
> WHAT A GOOD MAN YOU ARE.

Smooth was dumbfounded, as if a cudgel had come down hard on his temple. He immediately dialled Sufen's mobile, but it was switched off. Cascades of tears ran down his face and his legs were limp. Before long, he was letting out his pain more audibly. In spite of the fact she had told him not to come after her, he still trawled the railway station and the long-distance bus stations until New Year's morning arrived. When all his hopes had subsided into despair, it took some endeavour to drag himself home. Smooth lay face down on his mattress, so inconsolable that his teeth pierced his lips.

The sound of firecrackers outside gave him the sensation that perhaps the entire city was about to detonate. Who invented this New Year, this Nian? It was so inscrutable that Smooth had not a shred of affection for it. This sodding Nian had so far robbed him of three wives, so he despised the fucking season. His first wife, Daisy's mother, had eloped with another guy on the eighth day of the final lunar month, leaving him shamefaced and miserable. He was such a worthless cuckold that he couldn't keep her. Those who comforted him said that it was for the best, for he would no longer be held up to such endless humiliation. Daisy was only six years old at the time, so had no inkling of her mother's true character. Once abandoned, though, she cried all day long for her ma, causing her face to become puffy and chapped. That year, Smooth's heart broke.

Several years later, Plum's mother developed uterine cancer, being diagnosed on the twenty-eighth day of the final lunar month. She passed away on the twenty-ninth, exactly one year and one day later. From then on, New Year filled Smooth with apprehension to the point of terror. The ending of each year was like the creaking of the gates of hell.

Just as she fell ill, Orchid Zhao's business was flourishing. She planned to close the booth on the twenty-fifth so as to allow plenty of time to clean the house and spend the festival in leisurely fashion. By midnight on the twenty-seventh, she had still not completed all her orders when she collapsed to the floor, being unable to rise to her feet. Smooth rode her to the hospital, where she slept overnight, and the following day she had the biopsy. The examination established that the tumour was nearing an advanced stage. She had been feeling nauseous previously, though said not a word, and attributed her discharges of blood to having spent too long sitting on a stool. Besides which, her to-do list was heaving, and she deferred seeking treatment because she wanted to clear the backlog first.

In the year that followed, medical bills decimated their savings, but without a positive outcome. Unbeknownst to her husband, after dictating her last will, Orchid Zhao secretly took a massive swig of insecticide. Her attempt at suicide was observed by Goody who barked and barked until the corners of her mouth were bloody. A neighbour called Smooth back from the stage and a stomach pump and enema dragged her back to life. Three months later, on the twenty-ninth day of the final lunar month, she expired through natural causes. Smooth had been hoping she would last another fortnight until Lantern Festival. On the one hand, this was the off-season and there were no stages to shift, so she would have his undivided care. On the other, as everyone else was celebrating Spring Festival it was considered an ill omen to have anything to do with death and bereavement. For this reason, he shelled out more than a hundred yuan, burning incense for her deliverance in the Temple of the Eight Immortals.

When every other option failed, on the morning of the twenty-ninth Orchid was intent on being discharged from hospital. By evening time, she was noticeably frail and he took her back. She passed away soon after admission. He spent the New Year in such a chill mood that even the crevices between his teeth felt at risk of icing up.

This year eclipsed all the others in terms of heartache. There had been neither peace nor calm since the twenty-ninth of the previous month. First, the dog was murdered, then Daisy attempted suicide and finally Sufen left. Smooth could not articulate his stored-up frustration, nor the agitation in his heart. The death of Orchid Zhao seemed to spell the absolute end of whatever good fortune he could expect in life. Never again would he find such an industrious, virtuous, considerate and kind-hearted mate to complete his family. Her earnings exceeded his and she was good with Daisy. They were a family quartet as flawless as a pristine hen's egg. He was convinced that, given a few more years of concerted toil, they could buy an apartment of 120 square metres on Shangyi Road. Who could have predicted that the heavens would be so merciless, and that everything would be lying in waste within a year?

Once Zhao's mortal remains had been cremated, he slid into the red, owing others more than 10,000 yuan.

After being widowed, Smooth swore that he would never take another wife, preferring to raise his two daughters alone and then directing his efforts into finding decent families in which for them to marry. His mission would then have been accomplished. Nonetheless, owing to a strange combination of circumstances, Cai Sufen appeared. She was the one to flick the abacus beads of his life into disarray.

It all rested on his head now. He had not been resilient enough when faced with the allure of a temptress and had relinquished his arms and laid himself at her mercy. Actually, his arms were kindling dry and ignited with the lightest spark of her strong passion. He now found himself submissive, as if a sleepy head had encountered a pillow.

Later, he even found this business comical. Had he been a secret agent, he would not have been able to resist a seductress. Even the flimsiest of honey traps would have ensnared him into divulging names and cipher codes. In short, he regretted having bedded Sufen.

His initial thought was that she was too pretty to be reliable. On top of that, she was more educated than him and spoke differently from anyone close to him. He knew absolutely nothing about her background, so sensed that he was vulnerable to her wiles. At the outset, he had kept his guard up. As time progressed, he realised she was a fine woman. She could shoulder hardship and tolerate loss, never being fussy or inclined to gossip. She was even more broad-minded and generous than Orchid Zhao, not least because she didn't rise to Daisy's bullying, insults or public approbation. Sufen bit down on it all and cleaved ever closer to her husband. This gave him reassurance. On knowing further details about her personal history, he recognised her mettle. She was the sort who could be depended upon for a lifetime, whereas he himself was prone to doubt and could not believe that such an exceptional woman had chosen him. It was as though a fox fairy in an ancient drama had metamorphosed into female form and, while dwelling in the realm of humankind, had fallen desperately in love with a mortal man before disappearing.

Her departure was an aching tragedy. No audience would be left unmoved. To his mind, Sufen often appeared to be playing out the role of a fox fairy. He worried constantly about how midway through their affair, she might, like Daisy's mother, be spirited off by another person. In the end, it was not seduction that led her away, but fear and anger. He was at a loss. Their relationship had been sacrificed all because he had not been firm enough with Daisy.

One thing that did startle Smooth was how Sufen hadn't taken any extra cash with her. She pocketed the several thousand yuan presented in the pay packet the day before yesterday. As her own earnings had helped to subsidise the housekeeping, Smooth had wanted to place her in charge of all the domestic finances. This didn't sit well with her, for she thought that this family would be complicated to manage, and Smooth declined to labour the point.

When Sufen left, it was without removing a single blade of grass or scrap of wood belonging to the household. All she packed were her cosmetics and fresh clothes. As Smooth dwelt upon this, his guilt grew. Such a decent woman and she had given six months of her life to him, which was probably the most arduous period she ever braved. There were times when she bore her responsibilities like a beast of burden, never uttering a word or sighing. He was of the view that he owed her too dearly and had done little to nurture or protect her. He always had the sensation that his life was a protracted affair. In truth it was short, so short that he couldn't spare the time to buy her so much as a hairpin. Spousal affection had been extinguished like an oil lamp. The oil had run dry and the wick burned out. How could he not weep?

As soon as he finished reading the letter, he texted Daisy to tell her that Sufen had gone. This was not the message he had intended to send, but he thought that conveying his wife's wishes might avert another suicide attempt. When he went out to look for Sufen, he was actually also hoping to find Daisy. Smooth scoured the railway station, long-distance bus stations, the city moat and other public places that she could have frequented. Even on his return home early on New Year's morning, her mobile was switched off. He had twice exhausted his battery overnight, calling his daughter and then his wife. He even dialled Plum. The fact that her phone appeared out of commission suggested that she had severed links with the Diao family altogether.

The firecrackers continued until 8 or 9 am. He answered a call without glancing at the number. It was Big Army. He was keen to upbraid him, but since it was New Year he listened to what he had to say in a grisly silence. He was offering a seasonal greeting.

"I'm fine, not dead yet," was all Smooth could reply tersely and without emotion.

"Aren't you still angry with Uncle Scar pressing for money?" he asked, obviously with a smile. "I called him last night and told him not to bother you, and that I'd settle up with him when I come back. Just a few pennies. Is that worth acting like a landlord over and going rattling for money on New Year's Eve?"

"Don't go talking big again and again," Smooth snapped. "Oh Brother, my dear brother. Just a few pennies? If you really had the money, why did you scoot and bring this misery on your family?"

Big Army went on laughing and jesting for a while before hanging up.

Once again, Smooth tried to get through to Sufen. No reception. He dialled Daisy. The line was no longer dead, but nobody answered.

55

AFTER SHE FLED THE HOSPITAL THAT AFTERNOON, Daisy idled away her New Year's Eve around the Bell Tower and the precinct of the Big Wild Goose Pagoda. To have appeared on her classmate's doorstep would have been embarrassing. Same with the home of her maternal uncle. She could not abide the snobbery of that side of the family, who deplored this niece on account of her trike-pedalling father, and only appeared vaguely content when she brought them an expensive gift. So she checked into the five-star hotel where Big Army had stayed. Since it was the New Year, why not splurge and show some class? Anyhow, if she didn't use up her father's savings, it would only go towards other women.

The upscale hotel was truly plush. On first checking in, she adjusted the temperature control to 26C, then took a bath until she started sweating through every pore. The wind outside caressed, patted and then whipped at the window of the high-rise tower as though channelling the laments of angry ghosts. With fireworks soaring endlessly through the sky and firecrackers erupting, flames appeared in the panes of her French windows. These reflected against the glassware and mirrors inside the suite, invoking a singularly grotesque spectre. She lay in the foaming tub, washing the dust gently from her face. The particles felt grainy and her tongue seemed to have been invaded with sand. Facing the tap, she rinsed her mouth and spat the water out, for it was no more drinkable than the rapids of the Yellow River. The need to cleanse her palette confirmed just how pernicious the bracing winds of the Western Capital were on nights like this. They could contaminate any orifice with a welter of debris. Having been sealed thoroughly against all the elements, the interior of the room assumed the ambience of a moist and balmy spring.

She inspected her body in silence, paying attention to every joint and digit. She wondered about how she compared physically to others she knew. Apart from her inherited face, every centimetre and millimetre was similar to that of Princess Wu. How then could she have found an "upper crust, generous and sumptuous" suitor, while she was this picture of abjection? Portion by portion, she massaged herself and realised the difference. The texture of her skin came from Smooth Diao, as did the hairs on her arms, legs and even buttocks. They were rough and pronounced, and when rubbed, felt like sandpaper. Princess Wu, by contrast, was large-jointed and broad-hipped, with skin moist and smooth like satin. This Daisy had experienced for herself when they bathed together. Her own skin, by contrast, was just like Smooth's. Her shoulder blade smouldered maroon as his would after hauling weighty loads. Although she was not short in stature, her legs bowed too. Maybe her obedience was to blame. In the past, she had followed him to the theatres and gladly helped to carry props and boxes. Her legs slowly assumed the appearance of those skivvies as she copied their work habits. The more she studied these limbs of hers, the more she reviled Smooth. At last, she squirted shower gel manically so that the tub became a mass of bubbles and her loathsome body was engulfed with foam.

Afterwards, she lay naked on the bed and smeared her whole form, little by little, with the complimentary skin creme. Those rougher areas she covered in layer after layer, as though she were applying furniture wax. Most of the TV channels were broadcasting Spring Festival Gala shows, and she had wearied of this fare long ago. All the participants wore ecstatic expressions, as if today were the apogee of merriment. For her, each New Year had brought worse hardships and ire. She surfed through more than a hundred channels before repeating the process. Finally, she paused on a programme discussing cosmetic surgery. It was pure sorcery. They could transform a plain hobbledehoy into an angel. This was no myth, for she had seen it with her own eyes. Upon enquiring, she learned that to effect a tangible change in one's facial physiognomy would cost a minimum of hundreds of thousands. This was a game for the rich. As the daughter of lowly Smooth Diao, fate had consigned her to being an ungainly old maid for life.

At midnight, the New Year's bell pealed and the firecrackers ricocheted like artillery in a historical drama. It seemed that thousands of rounds of gunpowder had been discharged all at once, and the building beneath her feet began to quiver. Some of the more powerful rockets burst outside her window, though the panes were unscathed and only smuts were left on the surface of the glass. The savage and wanton bombardment went on for hours before the Western Capital was finally restored to its characteristic repose, save for a few stray "volleys".

Hunger struck Daisy all of a sudden. She stood up and foraged around inside the refrigerator for anything she fancied. There were potato crisps, imported cookies, chocolate, yoghurt, fruit juice, small bottles of foreign wine and cans of beer. Although she knew that everything was pricey, she nevertheless uncorked a mini wine bottle and enjoyed it in leisurely fashion with handfuls of crisps, chocolate and the odd dash of fruit juice. More than once she contemplated turning on her mobile, but didn't. She spurned contact with the world and hoped that the world would return the favour. Daisy did not need others, and vice versa. She submitted to resplendent isolation.

The hotel phone did then ring. Her first reaction was that it must be Smooth. Then again, how could he know she was staying here? She picked up the receiver and was about to speak, but was pre-empted by the voice at the other end saying, "Excuse me."

It wasn't her father, and she so she murmured, "Yes."

The voice cut her short again. "Sorry to interrupt you," it said. "Our general manager has prepared New Year's dumplings for his guests. Would you like some? We can have them sent to your room."

All at once, she came over rather light-headed, as this was exactly what she thought she needed. How could a business like this be so considerate?

"Thank you, please send them up," she answered.

"No problem at all. Happy New Year!"

"Happy New Year!"

She crawled out of the bed, pulled on her pyjamas and

rearranged the tea table so that it could accommodate the dumplings. A while later, the bell rang and she opened the door to the waiter, who was pushing a serving trolley. The trolley itself was a miniature dining table, laid with condiments such as soy sauce, vinegar, hot pepper, even garlic, and a bowl of soup from the dumpling pan. She thanked the young man.

"Miss," he replied, "once you have finished, please push the cart back outside. Thank you. Good night!"

"Thank you. Good night!"

As soon as the server was gone, she flung herself on the bed, yelping "Yeah". She reached for the wine and snacks from the bedside table and consumed them together with the dumplings. As Spring Festival was here, she was itching to sing and dance.

The gale outside was still blowing, but she was shielded snuggly indoors. She went so far as to peel off her pyjamas, and in the nude polished off two of the bottles of wine, a small bowl of dumplings, a canister of potato crisps, a packet of cookies and a can of fruit juice. One minute she was chuckling, the next she was grizzling. Not knowing how she really felt, she prostrated herself on the sofa until the following morning.

When she woke up, she was still naked and felt a little chilly. Her nose tingled with the first signs of a cold. She rolled herself from the sofa onto the bed, swaddled herself and wanted to drift off. The mood didn't take her, though, and so she flicked open her mobile, now having the urge to keep abreast of what had been happening outside.

Ping! Ping! Ping! Hundreds of messages popped up on the screen. There were New Year's greetings from classmates, and a lot of the others were headed with Smooth's name. She was too lazy to sift through them all and so she searched for titbits of gossip. Princess Wu had sent honeymoon snaps from Australia by the hundred. Among them was one in which her husband had accidentally bared his buttocks while changing his shorts after swimming. His ungainly appearance was enough to split anyone's sides with laughter. That tough and blunt-tongued Wu had nicknames like "Raw Sweet Potato" and "Hairy Winter Melon". It was not unlike Princess Wu to casually share with her girlfriend such an unflattering image of her other half. Her crudity and rashness were all too evident, though she could never be made to mend her ways.

There were messages from Mr Noodle Head as well. He was sending his seasonal regards and asked why her mobile was not turned on. He told her that he would return to the Western Capital on the third day of the New Year. How dull and pedestrian was he! Was your homecoming of any consequence to me? Anyhow, there was not one positive note among the impressions she had formed of this fellow, and so she deleted his messages straight away.

Once the texts from classmates had been dealt with, she turned to those from Smooth. She discovered the truth of Sufen's departure. Where had she gone? Daisy scrolled back through his other texts with curiosity, and pieced together the narrative in the order it unfolded.

"Daisy, where RU?"
"Daisy, UR Dad is looking 4U outside. Please reply."
"Daisy, 2nite is v windy. U might catch cold out."
"Daisy, Dad is looking 4U. Where RU?"
"My child, many guys R letting off bangers 2nite. Some R crude + rash. One blew his finger off. Beware of that type."
"Daisy, wherever UR, mind those bangers."
"Daisy, if something is bothering U, please come home + tell Dad. Don't do NEthing dumb."
"Daisy, it's blowing a gale. Don't go out. A board blew down + nearly hit me."
"Please come back. CS is gone. Never coming back."
"Please come back, Daisy. Dad is so tired."
"Please come back. It is just us 2 now"

Daisy sat up on the bed with a start. Had Cai Sufen really gone? Or was it a plot Smooth had hatched to coax her back?

She then checked messages from strangers. Most of them were "copy-and-paste" jobs for the New Year. As she was about to delete them, she was taken aback to see a text from her stepmother.

Daisy, I shouldn't have left this message for you. Your pa is really so pitiful now, and I felt I needed to share a few words with you. I always knew you hated me. I shouldn't have come along and disrupted your life. I really had no other place to go. Your dad might explain the story behind that later on. Thankfully, you and your dad let me live with you for more than six months. I felt sad on leaving tonight. He is a good man. It's not easy for him to shift stages as the breadwinner. He hasn't told you but he has severe piles, and a prolapse. All this he buried in his mind. No matter how sad his life is, he won't complain. You should understand how hard it is for him, and be kind. Don't look down on him. If it wasn't for the family conflict and my own jinx, I would stay with him for the rest of my life. He is honest and reliable. I never had to worry about strangers calling at night or him causing trouble for us. A pity that I didn't have such good fortune. I've brought my jinx to you, so had to leave. You're his daughter and he loves you more than anyone in this family. When he saw you hanged, he collapsed. Right then, I knew the meaning of the saying "kids are a piece of flesh that's fallen from their parents' bodies". Parents love their kids more than anything in this world. Please go back quickly. Don't force your dad to search everywhere. It's very windy out and cold. He's caught a cold already for you and should be in hospital. Go back, Daisy. Plum is gone. I've gone too. You can live calmly with your dad. He is a good man and you should love him. Maybe some of my words don't sound too nice. I mean no harm. I only hope you'll be kind to him. Sorry, my phone has no power. I am ditching this number. I am leaving the Western Capital for good. Peace and happiness be with you and your dad. Hope you find some nice in-laws soon.

— CAI SUFEN

For years, nothing had truly left Daisy so moved. On reading Cai Sufen's message, she was somewhat touched. She tried to call back that number, though it was out of service. Smooth soon made contact. She wanted to answer, but did not. Were her mobile left on, that would signify to him that she was safe and unharmed. Later, he called several more times. She simply typed the three words "I know now" without picking up the call. She had planned to live cosily in this hotel for a number of days, gulping up a few thousand yuan. After looking at their text messages, this scheme lost its appeal. She could not identify precisely what was discomforting her. It was just a general feeling of being perturbed. Daisy succeeded in brazening out her exile until midday, when she handed back her key. Still, she didn't return home directly. Instead, she sat in a coffee shop, sipping cappuccino and fiddling with games on her mobile phone until nightfall.

    Throughout that day, Mr Noodle Head had barraged her with phone calls, which she left unanswered. She was annoyed to see he was trying to ring again, as she was almost home. "What's up?" she answered coldly. He moaned that she had ignored him for the whole day. She hadn't the energy to explain why and so waited for him to say his piece. He then corrected himself, stating that he would in fact be back in town on the fourth day of the New Year. He intended to visit her and discuss a matter of some importance at the earliest convenience. She neither accepted nor refused this request, only asking if there was anything else he wished to say. When he declined, she hung up. Humph! A matter of some importance! What important matter could a shoddy bootlegger possibly need to discuss with her? Anyhow, nothing he could say interested her to the least degree.

WHAT A FUCKING NEW YEAR! Damn it! It seemed that misfortune had dogged his family for eight generations. Bloody, fucking calamity running through the ages! Smooth could not hold on any longer. He had a raging fever and was forced to stagger to the hospital alone on the evening of Daisy's return.

The high temperature had addled his thoughts, and he slumped to the floor upon entering the hospital foyer. He could vaguely recall being carried to a ward and then being transferred to an operating table. Later, he fell unconscious. He did not come to until the next morning when he found himself in bed with a drip feeding his arm, an oxygen tube in his nose and an arsenal of other instruments to his side. Wires from the instruments were fastened to his head, chest, wrists and ankles. He realised that this ensemble was reserved for patients in a precarious state. Before Plum's mother had died, she too had a similar arrangement. Was he about to die? Actually, that thought wasn't as unwelcome as it sounded. Maybe the heavens had chosen this exit route for him, and he would be dispatched in the best time and with the greatest efficiency.

There were more than ten beds on this ward, yet he and a child were the only inpatients. The kid was surrounded by at least twenty relatives, and their fussing woke Smooth up. When they noticed he had regained consciousness, everybody stared in his direction, and another child ran out to shout the news to a nurse. The consultant and the nurse appeared together, the former probing the patient about how he was feeling. "Not bad," came Smooth's response. He couldn't open his mouth fully, for it was parched, and he worried that the doctor may not have heard his reply. When the question was repeated, he reiterated those two words with as much stress as he could place on the syllables. The consultant told him he had been careless. How could a prolapse be left untreated for so long? He asked if there was no next of kin accompanying him, to which Smooth shook his head slightly. The doctor continued by saying that if he was hungry, porridge or suchlike was suitable. He neither nodded nor shook his head, for he wasn't sure where food could be obtained here. Smooth's belly was a touch empty.

An old man seated by the child wanted to know if chicken soup was all right for the patient. The doctor asked whether it had been seasoned with pepper or ginger, to which the codger answered "no". It was acceptable, so he brought it over to the stranger in bed. Smooth had thought he was going to feed it to the kid, but the fellow offered it to him.

"You can drink this bowl of chicken soup," he said. "My grandson hurt his hand on a firecracker last night. We cooked him this, but he only wants KFC. You see what kids are like. Such a shame."

Smooth came over a little pensive and shook his head. The old man approached the edge of the bed and proceeded to spoon-feed it to him. He was curious to find out why he had no family with him and where he came from. There was no answer. As the spoon hovered in his direction again, salty trickles moistened the corners of his eyes. The old man no longer pried, but made sure he consumed the whole bowl.

The child's relatives were pleased to see Smooth finish the meaty broth. He, on the other hand, was slightly embarrassed. From the way the huddle spoke among themselves, he could discern that there were paternal grandparents, parents, uncles and aunts, a maternal grandma and a maternal uncle. All of them had chosen to spend New Year with the injured youngster. This warm, sweet, harmonious scene of reunion reminded Smooth of Sufen, Plum, Daisy, his deceased second wife Orchid Zhao and even his first wife Tian Miao, all gone without a trace.

How could his family have disintegrated like this? He remembered his father once say that as man was acting, the heavens were monitoring. Yet, what had he, Smooth, done to deserve this retribution? Almost everyone had left him. Lying back on the bed, he dialled Sufen's and Plum's mobiles on the off chance that one of them might pick up. But both lines remained closed like the curtains after a theatrical performance, never to reopen.

He stayed in the hospital until the fifth day of the New Year. Irrespective of what the doctors and nurses advised, after finishing his IV, he was keen to pay New Year calls. There was one person he was bound to visit, regardless of the circumstances. That was his old primary school teacher with whom he had kept in contact for nearly thirty years.

The teacher's surname was Zhu, and he lived in a narrow alley behind the Confucius Temple inside Duanli Gate. His window faced the rear entrance of the renowned Forest of Stone Tablets Museum. Not far away was a site called Horse-Dismounting Post. This was where the noted ancient Confucian scholar Dong Zhongshu was buried. His teacher often frequented this spot. In recent years, whenever his wife said he was out for a stroll, that would be where he had gone. The couple were childless. Some attributed this fact to his wife, who had passed away the year before last, leaving him all alone.

The doorway to Smooth's teacher's home was rather narrow. Every year, the old man would hang up a pair of couplets for New Year written in his own hand. This custom had fallen into abeyance since he was widowed, and now the entrance appeared cheerless and stark while other residences had their calligraphy on red paper and scarlet lanterns.

His door was left unlatched. Whereas neighbours had replaced their wooden doors with metal ones, he maintained the old style. Smooth had helped him patch it up on a number of occasions, and it was now reinforced with riveted bolts and iron bars on the back.

It was an aged, one-and-a-half room residence. His teacher claimed to have lived here as far back as he could remember. In the recent past, those around him had "enlarged their cages and changed birds". In other words, neighbours had relocated to larger apartments while the old man could not bear to desert this place. From his dovecote-like attic, he could study everything that was happening in the vicinity of the adjacent museum. He masticated over this experience and would jot down his observations for future scrutiny.

The moment his visitor opened the door, he knew who was coming. "Smooth!" Teacher Zhu exclaimed.

He called down to him from the attic.

"Teacher, your student is here for a New Year's visit. Sorry, I'm late." As he spoke, Smooth negotiated the unsteady wooden stairs with the missing plank.

When he reached the attic, Teacher Zhu was reclining on the bed, reading a book. The room measured only four or five square metres, being just spacious enough to fit in a narrow desk and a small bed. Piles upon piles of books were heaped on the bed, leaving a sliver of a gap on which Zhu could rest his thin, fragile body.

Perhaps his teacher had not been to the barbers for a long time, for his hair appeared to have been ruffled into place using his fingers. Each strand seemed stiff and erect like newly shorn steel wires. Even though he was now seventy-three, the top of his head was fully covered. It was just hard to pick out dark hairs among the mass of grey. What was more, his forehead was wide, his face square, his chin large and lips thick. All in all, his appearance was decent and upright.

His teacher sat up when Smooth entered.

"Just lie back as you like, Teacher," Smooth urged.

"I've been like this all day. Ought to get up and sit straight for a while."

Smooth laid out his New Year's gifts on the desk. There were always the same four components: crystal cakes from De Mao Gong, marinated beef from the Old Tie Family restaurant, braised peanuts from the Hui Muslim Quarter and a red bottle of Western Phoenix brand grain liquor. All of these were his teacher's favourites, and Smooth had been bringing the same consignment for dozens of years. Originally, the cost had been just a few yuan, then it rose to a few dozen and now it cost a little over a hundred yuan. Each time he came here, his teacher's wife would present him with something in return so that he would never be made to leave empty-handed.

The visitor apologised because he knew he should have come on the first day of the New Year. His teacher asked what had prevented him. Little by little, Smooth unpicked everything that had transpired at home. When his first wife bolted, he felt able to share that tribulation with his teacher and his wife. He consulted them about his remarriage, and they even came to Orchid Zhao's memorial service. Since his teacher had only been recently widowed, he thought it best not to inform him about marrying Sufen. Now she had left him, he came over a little guilty for this omission. After listening to this narrative, Teacher Zhu sighed. "Just grind away slowly as you do. There's no alternative," was his take on the situation. "At least you've never failed or cheated anyone. Time for a sip?"

In previous years, when he had made his New Year's visit, Zhu's wife would prepare a couple of dishes and let them drink as they pleased. The year before last, owing to his bereavement, they abstained from alcohol. "I do want to share a sip or two with my teacher," Smooth maintained. "But this is a bit embarrassing. I've got haemorrhoids and have been on an IV drip…"

"Then don't try. Health is paramount."

"Well, Teacher, let me watch you drink." With these words, he opened the marinated beef and braised peanuts, and unscrewed the liquor. Zhu asked him to give him some of the crystal cake too, for this he was partial to and it happened to be one of the oldest and most traditional sweetmeats in the Western Capital. Nowadays, the young do not care for such things, though Smooth and his teacher did. He remembered how, when he was in primary school, his teacher's wife had offered him one of the cakes, which he ate with delight. He could still bring to mind its shape and consistency. It was one of those treats that once picked up, half the pastry coating would flake off back into the box. His teacher's wife did not discard the fragments. Instead, she left them in there as she refastened the whole package and tied it with the paper cords.

Teacher Zhu didn't reach for the beef or peanuts first. He picked up a crystal cake instead. "Can you eat this?" he asked.

"Yeah, sure."

Smooth didn't aim for a whole cake straight away. Rather, he gathered up the flakes of pastry fallen from his teacher's cake and slowly chewed on them. Only then did he allow himself to prise a whole one from the box.

"Really delicious," was his teacher's verdict.

"So tasty."

"I've seen a few for sale on the street."

"Not so many these days. I had to go to the Muslim Quarter."

"I'm seventy-three and my teeth aren't what they used to be."

"Doesn't matter. You still seem good on it."

"As the local saying goes – at seventy-three and eighty-four, the King of Hell will invite you to explore."

"Don't upset yourself, Teacher. The King of Hell surely isn't angling after you. You'll make a hundred at least, I'm sure."

"When my wife was alive, I was willing to continue without any sense of shame. Now she's gone, it's really too lonely here." He took a tiny slurp.

"Teacher, if you worry about your shame, I must be living a truly shameful life. I have no face."

"No, Smooth, you're not. You live honestly and work honestly. You've supported a big family, taking care of those you should have as well as those you shouldn't. Nobody can match your honest way of life and your work ethic."

Smooth all at once found himself on the brink of tears.

"But even my own daughter looks down on me. How can I get by on honest living and honest work alone?"

"That's another story. You should talk with her more. Daisy has the misfortune of being single, so that's warped her temper. You should just give her more attention."

"She looks down on me, though. Totally looks down on me. She won't share a single word with me. I do want to talk with her, but before I can finish a single sentence, she's shooed me out of her room. Don't you see what a wretched life I lead! Huh, these days if a guy is considered useless, even his kids treat him as nothing." Smooth bowed his head.

"I can't have you calling yourself useless, Smooth. You're as good as any man."

"You've never given me the cold shoulder. Every year when I come, you give me words of encouragement. In truth, your student's life is wretched. Sometimes, I'm no better than a dog. I'm losing face for you. Teacher, do you have another student as bad as this?"

"I am not afraid of others laughing at me because of you. I taught for more than forty years. Thousands of students have been through my hands. But how many of them remember their teacher? Only you, Smooth."

"There might be others."

"No, really, no others. Since I retired, fewer and fewer come. This year, you are the only one."

"They're all heartless," Smooth snapped, feeling how unjust this was on Mr Zhu.

"You cannot say that, Smooth," he replied calmly. "This is normal. A man always remembers the person who has been the most important and useful to him. A primary school teacher is like the foundations of the Big Wild Goose Pagoda. You're buried under the ground, so why complain if those at the summit can't see you?"

"Teacher, I did hear that some of your students have even gone to Beijing and become ministers."

"I don't remember. I've heard such talk, but can't recall who those people are."

"Among the lot, I, Smooth Diao, am maybe the lousiest loser. I pedal a tricycle for a living, but still you've never shunned me. I remember one summer break when I was in primary school, I had the job of carrying the night soil from the privies to the vegetable fields. I ran into you squatting over the hole and was so scared that I dropped the bucket and ran away. I was panicking so much about how you'd feel. But you called me back and showed me how to reposition the carrying pole so it was level. You never shunned me once."

"I'd forgotten that. When did it happen?"

"In the fifth grade of primary school. There was another time when I was in junior high school. That was the summer break, too. I'd got hold of a trike and was making money by carrying people. I bumped into you and your wife and was so scared that I pulled down my hat to cover half my face. Even then, your wife recognised me. I felt so ashamed, I wanted to bash my head against the city wall. However, you asked me for a ride and I took you to the Small Eastern Gate. You stuffed five yuan into my hand. Back then, that was worth as much as fifty yuan today!"

"I can't remember that either. How come you do?"

"All these tales perhaps lose face for my teacher. Still, you don't seem to mind that my memory runs so deep."

His teacher chewed the peanuts one by one with measured speed. He appreciated every single drop of the Western Phoenix liquor. "Why would your teacher ever have reason to detest you? Nobody is two-dimensional. Your teacher would never use sayings like 'he is not a good soldier who does not want to be a general'. If everyone were a general, then who'd be willing to be a soldier? The key point is the virtue of a man. If a man lacks virtue, he might even be incapable of carrying night soil or pedalling a tricycle. He may deliberately decide to spill his buckets on the street. Or he might rustle a goat when he should be carrying passengers. Such guys are losers. You know, Confucius had seventy-two disciples. He was aware of what each of them could do and taught them according to their capability. One of them was called Zi Lu. He obviously had no wisdom and was not destined to be a general. Confucius was sure he would die a horrendous death. Lo and behold, he was murdered, cut up and pounded to a pulp. What a wise teacher Confucius was! A few days ago, I read some words from a university professor quoted in a newspaper. He said that he classifies his former students only according to how much money they are able to earn in one year. Isn't that a crock of shit? How can he even call himself a teacher?"

"Making money is a talent," Smooth added. "In this day and age, kids think their dad is nothing if he has no money. Meanwhile, there are damned shits who shimmer with glamour. Teacher, you know that sometimes I find myself thrust into a corner. If bank robbery didn't carry the death penalty, I might try it." After saying that, he too took a small gulp of liquor.

His teacher struck the bottle of liquor so its contents splashed out all over the table. In his shock, Smooth didn't dare swallow what was inside his mouth.

"Nonsense? What nonsense!" his teacher declared earnestly. "Are you really going to rob a bank? Hah, does this sound like something that has come out of your mouth? I've known you for decades. This is the last thing I'd want to hear you say. Never, never do that. Don't even entertain such a thought."

"I was just making an analogy," Smooth explained hurriedly.

"Even an analogy of that kind is unsettling. It's put me on edge."

"Just an analogy, Teacher."

"Enough of that. Don't you have any better analogies to hand?

You want to rinse all of this stuff clean out of your brain. My student, Smooth Diao, is a fellow who lives by his labour, a clean, upstanding and decent soul, he is nobody's inferior..." His teacher got this all out without pausing for breath. He then hacked and hacked.

Smooth patted his teacher's back instinctively. "Teacher, that's all my fault," he apologised. "I just said these things for effect. I don't have the guts to be a robber."

"The more you talk about it, the more likely you are to want to bend that way. Jabbering away about crime may stir up other people's criminal motives. In that case, you do harbour a moral responsibility."

His teacher's wife had always regretted how single-minded and headstrong her husband appeared to be. Many students and their parents were reluctant to visit because they couldn't handle his manner of speaking. Even so, this was the first time he had been so fierce to Smooth. No wonder Daisy shied away from Teacher Zhu when he tried to bring her over. For a few years, Plum did come on these visits before changing her mind. Today, he had witnessed for himself his teacher's single-mindedness.

When Smooth found Zhu was agitated, he said, "Yes, you are right, Teacher. I must correct this fault myself." He then prepared to leave.

Teacher Zhu did not try to detain him any longer. "Your waist is crooked again," he pointed out as Smooth was going through the door. "I don't believe yours can be any worse than mine. Haul yourself up straight and you'll be fine."

Smooth left with his spine sheer as a bolt.

His teacher and his wife would repeat this observation whenever he went out of the door. They told him to keep his back erect. Where a man's back was concerned, they said, straightness mattered. If you started to slouch, that would become your permanent posture. Every time Smooth walked out of their house, he would adjust his back in this manner. Today, as he flattened out his backbone, there was a dead ache. He resumed his former posture as soon as he was beyond his teacher's sight.

57

Upon returning home, Daisy didn't say a word to Smooth. She didn't even return the glances he occasionally directed at her. She knew that it wasn't through his volition that Plum and Sufen had gone. They were simply unable to stick it out here, so had gathered their belongings together dejectedly and left.

Sufen's message to Daisy had been rather lengthy, and, to be candid, she couldn't read it without feeling somewhat affected. And yet, once back home, here was the all-too-familiar horror of the shabby, downcast hovel, complemented perfectly by Smooth's hangdog look of cowardice. To encounter these sights again was to instantly disinter the frustration, despair and futility in which she had been raised. It all flashed demoniacally through her mind's eye. The principal reason why this family could not better itself as others did was Smooth's compulsive attachment to women. His life had been pitiful, miserable and regrettable enough from the outset, but he chose a succession of companions who intensified that misfortune. Even though the women were gone, anger still sizzled in Daisy's brain and she knew that Smooth was the cankered root of this unsavoury stench.

Smooth stood before Daisy, his body kinked into an S-shape, and seemed to want to say something. She climbed the stairs without pausing to give him the chance. Later, she heard the clack of the gate. If it was her father, he would be going and not returning for the whole night. She surmised that he had left in search of Sufen, for her intuition told her this was no garden variety slut whom he could easily turn his back on. Had she not been press-ganged by the circumstances of life, she would not have considered Smooth a match. Once this type of woman decided to leave, it would be permanent. No matter how much it pained Daisy's father to let her go, she would have covered every trace, so his search was fruitless.

Daisy was all at once irked by how barren and cheerless the house had become. She cranked her stereo up to the maximum volume until her ears started to ring. As there was no response from beyond the adjacent walls or downstairs either, she was deprived of the pleasure of being a provocateur. Once more she was lonely.

How Daisy yearned to have Plum spring out and try to take her on. The pipsqueak was bound to lose, but the way she overestimated her prowess in these cat fights gave them a rather piquant aftertaste for Daisy. Sometimes there was satisfaction to be had in needling the touchy little bitch. Such a pity there would be no more of this. By now, Plum may have been installed as a housewife on a brick bed in some country courtyard in the deepest mountains.

Sufen was an exceedingly shrewd woman. In her absence, it dawned on Daisy that she had been the true "computer", mastering the controls of the household. She had challenged her stepmother unremittingly without Sufen ever trying to turn her tricks back on her. At the beginning, she thought that perhaps she was intimidated by her. Now she knew that there must be something monumental in her heart that caused her to remain emotionally costive and unflappable. Once her trigger had been located, some primeval power would be released against which there could be no defence. It would prove all-conquering, and confirm that Sufen was among the most perilous type of female.

By contrast, Plum had a hair trigger. Even the act of teasing her could cause her to discharge. Daisy actually even regretted not having pushed Sufen to the point of infuriation. Had she done so, the duel might have taught her a few supplementary tricks. Such a shame she was gone and this nest was vacant. Daisy returned to her thoughts of being lonely, empty and bored. Life lacked spice and animation under these grubby eaves with Smooth. It was her personal hell. Sooner or later, she might be driven insane.

She then curled up at home for a whole day and night, not wanting to encounter anybody or venture anywhere. On the evening of the second day of the New Year, Smooth had yet to come home.

It occurred to her that there might have been a mishap. She didn't want to call him directly on his mobile. Sufen had mentioned the severity of his haemorrhoids and the necessity of hospitalisation. Had he voluntarily admitted himself?

Each time Smooth needed medical advice, he would visit the hospital nearest home, and nowhere else. Daisy made enquiries and found that this was indeed where he was staying. She had intended to pay him a visit, yet winced at the notion that others might identify her as the daughter of Smooth Diao, the resident trike pedaller. Despite not being so conspicuous in appearance or manner, her father was known by reputation about Shangyi Road. He was even fond of reminding the neighbours who he was. To this end, he printed off these weird, grandiloquent business cards and handed them around. His skill set included stage shifting, cargo delivery, taxying people to and from the station, home clearances and removals, and pipeline dredging to name just a few. It appeared that his job remit had him busier than the secretary general of the United Nations. He would issue these cards on any occasion. That some folk flung them in the trash the moment his back was turned was no deterrent, for he believed these adverts could raise the profile of his business and open the sluice gates to let money pour in.

Daisy was convinced that Smooth's name cards might be circulating around the hospital ward, and raising the odd grin. Hence, she was unwilling to be noticed in this type of environment. Furthermore, she was unwilling to yield to Smooth, with whom she had not spoken seriously for ages. Especially upon Cai Sufen's arrival, any words they exchanged were said in the heat of a quarrel. Now that these sluts were gone, she still could not bring herself to bow her head before him and utter anything that could be construed as losing face for her. Still, Smooth was her father, and an inpatient right now. For her to shun him was nothing less than improper.

And so it was that same evening, Daisy strolled towards his ward. Much of her face was covered by a woollen hat.

The ward was massive, and Smooth its only occupant. He rolled himself up and coughed from time to time. She brought him food and a little milk, and asked what the matter was.

"Nothing serious," was all he could mouth in reply.

She continued to sit on the bed for a while without saying anything else.

"It's New Year and no one's cooked for you," he reflected. "Just try to rustle something up for yourself."

"Don't worry like this."

Daisy then noticed how his feet were trembling with the cold. She went out to buy a plastic hot water bottle, which she filled and then prodded into place.

He said there was no need to go to that expense as they had a perfectly good one at home.

Daisy still said nothing and then left.

Smooth paddled around in search of the hot water bottle with his feet. He now felt far warmer and thought his cough was better. With a little effort, his legs could be extended out straight. In this spring-like warmth, he sensed a kind of jollity that flowed through his heart. Apart from her demands for money, his daughter had kept a steely silence with him, and would flare up the moment they began to speak face to face. Today, she had showed concern towards him, even a touch of consideration. There was to be recompense, then, after the loss of Plum and Sufen.

With the ward almost deserted at night-time, he lay there alone. He had wished to go home to rest, but the doctor maintained that this condition was unlike others. If not attended to judiciously, there was the real danger of high fever.

Soon after Daisy had gone, the spectral figure of Third Skin appeared.

Smooth asked him why he hadn't gone home for New Year.

"Went... went back, and came back," he replied after a pause.

Smooth was eager to know the reason and thought it might be the result of a domestic tiff. Third Skin nodded his head absent-mindedly. He then wanted to know how he had heard he was in the hospital. This intelligence he had learned from Daisy, though when Smooth wanted to find out more, he was interrupted.

"If you're in the hospital, how come my sister... sister-in-law is not here to look after you?"

Smooth was silent for a long time.

"Where is my sister... sister-in-law?" Third Skin asked.

"Gone," Smooth answered, trying to appear unruffled.

"Gone where?" His tone was urgent.

"I don't know."

"How could you not know where my sister-in-law has gone?" Third Skin demanded, his tone now more urgent than before.

"I genuinely don't know."

The young man was so anxious that it appeared he wanted to burrow his hands down Smooth's throat and yank out the truth. "You're lying," he panted. "Can she... grow wings and fly away?"

"She did find her wings and has flown."

With delicate spectacles balanced upon his nose, Third Skin seemed habitually bookish and gentle. Right at this moment, any semblance of gentility evaporated. His eyes darkened to a sullen red and with a desperate, belligerent air he retorted, "Impossible, you... where are you hiding her?"

"How could I hide a full-grown woman like her? She really has gone. I'm telling you the truth. She walked out on New Year's Eve and told me she's never coming back." He then went on to pick over a few of the details.

As he listened, a wail began to rise up from within Third Skin as if his tendons were being drawn out by a torturer. He slid down and cradled his head in his hands.

Smooth started to come over a little peculiar. It was his wife who had gone, so why should his workmate be so bothered?

He had heard others cracking jokes about Third Skin and Sufen, and took it only as workplace ribbing. Those chaps on his team couldn't get through a whole day without some lewd banter. There was nothing out of character about that, but Third Skin's demeanour this evening made him a trifle dubious.

"What's wrong with you?" Smooth sounded unhappy.

Third Skin immediately appeared conscious of something. He rifled for some weak pretence. "My wife ran away too," he admitted. In fact, that happened ages ago.

"Yours too? Why indeed?"

"Who knows why? Anyhow, she did. Gone." He took hold of Smooth and the two single men let out their distress.

Without Smooth realising it, they were crying for the same person and had been talking about the same person. Smooth was under the impression that they were crying for their respective wives. Third Skin turned to praise his sister-in-law – how she was a good woman, and a rare catch, how she was the best of womanhood and the sort that is all too hard to find in this world. Smooth appreciated these sentiments and believed that he was giving voice to a number of those emotions that were tangled and teeming within himself.

Third Skin was intent on staying there and waiting on Smooth. The pair shared something in common, and both of them having company would expedite the protracted periods of loneliness. These they filled by reflecting on Sufen.

Even the nurses noted Third Skin's ability to tend to a patient. His tears were an elixir that brought on physical and psychological healing. But all the while he took care of Smooth, Third Skin was pining again and lost his appetite for food and sleep for days. His eyes sockets sank deeper, encouraging Smooth, paradoxically, to end up consoling him. He told him that it was something beyond human control, like the patterns of the rain or one's widowed mother wishing to remarry. Gradually, the two men were able to joke once again.

"I'd feel so content if I could find a woman like my sister-in-law," Third Skin confided.

"If you can bring her back, she's half yours."

"For sure?"

"You spend all that time at work together. Isn't that half enough for you?"

"A different thing. A different story."

"What different story?"

"I'm talking about something else."

"Well, as long as your sister-in-law is game, I have no objection." Smooth was quite self-confident in his tenor.

Third Skin said nothing.

58

DAISY FOUND EVERYTHING MEANINGLESS AND BANAL. She had never contemplated how being without Plum and Sufen could make her life so bland and lonely. In the past, roughing Plum over and cursing Sufen allowed her to work up a hearty appetite. Sometimes, she was able to gnaw on four marinated pig's trotters, which she had heard would not lead to weight gain, but could add definition to one's features. In the past few days, she had purchased the same number of feet, though after three days of nibbling, half were still untouched. Life was wearing her to death. She jabbed away at the buttons of the TV remote control, one of which sank inwards and would not spring back again. How she wished for a pet dog or cat, so there would be some distraction from this idleness. She lay on her bed, tossing to the left and to the right. In the end, she lay down with her head dangling over the edge of the mattress and her legs splayed upwards against the wall. Unable to fall asleep, she remained there, dumbfounded.

For whatever reason, she now thought of Shusheng, that guy who had taken her virginity. It had only lasted a few minutes, but she could never banish him from her mind. As time pressed on, the image of his face became more and more distinct. He was a native of northern Shaanxi, with a high nose bridge, broad lips, the musk of perspiration and the intrepid instinct of a tiger. At first, he had been so timid and shy. Perhaps it was her hints that had stirred his courage and launched him on this surprisingly valiant and assertive course. This was what left a lingering aftertaste for Daisy.

There were many times subsequently when she became bored,

and she was desperate to have somebody break into her home and service her again. No one came. Her only visitor was Mr Noodle Head, and she would rather die in the throes of such ravages than play this game with him.

While she was puzzling over Tan Daogui's peculiar hair, he tried to call her. Daisy had no intention of taking the call, but he was extremely persistent and once she failed to answer the first time, he tried twice again in quick succession.

"Happy New Year, Mademoiselle Diao," he crooned at the other end.

"Happy New Year," she replied.

He told her he was already back in the Western Capital, to which she asked, "Why so early?"

"It's the fourth day of the New Year. I told you this was when I'd return."

She had quite forgotten his plans.

He then suggested a meeting. Despite having no interest in him, she agreed, as meeting up couldn't be any more depressing than the situation at home.

By coincidence, the place he chose for their date was the same hotel where she had spent New Year's Eve. She was primed to say no. Then he reminded her how one could eat, swim and take tea there without having to expend the least effort. Her reluctance was tempered with glee, as she couldn't conceal her enthusiasm for the venue.

Tan first arranged a spot of swimming. His lizard-like eyes were trained on her thighs, while she was apt to compare his flabby body, especially when submerged, to the flesh of a sow's breast drained of milk. There was a bloodless whiteness to his skin, as though it had been bleached. More than once, he knowingly relaxed his muscles in the water and let his excess baggage sag free. Inch by inch, his single tuft of hair came to float on the surface of the water, while beneath there was a pale and stout jar-shaped carbuncle. Daisy allowed herself to laugh and realised why Princess Wu always thought him so comical. After their dip, Tan led her to a cafe for a latte, and shared his momentous decision with her. His companion was both left stunned and speechless.

Tan wanted to marry her.

Psychologically, and in every other respect, she was unprepared for the proposal. She should have refused outright, and yet one could not deny that Tan was a one-off. He supplemented his first proposal with something even more stupendous. He would take her to South Korea and there she could have whatever cosmetic procedures she wanted. "Don't you like Audrey Hepburn?" he asked. "Why not try to look like her? Then Princess Wu can see how Old Tan spends money on his beloved. You can look ten times prettier than your friend."

Daisy's heart was at once astir. Tan had kept this stratagem well-hidden, and she realised that he was keen to take a potshot back at Princess Wu. Yet still, being surgically enhanced in South Korea was the dream she had lodged in her bosom for years, never wanting to risk sharing it with others. As the daughter of Smooth Diao, providing she had enough to eat and wear for every season of the year, the greatest contentment she could conceive was to be able to wake up still giggling from what she had dreamt about. How could her dreams extend to cover a full facelift? Tan had thoroughly conquered her and her lips were aquiver, not knowing how to put into words a response. Loath as she was to be manacled to a lump like him, she could not jettison her dream of being made beautiful. From now on, Tan would try to mould her to his purpose, but not before she had moulded him to hers. If she ordered him to stand, he might bank on never sitting down again.

Although she didn't want to follow him to his suite, she went reluctantly so as to avoid dampening his expectations.

He strode into the bathroom, and when he came back into the room, he had already changed into pyjamas. Then he set about trying to hug her. She was repelled because this came across as so keen and needy. Hugging was not where this would end, and Daisy could detect his quickening breath as well as noticing a slight twitch in his pyjama bottoms. Tan proceeded to press her down onto the bed. As if on cue, his tuft of hair slid down and covered her eyes. She was still wriggling uneasily, but he appeared fired up. "You're sure to be ten times prettier than Wu," he promised, reiterating his resolution. "Twenty times, even thirty..." She could not resist him any longer, and the "straggly rice noodles" swished rhythmically against her face.

Tan did indeed keep his word. After they had finished on the bedspread, he phoned a travel agent friend of his and asked how quickly tickets to South Korea could be booked. He had customers scheduled to fly out on the 15th, so a special arrangement could be fixed.

While filling out the paperwork, Daisy did not leave Tan's side for one minute. She even rather regretted how she had caved in so fast that evening. She shouldn't have given him what he wanted until after the surgical procedure, or at least have waited until they were in South Korea. She had heard it said that men were essentially animals. The more you can suppress the urge to surrender, the greater their appetite will grow. As his appetite swelled, so too would his appreciation of your value. Such a shame she was an amateur in these matters and let herself go at the critical moment. Since Daisy had fallen into that mantrap, she could only persist. She consented to live with him and the couple were never apart. As soon as she reclaimed her passport and boarded the plane, she exhaled with relief.

59

SMOOTH AND DAISY'S PATHS did not cross after he was discharged. When he called her on the phone, her tone was less savage than it had been before. She just told him that she was staying at a friend's home for now and would be back in a few days. Providing he was assured of her whereabouts, he never became perturbed about brief absences of this kind.

As his thoughts brewed away, Smooth's attitude to Daisy inclined towards guilt and remorse. Other children had fathers who were practical and led decent lives without food and clothing posing a concern. He thought himself less than presentable and was dogged by the sensation of having lost face for her. What was more, he had been occupied day and night, never having had the leisure to spend twenty-four hours in her company. Neighbours of theirs had invested in cars, which they could take out on tours. There were those who had visited Beijing, Shanghai, Guangzhou and Lhasa, and regaled the community with their travel exploits. The most he could stretch to was to pedal her to the city limits for a spot of sightseeing. Long, long ago, though, folks had started to wrinkle their noses at this type of excursion. They regarded it as "demeaning", "face losing" and "undignified".

Right now, what twisted his innards most was the matter of Daisy's betrothal. She needed to find a decent family in which to marry, and with her mounting age and so many failed attempts, there was no underestimating the urgency. On the evening of the fifth day of the New Year, when he visited his teacher, he had been intending to solicit his advice. He had taught so many children over the decades that there must be a suitable connection somewhere there. Still, having witnessed for himself the old widower's daily struggle to keep himself kempt, he couldn't broach such a cause there and then.

On the sixth evening of the New Year, he paid a visit to Chief Qu. He thought it timely to thank him for his support throughout the past months. Also, he must press the issue of Monkey's injury. The chief was characteristically polite, emphasising that since the troupe was a state-run unit, official procedures would be observed. He had planned to raise the topic of Daisy's singleness, but again it appeared inappropriate. How could he presume that an eligible son-in-law would be orbiting somewhere among those of Qu's rank and class? Each time he came to visit the chief, he was handed gifts in return. Smooth had planned to sneak away while he was in the bathroom, but ended up being handed a leg of lamb. A relative had sent it from northern Shaanxi and with only the two of them at home, it was more than the Qus could hope to devour themselves. Were it not eaten soon, the meat would turn rank. There could be no way of declining the joint.

Tonight, Smooth had a roster of other calls to pay. He seldom had any contact with Director Jin save for when he was shifting stages for her productions. It was rumoured that she had lost her marbles. And so he measured his actions carefully when in her company, mindful that he could offend her inadvertently and provoke a humiliating, excoriating tirade. During the preparations for *Peach Blossom Cheeks*, she had been particularly hostile to begin with. She found fault in every facet of their work. He was as angry as the rest of the crew and slights like "night ogre", "paunchy pig" and "stinky mare" flew about. In the end, though, they found themselves uncommonly moved by her compassion towards Monkey. They had never anticipated that she should have such regard for a hired hand. Anyhow, Smooth thought a courtesy visit was obligatory on behalf of his team.

As for what gifts were fitting for Director Jin, Smooth found this something of a conundrum. He recalled that she was fond of grazing on snacks, so went to the supermarket and bought two large bags of savoury and sweet nibbles, together with a carton of milk. The 200 yuan meant nothing, as it was a gesture of camaraderie. When he knocked on the door, she answered a little perplexed and even asked if he was at the right address. When he told her this was a New Year call, she invited him in.

Smooth had been in the homes of several disorganised women in his time, though Madame Jin really took the biscuit. He couldn't even find a place to stand amid the clutter. Everywhere was strewn with a miscellany of opened books, scripts, LaserDiscs and photos. A DVD of Sichuan Opera, with which he was quite familiar, was playing on the TV. He had shifted a fair few stages for dramas of that ilk.

The coffee table before the sofa was heaped with torn open sachets of snacks, from salted broad beans, to puffed rice, to desiccated clods of what had been steamed buns, and soda crackers. A succession of packets of pot noodles had been shoved carelessly into the wastepaper basket under the table. Their smell wafted about the room, one that was very familiar to manual workers like him.

To his greater surprise, the walls of her home presented a collage of pinned-up leaves torn from scripts and handmade charts. On closer examination, these turned out to be hundreds of diagrams, scenery designs and progress plans, all relating to *Peach Blossom Cheeks*. The material showed how intensively she had plunged herself into a drama she knew already. It had been marinating away in her mind, and she even received dispatches at home about every evolving dance number, no matter how minor. No wonder she earned the nickname "She Who Lives Without Having a Life" after the character in *Outlaws of the Marsh*.

Director Jin was a loose-lipped woman, and no words ever fazed her. She could even come up with expressions that no man dared utter. One time, she claimed that she "couldn't find a clean pair of knickers" because the drama was occupying her every minute. Through hearsay this was adulterated to "Director Jin doesn't wear knickers!" Only those who had entered her lair could grasp that she truly was a "drama nut" and a "drama hag". Beyond the stage, she had scant aptitude for social graces. Little wonder that three husbands had abandoned her in turn, and she herself characterised their departure as "fleeing from darkness into the light". On this score, Smooth could appreciate the old proverb that "one miserable soul loves the company of another". Three women had left him one after the other, each separation bringing with it the urge to go out and hitch a noose. Presently, though, the director spoke jovially and zestfully, as if her sufferings were a series of frolics that had befallen some other hapless sod. Smooth now began to have the measure of this grand dame. She was broadminded and resilient in ways in which men could seldom let themselves be.

"Smooth, what's your game?" she asked. "I thought you'd got the wrong door."

"I've come especially to see you."

"You see, there isn't a place to sit. Just perch here." She swept aside some of the flotsam on the sofa, leaving a pinched gap.

"You have the bearing of an extraordinary director, Madame Jin. That much I could tell the minute I stepped in here."

"Tell me why."

"You take things so seriously. There aren't many people who are that way inclined nowadays."

"Don't talk like that. I'm a lazy sow. I don't know how to conduct myself as a lady. When the dress rehearsals were done with, I went over to my mother's house. I slept there and have only just got back this afternoon. You see, this place is just how it was before New Year."

"You're too tired, too put out. You should allow yourself a good rest."

"You're working hard too. For my money, stage shifting is the toughest job in the world. You have to work around the clock when needs must and if you're not in good shape, you're buggered. I think you're capable and brainy with it, Smooth, and halfway to being an artist yourself. What you don't know about the stage isn't worth shit all. If you could put yourself up for a title, you ought to warrant being a senior stage technician. That's on a par with being an associate professor. In fact, you deserve it more than others who've been promoted already."

Smooth could not bear to hear any more words of praise. Every fresh compliment made him want to rise to his feet and bow with his hands crossed in front of his chest. More remarkable was that these words came from Director Jin. Who was she, after all? She was someone who jetted around the country and ate and drank up drama rehearsals. To be dauntless in one field seemed like human nature to him, but what people feared was being starved of recognition and praise. As long as one's efforts did not go unnoticed, it was possible to bend to whatever task was required.

He thanked her again and again for her understanding. Maybe he had come over a little flattered, and was eager to share a few artistic observations with Madame Jin. He even accompanied their discussion with hand gestures to illustrate stage directions in *Peach Blossom Cheeks*. His gesticulations had not apparently clarified any of his points, so he promptly changed topic. Smooth tried to encourage her to pay more attention to her health. "Your continued well-being really is an asset to the country," he opined. "You can't just make do with snacks and instant noodles. They do your health no favours. If you got sick, that would be a real loss to the drama world and the country as a whole."

"Don't concern yourself with what the whole country wants. Come on, what else are you after?"

"I've no other motive. I just wanted to visit you for New Year. Thank you for your kindness. You gave Monkey a generous amount of money and showed generosity to us as employees. I just came over to thank you. Nothing else. Just to show our gratitude."

Director Jin, who was rather touched, replied, "Well, I accept that. Thank you, Smooth. We are finely matched partners. When I prepare for dramas, I can only face the task when I know you're there to help with the heavy stuff."

"Thank you for thinking so highly of us, Director Jin." He bowed several times before departing. Had his confidence in stage shifting ever begun to wane, today's two visits restored it fully. Tough as it all was, his contribution was valued. On top of that, stage shifting had sustained his family for years and few ordinary folk could match his dedication.

On leaving the apartment, he remembered one subject that had not been mentioned. Each time during rehearsal, she would describe the emotions of the characters in meticulous detail. Especially when it was a love story, her commentaries would provide a vibrant sensual palette. She observed how to evoke enticement, how to ogle, how to infer love at first sight and how to capture everlasting ardour, to name a few examples. It appeared that she was an auteur when it came to romance and matrimony. He wondered if it was fitting to bring Daisy with him and seek pointers on secrets and spells she could master. He had been desperate to open his mouth, though feared they were not so intimate that every barrier was removed. In the end, he believed he had been sensible to stay quiet. Those three men Director Jin had lived with "fled from the darkness into the light", suggesting that her knowledge was theoretical and didn't hold much authority in the real world.

Smooth's round of visiting was not yet over. There was one person he called on every year, yet of whom he was now wary. He had persecuted the team and behaved as if they were less than human. The King of Hell was easy to handle compared with pesky little spirits. That was Iron Kou to a tee, and the only reason Smooth did not refrain from visiting him was out of fear that he could use this as a pretence for being testy in the future. The truth was that most of his work came via Kou. He had already bought New Year gifts, but on reflection chose not to go. Should continuing with stage shifting entail being reliant on Iron Kou and his contemptuous ways, he would rather give in. He would sooner change job than continue to accept his crumbs.

Unexpectedly, the following day, Iron Kou phoned him. Tonight was scheduled to be the premiere of *Peach Blossom Cheeks*. The actor playing the dog had gone down with a high fever. He asked Smooth if he was willing to be the stand in, to which he replied that he didn't know how to perform such a part. Easy. The mutt ate poison and simply had to shamble a few circles about the stage before slumping down dead. Smooth was aware that this animal was a village dog that the heroine insisted on bringing with her to the city. The hero Cui Hu approved, but after a few days his own mother commanded that a servant poison it covertly. Iron Kou said that the salary was thirty yuan for playing the dog, so coupled with his nightly fee, his earnings would be doubled. He restated the offer and for want of anything else to do, Smooth agreed.

60

SMOOTH HAD DONE STAND-INS FOR THE OPERA TROUPE BEFORE. A few years back, just before the first performance of *Snow in Summer*, they found that the actor cast as a *yamen* runner had gone missing. It turned out that he'd rowed with his wife in the afternoon and then got sozzled. He had tried to make his way back to the stage but fell over in a stupor, never to regain his legs. When no replacement could be found, somebody proposed Smooth. That troupe was already using him to play a victim of execution in the same play. This was actually as a stand-in for the wronged heroine Dou'e. To be precise, the actress had developed backache and as it was too agonising for her to lie down flat, a substitute had to simulate her dead body. This was not a role for a trained actor, though the dying scene should be pulled off swiftly and neatly. Five seconds was all that was needed to dash from the back of the stage to the front and pitch to the ground in a mantle of white silk. To pull this off required perfect synchrony between the director, the music, the simulated thunder and lightning, the snow machine, those generating the sound of the wind and the scene-changing personnel. Any section or member who was off-cue in those crucial moments would cause a visible mishap. The "beheading of Dou'e" was meant as the climax of the play, so any glitch would mar the atmosphere and impact of the tragedy.

Prior to the performance, Smooth had taken a piece of white silk in his hands and practised rushing to the front of the stage and lying down dozens of times. His elbows and knees were left bruised.

In the end, the first performance was a hit. Afterwards, everybody praised Smooth for his stand-out turn and said that he had been a "convincing corpse". He had lain absolutely motionless on the ground with the silk dancing on the snow and wind.

On account of his brilliant job as Dou'e's body double, he was the troupe's first choice when a substitute *yamen* runner was needed. It happened that their roles didn't overlap. The *yamen* runner appeared in the act before Dou'e's decapitation. There were four men of that kind with official clubs in their hands. They had to mime the gesture of opening the door until the corrupt officer sentenced Dou'e to death and the judge declared the court session over. Smooth had seen countless performances, so was quite familiar with walk-on roles. To mime the gesture of opening the door, four of them had to cluster on the stage and then rotate as if performing the real action. This was very straightforward, as simple as writing out the number "1" on paper. It didn't even require the player to know what a number "2" looked like.

They rehearsed the scene once and then Smooth and his three fellow runners retired to the dressing room, where one of them helped him with his make-up. He first painted two slanted eyes, both of them even having a speck of white sleep in the corner. Next, he added a protruding lower lip and glued a tuft of hair onto his left cheek. As soon as he was finished, he concealed Smooth in a corner so that nobody would spy his eccentric appearance until he crossed the stage wielding a club.

On seeing Smooth act his role as *yamen* runner, the stage crew dissolved into giggles. This even made the orchestra temporarily lose their place in the score. Nevertheless, Smooth tried to appear serious and earnest. The harder he tried, the greater the comic effect. Ultimately, even the actress who played Dou'e couldn't help but break into a chuckle as her hands were clamped between two bamboo stakes. Fortunately, she had her back to the audience. After the curtain, Chief Qu criticised the "make-up artist", scolding him for being insufficiently solemn and letting in-jokes slip in. Come what may, this was the beginning of Smooth's foray into acting.

A number of bit parts came his way and he would often fill a small vacancy. Mostly, he took on slain corpses, be they villains hacked or blasted to death the moment they trod onstage or bodies hanging midair. The year before last, there was a large commemorative evening party featuring a selection from *The White-Haired Girl*. He had to play the girl herself as she picked wild fruit. The directions called for her to seize hold of some vines and inch along them so as to cross a deep gulley. The actress did not feel intrepid enough to venture across herself, so somebody reasoned that perhaps Smooth would be a game stunt double for a fee of 200 yuan. He wriggled into the heroine's dress and donned a frowzy wig. Screeching out "two hundred", he charged with his back to the audience and managed to negotiate the gulley. Playing a dog, however, was a completely new adventure for him.

Canines were a mainstay of the stage, for Smooth could name perhaps twenty plays that featured one. To act the "clever mastiff" in *The Orphan of the Zhao Family* was an acrobatic challenge, as it called for skills such as turning somersaults. "Tiger hounds" like those in *A Journey to Turtle Mountain* were ten-a-penny. These were usually the loyal pets of dandies or playboys and would lash out at the poor, wound people or cause all kinds of strife. The hero would typically dispatch them amid a series of rolls and tumbles, accompanied by plaintive howls. The animal in *Persuading a Wife by Killing a Dog* was quite simple. It just padded onstage, barked a few times and then was chopped to death by Cao Zhuang, ending its life with a "backwards flip".

Even though *Peach Blossom Cheeks* was a fully fledged opera, its dog had greater stage time. The amount of crawling the actor had to do was punishing, but to Smooth's relief, the present director was lenient and didn't demand any special manoeuvres. It should simply run after its owner and roll on the ground a few times to show it was happy. The pet would only eat out of Peach Blossom's hand. In the end, this was the cause of its demise, for the mother-in-law had spiked the food. The heroine took hold of the dog and sang a twenty-four-line aria before she was prepared to have it buried.

Once Smooth was cast, he went to the stage in the afternoon to rehearse the dog's gait. It was quite a chore. What appeared facile was shown with a little practice to be tortuous. No human could act effortlessly in this position, for it not only made one's waist and back sore but also induced throbbing headaches. Especially when it pursued Peach Blossom and dashed around the peach orchard, those were routines fit to kill a man. Smooth drilled himself assiduously, yet his wound down below was far from healed and all that crawling brought on twinges of pain. He would have to be disciplined and tolerate it for the sake of getting through the rehearsals.

The premiere of *Peach Blossom Cheeks* at last began.

Dressed in his doggy garb, Smooth scrambled at the foot of an earthen slope centre stage, waiting for his turn to really begin.

Apart from his own acting, his chief concern today was for the audience to applaud as soon as the curtain rose and the set was revealed. Director Jin said that if no one in the stalls clapped, then they really had buggered up the design. There had been raptures during the rehearsal, but this was the first actual performance. He knew that Mound had been the instigator then. Today was a different affair.

As the curtain receded, Smooth instinctively drew his paws before his chest and wanted to be the first to clap. Since he was onstage and in part, that would be absurd. Just as sullenness set in, there was an almighty surge of sound like a tidal bore ripping through the auditorium. The clapping and whistling from below even overwhelmed the melodies of the orchestra. Was it the set they were applauding? He became nervous that there had been some minor slip-up and that the audience were clapping in an act of mockery. With his animal head in place, he didn't have the field of vision to be able to gauge the truth. He could only peer at the facial expressions of those in the wings. Once he knew that the mood was one of excitement and expectation, he realised that the response was positive. As the hero was not yet onstage, it must be the setting that had won their approval. His confidence now fortified, his canine shenanigans would be stellar tonight.

Eventually, the dog did make its entrance. It too won a storm of applause. Smooth could be certain that this appreciation was all for him, since as soon as the creature craned its head, there was clapping and laughter as if a dam had been breached. The dog acted of "its" own volition and no human trainer instructed it to shake its head knowingly on the earthen slope. Again, there was a maelstrom of applause. In a split second, Director Jin's maxims of "role understanding" and "role creation" sank in. He was at once a genuine dog. His demeanour became so lovable, so docile and so natural that when the animal died and Peach Blossom held it in her arms and cried, he too was weeping inwardly.

He had won everybody's approval. "Well done, Smooth," Director Jin said. "On the nose!" Her thumbs were raised too.

"Director Jin," he hazarded in return. "Tonight, the audience did cheer for the setting."

"Yes, I saw that. A great job."

Iron Kou's words of praise he sensed were spoken with sarcasm. "What a nice dog!" he commented. "I'd never expected that you'd make such a fine mutt. Capital stuff."

The premiere had exceeded expectations, with the audience reluctant to leave even after three curtain calls. A few of the fans jammed onto the stage to have their photos taken with the leading man and leading lady until late into the evening. The players began to grow impatient and tetchy before the last admirers would leave. The clamorous scene finally dispersed.

Smooth had been propping up part of the peach blossom scenery. Towards the end of the play, he had to dash over to prevent it from falling. Since there was no time to fix the fake flora into place with the iron pier, he had to make do with his hands. There was an elevated platform to the rear on which the "dead" peach blossom was supposed to dance. This sequence lasted for only three minutes, but after the curtain call, the audience wanted to use this as a backdrop for photos. Smooth was left gripping it in place for more than half an hour. Several times he wanted to crick his neck and see what was going on out front, though others scolded him, even using vulgar words, to tell him to tighten his belt lest anything unseemly be exposed. Those who witnessed these events found it a hoot.

The stage lights were not extinguished until very late. When Smooth left the backstage, he ran into Mound. He asked him why he had come so soon, and his underling admitted that it was to clap for the setting. "Director Jin said if there was no applause, then we'd clearly buggered up the scenery," he remarked. Smooth was touched that he'd made such an effort and asked about his arm. It was fine, and he was able to move it around as normal.

"Was it you inside the dog costume?"

"How could you tell?"

"I saw through it. The guy who was doing it before was quite nimble and agile. You were as clumsy as a bear. Don't you know how I worked it out?"

"How?"

"The old dog would twist its backside with ease and quite gladly. When you did it, you paused. I realised that the pooch must have piles!"

"Go fuck your mother's cunt!"

That night after coming home, Smooth contemplated the role of the dog for half the night. For one thing, he must try to put everything into it. The following evening, Mound claimed that there was much more vigour to his second outing. He persisted in his study once he was back in the house later on, ambling back and forth a few times to imitate the pace of the dog, and chewing over what flourishes he could add to the motions. Night after night, the audiences were enthusiastic, and the stalls were packed out. Smooth was so elated that he even pedalled his teacher over to watch. Mr Zhu was not overly enamoured with the production. On the way back, he described it as "too boisterous, too gaudy. As for the setting, the sauce seemed better than the fish. Too flashy. If Cui Hu's mind had been filled with that, he'd never have composed his masterpiece." So many viewers praised the play. His teacher was the only voice of dissent. Smooth reasoned that this was a symptom of his advanced years and he had simply fallen behind the times.

Just as he was becoming submerged and intoxicated in his canine caper, Smooth heard that the regular actor for the role of the dog had recovered from his fever. Tomorrow evening he would resume the part, making tonight the last chance to have a glorious denouement. The popularity of the show caused so many of the cast to exaggerate and try to make the most of the scenes in which they featured. They wanted their lyrics, gestures and singing to win a deluge of applause. This was Smooth's final opportunity to prove himself the antithesis of an underdog. And so, tonight, the dog prickled with a sense of frenzy from the second it first appeared. It shook its head when it should not have done. It twisted its posterior at an inopportune time. When it tailed its mistress around the stage, it even made facial expressions at the audience. These points might be deemed too insignificant to even mention. What did matter was what happened when it died. Peach Blossom sang a line recalling how loyal it had been. Despite being sprawled inanimate in her arms, the dog's body swayed to her doleful, beautiful strains. It had sunk into the very fabric of the plot. The actress playing Peach Blossom bumped it lightly as a reminder not to move. Still, it rocked contentedly. He had never before lain in such warm arms and lapped up such praise. More than twenty lines of Shaanxi Opera sung in slow tempo were all dedicated to him. When in normal life did anybody reserve so many words for him? Most of the time he only heard injunctions such as, "Smooth, go and do it" or, "Smooth, do you look through your eyes or breathe with them? Can't you see what you've done?" Even when he was being praised, the compliments were always rather curt, like, "Well done, Smooth. We're sure to book you next time." In more than fifty years on this Earth, it had taken him playing a dog to end up here. Now he was hearing a hymn of praise on the significance of life, infused with pitiful love and heartbroken affection, condensed into the shape of an opera lyric.

Throughout his existence, Smooth had been looked down upon and scolded. He had never lived a single day nobly or with pride and dignity. He was now supping his fill of nobility, pride and dignity. This pleasure had musical accompaniment, and he couldn't resist keeping time with the rhythm by tapping his feet. Then, without warning, there were guffaws assaulting his ears. It dawned on him. He was on a theatre stage acting the role of a dog. His anus now ached. How could people laugh like this? Was it because his tail had fallen off when he shifted his bum just now? The dog stretched out a paw to feel. Only then did he remember that the animal was meant to be dead. As the performance was so much grander than the sky, he knew that this was a terrible calamity reaching up to the clouds.

Iron Kou kicked his rear end three times following his stage exit. "You son of a bitch," he squawked. "You're dicing with death, dicing with death. Crazy, you're a crazy mutt." He wanted to inflict more violence, but Chief Qu stopped him. This contempt for him was obviously shared by everyone backstage.

Chief Qu interrogated Smooth about what had happened. He claimed to have fallen into a trance, and was extremely apologetic, even branding himself a "damned shit". Smooth had thought he would encounter Director Jin, too. It was better to have her reprimand you to your face with the most rabid curses than to be ignored. He heard that when she saw the dog begin to disport itself onstage, she kicked over her own stool and stormed off. Smooth believed he ought to apologise in person straight away, though the set changes needed to be dealt with immediately.

Following the performance, Iron Kou informed the meeting of staff how Director Jin had charged out through the backstage with her eyeballs red and her hair standing on end. Her bearing was akin to a marauding tiger fresh from the mountain slope. The acoustics section had prepared a mike for her to address the gathering. This she gripped for an age before speaking. The whole stage area and orchestra pit were so silent that the sound of a falling pin would surely echo. Smooth had seen his share of after-show emergency meetings. This was different because of the all-pervasive solemnity. He thought that if Director Jin had a rifle to hand, he would be blasted into oblivion in seconds.

Smooth cowered behind the peach tree, trying not to be noticed. His whole body trembled. If there were a fissure in the ground, he would happily take that as his warren, never to be seen again.

After a lengthy silence, Director Jin spoke up. "None of you must take tonight's fiasco as a simple accident," she started off. "No, it was something that was bound to occur somewhere along the line. Accidents are inevitable. That glut of applause was the catalyst. We all went crazy on it. It's not just that one dead dog acted up. Smooth? Where is Smooth?"

Smooth was so terrified that he remained barricaded behind the piece of setting. He could no longer reach his full height due to the curvature of his backbone.

At the sight of his posture, someone chuckled. Soon, everyone was laughing.

Smooth did not know what was so funny. Maybe he had done

something clumsy again. As he unconsciously reached one hand behind himself to touch his bottom, there was even more wanton hilarity.

"I'd never taken you as one with comedic talent, Smooth Diao. This has been revelatory. I still can't comprehend it. You're quite familiar with the stage and no street bum, so how could you make such an almighty cock-up? It's intolerable. I could only think that you'd gone temporarily mad. There's no other explanation for this most terrible, shameful, nauseating and ugly display. You can't even exercise self-control when you're cast as a dog. Too sad, too sad…" She then cursed him with the most excoriating words imaginable. As he was listening to her, he experienced a booming, cavernous sensation inside his brain. He followed nothing of what this gorgon was saying. He only saw her podgy lips open and close, juddering somewhat as they did so.

Acting the dog had brought so much humiliation and sadness. He determined never to take on such a role again.

That dog, a real son of a bitch.

In the evening, he returned home. He couldn't remember exactly how. Another brain-taxing ordeal awaited him there. Daisy gave him formal notice that she was travelling to South Korea with somebody and would stay there for two or three months. When he asked her the reason, she replied "cosmetic surgery". Alongside her stood a man with a solitary tuft of hair draped across his head. He was perhaps only a few years younger than Smooth himself, yet his figure was far fuller and his complexion shone as if coated in grease. Smooth then understood what was afoot.

He had been dreaming day and night that Daisy would have a man to keep her company. Only, when it came about, he found he could say nothing.

Overwhelmed by the awkwardness of the situation, he dared not enquire about further particulars, only murmuring that they should be mindful about safety.

Daisy went out of the gate on the stranger's arm.

The bottom had fallen out of Smooth's heart. He paced one circuit of the room as if bereft and then chased after them, asking, "Do you need any money?"

"No, don't bother about that," the man replied.

Daisy leaned her head against his shoulder in an exaggerated gesture and they left together.

On his way back in, Smooth closed the gate in a state of numbness, and slid down with his back against the metal panel. Earlier, when they had the debriefing in the theatre, his legs were already fit to give way. He tried to hold on and hold on while in company. Now his resolve was gone.

61

EARLY ON THE MORNING of the fifteenth day of the New Year, Third Skin came knocking at Smooth's gate. His pounding was so urgent it sounded as though he were trying to escape from a blaze. Smooth opened up with a quilt wrapped around his body. The young man let himself in, anxious to report the dream about Sufen he had the previous night. In it, she had taken holy orders as a nun. Smooth at once brought to mind the lady Serenity in that temple in the southern suburbs. Every other conceivable place had been considered, so why had this one been overlooked? He dressed himself and the two men headed over there on a bus. They found her dwelling next to the religious house.

Serenity was tight-lipped at first, but soon disclosed the truth. Sufen had appeared there in the middle of the night on New Year's Eve and left three days later. When they asked where she had gone, she could only say for certain that it was a faraway destination and, in all likelihood, her objective was to become a nun. Sufen had chatted with her about the religious life during that period, and admitted how she believed that she had led a sinful existence and needed to redeem herself. Serenity assured them of how she had told Sufen that this was no easy path. Her sin could be expiated as a laywoman. Even so, she was determined, and reasoned that she must select a remote habitation. No precise location was ever specified. She only asked Serenity to keep her confidence on one matter. She must not divulge that she had visited her. Nevertheless, given the perturbed and distressed state of the pair, Serenity felt that this scrap of information should be shared.

Her words left them little the wiser. A "faraway destination"? Now where could that be, and which direction? They discussed this with Serenity for some time without her offering anything further. She only said that fate must take its course. If fate determined that Sufen were to return, then she would indeed do so even if she had ventured to the farthest end of the planet. Should fate withhold its blessings, they might never encounter each other again, even if they were living in the same neighbourhood.

Third Skin started bawling after they left Serenity's home. Smooth thought it peculiar that he should be showing such emotion when it was his own wife who had walked out on him. Third Skin's behaviour seemed to add to the suspicions that were fostered more than ten days earlier.

Smooth repeated the question he posed back then. "What's the matter with you?"

"She's such a lovely sister-in-law," replied Third Skin. "How could she disappear like this? I... could never hope to have a better co-worker."

He said nothing more. The two men were sullen throughout the return journey. Third Skin was keen to go to his boss's house and sit there a while, though Smooth said it was impractical for he had tasks to do. And so they parted company.

Night had fallen by the time they reached their respective homes. On departing that morning, a few snowflakes started to fall. Before long, they were falling heavily, coating the whole of the Western Capital in a deep veneer. Amid this interminable expanse of silvery white, the sparkles and flames of the Lantern Festival tantalised. Soon, the city glowed red once more from the radiance of lanterns and lamps. Fireworks and firecrackers jetted into the air from everywhere, composing a chromatic haze before disappearing. A murky calm was restored.

Smooth normally had a predilection for this type of extravaganza. Several times in the past he had climbed the city wall to survey the annual pyrotechnic display. Tonight, he was phlegmatic. He just wanted to stay at home, shielding his ears and eyes.

He now realised that he had gone a whole day without food or refreshment. In his hunger, he traipsed into the kitchen with the intention of preparing a meal. The tap had seized up with frost and the wok and stove, which were icy to the touch, dampened his willingness to start a fire for cooking. Instead, Smooth bought a few baked flatbreads and cartons of instant noodles from outside. He had been salivating over sausages, though the stores that sold them had raised the price by a dozen cents to milk the seasonal demand. Back home, he doused the bread in the soup from the noodles and improvised by tossing in some pickles. Once full, he felt the onset of regret. Lantern Festival was here and he should have taken better care of himself. How could he maintain in private the sort of bad habits he practised while still on the job? It occurred to him that it was indeed true when people criticised him for living so wretchedly.

Afterwards, he went upstairs to look inside his daughters' rooms. Plum's bedroom was unlocked just as she had left it, and appeared to be abandoned for good. Through the window he could spy that Daisy had rolled up her quilt and covered it in a polythene sheath, suggesting that she would be gone for a long time. As he stood on the upper floor balcony, he tried again to reach Plum on the phone. He had lost track of how many times he had called since her departure. A few days ago, her mobile had been merely switched off. Now, the number was out of service. There was the sense that their two fates had now forked apart irretrievably. He couldn't welcome this estrangement. Having spent years as her guardian, the fact that she was not his natural born child became an irrelevance. However, she might be thinking otherwise. Hence her disappearance.

He then called Sufen with the same outcome. Tears flowed down his cheeks. There was nobody around watching him, so he let them flow freely until they had drenched his collar before forming into icicles.

He entered his own bedroom and found it a frigid cellar of a space. His legs and feet especially were nearly numb with cold. He turned on the electric heater and propped up his legs so they were virtually in contact with the grille on the device. Presently, his extremities were touched by an incendiary heat, while the rest of him froze.

With the heater turned on, it was guzzling away precious electricity. That was unbearable. He switched it off and set about lighting small fires on scraps of waste board to thaw the pipes.

Smooth boiled the kettle and then huddled on his bed with a hot water bottle.

He dropped off straight away, not even being mindful of the hour. In his dream, he could perceive Cai Sufen adrift amid the limitless oceans, so he grappled after a piece of wood to pursue her. His raft turned out to be a plank bed. Ever since he was a child, he had longed to be a seafarer, but in five decades he had barely left the Western Capital. Now he found himself trying to reach his wife across the ocean.

To begin with, the sea was calm and flat. Sufen grinned, and he had the impression that she was waiting for him to catch up with her. As soon as the winds rose, though, the waves banked up high above his head, and she drifted ever further into the distance. Try as he might to paddle, his own craft remained stationary. The seawater was now choking him. It was so bitter and salty that he wanted to wretch up the contents of his stomach.

Just as Sufen was about to disappear into the distance, Third Skin appeared on a bed identical to his own. It too refused to budge, only he had the benefit of an elongated bamboo pole with a hook at one end. They extended it together so that it reached the edge of Sufen's boat. Still, they occasionally lost sight of the vessel. At last, they caught hold of its rim and it inched nearer and nearer. Then, as they stretched out to take hold of Sufen, a huge wave pitched over between her and her would-be rescuers. The waves overwhelmed Sufen and her boat, leaving not a trace. Only their two plank beds continued to float. Smooth uttered a spirited wail, followed by Third Skin whose bellowing sounded like a decrepit old ox. Their cries mingled and drowned out the racket of the waves.

Sufen was gone for good.

He awoke in panic.

How come it was damp under his body? Had he wet the bed? Impossible! He hadn't done that since he was eleven or twelve years old. He turned on the light and lifted the quilt to check. It turned out that the hot water bottle had leaked. Almost a bagful had seeped out, drenching not only the matting beneath and the coverlet, but making his cotton underwear stick clammily to his body. He was stunned. He was so angry that he felt the need to curse somebody. And yet he didn't know who to take as a target.

Up until now, it hadn't registered with him how chilly the bedroom was. The stray splashes of water that had trickled into the basin when he was filling the bottle had solidified into ice. Once his clothes were changed, he considered going upstairs to claim a quilt belonging to either Daisy or Plum. Then again, was this entirely appropriate? What if they happened to return home? Both of them had complained about his musty body odour.

One day, when the weather had taken a sudden turn, he had pulled down Daisy's quilt that she had left hanging on the rail to dry. When his elder daughter came back, she pulled off the cover and washed it in disgust. What marvellously sensitive noses young people now possess!

On second thoughts, as their father, he shouldn't interfere with their personal bedding. He placed his own quilt on the warmer to dry and then tried to heat himself up by running around the room.

This proved effective. Stage shifting work always took place at night. Sometimes it was excruciatingly cold at that hour, even in spring and autumn. This jogging about a confined area served both to generate body heat and clarify his jumbled thoughts. Following this exercise, his frozen frame gradually revivified and his mental agility improved, to the extent that he could even begin to contemplate the intricacies of his life. In the past, ordering his personal affairs posed no intractable problem. He had indeed been as wretched a soul as others had described. For the rest of his mortal span, he could do well to plan and be methodical.

Stage shifting robbed him of the ability to distinguish night from day, and all that begging after unpaid fees made it no long-term career. When all was said and done, he had reached his fifties. Those ideals he clung to in his childhood sprang into focus, not least an incident from his third grade in primary school. Teacher Zhu asked each of his pupils about their aspirations. When it came to Smooth's turn, he screamed at the top of his voice, "To be a retired cadre!" His answer caused everyone to giggle. Zhu asked why that should be, and he explained that in his community there lived one such man. When others went out to tend the fields early in the morning, he took a couple of caged birds to the bend in the city moat. As those feathered companions basked in the congenial atmosphere, he performed a regimen of physical training that began with pounding his back repeatedly against a tree. Once this was done, he withdrew to a deckchair in the sunshine, whereupon he sipped tea and sampled newspaper articles choicely as if he were nibbling upon a marinated goat's hoof bought in the Muslim Quarter. During the afternoons, he would take a camp stool to the moat so as to listen to operas, try to catch fish or pocket chirruping insects. Strolling back in the evening, he would tune his hand-held transistor radio to listen to the evening news. Next, the captured insects were spread out as his private chorus. Then followed a discussion with them as to their virtues and demerits. He wanted to know which among them they thought "chirped crisply" and which had a "reckless chirrup", denoting it was dumb. The key point was that, in this company, he appeared to be the wellhead of all wisdom. The cadre once related how Lin Biao had fled by plane and plummeted to his doom in a place called Ondorhaan, or something of the sort. Sure enough, a few days later, Smooth's teacher covertly removed the picture featuring Chairman Mao alongside Lin, his closest comrade-in-arms.

Even Smooth's pa said that the life of a retired cadre was the model way to live. And so Smooth installed this as his fantasy of what he wanted to achieve in the future. He could still remember everyone around him laughing at length. Other classmates maintained it was their ambition to be a scientist or an author. Those with more modest goals hoped to at least join the army so they could help vanquish American imperialists and Soviet revisionists. He had blurted out an idea that the others regarded as neither fish nor flesh. Fortunately, Teacher Zhu decided not to criticise him. He instead broke into a smile. "Smooth's idea is canny," he commented. "The life of a retired senior cadre might be regarded as refined. That's how an old person may choose to live. However, for the young, it's not an option."

He could remember how Teacher Zhu later pressed him on the subject. "If only I could allow my father to have a life like that, it would be enough," replied the boy. "My dad's older than that man and he still has to lead me out when I carry the night soil and water the veggie fields." Teacher Zhu said nothing, and patted Smooth's head fondly.

In retrospect, the life of that retired cadre was nothing short of wonderful. It was the picture of how a city dweller should spend his days. Smooth could reflect on how he was no better off than Big Hook or Monkey or Mound or Third Skin, all of whom had entered the city as migrant hands. His father related to him how the Diao family clan had been residents of the Western Capital for generations. Their home had originally been in the downtown area until they relocated to outside the city wall. It was fortuitous that the wall was now no longer the boundary point it had formerly been. Shangyi Road had been absorbed into the inner cabbage heart of the metropolis. He was of timeworn city stock, so was bound to warrant the lifestyle of an urban fellow. Back in the day, although his father carried night soil and watered vegetable fields, that didn't prevent him from keeping two thrushes of his own. Look at Smooth Diao today. How could he rely on pedalling a trike for his crust?

He believed he should savour the quality and swagger of a city dweller. What about making money? In the past, he slogged away to try to become established and to scrabble a living of his own. Later on, he had to persist in this course to support his parents and, further down the line, to seek a cure for Plum's mother, then support Plum through college, and allow Daisy to lead a contented and decent life like the other girls in the community. He even had to think ahead about the dowries of the two daughters. And then Sufen came along. In all this time, he was short of money and had to try whatever he knew to earn extra and feel assured that there was grain in the cupboard. Now he seemed to have a little respite from chasing banknotes. All of them had gone and he appeared to be left with no dependents. Wanting for nothing himself, his vigour for earning was diluted. Actually, he had saved a little private money of his own, though this was his greatest secret. That 100,000 yuan was set aside for when he became old and could not work.

He was truly exhausted. Smooth did not want to continue with stage shifting as a career. He would make do with pedalling his trike, carrying either people or cargo. That was small money, but readily and cleanly made. No catches. There was no need to tax his brain or exert himself to deal with so-called artists in all their paranoia. Each without exception was deranged – cold one moment and convivial the next, chuckling one moment and inconsolable the next. Any normal person would be driven crazy by them. Was there any need for him to kiss their cold backsides with his warm face? Once he had reached this resolution, he was at peace. As daybreak drew near, he was so worn out that he curled up beneath an overcoat and slept until dawn. He then went to the street to buy a newspaper, some tea and a pair of reading glasses, before swinging around the Muslim Quarter where he purchased a caged song thrush for 150 yuan. Smooth returned home, having realised his childhood ideal: he had officially started the life of a "retired cadre".

In his house there was a deckchair left behind by his father. It had a rectangular wooden frame with white canvas stretched across the middle. Smooth fished it out, opened the contraption and tried to make it stand, though it slid down flat. He then went to a market where they sold similar chairs made from bamboo. On bringing one home, he brewed tea, using a lidded porcelain cup that had been found backstage after a visiting Beijing Opera troupe had departed. Smooth unfolded the newspaper, balanced the spectacles on the bridge of his nose and even crossed his legs. He began to read the paper, going so far as to enunciate out loud the title – *Hua-shan Daily*. At first, he spoke in a murmur before recalling that the retired cadre had never uttered a sound. He just read and turned the pages in silence, sometimes folding it shut, closing his eyes and mediating for a while before opening it again and resuming. Smooth imitated the very manner of the cadre and thus adopted the elegant lifestyle mentioned by Teacher Zhu.

A few days later, Big Hook, Monkey and others came visiting. Big Hook told him how he had brought his wife and child to the city with him, and asked if it were possible to arrange for her to do some odd jobs among the crew. He also mentioned that whatever Sufen had done, she could do likewise.

Smooth peered at Big Hook, his protruding eyes visible above the frames of the glasses. Dozens of years may have passed, though he could still bring to mind clearly how this was the selfsame expression that the senior cadre directed at those in his presence. It was a rather dignified demeanour. Mimicking the tone and look of the old man, with his perfectly arranged syntax and word order, Smooth explained, "I, too, need to have a good rest. I've been doing this my whole life, it seems. It's high time for me to offer my post to someone more capable. You carry on shifting stages if you like, but as for me, I am retired."

At first, Big Hook thought he was joking. Later, he discovered that Smooth was entirely serious. What a git!

62

It had not been Big Hook's intention to bring his wife and child along with him. His other half, Laurel Zhou, nagged him, pointing out that since she stayed at home, she could only eke out the essentials of life. She relied on her hens laying every day, on being able to fatten two sows a year, harvesting some fruit and vegetables, in addition to several hundred pounds of wheat, a few green beans and soya beans. Ends just about met. However, theirs was a household where, if one corner caught fire, eight other places would billow smoke. Even their meagre savings could be singed away through various daily expenditures. The scant income Big Hook earned maintained his parents and had to cover his wife's and daughter's necessities. Just a little was left behind to salt away for their girl's operation.

When she was only two years old, their daughter Lily had the misfortune to pitch over into the stove by which she was warming herself. Her face and neck were burned and fused partially together. They had been saving money for restorative surgery, though to date had never been able to accumulate enough. In order to prioritise Lily's treatment, they dared not risk having a second child. Once her face had been restored, they could try for another baby.

Year in, year out, they found themselves in no position to afford the surgery. By now, Lily had reached the age of fourteen, and Big Hook's parents tried to persuade them to give up, convinced that the accident had been a matter of fate. As the operation could refine her deformed features without ever making her beautiful to behold, they reasoned that there was no need to spend hundreds of thousands on such procedures. Indeed, it could be a case of second time lucky. Were they to have another child, the heavens might bless them with a boy of handsome appearance. Should it be another girl, raising her would prove far less costly than their plans for Lily. There was no need to stubbornly dismiss alternative ways. For a time, even Big Hook wavered in the face of his parents' coaxing and Laurel was the one who stood firm. In her mind, that would amount to a grave injustice and a sin. After all, it was she who should have been taking care of the girl when she was injured.

Back then, Big Hook was a migrant worker and she was left at home. Laurel had been feeding the pigs when she heard the child's cries. She ran directly indoors, but by the time she could haul her from the stove, the girl had already sustained horrific burns. At that moment, her heart seemed to have been run through a mincer, leaving not one single scrap intact. From then on, she feared having another baby. As it happened, later on she did fall pregnant by chance. A terrible nightmare stirred her awake one night and appeared to induce a miscarriage.

By the age of five or six, Lily started to ask her mother almost daily, "Mum, when are you going to make my face pretty?" Laurel would weep and promise that it would be sorted soon. Still, many years passed and they had not beautified her. This year she believed that, come what may, she mustn't disappoint their child any longer. And so, during the New Year period, Laurel set about pestering Big Hook to allow her to accompany him to the city. For one thing, this would be an opportunity for her to earn a little extra. For another, she could cajole her husband and press him to pursue the girl's surgery. Any window for postponement had now passed as Lily was acutely conscious of her looks. She would always sob alone in secret, and there were times when she couldn't face living. One day before New Year, some of the kids in the village reacted to her with fright and hurled abuse at her from afar. "Go away stinky scar, go away stinky scar," they shouted. They even pelted mud and pebbles at her. She was so distressed that she stood by the wellhead and wanted to jump down the shaft. If her mother had not experienced a pang of premonition and rushed over there straight away, Lily might have been lost to the pit.

This year, Laurel Zhou was inured to anyone's coercion. She

even argued with Big Hook and threatened that if he didn't take Lily and her to the city, the two females would set up home on their own. Anyway, as long as he deferred the facial operation, she would go on making a spectacle of herself. She threw a tirade on Lantern Festival, leaving Big Hook with no option but to comply.

Lily followed her parents, her head wrapped in a flowery turban. Laurel also slipped a mask over her face, so that only her eyes were left exposed. Ever-anxious to hold his head up among others, Big Hook had not mentioned his daughter to those around him. He tried to keep her existence under wraps even after they reached the city. It was a positive thing that his wife had argued with him on the phone at New Year and forced him to find them a room in the city. It was not that he was unwilling to pay for the surgery. He had consulted a number of hospitals about the issue and been told that 200,000 to 300,000 yuan was needed for basic reconstructive work. To date, he had saved seventy-odd thousand, and a plan was taking shape in his mind. If they could have her treated before the age of eighteen, that might boost her marriage prospects in adulthood. Even so, Laurel Zhou had become pushier in recent years and resorted to every method this New Year, save for pulling out a cleaver and engaging him in an armed brawl. Actually, before departing the Western Capital this time, he had made enquiries about rental rates in case Laurel made a sudden beeline for the city. He sought after accommodation in a community close to Shangyi Road. In order to minimise future hassle, he chose to rent from an old landlady who lived alone and was partially sighted. Only one-and-a-half rooms were up for rent, these being dark, humid and pricey. He cut a deal for 800 yuan a month, making a verbal agreement with the owner so as to avoid the involvement of others. She stipulated that they pay one month's rent in advance as deposit. Even then, he thought Laurel could yet be dissuaded from trying to relocate there. When he brought her to the community, he worried that someone else may have pinched the apartment. Fortunately, it was still empty and Laurel and Lily thought it acceptable. Thus, they settled down.

Big Hook was unprepared for how much Smooth had changed. He couldn't even recognise him at first. He now put on airs in his presence. Ten years of experience under him had taught Big Hook that Smooth would be sure to cave in and allow Laurel Zhou to join the stage-shifting crew. His soft spot as a boss was his meekness, which had caused so much extra profit to slip away over the years. Still, without Smooth there would be no team and no openings for business. Many of them had tried to break away and form their own gang, but received no recognition or job offers once the employers realised Smooth was not among them. In the end, they all had to return obediently to him to be assured of a living.

With a pair of spectacles perched on the bridge of his nose, a newspaper in his hands and a lidded bowl of tea alongside him, Smooth repeatedly declared himself retired. In the eyes of Big Hook, he had gone doolally.

Through contacting Monkey, Mound and Third Skin, he learned that their boss had suffered a horrendous ordeal. Cai Sufen had bolted on the evening of New Year's Eve. Whenever her name was mentioned in the basement where they lived, Third Skin would cry volubly. "Wasn't it you, you son of a bitch, who stirred things up and broke their family apart?" Monkey asked. Third Skin swore that it was not so, and he defended Sufen as a thoroughly decent woman who had only Smooth in her heart. Maybe the domestic strife had caused her to run and it was no fault of his? As a matter of fact, everyone was certain that Third Skin had been harassing her. Big Hook even scolded him for being so ungrateful as to have done that to his own boss. But Third Skin could not exercise self-control and continued to bother Sufen. While they were drinking, they interrogated him again in detail. He swore that, had he done anything untoward with Ms Cai, then his cock ought to fester and be chewed away by maggots. They all thought this oath was too mild, so forced him to extend it to cover his father's cock as well.

Later on, Mound suggested that Smooth's eccentricity may be somehow connected with the performance on the fourteenth. That evening, he had been acting as the dog and his behaviour came across as deranged, since even after the hound was supposed to have died, he still twitched and stirred nonchalantly. Director Jin and Iron Kou had almost gulped him down whole.

The men spent until midnight discussing what was to be done about their stage-shifting work. They concluded that, were they to have any future in the field, they needed Smooth as their leader.

Without him, they could achieve nothing. They resolved that Big Hook and Monkey should go on their behalf and try to reason earnestly with him. If they could not talk him around, then no one else had a hope.

Early the next morning, Big Hook and Monkey dropped in at Smooth's home. The outer gate was locked and upon dialling him, they were told that he had gone to the local fair in the Muslim Quarter. Big Hook asked for the location as they too would like to have a look around. Smooth said now was not the time to meet and, given the size of the market site, they would never be able to find him even if they came. They were steadfast and Smooth, perhaps finding no other pretence to refuse, informed them that he was inside a store that sold calling insects. They quickly ferreted him out.

In spite of more than a decade's residency in the Western Capital, none of them had heard of this huge market that sold insects, fish, birds and flowers. It was situated in the cabbage heart of the city and the name – Western Granary – may have referred to how the area housed a granary from the Qing Dynasty onwards. Now it was occupied by working units and households, with the two intersecting streets being festooned with various living creatures. There were more than a dozen species of bird alone, some of which they had never heard of or seen in the countryside. Mynas and parrots could be priced up at thousands or even tens of thousands of yuan per head. Then there were the pet dogs, snakes and pigs. Their eyes widened. Especially curious were the maggots used to feed the birds and fish. Drawer after drawer was jammed full of their wriggling forms, and one could observe exactly how they were nurtured.

The group walked along, inspecting what was on offer at every doorway. So many stores sold therapeutic walnuts, a pair of which could fetch thousands of yuan. In their daily lives, they had noticed certain citizens rubbing them and flexing them around in their hands, though could never have envisaged that the price could be so steep. The labourers were stunned and smacked their tongues to see labels quoting 10,000 yuan, 15,000 yuan or even 20,000 yuan.

They finally honed in on the calling insect shop mentioned by Smooth. It was bristling with the same range of creatures that could be heard on the paths of the distant countryside at night. A row of stores stood before them, each with an identically narrow door and boxes of assorted size in front. These contained diverse species of calling insect. Some of them they recognised, like the mole cricket and the grasshopper. Others they had encountered before without being aware of their names. Every specimen cost dozens of yuan, with a few running into three figures.

They entered the establishment to which Smooth had directed them. It was dim inside since all the lights were extinguished. Concealed in there was a huge, vibrant world where calling insects were displayed alongside ornamental jars for containing them. As busy as the store was, Smooth was nowhere to be seen. Then, Monkey elbowed Big Hook and indicated that he should take a closer look at the gentleman next to him who was selecting a jar. Big Hook did so and noticed he was clad in a beige windbreaker, a black bowler hat and cap-toed leather shoes. His attention was occupied by a rack of insect homes. Before Big Hook could figure out his identity, Monkey had already mouthed "Smooth". Was that who it was? Big Hook couldn't conceive of the idea. He craned his head towards the counter and then peered around. Sure enough, it was Smooth. Underneath his outer garments, he was even wearing a white shirt and a red tie. "What a git," Big Hook said, chuckling. "All done up to the nines."

Big Hook stood behind Smooth and covered his eyes with his cold hands. His victim knew who was there and shook his head and sneered, "Dirty paws." He wrested his mitts away and then resumed the process of selecting his purchase, studying meticulously and gazing, even squinting with one eye as if aiming a rifle. His devotion, concentration and the expression on his face conveyed that he was no longer one of their peers. His erstwhile colleagues felt it difficult to associate the gentleman before them with the Smooth they had known. A canyon had opened up between them.

In the eyes of Big Hook and Monkey, he had assumed the air of a true city dweller, but in reality he was nothing more than a poseur.

"So you want to fiddle about with insects now?" Monkey asked suddenly.

After a protracted silence, Smooth only let out a hum.

"Where's the fun in this?" Monkey persisted. "If you really like them, there's no need to shell out like that. We can go home and catch you some."

"Then go home and catch some," Smooth answered disdainfully.

"So what? You don't believe me? Don't think I can do it?"

"You go home and catch some then," Smooth repeated as he continued to scrutinise the jars on the counter.

"If you really want them, yes, I can go right now and catch some."

"Unless summer has come early this year in your hometown, how can you find calling insects?" Smooth shot a haughty sideways glance at Monkey, who then realised that these creatures only emerge into the open in the late spring and early summer. "Where do they get these from, then?" he asked.

"Even people can be cloned nowadays. How can it be so hard to produce a few summer insects in winter? You ask such ridiculous questions. No wonder people around here look down on you as a country bumpkin."

Big Hook and Monkey were taken aback by Smooth's manner of speaking.

"What kind of people play with these?" asked a curious Monkey. "And how can you be that way inclined?"

"You really are ridiculous. What kind of people keep these? The Western Capital is full of professors and senior cadres who raise them as pets. You think they are toys for city layabouts?" He continued to examine all the porcelain bottles and earthenware jars, even turning them upside down.

"Are you really so minded?" Big Hook asked.

"Why not? I've dabbled with them before, only these past few years there hasn't been the time."

"And you have the time now?" Monkey wanted to know.

"Why should I be short of time? I'm retired now. I have time by the bucket-load."

"Don't puff yourself up. You're not a senior cadre, so how can you say you're retired?" Big Hook's speed of talking accelerated as anxiety set in.

"You've only got a fart's-worth of knowledge. In the city, you can even step down from a community factory and call yourself retired. Are you such a country bumpkin that you don't know that?"

"Well, well, so you're retired. No more stage shifting for you then?"

"None."

"Why on earth?"

"No reason. I just don't want to do it any more."

"Everybody has come back, so how can you throw in the towel?" A hint of menace was discernible in Big Hook's voice.

"I didn't ask you to come."

"Hah, how can you say that? Did you tell us before New Year that we shouldn't return afterwards?"

"Did I tell you before the holidays that you must come back after New Year?" Now Smooth's own voice was raised a little as well.

In hindsight, Smooth hadn't in fact said a thing on this score. At this time of the year, they all raced back of their own volition.

"Are you really calling it quits?"

"Of course. You carry on by yourselves if you want to, but don't come chasing after me later on."

"What the heck's happened to you?"

"Nothing. But anyway, I must tell you today. If I keep on at it any longer, I'll end up a scabby bastard."

Smooth was resolute and showed no sign of budging. Big Hook and Monkey gaped at each other, fully conscious that this was not the ideal place for a conversation of this sort. They stayed a little longer and, as Smooth appeared so very indifferent to them, turned around and went off in a sulk.

63

SMOOTH WAS RESOLVED to lead the life of a modern city dweller. Of all the residents in his neighbourhood, he was the only one who worked around the clock. This did not emancipate him from an existence that was shameful and, at best, had no honour. He was even worse off than Uncle Scar who had spent a lifetime gambling, not to mention those idlers who fished, promenaded with their birds, played chess or merely loitered around. Take, for example, Huge Treasure. He and Smooth were the same age and had attended primary school and hauled night soil together. Thereafter, Huge Treasure didn't have to pedal a tricycle, nor did he take up hard labour. Without looking deeply into anybody's eyes, he rented out rooms for a living. He even regarded the Village Head as a nobody.

Every day, Huge Treasure squatted by his gate and watched on as others gave battle on the chessboard. Save for his annual round of rent collection and monthly gathering of electricity and water fees, he was permanently spectating, chatting, playing or cursing the chess aficionados. Sometimes, in the course of swearing and squabbling, he would smash the chessmen into the face of his opponent, or vice versa. Crucially, he had married a charming wife, who would carry his meals to the board and very politely invite him to take his fill. In spite of her country roots, she carried herself as an urban lady, for she permed her hair, shaded her eyebrows, painted her lips and clipped on two walnut-sized earrings. Huge Treasure claimed that he wouldn't swap roles with a governor. That would be too damned troublesome and vexing.

As a point of fact, at the time the government issued its policy forbidding the erection of extra storeys, Smooth's home had the same floor space as Huge Treasure's. Ever-obedient, Smooth obeyed the letter of the law. Huge Treasure, though, wouldn't be bossed around and so added more floors as he saw fit. If anybody did come along to interfere, he would sink an axe into his gate panel and no one dared ask further questions. By this means, he gained eight more rooms than Smooth and netted an annual income in excess of 100,000 yuan.

Now, Smooth decided that he would aspire to emulate Huge Treasure. If Plum wasn't coming back and Daisy's marriage had gone ahead, he would surely extend his house. He owned an axe as well, so could plant that in his gate should he ever be challenged. Come what may, Smooth was ready to trade in his tricycle and adopt a leisurely ethos embracing fishing, raising insects, carrying caged birds to the park, playing cards and listening to opera. He would surely prove as adept as anyone in these matters.

Calling insects were truly peculiar creatures. Smooth bought seven or eight species of them in total. There were crickets, grasshoppers, golden chimes, golden bells, tower bells and horse bells. Previously, he had kept crickets and grasshoppers, all of them caught in the allotments, and easily fed on vegetable leaves and plain water. The storekeeper told him that those he bought ought to be given a diet including slivers of apples, bananas and pears. Moreover, they favoured a warm environment, and the balmier the temperature, the livelier they would chirp. So, when Smooth arrived home, he reconfigured his stove. It had been out of commission for ages, but fortunately the iron pipes were intact and he had dozens of coal cobbles heaped in the corner by the wall. With a little effort, the room became ambient.

Smooth drew the window curtains closed and turned off the light to darken his surroundings. The insects, perhaps believing that dusk had come, began to break into song. Their owner reclined on the sofa, shut his eyes and listened to those soloists competing for his attention. He could start to distinguish their calls. The one with the bright, resonant sound was the cricket, and its high-pitched skreigh continued until the householder clapped his hands. The less clarion, muffled, off-pitch sound belonged to the grasshopper. As for the steady and firm, thick and metallic drone, that was the golden chime. The sound that seemed to be falling in pitch, pace and gusto was the tower bell. This had been the name the retailer used, though Smooth felt that "falling bell" was more apt. No great distinction could be registered between the golden bell and the silver bell. Their chirps were so crisp and rounded that they might have been jangling bells that one would be willing to strain to hear. The bodies of the two were quite different, however, as one was golden yellow and the other a shade of platinum. Since the former was twenty yuan dearer than its counterpart, the shop owner likened them to a queen and a concubine. Should Smooth purchase both, he would have two archetypes of womanhood. Unable to shake off the temptation, he complied and the pair accompanied him home.

The most unique chirp came from the horse bell, which appeared to jingle and jangle, neither too quickly nor too slowly. It was as if the insects were half dead and half alive, their noise giving the illusion that a horse or a mule was approaching. As a boy, Smooth had trailed many beasts of burden close by their hind quarters. At that time, the cart was the only means of transporting tools and crops around the allotments. The sound drew him straight back to those plots he had guarded in his youth. He savoured their singing until later at night, then moved from the sofa over onto the bed where he slept. That night, he convinced himself that he was lying in those bygone fields. Halfway through, he awoke with a start, just as if someone had tipped him back into that shack amid the cucumber patch.

The next morning he got up and strode out to buy soya bean milk, fried dough sticks, omelettes and a newspaper. He had already taken out a subscription at the newsstand, but it would be the beginning of the next month before deliveries would start. A mailbox was now installed outside his gate. Even Uncle Scar had one of these. He liked to sit on the deckchair and read his newspaper, copying the retired cadre who had once been his neighbour. That was what he understood to be the "official" method of doing things. While drinking the soya bean milk, he put on his spectacles and began the routine.

Unexpectedly, Monkey came over early in the morning. Smooth did not offer him a seat, even though he balanced his own thin buttocks on the edge of the sofa. Neither did he offer him food, despite having stuffed his own face with the omelette.

From over the top of his glasses, Smooth focused on Monkey's hand. There was an obvious gap where the middle finger had been amputated.

His guest noticed what he was doing. "I'm afraid I can no longer give anyone the middle finger," he said.

"But you can still flick your other middle finger and tell them to 'go fuck themselves'," Smooth countered.

Monkey discerned that there was something different about Smooth. Formerly, had anyone joked about those with physical defects, Smooth would never join in. Today, without warning, he had made light of his lost member. Monkey came over somewhat edgy. A plan had been hatched the night before for him to visit the next morning. It was agreed that Monkey should ask him to be their leader again, using his severed finger as the ace in the hand.

"They haven't paid me all the compensation I'm due," explained Monkey.

"You can go over and claim it."

"If you don't go there, what am I to do?"

"You mean you can't even eat or take a dump without me holding your hand?" Smooth sported an attitude of coolness and flicked over the pages of his newspaper as he spoke.

"You really don't want to be responsible for this?"

"Really I don't."

"What's brought this on?"

"I just don't want to."

"So when it comes to one simple matter, you don't want to be responsible for it, and then you throw away all responsibility?"

"Why should I? Did someone issue a letter of appointment? Was I chosen by popular vote?"

Smooth's words left Monkey feeling choked.

"Get a move on and sort out your own crap. We reached an agreement with Chief Qu about your finger before New Year. If you don't want to go, does that mean you're waiting for someone to shit the cash into your mouth?"

Monkey was finding the conversation excruciating and had to beat a retreat after sitting there only briefly.

The minute Monkey left, Smooth was infused with a delightful sensation of the "far from court, far from care" kind. Although he was not really an official, dozens of people were under his charge and swallowed up his attention day and night. Now he was cut free, were someone to have their leg sawed off, that would be no concern of his. Right now, he was seized by the urge to sing an operatic aria composed for a female singer:

> *My dad sold me because he was greedy for money,*
> *Unwilling to be a slave, I duly fled...*

As he trilled away, he trawled through his recollections. For dozens of years, he had kept company with opera troupes and filled a number of boxes with posters he had collected from productions. At first, he found them pretty and eyecatching, so kept hold of them as he thought it a pity to see them discarded and strewn across the ground. As time went by, he became a habitual collector and even decided to have his posters embellished with signatures from the star players. The year when the movie actor Ge You came to the Western Capital to top the bill in *Looking West Towards Chang'an*, as the builder of the stage, he found the chance to cadge his autograph. When the renowned comedian Chen Peisi appeared in *Balcony*, Smooth got him to sign a poster too. Similarly, when he shifted the sets for a modern drama starring the iconic Pu Cunxi and Sun Dandan, he made certain that their autographs were obtained too. The time had come, thought Smooth, to apply himself to curating this hoard.

The insects chirped inside the room, and outside in the courtyard the birds twittered. Smooth himself began to hum as he opened the boxes and rummaged through their contents. Some posters had become stuck together and resisted being peeled apart. He applied a gentle tearing action, tilting the pages as the gap grew wider. Almost every image took him back to some situation in which they were shifting stages, dismantling platforms or watching rehearsals. There were instances when he gawked on from the wings, and other times from among the lighting fixtures. He might fiddle with the spotlight, adjust items of set and brush past the high-flyers. A few hours passed, yet he had examined barely a dozen posters. He didn't want to skim through them since he had so much free time. This was a task to be done at leisure. He should unfold them unhurriedly, appreciate them unhurriedly, reorder them unhurriedly and savour their pungent aftertaste.

The significance of his collection now sank in. This was perhaps what set him – a city dweller – apart from Big Hook, Monkey, Mound and Third Skin. They had never displayed any interest in such ephemera. Mound even snorted when he saw what he was doing, remarking that the sheets were too rough to be used as bog roll.

Smooth pored over the posters with the greatest of satisfaction and interest until it was dark outside. His back ached and his waist stung with pain, so he composed himself and went out onto the streets to watch some chess games. A round booth beneath a street lamp housed perpetual tournaments. He had the impression that regardless of whether there was rain, wind or snow, the players never dispersed. Sometimes he would return at the ungodliest of hours from shifting stages to find chessmen still being slammed around. He was rarely in the neighbourhood, since the stage ate up most of his time. Duly, those stalwart players felt it something extraordinary to spy him coming their way.

Smooth was certain that Huge Treasure spent his entire waking life watching these games, so he drew to his side and observed the matches. Yes, he was always a bystander here, though not without coming unstuck on occasions. His mouth was ill-disciplined, he was garrulous and prone to dive in and move the players' pieces for them. That was a liberty too far. Should his move be well-judged, that was wily of him. If it were not, the hot tempered would pounce, pulverising Huge Treasure with their chessmen. His forehead and the bridge of his nose retained the vestiges of these past assaults. Nonetheless, he continued to watch, comment and stick his paws in. This was just him being overly fond of this lifestyle, or that was how he phrased it.

Smooth crouched down by Huge Treasure and heard him being cursed by different tongues. "Shut your pussy trap." Then there was, "Is your mouth really a mouth or a cunt? Button it!" Even, "If you dare fiddle with the pieces, I'll hack off one of those pig's trotters you walk on!" This was to no avail, as Huge Treasure could control neither his pussy mouth nor his interfering hands.

Smooth continued to watch for a while before starting to lose interest. He stood up and wanted to grill Huge Treasure about the ins and outs of adding storeys to his home. This he found hard to broach, and as he was about the leave, the current game ended in stalemate. While the players were reassembling the pieces, Huge Treasure was the one to volunteer conversation. "Hey, Brother Smooth," he said. "You've been building stages for years. Must have made a fortune from it, I bet? You're so busy that whole years seem to spin round without us seeing you. You've made a packet, so how come you don't treat your brother to a foot massage or a screw?" All the folks around them laughed.

Smooth knew he had to hazard a chance now. "Fine, I'll take you for a foot massage," he promised. "Let's go."

"Let's go," Huge Treasure echoed. He stood up and followed him off.

Huge Treasure detected that there must be some hidden motive behind the invitation, so suggested they bathe at the spa instead. Since he had extended the offer in the first place, Smooth found it impossible to refuse the revised arrangements. He followed Huge Treasure to the spa, knowing full well that this was a man who would exploit any available pretence. When Smooth asked him a question, he would give only half an answer. For the sake of a considered response, he would extort a massage out of Smooth.

Huge Treasure told him there were a few Russian girls at this particular spa and said he fancied a taste of the exotic. Smooth disagreed and was rebuked for being a "stick in the mud". Stick in the mud or not, gambling and whoring were both pastimes he steered well clear of. He was then mocked as a "good-for-nothing dick" and Huge Treasure said it wasn't as if he had to keep his hands clean in anticipation of running for the presidency or anything. Even if he were a "good-for-nothing-dick", Smooth couldn't compromise his principles. "You've screwed plenty of women in your time," Huge Treasure surmised. "What's one more?" Smooth maintained that such comparisons were ill-judged, for Huge Treasure was talking about whoring, which he never indulged in. The two of them argued fruitlessly for a long time. In the end, Smooth couldn't dissuade him and so absented himself after slipping him 300 yuan.

The business of going bathing had truly riled Smooth. All he got in return was the scantest outline of how to build more rooms on a residence.

As the new college term was about to start, Smooth reasoned that Plum must be back in Shangluo and he should check in on her. From the depths of his being, he pined for her to return. He had raised her since the age of five or six and it pained him to be parted from her like this. If she were to return, her room would be awaiting her. Their reunion turned out a sour disappointment.

Smooth had dressed up as well as he could beforehand. He wore the beige windbreaker and blue suit her mother had tailored for him years ago. His clothes were ironed and his leather shoes buffed. Still, Plum requested that he leave the campus, adopting a manner that could not go unnoticed by strangers. Her words were jagged, and she asserted that she would never step into the Diao family home again, suggesting that Daisy was the culprit. Even so, Smooth felt bloodied by how ready this daughter was to write off the sweet experiences of the past.

He enquired about the situation between Plum and Zhu Mancang. She informed him off-handedly that they were already married. He was stunned and asked why they had moved so fast. She maintained that she had been forced into a corner on New Year's Eve. What was she to do? Give herself to a human trafficker or place herself under the thumb of a cruel landlord like Huang Shiren? What is more, she and Zhu had signed their marriage licence in his hometown on Lantern Festival. Her words sank in like daggers and hooks, being so sharp, rough and stern that they assailed his body. He could only shrink in retreat. His verdict was that her heart had been truly mauled by the ordeal and his heart was mauled as well. He had prepared several thousand yuan as a gift for her and when it came to presenting the money, she rejected it in one stroke. Her brusqueness left him with no space to re-enter her affections. Smooth even struggled to know how to graciously retract his hand and the cash gift it held.

He left.

He had visited Shangluo a number of times on account of Plum.

He had found the place scenically beautiful. Now, it appeared dusky and downbeat, with even the rocks on the roadside being perceptibly more scarred and erratic. As the bus was passing through the Qinling Mountain tunnel, Iron Kou phoned continuously. Smooth did not want to answer, though Kou persisted until the passengers around him were so irritated that he felt compelled to pick up. Iron Kou, retaining his usual stentorian tone, declared stiffly and crudely that there was an evening party that needed stage shifters the next day. "Twenty hands are required. Six thousand yuan is the offer. You can take your crew to the theatre early in the morning. If you're late, you'll miss out."

In normal times, Smooth would have spouted a stream of gratitude. Today, he could only muster two words far stiffer than Kou's: "No time."

He hung up contemptuously.

64

MORE THAN A FORTNIGHT HAD PASSED since New Year and the stage-shifting team were still idle. Big Hook discussed their predicament again and again. The consensus was that the crew could not carry on without Smooth at the helm. They came across as a slack, profane and disorderly rabble, like a rampant horse that slipped its bit as soon as the rider dismounted.

Iron Kou had contacted Smooth by phone, but when he dangled a job before him, he stated flatly that he had no time. He then turned to Big Hook, first cursing his gaffer for being so puffed up in his dealings with him. Kou claimed that from now on his deputy could have first refusal on any job. As for Smooth, he could slink away to wherever he felt snug.

Once he had weighed up the options, Big Hook's dander fell. He realised that Iron Kou was a bastard to deal with. At the same time, he had good reason to decline. To accept what Smooth had cast away was tantamount to ratting on a friend. To compound things, he couldn't deny that the team was unruly. Too many problems were piling up in his mind. It was not as though he could afford to plead with others for leniency, beg for mercy or yield in a posture of obedience. Smooth did take a slightly greater cut of the money, yet this advantage was eroded by the necessity of having to sweeten others. Big Hook was afraid to accept the fee for the task, even if it was waved before him. Had he the luxury of cash in hand, he couldn't wield the crop so fiercely and might end up being skinned.

There was no question about it. Big Hook craved a crew of his own, and more income would not go amiss either. A few years back, he had confronted this dilemma in his mind. Taking the lead was not his style. Stage shifting differed from other professions in that nothing could be counted on and there were no hard and fast patterns or examples to use as points of reference. One could never predict what an artist or an actor was thinking. Should a fake tree be required as a prop, the root ought logically to be directed vertically downwards. These impresarios were inclined to study the creation up and down, and from left to right. They would then ask the set dresser to suspend it so that the full effect could be observed. One look at it the following morning and they would request that the trunk be laid horizontally because it appeared more arresting to the eye than when floating above the stage. In the end, they might decide it looked best "planted" in a naturalistic fashion on the stage, but not until their vacillations had tortured the stage shifters to death. Were it not for the emollient character of Smooth, Big Hook would have tried to settle the matter with his fists, socking it to those knobheads. Were he to take Iron Kou, the stage manager, as an example, many had been the time when Big Hook was sufficiently incensed to bound over and crush his balls. Smooth would rather sacrifice his own bollocks than let his men lay a hand on someone else. That took some tenacity and well-honed tolerance – something that Smooth had in spades, but Big Hook lacked.

Big Hook also egged on Monkey, trying to make him accept the mantle of leader. He replied that he was only a primate, and capering up and down midair was all he was good for. He did not have the decency to be seen as the face of the team. Big Hook then began to deride his workmate. Usually people liked to brag, boasting of how they could peel spring onions with only one bare finger. As they bragged, the guys would claim they had the lifting power of a jack or could chisel diamonds with their bare hands. However, once there was an actual weight to be shouldered, their steely bowels could only lay soft eggs.

Big Hook and Monkey were ensconced as the second and third in command, respectively. In their daily work, the pair would needle each other so as to inflate their own egos and fan their sense of indispensability. But the moment some tough nut was encountered, they would become as soft as shit. Mound quoted a term Chief Qu had used to describe Smooth to Director Jin. Smooth was the "living soul" of the team. Without him, they genuinely had lost their spirit.

The long and short of the predicament was that they needed Smooth back as leader. Monkey had tried to persuade him, but to no effect; Mound and Third Skin similarly. Big Hook turned it over in his mind and knew the onus was on him. He self-consciously avoided mentioning work and only told Smooth that he had brought his child to town and she was staying in the Renters Village nearby. His friend was welcome to visit them.

Smooth could not decline in principle because there was a youngster involved. So he proposed that Big Hook bring the kid to his home, though he said that was impractical. Smooth was curious to know why this should be and was told that if he came along, he would understand everything. He laid down his poster collection and followed Big Hook.

Out of courtesy, Smooth wanted to buy some fruit, but Big Hook wouldn't have money spent on their behalf. Smooth maintained that this was all about meeting his younger brother's wife and his niece. He even joked that if he were to come across Big Hook alone, he would go to the trouble of stuffing a carrot into his mouth.

Early in the morning, he informed his wife that Smooth could be coming over for lunch and Laurel Zhou went to the market to purchase vegetables and a little meat.

When Smooth entered with his fruit, Laurel was trying to flatten her hair with damp hands. This was how country women tried to smarten themselves up for visitors. The result would be neat and pretty, definitely no longer messy.

Laurel had heard Big Hook mention Smooth before, so she knew that he was the head honcho and a true citizen of the Western Capital. He was pleasant enough and easy-going, but apart from being able to turn a steady penny through regular graft, there was nothing eminent about him. Today, Laurel met the man himself. Had she not been told he was a native of the city, she would never have taken him as such. He did indeed wear a windbreaker, a suit and tie, and a bowler hat. Nevertheless, the wasters in her village were also fond of this type of get-up. Her neighbours back home favoured Stetsons like in the cowboy movies. The brims of those hats were invariably upturned, whereas Smooth's drooped humbly downwards.

Smooth was even a touch timid to meet Laurel, not venturing to look at her in a solemn manner even after being in their home for a while. His large but dull eyes were fixed on Big Hook as he spoke.

Big Hook was in no hurry to have Smooth meet his daughter. To be frank, he had been reluctant to mention Lily unless it was absolutely necessary. He neither wanted to be laughed at, nor be regarded with pity. He hit upon the idea after several days only because he was in a bind. He himself thought this the trump card. Smooth, he knew, was a tender-hearted fellow, so his weak spot left him prone. He yearned to arouse Smooth's sympathy and knew he needed him to take the lead so they could be assured of making money. If Smooth were amenable to his wife joining them, that made Lily's surgery more likely.

"Where is my niece?" Smooth asked.

"She'll come and see her uncle later," Big Hook answered.

"How much is the rent here?"

"Eight hundred yuan a month."

"Why so steep?"

"I know it's steep."

"Why rent it then?"

"No choice."

"How come?"

Big Hook told him he had no choice without elaborating on the details.

They chatted away for a time. Big Hook injected Lily into the situation whenever the chance arose. "I don't care if you laugh at me," he vowed. "My child is quite miserable, and she has no face to meet others. This is why I have to rent a place like this."

"How come she doesn't have the face to meet others?"

Big Hook then asked his wife to lead Lily over from next door.

Lily was reluctant. "Look," her mother said. "Your dad has invited someone over to help and make you pretty. You must let him see you."

Lily agreed once she was told that the visitor had come to assist with beautifying her face. Even so, she insisted on covering it with a scarf. After coiling and twisting her body for an age, she raised the tiny edge of the covering timidly before this strange uncle. She then pulled it back to conceal her face again as soon as the guest could see it clearly.

As Laurel found the girl was so abashed about removing the scarf, she went ahead and pulled the entire thing away so he could take in her whole appearance.

"Golly!" Smooth exclaimed. The child ran back into the next room.

"What happened to her?" he asked hastily.

Big Hook told Smooth the details of the story. Laurel went out to console the child and then returned. With her nose and tears running, she again described the accident. They noticed how Smooth tried to dab his eyes dry discreetly as he listened.

From the beginning until the end, Smooth breathed not a single word about him returning to head up the stage-shifting crew.

As Big Hook saw that figure with his hands in his pockets grow more distant with each step and finally leave the Renters Village, his heart was sombre and melancholy.

65

ONCE BACK FROM RENTERS VILLAGE, Smooth could not settle. The deformed, ungainly and globular face of Big Hook's daughter flickered and flashed in his mind. He had seen burn-scarred kids before, but never one as serious as this. For him, it was all the more terrible because she was a girl. In any case, he was deeply touched by the efforts of Big Hook and his wife. The couple tried to make money so that they could afford plastic surgery for her. At the very least, they should try to reconstruct her appearance so that she might be able to look straight at the world with decency.

These thoughts made him insensible to the vibrations of the crickets and grasshoppers, and also those gaudy posters he had spent the afternoon and evening leafing quietly through. He went out for a walk. By chance, the top of the city wall was open that night for the annual lantern display. Trailing the crowds as they swept along, he found there were simply too many pedestrians to gain a good vantage point. Everyone was clustered and advanced virtually chest to back. Through all that pushing and shoving, he was borne up from the Duanli Gate and then down again on the pavement at the South Gate. The loss of one of his brogues in the scrum meant he had to limp home.

The next morning, Smooth was awoken by a banging at the door. He looked at his watch and it was past nine.

He swayed to his feet and went out into the courtyard. A battalion of ants was on the move, heading to a new home.

The insects teemed in through one exterior wall of the yard and then exited through another. Their troop was long and broad.

Smooth leaped from his doorway towards the gate with one big stride lest he might tread on them.

When he opened the gate, Big Hook and several dozen or more besides were there, their heads jammed together like bobbing buoys.

"You're intent on me having no peace and calm, aren't you?" he winced.

"You may be able to live in peace and calm," Big Hook retorted, "but what about your brothers?"

"Well, all of you should come in, I suppose," muttered an impotent Smooth. "Take care. There are ants under your feet."

66

Smooth was again press-ganged into service by his brothers.

He could not bear the way they incited him. In fact, it made the blood rumble uneasily through his body. Each of them was invited into his home, whereupon they devoured all kinds of New Year's treats, including melon seeds, peanuts, sweets and crystal cakes. A tray was also broken in a scuffle over who should have the last crystal cake. When they were gone, the debris on the floor gave the impression that an army of ants had marched through the room. Smooth was, nevertheless, rather elated.

While tidying up, he brought to mind the opera plot concerning the ancient sage Zhuge Liang, who was beckoned over three times by Emperor Liu Bei. As delight welled through his brain, he broke into song and started flexing a broom in impersonation of Zhuge Liang lightly swishing a goose feather fan. One beat, two beats, three beats, four... he took up the merry adagio from the Shaanxi Opera:

> *I, Zhuge Liang... meditate... on Sleeping Dragon Mountain,*
> *Behold... all those boisterous soldiers... under heaven.*
> *Knives flash... swords wave... who would, who could put*
>   *down all these*
> *If I refuse to go... I defy the will of heaven, I... must be*
>   *blamed.*

Oddly enough, as soon as Smooth agreed to head up the team again, offers of stage-shifting work materialised. The first came from a county opera troupe that had invited a nationally famous singer to participate. The cost was purported to be upwards of ten million yuan, and the settings, props and lights filled eight trucks. Smooth and twenty others spent the whole night unloading them.

The next day, when the stage-shifting proper commenced, Smooth discovered that the director, stage designer and head of lighting were all the same people they had cooperated with on *Ode to Golden Autumn Fields*. There, too, was the director general. Last year, he had a moustache and a comb-over hairstyle upon his otherwise bald scalp. Today, all the flesh around his head and chin was bald and appeared to have been lubricated with grease. A pair of old-fashioned, copper-framed glasses sat on his nose, though one of the arms had been lost and so a hemp thread was in place to fasten them to the back of his head. He wore a suit in the style of the Tang Dynasty and appeared like a hangover from pre-Qing times. To Smooth's recollection, his voice had been high, clipped, slightly fierce and quick. Now it had modulated into something lower, softer, smoother and more clement. Notwithstanding his outward transformation, Smooth could tell who it was on first sight. When Big Hook, Monkey, Mound and Third Skin spied him too, they confirmed that it was most definitely that crooked shit. Their eyes glistered, for this crappy company owed them tens of thousands of yuan from the previous year.

Against his initial judgment, Smooth called Iron Kou and told him that the toerags had resurfaced. Kou listened with interest, but warned them not to act rashly, as beating the grass might startle the snakes to flee. He would come and assess the situation first. Iron Kou did so and then confirmed their suspicions. He called the man over to the side of the stage, with Smooth, Big Hook, Monkey, Mound and Third Skin following behind.

"Director Feng," said Iron Kou, coming straight to the nub. "Do you still remember me?"

The director general slid his glasses up his nose and shook his head at him as if he were a stranger.

"Let me jog your memory," Iron Kou said. "Last year, we helped set up an evening party together. You were the director general and I was the stage manager."

"I've done so many parties. I wonder which one you mean?"

"*Ode to Golden Autumn Fields*. It was held right here in the Western Capital. At that time, you had a fine bit of topiary above your mouth and favoured an army overcoat."

The fellow whom he had addressed as Director Feng was compelled to abandon his act. He patted his head three times in succession and admitted, "Oh, oh, oh, I've got it. I've got it. There was a party of that kind, and a very successful one."

"True, it was successful. Only you were very unfriendly to us in the end. You did a runner without paying most of our labour fees. That's not how it's done in our circle."

Director Feng was acting without his typical reserve, and he too became excited. "If you hadn't mentioned it, I wouldn't have felt at all angry. Now you have brought it up, my stomach is churning with rage. Don't you know I was cheated too? I only got half my fee, and I wanted to curse as well."

"Who on earth put you up to this, then?" Kou asked.

"The general stage manager. You've forgotten him? Short and stocky chap."

"Where is he now?" Smooth could no longer resist stepping in.

"He disappeared right after the party."

"You're a bunch of cheating ghosts. You're all in cahoots."

"How can you talk like this? I fared no better than you did. I'm also a hired hand working for a third party. I'm a victim as well." He made a point of stressing the word "victim".

"Then why did you scurry away right afterwards like you did?" asked Kou.

"Us scurry away?"

"After the party, you were all gone," pointed out Smooth.

"The folks in charge left, so why would we hired hands linger about? Shouldn't we go and chase after them? We heard that you local guys were also owed money, so should we have hung around waiting for you to beat it out of us?" The man outlined his excuse with intricacy and finesse. It seemed that the wrongs meted out on him far surpassed anything others were enduring. "How much do they owe you? Don't you know that we're owed more than a million yuan? I treated it as a contribution made towards the development of the cultural sector and ethics of the Western Capital, you know. But we must root out the fraudster. Let's search him out together.

Whichever of us finds him first can notify the other. We mustn't stand back and let the bad lead charmed lives while the good suffer."

Iron Kou went to the enterprise that had sponsored the party, his hope being that they would take a stand and that Director Feng could be investigated through the public security agencies. However, the boss of the enterprise cautioned that they should not underestimate what they were up against. Those bastards had formidable social and political ties, a mass of twisted roots and gnarled branches. Anyhow, he wanted to sever all involvement with these types. Iron Kou had no further recourse and so Smooth and his team could only glare powerlessly at their adversaries.

What mattered most at the present time was to avoid further traps.

In spite of having invited a big shot over, the concrete business was still the preserve of the head of the troupe. Set alongside the invited notables, he appeared decidedly small. He too had a storehouse of pent-up grievances. His surname was Blue, so Smooth addressed him as "Chief Blue". As they shifted the stage in the middle of the night, Smooth took the chance to chat with him.

"You're making waves this time," he began. "Not even provincial-level troupes are prepared to try to launch a show on this scale."

"Who knows what is going on? Anyhow, the investment in this is massive."

"Ten million at least, I suppose?"

Chief Blue shot him a surprised glance. "And how did you reach that figure?"

"I've been shifting stages for over twenty years. From the arrangement and scale of a production, I can reckon the size of the budget to within eighty or ninety per cent of the full figure. How did you even get in touch with those guys?"

"Who am I to know? I'm only in charge of the nuts and bolts. Others are responsible for communication and sponsorship. Our sole remit is to deliver a quality production."

"What kind of play is it?"

"The story is about how someone sinks a mine in the hope of becoming rich. There are a few folk songs in it, but I don't catch what they are trying to express. A huge scale, a vast cast, plenty of settings and lights in striking colours."

Smooth and his men spent a solid seven days completing the shift. The steel scaffold at the rear of the stage soared high from the platform, and the apron of the front stage extended all the way to the auditorium. The hanging curtains were raised and a long cover ran from the back to the front. This could be illuminated. When dark, it simulated the bottom of a coal mine and when lit up, it was a crevice in a valley. During the performance, there was a scene in which a firedamp explosion occurred and the cover broke into fragments, representing small pieces of falling rock. The effect was quite shocking.

There could be no doubt that the stage was overloaded with bodies. The number of actors alone totalled two hundred. About a hundred extras had mounted the steel scaffold towards the back of the stage, arranged in terrace fashion, so the audience could only see the feet of those in the back row. Then there were several knots of additional walk-on players, who Chief Blue remarked had been hired locally and were paid 120 yuan for the day, including a free meal and board. The director was adamant that this evoked an authentic sense of the organic locality.

In the first rehearsal, the director called "cut" when he noticed that one of the walk-ons had a gammy leg. He scolded Chief Blue for not being assiduous enough in the vetting process and emphasised that this was high art and not a jaunt around a fruit and veg market. Blue explained hastily that it was hard to recruit male walk-ons for 120 yuan and there was a dearth of men suited to play miners. The director relegated the lame-legged fellow to the back row, where he remained stationary.

When it came to the leading players, there were virtuosi invited from afar with promises of 5,000 yuan a day for rehearsal and then as much as 100,000 yuan for the final performance, with 50,000 yuan being the baseline. Chief Blue was anxious for the performance to come around so he could dismiss those "gods of the plague" at the earliest juncture.

The troupe issued the tickets in the afternoon of the day before the show. They concocted advertisements with slogans such as "National First-Class Production Team" and "Earth-Shatteringly

Emotional Performances". In order to achieve the appearance of a full house, they negotiated with the theatre and gave out 500 free seats in addition to the 1,200 regular tickets. Unfortunately, when the night came, the auditorium was barely one third of its full capacity.

The second the curtain rose, the audience were in awe of the bespoke stage settings, the acoustics, lights and electrical devices. They applauded incessantly. Nevertheless, once the first act was over, people gradually slipped out of the theatre. As soon as his tasks were completed, Smooth crouched backstage and took in the drama. Part of him was keen to observe the impact of the stage they had built; simultaneously, he was eager to try to discern why so much money had been thrown at this one performance.

The stage shifters called the special moveable settings "magic gadgets". Since they were familiar with how these operated, there wasn't much novelty in seeing them deployed live. He even noted how the audience was less than enthused by the constant changes of setting. In fact, the climatic firedamp explosion that left the top of the stage scarred and battered didn't raise the lightest ripple of applause. At the two-thirds mark, more paying customers had left.

The performance was not presented under the banner of a drama. They called it a "folk opera" in spite of the arias being composed by hacks in Beijing and the recording being made in the capital, too.

For Smooth, it was an opera. The plot focused on a poor community where a mine was sunk successfully thanks to the leadership of an official they hailed as "Saviour Wang". It featured a romantic storyline, uniting a miner with a local woman with a talent for singing folk songs. He was among those buried in the explosion, only to be finally revived by the sound of female songstresses. "Saviour Wang" commanded the rescue mission in person and also joined the chorus of folk singing. In the end, every collier was saved. The stage was now taken over by a visual effect showing coal cobbles rolling out from the mouth of the mine and banknotes rolling back towards the people. By the finale, all of the characters celebrated their new-found affluence by thumping away at waist drums. Some two hundred drummers paraded off the stage and into the auditorium, the performance continuing until everybody's eardrums were throbbing. The fantastic and grandiose array of folk drummers did earn a round of applause.

Smooth took soundings from a few veteran opera buffs. Each cursed the stage show more vehemently than the last one. He heard comments like, "This is literally burning money." A bespectacled critic dismissed it as, "Yet another hollow shell masquerading as drama." Then one lamented how, "Grandsons never feel heartache when they realise they're wasting their grandpa's savings." Smooth couldn't bring himself to listen to any more, for his greatest worry was that his labour fees might be in peril.

Chief Blue apparently lacked cunning. He had paid the first instalment of their fee and promised them the rest once the rig was dismantled. The authorities had planned on holding three more evening performances, though Smooth was sceptical that even one more was feasible. After the show, he went backstage and shadowed Chief Blue so as to understand what was required for the next evening. Of course, he was desperate to see what spin those national-grade bigwigs would put on the fiasco. Contrary to his expectations, they were lauding their own success amid jets of champagne and copious amounts of hugging, with tears enamelling their eyes. Even a confused Chief Blue was given the bumps.

"You just get ready," the director bellowed. "We're heading for the nationals. What's been achieved in a small county is going to create a miracle."

One man, who was perhaps a personage of stature in that county, asked why so many ticket-holders had left during the performance.

"This is a question of outlook," the director responded. "Once you move it into the setting of the grand national theatre, then all of these glitches will be ironed out. Sir, you just put your trust in our artistic judgment. Be assured that everything went off to pat. Splendid."

The hired walk-ons didn't care what was being gushed about before them. They nabbed as many pork baps as they could for a night-time snack. Next, Smooth heard Director Feng inform Chief Blue that they had fulfilled their task and were going to a different province where another great performance was awaiting them. Later still, he observed Director Feng asking Chief Blue where he could check the total takings. Blue led them away with his head tilted towards the ground in embarrassment.

Smooth now set his sights squarely on Chief Blue. He was not afraid of them doing a flit this time because there were still eight truckloads of gear waiting to be dismantled.

The longstanding members of his crew all adjudged this production a bomb. As an empty theatre could be foreseen tomorrow, those liars had obviously fleeced the county troupe. Only Big Hook's wife, Laurel Zhou, was the least bit impressed. She said she had never believed a stage show could be so magnificent and that tomorrow evening she was bound to bring Lily with her to watch it. Big Hook scolded her for being short-sighted. She hadn't seen a professional play before and all this time her tongue was wagging, she made herself a laughing stock.

When Smooth agreed to resume shifting stages, he told Big Hook that Laurel Zhou was welcome to join them. She was grateful for the opportunity and just now when the troupe were handing out pork buns, she laid her hands on three. One she gave to Smooth and the second to Big Hook. The third she grasped herself, not bearing to tuck into it. Smooth returned his, asserting that he was too tired to have an appetite and Laurel should save it for Lily. She was so touched by this gesture, she had to hold back tears.

The next evening, as predicted, the audience was paltry. Chief Blue said that 2,000 tickets in total had been distributed, but when the bell rang to signal the start of the show, fewer than a hundred seats were occupied and these audience members seemed to be residents of the county. Halfway through the performance, the authorities and Chief Blue reached the decisive conclusion that tomorrow's show must be canned. Doing that would save hundreds of thousands of yuan in costs. Smooth had foreseen this outcome beforehand and in the afternoon sent a text to a few in his crew, asking them to be on hand in the evening. When the show started, Smooth realised that a late-night shift was likely. His men had only just finished their suppers and gathered outside the theatre. Chief Blue then informed them that they must pull an all-nighter to take apart the stage.

Given the desultory outcome, Smooth was scared that Chief Blue would welsh on what was owed them. Typically, if a show thrived, the chief in question would be effusively generous. In the opposite situation, they should expect some kind of deductions because the chief usually harboured the greatest anger. To their relief, Chief Blue turned out to be a man of calm composure, and he showed Smooth sincere politeness. Where the stage itself was concerned, he never abandoned his post during the process of the dismantling.

Smooth asked that Mound, Monkey and Big Hook follow his example by monitoring Chief Blue's moves. The job took a whole day and an entire night. When those eight trucks of set were almost fully loaded, Smooth made a point of sticking to Blue's tail. The chief could tell what was on his mind. "Take it easy, Boss Diao," he said. "We've had our ox fall down the well and there's no use scrabbling to grab a strand from its tail. We won't niggle about your labour fees. Don't expect one cent less than you are due."

Chief Blue kept his word. After he had tied the canvas down on the back of the last truck, he called the accountant over and settled the bill. Not only did he not short-change them by a single cent; he threw in an extra 1,000 yuan. "What you've put on the line means much more to you than those hard-hearted big shots. You've been busy for more than ten days, yet each of you has harvested less than two thousand yuan. Those actors earn more than double that for just one morning rehearsal. You can take this grand as my gift and treat yourselves to a midnight feast."

Smooth was experiencing a touch of congestion on account of the weather. His nasal mucus felt as if it had frozen solid. However, he was touched and warmed by the chief's actions. He asked Big Hook to check in person that all the ropes on the trucks were fastened tightly since they had to travel a great distance.

67

ONCE THE WORK BEGAN TO ROLL IN, the number of tasks spiralled. As the team were building a stage for the Shaanxi Opera troupe again, Monkey prodded Smooth to raise the issue of his compensation with Chief Qu at the earliest opportunity. Smooth scolded him frostily, saying how he normally acted so boldly that he seemed able to pound a gong with his tail. Now, how could he be so cowardly that he wouldn't even dare hit a marching drum with his fist? He was a hero, but only behind closed doors. Monkey admitted as much by repeating "yeah" to every charge. Even so, he cajoled Smooth into doing the favour.

Smooth remembered the advice of Teacher Zhu and his late wife. Should he go back to stage shifting for the opera troupe, he must always keep his spine straight. As far as one's backbone is concerned, if you condition it to remain erect, it will comply. Slouching will lead to a permanent hunch. Smooth would observe this guidance strictly from now on.

Of course, Smooth went to the chief first.

When he entered Chief Qu's office, a renowned actress was rapping her hand on his desk.

"Why?" she demanded to know. "Why did you arrange a part for her but not me? What is the reason? Old Qu, tell me why."

Smooth knew this actress, whose surname was Deng. Years ago, she had played the wife of Lin Chong in *Being Driven to Revolt*. In more recent times, her stage appearances had been sporadic.

"Don't get aerated," the chief replied slowly and in a placid tone. "Who gets to play what role is not up to me. There is the director, the professional section, the arts council and the youth league committee. The different levels must hold discussions with each other on this. It's a good thing you still want to act, though we must find a role that suits."

Before he had finished his explanation, she interrupted with a series of sharp pats against the desk. "Enough of that, Chief Qu, enough. No need to put on a show in front of me. What about the director, the professional section, the arts council and the youth league committee? If you just let them ride roughshod over you, then what's the point in having a chief? You always assign the heroine roles to that pussy-for-hire. Do you want others to live or not?"

"Hey, hey, stick to the topic. Don't go flinging curses at other people. Playing the heroine entails making a major contribution to the troupe. She must sweat all day long in rehearsals. That effort goes uncredited, but at least she's exerting herself."

"Well, well, Old Qu, I can see now that you're the rotten root at the bottom of all this. No wonder they say you're having it off with her. You seem to be incriminating yourself."

"If you say it's true," Chief Qu grinned, "then there might be an ounce of truth in that."

"So you're admitting it now, Old Qu? You just admitted you're banging that slut."

"A minute ago you said that everyone was alleging that. If everyone is in agreement, then who I am to deny it? You shouldn't wag your tongue without restraint, shouldn't curse who you see fit and shouldn't scowl at others. How can you blame folk who scowl at you in return?"

"Whoever wants to scowl at me, let them. This old dame's got a temper, so what? Your old dame made the most of it when she was in her prime. If I wanted to get it on with your farting director, any bloke in the professional section, the arts council and the youth league committee too, none of them would have turned me down. As for you, Old Qu, you are not a hero like Xu Yunfeng or Li Yuhe."

"So I'm a traitor like Pu Zhigao and Wang Lianju?"

"Who do you think you are?" the diva Deng chuckled.

Chief Qu had noticed Smooth step onto the threshold, but then retreat when he saw he was not alone. The chief's door and window were constantly wide open, even in the depths of winter. This ensured that everyone could hear clearly what those inside were talking about. It was said that in the later stages of the Cultural Revolution, there was a very strident chief in the troupe who was fond of giving lessons in politics and ideology with the door and window firmly shut. Eventually, he was expelled and punished for his dissolute lifestyle, so every chief thereafter observed this habit of openness.

Maybe Chief Qu was eager for Madame Deng to leave, for he called Smooth in and asked him his purpose.

As Smooth was outlining his business, the lady stayed put, flopping back on the sofa, crossing her legs and then rocking them in a distracting manner. Smooth was almost asphyxiated by the scent of her cologne. A packet of wedding sweets and melon seeds had been left anonymously on the desk, so Madame Deng opened it and started to munch away.

Smooth could not say his piece without nonstop interruptions from her. "Thirty thousand for one finger? What do you think our troupe is now – a bank?" she cawed. Smooth was antagonised by these words and wanted to kick those stumpy, rocking legs of hers.

Without hesitation, Chief Qu called over Iron Kou as he was certain that he should be involved in the discussion. On hearing this, Smooth became perturbed. A few minutes elapsed and Kou came into the office and started flirting with the actress from the very first moment. "Oh, Sister Deng, you're here too! You've really caked on the powder and rouge today, haven't you?"

"Without caking it on, how would this dame have the nerve to step into a leader's office?"

"You're already on Chief Qu's sofa. Wouldn't you feel more comfortable sprawled out on his desk?"

"I wanted to perch on his thigh. Alas, I'm already over the hill and can't pull those sorts of favours any more."

"Well, well, we're going to have a small meeting now," said Chief Qu. "I know what's on your mind."

Madame Deng made it look like she had no intention of leaving. "All this palaver about one shitty finger?" she scoffed. "You make it sound like a Politburo reshuffle. You carry on with your business and I'll get on with mine. I'm not done yet."

Chief Qu felt embarrassed about the prospect of driving her away once more, yet resumed his discussion with Iron Kou and Smooth.

"What amount do you think is proper?" he first of all asked Smooth.

"Monkey made enquiries with many people. He thought that if the troupe could spare a hundred grand, that would be in order."

Before the chief could respond, Madame Deng had stood up from the sofa in a mien of exasperation. "What a monster!" she exclaimed. "Some shitty stage shifter loses a finger on the job and he wants to wheedle a hundred thousand out of our troupe! Dreaming about money has made you go loopy! Are you the one they call Smooth or something? Ha, yes. You are Smooth, Smooth Diao. Smooth by name, Smooth by nature. Now you've even come to blackmail our troupe. You are the King of Hell and we are the ghosts you eat, never minding if we are fat or lean. Do you think our troupe is a finance department? A tax bureau? Do you think Chief Qu is an oil or coal tycoon? No way. If you keep on pestering the whole troupe, we will all fight back together!"

She had poked into a subject that was nothing to do with her and even pounded the table and risen in defiance. Smooth was now so furious that his teeth were on edge and he didn't know what to say in return.

"Whatever the situation, there ought to be set laws and regulations," Kou continued. "We can't arbitrarily give you any figure you request. I've consulted lawyers, and their opinion was that thirty thousand yuan was adequate."

"Adequate!" declared Madame Deng. "A finger for thirty grand! A whole set of ten would be three hundred thousand. Does a thumb warrant double? Then there are ten toes. Worth another three hundred thousand? Why not throw in other parts of the body? How much for a nose? An eyeball? What if a hand or leg is left disabled? And what if someone dies? The families of plane crash victims get less than a million. How dare you calculate like this! Your name is what, is it Diao? Ah yes, Smooth Diao. That's enough, absolutely enough. A man shouldn't want for more when he is given more. Don't stir up trouble here. Get on with your own stuff. Chief Qu has enough to attend to, without you loitering around, annoying him."

As she was talking, she drove Smooth backwards as if she were warding off a beggar. He had come directly from the stage and was wearing a blue overcoat that made him look as mangy as the skipper of a trawler. Today, although his spine was upright, he found himself confronted with this diminutive female whose face was plastered with more layers of cosmetics than when she was on the stage. He was now bold and disdainfully contrary. "Don't touch me," Smooth snapped. "I am talking with Chief Qu. Does that have anything to do with you?"

Smooth flexed his shoulders and menaced her into retreat. The woman had accumulated pent-up anger aplenty and now became even more agitated. "So what, what do you want to do?" she challenged him. "You're only a poor shit of a stage shifter. Has this dame lost so much glamour that even the maggots from down the sewer want to take her on? Do you dare do that again? How dare you try to push your old ma!" With that, she lunged towards Smooth and raised her hand to swipe him. Chief Qu moved to block her charge.

At this second, Director Jin happened to walk in. "What's up?" she asked in puzzlement. "They're even resorting to kung-fu now?" She was cut short by Madame Deng who seized the chance to kick Smooth. Her toes dug right down into his crotch and he covered that region with his hands as he sank to the floor.

Director Jin's face changed at once. "Deng Jiuhong!" she snarled. "What's got into you? How can you go kicking Smooth like that?"

Deng Jiuhong. Smooth at last could put a name to this clapped-out has-been of a leading lady. Deng Jiuhong.

"Why not ask him how his nuts came to collide with his old ma's toes? Hey, how can I not be angry? This old dame was talking with Chief Qu, when this shitty stage shifter butted in and tried to blackmail a hundred grand out of our troupe. How could this old dame not make a stand and speak out on behalf of the troupe? Haven't you seen how the morals of society have been tossed away? How can I go about with one eye open and one eye closed? Public morals are tumbling further every day, and blackguards and their wiles are holding sway." Deng was now speaking in a solemnly judicious tone, and the last two sentences were a rhyming couplet lifted from a stage drama. She enunciated the rhyme as she said it.

"Don't say 'this old dame this' and 'this old dame that'," insisted

Director Jin. "You must be a year or so younger than me, so how can you refer to yourself as that?"

"It's what I want to do, so why shouldn't I? If this old dame wasn't growing older, how could she deal with all the bottled-up annoyance around her? Now even a lousy stage shifter takes it upon himself to push me around. In the past, this stinking shit wouldn't be considered fit to tie my shoelaces. You tell me, tell me, where is the justice in this world?" Without placing her finger on a specific injustice, Deng began to wail loudly at how wronged she was.

"Well, well, Smooth has done nothing to you," observed Chief Qu. "You're the one who kicked him. What more do you want?"

Smooth's groin still smarted at the point of impact and tears of pain filmed his eyeballs. He noticed how Deng was wearing red leather shoes that tapered into a kind of awl shape at the toes. He had seen shoes with tapering toes before, but never ones with such a sharp point. The tip had bored into his knackers like a nail.

Deng moaned and protested, even becoming breathless in the process. The chief arranged for some staff to carry her home on piggyback.

Smooth squatted as he waited for the agony to subside. Director Jin pulled his leg by saying, "Check your 'man eggs' Smooth. Have the yolks been splattered out?"

Male or female, what kind of creature was Jin? Smooth had been courteous to her, but was relegated to the position of a dog, then scolded by her. He never wanted to engage with this deranged bitch any more.

Smooth slowly rose to his feet, keen to resume his conversation with Chief Qu about the compensation for Monkey.

They were still gossiping about Deng Jiuhong. She had been living in pitiful straits these years. Her husband had divorced her and her mother was bedridden with paralysis. Worse still, her son-in-law had left her daughter. The trio of women had a miserable lot.

Smooth let out a cough and Chief Qu shifted the topic back to Monkey's compensation. He was not unpleasantly surprised at how Director Jin stood on his side of the argument. She emphasised that this was a human finger at stake, a part of a fresh and healthy body. Needless to say, that body belonged to a man who lived by his hands, so 30,000 yuan was far from sufficient. Jin maintained that whoever considered it adequate was talking hogwash. If the troupe stopped at 30,000, she would dig into her own pockets and provide the extra. As the director of the production, she could not shirk responsibility.

Her sentiments touched Smooth. This woman, in his eyes, was certifiable, only she hadn't yet been sent to the nuthouse. Once she was on the stage in rehearsal, she would jettison all ties to this world, focusing on the artistry as though it were more important than her immediate family. If anyone ruffled a single hair on her head, even unintentionally, she could rally like a lioness and fight to the death. That night when Smooth was acting the dog and got carried away, her trembling and sense of fury were so intense, he believed that only wrist and ankle restraints would be enough to pacify her. Today, however, the lioness had become as winsome as the Bodhisattva in a temple. From beginning to end, she had spoken out on the side of Smooth and Monkey, showing no inhibition about dogfighting verbally with Iron Kou. Deep down, the respect and esteem he formerly had for her were revived. She began to cough as she talked excitedly, so Smooth bent down to offer her a cup of hot tea with both his hands.

This was not the true motive for her being there today. She had come to talk about how the rehearsals for *Peach Blossom Cheeks* could be refined and just so happened to stumble in on this discussion about Monkey's compensation. She and Iron Kou argued with each other mercilessly as Chief Qu listened on in silence. This was his personal style of leadership and the mode in which the troupe operated. Whenever a meeting was in process, his door was always wide open and whoever came after him could chip in after a minute or two if they chose to be so bold. Nobody was truly bothered about such interruptions, since according to Chief Qu's ideology, there should be no secrets among the troupe and it would do no harm to listen to grassroots opinions. Those who visited his office seemed to sprout mouths all over their bodies. The only meeting not held like this in the troupe was the professional titles evaluation conference. That was because, for several years in succession, the event always ended up being derailed. A few members of staff were inclined to sit down throughout the proceedings and refuse to budge when they were asked. Staging it outside became essential.

Sometimes when he came to the chief's office, Smooth could pilfer a little tea without its owner straightening his mouth in disapproval, becoming less easy-going or curtailing his chatter. Today, Director Jin had been at loggerheads with Iron Kou, so Qu cut them short. Iron Kou then left with a flick of the door handle and said that it was all too easy to behave like Li Hongzhang, the paragon of compromise. Chief Qu asked Smooth to leave on the proviso that he would be in touch later. He did as he was told.

As he was walking away, he heard Director Jin gabbling on. "Old Qu," she implored him. "He makes his living by his hands, so thirty thousand is far from enough. One finger must be worth more than that. We should be mindful about not duping those hardworking souls..."

After a period of time had passed, Chief Qu sought out Smooth and asked whether 50,000 yuan was acceptable. Actually, Smooth had talked it over with Monkey and others. They were of the opinion that people like Chief Qu and Director Jin had been compassionate towards them and remained ever-conscious that they had been working with this troupe for years. That figure would be OK as a baseline. Nonetheless, Smooth straightened his back and assumed a negotiator's stance on the chief's sofa. He bargained away, wanting to push for another ten thousand.

"How about we settle for sixty grand?"

"Sixty thousand is a deal."

It was evident that there must have been some prior discussion on the compensation.

The day Iron Kou gave Monkey the money, he couldn't resist slipping in some callous words. "Would've been better if your dick was chopped off," he hissed. "Then you could've squeezed us for six hundred grand!"

"This fist really wants to scatter a few of Iron Kou's teeth," he growled in anger when he returned to his brothers.

While everything was unfolding on schedule, Smooth was confronted by another jolt at home. Big Army Diao was back under his roof. Having previously weighed over a hundred kilos, he was back to being as lanky as a hemp stalk. His condition was so grave that eating and drinking were rendered impossible.

68

It began a few days before Tomb-Sweeping Festival. Smooth answered the phone to find himself unexpectedly speaking to a member of staff at a police station in Zhuhai. The voice asked whether he was Smooth Diao, and then if he had an elder brother by the name of Big Army Diao, both questions eliciting an affirmative response. Next, they enquired whether it was convenient for him to come to Zhuhai without delay. His brother had pancreatic cancer and his days were numbered. As nobody was there to tend to him, they hoped he could fill that role. Smooth didn't hesitate.

This was the first time in his life that he had trekked far from the Western Capital. The police station directed him to where Big Army was being cared for, and he arrived to find his brother in an almost subhuman state. Smooth even felt scared to admit that what he beheld was actually the same Big Army who had stayed with him in the run-up to New Year. How could his appearance become so desperate in such a short space of time? His hair was long and unkempt like tarragon in autumn, and his face as drawn and thin as a palm leaf. What had formerly been the landmark on this palm – the proud, high-bridged nose that girls once found tantalising – was tilted to one side. There had been women who told him outright that it was this organ that ensnared them. "Brother Big Army, can you guess what made me fall into your trap?" they would ask. "It's that hooter of yours. So erect, so sexy and so charming." Smooth could even recall seeing them kiss his brother on the nose in public when there were others around. His angular nose, which had once been as steep and precipitous as the western peak of Mount Hua, had collapsed into a tumbledown, untended old tomb. The base of the peak appeared to have given way so his nostrils slackened and receded from the bone, crumpling down towards the corners of his sunken mouth. His whole face, including the extremities of his lips, had a concave appearance. Those two eye sockets had slumped as deep and dark as unfathomable pits. Inside them, hollow lights still shimmered and scanned Smooth's face in such a way that his hair stood on end. How could this be? How could Big Army have ended up like this?

Smooth bent forward and intoned, "Brother."

In what little light remained in those two dark pits, he could make out tears.

Smooth wanted to find a tissue to dry his elder brother's eyes, but there were none by the bedside. Finally, he managed to find a used paper hanky, but phlegm had hardened it to the texture of a scab.

"Brother, what's happened to you?'

Big Army said nothing. He shook his head gently and sighed.

Smooth cried, loudly in fact, and couldn't hold himself back.

At last, Big Army opened his mouth. "Don't cry, i... it means enough to be able to see you. In this world... I have... you... only dear you..."

Even though Big Army neither choked nor snivelled, tears ran from the edges of his eyes. Smooth couldn't remember ever having seen his elder brother weep. In their childhood, Big Army had been so mischievous. In the vegetable patch, he singled out their neighbours' best watermelon that they had been leaving for seed and gouged a little plug out of the skin. He and Smooth shared the pulp he spooned from it, before Big Army dropped his trousers and filled the hole with the loose contents of his bowels. Having covered up his prank and not severed the stalk, the fruit grew on, though rotted away from the inside. Since the two families were at odds, those neighbours played tricks on the Diaos, nicking their hot peppers, aubergines and tomatoes. The rotten watermelon became a new focus for hostility.

Smooth's father did not want the trouble to snowball, so when the neighbours threw the rancid fruit over their gate, Mr Diao picked up the handle of a spade and made Big Army and Smooth kneel down in the middle of the courtyard. Smooth was so terrified that he peed his pants. Big Army, on the other hand, bore the full brunt, admitting that he was to blame and it had nothing to do with Smooth. Their father grilled his younger son in order to discover whether he was an accomplice. Big Army reiterated that he knew nothing of it and that night, while he was sabotaging the fruit, Smooth was as fast asleep as a dead sow. Their father then asked if this was the whole truth and, looking at the spade handle held up high in the air, Smooth nodded his head. His father let him stand and watch to one side as he began to belt Big Army. The punishment was vicious, and sometimes a blow from the handle would make him stagger forward a few steps. Still, Big Army did nothing to dodge the beating, returning after each strike to his former spot in preparation for the next. At that time, Smooth was only in the third year of primary school. His understanding of phrases such as "dash ahead regardless of safety", "better to break than bend", "die before you surrender" and "face death unflinchingly" were all founded on the example of his elder brother Big Army's behaviour.

Smooth had never seen his brother cry. No wonder then that the streams of tears before him brought on a sense of despair and brokenness.

It was only now that Smooth learned that, for all these years, Big Army had not been living in Macau itself. Instead, he had rented an apartment in nearby Wanchai District, Zhuhai. His landlady told him that Big Army was seldom in residence, for most of his time was occupied gambling in Macau. Upon becoming ill, he shambled back here, never to leave his home. Smooth asked the whereabouts of his wife. The landlady admitted that she wasn't entirely sure to which, if any, woman he was married, since he brought so many of them over. Smooth was keen to know if there was one named Marti. The landlady shook her head and said that all she knew right now was that Big Army owed her four months and seventeen days-worth of rent. She implored Smooth to move his brother at the earliest opportunity because if he died in that apartment, it would be awkward for her to find a new tenant. She wanted to cut a deal whereby, if he could be relocated in a day or two, she would waive the outstanding seventeen days. Smooth decided his elder brother was best off coming home.

Big Army would not comply. Seeing his brother for one last time was sufficient, he said. He grabbed the edge of the bed, and as the landlady helped to pry his fingers loose, a nail was snapped.

Eventually, with her assistance, Smooth hauled Big Army onto his back and into a cab. They reached the Western Capital by train. A few of the neighbours spotted the piggybacking Smooth, and word of Big Army's return swept around the alleys. Uncle Scar could not believe how, after an interval of three or four months, such a strong and macho man was "nearly ready to have the coffin lid nailed shut". In the evening, he came to knock at Smooth's door, for Big Army still owed him hundreds of thousands of yuan in gambling debts. He was astounded to clap eyes on the withered body of the "living mummy".

Big Army lay there mute.

Uncle Scar sat around idly, but his eyes focused on the sick man's neck, wrists and fingers.

Big Army was wearing a neck chain, had a gold ring inlaid with jadeite on one of the fingers of his right hand and a jade bracelet around his left wrist.

Uncle Scar stared at these effects avariciously. So intent was his stare that his eyeballs almost became bloodshot.

Maybe he coveted them for too long because Big Army was struck with embarrassment. He sighed a futile sigh and reached his hand to fumble for the chain and pendant around his neck. Smooth had heard from Daisy that it was worth hundreds of thousands of yuan. His big brother gave it to Uncle Scar and then pleaded breathlessly, "Even... even now... don't pester... Smooth any more..."

The older man accepted the chain, but was not ready to depart. Like a spotlight, his focus switched to Big Army's hands with their ring and bracelet.

"I should... leave something... to Smooth to remember me by," whimpered Big Army.

"I don't want it. Brother, since you owe him, give him it all." Smooth left the room sadly.

Big Army finally closed his eyes, with Uncle Scar still fixated upon him. Upon shutting his lids, he stretched out a trembling hand to the old man, who first removed the bracelet.

That item of jewellery was easy to remove as his podgy hand had become so shrunken and drawn that it resembled a chicken's paw. As for the ring on his right hand, its new owner had to exert considerable force.

Despite the rest of Big Army's body becoming dehydrated to the point that he lay there like a shrivelled, frost-stricken radish, his knuckles had not receded. As a matter of fact, that finger with the ring was swollen and distended. In order to remove it, Uncle Scar really had to sweat. In the end, with the aid of his omnipresent ear pick, he succeeded bit by bit in poking and pinching it free. A bruise was left behind on the bloodless digit.

On obtaining the ring, there was no hint of satisfaction on Uncle Scar's face, which never seemed to shine even in the sunlight and was pallid like white lime. He merely patted Big Army's chest. "Have a good rest. Your uncle is leaving now," he said, before standing up and swaggering away.

Big Army's eyes remained closed for a long time after his departure, yet his teeth had been chattering throughout.

Smooth had arranged for his brother to rest in his own bed. On their way back home, Big Army pronounced that he would absolutely not go to the hospital, nor did he want his little brother to go throwing his hard-earned money after a lost cause. Smooth agreed, though on returning to the Western Capital, he made enquiries everywhere about veteran practitioners of Traditional Chinese Medicine. This was his last and best option, for he could not endure seeing his elder brother prostrated in bed, awaiting death.

Smooth invited over a senior doctor of Traditional Chinese Medicine. He was purportedly adept at curing cancers of the liver and pancreas and hailed from the foothills of Mount Hua. He had heard of his reputation through one of the leading actors in the troupe, who claimed that he was able to rescue patients who the big hospitals had dismissed as incurable. Holding on to a slim ray of hope, Smooth rode the bus for over an hour to escort the gentleman from Huayin County.

This doctor was "senior" in title only, since he must in fact have been in his thirties. He seldom said a word and exhibited an aura of great experience. He spent more than half an hour feeling Big Army's pulse and just as much time in writing out the prescription. He would ponder and calculate at length about which herbs to prescribe. His conscientious and responsible manner gave Smooth great optimism. Several times he asked him if there was any hope, to which the doctor wouldn't offer a full answer, simply seeking more details about the state of his illness, his diet and bodily functions. At last, the physician outlined how to decoct and drink the herbal brew. Worried that he might be unable to remember everything, Smooth made copious jottings in the notebook he used while stage shifting. He was still asking the expert whether Big Army could be cured as he prepared to open the door. The "senior doctor" would do no more than offer up one ambiguous sentence: "It all depends on his fortune and luck." Smooth paid him 2,000 yuan and sent him on his way with profuse thanks.

Daisy returned abruptly on the fourth day of Big Army's confinement.

She was escorted back home by Tan Daogui, the brand name liquor agent.

At that moment, Smooth had just come back from purchasing Chinese herbs for his brother. A female voice addressed him as "Dad" and he turned around to find a woman behind him arm-in-arm with a man. He didn't recognise them and thought they might have hailed him by mistake, so he continued to amble back home. On being called again, it at last dawned on him it was Daisy. But it was not her likeness he saw when he turned around again. The lady laughed, cupping her chin with her hand as she did so, presumably out of fear that her face might be disfigured by the flexing of its muscles. In a fraction of a second, he knew her as his daughter. She had gone off with somebody to South Korea to get cosmetic surgery, and the difference in her appearance might have been the result of that beautification.

Smooth took a studious look at the woman before him. It was Daisy, and the transformation was indeed profound. Smooth had never before conceived that surgical procedures could transform the appearance and even the facial structure of a person. For starters, she once had a hump of a nose that was somewhat like Big Army's in former days. Now that nose was too high to be a product of nature and radiated incandescently, perhaps because the skin had been drawn too tight. Before, her face had been long with a narrow forehead and chin, somewhat akin to the shape of a weaving shuttle. Her hair was restyled so that the fringe hung down to her eyebrows, concealing the forehead completely. From having formerly owned a goose's egg of a face, somehow she now resembled her favourite actress, Audrey Hepburn. Smooth, after all, was a city dweller and so had watched many movies since childhood. He was familiar with those leads from home and abroad. Moreover, Daisy pinned photos of the Hollywood film star on the walls and even slipped one into her purse. Still, Smooth could not fully comprehend why she had redesigned her face to look like that of a foreigner. It appeared rather weird from any angle and not one of her features was authentic. This was the manufactured Daisy, not the genuine article.

To his relief, her temper had changed too. She had ceased to sport an expression of indifference whenever she met him. Daisy even began to call him "Dad" again, which delighted Smooth. As they were about to enter through the gate, he told them the truth about Big Army in case she was still seething at her uncle. Contrary to his assumptions, all those unpleasant machinations seemed to have been forgotten. "It's so fortunate I didn't follow him to Macau," she reflected. "Had I done that, I would have missed out on finding the best husband in the world." As she spoke, she pecked a kiss on Tan's podgy face, which left Smooth feeling a touch uncomfortable.

Daisy went inside to see her uncle. Facing his niece was like studying a pupa that had spontaneously been transformed into a butterfly. Big Army's uneasiness defied words, and Daisy's brand of consolation was now both generous and broadminded. She told her father that in recent days she had been planning to leave the Western Capital and relocate to the northeast with Tan to set up a company to sell brand-name wines. She also reported that only the first stage of her plastic surgery had been completed, so her husband would arrange the second and third, until she was indistinguishable from Audrey Hepburn.

Smooth smiled. "If you are her double, then what has become of my daughter?"

"Isn't it good that your daughter resembles Audrey Hepburn?"

"Is it really such a good thing that my daughter resembles others?"

"My husband had planned to fashion me into the new Hepburn to infuriate Princess Wu. Wasn't that so, hubby dearest?"

"Why try to make Princess Wu angry?" asked her father.

"You don't understand, Dad. Isn't that so, hubby dearest?" With these words, she kissed Tan again. Smooth felt dizzy on hearing her call him "hubby dearest" so often.

"Have you got registered?" he asked in a hushed voice.

Daisy laughed at him for being so behind the times and wondered out loud who really needed a slip of paper in this day and age?

Smooth was of the opinion that it was still better to have their union formalised, upon which Daisy mentioned they had bought an apartment in Dalian.

"You're not coming back to live here?"

"No, Dad. You can take care of yourself now. Further down the line, when you get too old to look after yourself, I'll take you to Dalian. It's by the sea. The air and the environment are wonderful there."

Once Daisy had finished, she took Tan's arm and went away. She gave 10,000 yuan to her father, stuffing the money into his pocket when he tried to refuse it.

Smooth escorted Daisy out of the gate. There was something in his eyes that he couldn't hold back, and it trickled out slowly. Once Daisy was out of sight, he crossed his hands before his chest and mouthed "heavenly blessings", then turned slowly back.

During the period when Smooth was fetching his elder brother home and then searching out doctors, a good many troupes from outside came to the Western Capital. Theatres rang Smooth, requesting that he prepare to shift a stage. He passed the jobs on to Big Hook and Monkey, but whenever he wasn't present to mediate between the two, they butted heads. Quarrels flared up easily and nobody accepted the way they allocated tasks. Big Hook was enraged and so came to complain to Smooth, pleading for him to return to work soon. It was obvious that he couldn't abandon the house since there was a patient to be waited on and the process of decocting herbs required minute care and attention.

The boiling stage alone called for twenty-four hours of absolute diligence.

Big Hook proposed that his wife, Laurel Zhou, could be commandeered. She was a seasoned carer who had looked after his grandparents when they were alive and arranged their funerals properly after their deaths. Since there was no viable alternative, Smooth let her take on the role.

69

IN THE BEGINNING, Laurel Zhou came to the house early and left late. As Smooth's workload intensified, he could not make it back at night and she had to become a live-in carer.

Smooth permitted her to dwell temporarily in Plum's old room, but this left nobody to supervise Lily. Once Big Hook informed Smooth of this, the child joined her mother. Since their rented room was now empty and the costs were punitive, he ended his lease and the whole family made Smooth's home their residence for the time being.

Laurel Zhou showed herself to be an attentive nurse. Big Army was Smooth's elder brother and Smooth had been her husband's boss long before she too became his hireling. Big Hook always impressed on her that Smooth was a friend for life. And so she was meticulous towards Big Army.

The patient did feel embarrassed at having to be bathed. Just like her paralysed father-in-law, his buttocks needed wiping twice daily with a warm towel. Whether the herbs were having an effect or this was the consequence of her diligent care, Big Army's condition appeared to improve. One day, he even climbed out of bed and walked a few steps with Laurel as his support.

Nevertheless, Big Army's stroll through life was coming to its close. Despite having been one head taller and a shoulder's breadth wider than his carer, he sagged down on her like a laundered quilt being hung out to dry in the sun. Any part of his anatomy that she didn't prop up would slouch towards the floor. She did her utmost to sustain him, but finally he lost the ability to speak, and his eyes took on a dazed appearance. The "senior doctor" of Traditional Chinese Medicine was invited over again. He said that there was nothing that medication could do for him and this was the will of heaven. Even if an immortal were to come down and intercede now, it would prove fruitless. Big Army would have another week at most and they should prepare for his passing. The doctor accepted only 1,000 yuan for this home visit.

Smooth's schedule had become jam-packed, though he consciously held back from visiting the stage on the pretence that he should be there for his brother. He first of all prepared the funerary hat, clothes, shoes and socks, then sat beside him to deal with the contents of his bedpan. He watched and caressed him as he waited, powerless for the lamp of his life to run dry and flicker out.

He could recall how his brother's life had been saturated with glamour and colour. From childhood, the two of them had been an incongruous pair. Smooth toiled away in silence and had endless chores to accomplish, while his elder brother always seemed to be whistling a tune to the accompaniment of his boisterous flatulence. His brain must have been grooved intricately to the effect that he could stir others to toil while he himself sat back and savoured fine dining. How Smooth had wished he could emulate his brother's charisma, but never learned how he pulled it off, and so instead he had to persevere honestly and sheepishly.

These days, his thoughts turned repeatedly to the time he followed his elder brother to keep sentry duty at the vegetable fields. Their father was still alive back then and was always convinced that Smooth would run into bother if he stayed over on his own. In the past, incidents had occurred there. Vegetable thieves once jabbed out the former watchman's eyeballs with a knife. Their father then resolved that Big Army must be his companion. The elder brother agreed without pause for thought, since he could bask in his own freedom out there without the need to go home every night. But how could someone of Big Army's stripe play the level-headed watchman after nightfall? He struck up a bargain with Smooth. If he let him go and play mahjong at night, he would pay him sixty yuan. In other words, two yuan per day for every day of that month. Smooth was more than pleased with the idea, for he could make an extra two yuan that he didn't have to hand over to his father to manage. There was one further advantage to his brother's arranged absence. Big Army was tall and heavy. The narrow bunk in the felt-roofed shed could not support his bulk. Needless to say, as soon as Smooth himself lay down, his brother pitched into a death-like sleep. In that state, he wouldn't have known if someone kidnapped him, let alone have the wherewithal to monitor the fields after dark.

Smooth kept a dog, which took an immediate dislike to Big Army. It too slept in the shed, but was disturbed by the elder brother's nocturnal habits. He would snore, grind his teeth and fart, the noise being so raucous that the hound could not slumber. In line with his promise, Big Army gave Smooth the sixty yuan at the specified time. On occasions, if he were in a good mood, he would boost that to eighty or even one hundred. Smooth hid this secret from their father.

Their subterfuge continued until one snowy night. Big Army came after his younger brother in a hurry, requesting 500 yuan. He had amassed a gambling debt and it needed to be settled that very night by whatever means possible. Big Army knew that Smooth stashed away personal savings in a split seam of his cotton-padded clothes. He had once noticed him stuffing some notes in there. Smooth had no intention of giving him the money, but when he noticed that Big Army had taken off his watch and overcoat as surety, he realised that money must be found to redeem these articles. The younger brother's heart softened and he parted the broken seam willingly. As he then flattened out the creased banknotes, Big Army promised that he would receive double that amount in return.

By his calculations, Smooth surmised that he had been given 420 yuan in the course of six months. Now he was having to relinquish fully 500 yuan. This was a game of diminishing returns. Come what may, however, Big Army was his elder brother. When he was being bullied as a kid, it only took Big Army to put in an appearance for the wild aggressors to disperse like frightened rats, no matter how many they numbered. Tonight, his brother was cornered like the well-known opera character Yang Bailao, who owed her landlord a fortune. How could he refuse to extend a rescuing hand?

Naturally, Big Army paid him off later with more than 1,000 yuan in notes. He had plainly forgotten the exact size of the debt and ended up reimbursing him for twice the amount. Anyhow, this had all been the spoils of gambling and was like him tossing Smooth a little morsel of tasty chicken. Word had it that when Big Army was flush with winnings, he would even lavishly tip the tea servers in the gambling den. His younger brother, of course, was party to this bounty too.

Smooth directed much thought to the issue of his brother's generosity. Obviously, this was not a habit that he could acquire. It was said that people judge the generosity of a man according to his attitude towards money. When Big Army's pockets were full, he liked to dole it out ostentatiously in public without counting. He would only bandy about rough estimates and make gestures as he did. Meanwhile, when Smooth had a mite to set aside, he would find a private corner and count the notes merrily again and again. He was so frugal that he would fish out the torn-edged notes and go back and ask those who had given him them for a replacement. He would then hide his wad straight away as though he feared a pair of thievish eyes were observing him from behind.

While tending to his elder brother, Smooth also pondered about his deceased second brother, Fortune. Here was another guy who knew how to imbue every moment of life with pleasure. Smooth thought of those years when their father asked them to carry night soil from the government units in the city. He never understood how, but his brothers always had sweets or flat cakes, coins or small denomination notes to hand. These they would deploy to bribe Smooth into clambering down the shit holes and scooping out the waste. They then coaxed him further to haul the load out of the gate. To be seen carrying such matter, the two boys felt was undignified. Once they reached the fields, the pair of them would sit on the ground and play as Smooth made sure that a quantity of fertiliser was dripped onto every last seedling. He was prepared to be exploited like this because he was sure that they had items with which to encourage him. After a period of time, what he squirrelled away he would loan back to them and so he had to begin the process of saving bit by bit all over again.

When it came to being protected, Smooth had no worries on that score. As something of a weakling, the neighbourhood children liked to set upon him in their gang fights. Whenever he was in danger, his brothers would risk their hides to save him, dashing over from wherever they happened to be. They could beat anybody into submission until they ended up on their knees, pleading for mercy.

His second eldest brother later turned to drugs and shrivelled to the size of a hemp stalk. There was a time when the trike-pedalling Smooth was browbeaten by a man selling beef. Fortune Diao reared up and thumped the chap in the mouth, only, owing to him channelling too much force into his fist, the two of them ended up flat on the ground, unable to get up.

Smooth allowed himself to chuckle at these memories. Laurel Zhou asked him what he had found so funny. He told her he was reminiscing about his past exploits with his brother.

"I've heard people say that Big Army was the type who could eat a lion or punch a tiger," she commented. "How come he never found himself a wife?"

"He could have had eight or ten of them if he wanted to. He was the one who ruined his own good life." Smooth's voice was maybe a little too loud, for Big Army promptly opened his eyes and stared at him and Laurel, neither of whom he now seemed to recognise.

According to Smooth's own impressions, by the time his elder brother reached the age of seventeen or eighteen, he had become a gallant gentleman of arresting appearance. Every night when they kept watch over the vegetable fields, Big Army would go gambling and lead girls from their community to frolic in the wild meadows. When all this began, Smooth was a green hand and convinced himself that his brother must be abusing those girls somehow. Deep in the night, he made them wail in a peculiar manner. Once, Smooth even went over and pulled Big Army off the female he was pinning to the ground. "You're a nutter," the girl cursed him. Later, Smooth understood what was going on and he came to loathe his brother's habit of working his way through a new woman every day. However, owing to his seniority, this was a criticism he couldn't share out loud. To date, he never divulged the identities of his conquests. Unless the girls had shared their experience with others, there was no chance of Smooth being the one to blab. He regarded these assignations as dirty and cheap. To speak of them would be to soil his mouth.

And now Big Army, whose entire life had been saturated with

glamour and colour, had reached the end. Once such a man collapsed, he was out for the count. Smooth admitted that he had never seen his brother shed tears, yet in the space of a month or so since he brought him over here, he had witnessed him cry more than ten times. His elder brother had been turned from a firm to an overripe persimmon. Smooth did ask about Marti, the young socialite. Big Army only shook his head. "Never mention that... nobody's straightforward," he rasped. "I felt guilty about her, she left... she should... I didn't... even leave her a penny..." He started to wail out loud with regret.

Smooth had been readying himself for the task of dressing his brother in his shroud as soon as he drew his last breath. When death came, the body would start to stiffen and become hard to manipulate. Years ago, Smooth had a sideline in dressing corpses and performing funerary customs for a fee. Just as he was adjusting Big Army's cloth, he suddenly regained consciousness. Not only did he know who Smooth was, but Laurel Zhou too. She described this as being the final radiance of the setting sun.

Intermittently, Big Army shared some last thoughts with him. Had the listener no background knowledge of the dying man, not even a ghost would be able to decipher his words. Fortunately, Smooth could assemble the clues. More than thirty years ago, Big Army had run away from home and spent a fortnight wooing a girl in the deepest mountains. His father responded by beating his legs until they nearly broke. Regardless, Big Army impressed it into Smooth that the whole episode had been worth the suffering. The beauty of that girl could not be expressed in words, and he had never seen such a tender, fresh and charming person in the Western Capital. For a while, he dwelt on this "crystal spring", and then shifted to calling her a "melt-in-the-mouth peach". Anyhow, he drew numerous comparisons without ever precisely pinpointing the charm of the girl.

As soon as Big Army mentioned Zhen'an County and said "more than thirty years ago", Smooth understood the topic. He was aware that, during his pre-New Year trip, he had gone out in search of the woman. In Smooth's eyes, his life had been consumed by whoring and seeking carnal pleasure, so visiting another female didn't warrant any fuss. To his surprise, Big Army's infatuation was sincere and consuming, for she was on his tongue the moment before he left this world. Although he was past the stage of being able to articulate clearly, Smooth grasped what was behind his words. He explained that the woman was now so pitiful. Her son had fractured his spine in a mining accident. The whole family was in despair, and he hoped that Smooth could lend assistance. Big Army stressed repeatedly that she was to be found at Black Kiln Ditch in Zhen'an County. Her name was Peach Blossom Yang...

Big Army died in the second half of the night, cradled in Smooth's arms. At that time, he was seemingly cold all over and tried to inch closer into his brother's embrace.

In the preceding days, Smooth slept alongside him, and if there was any sound or movement, he would rise immediately to address the problem.

Finally, Big Army failed to stir when he wanted water, nor did he wish to turn over his agonised body. He merely wanted to lean nearer to Smooth, who bent over him and shouted, "Bro, Bro. What's up? Tell me." Big Army was already dumbstruck and released a paff of wind from down below. This was no longer his customary ebullient emission with all the crispness of cannon fire. It crept out of him quizzically.

Once again, Big Army leaned further into Smooth's embrace. Perhaps this was his haven of safety and calm. He passed away with a pronounced lurch of the mouth.

70

AFTER BIG ARMY'S FUNERAL, Smooth took to his bed for three full days. Laurel Zhou oversaw his every need, just as she had done with his brother. He felt rather bashful about all this concern and told her she was free to move on and that he didn't need a carer. Besides, he informed her, there was no shortage of folk around in his time of bereavement. She could direct her energy into her own work. Laurel did not respond. In the evening, Big Hook came for Smooth.

This took Smooth off guard. He had been contemplating renting out the spare rooms, though hadn't devised a plan yet. In fact, his house contained only three bedrooms. One of them was his and the other two belonged to Daisy and Plum. In spite of the fact they had technically left home, he was unsure if it was proper to let their rooms out. He began to consider if it was necessary to discuss the matter with them. Both had their grievances with him, so it might seem like he was trying to drive them out if he did this on the sly. Big Hook, however, had been so bold as to move in first and put off asking for permission until later. He related to Smooth how he had handed back the key to his rented room. Smooth then realised that since he could not send the mother and daughter packing, he must let them stay irrespective of any misgivings he had. He notified Big Hook that the arrangement should remain temporary. Once they had found somewhere else suitable, they should depart. He said that frankly there was something peculiar about this home. If matters did begin to run awry here, then their peaceful lives would be bound to be a thing of the past. Big Hook agreed to the terms implicitly, and in the evening, he moved in without trying to conceal what he was doing.

Events then took on a bizarre twist. No sooner had Big Army been laid to rest did Smooth hear that Teacher Zhu was on his deathbed. On receiving the phone call, he wasted no time.

When he got to the apartment, Zhu had already started to cough so hard that he was gasping for breath. His teacher suffered from asthma, which purportedly stemmed from the cold conditions of his early life. At the time of his birth, the Western Capital was engulfed in war. He came into this world in an air-raid shelter and referred to his malady as "puerperal fever". Teacher Zhu adopted the tradition of taking medicines each summer to try to stave off illness in the winter. More than seventy years had passed and the root of his condition had not been lanced away. Finally, and with no warning, it was about to claim his life.

Teacher Zhu knew everything about his condition. He also appeared resigned to what it was about to do to him. Before Smooth came, he had actually made full preparations and had even bought a shroud that now lay on his bedside table. As Smooth lifted him onto his back, Zhu asked him to fetch the winding cloth.

"Teacher, we are going to the hospital. You're not seriously ill. After they've given you a once over, you'll be fine."

"This time, that's not how it'll be. I know that the King of Hell... is insisting on inviting me... he gave me a reprieve... a few times. I'm already fully... fully seventy-three years old. Confucius only... only lived to this age. What virtues do I possess... to live longer than him? Enough... I have lived long enough."

As he had predicted, a dozen days later, Teacher Zhu found himself choking and passed away with his throat flooded with phlegm. The first two days after his admission, Smooth had been his carer. When he rallied on the third day, he suggested that Laurel Zhou could take over, enabling him to go and help shift the stage. On the seventh day, he began to deteriorate again. "Smooth, Smooth," he called out repeatedly until his pupil returned to resume his nursing duties.

In the evening, Teacher Zhu grasped hold of Smooth's hand. "There is something which concerns you that I feel guilty about... Smooth," he said.

"As the saying goes, 'a student may have guilt where their teacher is concerned', so how could the tables be turned?"

Teacher Zhu slowly filled him in on the details.

He related how following his imminent demise, there would be no kinsmen left in his family. When his wife was still alive, they discussed to whom they should bequeath their small apartment. There were two options. One was to leave it to the primary school where both of them had taught for years. The alternative was to leave it to Smooth. These two possibilities occupied the old couple's minds until the wife died. Then Teacher Zhu was left to figure it out for himself. If Smooth's life was actually so poor and downtrodden, then without any dithering he ought to name him his benefactor. The problem was that each time Smooth visited his teacher's home, he would tell him how he was able to make money, lead a crew of a dozen or more men and was the de facto boss. To allow someone in a managerial position to inherit his estate would be inappropriate. Having just enough money was fair and decent, so what was the use in blessing him with a small fortune? Should Smooth be solvent, couldn't he turn a living by honest labour? Even as he lay on his deathbed, Teacher Zhu still had not plumped for an heir.

Who was it proper to transfer his property to? His estate was estimated to be worth in the hundreds of thousands. There was no shop frontage beneath the apartment and it was accessible through a small alley, so that the total living space, including the dovecote attic, was thirty square metres at most. Its value stood at between 400,000 and 500,000 yuan. Teacher Zhu and his wife believed that if they donated the home to the primary school, then the proceeds could provide subsidies for the children of migrant farmers who had come to the city to work. Also, they could use it to build a small library.

However, their investigations revealed that the amount was not even sufficient to upgrade the existing library. The government was not able to match the donation and facilitate such a project, so there was a real danger that the money could disappear after their passing. Some time ago, it was alleged that the headmaster who was in charge of school finances had been arrested for embezzling public funds. Could their tidy legacy end up in the pockets of a crook? If so, wouldn't they feel more peace of mind leaving it to Smooth?

After thinking about it back and forth, Teacher Zhu disclosed to his pupil what the couple had been considering previously before supplementing this with his current reservations. His thrust was quite clear. If Smooth judged himself in great need of money, he would invite a solicitor to come to the hospital and draft a legal document, leaving the property to him.

It was not that Smooth didn't want the house. Half a million yuan was no mean sum to him. If he had already decided to make him the heir, he had every reason to agree. His teacher had no next of kin and he was not averse to becoming wealthy, so why not say yes? Since his teacher had spoken to him in this manner and Smooth was not incapable of earning money himself, how could he accept the old man's home free of charge? Were he to do so it would be something shameful, just as his teacher had said.

Smooth answered flatly that he must decline.

"Thank you for all the care you have given me and my wife over these years. I thought it was only right to offer the house to you."

"Taking care of you two was my duty as a student. If I were to become the owner of your home, what kind of a person would that make me? I wouldn't even be worthy of public gossip."

The more Smooth talked in this manner, the more Teacher Zhu wanted him to inherit. In the end, there was a blunt rejection. To compound matters, Smooth went to the school and sought out the headmaster, informing him of Zhu's intentions. Forthwith, the school contacted its solicitor, who dropped in at the hospital and handled the relevant procedures. Teacher Zhu added one extra clause to the document: "Smooth Diao retains the right to examine the details of how the money from the legacy is used."

Teacher Zhu passed away the night the bequest was finalised.

Smooth regretted his failure to stop the doctor from performing a tracheotomy on the old man. Since he could not clear the phlegm from his throat, the consultant was determined to make an incision. Zhu waved his hand in disagreement, though Smooth had heard that such a procedure could be lifesaving. The neck was opened up, but his teacher died soon afterwards. It had been a grave mistake to have allowed them to cut him like that in his last moments. He was beset with guilt.

Naturally, his teacher's donation attracted a lot of attention at the school. The district bureau of education sent dedicated personnel over, so there was no need for Smooth to arrange the funeral and related affairs.

Smooth just followed his teacher's body to which no one else administered care. From sliding on the shroud, to sending his corpse to the mortuary, to making sure it was transferred to the crematorium and put on ice, Smooth acted alone. He arrived especially early on the morning of the memorial ceremony and found his teacher's body ahead of time. Smooth duly stood vigil until it was pushed to the chapel of rest at 8 am sharp. He was particularly attentive since a mishap had occurred when his elder brother was to be cremated. The staff made him wheel out the wrong corpse, so that once he had arranged the bier and then removed the red cloth covering the face, he found it was not Big Army. He hurriedly returned the body and notified the staff that there had been a mix-up. They nagged at him, maintaining that this simply could not happen and he must be the one at fault. If he was so sure, he should go and pick out the body he thought was actually his brother's.

That morning there were twenty-odd corpses, all made up and waiting to be burned. Each one was wrapped in a scarlet quilt with a cloth of the same colour draped over their faces. Big Army ought to have been easy to pick out owing to his huge stature. The trouble was that the terminal illness had reduced his frame to forty or fifty kilos. Hence, Smooth had to remove a number of cloths only to discover that none of them was him. There was one that appeared to be larger than the others, though this turned out to be a woman with pouting crimson lips. Smooth was so taken aback that he broke into a cold sweat. He nervously patted his chest again and again. "Brother, where are you?" he squeaked. "Don't scare me. You know I'm a chicken."

And so on the day of Teacher Zhu's cremation, Smooth made an issue of punctuality. However grand and solemn the ceremony others had planned might be, he would claim sole possession of the deceased and see that the send-off was trouble-free.

When Smooth wheeled the body of his teacher lugubriously into the chapel of rest at the allotted time, his own heart was half frozen. Only a dozen people lined the room. The school leader who had been sent was a deputy in rank, and just four or five former students were also present. Smooth had informed several of his classmates about Teacher Zhu's death and anticipated that plenty of mourners would come. The chamber appeared dreary and bleak. As he studied that thinnest of cheeks – only two fingers wide – and that mop of white hair, Smooth wept inconsolably.

Once the ceremony had ended and the others left, Smooth pushed his teacher to the oven and launched the stretcher inside. His mouth was open as the staff sprayed the corpse with oil, reducing his teacher to a fireball with a few simple splashes. The day they cremated his brother, Smooth had the sensation that his own flesh would cave in as he heard the crackling sounds from within the oven.

After a long wait, his teacher had been transformed into a heap of ash. Smooth shovelled the ash out and into an urn. A few chips of bone protruded, which he flattened down with his palm. He then travelled to the burial lot of his teacher's wife in the suburbs and deposited the cremains there.

He had done the same for his elder brother, Big Army. The difference now was that his teacher's tablet had been erected at the same time as that of his wife. Big Army's memorial had to be constructed following his internment. He was now at rest, flanked by their parents on the left side and second brother Fortune Diao on the right. Since his brother's death was drugs-related, he had to handle the post mortem affairs largely alone.

Fortune's putrefying corpse was found one summer's day in an abandoned warehouse in their neighbourhood. The police conducted an autopsy, and then Smooth had to wrap what was left in plastic and sling it over his shoulder. He remembered that nobody attended the cremation. Big Army was in Macau and could not be contacted. He also remembered that there had been a downpour that day. Clad in a raincoat, he scooped the soggy ashes into a hollow in the ground.

As soon as his teacher's remains were properly arranged, he kowtowed three times and burned hundreds of notes of touchpaper. The denomination printed on them ran into hundreds of millions of yuan. He mused silently that all that cash was enough for his teacher and his wife to build a college in the afterlife.

The day he burned touchpaper for his elder brother Big Army, he also burned identical fake banknotes for Fortune. "Big Brother, Second Brother," he murmured, "if you still like to gamble and do drugs, please suit yourselves. When you run out of money, send me the word in my dreams. Your younger brother is sure to burn more of it for you. This type of money is quite easy to come by."

71

Laurel Zhou had helped Smooth to care for his elder brother for more than a month and then attended to his teacher for a dozen days. He paid her 3,000 yuan, but she would not accept the money even though he crammed it into her hands.

"You're making me lose face," Big Hook blurted out angrily. "Our whole family is living in your house for only three hundred yuan rent. We offered a little help in return and you are trying to shame us by giving us cash. Is that fair, Smooth?"

In spite of Big Hook's response, Smooth continued to press the payment. "You don't have it at all easy," he said. "You need to take care of Lily's face and have so many other expenses. Take it for the sake of your kid."

The couple had to acquiesce.

Laurel Zhou had been taking Lily into the city for surgery for almost six months. Those two procedures had no tangible effect in the eyes of others, though Lily saw hope looking back at her in the mirror. She believed that her mother was the most alluring woman in the world and demanded that the doctor sculpt her features to be more like hers. To one side of the mirror she pinned up a photo of her mum taken when she was fifteen.

Laurel claimed she had never heard Lily sing, but in recent days she began to warble away in a low voice. The song went, "There is a village girl named Xiao Fang, so tender and graceful, her pretty eyes are large and her pigtail long and bunched..."

Her mother knew that each operation inflicted great pain. The doctor had to graft skin from Lily's thigh onto her face. By his estimation, at least a dozen such operations were needed to complete the reconstruction. On hearing this, Laurel was struck with such angst that cold sweat covered her body. Even so, Lily shrugged it off by saying it was no worse than being nipped by an ant, and she'd be prepared to repeat the procedure twenty or thirty times if necessary. Every time her daughter spoke like this, she nearly cried. The tears had to be withheld, however, and she flashed a calm, fond smile in return. Deep down, she feared that the sight of her crying would make Lily suicidal with despair.

When Lily was eleven years old, she had lashed a noose around her neck after being criticised by her mother. Laurel remembered that this was when a county opera troupe had come to their village to perform. Together with other kids, Lily squeezed her bottom onto the arch above the stage. Many in the audience stared at her and wagged fingers, being more interested in her distorted appearance than the performance itself. Such was Laurel's embarrassment that she tugged her girl home by the ear. Her tongue was particularly salty. "Don't you know how you look to other people?" she yelled. "I told you to steer clear of crowds. You may not feel ashamed, but I do."

That evening, Lily attempted to hang herself. Had she not been saved in time, a young life would have been snuffed out at the age of just eleven.

Ever since Laurel took Lily to the city, she could sense her mood lifting. Especially after the first operation, she wasn't the same girl. She cooked, washed clothes, and did all her business in a neat and orderly fashion. Every vegetable the child prepared was chopped finely, and even the porridge she cooked was sticky and moreish. The family seldom ate meat so as to save money, and she took pains to vary the ingredients and recipes to tantalise her parents. As she witnessed how arduously Big Hook threw himself into his job, whenever her mother brought a little meat home, she would tip her share into his bowl as the reward for being the breadwinner. Big Hook would not eat this gift and, as a matter of fact, a few pieces of meat landed on the floor as they were levered back and forth between different bowls. Lily then began to chop the meat into mince and mix it into the dishes she gave her father. Sometimes she did the same for her mother, but never herself. She was conscious of how her parents were saving money for her facial surgery, so couldn't dare eat more than her due.

From moving into Uncle Smooth's house, Lily's temperament became far more balanced. She remembered Uncle Smooth's aghast expression upon first meeting her. That was the same look she received from everyone in the Western Capital. Their former landlady had never seen her full face before she left. Uncle Smooth now clearly did regard her as an ordinary and normal girl, for there was no surprise or pity in his eyes. He treated her as her parents did, and so she soon forgot that she was supposed to be the most hideous-looking girl in the world.

During the time when Smooth's elder brother was being cared for, Lily would lend a hand with the cooking, washing terry cloths and bed sheets, and many other chores. And yet she never entered the sickroom lest she terrify the patient.

Lily fed the calling insects that Uncle Smooth raised, she cleaned and swept upstairs and downstairs daily. Frenetic as this life turned out to be, she still had the urge to sing and giggle. Laurel had heard from her husband that shifting stages was a tough lot, though she had underestimated the weight of his words. Folks in her village claimed that the three hardest professions were rowing boats, forging iron and making tofu. From what she had observed, these hardships were slight compared with Big Hook's labour. For starters, stage shifters had to work around the clock, insensible to day and night. Besides which, the toil was heavy, with none of the iron boxes containing lights, rubber-coated wires, copper wares and costumes, weighing less than fifty kilos. A hundred kilos was not rare either. In addition, they had to scale heights and depths.

Laurel herself was allocated the job of clearing up the costumes and props with Third Skin, which was relatively light and straightforward work. Big Hook had it far harder, for he almost always had to take the lead and shoulder the heaviest boxes. Once, she saw him nearly tumble off the ladder while he was lifting two moving lights. Laurel had assumed that as the boss, Smooth might take matters easy. Quite the opposite. He did no less than anyone else. In spite of being in his fifties, he, like Big Hook, climbed the lighting tower with one box on his back and another in his hand. His legs trembled mid-air and Zhou watched from below with her heart in her throat.

The crux of the situation was that it was not easy to wait on others. The director, the head of the lighting division, the scenery designers and all types would scold and swear at people. Smooth was basically like a vegetable for the pot. Whether he was cubed or cut into rounds was at the whim of his superiors. Or, as country folk would say, the job was lowly and a bitch.

Certain moments were heartening. When the stage shifting wound on into the second half of the night and co-workers went to take a rest, the labourers who took on the heaviest duties became garrulous. For one thing, they had many feelings bottled up and needed an outlet. Also, the joking helped to chivvy them on so they wouldn't nod off while working.

Laurel couldn't attune her ears to the workplace humour at first. As Big Hook had been away from home for many years, she usually refrained from joking with men. If a woman in the village flashed a gleeful face to a ruffian, they could easily take liberties and be unabashed about reaching out a greedy hand. Here, though, she showed no irritation at funny remarks and felt protected by having Big Hook to hand. As time wore on and the jokes grew bluer, she let herself unwind. She even learned why her husband was nicknamed "Big Hook". Early in their marriage, fellow villagers would address him as such and she came over rather embarrassed. Having no basis for comparison, she asked him if this was true. He explained that he dwarfed every other guy in the village, in some cases his was twice as large as theirs. Laurel was unsure how this nickname had made its way over here, since she heard them call him that name from the minute she joined the team. She cursed her husband for being so brazen and nattering about their private business. Big Hook told her how in the summer they all slept in the same place and it was too hot to wear a stitch. Was he supposed to tuck his monster manhood between his thighs so others would not gossip about it? As Laurel became familiar with everyone, they began to joke with her about his prize asset. At the start, she was coy and tried to recoil from the conversation, but later on she let it go. On top of that, she was in a rather buoyant mood recently, so she could afford to act brassily around them and soak up their filth.

For example, Monkey once cracked a joke. "How lucky my

sister-in-law is," he observed. "You've had a bite of the best thing in the human world."

"If you're game, I can let you have a bite of it too," she replied.

Her answer choked Monkey senseless.

Mound came over to harass her as well. "Hey, sister-in-law," he said. "We tried to measure Brother Big Hook's todger with a length of rattan. It was as long as five-and-a-half matchsticks, but I heard when you measure it, it's seven-and-a-half. What's going on?"

"It's just like your head," she quipped back in a trice. "The hat you wear in winter won't fit in summer. It grows with the heat and shrinks with the cold."

Big Hook listened, beaming all along. Occasionally, he would nag at his wife, though it was hard to tell whether this was out of admiration or complaint. "You see what a humorous piece of shit you are!" he would say.

Smooth would smile with joy too, but never utter a word. Laurel was more than ten years his junior, and as she was also his tenant, it was improper to joke with her.

One day when they were working late into the night, the bawdy jests about Laurel began to fly again. She lashed back with remarks that were pricklier, spicier and sexier. Everybody fell to the floor laughing. While they were choking to regain their breath, the crew wanted to see how Big Hook reacted. They found him sprawled on the ground motionless.

"Playing dead!" Mound shouted. He moved forward and touched him. His body was sweating all over while his feet and hands were as cold as ice.

"Brother Big Hook!" Mound shouted.

Everyone gathered round. He was deathly unconscious, and Laurel herself was so startled that she collapsed too. Luckily, as Smooth was experienced at waiting on very sick patients, he knew he should pinch Big Hook's philtrum and call out his name at the top of his voice. Soon he came to, unsure as to what had happened. Smooth said that it was better to send him to the hospital, yet he insisted he was fine and he'd just dozed off momentarily. Laurel Zhou agreed with Smooth, but Big Hook rose and paced a few steps, saying they were overreacting and he was just fine. As he was fine, there was no need to get the hospital involved. Smooth exempted him from heavy work and told him to oversee others as they hung up lights and painted curtains.

Not long after this incident, the Shaanxi Opera Troupe received word that they would go to Beijing. *Peach Blossom Cheeks* had been selected as one of the highlights of national opera. The scale of the stage shifting was intimidating, and a number of separate productions had been chosen for the gala. This meant that the schedule for assembling and dismantling the stage was extremely tight. It had to be completed in a day and two nights. If the troupe hired temporary hands in Beijing, they might cause a delay since they were not familiar with the set-up and could turn out to be difficult to deploy. At last, the troupe reached the decision that Smooth should accompany them with ten strong and able hands.

This was the rarest of opportunities for Smooth and his associates. Previously, the troupe had travelled to Shanghai for a performance, and Smooth had suggested to Chief Qu that several of his team accompany them there. If the in-house designers had their duties extended to include shifting stages, the oxen might not pull an equal load to the horses, so to speak. There was the real potential for matters to run awry. Those arty types would probably be too busy window shopping to take the heavy work seriously. Likely, they would act as if they were stubborn oxen and refuse to budge because they were used to carthorses doing all the legwork.

On that occasion, Smooth even boasted his men were willing to go for free, simply because they wanted to do the best job for the sake of Chief Qu. The chief was having none of it. Scarce as the chances of working in Shanghai were, it was impossible for him to take temping stage shifters like them in lieu of the permanent staff. This time, though, the situation was different. Doing battle on the most adverse of slopes, they needed the reinforcement of Smooth and his men. Director Jin was unwavering on this point, so it was agreed.

Smooth enumerated the merits of his team again and again before selecting ten for Beijing. He was reluctant to bring Big Hook because his funny turn left him shaken. Nonetheless, Big Hook was bent on going and knew the job depended on him. Smooth relented.

In the middle of the night, Laurel Zhou came to see off Big Hook and Smooth after they had loaded the trucks and were ready to leave the Western Capital. Her eyes teemed with tears. "Brother Smooth," she pleaded. "I'm afraid there's something wrong with him that hasn't been found out. He's so stubborn and won't get himself examined. I'm begging you to look out for him." She repeated these sentiments several times.

"Try to stay calm. There'll be no heavy graft for him," replied Smooth.

As they were sitting in the driver's cab, Smooth could make out Laurel Zhou in the rear-view mirror. She was tailing the truck and even broke into a sprint.

72

Smooth was indeed stoked up, and Big Hook too. They had never been to Beijing before, let alone to the national highlights gala. In the words of Chief Qu, they were "presenting a gift to the people of the nation's capital on behalf of their kindred in the Western Capital". Should face be lost in the process, the resultant shame would be monumental. Smooth knew how keenly that burden rested upon him.

There were more than 160 members in the group, and the names of Smooth and his assistants were listed in the brochure. They were categorised in a special way as "Stage Design Team Two". Smooth naturally headed the crew with Big Hook chosen as his deputy, much to Monkey's annoyance. In front of Mound and Third Skin, Monkey complained that in that case, they should leave Big Hook to do all the shifting by himself.

Most of the staff of the troupe travelled by train. Smooth and his men were supposed to escort the four Cummins trucks to Beijing. Taxing as this was, they were content to take in more of the scenery. Their route would take them through various provinces.

Half the night had passed by the time they departed the Western Capital. Smooth, Big Hook and Monkey all boarded the same truck. There were two rows of seats in the driver's cab. Three people could sit at the front, including the driver, and should one of them wish to take a nap, there was room on the row behind. Smooth encouraged Big Hook to lay down as soon as they were out of the city, for he worried about his health.

The trucks rumbled along sluggishly. Quite apart from the

frequent traffic jams, haulage vehicles were not permitted to enter urban districts. Beyond the highways, there were only fields and monotonous torrents of vehicles. Their enthusiasm for the scenery fizzled out.

The previous night when they were loading the trucks, Iron Kou opined, "This is like a publicly funded junket. Have none of you ten ever been to the capital?" They looked at each other and shook their heads. "Each of you will be given eighty yuan a day as food allowance," he added. "On the way, you can take in the views. There's another fifty yuan for escorting the gear on top of the stage-shifting salary. Has there ever been such a good thing under the heavens? This is what people call having your cake and eating it."

All of them expressed satisfaction with the deal. On the road, though, most of the time all they could see were the signs notifying motorists that it was fifteen kilometres, fifty kilometres or even a hundred and fifty kilometres to such-and-such a place. Still, they had set out on a long-distance road trip and could at least boast that they had travelled through other provinces.

The first night, they rested on the border between Henan and Hebei. It was already past 10 pm when they arrived, and Smooth couldn't make out their exact location. He only heard a driver give the name of the place as "Handan". He recalled that in primary school he had learned an idiom that went, "Learn to walk like the people of Handan." Third Skin was so excited that he unpacked the origins of the phrase for everyone.

The drivers had a fixed place to eat and rest. Smooth took everyone to get some supper from the stalls at a night market. Beforehand, he called Chief Qu to issue an update. The four trucks and ten personnel in Stage Design Team Two had arrived safely in Handan, where they would stay overnight. He reassured the chief again and again that he would deliver the trucks and their occupants intact to Beijing.

No matter whether they were sitting in the truck, eating or resting, Smooth paid particular attention to Big Hook's well-being. He experienced no twinges or sensations of discomfort, and each of Smooth's enquiries received the response that he was fine. The others made jokes by addressing him as the "Head of the Hookers". Mound said that "Deputy Group Head" or "Group Deputy Head" had a better ring to it because the former made them sound like a pack of rent boys. Monkey proposed "Deputy Hook" and this version stuck. However people chose to address him, Big Hook never stopped beaming. He appeared like he had become a different person after his first fainting fit. He was less talkative, though still liked to keep company with others and was even rather conciliatory towards Monkey, who typically directed his jibes at him. Knowing he was fond of barbecue, Big Hook gave him a few of his twenty skewers.

It was so hot that they might as well have been in an alley full of food steamers. After sitting in the truck for a whole day, their buttocks developed heat rash. Thankfully, Smooth had brought some of the talcum powder he applied to his piles. Following their nightly shower, he asked each of them if they wanted a dab. They then came over cool and cosy down there.

Smooth arranged for Big Hook to sleep in the same room as him. He woke up a few times to monitor his condition. The sound of his thunderous snoring was reassuring and he could close his eyes again.

The next morning, he intended to check on Big Hook once more, but his bed was empty. He dashed out in a hurry, fearful that something bad had befallen him.

Big Hook was to be found inspecting the vehicles. He claimed to have had a dream that night in which the four truckloads of settings were stolen and the performance floundered. The expressions of everyone in the troupe were crumpled with anger for they had truly lost face for the people of the Western Capital. On returning to the city, their troupe was disbanded and they ended up being exiled to their hometowns, banned from ever returning. Their stage-shifting days were done. Crucially, there was no means of funding the corrective surgery, and his wife and daughter cried in desperation. Their misery frightened him awake.

Smooth patted his thigh. "This is a good omen, I guess," he said. "The reality often runs counter to what we see in our dreams. It means our performance will be a sure-fire triumph. Didn't you know that?"

They set off after breakfast. Smooth let Big Hook lie behind, occasionally changing places with Third Skin. He himself remained at the front, purposefully allowing Big Hook all the leisure he needed. Part of him was anxious that his friend would be stricken down again. At the same time, he hoped that he might be properly rested in order that he was fit and capable, so as to be able to direct the other stage shifters in commanding tones. To be honest, his haemorrhoids were beginning to tingle. Whenever Big Hook invited him to take a rest, he insisted that he was too busy drinking in the landscape outside. He duly dozed on his seat just like a snapping bug.

Eventually, dusk found them in Beijing. The driver told them that they had arrived. By law, they were compelled to wait in the parking lot outside the fifth ring road because heavy vehicles could only enter the downtown area after midnight.

They sat there in the gigantic car park and waited for that time to come.

In spite of their exhaustion, everyone was somewhat giddy. They had reached the national capital. Big Hook was so fired up that he began to play Chinese chess with Monkey and Mound beneath a street lamp. The chess set was his, and they often whipped it out for a few games in the slack times during stage-shifting jobs.

Smooth passed on the news of their arrival to Iron Kou, and said that the four trucks and staff of Stage Design Team Two were now waiting in the car park outside the fifth ring road. He was displeased not to hear a single word of response. They had accomplished a brilliant feat, so how could he not even offer a reply? On second thoughts, why had he reported the news to him? It was Smooth who was acting humbly and with servility. He shouldn't take any notice of Kou, being content just to be able to lead his crew here without having to encounter his mug. Thinking of this, he straightened his backbone.

Smooth only now realised that he was experiencing full-blown haemorrhoids. He reasoned that come what may, he must have the operation on their return. Smooth headed for the washroom, where he spread some talcum powder on his posterior. He came back and advised everyone to take forty winks. Once they entered the city, they would have to tussle hard.

Seasoned as they were, they knew they needed to "chew a sleep". They always used this phrase when they were in need of a brief, refreshing doze. They spat out the word "chew" through gritted teeth as if readying themselves to gnaw on tasty pig's trotters or beef tendons.

Two accessories were obligatory during those years of shifting stages: a winter overcoat and a sleeping mat for summer. The mat was a one-foot-wide tube that they could unroll, spread out on the ground and lie down upon whenever and wherever they found themselves. Huge as the car park was, the space to sleep was decidedly limited. Vehicles whizzed by incessantly and it was hard to avoid them standing up, let alone on one's back. The best and safest spots were beneath the trucks. Of course, other people's lorries were off limits since one had no idea when they might gird into motion. Their own four Cummins trucks had spacious underbellies, and they determined the time of departure themselves. So they all probed around under there and savoured the most splendid "chew" of their lives. On finding that they were embracing this rather too enthusiastically, Smooth crawled out from below and decided to lean against the driver's door as he napped. That eliminated the risk of the driver coming back and starting the ignition without warning. He had to prevent his brothers from being crushed into meat patties.

Around half past midnight, Smooth received the instruction from the advance party: "You may enter the city now." Their excitement was rekindled.

Smooth called the drivers over. As the engines of the four trucks began to roar, he waved his hand solemnly, like the great commander in a movie. "Charge!" he ordered.

And so, Stage Design Team Two bringing *Peach Blossom Cheeks* over from the Western Capital marched into the national capital, confident under the personal leadership of Smooth Diao.

73

ALL WAS NOT SO SPLENDIDLY BRIGHT as they had anticipated. As they crept into the heart of the capital, it seemed to be in hibernation. Despite the blaze of streetlights and the occasional twinkling of neon from a hoarding, the traffic was sparse and pedestrians few. The buildings nestled in the tranquillity of their shadows. After taking seven or eight turns and finding the theatre, they came across a team of stagehands dismantling a platform. More than one Cummins truck was parked by the stage door, forcing them to wait in their vehicle on the roadside.

Smooth and his crew had encountered their peers and were curious to inspect this operation. To their surprise, two men carrying pieces of set barred them from entering.

"What are you doing here? What business do you have?" quizzed one of the strangers.

On hearing his clipped Mandarin, Smooth attempted to affect a more standard pronunciation. "We've come to take over the stage," he said haltingly. "We're the crew from the Western Capital working on *Peach Blossom Cheeks*."

"What crew? What crew?"

"The crew from *Peach Blossom Cheeks*," Smooth repeated.

The other fellow explained the meaning of the title to his pal. "It means that somebody's face is flushed like a peach."

"Why not call it *Chinese Rose Cheeks*?" he retorted. "The rose is the emblem of Beijing City."

The first man assumed a more amiable tone and asked, "Do you need a stage shifting?"

"No," replied Smooth. "We've brought our own shifters."

From then on, the two hands appeared oblivious to Smooth and his men, but curtly blocked the way once they tried to enter to the set. "You think you're guards from Zhongnanhai?" he asked. "Think you can breeze about and prod wherever you like? This is the capital city, and you should know the rules. The troupe from Tianjin are still here. What are you after?"

"We just thought we could stroll about and see what we're up against."

"Who are you? What are you?" The man's face was stony stern.

"He's our leader, our head," interjected Mound. "We just want to check out the stage."

"What? What did you say? A leader? A head? How dare you put on such airs in Beijing! Leader? Head? What rank? In this theatre, you can stick out your hand and snag three government ministers in a single evening. You have the nerve to claim you're somebody. Just sling your hook and find some place to sit and wait."

Smooth and his companions were put in an uneasy spot.

"Dog's bollocks!" shrieked Mound. "Even stage shifters in Beijing speak proper Mandarin."

"You fucking cretin," cursed Monkey. "Mandarin is the local language here. You expect them to talk in Shaanxi dialect?"

"I can follow the Mandarin they speak on the TV news," confessed Mound with a smile. "But them. They talk like they've rammed a date stone in their mouths and can't move their tongues."

"We're the outsiders here," hissed Smooth. "Just keep your pussy traps closed and don't cause trouble."

They had been supposed to take over the stage at 2 am, though the previous troupe had still not finished dismantling their set. The update from the office estimated that it might drag for on another couple of hours. Smooth told his men to take a rest where they were. The completion time was later revised to 4.30 am. In actual fact it was 5 am before the site was theirs.

Until that point, they had not been aware that the theatre was a clubhouse attached to a factory. Although better suited for hosting conventions, once some challenges had been overcome, it could function as a theatre space.

Iron Kou, who appeared at this moment, cursed the office staff at their troupe. When they came over a month ago to draw lots, they had managed to select this godawful hole. Their hands must have been slathered in night soil.

The stage was substandard and worn. On top of that, the previous troupe had overrun their allocated shifting deadline, making the task more daunting.

Smooth and his team began to offload the truck at 5.30 am. By the time the most basic equipment had been brought out, it was already 8 am. The dozens of additional personnel sent by the troupe did not appear at the theatre until this time, leaving all the key components in the hands of Smooth's men. He called them all over for a pep talk, reminding them that nobody should slacken or blunder when the crucial moment came. He used a line he had often heard in old movies: "Cometh the hour, cometh the man."

What gave Smooth the greatest cause for worry was Big Hook's health. He had been watching him intently all the way here without finding anything obviously amiss. Now that the toughest contest had begun, he reminded Big Hook not to strain himself too much and to think carefully about his body. To begin with, he arranged some lighter chores for him, though he refused them, saying that this was the type of stuff that should be left to Third Skin and women. He had a penchant for working high above the ground, and Monkey loved to goad him into competing head-to-head. Since Big Hook was unwilling to yield, he chose to carry the lights up to the gantry on the second tier. Smooth monitored everything he did and encouraged Mound to do likewise.

Even though there were dozens of lights around the venue, most of them were domestic bulbs used for when meetings were held. Maestro Ding inspected them and declared that none were usable and they must rely on those they had brought along themselves. That amounted to nearly 300, all of which now needed to be installed. The task was epic, and Smooth and the team faced it with gritted teeth, knowing full well that this was a national-level contest. As the stage lacked professional-standard equipment, they had to upgrade everything connected with the set and its illumination. The professional staff in the stage design section found the work a chore. Smooth prodded his crew on as best he could.

Around 10 am, Chief Qu, Director Jin and the others arrived by train. They hastened over to inspect the stage assembly. Iron Kou reported that the whole affair was sub-par and there was no prospect of setting the stage in time, let alone putting on a competitive performance the following evening. The chief then called out for Smooth.

In fact, Smooth had already descended from the front light slot when his two superiors arrived. He did not go towards them because he saw Kou was giving his evaluation. His former sycophancy had abandoned him and he was not about to apply his warm face to anybody's cold arse cheek. This was now his resolution and his backbone would remain proud as a bolt as long as he was pursuing the task at hand. The problem was that as Qu was calling out his name, he needed to quicken his step and respond, for the chief had always been considerate towards him. Smooth still wore his blue overcoat of old, which had become adhered to his clammy chest and back. This was, as he put it, their costume. By keeping the coat on, he protected his flesh from possible cuts and snags on turned edges or bent frames, be they iron or wood.

"Thank you for your hard work, Smooth," commended Chief Qu.

"I'm just a labouring hand," he demurred. "How could I hold myself up as more industrious than Chief Qu or Director Jin? You've travelled on the train through the night and came here in person as soon as you got to the city." Right then, he felt a pang of regret, for he had involuntarily slipped into flattery.

Director Jin smiled and patted him on the shoulder. "Hey Smooth, don't kiss my backside," she said with candour. "Tell me, can you finish the set on time?"

Smooth had intended to say something terse to display his resolve. On noticing how Iron Kou was staring, he honeyed his words. "Director Kou must have told you this job is a hard call. Fair enough, this place would do fine for an evening party. As for an opera, especially Director Jin's masterpiece, the obstacles just pile up."

The short-fused director addressed him pointedly. "Well, no more of this nagging. Tell me straight. Can you hand the stage over to me tomorrow morning for the rehearsal at eight or not?"

"Depends on what sort of finish you want. If you want something refined and delicate, I'm afraid there's not a chance."

Before Smooth could complete his words, Iron Kou butted in. "It's not an issue of being refined or delicate. We can't hope to achieve even the barest outline of a set."

Director Jin fixed her eyes on Smooth and asked, "Can it be done or not, Smooth? You tell me. It's impossible to alter the venue now, and withdrawing from the contest is out of the question. This all rests on when you can hand the stage to us."

Smooth was in no frame of mind to enrage Iron Kou, though was keen not to let Qu and Jin down as they had arranged for his team to be here. As Director Jin had fingered him, he should take the rap for them.

"Smooth, this time your crew was brought over especially," the chief reminded him. "The time is indeed limited and the job a burden. Had we thought it would be a doddle, we'd have relied on the in-house design team to handle it. You're an old hand. One quick look at the stage is enough for you to estimate how long it will take. Give the director a definite answer. When can you hand over the stage? This affects the entire troupe."

Smooth paid no notice to how Iron Kou was winking at him. With an expression that seemed to say he was making a military pledge, he vowed, "Give me twenty-hour hours. We're sure to be finished this time tomorrow."

Director Jin was the first to clap in response. "There's Smooth for you. Old Qu, if the performance is a hit this time, the top prize should go to him."

"Top prize or not," said Smooth, "as long as we can escape a rollocking from Director Jin, the Buddha has blessed us."

Smooth saw how Iron Kou was shooting him the flintiest of stares. He knew that Kou was at odds with the office of the troupe and was trying to bring embarrassment upon them. Furthermore, if he focused merely on the difficulties entailed in shifting stages, the chief and the director would be compelled to flatter him. Then, Iron Kou could showcase his aptitude for working under pressure. But unexpectedly, Chief Qu and Director Jin just talked with Smooth, coaxing him into this pledge and giving him the kudos. All of that was naturally to Kou's annoyance.

After the pair left, Iron Kou immediately flared up. "Smooth Diao, what a shitty prick you are," he fumed. "A shabby stage shifter thinks he's somebody now. Toadying, flattering and backbiting in front of the leaders. Such a no-good leech! Be careful your waist doesn't give way. What a creature! Boasting like that. Damn your mother! Can you pull it off in twenty-four hours? You son of a bitch. Could you do it alone? If you can't hand the stage over in twenty-four hours, I'll break your fucking dog legs!"

Smooth wanted to lash out. He swore that he wouldn't grovel around at work like he was anybody's grandson, not least for Iron Kou. He even thought that if the bastard tried to bully him again, he would punch him in the mouth in front of the whole troupe. For the time being, he resolved to restrain himself. After all, they were in a foreign land, and the capital city, to boot. Those in charge of the theatre had him in their sights and he should be sensitive as to their reputation and influence. He then tried remaining patient as a strategy.

"Director Kou, please don't curse me any more," he said. "I'm just a hired hand. I've come to help do what's best for the troupe. I'm no expert recruited from outside. Just a human being. We're in a tight fix. Only twenty-four hours to spare. Even if it is remotely possible, how do we help ourselves by saying it's impossible? I want more time, too. One more day would mean more money for us. But that's beyond our control. If you think I've been a blabbermouth, there's no need for us to speed up the process. As long as you can explain what has happened to Chief Qu and Director Jin, those of us who put in the legwork can simply leave and give up on the money."

Since Smooth had been so firm and brusque, he didn't dare risk the deadlock. If matters really reached an impasse, he couldn't afford to shoulder the blame. He resorted to cursing once again. "Hey Smooth, given you're so capable, try peeling a spring onion with a single finger. You speed up. If you can't hand over the stage within twenty-four hours, I'll have no need to bust your legs. Somebody else will do it."

Smooth wasn't prepared to argue with him, so he told Big Hook, Monkey, Mound, Third Skin and the others separately that they should speed up with what they were doing. All of them gave him their guarantee in a hushed voice: "Rest assured, they'll be no problem on my part."

Smooth's greatest source of consolation lay in his team members. Usually, there would be quarrels and friction among them. There might even be full-blown clashes. And yet, when it came to consequential events, there was absolute clarity. The boss's words may have lacked the grandeur of an emperor in an opera, yet every syllable carried weight, and none of his men would dare transgress order and rank. Most particularly in the rushed and critical moments, none of them dared be the one to blunder. For a dozen or more years, the secret of Smooth's leadership resided in adhering to the same three points. The first was to assume the lead, talk less, command less, and take on whatever was heavy and hard. When others faltered or fell short, he would step in and redo it. After a few rounds of correction like that, nobody dared let standards slip. The second point was to be magnanimous and take others as his brothers. If any of them needed help in matters large or small, he was sure to gird himself in their aid. Even a headache or bout of fever warranted his solicitude, and he was not averse to supplying a cooling ice lolly, a handful of painkillers, a marinated pork bun or talcum powder if somebody's backside had prickly heat rash. These little caring gestures were like the melon seeds they cracked with their teeth – not sufficient to fill their bellies, but welcome enough to cheer their hearts. The third was to avoid being greedy. As the head of the group, he was entitled to a slightly bigger cut, though his share was gleaned by racking up extra mileage and through extraordinary measures. Were he to reward himself indiscriminately, that would be tantamount to scratching welts in his blood brothers' backs with his money-grubbing claw. This they simply wouldn't tolerate.

Stage-shifting jobs were plentiful in the Western Capital. Try as the selfish, grasping and ruthless might to establish their own outfit, they would founder after just one or two assignments. At crucial junctures, Smooth was the one who brought cohesion and supplied the centripetal power to his team. Chief Qu and Director Jin were fully conscious of these merits and so would turn to him in their most desperate hours. He knew the degree of responsibility that lay on his shoulders, but would not let it show in his expression. He only accelerated his pace, carrying two lights to the ceiling slot at a time, whereas ordinarily he would take one. Right now, he was not simply shifting lights. He had a coil of cable draped around his neck, causing his legs to tremble as he climbed the ladder. On seeing his determination, all his brothers redoubled their efforts.

Big Hook was transporting lights to the second gantry on the ceiling. These were all automated lamps, some of them weighing fifty kilos apiece. Together with the light on his back, he too wore a necklace of cable and was gripping a roll of iron wire in his mouth. Smooth warned Mound to pay more attention to him. Big Hook responded that there was absolutely nothing out of whack with him, and he should be mindful of his own ailment down below.

For reasons unknown to himself, Big Hook was truly exhilarated by the present task. He not only channelled more brawn into his work, but maintained his interest in jousting tongues with Monkey. For his part, Monkey had scaled a six-metre-high ladder, and now had his legs clamped tightly around a steel pole so he could fix the ceiling lights.

"Monkey, are you pole dancing?" Big Hook shouted from the second gantry.

"Just putting on a show for Chief Hook."

"Did you lash the pole with your tail or with your todger? If it was your todger, you'd best wrap it round a few more times so it doesn't slide off."

This made everyone roar with laughter.

"If I had Chief Hook's asset, I'd tether it to the beam and swing around nonstop."

The laughter was now more bilious. The staff from the troupe didn't know the in-joke about Big Hook, so the babbling Mound filled them in. From then on, everybody at the stage called him "Chief Hook" and referred to Smooth's team as "the Gang of Hookers".

The in-house staff were less than happy at the outset. They followed Iron Kou's example by calling the office workers a waste of space and blaming them for having made a shower of drawing lots. Or else, they nagged about the leading players jetting in or being pampered on the soft sleeper, while their own dormitory was a toilet. They all said that Chief Qu had spoiled those folks. It might be better if they roosted on the Sichuan pepper tree where they could gorge themselves to death on the tangiest and most delicious corns. Some commented that the leading lights were the only ones set to reap any benefits from victory in the competition. They were eligible to receive prize money, a raise in pay and other perks. All of them already had senior professional titles, owned smart apartments and would need a train to carry all their certificates of merit. What did the rest of them have? They would always be the potatoes, sweet potatoes and rough cuts of radish used for padding out the "steamed bowls" beneath the glistening meat. Under such incommodious conditions, they had built them a stage to perform on, helped them to win a corsage and applause. These grafters would still be shown base ingratitude, belittled and treated as if they were unworthy to lace their shoes. What had the in-house team gained? What were they toiling for? A number of the agitators became more enervated and finally just sprawled out on the carpet and said they were on strike.

Smooth's crew, however, couldn't down tools and wouldn't even spare the breath to vent their longstanding grievances.

Mound had a big mouth. As he carried a newly imported spotlight up the stairs, he was tired and hoary, yet still hectored his leader, firing off questions like, "Hey, Brother Smooth, what are we actually working for here?"

"For your mother's pussy. Look sharp and get back to it!"

74

THE SUMMER IN BEIJING seemed hotter than that in the Western Capital. The lack of air-conditioning made the theatre positively kiln-like. Before noon, more than forty personnel came along, all of them near naked with a wet towel slung over their shoulder. At the beginning, there was much gassing and prattling, which soon subsided as everyone became fully occupied.

The "nit pickers" in the troupe, who liked to make cynical remarks and were normally only content to work after a decent whinge, knuckled down rather well. Their customary fare was to jabber sarcastically, especially about the leaders. Leaders, high or low, were the prey for their criticism, with Chief Qu being the most unfortunate. It appeared to be a custom, a fashion or an ingrained trait to berate those in authority. It was as if somebody who didn't dare criticise the leaders lacked talent, was incapable or maybe gutless. After some repackaging, the lyrics from traditional operas that were sung by expostulating officials and imperial censors became their cannonballs. Fortunately, the victims of their tongues had grown accustomed to this carping manner and style. On the other side, the backbiters were stirring for the sake of stirring. As long as their diatribes were not discomfiting to the leaders, and both excited laughter in the team and catharsis in the stirrer, a kind of equilibrium was achieved. The daily routine would continue unimpeded.

When Smooth and his ten titans, each tasked with one field, found themselves at zero hour and were working ardently, they acquired this foible too. On the stage, there was a sashaying rumpus of slick and bare backs, with not one human voice to be heard among the clang of lights, props, settings and pliers. Soon, a fairly formal outline took shape on the empty platform. Even the theatre managers lauded them as "a hardy gang from the northwest who could brook the stiffest adversity". On such a scruffy stage and in such a tight window, they had made the preposterous feasible. No wonder Li Zicheng, the leader of a peasant rebellion who became emperor, was born in their part of the country.

Chief Qu turned up after 1 am and was taken aback that the stage shifting had proceeded so rapidly. In his estimation, the set ought to have still been a pig's breakfast. To have had even half of the lights installed by now would have been a feat. To his surprise, the hanging fixtures were all in situ. The viewing screen had been tied to the battens, and even the greater platform was now being assembled. His faith in the men themselves was firmly restored.

Nevertheless, an odd niggle or two persisted in his chest. He couldn't quite conceive how the following evening's performance could arrive on track.

Even then, he had not envisioned the sheer plethora of hurdles this time. Not only was the venue seedy, but the living quarters were substandard. When the staff members from the troupe reached the hotel, the previous occupants of the rooms had not yet checked out, leaving sixty of them waiting until 2 pm before they had accommodation. Those concerned were deeply displeased, though the troupe had been given no means by which to pre-book the rooms at a discount the previous day. Also, as their train had arrived so early that morning, it was tricky to execute everything in succession. The last member did not check in until 2.10 pm.

Owing to the limited budget, there was no central heating, and each room relied on its own air conditioning unit. In half of them, the machine could be heard gasping away without any soothing breath to accompany it. The hotel had supplied some aged electric fans to solve the dilemma, only the heat their rotors generated intensified the stifling conditions, leaving a few of the leading players fearing for their throats. And so Director Jin advised that special concern be paid to the actors and actresses with singing roles.

The male and female protagonists had come the previous day,

causing Chief Qu to recommend that the office arrange for them to be put up in a better grade of establishment. This morning, when the supporting actors got to the hotel, they nagged about its condition and the fact that they couldn't check in immediately. The chief then had to direct the office to upgrade them as well. As the finance officer fumed over the figures, Qu decided to borrow a pet phrase from Smooth. "Our ox has fallen down the well," he said, "so what's the point of scrabbling to grab a hair from its tail?"

In the opera field, the vocals and bearing of the actors held the greatest sway over audiences. If the players were hoarse or mute or downcast, even the best-planned of performances would end in catastrophe. No matter who objected, they must give the highest consideration to keeping the actors ebullient. Those players who ate the choicest fare had earned their privilege in this circle. Having been head for several years, Chief Qu espoused the philosophy of gently kneading the stars' bodies so they were "cosseted to sleep". This had earned him a myriad of nicknames such as "Chancellor Li Hongzhang", "Soft-Boned Qu", "Calcium-Deficient Qu", "Snapping Bug" and "Old Amah". In spite of all the undesirable tags he accrued, he still had to gently coax particular people. Under the heavens, his stood out as a special profession. If you couldn't handle the business of revering actors as you would your "grandparents", then they would bring you such regret that you had no more tears to shed.

However, no sooner had the problems of the actors been settled, then someone from the band, say, would raise objections. Today, the timpanist demanded that his room be upgraded too, for in his mind he played a role in the opera as vital as the conductor himself. Overseas, a conductor would be entitled to his own suite backstage and savour superior treatment to the leading actors. Were there to be no suite available, the least he could expect was to not share a bedroom and be given a fully functional air conditioner. Was this not a demand too far? "No, we'll sort it out for you at once," came the reply. Next, the banhu fiddle player and the first violinist weighed in to explain why they too deserved to be upgraded. Chief Qu complied with these "grandpas" of his. It must have been 8 pm before every last demand had been satisfied individually. Afterwards, the members of the office led him to pay a visit to the senior and veteran experts who had been supporting the troupe for years. He presented them with invitation cards and tickets, and asked them to be guests of honour at the following night's performance.

Once everything had been settled, Chief Qu was ready to check the stage. Without warning, Director Jin called him on the phone and said, "Old Qu, come here right now, I can't cope with your 'grandpa' and 'grandma' any more." It turned out that the director had arranged an evening consultation with the leading actor and actress, hoping to fine-tune their artistry. She allowed the situation to veer out of control so it became a slanging match. He had to hasten over there.

When Chief Qu appeared at the hotel, the two players were sparring away over whose role had precedence.

The germ of the disagreement was spawned in the first rehearsal. Under normal circumstances, it should have been Cui Hu who was the de facto protagonist. With a little scrutiny, it became evident that the playwright had penned more lines for Peach Blossom, thereby plumping out her role. By the opening run-through of the song lyrics, there were mutterings among the crew about who had top billing. At first, the writer was coy and didn't issue a character list. He merely reflected that the opera was in development, and whoever could muster the mightier singing and acting performance should be considered the principal on the stage.

Matters further unfolded during the rehearsal. Certain busybodies goaded the male lead and in other instances the female lead, almost bringing about a theatrical miscarriage. Even though neither player mentioned their grievance out loud, the chief and the director were well aware what sore spots were being nurtured. At the "troika" rehearsal, the leading actor had been put on an IV drip early in the morning and brazened out his condition. In the midst of this, Chief Qu had whispered something in his ear and the young man promptly removed the needle from his arm. Exactly what he had said was a point of much speculation. Smooth even asked the chief about it, but was fobbed off with a grin. If there were secrets in the troupe, then this was surely the largest one of all. Were it to be disclosed, the rehearsal or performance would grind to a standstill in an instant. What he had, in fact, uttered was quite simple: "Having discussed it with Director Jin, both of you are joint leads. On the captions on the screen, though, the hero is the protagonist." With this timely sleight, he had alleviated the "sore spot".

However, that was not the end of the saga. Chief Qu had promised discreetly to resolve another difficulty for the female lead. She employed a babysitter, who had no dormitory bed in which to sleep. Flouting the official rules with a nod, the chief promised to arrange modest lodgings for the girl. In return, he persuaded her that the name of the hero should be given higher billing, even though they shared equal eminence in terms of the drama. He hoped that she would have regard towards the overall interests of the troupe and be prepared not to haggle over every trifle. In order to secure that single room, she assented without even having to nod or shake her head. Nonetheless, when they came to Beijing, the ranking of the leads was no longer small beer, but had escalated into a prize fight.

Usually, there would only be one first prize available for the protagonist in a single production, and the person in second place would be relegated. In addition, both actors attached extreme significance to receiving that certificate of merit, for it carried much credence both inside and outside the sphere of drama. As a result, their altercation was intractable and reconciliation hard to conceive. Chief Qu had been cock-a-hoop about being at last invited to Beijing. How could they dare imperil the occasion? Gauging from Director Jin's exasperation on the phone, the chief could tell that it would be far less straightforward than he thought.

Qu entered the hotel to find the director packing her belongings and preparing to return to the Western Capital. She said it was impossible to carry on, for she was not about to kowtow to anybody. Fame and acclaim had enveloped the hearts of those people like smoke until they were stained to the darkest hue. There was not one inch of room left for art in this fiasco. She announced that this was her farewell to art, and she would go back to selling braised pig intestines with flatbreads. Madame Jin cursed that art had been reduced to an old whore, utterly rancid with nothing tantalising about it. Art had reached its nadir and people must content themselves with ugliness. She was thus bidding adieu.

"Director Jin, just rest for now," the chief reassured her with a smile. "Get ready for tomorrow morning's rehearsal and let me settle things here."

He then arranged for some colleagues to keep her company and buy her a few snacks, while he took over as mediator.

Chief Qu spoke with both of them separately for more than an hour. The leading man demanded that the first eight lines of his antagonist's lyrics be expurgated. He claimed that they left him vexed and that he couldn't perform his own number effectively afterwards. He even forgot his words. In fact, those eight lines were one of the highlights of the production. The singing of each meter brought a euphoric response from the audience and this was what baited him so. Beyond that, he required that twelve lines of his that had been edited out must be restored. Unless they obeyed, he had no wish to "wait on" here. He was due for another IV shot and his throat was inflamed.

The heroine was receiving IV treatment in her room as well. She was emphatic that the top billing be hers, as out of the 382 lines of the libretto, 134 belonged to Peach Blossom compared with just 116 for Cui Hu. She counted again and again to determine that there were 28,146 words in the opera, with 9,425 assigned to her and seven words shy of 9,000 for him. Outnumbering the leading man in lines and words, she was the genuine protagonist.

"The plot of the opera was inspired by four lines of Cui Hu's poetry," the chief explained. "It's improper not to list the hero first."

"But the title is *Peach Blossom Cheeks*, not *Cui Hu's Cheeks*," the leading lady countered. "If her name is in the title, and she's not listed first, won't that confuse the audience?"

Now cornered, Chief Qu raised the promise of the room. That had been made on the condition that she would compromise.

She took him unawares by kicking back with, "I don't want it. I'll return that shabby hole when I get back, Old Qu. It's leaking. You're treating me like a beggar!"

Chief Qu cracked his knuckles as a means of displacing his anger. He succeeded in keeping a lid on his temper, and resorted instead to trying to convince her by using reason inflected with emotion. Whether his persuasion was as delicate as the spring breeze or meticulously measured, the two players would neither relinquish their terms nor entertain the notion of yielding.

Finally Chief Qu, or Qu Yangzheng to use his full name, blasted off for the first time in his life. His temper was so incendiary that he astounded even himself, smashing a teacup that belonged to the hotel. Different versions of his destructive gesture were bandied about. There were those who said he did it at the outset as a trigger, while others maintained it happened at the end. Yet others were sure it occurred somewhere in the middle of the exchange. Whatever the truth was, the cup was smashed into pieces. Another rumour held that Qu Yangzheng's hand was gashed in the process. A few days later, the office of the troupe did indeed pay out an extra sum. More than fifty yuan was debited for a replacement cup.

Several folk from the headquarters of the troupe had been eavesdropping in the corridor. All they could really make out were Chief Qu's final high-pitched words of reproach: "... go, go on with your troublemaking, all for the sake of a bit of personal fame and money. Go on with your troublemaking, regardless of anything and caring about nothing. But today, I, Qu Yangzheng, have stated my attitude clearly and frankly. As chief of the troupe, I have made my decision. First, not one word of the script will be altered. Second, as for the lyrics, no additions and no deletions. Third, as for the opera, everything is kept in its original form. Fourth, the rehearsal will begin at ten-thirty tomorrow morning, and nobody is allowed to turn up late or leave early. Fifth, the performance starts at seven-thirty, so everything must be perfect with the quality and quantity guaranteed. Of course, if you want to make a scene, you can do it boldly and in public. If you have the guts, you can go make a spectacle in Tiananmen Square. But I must be clear about the issue of gain and loss – the national team and our troupe comprises more than a hundred people, and you will be liable to pay every last cent of loss incurred. Besides, you will be severely punished. You don't believe me? Perhaps your employment will be terminated. Let's make the loss complete. Go ahead, waste those twenty years of your youth that you've used up, waste both your fame and finances. Make like the hens that fly away from the coop, leaving all the eggs broken. You're still fighting over the prize. I shall crush your rice bowls into dust. I, Qu Yangzheng, am absolutely ready to do what I've said. You all know that I've barely three hundred days left before retirement. Yes, Qu Yangzheng is about to bugger off. I've been trying to mediate differences at the cost of principles for years. I don't want to carry on and daren't carry on like this. If I, Qu Yangzheng, have to carry on, I'll led the troupe to its doom. It's up to you. Please yourselves."

After he was done, Qu Yangzheng left the room with his hands clasped behind his back. He never usually did this, but now he seemed to rely on body language to stress his authority and resolve.

Not long after his departure, the news reached Director Jin. "Old Qu," went the message she sent him back, "I hear at last you shat a brickbat."

After being driven into a corner and with people showing their strongest suits, contrary matters untangled themselves in no time. Chief Qu suddenly came over quite relaxed, infused with a briskness that he had never felt since taking charge of the troupe. Should the whole thing be a washout, they could simply call it a day, pack up and head home. In that case, he would be justified in discharging dozens of years of repressed spleen.

He went to the theatre and sat in the auditorium, his ravelled-up mind gradually regaining equilibrium when he saw how conscientious the set dressers were.

Iron Kou had been smoking outside the stage exit. Upon hearing the chief was there, he quickly stubbed out his cigarette and came over. Again, he reported the difficulties. Forty-three battens were required for the performance, but the theatre had thirty-five at most and two of them were broken and unusable. He moaned about how such a dive of a venue could exist in the grand, dignified capital of the nation. He complained that the guys in the troupe office didn't know how to conduct business. How could they have plumped for such a dreadful stage not capable of being dressed properly? On top of that, the battens were manually operated and seven of the set pieces couldn't be hung up. Chief Qu made no response and just asked where Smooth was to be found. Someone shouted in the direction of the ceiling light slot, "Smooth, your Uncle Qu is calling you."

All the people on the stage, though worn out, cackled.

A little later, Smooth appeared. He was wearing only shorts, having shed his blue overcoat. Perspiration was trailing down from every gulley, furrow and fold of his body. His legs, which he normally dragged behind him, now appeared even more of an encumbrance, as if someone had lassoed his heels and was tugging them hard from behind. On making eye contact, he became embarrassed and covered his exposed chest with his hands.

"General Manager Diao, remove your hands," one chap joked. "Chief Qu isn't bothered by your pancake breasts."

Even Chief Qu found this amusing.

Smooth walked over to the chief and realised that his hair looked like it had just been drenched in water. The sweat had scoured Smooth's dust-covered face into black and white stripes. On taking a closer look, there were fine, bloody scratches incised all over his face, arms, chest and legs. One of his toes was bandaged with toilet paper sodden red.

The chief asked him what the matter was.

"A toenail got torn loose when I was climbing just now," he replied in a remarkably light tone.

Qu's heart leapt, and he asked whether it was serious.

"Nope, only a cricked nail. I pressed it back down and tied it fast."

The chief wanted to inspect it but Smooth refused, again downplaying the injury.

"Seven settings still can't be hung. What should be done about them?" Chief Qu asked him. This time Smooth avoided looking at Iron Kou, for to pause and give credence to him would be counterproductive now. He thought that Qu had invested great trust in him and so he must tackle every tough nut in order to repay him. Maybe that was what was meant by the saying, "A gentleman will lay down his life for the sake of his patron."

"Chief Qu, be assured," he answered. "I know a way to deal with those seven settings. When all the lights are in position, Big Hook and I will give them our special attention, and not leave you wanting. This is a national-level competition, and I realise its significance. Sir, just go and have a rest. Tomorrow at ten-thirty, we'll be certain to hand the stage over to you."

"Smooth Diao, don't just give us some lip service," Iron Kou interjected. "None of your bravado. If you can't give us the stage at ten-thirty, Director Jin may well skin you alive."

Smooth bottled his anger and didn't respond.

"No more talking. Just see that it's done as Smooth said," concluded the chief.

Iron Kou looked at Smooth with a weird grimace. Smooth immediately turned his face to one side. After all, he wasn't so brave as to goad Kou into making a fool of himself. Chief Qu had given him his support in the sight of so many others. Now, he grasped the meaning of the saying, "Bearing a responsibility as weighty as Mount Tai".

The toe with the lost nail was swollen and it stung. Even though he was afraid to let it touch the ground, he nonetheless stamped that foot down hard. The stage gantry was the hottest, most humid zone. He dangled in that spot, which was considered the worst hazard of all.

Chief Qu chose to stay at the stage, for he felt greater comfort sitting there than returning to the hotel. In fact, whenever an important performance was in the offing, he would keep a nocturnal vigil at the theatre. In recent years, he had sensed the onset of old age and his diminishing stamina limited the number of late nights he felt he could take. Anyhow, tonight, he must stay among the company. Had he tarried at the hotel, melancholy would have set in. Irrespective of whether the performance could go ahead the next evening, the stage still had to be constructed first. For so long in his chosen career, he had attended a slew of opera galas. He was certain that having the stage finished to perfection was the best way to guard against mortal blows. Sometimes, a minor mishap could derail a performance. Picking faults in the presentation was one way that the pedantic could dismiss an otherwise inspiring display.

With Chief Qu assuming personal command, even Iron Kou became more obedient and, naturally, many of Smooth's and Big Hook's ideas were implemented. They tried their best to tie forty-three set pieces to thirty-three battens and solved challenges such as how to switch, lift and drop the settings, especially those that were load-bearing. Even the managers of the theatre were astounded by Smooth's ability to accurately estimate weights with his eyes, hands and head. By scanning with his eyes, picking objects up or bumping his head against them, Smooth could guess their mass to within an ounce. The managers had never met a group of stage shifters so familiar with the rigours of their craft, and every point in the process shone with a knowing flair. From the positioning of the lamps, to their screwing into place, to the fixing of wires and plugs, and the balancing of the holders, they could install a row of upper lights with machine-like speed and precision. And yet this was actually the result of human labour. Their forte was working at heights. The men could scale and ascend, turn and rotate freely like acrobats, in defiance of health and safety. Little wonder then that "Monkey" had acquired that nickname.

When the theatre managers learned that the men were not the in-house professionals, but largely made up of migrants from the countryside who had honed their skills over years of experience, they showed them ever greater respect. They even permitted them to experiment with outlawed practices with the battens. Consequently, the shabbiest of gear was able to operate safely with a full load within a tiny window of time. Even Iron Kou covertly admitted that, "Those sons of bitches under Smooth have worked like supernatural beings out here."

At 10.30 am sharp, the stage was handed over to the director.

Smooth made a point of going up to her and reporting, "Director Jin, the broth hasn't been allowed to spoil. With Chief Qu leading at the front, how could we cock up your business? But this stage is a real bitch, the toughest nut I've ever had to crack. It's fortunate the chief showed so much concern and stayed up the whole night. When a leader does that, it lightens the load and we just slog away."

Smooth had intended to praise himself, but as soon as he put his tongue into gear, he ended up praising the leader instead. He was powerless to alter this old habit and could only take it as a relief that he was celebrating Chief Qu who lapped up his compliments rather than having to suck up to that fucking Iron Kou.

Director Jin, who was busy discussing the two protagonists with Chief Qu, could only murmur, "Oh, OK." Smooth withdrew edgily to the side.

What vexed the pair of them most was the tension between the two leads. Everything would be fine if they could only manage to appear at 10.30 am. If not, the trouble would be incalculable.

Chief Qu reminded himself again and again to remain composed. Still, he found himself a little flustered, for this was an onerous matter. At the same time, he had prepared himself psychologically and knew that if they really did refuse to perform, he had drafted a speech in his mind that he would deliver in front of the entire troupe. Should a pustule fester, it is best to leave it to worsen. Desperate remedies can then be applied to the root so that the troubles and anxieties do not become chronic.

It was gone 10.30 am, then 10.40 am, and the two demigods had yet to appear. Every pair of eyes in the theatre was trained on Chief Qu, all eager to know if the performance had been aborted or not. The news of his outburst last night had done the rounds in the troupe. Somebody posted a message on WeChat, stating, "Old Qu took a load of calcium supplements once he came to the capital. Now he is truly stiff."

In spite of having heard this tale already, Smooth shared everyone's feeling of suspense about today.

Chief Qu's hair had gone grey a few years ago and now, perhaps because of the blaze of stage lamps, not a single black strand was visible on his scalp. Someone sighed and mused that Old Qu was indeed elderly, and with age came swiftness. He was as quick as the proverbial white colt passing by a crevice. His white hair, though bedraggled and fluffy, possessed a grace and elegance of its own rather like those sepia photos of artistes long since faded away.

More than a hundred sets of eyes were now directed squarely at him.

Smooth was profoundly troubled about what would happen to the white-haired senior.

Chief Qu glanced at his watch a number of times until it was five minutes to the hour. He decided they would wait until eleven and take that as confirmation that they weren't coming. He would then share his major declaration.

As the futility and despair of the situation was becoming apparent, the demigods finally arrived. They entered through two different side doors, their heads held high, unwilling to look at any of the assembled.

Everybody was dumbfounded. Some were clearly still spoiling for a grand altercation.

Although they were late, the chief experienced a sensation akin to a thousand-pound rock impacting on the floor. Great it was that they had come. He now even felt a slight warmth towards these two youngsters and came close to tears.

In the end, these two kids had not robbed him of his face and honour. What did it mean for one to lay aside self for the sake of the troupe? Here was that spirit exemplified. The male lead was a little over thirty and she was twenty-seven or twenty-eight. It was natural that all the plaudits heaped on them by the world affected their very gait as they walked. Anybody else in their position would behave the same way. Imagine that. The two of them enjoyed the admiration and flattery of thousands upon thousands of people all day long. That would surely be an impediment to keeping calm, sober and self-controlled, and to having an accurate perception of their own weight in the world. Even those great figures in history had their judgment impaired by the cheers and plaudits of the massed millions. Here they were, a couple of youths who had been elevated because of their singing and acting abilities. For certain, these past few years had entailed effort, and they gave it their finest.

As the chief, Qu had great perspicacity and knew the travails of being a lead player. They were surrounded by jealousy and intolerance, with some folk even itching to see them slip. Chief Qu could peer into the heads of those who had ulterior motives and affected manners. Years of brushing around the theatre world had endowed him with a certain degree of adulation towards authentic talent. Were one to be intolerant, hard-hearted and dismiss those who made slight errors, then there would be no room for saplings to grow, let alone towering oaks and artistic masters. Any good troupe could fall into discord and disband. This was a sign that they had rules and a bottom line that was not meant to be breached. As long as these kids showed up, Chief Qu was prepared to act as their "protective umbrella" and "backstage retainer". He was not afraid that others would accuse him of being weak-boned and unprincipled, or scold Qu by comparing him to the Qing regime or its leading minister, Li Hongzhang. Is it not only natural that the young make mistakes? The fact that they had come indicated that they realised they had been in error and he still owed them his support.

When the rehearsal began, Chief Qu passed a secret memo on to the office. "Buy porridge rather than greasy vegetables dishes.

Some egg custard too. Take them backstage for these two youngsters. They're still receiving IV treatment."

The director of the office smiled and said, "I see the chief is still wanting to massage them."

Chief Qu kept silent.

75

SMOOTH AND HIS MEN WERE SWIMMING IN ADRENALINE. Prior to the rehearsal, Director Jin had asked the actors and actresses to clap in gratitude to the stage design crew. She specifically mentioned that they should applaud Group Two. Smooth stood up in a rush and interposed that they were mere labourers who worked hard. Their success was down to the leadership of their chief.

The assembled all laughed, and it was joked that, "General Manager Diao is quite the politician now."

When the rehearsal began, Smooth and his men were still occupied, for there were other tasks to be completed. A few of the pieces of set had been knocked apart and needed fixing, while others required an extra lick of paint. Director Jin was not absolutely satisfied with certain installations, so they had to be re-positioned in the course of the practice run.

The in-house stage shifters were drowsy and had begun to nod off at the edges of the stage. As for Smooth and his team, they had become accustomed to late nights, so were pumped up by the pounding of the drums and gongs.

What cheered Smooth particularly was that Big Hook showed no signs of illness or strain. They had stayed up the whole night and he, like Smooth, took on the most taxing roles and worked most doggedly. He would smile back at everyone who called him "Boss Hook", without a glimmer of annoyance. Apparently, that nickname implied a measure of responsibility.

One issue that was inescapable was Smooth's haemorrhoids. Each time he developed a prolapse, he had to go to the lavatory and use some bumf to push it back in. To his relief, his condition remained secret, for he would be mortified if others ever found out. Every last one of them was busy, so if his brothers were in the know, it would cause more palaver. He simply had to grit his teeth and press on. This was a means of circumventing the agony, for at present he couldn't risk splaying his legs too far apart. For better or worse, there would only be a couple more days like this. He had resolved that when he returned home, the condition would be tackled at its root.

As the rehearsal panned out on the front stage, at the rear there was discord over how to arrange the setting. Since all the battens were manually operated, there were not enough hands to move and change the set pieces. Performances in the Western Capital relied upon forty-three battens being operated by two personnel who did no more than press buttons. Now, eight members of staff had to work the mechanism simultaneously, and without adequate safety measures. Besides which, the layout of the theatre called on them to tweak the configurations of the freestanding settings and the props placed both high and low. Most of the employees found themselves ill-adapted to this new layout, not to mention the extra shifting and moving of sets that affected everyone. Hence, when the stage manager Iron Kou materialised in their midst, he was barracked with roars of objection. He too was helpless and tried to marshal those around him, but discovered there were still so many jobs left unassigned. It was not that the crew were workshy. Rather, they were awash with outstanding responsibilities. Furthermore, being an exalted performance of massive import, many were petrified of coming a cropper and slyly chose minor tasks to avoid the more consequential ones. Smooth and his core crew duly found themselves with the most unyielding of nuts.

Smooth was incensed, for he assumed that the son of a bitch Iron Kou was surrounding himself with pushovers he could easily bully. And still there were those two tasks that Director Jin thought to delegate by name. A kind of honour and trust must be invested in them.

One was to track the spotlights, which was the trickiest bugger of a nut. For starters, it was sweltering in that light slot, being perhaps fifty or sixty degrees. That would surely worsen when all the bulbs were on. Yesterday afternoon, when Smooth was installing lights up there, he had even peeled off his underpants. Thankfully, no one else was around, so he could tear into his job with a cosy abandon.

Tracking the spotlights was of crucial importance since in the key scene, two lights had to be operated in tandem. Two men had been taking care of this yesterday. The one who made the most accomplished attempt and was earnest in his manner succumbed to heatstroke. His fever was said to have rocketed to over 39C and he was blathering nonsense. The poor chap was still lying on the ward right now. His counterpart, whom Director Jin held in no esteem, was disdained for having let his hands tremble and shake relentlessly, thereby unsettling the mood of the performance. It was obvious then that the director should let Smooth and Big Hook take over. The two were dab hands, and she had praised them before for undertaking this self-same duty.

There was no reservation when it came to Smooth. Big Hook, by contrast, was a source of concern for his gaffer. After all, the temperature was stifling up there and they might begin to feel suffocated. Before Smooth could veto his involvement, Big Hook had answered the call. He had previously thought about switching him with Monkey, but it was too late in the day. Manipulating spotlights was Monkey's proud preserve, yet on this occasion, Maestro Ding had singled him out for other duties. He was to be in sole charge of operating the lighting console, so every automated movement was at his fingers' behest. This extra responsibility was taken by Smooth as a corsage of honour for both himself and Group Two. The thirty-three manual battens had to fall to Mound and Third Skin to flex, for Smooth could entrust the task to no one else. In terms of mental acuity and perspicacity, those two surpassed Smooth and Big Hook, so the two spotlights must be theirs to point.

The morning rehearsal was limited to key scenes and those that hinged upon scenery being altered. When an impending scene employed tracking spotlights, the director would reiterate how the actors should conduct themselves sensibly. Her motive was to try to further acquaint Smooth and Big Hook with the demands of the stage and the components of the plot. Mercifully, both had seen it acted out in the course of their time on the production. The stage and the plot were familiar enough, so Director Jin simply brayed an affirmative "OK" from below. "Smooth," she cried, "I'm hoping that tonight we'll not only see that you have the routine timed to perfection. You must make your pair of lights breathe and interact in a lively fashion. Understand?"

"I see, Director Jin," he replied. Then, turning to Big Hook, he jested, "Demonic possession – that's what it would take to bring these lumps of iron to life! How can we make them 'breathe'?"

An additional task she allocated them was to push the iron frame. In the closing scene in which Peach Blossom turns into a ghost, the female lead was meant to float back and forth in the air like a dainty peach bud. No matter how hard he tried, Cui Hu couldn't catch her. Peach blossoms fluttered and waltzed through the sky as sad songs lingered until the curtain fell.

The levitating and wandering ghost was in fact made animate by the iron frame being moved. The frame itself, which resembled a crane arm from a film set, was concealed behind a black seamless curtain. It could be lengthened or shortened and extended or retracted. The actress who was playing the heroine was suspended at the top of it with a series of lights following close on her tail. She was decked out in a glorious costume in the shape of a peach bud, and once the frame was in motion, she appeared to be treading on the clouds like a fairy.

The iron frame turned out to be so heavy and unwieldy that it was a chore to operate. Too much variation in movement was called for. Smooth and his fellows had used it before as the troupe tried to avoid hiring extra hands from outside for the sake of regular performances. On such occasions, the credits would be typed out as "Special dynamic stage effects courtesy of the resident stage design troupe". This time, Director Jin just doled out this duty to them, so Smooth approached it as a burden and an obligation.

The gadget proved extremely challenging to handle. It called for brute force and cooperation together with artistic grace. The iron frame alone weighed more than two tons, which was necessary in order to ensure the safety of the actress when it rotated with her in harness. This challenge might have been remedied with an engine, but such a contraption would create a din. In one scene in the opera, there was a spectacle of the uttermost tranquillity that was enacted without the accompaniment of music. As Director Jin put it, silence here was far more eloquent than speech. It should be so tranquil that a needle falling in the auditorium would be registered by all present. By the opposite score, in several other scenes it was stipulated that there should be a radical rising and falling effect in conjunction with the varying rhythm of the score. Technology could never appreciate the vicissitudes of artists, so controlling and feeling human hands were essential.

Every time the rehearsal reached this point, the director would call for those operating the iron frame to act as artists as opposed to stevedores. The device must be able to breathe. That was how she always characterised the behaviour of the articulated parts of the set, whether it be scenes having to be changed or lifted or dropped, or lights being switched on or extinguished. Each should have a sense of respiration. Once one understood the action of breathing, one comprehended the essence of art. The loftiest realm of art was breathing.

Could Smooth perceive breathing? Every time he heard this spiel, he wanted to giggle. Who wasn't able to breathe? These artistes loved to spout bullshit. Eight or nine guys mounted on that frame. Try telling them to breathe when they're practically suffocating to death!

Nevertheless, Smooth and his team practised and practised. At first, they strapped in the actress according to the stage directions. As she grew impatient at being fastened to the top, Director Jin permitted the players to take a break. The shifters then continued with Third Skin as her proxy. He weathered this ordeal until, at last, he screamed that he was dizzy and ready to heave.

It was 6 pm by the time Smooth's gang had finished every last errand. The stage supervisor inspected the set and told them to clear the area one last time. Only an hour and a half was left before the curtain-up. Smooth told his men to take a breather and conserve their energy. "The finest blade needs the best steel sharpener," he said.

He himself chanced upon a carton used for packing lights. This he flattened and used as a ground sheet at the front of the lighting slot. Sleep would not come for he had the spirit of a soldier gearing up for battle. What he and the team had done zipped across his mind's eye like a canister of movie acetate spooling through a projector. Any potential weak links were noted, for he must see his brothers had every assistance on the job. Nobody should fumble or lose their composure during the performance.

He called Big Hook over and they pooled ideas. He dared not contemplate a power nap until every flaw had been discussed. Big Hook said this was no place to doze since there was the danger they would not wake up in time if left to their own devices. He recommended instead the side stage, since there was a fair amount of hubbub around, enough to ensure that they had a wake-up call. Smooth agreed and so they and their colleagues retired over there and nodded off in a propped-up posture.

There and then he dreamed that the performance had drawn to its end. This despite having been asleep for a mere matter of minutes. He pictured that it was Big Hook who was pinned to the iron frame and that the wolf whistles and applause of the audience lapped the stage like a tide. He was so agitated that his hair prickled on end and his body felt moist with cold sweat. Someone shook his arm, and he awoke to see Big Hook. He informed him that the performance was about to begin and Chief Qu was in the process of coaching the others backstage.

76

The commencement bell rang at last. Its peal was allowed to resonate for a protracted period so as to make certain the audience was subdued. Smooth and Big Hook gripped a canvas depicting a house. This was the largest canvas of its type in the whole production and, being richly evocative of the architectural style of the Tang Dynasty, it formed the screening wall at the Cui family mansion. Since the frame was tall, heavy and cumbersome, Iron Kou singled them out to be its custodians.

The opera began with a five-minute prelude, leaving fifteen seconds to position the set for Act One. Should any of the crew still be visible on the stage when the lights came on to the accompaniment of the opening number, that would be regarded as a cock up. It would be taken into account when the judges were casting their votes. Not observing strict stage manners or being less than proficient with the logistics of the stage were shortcomings associated with amateur productions.

Smooth grasped hold of his piece of set and waited in the wings. He made sure to scan the route they would have to take across the darkened stage, figuring out how to sidestep the pillars and the corner of the platform and get the house into position with a single stride. They then had to marry the iron pier to the iron angle at the foot of the piece, and swiftly withdraw from the stage area. Director Jin had stressed that the pair should pay particular attention to how they breathed as they installed the set. And so Smooth composed himself and tried to discern how exactly he was breathing. Comical as he felt this was, he did his best to effect the change. All of a sudden, he caught a glimpse of Chief Qu who was also struggling to support a flat piece of scenery against his thighs. His hands were shaking visibly and Smooth had the sense that both his and Director Jin's hearts must be ready to explode with the tension.

The prelude drew to an end, and the lights dimmed. "First setting, go, go!" the stage supervisor whispered authoritatively. Smooth and Big Hook bore their charge onto the stage in the darkness. Black as this area was, the stage was dotted with tall and short props in a kind of honeycomb pattern. They carried the house to its position while imagining they were treading across a perfectly flat plane. The entire process came off as so casual, seamless and unforced that they might as well have been sleeping or eating. As the lights came on once more, the two of them withdrew discreetly behind the side curtain. The stage supervisor flashed his thumbs at them as he knew that this tall, teetering canvas was tricky to handle. Smooth then realised something peculiar. He had discovered the sensation of breathing that Director Jin had enjoined him to search out.

Apart from the actors who were onstage, the remainder of the company rested in the wings, monitoring the performance and how it was going down. It occurred to Smooth that everybody shared an air of trepidation, since they were so anxious for their work to earn recognition here in the capital.

He had been in this field for such a long time that he fully comprehended the kinds of quirks to which those in the theatre were given. In normal times, they may appear slack and ill-disciplined. Occasionally, they wouldn't give a turd what the emperor was decreeing. However, when they reached a critical phase, they could adjust their breathing to the same rate. Those who were fond of cynical and snide remarks would alter beyond recognition. Their vocabulary became as scintillating as the blossoms on a lotus and their eyes flooded with concern. At this very moment, nobody cursed Old Qu, the director, the office, the business section, the despotic leads, their lack of professional titles, representatives, committee members, apartment rooms, the Plum Blossom Prize, nor any other honour or accolade. Apparently, all personal grudges and interests had been voluntarily surrendered to the four winds, and instead, they focused on one common interest: collective glory.

Whoever dared to bring shame on the troupe or even made the tiniest hiccup would offend the entire company. Any individual gripe had to be gulped down and stored away for the time being.

Smooth and his men were instinctively afraid about their own areas of responsibility. Such was their circumspection that they took to walking on the balls of their feet around the wings. By breathing artistically in the darkness, Smooth and Big Hook had been able to negotiate the first setting to perfection. Next, the two of them gently and cautiously climbed up to the lighting gantry on the ceiling and braced themselves to take custody of the spotlights.

As it happened, these parts of the rig were not scheduled to be used until Act Four. A breather was conceivable in the meantime. Nonetheless, Smooth believed that when more than a hundred people were exerting themselves in the cause of art, it would have been odious for him to leave the backstage and get some fresh air. The pair each doused their flannels and carried two bottles of mineral water apiece up to the lighting gantry, where they awaited orders.

The gantry was situated in the front dome of the auditorium. Whereas the principal stage slot in theatres was spacious, capable of housing scores of lights, today they were in a clubhouse. The present slot could accommodate no more than a dozen lamps, and any supplementary ones had to be suspended on lights outside the fitting. The whole gantry measured eight metres in length, yet was only 1.5 metres in both height and width. Once they entered it, operators had to bend their backs to be able to move. That was no big deal for Smooth, but the six-foot Big Hook had to adopt the pose of a shrimp. Worse still, the searing atmosphere in there made the occupants breathless.

As it happened, during the lunchtime rehearsal some of the lights were switched off. Now, all of them were at full blaze and the platform became baking hot. Since there were no holes for ventilation, the scorching steam mounted up and the pair were gasping for fresh air.

Smooth was still in anguish about Big Hook, but he assured him he could cope with the conditions so long as he could lie down there and didn't have to make any movements. He was, in fact, lying on his side, waiting for the scene in which the two spotlights were used. Soon, both of them were perspiring heavily. All of the stage design group had been kitted out in black uniforms for the evening performance. Black in order to absorb the light and to make the staff operating the sets invisible to the audience. The cloth was rather thick and impermeable, so was unbearable to wear once the temperature soared. Smooth removed his outfit and then wrung it out, releasing copious amounts of sweat. "You'd better take yours off too, Big Hook," he advised. "Wring it dry so we don't shimmer in the stage lights when we're at it."

Big Hook stripped off and twisted his clothing, placing it to one side to dry.

In the finale, both of them would have to carry Peach Blossom. For the time being, they wore only underpants. As the fabric was soaking, Smooth's backside became sore. He tugged his smalls down, exposing his posterior to one of the lights.

Big Hook was shocked. "Oh, heavens," he cried. "How could you let your arse get into that state?"

"Old war wounds. Nothing serious."

"You'd better sort it out sharpish."

"I'll fiddle it back into place once we're down in the wings."

He asked Big Hook if he would take his off too, reasoning that there was nobody around and actually it felt more comfortable being nude. Big Hook did so and squeezed out all the moisture. Droplets of sweat pittered against the bulbs, causing a crackling sound. The two men looked at each other's crotches and chuckled.

"You're humongous," Smooth gasped. "No wonder they call you Big Hook."

"It's natural for a bigger man to have everything in proportion. But yours is a bit of a tiddler."

"Only used for peeing now, so what's the point of extra inches?"

"You don't think about finding another missus?"

"No."

"You're only in your fifties. Why not find another?"

"No. It's too brain-racking."

"How come?"

"It's not really brain-racking to find a wife. I just don't want one."

"What if someone made a move on you?"

"Who'd do that? Are they blind?"

"Ha ha. Didn't Cai Sufen come voluntarily?"

"Enough of this. I wouldn't want one even if they came off their own bat. My mind is made up. Living alone brings fewer worries."

"If someone decent did come along, you should accept. That's the way of the world when it comes to men and women. If you don't accept her, maybe she'll end up left on the shelf. Some bastard could take her and screw her over. If a decent bloke took her on, that would be virtuous of him."

Smooth did not pay much heed to what Big Hook was saying that evening. Months later, those words came back to him as something eerie and prophetic. Still, Smooth swore off remarriage and wouldn't budge. To date, three wives had each broken his heart, so he couldn't venture there any more. He thought he had a jinx when it came to women. Whoever he took in would come to misfortune and have a sorry lot. He was determined to spare anyone else from that fate.

The performance below was met with hysteria, the applause being rabid from time to time. Smooth and Big Hook, too, could partake in a form of glory. As Act Three began, they stopped conversing. They simply had to watch the performance so that they retained that warmth and emotional connection. As the current act was rather long, the pair rose to their feet several times to keep limber. Each time they realised that umpteen numbers still had to be performed. It appeared that the actors were drawing on every sinew, since their pace of talking was highly measured and their speech became a kind of drawl. Smooth and Big Hook found the wait interminable. Then, finally, the act came to its denouement and the stage lights darkened to the sound of enthused applause. Now their chance was afoot.

The hands that clasped the handles on the paired spotlights had grown sticky. As the background to the stage was dyed Prussian blue, the brittle gleam of moonlight bit by bit reconstituted the scene into the poetic idyll of the Tang Dynasty. Their waists ached from bending for so long. And yet at this time their minds could stretch no further than processing the stage directions Madame Jin had given them in rehearsal:

...finally, attention, finally, Peach Blossom is going to run out from these tall walls. Attention, first light. In the fourth bar of the music, in the long fourth, begin by tracking from behind the third curtain. Zoom the aperture from small to large. Welcome her with passion... no, embrace her, a country girl so cruelly bullied by the noble aristocratic family... follow, follow closely. She is going to trot. Now she is trotting. Round the stage, a whole circuit, speed up. The light should enfold the girl like the girl is its own daughter. Keep steady, more steady – dash, follow the helpless girl as she dashes forward. She sinks to her knees, suddenly down on her knees, bounding down the cliff. Now hold it. Zoom the aperture small, smaller, smaller, smallest. We only want to see the pinched and helpless face of poor Peach Blossom. Attention, second light. Focus your beam on the spot where she entered just now. Cui Hu screams "Peach Blossom!" from inside. The whole orchestra swells. Attention! At the fourth bar of the five-five-five-five rhythm, switch on the light at its strongest projection. Let Cui Hu appear panic-stricken as he rushes in. His sweetheart wouldn't obey the rules of the family, and so she was driven out by the evil mother. He chases her. Follow, follow Cui Hu closely. He makes a tough kung-fu-style somersault, then screams "Peach Blossom" and follows her again. He finds Peach Blossom. Both move back, back, back, back more, back again. Hold the light, keep it steady. Both dash forward. Zoom the aperture. Hug, hug tightly. Attention, attention, the two apertures must be synchronised perfectly. Don't cast one bit of shade from being wrongly positioned. Fix, fix, fix firmly. Don't wobble the tiniest bit. Just a beautiful death. Next, slowly, slowly follow the plaintive notes of the erhu violin as the hero and heroine are torn apart, gently separate, separate, breathe, separate, breathe, separate some more, breathe again, like the still surface of a lake reflecting moonlight... flow, let the lights flow sinuously along with the hero's performance. Breathe, the lights must breathe, like satin, unfolding softly and gently, unfold, unfold some more. These are two pieces of flawless satin, so gorgeous that they make people intoxicated, breathless... breathe... again breathe...

Smooth and Big Hook ran through the motions as they were described in rehearsal. The act lasted approximately twenty-eight minutes. The two of them held their spotlights steady until they had conveyed the hero and heroine to what Director Jin called the "Ever-Bright City of All Nations" and the "cosmopolitan, poetic and youthful Great Tang Dynasty". As the applause came from below like a dam being breached, they both pounded their waists and lay down serenely. Too perfect, they had pulled it off all too perfectly and thoroughly convinced themselves of their own achievement. They had seemingly fulfilled Director Jin's admonition that they mimic "two pieces of satin". It was flawless to a degree that glamour was added to art and could never be an impediment to it. This self-confidence was justified since they had truly breathed art tonight. Like two drowning men fished from the brine, they sprawled there for an age. Still forty minutes to go until the curtain went down, so they could gorge on their feelings of artistic accomplishment.

"Any discomfort now?" Smooth asked.

"It's fine."

"You see, I've been so fearful about your bastard health."

"I know. It's nothing. I must be stronger than you are."

"If there's nothing amiss, that's fine. Hey, Big Hook. Such a wonderful play. How do you think the audience would react if they knew there were two men in the buff operating these spotlights?"

"They'd be sure to storm out, hand back their ticket stubs and demand a refund."

"Do our naked bodies look that ugly?"

"If anyone saw your arse, they'd be put off eating for life."

"True enough. Your dick is scarily big, mind. Like a donkey's. Let's get dressed and go down and wait for the end. There's still a tough battle to come."

77

When the performance reached this moment, victory was surely at hand. Nonetheless, everyone both front of house and backstage was in the grip of an enervated tension. Talk was sparse as they readied themselves for their contribution. After Smooth and Big Hook descended from the gantry, the stage supervisor showed his thumb once again and purred softly, "Director Jin is extremely satisfied and said you must be true artists." The duo appeared as if they had supped honey and the residue was still beading the corners of their mouths. They were hesitant to display their pride and feared becoming slack. Their best policy was to show modesty and keep subdued. Where shifting stages was concerned, once you turned haughty and relaxed that was inviting a debacle to your door. Smooth and Big Hook went backstage and slaked themselves until they wanted no more. They then masticated over with Mound, Third Skin and the others how the three minutes of steering the frame would run in the finale. At last, they heard the stage supervisor calling them into position.

The climax was upon them.

While Cui Hu was on a recreational tour outside the ancient Western Capital with some fellow poets, his mother expelled Peach Blossom from their home. Upon his return, she coerced him into drawing up divorce papers. Such was the young bride's despair that on the way back to her home village she took up a piece of white gauze and fashioned a noose. Her life came to an end, swinging from the branches of a peach tree.

When Cui Hu arrived at Peach Blossom Village, he encountered the same narrow gate as at the beginning of the play. Tears ran down his face as he penned his immortal love lyric:

> *In this house on this day last year, a pink face vied*
> *In beauty with the peach blossoms side by side.*
> *I do not know today where the pink face has gone;*
> *In vernal breeze, still smile pink peach blossoms full-blown.*

In preparation for writing the four-line poem on the stage, the bigwig who was playing Cui Hu, the hero of the play, had taken tutorials with a master calligrapher and practised hard how to form these characters of the composition in cursive script. His calligraphic skill added an unforeseen burnish of refinement to the finale. Whenever his turn came to play this scene, the audience would catcall in a frenzy. Tonight, when the brush came into contact with the paper, there was unremitting clapping and cheering. His grace, mature artistry and rhythm in the execution even prompted Chief Qu, who was standing at the side of the stage, to exclaim "Phenomenal" out loud. All those in the wings applauded.

As Cui Hu was chanting and writing, the spectre of Peach Blossom began to levitate thanks to the tilting iron frame. Smooth and his supporters, who had been waiting behind for so long, initiated their most artistic creation to the letter of Director Jin's instructions:

> Be alert. The poem will be sung three times. First by Cui Hu, then by the male bass chorus. The third time, the first two lines will be sung by a mixed duet, to be succeeded by the full chorus from the third line. Attention those brothers who operate the iron frame. When Cui Hu reaches the third line, you start to inhale. Note, you should hold your breath. When the last word of the last line – "blown" – is sung, there will be a pause and the lights come on. The moving light should start from the face. No, the very tip of her nose. Then zoom in gradually, little by little, until the light covers the actress's entire peach bud costume. Get moving. Go. The peach bud should begin to float in the air, float, float, nearer. Push the long rocker arm forward, push, push it before the very eyes of Cui Hu. Pay attention now. Draw nearer, nearer, still nearer. When the

rocker arm is about a metre from Cui Hu and while he is stretching out his arm to hold her, just as his fingers are about to touch Peach Blossom, pull back hard. Be swift, be firm, pull, pull, firmly pull beautiful Peach Blossom away from her beau. Pull her so far away that it's impossible for him to reach her.

This was the first full run of the finale. All members of Stage Design Team Two, apart from Monkey who was at the controls, were bunched in manipulating the frame. As a matter of fact, this frame relied upon the lever principle. At the centre of the structure was a pivot, and the actress, harnessed at the uppermost tip of the rocker arm, was elevated according to human heft at the other point of the balance. According to the heights required by the director, different forces of manpower could be applied to the balance point. In order to make sure that it was safe and steady, the frame was protected by six people and moved back and forth. Two served as the ballast on the balance point, decreasing or increasing the weight from time to time. Big Hook acted at the lifter at the middle of the rocker arm, determining whether it was to rise or fall. Simply to make the actress float almost weightlessly called for the efforts of nine staff working below in perfect unison. Sometimes they were asked to run like they were taking part in a hundred-metre dash. At other times, they had to stroll as if padding across a cloud. At this moment, the entire space behind the curtain had been cleared. They were the sole people there, left to run back and forth, or to the left and right. All the nine were barefooted to reduce the creaking of feet on stage. The sound was light rather like a flock of sheep entering or sweeping out of a fold. When everything merged into a sonic whole, it was as if the earth's core was vibrating.

Director Jin's words rang in their ears all this time:

...Attention those brothers operating the frame. You are artists, not stevedores. You're not Smooth Diao's henchmen, you're performance artists. Breathe, breathe deep, dash, dash, propel the mournful Peach Blossom into the sky... fine, slow down, slow down a bit more. At this point, the movement should be like a Tang dancer swishing her fine, long silk sleeves. Can you picture a sleeve dance? It has the feeling of floating, or a graceful unfolding. It is the sensation of breaking loose from feudal fetters and entering the realm of freedom. Float, float up, float up high, higher, float like a fairy. Let our beautiful angel levitate. Well done. Sink down, sink down, sink, inhale, float up, float, turn, one more turn, one more. Fine, fall down, rise up, fall down, rise up, fall down again, rise up again...

In the darkened zone, among those nine people operating the frame, Big Hook had assumed the most gruelling role. Owing to his height, nobody else could take on his duties. Since he experienced his first turn, Smooth had managed to procure another six-footer, though this man lacked Big Hook's familiarity with the stage and indeed was something of a clodhopper. Big Hook was certain that only he could guarantee the desired effect and, as Smooth had seen not a hint of illness about him in recent days, he gave his consent. His job entailed waiting until the rocker arm was raised up, then crawling under it before lifting the rig higher, first with his shoulder and then his hands. The rig would be pushed up or down, to the left or to the right nine times in response to the variations in the music. These changes could be light or heavy, quick or slow. The effect might be as fierce as "tearing the silk towards the sky" or as light as "letting feathers drift" or "giving us a face-caressing spring breeze" or "imagining a fairy descending from the sky". The words, of course, were the expressions crooned by Director Jin. All the same, every last one of the movements relied on shoulders, arms, backbone, waist, the twisting of the buttocks, and tiptoeing like a spinning top as Big Hook did. To Smooth, he was a towering crane, launching the protagonist to the heights again and again. After garnering cheers and claps, he pitched her once more to a still more splendid land. As Director Jin would put it, they should let art come to an abrupt end with a strikingly gorgeous spectacle and the spell of amazement. The aesthetic effect would hover on the memory like a melody in days to come.

Finally, the grand chorus came to the last line: "In vernal breeze still smile pink peach blossoms full-blown." This was the third time it had been repeated. The choristers raised their voices to the highest pitch. Any more might have caused their vocal chords to crack. The ovation came with the spontaneity of beans hitting a hot wok, rainstorms breaking out or thunder rattling. The thunder then subdued and Smooth knew that the main curtain had been dropped, thus muffling the sound. They could let go of their artistic breathing. Every last one of them lay down or slid prone to the ground. They waited and did not rise again or vacate the stage until the cast had satisfied the curtain calls.

Smooth crouched on the floor on all fours, now puffing with effort. These three minutes had covered no greater distance than a hundred-metre dash, but it impressed upon them how tenuous their hold on life was. These breaths had become their terminal gasps. Four words alone in his heart encapsulated the feeling: "genuinely flawless, indeed perfect". It was truly, flawlessly perfect. Smooth thought he could hand in his mission report to Chief Qu and Director Jin. Stage Design Team Two had not lost face on behalf of the Western Capital in Beijing.

The cast made three curtain calls on the stage. The curtains swung closed and open, closed and open. Cheers and applause prevailed. Smooth had been associated with this troupe for so many years, yet this was the first time he had seen such post-performance fervour. In spite of being on his hands and knees and having no line of vision ahead of him, the enthusiasm was manifest and he could tell the audience were unwilling to leave.

When a performance was sub-par, perhaps half of the opera-goers would leave before the end and certainly would not stick it out until the curtain call. Only the best of productions could expect curtain call after curtain call.

The crew did not stand up until some of the audience had leapt onto the stage to have pictures taken with the leads. Big Hook, however, stayed on the ground, motionless. Smooth's heart started to thump and he hurriedly shook his friend, who still didn't move. He yelled out "Big Hook!" but there was no response and his legs had gone limp and feeble. Mound and Third Skin knelt over him too, shouting and jiggling his limbs. Just as Smooth was sure he was a goner, the body twitched to the nervous shouting of the numerous troupe members who crowded around. As the huddle grew larger, Big Hook turned over of his own accord and looked about. "Nothing serious, I'm fine," he muttered. "Nodded off, that's all." The onlookers broke away with some commotion.

Later on, Smooth cursed Big Hook. He complained that his pal was so inept he couldn't even choose a suitable time to die. If he were to peg it, why not do it that night as the play reached its crescendo? Why wait until the next day and exit with a whimper?

That damned Big Hook. He really had no sense of timing.

78

People were debating for a long time afterwards whether Big Hook was in a state of shock that night or had merely nodded off. He told others that he had been fatigued, and so many had heard his explanation that little credence could be given to the shock theory.

It was only fitting that the troupe should have a party that lasted half the night after their performance had been so gloriously well received. A repeat staging was scheduled for the next day, though nobody felt any trepidation about that. Opera performances relied upon word of mouth, with a successful premiere virtually ensuring a decent follow-up. As the actors and actresses were removing their grease paint, Chief Qu made a point of patting Smooth on the shoulder and saying, "Genuinely flawless, indeed perfect." Director Jin came over and echoed the same praise. Later, Smooth discovered that all members of the troupe had subsequently greeted each other with those same four words of congratulation that night.

After hours, the troupe habitually played cards, chatted or shared a tipple. Every one of them was a night owl and were usually in an excitable mood following a show. Tonight's triumph galvanised these emotions. It was said that a few experts had been heard to describe it as the best production in the selective performance category. The top prize seemed to be awaiting them. This thrilled Smooth and his team, and they intended to go out and buy some chicken feet and peanuts to be swilled down with liquor. However, by the time Mound had returned with these items, they had sprawled themselves out and could not get up again.

The next day was supposed to be a period of respite. The troupe instructed that none of its employees should go outside to take a stroll. Conserving their strength and storing up energy were vital in preparing for the final performance.

When Monkey, Mound and Third Skin awoke in the morning, they noticed that a lot of the staff had sneaked out. Several had left around 5 am to witness the ceremony for raising the national flag at Tiananmen Square. They were keen to have a little tour of their own, and Smooth agreed because they had never been to Beijing before.

After visiting Tiananmen Square, Big Hook suggested a wander around Dashilan Market. People in the troupe had mentioned that it was a place for bargains, and he wanted to buy gifts for Laurel and Lily. Monkey nagged away, saying that even though Big Hook was a man, he wittered like an old biddy. He went off for a solitary stroll, while Mound and Third Skin accompanied Big Hook. Smooth, meanwhile, was aching down below again and retired early to the hotel.

Around 3 pm, Mound called Smooth to pass on the news that Big Hook was dead. He had taken his final breath in Happy Valley amusement park.

Mound related in his account that having left Dashilan, he proposed a spot of sightseeing at Happy Valley. He had also heard from those in the troupe that this was a place of wonderment, and many of them planned to take it in. Big Hook joined the group and they simply looked around, watching others play without a thought of doing so themselves. Mound wanted to have a go on some rides, though balked when he saw the price. He couldn't bear to shell out money like that.

Next, as they took a few steps out of the gate, without warning Big Hook pitched towards the ground. A similar situation had occurred twice before. This time, they failed to revive him, and his slumber would be eternal. They carried him to the nearest hospital for first aid. None of it worked, and he was now lying in the morgue.

Smooth's head detonated with an almighty boom.

He wasted no time in relaying the tragedy to Chief Qu. Together with Smooth and the staff from the office, the chief raced over to the hospital to take charge of the particulars and his personal effects. He asked whether it was appropriate for him to be the one to call Big Hook's family. After discussing the matter with Monkey and the others who had quickly come over, they decided against contacting his older relatives. Supposedly, they were in such miserable health that they couldn't even walk out of their home village. They must inform Laurel Zhou, though, for this was a calamity as vast as the skies. Smooth couldn't take personal charge of everything.

Chief Qu immediately called the staff back home and asked those who were in the Western Capital to buy plane tickets. He then told Smooth to phone Laurel on the pretence that Big Hook was in hospital without telling her it was anything serious. He should say that all the crew were busy, and they needed an extra pair of hands to tend to the patient. She was to come at their behest.

"Is it really nothing serious?" asked Laurel. "Don't trick me, Brother Smooth."

"How ever could I trick you? He just had a turn and nothing more than that."

She wanted to know if she could bring Lily along with her, to which he replied, "Up to you. If you think it's for the best, go ahead."

"If she does come too, who'll pay? It might be pricey to go to the capital."

"Don't fret about that. Chief Qu was the one who invited you to be a carer. How could he make you two foot the cost?"

The box office was a sell-out and so the evening performance was set to proceed. Smooth once again carried the large set piece forming the house, operated the tracking spotlight and manipulated the iron frame together with his crew. Only, Big Hook's role had to be filled with a replacement. All of Smooth's team felt out of sorts and were inconsolable. He tried to comfort them, but found himself turning his head sideways to hide the tears that ran down his own cheeks like the pearls of a broken necklace.

Laurel Zhou was taken from Capital Airport to the morgue directly after the performance. Smooth had arranged for eight people to take care of her and Lily. Only then did he and the chief reveal the truth to her. Those eight were insufficient to prop up the pair of grieving women. They knelt down limply before the entrance to the mortuary. Forgetting that they were in the capital city and amid human civilisation, they banged their heads against the ground, wailing bitterly and mourning excessively.

Big Hook was cremated at Babaoshan Revolutionary Cemetery.

As Smooth was collecting his ashes, he cursed, "You shit! You may not have known how to die, but you did it in the right place. Don't you know where we are? This is Babaoshan in Beijing, where the greatest in the nation are cremated."

79

SMOOTH, MONKEY, MOUND AND THIRD SKIN went together to Big Hook's home village to make the funeral arrangements. Chief Qu and the staff from the troupe office followed on.

Big Hook's family was truly pitiable. When his elderly parents learned of their son's demise, it was as if the Earth had crumbled and the heavens collapsed. His elderly ma pounded her head against the wall and his pa unleashed a torrent of abuse, cursing Big Hook for being worthless, disobedient and un-filial. He had strode on ahead of them, cutting off their roadway and bridge to the future, laying waste to whatever merits and virtues the Zhao family may have stored up. Not until now did his friends learn that Big Hook's real name was Pumpkin Zhao. His father had given him the name out of superstition, figuring that as the only son in the family, the rope might snap at some weak point. If he owned an auspicious name, that could attract the attention of ghosts and demons. Naming him after a useless old pumpkin may cause those same evil spirits to ignore him. Nonetheless, this fruit had been plucked away midstream by a wicked ghost. His parents cursed the heavens, the Earth and the ghosts for being blind enough to have pilfered a crappy pumpkin.

After they had buried Big Hook's ashes, the four men knelt in a row and kowtowed in unison to Big Hook's folks before handing them all the money they had in their pockets and departing the village.

Long after they returned to the city, Smooth and his pals were still cursing Big Hook. They all bemoaned that he didn't know how to die properly. Had he expired on the stage, that would have been counted as dying in the line of duty. Smooth made enquiries. Were all the expenses to be added together, including the funeral bill, compensation for the death, welfare payments for the bereaved elderly and childcare fees for his daughter, the troupe could be liable for in excess of 400,000 yuan. Were he not to have died on the stage, it would have been better to pass away inside Happy Valley rather than outside its perimeter fence. He had closed his eyes just a dozen metres from that park, so absorbed none of its positive karma.

The hospital reported that the ultimate cause of death was a sudden heart attack. They confirmed that when Big Hook had dozed off, this was in fact a symptom of bodily trauma. The doctors termed it a "death prior to death". They went on to say that when a patient has coronary heart disease, they must undergo an immediate examination and have bed rest. In this case, delaying treatment proved fatal.

Whenever Smooth recalled the words of the doctor, he came over bereft and full of remorse. If anything could have been done to avert the attack, then he must share some responsibility. Having known that Big Hook's health was precarious, he should have overruled his protestations and insisted on him not travelling to Beijing. On second thoughts, it was such a rare opportunity that had he rebuffed him, Big Hook might never in his life have had the chance to visit the capital. He was his good brother, so he couldn't arrange for everyone else to come to Beijing and leave him behind. Besides, his family were in real want of money. To have travelled there, while forcing him to wait idly at home for days was not what he wished. There was no culpability in organising for him to join them. However, he shouldn't have been made to operate the tracking light or iron frame that night. These may have finally done for him. But since he had come, no one could dissuade him from taking on those tasks. The source of this misfortune had now been laid to rest.

After Big Hook died, all the staff from the troupe exhibited compassion, donating money that very evening. Smooth was fully aware that none of them was well off and sometimes they were not even given the whole salary they were due. There were occasions when they were desperate to pick up a knife for the sake of several dozen yuan of unpaid wages. That would be a sure-fire way to make Iron Kou shed some of his "black blood". He was a real despot of a manager with everybody, and were any small mishap to arise during a performance, he would penalise those he held responsible without blinking. Now, faced with the catastrophe of Big Hook's family, and in particular his daughter's plight, each of them grizzled. When they heard of how the couple had been trying to raise funds for the corrective surgery, people were even more liberal with their donations. Even Iron Kou coughed up 200 yuan.

Smooth knew that when they lost one of their own, troupe members could be expected to donate 100 yuan apiece, and then the family of the deceased should treat them to a meal. Director Jin gave 10,000 yuan, explaining repeatedly to Chief Qu that his death must be related to fatigue and that should be considered as a key element when adjudicating over the matter later on. The leading man and leading lady not only offered cash but also joined them at Babaoshan and bowed deeply as a mark of respect to their lost colleague. "Big Brother, may you have a safe journey," the heroine shouted as she wailed. Maybe the death of Big Hook had been a real jolt for them and caused them to forget about competing for the top billing or a prize? As it transpired, there was a double-yolker in the pot. Both of them were presented with the award for outstanding lead player.

Ultimately, Smooth and those closest to Big Hook found genuine consolation in the emotion and reverence the staff displayed towards his passing.

As a state-run unit, everything the troupe did had to be conducted in accordance with public sector regulations. These regulations specified that no additional benefits could be delivered in response to the death of Big Hook. If the troupe wanted to absolve liability, then they could do so. After all, he had not died in the workplace and, moreover, the troupe had stipulated that the staff should be resting in the hotel that day ahead of the evening performance. As second in command of the group, he had violated the rules of the organisation by leading others under him out onto the streets. His death had occurred suddenly after enjoying the pleasures of Happy Valley. What is more, he had a prior history of illness, and his employment unit had even actively sought to discourage him from undertaking this task.

When confronted with Iron Kou's cross examination, Smooth had to admit that all these points were true. He acknowledged that Kou had instructed him to tell Big Hook to stay at home if he was not in sound condition. The job in hand would be a tournament, not some country fair. On top of that, Big Hook was informed that if he chose to go to Beijing, any bills for medical treatment would fall on him, thereby relieving the troupe of responsibility. That son of a bitch Iron Kou dissected the situation in these very terms. There was veracity behind what he was saying, though no sensitivity about the timing. Smooth refused to resort to flattery. He would have been glad to spend the rest of his life without ever speaking to this arsehole again. Right now, he had no option.

Smooth asked Iron Kou if the two of them could find some place where they could speak in private. He then started to beg. He told of how Big Hook's family was destitute and needed every gram of assistance they could offer following their bereavement. His parents were sick and his daughter suffered from a severe facial deformity. Even then, Iron Kou's mouth was toxic. He ranted on and even raised his voice, saying, "Your guys broke the rules. They went loafing the streets and that's why he pegged it. He pleasured himself until he died, so how can you hope to extort the state over this? Providence cannot forgive this."

Smooth was speechless. He stood there for a time and then hurled his fist at Iron Kou's mouth. He had been spoiling to do this and now he had. Besides, the force of the blow stunned him silent.

"Smooth, you shit! You even dare to sink to violence!"

"Sure, I've wanted nothing more than to whack you, you monster piece of shit!"

Realising how things had soured irretrievably and that Smooth was enraged, Kou could only cover his mouth with his hands and flee.

Iron Kou crowed directly to Chief Qu, who then called Smooth over. He denied having delivered the offending blow.

"Chief Qu, how could I, Smooth, even think of punching Director Kou? Even if you offered me some guts of my own, I wouldn't be able to bring myself to do it. Why should I have punched him for telling the truth?"

Indeed, no one could believe the tale. Smooth was inclined to sidestep ants, so how could he batter Iron Kou?

Kou had to swallow the bitter pill in silence. In actual fact, he had now grown somewhat fearful of Smooth, whom he half expected to stab him in the back or dash his head with a brick. Petty fellows were fond of such tricks, so he desisted from stirring in the matter of Big Hook's demise.

The negotiations over compensation passed through multiple rounds under the supervision of Chief Qu. The troupe had hired a lawyer, and Smooth and Monkey obtained legal representation on behalf of Laurel Zhou. The package started at a baseline figure of 100,000 yuan, rising to 150,000 yuan, then 180,000, before settling at 200,000. By the end, staff members from the troupe had also given more than 60,000 yuan in donations.

Big Hook's parents appeared pleased with the settlement and once they had received it, they held Chief Qu's hands and uttered their profuse thanks.

Smooth visited the hospital as soon as he came home. He was more run down now that at any time in the past and was determined to tackle the root of his interminable condition.

A stage-shifting job was scheduled for right after their return. This time, Monkey was to head up the team, but he rang Smooth three or five times a day. These endless requests for instructions soon became irritating.

While Smooth was an inpatient, Monkey arranged for Third Skin to be his carer. His propensity to talk about Cai Sufen all the time sowed misgivings in Smooth's mind. He wondered, how could this lad be so hung up on my other half leaving? One evening, tears started to cascade down his face as he brought up the topic. By now, the doubts had snowballed and Smooth ended up telling him to fuck off.

During this hiatus, Smooth also accomplished a little unfinished business bequeathed to him by Big Army. He sent Mound over to Black Kiln Ditch in Zhen'an County in order to fetch Peach Blossom Yang's husband. He would now fill the vacancy in their stage-shifting team. Monkey complained that the fellow was too old, to which Smooth replied, "I know, but we have to take him in. They have a paralysed son at home, so need the income."

After a hundred days had passed since Big Hook's departure, Laurel Zhou brought Lily over, their initial spell of mourning being complete.

Laurel asked Smooth to admit her to the crew as well. She was capable and prepared to tackle any heavy job. Her main motivation was to be able to stay in the Western Capital and have Lily's face treated. Smooth agreed, being unable to say otherwise.

She continued to live in Smooth's home, seemingly without any intention of going elsewhere. Smooth wanted to raise the issue, but was fearful that in so doing, he might drive the pair away. For an orphan and a widow to spend so long under his roof was bound to become a subject for gossip. Smooth tried to broach the matter with subtlety, though Laurel never seemed to catch his meaning. Sharing a home with him, she demonstrated consummate consideration and care for her host. When they were about to go out to shift stages, she would jump on the tricycle ahead of time and boom, "Brother Smooth, I'm ready for a lift!" She appeared as though she were worried that he might not hear her. He knew that there could be no more procrastinating over the key issue.

He initiated a serious discussion with her by saying, "I know it's mean to ask you to move out. But if you stay here indefinitely, it might not be in your best interests. After all, you are a widow and I am a separated man. As time goes on, we might find ourselves drowning in other people's saliva."

"They can gossip as much as they like. Big Hook was content to let us live here, so he should be the one you bring it up with."

Laurel would sob whenever her husband's name was mentioned. Once her eyes were damp, Smooth could neither say nor do anything further.

After a short while, gossip did start to spread. It was said that Smooth had forcibly seized the widow of one of his underlings. That man had been worked to death. In response, Smooth tried to instigate a tougher line with Laurel. He told her that it was high time she found another home and that he ought to be continuing his life as a single man.

Laurel wept once again and bemoaned how she was cornered in

the Western Capital, and her only choice was to go the same way as Big Hook.

What could Smooth add when she spoke like this? The matter was duly abandoned.

Later, even Mound tried to joke with Smooth about the situation. "Brother," he piped up, "I suggest you should take on all of Big Hook's duties. Our sister-in-law isn't easy. You can just take it as learning from Lei Feng."

"Fuck off, and your mother's pussy too!" Smooth kicked him so he landed on his face.

Another time, Third Skin recommended that since Cai Sufen was never coming back, he should make an honest woman of Laurel.

"What if Sufen did return?" Smooth asked deliberately in response.

Third Skin hummed and hawed. "Return... return... in that case, let me take care of her."

"You motherfucking fart!" Smooth was furious with Third Skin.

Even Monkey's words seemed to cut both ways. "Brother, I think it's absolutely fine," he said with apparent reassurance. "You and Sister-in-Law Zhou can both try rowing the boat along with the current."

Smooth then decided to show her his hand.

He gave her one week's notice and promised to do everything to help her find alternative lodgings.

Unexpectedly, Laurel Zhou struck back with greater bite. "Brother Smooth, I have lost Big Hook," she asserted. "There is no way I can afford to lose you, too. You're a decent bloke and live all on your own. I, Laurel Zhou, am willing to follow you my whole life long and work like carthorses together and be driven like oxen. I think that when Big Hook fixed it for us to live here, he was placing his trust in us. It must have been the will of the heavens as well."

Whatever Smooth could have said would have been no spur to make Laurel leave. In addition, she invited Lily over and she knelt before him, imploring her uncle to assist them and not to force them out of the gate.

Smooth was too tender-hearted to expel the pair.

Later, Daisy came back too.

Once Daisy was home, this whole conundrum had to be settled.

80

DAISY CAME BACK ONE LATE-AUTUMN AFTERNOON. Tears corroded the make-up on her face as she announced that Tan Daogui had succumbed to catastrophic circumstances. He had been sentenced to ten years in prison for selling counterfeit liquor. His former wife was one of the "black hands" who had helped seal his conviction.

Smooth gazed at the "beautified" face of his daughter. Her nose was somewhat aslant and her cheeks pitched downwards. In appearance she resembled neither Audrey Hepburn nor the Daisy of old. Had no one pointed out who she was, those who knew her might pass her by.

Smooth was keen to know what had happened.

"I can't afford the cosmetic injections any more," she said. "They cost thousands every month."

Smooth said nothing and just helped her clean her room.

And so Daisy came back like the phoenix returning to its nest.

No sooner had she restored her "nest" did the sound of the music of the past reverberate once more. There was the same noise, the same pounding rhythm and the same screaming. The scream was unearthly and never ending. It was not singing per se, just an interminable wail that had no beginning and no end. Fortunately, Smooth had become used to it and was prepared to yield to that which he could not fix.

He suddenly recalled some lines from *Peach Blossom Cheeks*. Even though he didn't fully grasp the meaning of expressions like "immutable" and "mutable", he felt the compulsion to hum that part:

> *Even ghosts cannot prevent trees and flowers from budding and withering,*
> *One's fate is to be judged by the heavens' reckoning.*
> *Human life is full of paradoxes and tricks,*
> *The immutable always becomes mutable...*

As Smooth was humming these lines, Laurel Zhou appeared unannounced. Lily had just been for her fourth round of surgery and she was back to cook something for her.

When Laurel stepped through the gate, Daisy was on the alert and asked, "Who? Who is she?"

Smooth didn't reply and Daisy demanded to know if he had found another woman.

He nodded. That was a nod of assurance. A nod of such assurance that not the tiniest gap was left open for debate. Daisy raised her hand in fury and a potted plant ended up being swiped to the ground.

In the evening, an army of ants began its odyssey to a new home, passing via the house of Smooth. No one could tell where they had come from, nor their destination. But this was a magnificent troop, and it marched forward in an orderly and systematic formation.

The overcast sky foretold a downpour and the humidity was agonising. There was no fuss or mess, no upset or agitation among the ants, only the rustle of them marching. Smooth sat up once he heard their movements. He prepared some water and splashed it down alongside the insects, for he had been told that ants will die from thirst if they go too long without drinking. He also sprinkled sesame seeds and grains of millet as he saw that some of them had nothing in their front claws and were on the lookout for whatever could be lifted and paraded away.

He sat himself down and listened to the chirps of his calling insects while studying how the ants busied themselves. These creatures were hauling up and carrying away objects many times their own weight, yet still marched on so neatly and unhindered.

All at once, it occurred to him that it was self-esteem, solemnity and, moreover, stolid determination that prolonged their march. Had Director Jin spied this brigade, she would have made Smooth train his spotlight on them.

ABOUT THE AUTHOR

Chen Yan (born 1963) is a native of Zhen'an County, Shangluo, Shaanxi Province. He first rose to prominence as an essayist and the author of the "Xijing Trilogy" – comprising *The Late Blooming Rose*, *The Great Tree Transplanted to the West* and *Tales of the Western Capital* – a bold attempt to adapt traditional local opera for the twenty-first century stage. Mr Chen's novel *The Diva* was awarded the 2019 Mao Dun Prize, the highest literary accolade in the Chinese-speaking world. In 2018 he was appointed party secretary and vice chairman of the Chinese Drama Association. He also serves as vice chairman of the Writers Association of China.

ABOUT THE TRANSLATOR

Hu Zongfeng was born in Fengxiang County, Baoji, Shaanxi Province in 1962. He serves as president of the Shaanxi Translators Association and director of the Edgar and Helen Snow Studies Center. Between 2016 and 2022, he was dean of the School of Foreign Languages at Northwest University, Xi'an, where he has taught for more than thirty years. His acclaimed English-to-Chinese translations include *China at Last* by Burton Watson, *The Eagle and the Dragon* by Russell Duncan and *Disappearance* by David Dabydeen (longlisted for the Lu Xun Prize). He is the most prolific translator of the literature of his home province, having published English renderings of Jia Pingwa, Chen Zhongshi, Yang Zhengguang, Hong Ke, Ye Guangqin, Wu Kejing, Mu Tao and many more authors besides. His bilingual version of Chen Yan's modern opera trilogy was released by Shaanxi Normal University Press in 2021.

ABOUT THE TRANSLATOR

Robin Gilbank is originally from the North Yorkshire coast. He obtained his BA and PhD degrees from Aberystwyth University and his MA from the University of York. Since 2008 he has taught at Northwest University, currently acting as associate professor in British Literature and assistant dean in the School of Foreign Languages. Together with Hu Zongfeng, he launched the "Shaanxi Stories" series (Valley Press, UK) to promote the work of local authors in English translation. His other publications include *An Englishman in the Land of Qin* (2018) and *Exploring China* (2018), both translated into Chinese by Hu Zongfeng, with the latter being longlisted for the Lu Xun Prize. His essays on China have received the Feng Zikai Prize and the Wang Zengqi Prize.